The Struggle f

THE WESTERN ALLIES AND T

ARCHIVES AFTER THE SECOND WORLD WAR

When American and British troops swept through the German Reich in the spring of 1945, they confiscated a broad range of government papers and archives. These records were subsequently used in war crimes trials and published under Allied auspices to document the German road to war. In 1949, the West Germans asked for the documents' return, considering the request one of the benchmarks of their new state sovereignty. This book traces the tangled history of the captured German records and the extended negotiations for their return to German custody. Based on meticulous research in British, American, and German archives, *The Struggle for the Files* highlights an overlooked aspect of early West German diplomacy and international relations. All participants were aware that the files constituted historical material essential to write German history, and at stake was nothing less than the power to interpret the recent German past.

Astrid M. Eckert is Assistant Professor in the Department of History at Emory University. Eckert's dissertation on the history of the captured German records, which forms the basis of this book, won the Hedwig Hintze Prize from the Verband der Historikerinnen und Historiker Deutschlands (Association of German Historians) and the Friedrich Meinecke Award from the History Department of Free University Berlin. Her work has been supported by grants from the Fulbright Foundation, the German National Academic Foundation, the Fox International Fellowships at Yale, and the American Academy Berlin. She has published articles in *Central European History, Studies in Contemporary History*, and *Vierteljahrshefte für Zeitgeschichte*.

PUBLICATIONS OF THE GERMAN HISTORICAL INSTITUTE

Edited by Hartmut Berghoff
with the assistance of David Lazar

The German Historical Institute is a center for advanced study and research whose purpose is to provide a permanent basis for scholarly cooperation among historians from the Federal Republic of Germany and the United States. The Institute conducts, promotes, and supports research into both American and German political, social, economic, and cultural history; into transatlantic migration, especially in the nineteenth and twentieth centuries; and into the history of international relations, with special emphasis on the roles played by the United States and Germany.

Recent books in the series

Christof Mauch and Kiran Klaus Patel, editors, *The United States and Germany during the Twentieth Century*

Monica Black, *Death in Berlin: From Weimar to Divided Germany*

John R. McNeill and Corinna R. Unger, editors, *Environmental Histories of the Cold War*

Roger Chickering and Stig Förster, editors, *War in an Age of Revolution, 1775–1815*

Cathryn Carson, *Heisenberg in the Atomic Age: Science and the Public Sphere*

Michaela Hoenicke Moore, *Know Your Enemy: The American Debate on Nazism, 1933–1945*

Matthias Schulz and Thomas A. Schwartz, editors, *The Strained Alliance: U.S.-European Relations from Nixon to Carter*

Suzanne L. Marchand, *German Orientalism in the Age of Empire: Religion, Race, and Scholarship*

Manfred Berg and Bernd Schaefer, editors, *Historical Justice in International Perspective: How Societies are Trying to Right the Wrongs of the Past*

Carole Fink and Bernd Schaefer, editors, *Ostpolitik, 1969–1974: European and Global Responses*

The Struggle for the Files

THE WESTERN ALLIES AND THE RETURN OF GERMAN ARCHIVES AFTER THE SECOND WORLD WAR

ASTRID M. ECKERT

Emory University

Translated by Dona Geyer

GERMAN HISTORICAL INSTITUTE

Washington, D.C.

and

CAMBRIDGE
UNIVERSITY PRESS

CAMBRIDGE
UNIVERSITY PRESS

32 Avenue of the Americas, New York NY 10013-2473, USA

Cambridge University Press is part of the University of Cambridge.

It furthers the University's mission by disseminating knowledge in the pursuit of education, learning and research at the highest international levels of excellence.

www.cambridge.org
Information on this title: www.cambridge.org/9781107629202

© Franz Steiner Verlag GmbH, Stuttgart 2004
English translation © Cambridge University Press 2012

First published 2004 as *Kampf um die Akten: Die Westalliierten und die Rückgabe von deutschem Archivgut nach dem Zweiten Weltkrieg*
First English edition 2012
First paperback edition 2013

A catalogue record for this publication is available from the British Library

Library of Congress Cataloguing in Publication data
Eckert, Astrid M.
The Struggle for the files : the Western allies and the return of German archives after the Second World War / Astrid M. Eckert ; translated by Dona Geyer.
p. cm. – (Publications of the German Historical Institute)
Includes bibliographical references and index.
ISBN 978-0-521-88018-3 (hardback)
1. World War, 1939–1945 – Germany – Archives – History.
2. Germany – History – 1933–1945 – Archives – History.
3. Germany (West) – Foreign relations. I. Title.
D735.A1E45   2012
940.5314–dc23   2011044019

ISBN 978-0-521-88018-3 Hardback
ISBN 978-1-107-62920-2 Paperback

Contents

Acknowledgments *page* ix

Abbreviations xi

Introduction 1

1 The Confiscation of German Documents, 1944–1949 13

2 The First German Calls for Restitution 99

3 The Positions of the United States and Britain 169

4 Negotiation Marathon 219

5 Ad Fontes: The Captured Documents and the Writing of History 293

Conclusion 375

Bibliography 385

Index 417

Acknowledgments

Several years ago, this book was my German dissertation, submitted at Free University Berlin and crafted under the able guidance of Professor Knud Krakau, my advisor at the John F. Kennedy Institute for North American Studies. Steiner Verlag Stuttgart published it in German in 2004. During my period as a research Fellow at the German Historical Institute (GHI) in Washington, D.C., Christof Mauch, the GHI's creative and brilliant director at the time, was the first to bring up the idea of having it translated. I owe him much more than this idea and the encouragement to take it on. I already thanked many individuals in the German version of the book, and this gratitude to archivists, librarians, friends, and family has in no way diminished. I still think that this book would not have been possible without the help and support of Dr. Timothy P. Mulligan, the leading expert on captured German records at the National Archives, now retired. Over the course of the translation, however, I amassed still further debts, above all to Dona Geyer in Munich, who translated the manuscript from German. During the successive rounds of revisions, the senior editor at the GHI, David Lazar, taught me the real intricacies of Track Changes and, incidentally, some English grammar, too. I owe him many a straight sentence! Eric Crahan at Cambridge University Press contributed his professional skills and above all the patience to wait for us. The same holds for my colleagues at Emory University's history department who have been a model community of support ever since my arrival at Bowden Hall in early 2006. Acknowledgments usually close with a reference to the spouse who patiently endured the seclusion of the partner, his or her frequent absences, and monothematic conversations. I would like to think that it wasn't all that bad, but Brian is the better judge of that. I hope this will not be the last book I have the privilege of dedicating to him!

Abbreviations

Since some institutions in the British and American military bureaucracy used similar acronyms, some abbreviations listed here carry the added identification (Brit.) and (U.S.).

AA	Auswärtiges Amt
ACoS	Assistant Chief of Staff [Intelligence] (U.S.)
a. D.	außer Diensten
ADAP	*Akten zur deutschen auswärtigen Politik*
AFHQ	Allied Forward Headquarters [in Algiers]
AGO	Adjutant General's Office
AHA	American Historical Association
AHC	Allied High Commission
Ako	Archivkommission [of Auswärtiges Amt]
AmEmb	American Embassy
AMGOT	Allied Military Government of Occupied Territories
Asst.	Assistant
BArch	Bundesarchiv
BA–MA	Bundesarchiv-Militärarchiv
BAOR	British Army on the Rhine
BDC	Berlin Document Center
BfV	Bundesamt für Verfassungsschutz
BIOS	British Intelligence Objectives Sub-Committee
BJSM	British Joint Services Mission
BkA	Bundeskanzleramt
BMI	Bundesministerium des Innern
BMVtg	Bundesministerium für Verteidigung
BritEmb	British Embassy
BT	Bundestag

CAB	Cabinet Office
CAFT	Combined Advance Field Teams
CCG(BE)	Control Commission for Germany (British Element)
CDF	Central Decimal File [of the State Department]
CIA	Central Intelligence Agency
CIC	Counter Intelligence Corps or Combined Intelligence Committee
CINCUSAREUR	Commander in Chief, United States Army Europe
CIOS	Combined Intelligence Objectives Sub-Committee
COSSAC	Chief of Staff of the Supreme Allied Commander
CRS	Captured Records Section
DA	Department of the Army
DAI	Deutsches Auslandsinstitut
DBF	Deutsches Büro für Friedensfragen
DDMI	Deputy Director of Military Intelligence (Brit.)
DFG	Deutsche Forschungsgemeinschaft
DGFP	*Documents on German Foreign Policy*
DMI	Director of Military Intelligence (Brit.)
DRB	Departmental Record Branch
DRP	Deutsche Rechtspartei/Deutsche Reichspartei
DSIR	Department for Industrial and Scientific Research
DVP	Deutsche Volkspartei
EAC	European Advisory Commission
EDC	European Defence Community
EDS	Enemy Document Section [at the Brit. Cabinet Office]
EGA	Exploitation German Archives
EO	Executive Order
ERR	Einsatzstab Reichsleiter Rosenberg
EUCOM	European Command
EWZ	Einwandererzentrale
FAZ	*Frankfurter Allgemeine Zeitung*
FDRL	Franklin Delano Roosevelt Library
FIAT	Field Intelligence Agency, Technical (U.S.)
FO	Foreign Office
FOIA	Freedom of Information Act
FORD	Foreign Office Research Department
FRUS	*Foreign Relations of the United States*
Fü B	Führungsstab der Bundeswehr
G-2 (Intelligence)	Intelligence Division of the Army
GDR	German Democratic Republic

GMDS	German Military Document Section
GP	*Große Politik der europäischen Kabinette*
GPO	Government Printing Office
GSA	General Service Administration
GStA	Geheimes Staatsarchiv [Berlin–Dahlem]
GWU	*Geschichte in Wissenschaft und Unterricht*
HICOG	(Office of the) High Commissioner for Germany
HMSO	His/Her Majesty's Stationary Office
HQ	Headquarters
HRRI	Human Resources Research Institute [of the Air University, Maxwell Air Force Base, Alabama]
HStA Dü	Hauptstaatsarchiv Düsseldorf
HZ	*Historische Zeitschrift*
IfA	Institut für Archivwissenschaften
IfZ	Institut für Zeitgeschichte
i. G.	im Generalstab
IRR	Investigative Records Repository
JCC	Joint Consultative Committee
JCS	Joint Chiefs of Staff (U.S.)
JIC	Joint Intelligence (Sub-)Committee
KPD	Kommunistische Partei Deutschlands
LMDC	London Military Document Center
LoC	Library of Congress
LoCM	Library of Congress Mission
LR	Legationsrat
Lt.	Lieutenant
MCC	Ministerial Collecting Center
MDB	Military Document Branch
MF	Microfilm
MFAA	Manuscripts, Fine Arts, and Archives
MI	Military Intelligence (Brit.)
Mil. Gov.	Military Government
MinDir	Ministerialdirektor
MIRS	Military Intelligence Records Section
MIS	Military Intelligence Section [in the U.S. War Department]
NA	National Archives
NATO	North Atlantic Treaty Organization
NL	Nachlaß
NSA	National Security Agency

NSV	Nationalsozialistische Volkswohlfahrt
OAD	Offenbach Archival Depot
OAP	Office of Alien Property
OCCWC	Office of the Chief of Council for War Crimes
OKH	Oberkommando des Heeres
OKL	Oberkommando der Luftwaffe
OKW	Oberkommando der Wehrmacht
OMGUS	Office of Military Government, United States
ORR	Oberregierungsrat
OSD	Office of the Secretary of Defense
OSS	Office of Strategic Services
PA/AA	Political Archives of the Auswärtiges Amt
Pg.	Parteigenosse
PL	Public Law
POLAD	Political Adviser
PRO	Public Record Office
RA	Reichsarchiv [Potsdam]
RG	Record Group
RK	Reichskommissar
RKF	Reichskommissar für die Festigung deutschen Volkstums
RSHA	Reichssicherheitshauptamt
SA	Sturmabteilung
SCAEF	Supreme Commander Allied Expeditionary Forces
SD	Sicherheitsdienst
Sec	Secretary
SHAEF	Supreme Headquarters Allied Expeditionary Forces
SHAPE	Supreme Headquarters Allied Powers Europe
SOE	Special Operations Executive (Brit.)
SRP	Sozialistische Reichspartei
SS	Schutzstaffel
StA	Staatsarchiv
StS	Staatssekretär
SWNCC	State-War-Navy-Coordinating Committee (U.S.)
SZ	*Süddeutsche Zeitung*
T-Forces	Target Forces
TIIC	Technical Industrial Intelligence Committee (U.S.)
TLS	*Times Literary Supplement*
UA	Untersuchungsausschuß
UP	University Press
USAREUR	United States Army Europe

USFET	United States Forces, European Theater
USGCC	United States Group Control Council
USNR	United States Navy Reserve
VDA	Verein Deutscher Archivare
VDI	Verein Deutscher Ingenieure
VfZ	*Vierteljahrshefte für Zeitgeschichte*
VLR	Vortragender Legationsrat
VS	Verschlußsache
WASt	Wehrmachtsauskunftsstelle
WD	War Department (U.S.)
WDP	War Documentation Project (U.S.)
WO	War Office (Brit.)
WP	Wahlperiode

Introduction

On April 19, 1945, advance troops of the American Counter Intelligence Corps stumbled on one of the major trophies of World War II: the almost complete archive of the German foreign ministry, the Auswärtiges Amt. Stored in several castles in the Harz Mountains, the archive promised to reveal the secret history of Nazi foreign policy, to offer a glimpse into the minds of those who had helped plunge Europe and the world into an unprecedented war of destruction. But according to the boundaries negotiated at Yalta, the Harz castles were located on territory that technically belonged to the Soviet zone of occupation. Eager to snatch this major find from their Russian ally, British and American troops quickly removed this collection – all 400 tons of it – to Marburg Castle in the American zone. For a few more weeks, they managed to exploit the files in secret, suspiciously watching even each other, until British newspapers blew their cover. Thus began the struggle for the files.

This book is about the history of the German records and archives confiscated in the wake of World War II, and in particular about the long negotiations concerning the documents' return to (West) German custody. As the Third Reich collapsed, not only the archive of the Auswärtiges Amt but also hundreds of tons of files and documents from the registries and archives of Reich ministries, military offices, Nazi party organizations, and research institutes fell into Allied hands. These records were used in the first instance for intelligence purposes, war crimes trials, and denazification. They were variously cataloged and microfilmed, published or pulped. In some instances, their whereabouts were made public, in others they were kept secret. The documents divulged wartime secrets that made headlines in newspapers across the world and, later, allowed for more tempered publications aimed at the educated history reader. For a long time, the Germans were not sure which materials had been destroyed in Allied bombing raids

1

or by German officials themselves, and which had been captured and carried off by their former enemies. During the Allied occupation of 1945–1949, they were not in a good position to find out. However, once the two German states came into being, West Germans asked increasingly pointed questions about "their" archives. In October 1949, during one of the very first sessions of the Bundestag, a group of deputies demanded the return of these captured documents, at least those in the possession of the Western Allies. Despite the many pressing affairs confronting the nascent Federal Republic, the issue of the captured German records was deemed urgent enough to become one of the first items of business on the new state's agenda – so urgent indeed that the West German government under Chancellor Adenauer was at times even willing to alienate two of its key allies, the United States and Great Britain, over the matter.

The negotiations for the return of the records are an integral part of the early history of the Federal Republic. In the larger tableau of these early years, the demand for the return of the German records was one manifestation of the increasingly forceful strides toward the political emancipation of the Federal Republic from Allied tutelage. Regaining sovereignty was not merely a matter of reopening consulates abroad, resuming foreign trade relations, or being invited to join international organizations again. Nor, given their symbolic value, were the negotiations for the return of captured records just another foreign policy issue for the new Federal Republic. Among the captured records were the archives of the Auswärtiges Amt, which included materials dating back to the 1860s. They embodied the history of a once fully sovereign foreign policy. Regaining those records amounted to an attempt at regaining that lost sovereignty as well. In the microcosm of the re-established Auswärtiges Amt of the Federal Republic, the capture and continuing absence of the diplomatic records was an emotionally charged subject – all the more because its very own records had been used against the foreign ministry at the American "Ministries Trial" at Nuremberg. This devastating evidence was still in Allied hands in the early 1950s.

The files did not only represent sovereignty in the eyes of German officials; they also contained history. Not thought of solely as administrative paperwork necessary to rebuild the government bureaucracy, these records constituted the historical source material necessary to (re)write recent German history. Discussion about their return thus moved to another level: at stake suddenly was nothing less than the power to interpret German history. Who would write the first draft of "Germany under National Socialism" based on the original sources? The question of access to the captured records, especially the diplomatic files, fueled a debate over who could legitimately interpret Germany's disastrous course during the first half of the twentieth century. For the Germans, this issue was linked to the discussion of whether their national history was irreversibly tainted and of the place of National Socialism in the continuum of German history. The struggle over the records thus merged with the "rapidly growing need for historical self-assurance," in the new Federal Republic.[1]

For their part, the Allies too were keenly aware of the fact that new assessments of German history, including the origins of National Socialism, could be decisively influenced by possession of the relevant source material. British and American historians showed this awareness just as much as the political authorities. Clearly, historical interpretation was as central to the negotiations as the materiality of the files themselves. This study argues that the captured German documents played an important role for historical study in West Germany, Great Britain, and the United States. The establishment of contemporary history as a field of research in West Germany as well as in Britain and the United States was closely related to the relatively early accessibility of the captured German records, if "early" is considered in relation to state records under more typical thirty- or fifty-year rules.[2]

The main players in these negotiations were the Federal Republic of Germany and the governments of Great Britain and the United States. The French government took part in the talks as well but only because they were conducted within the framework of the Allied High Commission, of which France was undeniably a part. The U.S. State Department considered the participation of the French merely a formality, however, and a burdensome one at that. Although a French representative warmed a seat at each meeting with the West Germans and duly put a signature on the diplomatic notes, the French were not involved in drawing up the British-American agreements, nor were they privy to the many British-American disagreements on the matter. Their relegation to the position of a "junior partner" in this issue stemmed from the fact that the French themselves had not confiscated a substantial quantity of German records at war's end. What they did seize pertained mostly to the German occupation of France.[3] These spoils, however, were not enough of a pawn to obtain for the French an equal role in the negotiations, a fact that is reflected in the coverage of this book.

---

1 Jessen, "Zeithistoriker im Konfliktfeld der Vergangenheitspolitik," 153.
2 See also Eckert, "Transnational Beginnings of West German *Zeitgeschichte*."
3 Martens, "Frankreich und Belgien unter deutscher Besatzung und das Schicksal der deutschen Akten nach dem Zweiten Weltkrieg." Parts of the so-called Goebbels Diaries did end up in French hands – an exception to the rule that the French did not capture any highly important political documents. See Eckert/Martens, "Glasplatten im märkischen Sand."

American and British interests in the German records were as diverse as
the various government agencies holding them. The State Department took
a pragmatic approach to the issue of return in 1950, initiating a preliminary
survey to determine which agencies were in possession of German records.
Its generally supportive attitude toward document return was briefly affected
by the outbreak of the Korean War, which spurred a renewed interest in
German military records thought to hold vital information on the Red
Army. By autumn 1952, however, the State Department could point to a
policy paper that advocated, in principle, the return of the records to West
Germany. Yet both the American and the British governments had publicly
committed themselves to publishing a scholarly edition of selected documents on German foreign policy. This slow-paced endeavor put a check
on their flexibility in returning German diplomatic records. The British
government was hampered by even more impediments. Its Foreign Office
transferred jurisdiction on the matter to an interagency committee, which
was tasked to draft a return policy. The committee soon represented all the
departments that had an interest in retaining the records. It cited concerns
that British intelligence interests could become compromised; that domestic industries would lose access to German patents and research materials;
that German naval strategy documents, if they fell into the wrong hands,
remained a credible threat to British security; or, most bluntly, that the Germans had unleashed and lost the war and had to live with the consequences.
As the Foreign Office adopted an increasingly friendly and supportive policy toward West Germany, its new Cold War ally, a constructive solution to
the issue of captured German records was threatened less by the perceived
German presumptuousness than by obstruction in its own government
bureaucracy.

Only slowly growing aware of the complexities on the other side, officials
in Bonn at first considered the issue of document return to be no more
than a logistical problem.[4] West German diplomats could not imagine that
they were about to embark on a long and, at times, frustrating series of
negotiations with the Western Allies on a problem that could, perhaps
even should, have been peripheral to their relations. Had the British and
the Americans returned the records quickly, the matter would indeed have
been merely an organizational task, a footnote in diplomatic as well as
archival history. Yet the transfer of significant amounts of records only

---

4 Hanns-Erich Haack, [notes] re. Akten des ehemaligen Auswärtigen Amtes, Feb. 1, 1951, in PA/AA,
    B118, vol. 28. In this memo, the director of the archive at the new German foreign office is already
    contemplating specific possibilities for the future housing of diplomatic records, which he fully
    expected to be returned in the near future.

began eleven years after the end of the war. The diplomatic files of the pre-1945 Auswärtiges Amt were returned to Bonn between 1956 and 1958. The shipment of military documents from Washington began in 1958, with major deliveries continuing until 1968 and beyond. The arduousness of the negotiations over the return of records – mirrored in a long succession of inconclusive talks – stands out all the more because it took place in a period commonly characterized by successful and constructive German-Allied cooperation in areas such as security, commerce, the settlement of war debts, and the overall status of the Federal Republic. The delay in returning the records indicates just how strong the interests of all parties in these documents actually were. Uncovering these specific interests in the various and changing contexts attached to the negotiations is one goal of this study. Tracing these interests sheds light on power relations among the players involved and reveals much about the players themselves.

This study is neither an analysis of sources on a key period of German history nor a compilation of profiles of source material found in prominent archives. Since I published this study in German, I have regularly received e-mails with queries about the whereabouts of specific documents or files. What happened to Mussolini's private files after he was shot? Where are certain records of Army Group Center dating from 1941–42? Did the papers of the Historical Division of the German Army make it through the war? Readers expecting a catalog of locations of specific document collections or a series of accounts of their fates will come away disappointed.[5] Except in a few cases, I distinguish the captured records in this study only in general terms such as "diplomatic" and "military" records. This corresponds with the distinction applied by the actors at the time, above all in the correspondence of the foreign ministries. It was sufficient at the time to communicate on the political level which documents were then being discussed, and it suffices here for the examination of those negotiations. The issue of the return of captured German records was most intense during the 1950s, and the negotiations are being presented here along chronological lines.

The study opens with a look at Anglo-American plans for confiscating German records. This planning was accompanied – one could even say initiated – by the activities of British and American archivists who worked to raise awareness among the military of the value of archives and to secure the protection of such collections in war-torn areas. Even before victory in

---

5 Tracing the itinerary of particular documents or stacks of records can be highly illuminating and is at times quintessential to assessing the value of a source. See, for example, Grimsted, "Odyssey of the Smolensk Archive," parts I–III; Smith, "Hoßbach-Niederschrift"; Reynolds, "Fritsch-Brief."

Europe was achieved, British and American authorities in the Army and the
foreign ministries had already concluded agreements on archives that would
influence later discussions on the return of the archives to German possession. These well-intentioned plans for the confiscation and preservation of
archives were submitted to a hard test at war's end, however. The advancing
troops had other priorities than protecting archives, a multitude of Allied
civilian and military agencies competed for their share of German records
for various intelligence needs, and budding mistrust of Soviet intentions
propelled the British and Americans to whisk their finds away, out of the
Red Army's reach. Allied competition for the prime trophies among German records is thrown into stark relief in the case of the Auswärtiges Amt
files recounted at the opening of this introduction. At the price of diplomatic strain, the British Foreign Office and the American State Department
made sure to secure this collection for themselves, soon turning it into a
political weapon in the early Cold War blame-game.

The second chapter examines the context of the initial German demands
for restitution in 1949. Professional archivists were again the first to flag the
issue, this time on the German side. These archivists were in a peculiar
situation: those at the newly founded federal archives, the Bundesarchiv,
and the Political Archives of the refounded Auswärtiges Amt presided over
nearly empty stacks. The return of captured German records was thus
of vital importance to them. As the potential recipients of the returning
records, they followed the matter closely, frequently injecting their views
into the official negotiations. A closer examination of the new beginnings
of the German archival profession after 1945 reveals, however, that the
same archivists accusing the Western Allies of breaking international law by
retaining German records had played a role in the German spoliation efforts
in countries under German occupation during the war. The tension arising
from a past strategically blocked out by some of the archivists presented here
gives their part in the negotiations a particular savor. West German efforts
were eventually answered with an Allied compromise offer for a piecemeal
return of records, which Bonn rejected, sending the negotiations back to
square one. Chapter 2 thus provides analysis not just of the early negotiations
over return, but also of the early history of the archival profession in the
Federal Republic and the related question – so central in so many avenues
of life in postwar Germany – of the continuity between the Nazi years and
the early Federal Republic.

While the West Germans presented their demands, the American and
British governments coordinated their interests. The third chapter shows
how during this same time period the British and Americans eventually

came to agree on a common position regarding the return of German records following a drawn-out process of consensus-seeking that was often hindered by colliding objectives. The fourth chapter deals briefly with the legal status of the confiscated records, an issue that was a constant undertone in the negotiations. The intention here is not to determine which party advocated the "correct" interpretation of international law but to demonstrate the way in which legal arguments were used as political leverage. The focus then shifts to the negotiations proper: first to those over diplomatic records and then to the subsequent talks on military and Nazi Party records. That the Allies agreed to tackle the records of the former German Auswärtiges Amt first reflected the situation on the ground: the U.S. State Department and the British Foreign Office had these files under their own immediate jurisdiction and were therefore in a position to negotiate their return. Other documents were held by military departments where resistance to the entire return issue was at first stronger. Out of consideration for their own military establishments, the American and British diplomats had to postpone talks on these materials as long as possible.

The final chapter focuses on the historiographical dimensions of the captured German records for the community of professional historians in West Germany, Great Britain, and the United States. Bruised by the efforts of the Weimar Republic to use scholarship to refute the accusation that Germany bore responsibility for World War I, the Western Allies decided to undercut even the possibility that a new (West) German government might try to incite a similar debate about the German invasion of Poland and the beginning of World War II. A select group of British, American, and French historians converged on the English country manor Whaddon Hall to compile the multivolume publication *Documents on German Foreign Policy*, which chronicled the foreign relations of the Third Reich. The West German press decried the publication of the German diplomatic records abroad without the participation of German scholars as an extension of Allied re-education efforts. German scholars decried their exclusion as well, not only in the case of diplomatic records but also in regard to the vast microfilming project of captured German documents that got off the ground in the United States in 1955. Before any records in American custody were returned, a group of American historians secured the funds to film them in order to ensure their continued availability for research. These efforts were fueled not only by the prospects of research convenience but also by a more or less latent mistrust toward German assurances that the records, once returned, would be made accessible for scholars from Germany and abroad.

The history of the captured German records and their eventual return has for a long time been the insider knowledge of historians and archivists who had worked directly with those documents over the years. German archivists tried soon after the war to determine the fate of well-known archival institutions or specific inventories.[6] A great deal was learned in the early 1950s through information supplied by Americans on the administration of confiscated documents in the United States.[7] The return of the Auswärtiges Amt archive in the late 1950s, and the first deliveries of military and Nazi Party papers to the Bundesarchiv in Koblenz in the 1960s generated some more accounts of the matter.[8] The American perspective was presented for the first time at a conference hosted by the National Archives in 1968. The participants included archivists and scholars who had been involved with the administration and use of the German records in some capacity. The proceedings were edited by Robert Wolfe, a former archivist with the German records staff at the National Archives, and published in 1974.[9] Particularly illuminating are the contributions by Seymour J. Pomrenze and Herman Goldbeck. Both men were members of the Adjutant General's Office of the U.S. Army, the agency that administered the bulk of German military records until 1958. Based on their own internal files from the 1950s, they offered a summary of the policies guiding the handling of the records.[10] In a series of articles, Robert Wolfe later expanded on the topic of German records in United States custody.[11]

---

6 Benninghoven, "Reichs- und preußische Behördenüberlieferung"; Heinsius, "Aktenmaterial der deutschen Kriegsmarine"; Poll, "Schicksal der deutschen Heeresakten"; Rohr, "Schriftgut der obersten Reichsbehörden."

7 Epstein, "Zur Quellenkunde der neuesten Geschichte," which appeared in the *Vierteljahrshefte* of 1954. The first published guide in the United States – the 1952 *Guide to Captured German Records* compiled by Gerhard L. Weinberg und Fritz T. Epstein – only listed material that was available in research institutions and excluded German military documents held by the U.S. Army, which at the time were still listed as classified information. In 1959, the American Historical Association (AHA) published a supplement. See also Humphrey, "Microfilm Holdings of the Department of State"; Kempner, "Nuremberg Trials as Sources."

8 Philippi, "Politisches Archiv I, II"; Boberach, "Schriftgut der staatlichen Verwaltung;" Boberach, "Schriftliche Überlieferung"; Booms, "Bundesarchiv," 20–5; Kahlenberg, *Archive in West und Ost*, 27–30, 57, 137.

9 Wolfe, *Captured German Records*. See most recently Weinberg, "German Documents in the United States," 555–67.

10 In preparation for his essay, Pomrenze compiled a numerically listed collection of the material that can be found today in NA RG 242 (Collection of Foreign Records Seized): AGAR-S Record Series. Selected Documents Concerning the Conference on Captured German and Related Records. [Numerically] Compiled by Seymour J. Pomrenze. The collection contains only copies, no originals. It is, however, a useful introduction to this topic even though the provenance of certain documents is no longer discernible. I cite the series as NA RG 242, AGAR-S and the document number.

11 Wolfe, "Exploitation of Captured German Records"; Wolfe, "Sharing Records of Mutual Archival Concern"; Wolfe, "Short History."

Even as the years passed, the history of the captured German archives seemed to remain of interest primarily to those who dealt with records professionally. Studies of German historical scholarship have noted the absence of the captured records during the 1950s, but they usually do so only in passing or without full understanding of the Allies' intentions or of the details of the return agreements.[12] It was again a professional archivist who, in 1982, provided the first concise account of the history of the captured German records. Josef Henke of Bundesarchiv in Koblenz based his essay on the internal files of that institution and reconstructed part of the negotiations for the first time.[13] Other articles on the planning for the confiscation of records from the British perspective and on the fate of the Auswärtiges Amt archives later supplemented Henke's account.[14] The American wartime planning for the seizure of German archives and their initial evaluation features prominently in the fine study on "document diplomacy" by the Swiss historian Sacha Zala. In his book, Zala compares the politics of governmental document editions in various European countries and the United States, beginning with the Color Books of the First World War.[15]

Although the number of studies directly addressing an aspect of the history of the captured German records remained rather limited when this book was being researched, I could nonetheless turn to other bodies of literature for inspiration. This study has benefited from the remarkable increase of research published during the 1990s and later, on the confiscation of art

---

12 Benz, "Etablierung der Zeitgeschichte," 19; Conrad, *Verlorene Nation*, 228; Cornelißen, *Ritter*, 535; Kleßmann, *Zeitgeschichte in Deutschland*, 11f.; Kleßmann/Sabrow, "Zeitgeschichte in Deutschland nach 1989," 3; Kwiet, "NS-Zeit," 186; Schulze, *Deutsche Geschichtswissenschaft*, 238. Auerbach, "Gründung des Instituts," 535, attributes the duration of the return negotiations to the egoism of American historians who wanted to publish their own source-based studies before allowing Germans access to the records. On the other hand, Hockerts, "Zeitgeschichte," 12, writes that "shortly after the end of the Nazi regime, large amounts of its written communication were available to researchers." Similarly Schwarz, "Neueste Zeitgeschichte," 23f. However, no member of the Institute for Contemporary History, such as Auerbach, would have shared this view in the 1950s or early 1960s. On the contrary, the IfZ staff felt excluded from the sources for many years. Schöllgen, *Außenpolitik*, 10, gives the impression that the Auswärtiges Amt was able to "obtain nearly [its] entire archive, practically intact, from the Allied victors again," as if this had been a self-evident occurrence.

13 Henke, "Schicksal deutscher Quellen." See also Oldenhage, "Schicksal deutscher zeitgeschichtlicher Quellen."

14 Kaiser-Lahme, "Westalliierte Archivpolitik"; Kröger/Thimme, "Politisches Archiv"; Thimme, "Politisches Archiv." The third essay here addresses the origins of the quadripartite edition *Akten zur Deutschen Auswärtigen Politik* (ADAP) under German auspices. Roland Thimme was a former member of the ADAP staff. Roth, "Hans Rothfels," 70, note 99, calls Thimme's assessment of the ADAP years a "semi-official account" ("behördenoffiziöse Darstellung"), which is not correct but seeks to capture the tone and spirit of Thimme's article.

15 Zala, *Zensur*. Zala deserves credit for having pried loose the files of the State Department's Historical Office through a request under the Freedom of Information Act. These files benefited my work greatly.

and cultural goods during the World War II, and on the postwar restitution efforts.[16] Such studies have painstakingly reconstructed the German looting operations in occupied countries, especially the systematic expropriation of Jewish art collections before the deportation of their owners. Almost as an aside, such studies have touched on the role of German archivists in the administration of occupied countries. Cultural plunder might not have been their main activity, but some of them became deeply entangled in the pursuit of spoils of war. Some scholars subsequently set out to explore the roles of archivists during the war in more detail, producing studies that provided the springboard essential for this book to address the postwar history of the German archival profession.[17] It is this part of my work that seems to have had an immediate impact, in that the German Archival Association decided to make the wartime and postwar history of their profession the focus of its annual gathering in 2005.[18]

The subject of captured German records remains of contemporary relevance. The initial postwar negotiations on their return came only to a temporary halt in the late 1960s. Inventories, either microfilmed or as originals, are still being returned sporadically to Germany from Great Britain and the United States.[19] With the fall of the Berlin Wall, the opportunity arose for the first time to learn more about archival and other cultural treasures confiscated by the Red Army.[20] Sensational reports about secret police

---

16 Eichwede/Hartung, *NS-Kunstraub*; Freitag, "Restitution von NS-Beutegut"; Kurtz, *Nazi Contraband*; Nicholas, *Rape of Europa*; Petropoulos, *Faustian Bargain*; Simpson, *Spoils of War*; Volkert, *Kunst- und Kulturraub im Zweiten Weltkrieg*.

17 Kleßmann, *Selbstbehauptung einer Nation*, was one of the first to highlight German archival policy in the General Government as part of the German "cultural policy" in occupied territories. Also Umbreit, "Kontinentalherrschaft," 309–20. Specifically on archivists and archival plunder Heuss, "'Beuteorganisation'"; Kißmehl, "Kriegswichtige Zielobjekte"; Musial, *Staatsarchive im Dritten Reich*; Roth, "Klios rabiate Hilfstruppen"; Roth, "Höhere Form des Plünderns"; Stein, "Inventarisierung von Quellen." A few authors have traced the fate of specific collections from the war years, beyond the political turning point of 1945, and into the present. See Lenz, "Verlagerung des Revaler Stadtarchivs"; Grimsted, "Twice Plundered"; Grimsted, "Odyssey of the Smolensk Archives"; Grimsted, "Roads to Ratibor"; Schroll, "Spurensicherung."

18 Kretzschmar/Eckert/Schmitt/Speck/Wisotzky, *Deutsche Archivwesen und der Nationalsozialismus*.

19 For example, the British government sent German submarine documents to the Federal Archives in 1977 and German air force records in 1981. In 1994, the Berlin Document Center was transferred from American to German custody. In November 2001, the Federal and Military Archive in Freiburg received a substantial number of military situation maps from the National Archives that once belonged to the Wehrmacht command. In the spring of 2004, the National Archives returned documents from the Reich Weather Service. See Boberach, "Schriftliche Überlieferung," 56–8; Gießler, "Archivalienrückführung," 65–7; Henke, "Schicksal deutscher Quellen," 557–620, esp. 595–600; and Krüger, "Archiv im Spannungsfeld," 57.

20 Aly/Heim, *Zentrales Sonderarchiv*; Browder, "Osoby (Special) Archive"; Browder, "Update on Captured Documents"; Jena/Lenz, "Sonderarchiv Moskau"; Wegner, "Moskauer Zentrales Staatsarchiv"; Zarusky, "Russische Archivsituation."

files,[21] music scores,[22] personal papers, and other records long believed lost once again reminded the world of the scars in the archival and cultural landscape left behind by plunder and counter-plunder during the Second World War. Although documents have been seized and destroyed during war and regime changes for centuries,[23] the phenomenon took on new dimensions both quantitatively and qualitatively in the twentieth century, specifically during World War II. To rectify the situation through restitution, archival exchanges, microfilming, and access guarantees is, as one German archivist has correctly pointed out, a task that remains both unfinished and urgent.[24]

In the meantime, speculation about the content of German records that may still be locked away in British and American vaults does not die away, and at irregular intervals, attempts to recover important documents sunk or buried by the National Socialists make the news.[25] That the theft of documents, and hence the appropriation of knowledge that is vital to power and sovereignty, is not a thing of the past has been exemplified for the German context by the CIA "Operation Rosewood" of 1989–90. In this case, microfilms of the most important personnel files from the espionage department of the East German Ministry for State Security mysteriously made their way into the hands of the CIA and were not returned to the Federal Republic until 2003.[26] While the nature of the records and archives that were stolen over the centuries during war and conquest might change, the general implications of such exploits do not: the theft of records

---

21 The SD (Sicherheitsdienst) and the Security Police (Sicherheitspolizei), directed by Amt IV D (Occupied Territories) of the Reich Security Main Office, captured sizable inventories from the Deuxième Bureau and the Sureté Nationale in France, which fell into the hands of the Red Army at the end of the war. Most of these records were returned to France between 1991 and 1994 and a few more again in October 2000. See Grimsted, "Twice Plundered," 215–18; and Grimsted, *Trophies of War and Empire*, 296–9.

22 Brigitte Schulze, "J. S. Bach im Ost-West-Konflikt," *Süddeutsche Zeitung*, Jan. 28, 2000; Christoph Wolff, "Der Bach-Fund in Kiew," *Tagesspiegel*, Sept. 10, 2000 [Sonderbeilage American Academy]; Gail Fineberg, "Bachs Are Back: Family's Scores Found," *The Gazette* [Library of Congress], July 14, 2000, 6f.; Grimsted, *Trophies of War and Empire*, 270–7.

23 Posner, *Records under Military Occupation*; Stein, *Archive als Objekt von Kulturimperialismen*, 89f.; Zala, *Zensur*, 47f., 144–7. With regard to artwork, see Greenfield, "The Spoils of War."

24 Jena, "Rückführung deutscher Akten aus Russland."

25 The fascination with lost records might explain one underwater expedition to search for alleged sunken Nazi material: Walter Mayr, "Mehr als Fische und Falschgeld," *Der Spiegel*, Jan. 17, 2000; Karin Kneissl and Thomas Delekat, "Das letzte Geheimnis des Tolpitzsees," *Die Welt*, Jan 28, 2000; Ulrich Glauber, "Der 'Nazi Schatz' im Alpensee," *Frankfurter Rundschau*, July 10, 2000; Stefan Koldehoff, "Bei Mutti unterm Sofa. Handschriftliches Nazi-Dokument in den USA aufgetaucht," *Süddeutsche Zeitung*, March 20, 2004.

26 Helmut Müller-Enbergs: *"Rosenholz" – Eine Quellenkritik*, ed. by The Office of the Federal Commissioner, BStU (Series BF Informiert Nr. 28) available at http://www.bstu.bund.de/DE/Wissen/Aktenfunde/Rosenholz/rosenholz_inhalt.html (accessed August 2011).

empowers the thief and humiliates the victim.[27] Demands for return of records, archives, and other cultural artifacts are therefore always an emotional matter, too, as the ensuing pages should make amply clear.

For sixty years now, scholars have drawn on the documents and archives once collectively known as the captured German records to research aspects of German history from the Imperial period until the end of the World War II. Users of archives do not necessarily busy themselves with the history of the files they read when they research the history of something else. Yet whether citing the English or German edition of the *Documents on German Foreign Policy*, using the many T-rolls of microfilm at the National Archives in College Park, or traveling to examine the returned originals at the Bundesarchiv and the Political Archives of the Auswärtiges Amt, it is important to know that these files also have a postwar history, a "biography," in their own right. They stand for an unprecedented situation in which the "documentary materials covering all aspects of a nation's life during a whole era" had fallen into the hands of its wartime enemies. They remind us of the fact that it is not always the archive that shapes history but that history can come over the archive.[28] To think about the history of the files when writing history adds another layer to our complex task as historians.

27 This point is made, in connection with art theft, by Alexander Demandt, *Vandalismus: Gewalt gegen Kultur*, 43.
28 Quote in Perman, "Microfilming," 433; Fritzsche, "The Archive," 16.

1

The Confiscation of German Documents, 1944–1949

ALLIED PLANNING AND PREPARATION FOR CONFISCATING RECORDS AND PROTECTING ARCHIVES

Preparations for the confiscation and protection of German archives and active files were part of Allied planning for the invasion and military occupation of Germany. The importance of particular sets of records evolved in step with major political decisions about Germany's future. Until the fall of 1944, American officials had assumed the Third Reich would collapse militarily but its administrative structures would remain more or less intact. Accordingly, they believed that it would be possible to govern Germany indirectly through existing structures and that relatively few American troops would be needed for the occupation. As that assumption became increasingly untenable, the Allied leadership made the political decision to place the entire country under direct military rule.[1] With this change in plans, routine administrative records immediately became important because the American military government would fully replace German administrative structures. Similarly, once the Allies agreed to conduct war crimes trials, a variety of governmental and Nazi party records became of interest as potential evidence. The plan to denazify large numbers of Germans was another policy decision that cast a spotlight on German documents and records. Personnel records of all kinds would be decisive in reconstructing individuals' careers and actions during the years of Nazi rule.

The way the German records were treated as the Allied invasion progressed was governed by a mix of previously decided policy, ad hoc

---

1 Henke, *Amerikanische Besetzung*, 98–100, 109f.

decisions, and improvisation.[2] In turn, the initial experience of dealing with large quantities of captured records and safeguarding historical archives influenced the planning process. In close but not always frictionless cooperation, the British and Americans prepared to confiscate German records and evaluate them for intelligence purposes as well as to protect historical archives in the war-torn areas. Although the French were also keenly interested in the German records, the British and Americans did not include them in this planning.[3] The planning for the seizure of German records and archival material began in Washington and only slowly became at least somewhat coordinated. A number of American civil and military agencies and institutions independently defined their sometimes opposing interests in the German records. A report commissioned by the U.S. Army dated November 1947 lists no fewer than 121 Western Allied agencies and offices dealing with the captured records between 1944 and 1947.[4] The British often despaired when they looked to Washington, where wartime offices and agencies mushroomed and policy-making processes were difficult to comprehend.[5] The problem was not a lack of planning but rather a lack of coordination.

The British and American document hunters who followed on the heels of the invading armies remained dependent on the support of the Allied high command, the Supreme Headquarters Allied Expeditionary Forces (SHAEF), and later the military government. Only accredited officials were permitted to collect, evacuate, or confiscate archival materials and government documents. Combat objectives and troop safety took priority over seizing or safeguarding archives, however. The agreements that the Americans and British concluded during the closing phase of the war would play important roles years later in the negotiations on the return of captured documents. This chapter explains the planning and different interests of a select number of American and British institutions and traces the key developments concerning the documents until the eve of the first German call for their return.

---

2 Other accounts ascribe much coherence and systematic organization to the phase of planning and confiscation. See, for example, Pomrenze, "Protection, Use, and Return," 7–14; Kaiser-Lahme, "Westalliierte Archivpolitik"; Zala, *Zensur*, 163, 198, who also emphasizes the rivalry among various institutions.

3 Martens, "Schicksal der deutschen Akten."

4 Seymour J. Pomrenze, Archivist, to Director, Office of Records Control, Subject: Captured Records in Germany and Austria, Nov. 25, 1947, NA RG 242, AGAR–S no. 706, box 2. Ninety-one of these 121 listed agencies, offices, and departments were strictly American.

5 Kettenacker, *Krieg zur Friedenssicherung*, 242. Britain, too, saw a complicated system of ad hoc groups evolve during the war. Yet in comparison, these groups remained more closely tied to established administrative structures than did those in Washington. See Reusch, "Londoner Institutionen."

Civilian Preparations to Protect Archives in War Areas

Professional archivists, not military planners, were the first to ponder the issue of the German records. They were not interested in the intelligence value of these materials; their concern, rather, was to protect archives from destruction. A lecture by the archivist Ernst Posner in May 1943 triggered the initial discussion among American officials of the protection of archival material in war zones. Posner, one of the few Jewish archivists at the Prussian Archival Administration (Preußische Archivverwaltung) before the Nazis came to power, had fled Germany via Sweden to the United States in 1939 and found a new home in Washington.[6] Had he concentrated on only the historical value of archival materials in his lecture, his message would never have been heard outside of professional circles. Posner underscored, however, the potential utility of government documents to an occupying force: such records could become the key to a successful occupation under either direct or indirect rule. "The great importance of the records becomes fully evident, if, where the native authorities have fled or offer passive resistance, their archives, too, are unavailable to the invader," he observed. German occupation forces had acted with this point in mind during the war. The rapid seizure of documents and archives facilitated German rule and economic exploitation of the occupied countries.[7] Posner's argument became increasingly pertinent as Allied troops fought their way toward Germany and planning for the postwar occupation of the country progressed.

The archivists of the U.S. National Archives and the British Public Record Office were well aware of what the destruction of archives might mean. Solon J. Buck, Archivist of the United States, described the daunting task in Italy:

Not only property rights but human rights are involved, and evidence of citizenship, birth, and family relationships are necessary to restore them. The people of Italy have been deprived of full knowledge of what has been going on under the Fascist

6 Ernst Posner (1892–1980) was an archivist at the Prussian Privy State Archives (Preußisches Geheimes Staatsarchiv) in Berlin from 1921 to 1935. He was suspended in October 1935 following the passage in September of the Nuremberg Laws. He continued his research work on the *Acta Borussica* for the Prussian Academy of Science until 1938. Following the a six-week internment in Sachsenhausen concentration camp in the wake of the 1938 November pogrom, he managed to flee Germany to the United States by way of Sweden in January 1939. Thanks to his good academic contacts, he became a lecturer at American University that very same year. By 1940, he was assistant professor and by 1945, full professor. At the same time, he was recruited as an advisor for the National Archives, the Roberts Commission, and the State Department. Posner became an American citizen in 1944. See Giesecke, *Ernst Posner*, 12–14. See also Posner's own account of his career in the *National Archives Oral History Project: Statement Dictated and Written by Ernst Posner, October-December 1973*. I thank Dr. Gabriela Eakin-Thimme for this source.

7 The lecture was published as Posner, "Public Records under Military Occupation," quote on 223.

regime. If there is ever to be a re-education of the people, it can only be done through preservation of the records of the true actions of this regime.... The destruction of the evidence will only encourage a mythology. It seems to me that the Germans have been very systematic in their handling of the records of occupied countries.... They are keenly aware of the fact that loss of essential records in a modern industrialized country results in a far-reaching paralysis of its life, which serves the enemy's ends. Even when a war is over, a country may recover only partially from this paralysis and complete recovery, if it is attained, is a matter of years and possibly generations.[8]

British and American archival experts found it easier to cooperate with one another than with their respective militaries. Efforts to protect archival materials were not necessarily compatible with military objectives. Archivists tried repeatedly to explain to intelligence officers that a professionally organized archive lost its value the moment its finding aids were destroyed or the files were mixed up, even if not a single sheet of paper were destroyed. Hilary Jenkinson, head archivist in the Public Record Office in London, despaired over the ignorant zeal of the intelligence officers: "Any experienced Archivist should have been able to say what would result if uninstructed officers and other exploiters, each acting solely in his own sectional interest, were allowed unrestricted and uncontrolled access to Archives."[9] But so long as there was a war on, combat operations and the retrieval of militarily relevant information took priority over the integrity of archives and active files.

"Looking for what was salvageable": Early Attempts to Protect Archives. Ernst Posner's May 1943 lecture did not go unnoticed. Among those in the audience was Fred W. Shipman, the director of the Franklin D. Roosevelt Library in Hyde Park, New York. Engaged with the preservation of FDR's legacy, a matter close to Roosevelt's heart, Shipman enjoyed direct access to the president. Two days after receiving a summary of Posner's lecture from Shipman, Roosevelt read it aloud in a cabinet meeting and ordered that all necessary preparations be made.[10] Shipman's personal connection to the president opened several doors to archivists.[11] Their main task in

---

8 Buck to Capt. William D. McCain, Historian, 5th Army, July 24, 1944, NA RG 242, AGAR–S no. 229, box 1.

9 Hilary Jenkinson, Adviser on Archives, War Office, London, to Lt. Col. Sir Leonard Woolley, Archaeological Adviser, Memorandum [on] The Present Situation in regard to Modern German Archives, July 1945, in LoCM box 31. See also Bell/Jenkinson, *Italian Archives*, 18, 21f.

10 See Holmes, "National Archives and the Protection of Records," 110f.; Poste, *Development of U.S. Protection of Libraries and Archives*, 165f.

11 Gen. J. H. Hilldring, director of the Civil Affairs Division at the War Department, considered Shipman to be an "unofficial adviser to the President on the acquisition, use and disposition of archives and records" and therefore treated his inquiries with priority. See Hilldring to Maj. Gen.

mid-1943 was to contact other working groups dealing with the protection of cultural treasures in war zones. The American Council of Learned Societies had set up a working group on the issue in January 1943. The American Defense Harvard Group independently began to compile information on historic monuments and works of art in Italy with the aim of presenting the War Department with lists of objects deserving protection. The most important organization dealing with the issue of cultural properties was the American Committee for the Protection and Salvage of Artistic and Historic Monuments in War Areas, commonly called the Roberts Commission after its chairman, Supreme Court Justice Owen J. Roberts. This commission had been established in 1942 by a group of museum directors, archaeologists, art historians, and politicians to offer their expertise to the war effort. With the support of both the State Department and the War Department, the Roberts Commission became a clearinghouse for information on art protection issues. It had a major input on the development of a concept for the Monuments, Fine Arts, and Archives (MFAA) division, a unit that was integrated into the occupation government and tasked with the protection and restitution of European cultural properties.[12]

Despite such efforts, no precautionary measures to protect historical archival materials and active files had been taken by the summer of 1943. Working at full speed, archivists at the National Archives compiled information on archives in Italy.[13] The information arrived too late, however, to be of use during the Sicily offensive that began on July 10, 1943.[14] Only after southern Italy was firmly under Allied control did an MFAA sub-commission begin its work. Thanks to the lobbying of a number of civilian committees, protecting art works and cultural monuments effectively became a war goal by the autumn of 1943. A Civil Affairs Guide published by the War Department explained that the work of MFAA was "part of the objective of this war, which is to preserve our civilization

Clayton Bissell, ACoS, G-2, Feb. 15, 1945, NA RG 218, Records of the JCS, CDF 1942–45, entry 1, box 125.

12 On the formation and work of these various groups, see Hammond, "Protection," 86–88; Poste, *Development of U.S. Protection of Libraries and Archives*, 78–96; focusing on the Allied protection of artwork are Nicholas, *Rape of Europa*, 209–27; Freitag, *Restitution von NS-Beutegut*, 170–2; see also Coles/Weinberg, *Soldiers Become Governors*, 84–90; Roberts Commission, *Report of the American Commission for the Protection and Salvage of Artistic and Historic Monuments in War Areas* (Washington, D.C.: GPO 1946), 1–5, passim.

13 Holmes, "National Archives and the Protection of Records," 112f., Roberts Commission, *Report*, 41f.

14 See Ziemke, *U.S. Army in the Occupation of Germany*, 54: "The Italian campaign . . . had revealed the military commanders to be distinctly unwilling to risk tactical advantage or the lives or welfare of their troops to protect cultural intangibles."

from destruction."[15] At the National Archives, efforts were made to better prepare for later military operations. The archivists drew up lists of archives in areas where combat was expected. Ernst Posner's expertise was in particular demand, not least his personal familiarity with the leading figures in the German archival profession. He helped in the preparation of a number of War Department publications on German public administration and archival practices.[16] He also compiled an evaluation of German archivists that assessed his former colleagues' professional competence and, more importantly, political views.[17]

Just as important as the availability of expertise was the deployment of trained archivists to combat zones. At the end of October 1943, the Allied headquarters in Algiers requested an archivist from the United States and one from Great Britain.[18] Finding a suitable candidate proved more difficult than expected. In January 1944, the National Archives nominated Fred Shipman.[19] Shipman was discouraged by the situation he found when he arrived in Algeria in late March: "The greatest danger to records occurs in the first days after the fighting. Then the intelligence agent seizes documents, the troops are billeted in records buildings, and the populace pilfers." Because there was not enough microfilm equipment available, intelligence agents tore collections apart, Shipman reported, "and hurried [files] off to their home offices without giving all other interested parties an opportunity to see them." He also noted, critically, that there was not a single archivist among the members of the MFAA sub-commission, which, he complained, was "the product of the minds of museum experts."[20] Hilary Jenkinson, Shipman's British counterpart, arrived in Algiers at about the same time. He temporarily solved the problem of the lack of archival expertise in MFAA

---

15 Civil Affairs Information Guide. Field Protection of Objects of Art and Archives. War Department Pamphlet no. 31–103, May 12, 1944, 1. The MFAA subcommission was located in the Civil Affairs Division of the Allied Military Government of Allied Territories (AMGOT) and later at the Chief of Staff of the Supreme Allied Commander (COSSAC).

16 Ibid.; see also, Preservation and Use of Key Records in Germany. War Dept. Pamphlet no. 31–123; Archival Repositories in Germany. War Dept. Pamphlet no. 31–180; Posner is the author of the Military Government Information Guide. Information on German Records. War Dept. Pamphlet no. 31–217, Feb. 3, 1945.

17 Posner, Biographical Data on 72 German Archivists Functioning in Germany, Austria, and Various Occupied Countries, no date [November 1944], in PRO FO 1050/1406. Originally the list was compiled for the Council of Learned Societies, but was also sent to the State Department and the OSS. See Posner to Lt. Raymond Deston, Chief, Central Information Division, OSS, Nov. 30, 1944, in NA RG 200, Posner Papers, box 4.

18 Coles/Weinberg, *Soldiers Become Governors,* 88f.

19 Shipman, Memorandum for the President, Jan. 6, 1944, in FDRL OF 221, Folder Archivist of the United States, 1944–45.

20 Shipman, Memorandum for the President, Sept. 12, 1944, in ibid.

by delegating two British officers to serve in that division.[21] The British and American archivists differed in their priorities, however. Whereas the British were primarily interested in historical archives, Shipman wanted to see current registries protected as well. But he had to return to the United States in May 1944, and not until months later was an American archivist finally dispatched to replace him.[22] The Italian offensive had revealed the limited reach of MFAA. The archivists' preparations for archival protection had begun too late. The officers responsible for historical monuments had learned their lesson: "The MFAA role tended to become less that of a guardian than of an insurance adjustor assessing the loss, looking for what was salvageable, and attempting to forestall unwarranted claims."[23]

Preparing for Invasion. Using the MFAA sub-commission in Italy as a model, SHAEF established its own MFAA division. In an attempt to learn from earlier mistakes, MFAA officers, often referred to as monument officers, were awarded higher military rank in order to enhance their authority among the troops. However, problems in assigning MFAA a place within the administrative structure of the Supreme Command delayed the effective start of the work. It was not until an administrative consolidation took place that the work of the archive officers could fully evolve.[24]

The experiences of 1944 made clear the importance of records to everybody involved, from intelligence officers to planning staffs preparing for the occupation. This change of attitude did not, however, immediately benefit the archivists. Shipman returned to Europe in mid-September 1944

---

21 Capt. T. H. Brooke and Capt. Roger H. Ellis both held the position of Assistant Keeper of the Public Records. Jenkinson's instructions to the officers from April 30, 1944, in Bell/Jenkinson, *Italian Archives*, 37; see also Ellis, "Recollections," 266–68.

22 Bell/Jenkinson, *Italian Archives*, 12, 37f. The archivist was William D. McCain, in civilian life an archivist for the state of Mississippi and during the offensive the historian of the Fifth Army in Italy.

23 Ziemke, *U.S. Army in the Occupation of Germany*, 55.

24 The burden imposed by SHAEF's twofold function as the operative command center and the military government became more noticeable by the day. The situation was only made worse in August 1944 by the incorporation of the United States Group Control Council (USGCC) as a planning staff for the envisioned interallied control authority. The United States Group Control Council (USGCC) emerged from the German Country Unit of SHAEF and became the military occupation government after SHAEF was disbanded. Until then, it acted as a planning unit. The USGCC was then incorporated into the OMGUS. The British counterpart to the USGCC was the Control Commission for Germany (British Element), CCG (BE). For MFAA, the various reorganizations ended in a double association with SHAEF's Civil Affairs division (G-5) and the American Control Commission's Reparations, Deliveries and Restitution Division, which resulted in a counterproductive command structure. Not until USGCC was revamped into the Office of Military Government, United States (OMGUS) in September 1945, did the situation improve, especially once competition with the G-5 was eliminated. See Ziemke, *U.S. Army in the Occupation of Germany*, 55–7; with sources Coles/Weinberg, *Soldiers Become Governors*, 860–67; OMGUS Handbuch, 11–15, 26–30; Hammond, "Protection," 88f.

to advise SHAEF on archives and captured documents. Although he had been assured that each army would be assigned an archivist, only the First U.S. Army received one. That archival officer worked first in Belgium and then followed the troops to Aachen. The harsh working conditions quickly wore him out; he returned to the United States in January 1945.[25] What equally frustrated Shipman and Jenkinson was the lack of coordination in the confiscation and evaluation of records as well as the complete failure to implement any protective measures. Jenkinson complained that the various military reconnaissance departments in Washington, London, and at SHAEF

have insisted throughout that measures taken in regard to the treatment of modern Documents must rest in their hands: and that in fact this has resulted in little more than grandiose schemes for exploitation. So far as protection is concerned, no general scheme of procedure appears to have been devised and no generally effective measures taken. . . . We reach the end of the SHAEF period . . . without anything having been done in a comprehensive way to safeguard Archives during that dangerous period.[26]

As in Italy, the archivists' goals in Western Europe could not be reconciled with military exigencies, and tensions often ran high. During his three-month tour in late 1944, Shipman wanted at least to make provisions for the invasion of Germany. In cooperation with the Public Record Office in London, he compiled a list of archives in western Germany for SHAEF and another list of repositories in Berlin, and he pushed for a decision on who would be responsible for them.[27]

After the archivist with the First Army left in January 1945, the situation returned to its previous state: "We found ourselves without archivists in the European theater when our armies were racing through Germany."[28] Not until March could the National Archives place a permanent archival advisor, Sargent B. Child, in the USGCC. Child brought together a team of five archivists by the end of the year and cooperated closely with his British

25 Special Report to the War Department on MFAA Operations in both European Theaters of Operation – with special reference to post surrender personnel requirements, April 16, 1945, NA RG 331, entry 55b, SHAEF, MFAA Subject File, box 324. See also Poste, *Development of U.S. Protection of Libraries and Archives*, 169.
26 Hilary Jenkinson, Adviser on Archives, War Office, London, to Lt. Col. Sir Leonard Woolley, Archaeological Adviser, Memorandum [on] The Present Situation in regard to Modern German Archives, July 1945, in LoCM box 31.
27 Official General List of Archives in Western Germany. SHAEF 1945; Official General List of Archives in the Berlin Area. SHAEF 1945; both found in the Meekings papers, PRO 30/90/04 and 05. What impact this list had remains an open question. Ten thousand copies were distributed down to the battalion level and, according to Ellis, "Recollections," 271, "have never been seen or heard of since."
28 Holmes, "National Archives and the Protection of Records," 121.

counterpart, Major R. H. Ellis.[29] These archivists found themselves in an unexpected alliance with their German counterparts as they tried to protect archival collections from destruction, pilferage, and selective confiscation.[30] Their greatest achievement was the rescue of many archives – particularly historical collections – under inhospitable conditions, even though they often arrived after damage had already been done. Their help in salvaging and re-establishing German archives after 1945 has never been adequately acknowledged.

The U.S. War Department and the British War Office

Whereas the archivists concentrated their efforts on protecting and preserving archives, the military focused on determining the intelligence value of the records. In planning for the confiscation, immediate evaluation, and long-term use of German records, the War Department in Washington and the War Office in London sought to combine two tasks that were not entirely compatible: to gather both "operational intelligence" (information needed for combat) and "occupational intelligence" (information needed for governing Germany after its defeat). Another aim was added in the summer of 1945: to gather evidence for war crimes trials. All records confiscated by advancing troops were considered the common property of Great Britain and the United States. They were first evaluated in London at the Military Intelligence Records Section (MIRS) and then shipped to the United States because, the argument went, the country was shouldering the greater burden of the war, especially in the Pacific. The Americans did, however, accept British claims to German navy records, especially those dealing with submarine warfare. When Allied forces marched into Germany and the quantities of captured records suddenly skyrocketed, these newly established procedures quickly broke down. The volume of documents and the multitude of storage locations were from the outset more than the invading armies could handle. The difficulties were compounded by the interest of numerous governmental bodies in both Washington and London in the captured records.

The American army had little experience with using captured documents as a source of intelligence.[31] The British observed with some concern that

---

29 The five men were Harold J. Clem, Jesse Boell, Paul Vanderbilt, Edgar Breitenbach, and Seymour J. Pomrenze. Lester K. Born, head of the Ministerial Collecting Centers in Fürstenhagen near Kassel, joined the MFAA only later and worked until 1949 on reestablishing the German archive and library system.

30 The course of a typical day is described in Nicholas, *Rape of Europa*, 353f.

31 Brower, "U.S. Army's Seizure," 191–207, esp. 202–7.

the U.S. War Department could not produce an estimate of German troop strength until a year after the Japanese attack on Pearl Harbor. The estimate put forward in the so-called Pink Book deviated strikingly from British findings, which led London to conclude that the information the Americans used had apparently come from "unsound sources."[32] MIRS was established in May 1943 to coordinate British and American intelligence work. It was headquartered in London and had a branch office in Washington. At the same time, the U.S. Army established an office, the G-2 Document Section, to coordinate the on-the-spot evaluation of captured records and their transfer to London. There they would be combed for information that might be of use in strategic planning. Although the German records were considered reliable, they often arrived in London too late to be of use in operational planning and thus served primarily to confirm information received through other channels. Captured records were then sent to Washington for a more comprehensive and intensive evaluation. The trickle of documents that followed Allied victories in North Africa turned into a flood after the Normandy invasion. By June 1945, MIRS had processed at least 150 tons of paper.[33]

"Document intelligence" on this scale was unprecedented. From the time of the North African offensive, Lieutenant S. F. Gronich, the head of the G-2 Document Section in Algiers, found himself in a "constant struggle to try to prevent the combat echelons from destroying documents, allowing their personnel to retain them as souvenirs, or building up their own document libraries." Important sources were often kept by subordinate offices during transportation and never arrived at MIRS. The administrative proliferation of SHAEF, euphemistically called "complicated echeloning," compounded the problem. The system that had been developed for the evacuation of captured records to England thus broke down once Allied forces crossed the Rhine.[34] Military intelligence officials concluded in May 1945 that the "SHAEF Document Section and MIRS are so congested that they cannot handle further intakes at the moment."[35]

---

32 MIRS. History and Operation. London and Washington Branches, May 1, 1943 – July 14, 1945, NA RG 242, AGAR-S no. 1500, box 5.
33 Ibid., 12. The treaty establishing the MIRS (March 1943) is found in NA RG 319, Finke Files, entry 1037, box 55. On MIRS, see also Pomrenze, "Protection, Use, and Return," 14–17.
34 MIRS. History and Operation, 10, also for the preceding quotes.
35 Director Military Intelligence, War Office, Aide Memoire for Conversation with General Bissell, May 15, 1945, PRO WO 32/15550. The standard British work on the military secret intelligence service is thin on document intelligence. Correspondingly, there is little information on the MIRS in Hinsley, British Intelligence, III, Part II, 27f.

At the end of 1944, the task of MIRS was shifted from operational to occupational intelligence. That put MIRS in direct competition with the Document Section of SHAEF, which seems to have actively undermined the work of MIRS on occasion.[36] When SHAEF was dismantled in July 1945 and all offices were placed under the supervision of the Control Councils, MIRS split into two offices: the London Military Document Center (LMDC) and the German Military Document Section (GMDS) in Washington, D.C. As London increasingly concerned itself with only the transfer of military records to the United States,[37] Washington expanded the range of its activities. At Camp Ritchie, Maryland, the captured German documents were sorted and cataloged in preparation for use in studies of all aspects of German war-making. All of the measures undertaken at Camp Ritchie suggested that the Americans intended to retain long-term possession of all the captured documents.[38]

The Bissell-Sinclair Agreement. By early 1945, Allied officials were already considering what would happen to the German military records after V-E Day and their shared military headquarters, SHAEF, was dismantled. The agreement of March 1943 that had established MIRS and provided for the collaborative evaluation of the captured documents would expire with the dissolution of SHAEF. British and American officials nonetheless remained in broad agreement that the German records already seized should remain in joint possession. To prepare for a new phase of Anglo-American cooperation, officials in Washington suggested the two governments conclude a new agreement on the administration of the captured documents after Germany's surrender.[39] The result was the so-called Bissell-Sinclair Agreement of May 1945, which was actually an informal working paper and not a binding agreement. In the absence of more formal regulations, however, this agreement became the main reference after the first German demands

36 The British archival officer Maj. R. H. Ellis reported after a visit to the SHAEF Document Section: "MIRS as an institution does not seem to be *persona grata* with SHAEF Document Centre, who consider that the control and removal of Documents, and the supply of Intelligence to SHAEF, are entirely Document Centre's business. MIRS are not at present allowed by SHAEF Document Centre to evacuate anything." Ellis, Report on a Visit to G-2 and G-5 SHAEF, June 19, 1945, NA RG 331, SHAEF, entry 47, box 20.

37 LMDC was closed on Feb. 1, 1946; the small number of captured documents no longer justified the existence of the facility. See Chief, Mil. Intell. Service to ACoS, G-2, WD, Jan. 19, 1946, and Jan. 22, 1946, both in NA RG 319, entry 1018, box 1.

38 MIRS. History and Operation, London and Washington Branches, May 1, 1943–July 14, 1945, NA RG 242, AGAR-S no. 1500, box 5. See also NA RG 242, AGAR-S no. 703, box 2.

39 Brig. General P. E. Peabody, Chief, MIS, WD, to ACoS, G-2, WD, April 6, 1945, NA RG 319, Finke Files, entry 1037, box 55.

for the return of documents in 1949 and was cited particularly often by the British in their efforts to fend off these demands. This agreement thus needs to be examined here in greater detail.[40]

The agreement was brokered by Lieutenant-General John Alexander Sinclair, the director of the military intelligence department (DMI) at the British War Office, and his counterpart in Washington, Lieutenant-General Clayton Bissell, Assistant Chief of Staff (ACoS) at the War Department. It designated the jurisdictions of the British and American intelligence services and spelled out the function of MIRS during the military occupation of Germany. It also specified what sorts of documents would continue to be taken out of Germany and defined common interests in the immediate assessment of captured documents. The war against Japan had the highest priority, followed by "occupational intelligence" and the search for evidence for the war crime trials. The most important stipulation of the agreement was that the records were to remain in joint British–American possession, regardless of whether they were held in London or Washington: "Such military archives and documents shall be disposed of as mutually agreed." Should the agreement be unilaterally cancelled, the records were to be divided among the parties. This clause of the agreement prompted protests from archivists and was subsequently abandoned. Archivists had argued that such a division would tear holdings apart and thus render them worthless.[41]

The decision to centralize German military records outside Washington at Camp Ritchie collided with the stated objective of keeping and evaluating German archives and current administrative records in situ so far as possible. Sinclair, closer to the scene than his colleagues in Washington, warned against shipping all the military records to the United States. He pointed

---

40 The Bissell-Sinclair Agreement is reproduced in Eckert, *Kampf um die Akten*, 466–72. A comparable agreement also existed between the two air forces (Bissell-Elmhirst Agreement). It stipulated the division of seized documents into the categories of technical and strategic records, each side was guaranteed the right of access to all records. Whereas the British received the "operational files" and the personnel records, the technical material was sent to the Air Documents Research Office in Alabama (Maxwell Air Base). See [Elmhirst] Assistant Chief of Air Staff (Intelligence), Air Ministry, and [Bissell] ACoS, G-2, WD, Memorandum with Respect to the Handling of German Air Documents, Nov. 12, 1945, NA RG 319, G-2, entry 1018, box 1. Between the British and American navies existed only a verbal agreement from April 1944. German naval records were considered joint property but were deposited exclusively in the Admiralty in London, which was de facto the recognition by the Americans of British privilege to these records. See Guides U-Boats and T-Boats, ix; Brian Melland, Enemy Documents Section, Cabinet Office, Anglo-American Inter-Services Agreements relating to Captured German Military Archives, Nov. 7, 1950, PRO CAB 103/458. Melland, who worked in the Cabinet Office on the official history of the Second World War, compiled in this document all of the agreements on captured records known at the time.
41 A memorandum from June 1948 mentions the new stipulation: "A subsequent agreement provided further that the Department of the Army would maintain the integrity of the joint collection, allowing the British access thereto." Intelligence Division to Commander-in-Chief, European Command, June 11, 1948, NA RG 407, entry 371F, box 2.

out that MIRS and SHAEF were already overburdened and the collection points were overflowing with the tons of documents American forces had sent from Thuringia in advance of the region's transfer to the Soviets. Intelligence officials in London feared that the military staff at the U.S. War Department underestimated the seriousness of the situation. The masses of paper involved not only made an orderly evacuation impossible but the amount also did not bode well for a centralized analysis of the material on behalf of all interested parties. Sinclair therefore suggested that only records truly relevant to the war against Japan be sent across the Atlantic and that more evaluation be undertaken on the Continent. Apparently it was dawning on the British, too, that whoever held German records had privileged access to them. Sinclair suspected that the Americans were "looking mainly to their own interest."[42] The Allied Control Commissions on the Continent protested against the removal of *any* captured German records. They considered the materials vital for governing the occupied territories. The removal of military records remained a problem that British and American officials tried to resolve in a series of discussions. Those talks were repeatedly hindered, however, by the two sides' incompatible interests and occasional distrust.[43]

The cooperation between the military intelligence services mirrored the power imbalance between the British and the Americans. Washington was the seat of the Combined Chiefs of Staff and therefore the headquarters for military decision-making. The supreme commanders for the Pacific and European theaters were both Americans. These facts were used to justify the shipment of German military records to the United States. The stipulation that Wehrmacht records be sent to Camp Ritchie for in-depth evaluation obviously put the British at a disadvantage. The closing of the London collection point effectively denied the British intelligence services MI 3 and MI 4 access to the captured records. "No purely military captured German documents have been received in London . . . since the London Military Document Center was closed last March [1946]. MI 4 and MI 3 (the main sections concerned) state that no captured German documents have come to their attention since last winter," an American military attaché in London

---

42 Unsigned memorandum from MI 17, War Office, American and British Views of Handling German Archives and Documents, May 6, 1945; [DMI], Aide Memoire for Conversation with General Bissell, May 15, 1945, both in PRO WO 32/15550.

43 DDMI, Aide Memoire for DMI on German Documents, June 20, 1945, PRO WO 32/15550; SHAEF, Office of the ACoS, G-2, Main HQ, Minutes of Meeting Held at SHAEF, June 24, 1945, to Discuss Handling of Military Documents and Program for Research, June 28, 1945, NA RG 331, entry 11, box 8.

reported to the War Department in September 1946.[44] That explains, for example, why the British never saw the files of Foreign Armies East, the German army's intelligence arm responsible for assessing the capabilities of the Red Army.[45] The Russian desk of MI 3 would have been extremely interested in these documents because, at the same time that these files were being shipped to the United States, MI 3 realized that its information about the strength of the Red Army was "too scrappy and not sufficiently objective." It did not know much about Russian losses, weaponry, military production, senior military personnel, or tactics – in short, everything necessary to estimate the combat strength of a country that was still at least nominally an ally.[46]

Establishing Archival Protection. The difficulties in coordinating the seizure of records relevant to military strategy prompted the issuing of a series of directives and plans for the handling of German documents during the invasion and occupation.[47] Allied army groups set up special search troops, known as Target-Forces or simply T-Forces,[48] and soldiers down to the battalion level were equipped with information on handling enemy records.[49] Whereas the first directives issued by the intelligence services dealt only with identifying targets and confiscation procedures,[50] the pressure exerted by professional archivists finally prompted Eisenhower's headquarters in August 1944 to issue an order dedicated solely to the *protection* of archives.[51] From that

44 Col. M. van Voorst, AmEmb London, Office of the Military Attaché, to Director of Intelligence, War Department, Sept. 23, 1946, NA RG 319, entry 1018, box 1.
45 In a letter dated June 26, 1945, Brig. Gen. T. J. Betts, SHAEF, confirmed the agreement with Clayton Bissell that 100 tons of Wehrmacht records were to be evacuated to Camp Ritchie "as quickly as possible." The collection of records "Foreign Armies East" was also transferred immediately "without local examination at SHAEF." NA RG 260, FIAT Executive Office, box 40.
46 Maj. N. Ignatieff, MI 3, Top Secret, Exploitation of German Documents on the USSR, June 29, 1945, PRO WO 208/1862.
47 A summary in Pomrenze, "Protection, Use, and Return," 8–11.
48 Ziemke, *U.S. Army in the Occupation of Germany*, 314.
49 Civil Affairs Information Guide. Field Protection of Objects of Art and Archives. War Department Pamphlet no. 31–103, May 12, 1944, 1. Preservation and Use of Key Records in Germany. War Dept. Pamphlet no. 31–123; Archival Repositories in Germany, War Dept. Pamphlet no. 31–180; Military Government Information Guide. Information on German Records. War Dept. Pamphlet no. 31–217, Feb. 3, 1945. Archival Repositories in Germany, War Dept. Pamphlet no. 31–180. Furthermore, the pamphlets: War Department, Military Intelligence Division, The Exploitation of German Documents, n. D. [1944], NA RG 260, OMGUS, Executive Records of FIAT, box 35; SHAEF, Office of the ACoS, Priority Documents and Operational Instructions, n. D. [Dec. 1944], NA RG 331, entry 11, box 8.
50 SHAEF, Office of the ACoS, G-2, Intelligence Directive no. 8: Intelligence from Enemy Service Documents, May 7, 1944, NA RG 331, entry 11, box 1.
51 SHAEF, Adjutant General, to HQ 21st Army Group, Commanding General 12th Army Group, Commanding General 1st Army Group, Subject: Preservation of Archives, Aug. 20, 1944, NA RG 331, entry 47, box 21.

point on, archival protection became a declared objective of SHAEF and was mentioned in all further directives, including the occupation handbook: "It is the policy of the Supreme Commander to ensure the preservation from destruction, alteration or concealment of all German records, documents, plans or archives of value to the attainment of the objective of Military Government."[52]

To facilitate the work of the occupation administrators, SHAEF devised a plan code-named "Goldcup" aimed to bring the German ministerial bureaucracy under control. The plan was also intended to provide a basis for cooperation with the Soviet Control Commission. Although it was still unclear in the fall of 1944 which of the Allies would reach Berlin first, officials at SHAEF were preparing for the capture of the city. An advance contingent from the British and American Control Commissions was to collect personnel records and the records of the German ministries in Berlin or wherever the ministries had relocated.[53] In January 1945, 287 officers and nearly 900 soldiers awaited deployment for this task. Since cooperation with the Soviets was slow in coming, the Goldcup teams worked on their own and compiled hundreds of tons of records and microfilms by May 1945. The material was deposited in the Ministerial Collecting Center (MCC) in Fürstenhagen, near Kassel. Former ministerial personnel were interned in camps nearby and assigned the task of arranging the material.[54]

As no one could be certain in the summer of 1945 that a functioning Four Power government for all of Germany would exist any time soon, no decisions on the future of confiscated records were to be expected. Tired of the unsettled state of affairs, the British decided to deal with the matter in their own occupation zone. The Joint Intelligence Sub-committee (JIC), a committee of the British chiefs-of-staff, appointed a working group called the German Documents Panel in August 1945.[55] Panel members included

52 SHAEF Handbook for Military Government in Germany Prior to Defeat or Surrender, December 1944, part III, chap. XVI, sec. II, para. 1198, 291; with identical text in the directive of the same name for the Army groups from Nov. 9, 1944, NA RG 331, entry 18A, box 156. See also SHAEF, G-5, MFAA, Instructions for the Use of Mil. Gov. Officers of Archives mentioned in the General List of Archives in Western Germany, Dec. 29, 1944, NA RG 260, Executive Office FIAT, box 35. On the history of the occupation handbook, see Henke, *Amerikanische Besetzung*, 101, 106–8; Ziemke, *U.S. Army in the Occupation of Germany*, 83–90.

53 The tasks of the Goldcup staff are laid out in the memoranda Control of Reich Ministries and Ministerial Control Planning Teams, n.d. [early 1945], PRO FO 1050/406.

54 Ziemke, *U.S. Army in the Occupation of Germany*, 177, 248f., 263, 315. On the establishment of the MCC, see USGCC, Goldcup Operations Staff, Ministerial Control Memorandum no. 15, Subject: Establishment of MCC, Kassel, June 17, 1945, NA RG 242, BDC Directorate Files, box 10A. On the work in Kassel, see Born, "MCC."

55 The work group was to exist "pending the establishment of a quadripartite organization appointed by the Control Council." Its task was to work out binding guidelines for the British Control Commission allowing material to be removed from the British zones in Germany and Austria. If

representatives of the ministries dealing with Germany and Hilary Jenkinson of the Public Record Office. The panel made numerous far-reaching decisions, including the decision that all German diplomatic records sent to Britain were to be administered by the Foreign Office.[56]

To Jenkinson's annoyance, the German Documents Panel did not show much interest in archival protection and concentrated instead on coordinating the exploitation of the German records. American agencies used the panel to gain access to the collection centers in the British zone and sent representatives to the panel's meetings.[57] Indignant over the development of the panel "into yet another Exploiting Agency," Jenkinson began to block the initiatives of the working group. He complained that hundreds of intelligence agents were involved with the German documents but not a single archivist. The struggle for the files between the various agencies effectively voided the measures enacted to protect and preserve records because intelligence agencies did not play by the rules. According to Jenkinson, it was initially envisioned that documents would be taken out of Germany only when absolutely necessary and that the Document Centers had been set up to preserve, not exploit, archival materials. He implicitly criticized the "unprecedented" scope of the confiscations.[58] With Jenkinson holding firmly to strict professional archival standards, compromise became impossible. Paralyzed, the panel ceased its work in the fall of 1946.[59] Jenkinson's unwillingness to compromise and his tireless commitment did, however, pay off in many respects. He, for one, took a long-term view of the captured documents and was especially aware of their historical value. His hand is clearly evident in many decisions and directives. He intervened against a

necessary, it was to mediate between various offices that claimed the same records and draw up proposals for the long-term treatment of records remaining in Germany or transferred to Great Britain. Finally, it was to help sustain Anglo-American cooperation. It convened under the name German Documents Panel for the first time on Dec. 5, 1945, chaired by the Admiralty. See Joint Intelligence Sub-Committee: Treatment of German Archives, Records and Documents-Panel, JIC (45) 184 (Final), Aug. 21, 1945; Minutes of 2nd Meeting of the Political Working Party on Germany and Austria, Sept. 14, 1945, both in PRO FO 370 1190/L3471.

56 Offices of the Cabinet and Minister of Defence to Dorothy A. Bigby, Library, FO, Nov. 14, 1945, PRO FO 370/1191 L3588.

57 German Documents Panel. Minutes of 2nd Meeting, Oct. 17, 1945, JIC/1509/45; Minutes of Special Meeting, Nov. 6, 1945, JIC/1643/45, in PRO CAB 146/196.

58 Jenkinson to Sir Harold Anthony Caccia, JIC chairman, Memorandum [on] Modern German Archives, Jan. 19, 1946, PRO CAB 146/196. Jenkinson's reputation reached even as far as the Military Intelligence Division of the War Department in Washington: "You'll want to watch out for this guy Hilary Jenkins [sic], an archivist, in London, from the British museum [sic]. He gets in everybody's hair including the British. The War Office keeps him in check pretty well, but it is deteriorating in its position in London." Notes on discussion of captured German war documents with Colonel R. L. Hopkins and Colonel St. Clair, War Dept., June 29, 1946, NA RG 59, Lot File 78D441, Historical Office, box 23.

59 Clanchy to Caccia, Jan. 28, 1946; Jenkinson to Caccia, Feb. 5, 1946; both in PRO CAB 146/196.

stipulation of the Bissell-Sinclair Agreement that would have divvied up the German army records after they had been analyzed. As a professional archivist, he preferred to see archival collections end up in Washington rather than have them disassembled and dispersed.[60] His demand that all captured records be meticulously tracked led to the introduction of precise *Document Activity Reports* in the British Control Commission and the British Army of the Rhine.[61]

The search for information that could be used for strategic purposes, prosecuting war crimes, or governing occupied Germany does not ulti-mately explain the vigor that the Allies – the Americans in particular – displayed in seizing archival materials. The interest in obtaining military and Nazi party records was linked to a fundamental Allied war aim: to pre-vent Germany from ever starting another war. That point was stressed in the "Talisman" plan for the occupation of Germany drafted in August 1944: "It must be impressed on our troops that the securing of official documents is of vital importance to our plans to ensure that GERMANY does not embark on a Third World War."[62] The "Eclipse" plan prepared three months later was even more direct: "To leave [military] documents intact in Germany would give any future German General Staff the groundwork for creating a fresh military machine and the data for an examination of their errors in strategy and tactics in this war."[63] The confiscation of military documents thus meshed with the objective of disarming and re-educating the Germans. Shipping documents out of the country or destroying them was preferable in Allied eyes than leaving them in German hands. Consequently, the direc-tive JCS 1067 of the Joint Chiefs of Staff outlining policy for governing the American occupation zone addressed the confiscation of German doc-uments in connection with plans for "denazification."[64] Control Council

60 Jenkinson, Memorandum [on] Archives of OKH and OKW, April 13, 1946; DMI, MI 4, Memo-randum May 15, 1946; both in PRO WO 32/15550.

61 A complete collection of these reports was not readily available. I could locate only report no. 1 of the CCG (BE) and the reports nos. 1, 7, 9, and 10 of the British Army of the Rhine (BAOR).

62 Annex 5 to Talisman Memorandum no. 7, Enemy Documents Special Instruction, n.d. [Aug 6, 1944], NA RG 331, entry 55b, box 323, emphasis in the original. "Talisman" was the codeword for an occupation plan that required the survival of an intact German bureaucracy. The subsequent plan "Eclipse" from autumn 1944 assumed that all German structures would collapse and consequently proposed complete occupation. See Ziemke, *U.S. Army in the Occupation of Germany*, 100, 163–5.

63 SHAEF, ACoS, G-2, Eclipse Memorandum no. 7, Jan. 30, 1945, sec. IX: The Handling of Captured Enemy Documents, para. 112, 26, NA RG 331, entry 11, box 8. See also Shipman to Roosevelt, June 20, 1944: "It is generally known how the German General Staff, though abolished by treaty, continued to function and assiduously studied the military records of the last war to prepare for the present one." FDRL, PSF confidential, Folders War Dept., June 20–July 2, 1944.

64 "You will make special efforts to preserve from destruction and take under your control records, plans, books, documents, papers, files and scientific, industrial and other information and data belonging to or controlled by the following: (1) The Central German Government and its subdivisions, German

Order No. 2 (October 10, 1945) ordered the confiscation of Nazi party correspondence and the records of party-affiliated organizations throughout the whole of Germany. Control Council Directive No. 18 (November 12, 1945), which dissolved the Wehrmacht, was supplemented by Control Council Order No. 34 (August 20, 1946), which provided for the seizure of military records.[65] Concealing or destroying records were made criminal offenses in zonal regulations. The Americans took the matter seriously. In one of the first military court trials held, a woman from Kornelimünster near Aachen was sentenced in October 1944 to no less than six years imprisonment because she had destroyed the records of her local Nazi women's organization.[66]

CIOS: The Combined Intelligence Objectives Subcommittee

During the invasion of Germany, intelligence for combat purposes took priority over all else. This did not, however, preclude intelligence-gathering for other ends. To coordinate the activities of the British and American agencies engaged in intelligence work, the Combined Chiefs of Staff established the Combined Intelligence Objectives Subcommittee (CIOS) in London in August 1944. Institutionally, the subcommittee was subordinate to SHAEF. When SHAEF disbanded in July 1945, CIOS was succeeded by two organizations: the American Field Intelligence Agency, Technical (FIAT), and the British Intelligence Objectives Sub-Committee (BIOS).[67] These

---

military organizations, organizations engaged in military research, and such other governmental agencies as may be deemed advisable; (2) The Nazi Party, its formations, affiliated associations and supervised organizations; (3) All police organizations, including security and political police; (4) Important economic organizations and industrial establishments, including those controlled by the Nazi Party or its personnel; (5) Institutes and special bureaus devoting themselves to racial, political, militaristic or similar research or propaganda." Directive to Commander in Chief of U.S. Forces of Occupation Regarding the Military Government of Germany (JCS 1067), part I, sec. 6, para. f, April 28, 1945, in Holborn, *American Military Government*, 161. The corresponding directive for Austria, dated June 27, 1945, contains the same stipulation, see ibid., 181.

65 Furthermore, the Control Council issued Order No. 4 in May 1946 on the confiscation of Nazi and militarist literature. Although directed primarily at pamphlets and books, this order later sanctioned the already ongoing purging of public libraries and educational institutions. See Control Council Order No. 4. Confiscation of Literature and Material of Nazi and Militarist Nature, May 13, 1946, Amtsblatt des Kontrollrats in Deutschland no. 7, May 31, 1946, 151f.; and the revision of Order No. 4, Aug. 10, 1946, ibid., no. 10, Aug. 31, 1946, 57.

66 Ziemke, *U.S. Army in the Occupation of Germany*, 144; Henke, *Amerikanische Besetzung*, 182f.

67 The two successor organizations were incorporated into their Control Commissions and directed from Washington by the Office of Technical Services at the Commerce Department and from London by the Department of Scientific and Industrial Research. The well-tested cooperation between the Americans and the British continued intensively during the Cold War. See Maddrell, "British-American Scientific Collaboration."

organizations collected both military and non-military intelligence.[68] CIOS began its work as a clearinghouse for the intelligence services of all government agencies. Military concerns received the greatest attention at first, especially the war against Japan.[69] CIOS's focus shifted, however, as government agencies and private businesses became increasingly interested in German economic data and scientific research. A contemporary observer estimated that 90 percent of CIOS's activity was devoted to industrial-technical targets.[70] The successor organizations to CIOS became instruments exclusively of economic warfare. After the invasion of Germany and the establishment of military occupation governments, BIOS and FIAT both served private business interests in their respective countries.

The mission of CIOS and its successor organizations was to identify, evaluate, and – as soon as the military situation allowed – inspect political and administrative bodies, industrial facilities, and research institutions in Germany. While waiting for the opportunity to work on the Continent, CIOS teams in London began to compile target lists: a "Black List" of targets with immediate military priority and a "Gray List" of less important targets.[71] Government agencies provided CIOS with intelligence wish lists; if precise information about particular targets was not available, requests would be formulated in broad terms in the hope that CIOS teams might come across pertinent material while investigating other targets.[72] Disputes

---

68 Represented in CIOS were seven British and at least eight American ministries and institutions. See Gimbel, *Science, Technology and Reparations*, 4.

69 Literature on CIOS and FIAT is rare. With an emphasis on the forced evacuation of scientists from central Germany, see Henke, *Amerikanische Besetzung*, 742–76, on CIOS esp. 745–7. The most extensive treatment is found in Gimbel, *Science, Technology and Reparations*. As a rule, CIOS is presented as if it had been an instrument of economic warfare *exclusively*. However, CIOS began as a clearinghouse for the coordination of various intelligence interests and *only then* developed its main focus in the area of industrial research and development.

70 E. Ralph Perkins, Division of Research and Publication, to E. C. Wendelin, State Dept., Aug. 20, 1945, NA RG 59, Lot File 78D441, Historical Office, box 6. Perkins represented the State Department in the commission for the target lists and headed the CIOS team put together by his institution from April to July 1945.

71 According to Perkins, "a Gray List was also in the process of preparation, consisting of targets of less urgent interest than those on the Black List, but this was never completed before CIOS ceased operations." Perkins, Memorandum, Exploitation of German Political Archives for the Department of State, Aug. 20, 1945, NA RG 59, Lot File 78D441, Historical Office, box 6.

72 For example, the foreign ministries and their respective agencies for economic warfare expressed an interest in "all information relating to external German assets and holdings. . . . " This information was thought to be "probably located chiefly in banks, foreign exchange and clearing institutes and in the files of large industrial concerns [or] in the most unlikely places." See CIOS [Directive], CIOS/101/1/S, Mar. 16, 1945, Additions to Second Revision of Revised Directive to Field Team Leaders, Deputy Field Team Leaders and Investigators, NA RG 260, OMGUS, Records of the Executive Office. FIAT 1945–47, box 43. The economic agencies were the Foreign Economic Administration (United States) and the Ministry of Economic Warfare (Great Britain).

often erupted over priorities. The war ministries carried greater weight than civilian agencies, but the latter were sometimes successful in arguing that the targets of interest to them were essential to the war effort.

CIOS intensified its activities at the end of 1944. By that time, the committee had sent 197 agents to 115 targets. The more information it gathered, the longer its lists of targets grew.[73] CIOS agents worked in tandem with the so-called T[arget]-Forces; search teams often included both CIOS agents and T-Force members. The T-Forces were responsible for the actual seizure of documents; CIOS's job was to assess and forward the materials to London. This division of labor broke down under the pressure of the large number of targets, internal rivalries, and the general chaos of the invasion. As a result, CIOS created the Combined Advance Field Teams (CAFTs) in February 1945 to accompany Allied combat forces. The CAFTs were CIOS's solution to the overburdening of the T-Forces and to the lack of qualified personnel among the combat troops. The CAFTs were also more flexible in handling the transfer of targets within German territory.[74]

The Combined Chiefs of Staff and their intelligence committee, the Combined Intelligence Committee (CIC), were not always happy with the course of action taken by CIOS. In March 1945, they felt compelled to remind CIOS officials that the main objective was to win the war: "SHAEF and its subordinate units have primarily a combat mission and interest; other responsibilities, irrespective of their urgency and importance, must play a secondary role to combat requirements." In their zeal, CIOS teams apparently did not always worry about following their orders to the letter. The CIC understood that CIOS agents had to question German scientists and thus break the rules on non-fraternization but warned "that CIOS investigators may of necessity become too friendly with key German personnel in an effort to win their 'cooperation.' CIC is opposed to such an approach; 'cooperation' would be contrary to regulations ... on fraternization with German nationals." The CIC also voiced concern that CIOS agents might reveal Allied intelligence aims simply by the way they formulated questions during their interrogation of Germans.[75] Moreover, CIOS teams were criticized for not consistently maintaining registers of all captured documents.

---

73 Gimbel, *Science, Technology and Reparations*, 4.

74 In all, there were 28 CAFTs. They were not required to adhere unerringly to the order of priority presented on the target lists. "Targets of opportunity" became the focus of their work during military offensives. Gimbel, *Science, Technology and Reparations*, 9; CIOS [Memorandum], CIOS/118/8/S, Preliminary Outline of CIOS Plan for Rapid Appraisal and Assessment of Targets under Conditions of German Collapse, Feb. 26, 1945, NA RG 59, CDF 1945–49, box 5701; see also CIOS, Progress Report for 1945, June 4, 1945, PRO FO 371/46712 C2898/G.

75 CIOS, Revised Directive to Field Team Leaders, Deputy Field Team Leaders and Investigators, CIOS/101/1/C, Mar. 8, 1945, NA RG 260, FIAT, General Records 1945–47, box 43.

Although informed in April 1945 that SHAEF would soon issue an order prohibiting the removal of documents from "organized collections," the CAFTs were instructed only to keep removals at a minimum.[76] In other words, the order apparently did little to change the situation. A June 1945 War Office report noted tersely that "a large number of documents of interest to CIOS have been got away."[77]

CIOS became the gateway for civilian agencies to Germany. It provided them with accreditation and served as a means to influence the Allied High Command's decisions in setting intelligence priorities. CIOS had the ways and means to get the Allied High Command to set priorities according to its wishes that none of these agencies acting alone would have had. The target lists gave civilian agencies the possibility to participate in the competition for German documents, experts, and equipment. Nonetheless, it was more important for agencies and ministries to send their own people to the combat zones and occupied areas and to make sure they had the necessary logistical support to carry out their missions. No repository could be secured, assessed, and if need be, removed without staff, security guards, and transport. Without the backing of the military authorities, civilian staffers might find themselves "going hat in hand, begging, 'Brother, can you spare a jeep?'"[78] On account of logistics, then, the State Department and the Foreign Office worked through CIOS. They submitted their requests for the CIOS target lists and dispatched a joint document team, the State Department–Foreign Office Team, to work under the auspices of CIOS.

The U.S. State Department and the British Foreign Office

Officials at the State Department and Foreign Office became interested in German records as a source of intelligence and as historical documentation of the recent past. The ministries' wide-ranging intelligence interests touched on topics such as Germany's trade relations, its propaganda efforts abroad, the Nazi party's foreign organizations, and all forms of foreign collaboration with the Third Reich. The historic interests grew directly from the experience of the aftermath of World War I. The Auswärtiges Amt had been able to steer the so-called war guilt debate in the Germany's favor by publishing pertinent diplomatic records. This time, the Allies wanted to

---

76 CIOS, Instruction to all CAFT Members and Investigators, CIOS/113/4/S, Apr. 20, 1945, PRO FO 371/46712 C1671/G.
77 DDMI to DMI, War Office, June 20, 1945, PRO WO 32/15550.
78 E. Ralph Perkins, Division of Research and Publication, to E. C. Wendelin, State Dept., Aug. 20, 1945, NA RG 59, Lot File 78D441, Historical Office, box 6.

forestall any attempt to open a new debate over war guilt by controlling the German diplomatic records. The ensuing cooperation between the historic divisions of the Foreign Office and the State Department, which is of key importance to this study, culminated in the publication of an edition of documents from the captured Political Archives of the Auswärtiges Amt.[79] The project *Documents on German Foreign Policy* lasted from 1946 until 1958 and yielded ten volumes in English and seven in German. This project and the Allied historians involved in it would prove to be a major hindrance in the negotiations between Bonn, Washington, and London on the return of German diplomatic records. The following account of the Foreign Office and State Department planning thus gives particular attention to British and American interest in the records as historical source material.[80]

The Germans themselves had inadvertently demonstrated just how important records could be in ideological struggles. The Allies were slow to recognize the full impact of German *Kulturpolitik* (cultural policy) in the occupied countries. Each country subjugated by the Germans suffered not only military occupation and economic exploitation but also "ideological penetration" to ensure German cultural hegemony and to relegate it to its assigned place in Hitler's "New Europe." An integral element in the Germans' plans to reshape the Continent was the deliberate plundering or destruction of cultural treasures and the attempt to control, if not eliminate, the occupied countries' cultural heritages and, by extension, their histories and identities.[81] The staffs of the historical divisions of the Foreign Office and State Department were well aware of the ways the Germans had used captured records, such as the production of so-called white papers legitimizing German political actions and discrediting foreign governments and politicians who had opposed the Third Reich.[82] The white papers the

79 At the State Department, this division was called the Division of Research and Publication until it was renamed the Division of Historical Policy Research in 1946. It belonged to the Office of Public Affairs. From 1953 to 1959, the very same office was called the Historical Division and since 1959, the Historical Office. See Zala, *Zensur*, 100. In London, the Foreign Office Research Department (FORD) was not an autonomous division during the war. After the war ended, it was restructured and called internally the Library. See Reusch, "Londoner Institutionen," 353–64, 436. In the following, I use the names Historical Office (State Department) und Library (Foreign Office).

80 Zala, *Zensur*, 148–63, also covers the American plans for confiscating German documents. See also Zala, "Dreierlei Büchsen der Pandora."

81 Umbreit, *Continental Domination*, 362–76, quote on 362; Heuss, *Kunst- und Kulturgutraub*; Kleßmann, *Selbstbehauptung einer Nation*, chap. III; Musial, *Staatsarchive im Dritten Reich*, esp. the source in appendix 7, 189; Lehr, *Vergessener "Osteinsatz,"* 107–251.

82 The practice of defending current policy in papers (associated with different colors) goes back to the nineteenth century. Until the First World War, the publication of one's own records was used as a tool of domestic and foreign policy, but after 1914 the Germans started also to publish captured records. See Hamilton, "Historical Diplomacy;" Zala, *Zensur*, 37–47. Publications of

Auswärtiges Amt issued during World War II employed the full range of techniques to sway public opinion, from the reproduction of official documents in full to selective editing to the use of outright forgeries.[83]

Well before the outcome of the war was clear, the British historians Lewis Namier and E. Llewellyn Woodward called for the publication of German and British documents on events leading up to the German invasion of Poland in September 1939. They argued that the interpretation of the recent past should not be left again to the Germans, as had been the case after the previous European war.[84] Similar ideas were being voiced at the State Department's Historical Office by early 1944. E. Wilder Spaulding, the head of the office, understood the importance of the Axis archives. The Allies needed to ensure that the records would not be abused after the war "to justify the Axis and prove their 'benevolent intentions' and the 'conspiracies' of the United Nations." He feared that the State Department could lose the race for the files and therefore pushed to have the department begin participating immediately in the planning already underway for the confiscation of German government records. "The records," he predicted, "will play a vital part in the ideological battles of the future."[85] Spaulding inquired at the War Department about the state of planning and soon met Fred Shipman, who informed him about the proposals put forward by the National Archives and other bodies.[86] By the end of March 1944, the first instructions on captured records and archives were sent to the Allied headquarters in Algiers and to the U.S. ambassador in London,

records could also be used to delegitimize a preceding political system. On the publications by Trotsky, see Spring, "Russian Documents;" on Kautsky's *Deutsche Dokumente zum Kriegsausbruch* see Heinemann, *Verdrängte Niederlage*, 74–8; Jäger, *Historische Forschung*, 34–43; Zala, *Zensur*, 52–7.

83 Kröger/Thimme, "Politisches Archiv," 246; Zala, "Censorship of Diplomatic Documents;" Zala, *Zensur*, 44–6 with a list of white papers in note 90. At the Auswärtiges Amt, the division Pol. XI under the direction of Werner von Schmieden was responsible for producing the White Books. The one on Poland, however, was actually produced under the direction of the former German ambassador in Warsaw, Hans Adolf von Moltke. In 1942, Heinz Trützschler von Falkenstein became the head of Pol. XI. In 1951, Trützschler returned to diplomatic service and worked at Division II of the Auswärtiges Amt, where he was responsible for the negotiations on the return of captured German records. On the work of Pol. XI during the war, see the postwar interrogations of Trützschler and his notes for the Americans, NA RG 59, Lot File 60D24, Division of Foreign Activity Correlation, box 10, and NA RG 59, Poole Commission, MF 679, roll 3.

84 Lewis Namier, Letter to the Editor of the *Times* (London), Sept. 25, 1943, quoted in Rose, *Namier and Zionism*, 138; similar reference by Woodward in his autobiography, published in 1942, as *Short Journey*, 236–9, 243. Namier was a professor in Manchester, Woodward in Oxford. Both were advisors to the Foreign Office during the war. Woodward was also the editor of *Documents on British Foreign Policy, 1919–1939*. See Bialer, "Telling the Truth;" Hamilton, "Historical Diplomacy."

85 E. Wilder Spaulding, Chief, Division of Research and Publication, to C. Howland Shaw, Jan. 3, 1944, NA RG 59, Lot File 78D441, Historical Office, box 6. Spaulding still anticipated lines of conflict in future ideological battles to run between fascism and democracy. The Soviet Union and communism were not yet on his mental map as the coming ideological antagonists.

86 Spaulding to Dunn, European Affairs, Procurement of Axis Archives, Aug. 15, 1944, ibid., box 24.

John G. Winant, who represented the United States in the European Advisory Commission (EAC).[87] Spaulding expected that British and Russian troops would be the first to confiscate German records. Therefore, he wanted to establish a binding agreement on the joint use of such records through the EAC so that the United States would not end up empty-handed.

Spaulding's instructions to Winant were still rather vague at this point, however. Spaulding pressed for access to the Auswärtiges Amt records, the papers of leading Axis officials, and anything that "might shed light on Axis intrigue, ruthlessness and aggression since Hitler's advent to power and during the war."[88] Allied control of the captured documents was intended, first, to prevent the Germans from mounting a postwar propaganda campaign to defend the Third Reich's actions and, second, to publicize the Axis powers' war aims and violations of international law. Spaulding believed that the use of Auswärtiges Amt documents would not constitute a breach of the inviolability of embassy and consulate property because "only the copying of especially important records and not their confiscation is proposed."[89] He did not at that point envision the systematic publication of German documents. Early exploratory talks in the EAC revealed that the British had already considered the question of captured records.[90] In July 1944, Sir William Strang presented the military commanders a draft directive on the handling of German records that placed great emphasis on protecting and preserving archives.[91] Winant submitted his own draft directive in November. The American proposals were more conducive to intelligence gathering. Nazi party records, national (Reich) and state (Land) governmental records as well as the records of banks and industrial firms were to be targeted. The search for "scientific and industrial information" would

---

87 Cordell Hull to AmEmb London, John C. Winant, no. 2293, Mar. 25, 1944, FRUS 1944:1, 1481f. At the Foreign Ministers Conference in Moscow, the United States, Great Britain, and the Soviet Union set up the European Advisory Commission in London in order to accelerate joint Allied planning for the occupation of Germany. The British wanted to make the EAC a decision-making body for Allied policy toward Germany. Foreign Secretary Eden envisioned a type of political counterpart to the Joint Chiefs of Staff with the inclusion of the Soviet Union. Roosevelt, who was always averse to planning as long as the war was not yet won, emphasized the advisory function of the EAC and did not want to be committed to advice. Due in part to the lack of cooperation by the Russian delegate, Feodor Gusev, the EAC was at times not much more than a debating club. It was disbanded at the Potsdam Conference. See Henke, *Amerikanische Besetzung*, 99f.; Kettenacker, *Krieg zur Friedenssicherung*, 238–50; Mai, *Alliierter Kontrollrat*, 19–28; Ziemke, *U.S. Army*, 37–41; as well as the memoirs of the participants: Murphy, *Diplomat Among Warriors*, 227f.; Strang, *Home & Abroad*, 199–225.
88 Cordell Hull to AmEmb London, John C. Winant, no. 2293, Mar. 25, 1944, FRUS 1944:1, 1481f.
89 Ibid.
90 Winant, AmEmb London, to SecState no. 15410, May 3, 1944, FRUS 1944:1, 1484.
91 British Draft Directive on German Records and Archives, appendix to Winant, AmEmb London, to SecState, no. 16892, July 17, 1944, ibid., 1490f.

be given highest priority under the guidelines Winant proposed.[92] The differences in British and American views evident in Strang's and Winant's proposals were never fully resolved and led to occasional friction during the invasion and occupation of Germany.

The EAC did not in the end present a directive that could serve as the basis for an Allied policy paper.[93] It remained one of many futile EAC exercises, much as the EAC itself never gained a significant role in planning for the postwar period.[94] Neither prior to the invasion of Germany nor during the early phase of occupation was there an agreement among the major Allied powers on captured records. The agreements that were to play a role during the negotiations over the records' return, such as the Bissell-Sinclair Agreement, were ad hoc, bilateral arrangements. The consequences of the lack of a Four Power agreement were significant. British and American troops captured the records of the Auswärtiges Amt in April 1945. After that, the Foreign Office and State Department were no longer interested in establishing an Allied policy because, for the time being, they had won the struggle for the files. However, their trophy did not remain a secret for long, and the French and Soviets were soon arguing that Four Power control of Germany should also give them access to the captured diplomatic records. They could not, however, invoke any agreement acknowledging their right to access to the captured documents.

Preparing for Invasion. When CIOS in London asked the State Department in September 1944 to submit its input on the target lists, Spaulding saw this as an opportunity to incorporate the department's Historical Office in the planning on document confiscation and sent his colleague E. Ralph

---

92 Winant, Draft Directive no. 4. Securing and Examining Information and Archives, n.d. [Nov. 23, 1944], ibid., 1501f. Strang worked Winant's draft into his own and presented it to the EAC in May 1945. The definitions of archival material were made more precise, but the intelligence aspects had been removed again. See PRO FO 371/46712 C2082.

93 It reappeared on the agenda of the U.S. Joint Chiefs of Staff and the State-War-Navy Coordinating Committee (SWNCC) in June 1945. See SWNCC, Directive, Treatment of German Archives, Records and Documents, SWNCC 122/1/D, June 23, 1945, NA RG 59, Lot File 78D441, Historical Office, box 6; Joint Intelligence Committee, Directive, Treatment of German Archives, Records and Documents, JIC 2999/D, June 30, 1945, NA RG 242, AGAR-S no. 1413, box 3; John D. Hickerson, Acting Chairman, SWNCC, Memorandum for the Secretary of State: Treatment of German Archives, Records and Documents, July 27, 1945, NA RG 59, CDF 1945–49, 840.414/7–2745. The directive listed in the appendix is the version revised once again to correspond with JCS 1067/6.

94 Several of the ideas and definitions formulated in this draft directive were incorporated into the SHAEF handbook on military government and into later Control Council orders. See SHAEF Handbook for Military Government in Germany Prior to Defeat or Surrender, December 1944, part III, sec. II, para. 1196–1212.

Perkins to participate in the document hunt in Germany.[95] Perkins arrived in London in December 1944 and met members of the Foreign Office research department who had similar interests in the German diplomatic records. The historian Llewellyn Woodward reiterated his proposal to include German documents in an expanded version of the series *Documents on British Foreign Policy, 1919–1939*, which he edited. He argued that German responsibility for the war could thus be made amply clear.[96] The Foreign Office designated Robert C. Thomson, deputy librarian at the ministry, as the head of the team that would be dispatched to Germany as soon as the military situation permitted. Thomson had a crucial advantage over Perkins: he spoke German fluently. Perkins also recognized that the British had the advantage in the hunt for German documents. Their preparations were much further along than Washington's, and he knew he could not count on receiving necessary logistical support on-site in Germany. His only option was to collaborate with his counterparts at the Foreign Office.[97] This would not be the last time that the Americans thought the Foreign Office was far more efficient and professional in dealing with this issue: it committed more researchers, microfilm teams, translators, and clerical help to the hunt for documents than the State Department did, and British officials in Germany could communicate with London more quickly than their American counterparts could with Washington. Many at the State Department began to suspect that the British would have the pick of the German records. Perkins soon called his superiors' attention to the American document hunters' dependence on British microfilm teams. The State Department had neither the equipment nor the personnel to undertake large-scale on-site filming of captured documents; Perkins and his colleagues often felt they were at the mercy of their British counterparts.[98] As will be shown later, Anglo-American cooperation was not as frictionless as usually portrayed. The transfer of German Foreign Ministry records first from Marbug to Kassel, and then to Berlin, and, finally, to Whaddon Hall

95 Spaulding to Adolf A. Berle, Assistant SecState, Sept. 6, 1944, NA RG 59, Lot File 78D441, Historical Office, box 6.

96 Record of informal conversation, London, Jan. 16, 1945; present: Hilary Jenkinson (MFAA), Robert C. Thomson (FO), E. Ralph Perkins (State Dept.), Maj. Ellis (MFAA), Maj. Ross, Squadr. Ldr. Goodison, NA RG 59, CDF 1945–49, 840.414/1–2445.

97 Ibid. See also Perkins to Fletcher Warren, Office of the Asst. SecState, Jan. 24, 1945, FRUS 1945:3, 1099–1102, here 1101: Perkins hoped that "when the big moment comes we will not be caught unprepared. The Foreign Office is at an advantage in that they are so much closer to the field of action."

98 E. Ralph Perkins, Division of Research and Publication, to E. C. Wendelin, State Dept., Aug. 20, 1945, NA RG 59, Lot File 78D441, Historical Office, box 6.

in Buckinghamshire stemmed in part from the mistrust between the rival allies.

The joint working group, the State Department-Foreign Office team, was integrated into the CIOS structure. That was clearly the wrong place for the group because the diplomats' interest in the historical-political aspects of the German records was not served well by CIOS, with its emphasis on industry and technology. The State Department-Foreign Office team was therefore instructed to pursue its own agenda exclusively and not to do any work for CIOS.[99] In addition, it was to narrow its focus to "German international relations in the fields of diplomacy, politics and broad economic policies" and disregard issues such as war crimes, capital flight, propaganda, espionage, "fifth column" activities, and military matters.[100] The most important targets, according to the instructions the group received, were Hitler's papers and the records of the Reich Chancellery, Ribbentrop's papers and the current files of the Auswärtiges Amt, and all papers belonging to the Japanese embassy and the Nazi party's various foreign organizations. The State Department and Foreign Office were looking forward to the highly unusual opportunity to see how their own policies had been portrayed and analyzed in German Foreign Ministry memoranda.[101]

An incident that again underscored the urgency behind the preparations underway at the Foreign Office and State Department was the discovery of the final report of the Gruppe Archivwesen (Archive Group) that had been attached to the German military command in France.[102] Gruppe Archivwesen, established in July 1940, was composed of German archivists. One of its tasks was to draw up lists of German archival materials that had landed in Ferench archives over the centuries. The materials on these lists were to be considered German cultural properties that were to be returned

---

99 E. Ralph Perkins, State Department, and Robert C. Thomson, FO, Memorandum, Objectives for the Combined Teams of the British FO and the U.S. Dept. of State in Searching German Archives, London, Mar. 20, 1945, NA RG 59, Lot File 78D441, Historical Office, box 6.

100 E. Ralph Perkins and Robert C. Thomson, Memorandum. Objectives for the Combined Teams of the British Foreign Office and the U.S. Dept. of State in Searching German Archives, Mar. 20, 1945, NA RG 59, CDF 1945–49, 840.414/3–2045; abridged in FRUS 1945:3, 1102f.

101 Perkins/Thomson, Memorandum, Mar. 20, 1945, NA RG 59, CDF 1945–49, 840.414/3–2045; FRUS 1945:3 did not include the "Chief Objectives as to Persons or Offices [and] to Subject Matter" that the original memo contains. See also Woodward's list, in which he worked out the priorities for the time periods of 1933–39, 1925–32, 1919–24 and pre-1914, NA RG 84, entry 2531B, box 37.

102 The document had been found in Aachen in early February 1945 and sent by an American MFAA officer to SHAEF in Versailles, after which it was immediately forwarded to the Foreign Office. On the British side, the source is found in PRO FO 371/46799/C649; on the American side, in NA RG 331, G-2, entry 47, box 21.

to Germany.[103] The lists were to be used in the negotiations for a peace treaty with France. The Germans laid claim to these records in French archives with the argument that the materials were of German origin, an argument that in many instances had more to do with politics than archival provenance. Contested cases were always decided to the disadvantage of the French. Gruppe Archivwesen was also responsible for preparing an inventory of sources linked to German history, particularly German-French history. Although German archivists did not remove materials from French archives, the finding aids they prepared enabled non-specialists to do so. They thus opened the way for the German agencies engaged in cultural robbery. The Gruppe Archivwesen's final report lauded its achievement: "The results of this action will benefit science, administration, and politics and thereby the German people for a long time to come."[104] One archives scholar aptly describes the work of Gruppe Archivwesen as an act of cultural imperialism and the involvement of German archivists in France as "archival science's fall from grace."[105]

The Gruppe Archivwesen's final report appears to have given the British and Americans some idea of the opportunities created by unrestricted access to enemy archives. The report aroused great interest at the Foreign Office Library because it offered insight into German procedures of confiscating archives during military occupation.[106] The "archival protection" that Gruppe Archivwesen claimed it had provided "naturally passed into exploitation," Foreign Office officials noted.[107]

It was the final report of Gruppe Archivwesen that also pulled Robert D. Murphy into the pursuit of captured German records. Murphy was appointed by the State Department to serve as Political Adviser (POLAD)

103 Allied planning for Germany also contained the controversial concept of "restitution in kind," meaning the restitution for the loss of cultural treasures in the German-occupied countries using German treasures of equal value. Due to its uniqueness, archival material was explicitly excluded from any "restitution in kind." But the use of artwork for such purposes was highly controversial within the European Advisory Commission, too; after all, each piece of art was unique as well. American art experts in particular balked at the concept, which they argued would turn Germany into a "cultural desert," and grumbled that no difference was being made at the State Department between a Rembrandt and a diesel motor. See Kurtz, *Nazi Contraband*, 75–101, esp. 83–5; Kurtz, "End of the War," 114.

104 The final report is edited and prefaced in Roth, "Eine höhere Form des Plünderns"; the inventory had been edited by Stein, *Inventar von Quellen*; on the *Gruppe Archivwesen*, see also Heuss, *Kunst- und Kulturgutraub*, 260–9; Musial, *Staatsarchive im Dritten Reich*, 115f., 142–50; Stein, *Inventar von Quellen*, xxvi–lxvii.

105 Stein, "Archive als Objekt von Kulturimperialismen," 113. According to Stein, the importance of the restitution lists should not be overestimated. The fact that they were so extensive was due to the pressure on the *Gruppe Archivwesen* to justify its own existence as an institution and to demonstrate its "success."

106 Llewellyn Woodward, Library, FO, Minutes from Mar. 16, 1945, PRO FO 371/46799/C649.

107 J. Michael K. Vyvyan, Central Department, FO, Minutes from Feb. 27, 1945, ibid.

to the Allied Supreme Commander in September 1944. He was to become in effect the department's watchdog in the combat and occupation zones.[108] In early 1945, Murphy prepared plans on behalf of the American Control Commission for detaining German diplomats and ending German diplomatic relations.[109] What particularly intrigued him about the Gruppe Archivwesen's final report were the sections touching on "the enemy practice of manipulating history for political propaganda purposes."[110] He forwarded the report on to Washington the same day he received it, drawing attention to the Germans' view that control over archival materials would benefit German scholarship in the long run. Murphy apparently thought that the Americans could learn something from the German operations, in particular from the efficient cooperation between the military occupation authorities and the civilian members of Gruppe Archivwesen. He was quick to apply his new insight to the Allied cause: "Unquestionably, Allied occupational authorities in Germany will have extraordinary opportunities for the exploitation of the archives field. With this in mind, I have established a small committee in the Political Division of USGCC with the responsibility of taking an especial interest in all matters relating to the seizure and use made of German archives which come within the possession of Allied military authorities."[111] It is certainly not without irony that German treatment of enemy archives provided a model for Germany's conquerors.

In March 1945, the joint State Department–Foreign Office team left London for the Allied headquarters at Versailles. As the invasion of Germany progressed, the troops stumbled upon important caches of documents with increasing frequency. The quantity and quality of political records alone far exceeded all expectations. With each new find, the number of parties interested in the records multiplied. The captured material opened new, often unanticipated opportunities for research. The transition from invasion to occupation, from the hunt for documents to initial exploitation, put British and American planning to the test. In May 1945, on the heels of the State Department–Foreign Office team, a group from the Treasury

---

108 On the office of the POLAD, see OMGUS Handbook 98–100. In 1945, the British filled their POLAD position to the British Commander in Chief with Sir William Strang. See Reusch, "Londoner Institutionen," 378.

109 United States Group Control Council, Political Division, Top Secret, Plan for the Control of the Reich Ministry for Foreign Affairs, Jan. 13, 1945, NA RG 84, POLAD, entry 2530, box 1. The aim of the plan was "to survey and establish effective control over the Reich Ministry for Foreign Affairs (Foreign Office) and its branches."

110 Murphy to Brig. G. D. C. Heyman, Chief, G-5, Operations Branch, SHAEF, Feb. 12, 1945, NA RG 331, G-2, entry 47, box 21. He is referring to sections 5 (photocopying) and 6 (opening up the archives for inquiries and use).

111 Murphy to SecState, Feb. 12, 1945, NA RG 84, entry 2531B, box 37.

Department headed by Bernard Bernstein arrived in Germany to investigate cartel-like corporate networks and capital flight.[112] The members of the Safehaven Program under Samuel Klaus, who started their work in June, had a related task, namely to block the transfer of German assets to Switzerland. At the same time, Supreme Court Justice Robert H. Jackson, who had recently been appointed chief prosecutor for the planned war crimes trials, announced that captured German documents would be needed as evidence.[113] Murphy tried in vain to maintain an overview of and some control over the document hunters from the various civilian ministries and agencies.[114]

The members of the State Department and the Foreign Office felt hampered in their investigative work because they were always being called upon to aid the other teams.[115] The historical interests that the State Department–Foreign Office team originally wanted to pursue were overshadowed during the first phase of analysis as priority was given to gathering intelligence that had immediate implications for policy.[116] The State Department, for example, was eager for materials dealing with the collaboration of neutral countries with Nazi Germany, Nazi infiltration, and fifth column activities. The most urgent task for the assessment teams, accordingly, was to uncover "all remnants of the German political, military, commercial, and propaganda penetration machine in foreign countries."[117] Special attention was also given to the activities of international cultural institutions and German professional associations.[118] State Department officials were therefore quite excited by the seizure of records from the Deutsches Auslands

---

112 See Greiner, *Morgenthau-Legende*, 217–24.

113 Joseph C. Grew, Acting SecState, to Murphy, POLAD, June 23, 1945, FRUS 1945:3, 1111f.

114 Murphy complained about the "serious lack of coordination" between the various parties. Murphy, POLAD, to SecState, no. 438, May 31, 1945, NA RG 59, CDF 1945–49, 840.414/5–2945.

115 "From dawn to dark we here [at Marburg] are faced with the problem of coping with the infinite and varied crowds of people who come to see us, some with legitimate interests to satisfy and others with interests which by no exercise of the imagination fall within that category." Gardner E. Carpenter to Murphy, Aug. 18, 1945, NA RG 84, POLAD, entry 2531B, box 37. The director of the intelligence department "Foreign Activity Correlation" at the State Department, Frederick B. Lyon, blocked the sending in late 1945 "of another 'mission' to Germany on this matter [German diplomatic files; A. E.]. It is my frank opinion that too many 'missions' have been sent to Germany during the past eight months and that what we really need . . . is additional qualified investigators." Lyon to Riddleberger, Chief, Central European Affairs, Dec. 14, 1945, NA RG 59, Lot File 78D441, Historical Office, box 6.

116 Lyon to Riddleberger, Dec. 14, 1945, ibid.

117 Acheson, Acting SecState, Telegram (Paraphrased), [n. no.], Sept. 28, 1945, NA RG 84, POLAD, entry 2531B, box 37.

118 Clifton P. English, head of the document team, to Murphy, Projects which the Department Desires the Office of Political Affairs to Work on in Germany, May 4, 1946, ibid., box 100.

Institut and the Verein Deutscher Ingenieure (VDI, Association of German Engineers).[119]

As the Allied aerial bombing campaign intensified, the German government moved entire offices from Berlin to less-exposed locations. The deeper the Allied armies advanced into Germany, the more hectic these moves became.[120] The Bundestag representative Hermann Brill later noted: "The historical absurdity is that the German naval archive ended up in the Thuringian mountain village of Tambach, while the Archive of the High Command of the Wehrmacht ultimately landed in [the coastal city of] Flensburg in Schleswig."[121] Archivists evacuated valuable historical collections as well. The director general of the Prussian Archival Administration, Ernst Zipfel, was named Reich Commissioner for Archival Protection and organized the evacuations within the borders of the Reich.[122] Meanwhile, Allied intelligence services tried to keep track of the movement of records. The CIOS target lists were continually updated as new information became available. Still, Allied knowledge of German archival holdings was often sketchy. A June 1944 memorandum suggests, for example, that the American Office of Strategic Services (OSS) might not have been aware that the Auswärtiges Amt maintained an archive.[123] In January 1945, Robert Murphy was given a list of eleven locations where Auswärtiges

119 Acting SecState to Murphy, NA RG 59, CDF 1945–49, 840.414/5–2945. "Information described Murphy's A-33 May 29 concerning Deutsches Auslands Institut of extreme and urgent importance [to] Dept." Joseph C. Grew, Acting SecState to AmEmb London, no. 4502, June 6, 1945, ibid., 840.414/6–645. For the course of events of May 1946 leading to the VDI record seizure, see ibid.

120 On the moves of various divisions of the Reich Security Main Office, in which not only files from that office but also those seized in other countries were evacuated, see Grimsted, "Twice Plundered," 202–5, 215–17; on the moves of Auswärtiges Amt offices, see Kröger/Thimme, "Politisches Archiv," 249, 251–7; in addition, Heinsius, "Aktenmaterial der deutschen Kriegsmarine," 199f. In the 1950s, the Federal Archive attempted to reconstruct the movement of records. See Wilhelm Rohr, Übersicht über die vom Bundesarchiv in Koblenz festgestellten Auslagerungen ehemaliger zentraler Dienststellen in das Gebiet östlich der heutigen Bundesrepublik, 24 pgs., January 1957, BA/K, N1418, NL Rohr, vol. 14.

121 Speech by Hermann Brill (SPD) in the German Bundestag, stenographic report 3, 63rd session, May 11, 1950, 2311.

122 On archival protection during the war, see Henke, "Schicksal deutscher Quellen," 559–67; Herrmann, *Reichsarchiv*, 459–66; Musial, *Staatsarchive im Dritten Reich*, 96–107; Weiser, *Preußische Archivverwaltung*, 199–208. The often-quoted essay by Wilhelm Rohr, "Die zentrale Lenkung deutscher Archivschutzmaßnahmen im Zweiten Weltkrieg," *Der Archivar* 3:3 (1950): 105–22, was commissioned by Ernst Zipfel in order to redeem his reputation.

123 Thomas W. Dunn, Office Memorandum for Ferdinand Mayer, June 29, 1944, RG 226, OSS, entry 210, Sources & Methods File, box 445.

Amt files might be stored; only four were accurate.[124] With so little reliable information available to the Allied document hunters, much was left to chance.

Impressions of the Document Hunt

Key documents surfaced in the most curious places during the invasion and throughout the occupation. There were sometimes outright races for particular materials, and once found, such trophies were jealously guarded, even at the risk of diplomatic complications. Important materials were discovered in collections that had already been secured[125] or located with the information gained in interrogations of recently captured individuals. Allied soldiers came across documents that German officials either had not had the time to destroy or had consciously sought to preserve. Nazi functionaries, military leaders, and government officials offered their services to the victors, usually favoring the Americans. Buoyed by the hope of negotiating better conditions and eager to avoid falling into Soviet hands, they placed documents from their units or institutions into the hands of the Americans or promised to reveal where documents were hidden. Some of the records uncovered were of tremendous political importance and demanded immediate action.

The Nazi Party Membership File. Sometimes the GIs were just plain lucky, as in the case of the central membership registry of the Nazi party. These records, which would eventually become the heart of the Berlin Document Center, were celebrated as one of the most important finds in Europe. Bungling on the part of the U.S. Army almost resulted in the loss of the registry, however. Legend has it that soldiers of the Seventh Army found the membership records in a paper mill near Munich and saved them from destruction.[126] But according to reports in German newspapers licensed by

---

124 Latest Intelligence Regarding Location of Foreign Office Premises, Inclosure to Plan for the Control of the Reich Ministry for Foreign Affairs, Jan. 13, 1945, NA RG 84, POLAD, entry 2530, box 1.
125 One of the more well-known examples is the discovery in 1947 of the only surviving protocol of the Wannsee Conference in the records of the Auswärtiges Amt. A reconstruction of the events in Axel Frohn, "Das Dokument des Terrors," *Der Spiegel*, Feb. 9, 2002. The discovery of the secret protocol of the Hitler-Stalin Pact also belongs to this category. See Wendell W. Blancke, Memorandum, Top Secret, May 6, 1946, NA RG 84, POLAD, entry 2531B, box 100: "I myself came across the photocopy of such a protocol, complete with hand-drawn map for the division of Poland and an agreement for the distribution of influence."
126 According to Kurt Rosenow, 7771st Document Center, *Military Government Information Bulletin*, no. 105 (Aug. 11, 1947), 3f., 10, here 3, the membership cards were stuffed in sacks stored in the paper mill "to be opened by pop-eyed, mudstained GIs"; see also Beddie, "Berlin Document Center," 134.

the British and American authorities, credit was due not to the GIs but rather to the owner of a Munich paper mill.[127] Instead of shredding the documents as the Nazi party headquarters had ordered in April 1945, Hans Huber hid approximately eight million index cards – each one detailing an individual's membership in the Nazi Party – under scrap paper and reported his "treasure" to the American city commander of Munich at the end of May.[128] Although Huber substantiated his claim by producing three sacks of index cards, the Counter Intelligence Corps of the Seventh Army did not take immediate action. Months later, the U.S. military government's archival advisor, Sargent B. Child, could barely control his anger in his report to the Librarian of Congress on his visit to Huber's paper mill. Although "any damn fool" should have understood how important the material in the sacks was, Child wrote, no one had pursued the matter until Major William D. Brown, the newly assigned security officer of the Third Army, followed up on the matter four weeks after Huber had reported having the membership file. Despite the lack of interest on the part of his superiors, Brown was able to locate the paper mill. Another five weeks then passed without a response from the military government headquarters in Berlin and Frankfurt to the discovery of such obviously important records. Finally, Brown traveled to Frankfurt in September to get someone to listen to him and to arrange for logistic support.[129] Meanwhile, the index cards remained in storage in Munich, unsorted and thus unusable. At the Office of the Political Advisor, the anger was immense. The Nazi party membership registry was considered the most important document discovery in Germany. It came to be seen as the key to uncovering the underground activities of the Nazi party, to exposing Nazis abroad, and to proceeding quickly with denazification.[130] The fifty tons of index cards were transported to the Ministerial Collecting Center (MCC) at Fürstenhagen near Kassel in November 1945 and then forwarded to the Document Center in Berlin the following January. "This story," Child fumed, "along with Uncle Georgie Patton's exit would sound

---

127 Stefan Heym wrote a literary rendition of this episode in which the owner of the paper mill is named Bachleitner. See Heym, *Eine wahre Geschichte*, 51–76.
128 Gwyn Lewis, "What the Complete Records of the Nazi Party Show," *Sunday Express*, Oct. 21, 1945, 1; "Parteiakten in einer Papiermühle," *Neue Zeitung*, Oct. 25, 1945, 3; "Namen unter Abfallpapier," *Neue Zeitung*, Oct. 28, 1945, 4. The first report of the find was filed by the Associated Press, "Yanks Find Nazi Files Listing 8,000,000 Members of Party," *Washington Star*, Oct. 17, 1945.
129 Sargent B. Child, Advisor on Archives and Libraries, OMGUS, to Luther Evans, Librarian of Congress, Oct. 8, 1945.
130 Robert Murphy, POLAD, to SecState, no. 1296, Nov. 7, 1945; John T. Burnite, Office of the POLAD, to Herbert C. Cummings, State Dept, Nov. 15, 1945, both in NA RG 59, Lot File 60D24, box 1.

well [to the press], wouldn't it?"[131] Indeed, the Army had to contend with sharp criticism from the press and Congress because of this incident.[132]

Hitler's Last Will and Testament. Three copies of Hitler's personal and political testaments surfaced in November and December of 1945. Hitler had signed them on April 29; three messengers were ordered to take them from the besieged Führer bunker. The messengers survived, but not one arrived at his assigned destination.[133] The first messenger seized was Heinz Lorenz, a member of Goebbel's propaganda ministry. He was traveling as a journalist with Luxembourgian papers when the British arrested him. His capture helped Allies track down the other two messengers: Willi Johannmeier, Hitler's army adjutant, and Wilhelm Zander, an advisor to Martin Bormann. Zander had gone into hiding in the American zone under the alias "Friedrich Wilhelm Paustin."[134] Two of the testaments thus landed in British hands and one in American.[135] Although the texts of the testaments appeared in the Allied press by January 1946, British Foreign Secretary Ernest Bevin was in favor of restricting access to the originals and withholding official comment on the content of the testaments, thereby consigning them to oblivion. He feared that the originals "might in time become objects of great sentimental and political value to many Germans" and therefore suggested to the American secretary of state "whether it would not be wise to destroy these [three] sets."[136] The number of copies should be "very strictly limited" for the same reasons. The British copies, Bevin said, would be taken out of Germany and "safely interred in the British official archives."[137] Given that the texts had already been published, the State Department did not appear to be very impressed by Bevin's concern. It affirmed only that it would prevent the testaments from becoming better known in Germany by not encouraging further radio or newspaper reports about them. The State Department also reminded the British that once the occupation was over and Allied control over the German press lifted, there would be little Britain or the United States could do to prohibit publication

---

131 Child to Evans, Oct. 8, 1945, LoCM box 31.
132 Victor H. Bernstein, "Open Letter to Gen. McNarney: Make Nazi Party File Public," *PM*, Dec. 10, 1945. See also O. P. Echols, Director, Civil Affairs Div., to Lucius D. Clay, Apr. 8. 1946, NA RG 59, Lot File 60D24, box 1.
133 The events are described in detail by Trevor-Roper, *Last Days of Hitler*, 27–31, 236–241, 245–9.
134 Ibid., 29f. On Zander, see 1st Lt. Allen Fial, to ACoS, G-2, Third U.S. Army, Dec. 28, 1945, NA RG 59, CDF 1945–49, 840.414/12–2845.
135 The British Document Activity Report no. 7, Jan. 26, 1946, presents the copies taken from Lorenz and Johannmeier. NA RG 260, OMGUS, Records of the Executive Office of FIAT, box 30.
136 BritEmb Washington, Aide Memoire, Ref. G4/-/46, Jan. 9, 1946, NA RG 59, CDF 1945–49, FW 840.414/1–1246.
137 Ibid.

within Germany.[138] Meanwhile, the number of copies circulating in the United States was increasing rapidly. Hitler's testaments and his marriage certificate were the only captured documents presented to President Truman personally. Truman had a copy made for himself and offered Secretary of War Robert Patterson another copy as a souvenir. Patterson and Eisenhower suggested having the documents exhibited at the Library of Congress – a suggestion hardly compatible with the secrecy Bevin recommended.[139] In the end, the testaments were introduced as evidence at the Nuremberg Trial[140] and stored at the National Archives, where they were on public display for a number of years.

Stalin's Son. Quick decisions had to be made about a number of potentially sensitive documents. The materials documenting the death of Stalin's son Yakov Dzhugashvili in 1943 in Sachsenhausen are one example. The materials had been found in the so-called Schmidt Box that had been buried near Mühlhausen in Thuringia by a colleague of Ribbentrop's chief interpreter, Paul Schmidt.[141] Gardner Carpenter of the State Department-Foreign Office team was the first to inspect the contents of the box. He suggested spontaneously that the documents be handed over to Stalin as a humanitarian gesture, on the erroneous assumption that Stalin cared about Dzhugashvili.[142] The idea was given serious consideration at the Foreign Office and the State Department. There was talk of Truman and Attlee presenting the originals to Stalin at the Potsdam Conference as an expression of condolence.[143] Once the documents had arrived in London and could be examined more closely, the Foreign Office backed away from the idea. "You will see on examining the documents . . . that the background of the incident is unpleasant," a Foreign Office official told an American colleague at the U.S. Embassy in London.[144] The German records indicated that Dzhugaschvili had been shot while attempting to flee – usually a euphemism for cold-blooded murder. What was "unpleasant" about the

---

138 State Department to BritEmb Washington, Aide Memoire, Jan. 30, 1946, NA RG 59, CDF 1945–49, 840.414/1-1245.
139 The episode described in NA RG 407, entry 363, box 943.
140 Prozeß Nürnberg, vol. XLI, PS-3569 used as document Streicher-9, 547–554.
141 On the discovery of the Schmidt box, see section 3 a in this chapter and Zala, *Zensur*, 169–170; Kent, "German Foreign Ministry Archives," 121f.
142 Carpenter to Robert Murphy, POLAD, June 30, 1945, NA RG 84, entry 2531B, box 37; a description of the documents by Carpenter und J. I. Jones, SD-FO Team in Marburg, Discovery of Private Files of Dr. Paul Schmidt, June 13, 1945, NA RG 59, Lot File 78D441, Historical Office, box 6.
143 The discussion in PRO FO 371/46713 C3120/G.
144 Michael Vyvyan to Allison, USEmb London, Minutes, July 31, 1945, NA RG 84, POLAD, entry 2600A, box 30.

incident from the British perspective was that his death had been preceded by an argument with British fellow prisoners. Officials at the Foreign Office came to the view that Stalin would not be consoled by the reports and photographs. It would be "distasteful... to draw attention to the Anglo-Russian quarrels [among the prisoners] which preceded the death of his son."[145] They may have feared that any mention of Anglo-Russian quarrels might take on symbolic weight at the Potsdam Conference. A more serious concern may have been the thought that, as soon as he saw the records pertaining to Dzhugashvili's death, Stalin would probably ask questions about the volume of captured documents in Anglo-American hands. This concern was reinforced by an incident that occurred while the idea of making a humanitarian gesture was still under discussion. In response to the first hints about captured German diplomatic records in the British press, Soviet ambassador Feodor T. Gusev immediately demanded to see the materials in British possession.[146]

Behind the Lines. By May 1945, American and British troops had advanced far into the territory earmarked for Soviet occupation. In the southeast, George Patton's Third Army had advanced almost to the pre-1938 border of Czechoslovakia and stood ready to march on to Prague. As the city was, by agreement among the Allied leaders, to be liberated by the Red Army, Patton's troops remained at the designated demarcation line, which ran east of Carlsbad, Pilsen, and Budweis. The Fourth Armored Division of the Third Army set up its headquarters at Strakonice, southeast of Pilsen. Behind the lines, east of Strakonice, lay the headquarters of the Wehrmacht's Heeresgruppe Mitte (Army Group Center). American officers learned on May 11, 1945, that a German intelligence unit, reportedly in possession of extensive and detailed information about the Red Army, was also there. The British and Americans had only sketchy military intelligence about their Soviet allies at that time. Therefore, a small American intelligence unit was ordered to locate the Germans and to secure the material. The mission was not without danger but proved to be well worth the risk. The Americans returned to Strakonice with "two truckloads' worth" of material. The captured documents were sent immediately to Frankfurt.[147]

---

145 Ibid. See also Murphy to Carpenter, Sept. 6, 1945, NA RG 84, POLAD, entry 2531B, box 37.
146 "Hitler secrets sent to London," *Daily Express*, May 29, 1945; "Allies Record Nazi Secrets. Germany's most secret docs are safe in Allied hands," *Sunday Chronicle*, June 24, 1945; Soviet Embassy London, Aide Memoire, June 19, 1945, PRO FO 371/46713 C3351/G.
147 Jacobs, "Operation Strakoniče" (with map). Harry A. Jacobs was a member of the Order of Battle (O/B) Team 24 of the Fourth Armored Division, which undertook the mission. The records

This expedition was not the only one of its kind. In February 1946, American agents carried out an operation to gain possession of a cache of documents that included the pre-war private and official papers of President Edvard Beneš, an operation that, as one official acknowledged, bore "certain marks of hijacking."[148] In 1938, Beneš had resigned in protest against the Munich Agreement and escaped to London, where he had headed the Czech government-in-exile. He was temporarily reinstated as president by the National Assembly following his return to Prague in 1945; at the time of American expedition, he was the Western Allies' preferred candidate in the approaching presidential election. To remove documents from the territory of an ally was a delicate operation to say the least, and absolute secrecy was essential.[149] The thirty-two boxes of material that the members of the Army's G-2 Documents Section retrieved included not only Beneš's papers but also the secret files of the protectorate government of Bohemia and Moravia from 1940 to 1945; Gestapo and Security Service (SD) files, including lists of SD informants and an address list of SD offices; records from regional SS-units; and an inventory of "treasures in certain Bohemian castles."[150]

The Americans owed this find to a chain of informants. An SS man being held by the French had told them of a hidden depository in a mine shaft but warned that the mine was booby-trapped with explosives. Since the French did not have the necessary personnel and equipment to defuse the explosives, they turned to the Americans. On February 10, 1946, a commando unit crossed the demarcation line near Strakonice. Among the fourteen members were two French soldiers, the German informant, and a *New York Times* correspondent who had gotten wind of the affair. Three days later, they returned with the documents, but three members of the group had been captured by Czechoslovak police and were being held in Prague. According to a later newspaper account, one of the American soldiers involved in the operation shot at a Czechoslovak soldier.[151] The American ambassador in Prague, Laurence A. Steinhardt, at first denied having any knowledge of the operation. Robert Murphy's staff was working in the meanwhile on

---

were combined with those of General Gehlen's "Foreign Armies East" and shipped to the United States.

148 J. D. Beam, Office POLAD Frankfurt, to Robert Murphy, Berlin, no. 18, Feb. 15, 1946, NA RG 84, POLAD Frankfurt, entry 2544, box 1. This and the other telegrams were classified as "Top Secret & Urgent."

149 Ibid.

150 Beam to Murphy, no. 22, Feb. 18, 1946, ibid. The telegram no. 18 (Feb. 15, 1946, NA RG 84, POLAD Frankfurt, entry 2544, box 1) speaks of an "inventory of treasures in Bavaria and Moravia." It was not possible to verify either reference.

151 "Czechs to Regain Papers Army Took," *New York Times*, Feb. 24, 1946, 29.

an account of the incident that would be acceptable to the Czechoslovak government. If pressed, American officials were to explain "that secrecy and raid technique were necessary since [the] depository was heavily mined, contained a large quantity of gasoline for destruction of the documents, and was under surveillance by German agents who were prepared to blow it up to prevent capture."[152] Just how German agents would have been in a position in February 1946, nearly a year after Germany's surrender, to guard or destroy a hidden depository near Prague without being detected remained Murphy's secret. In the end, the Americans could not avoid offering an official apology after Foreign Minister Jan Masaryk publicly pointed out that Czechoslovakia was a member of the alliance and that the war was over.[153] American diplomats thereupon portrayed the incident as an attempt to protect Czech lives and rescue important documents belonging to an ally.[154] In March 1946, the documents were turned over to President Beneš with the assurance that the American military authorities had not retained any of the retrieved materials. An incident that could have resulted in an embossing diplomatic imbroglio ended instead with the Czechoslovak military attaché exuberantly commending the Americans for a job well done.[155]

The American decision to cooperate with the Prague government was motivated less by altruism than by the recognition that the captured documents were of no use to either the State Department or the Army. "As far as our own interests go, it was hardly worth the risk, trouble, and international complications involved," a member of Murphy's staff concluded.[156] The most important items among Beneš's papers, the staffer speculated, had probably been removed sometime earlier. The light that the remaining papers cast on Beneš's international contacts was of strictly historical relevance. It is easy to imagine, however, that American officials nonetheless read the lists of SD informants, the SS Gestapo records, and documents on hidden art treasures with considerable interest before turning them over to Prague.

---

152 Beam to Murphy, no. 19, Feb. 15, 1946, NA RG 84, POLAD Frankfurt, entry 2544, box 1.
153 "Czechs to Regain Papers Army Took," *New York Times*, Feb. 24, 1946, 29.
154 "Public warning or negotiations with Czech authorities would have resulted in loss of this material as well as Czech lives." Beam to Murphy, no. 22, Feb. 18, 1946, NA RG 84, POLAD Frankfurt, entry 2544, box 1.
155 "Lt. Gen. (Ambassador) Palecek . . . expressed to me his admiration of the capable handling of this matter by the American personnel involved as well as for their courage in extracting the documents from the cunningly devised explosive system designed by the Nazis . . . ." Murphy to SecState, no. 864, Mar. 24, 1946, NA RG 59, CDF 1945–49, FW 840.414/3–2446.
156 Perry Laukhuff, Memorandum for Robert Murphy, Feb. 27, 1946, NA RG 84, POLAD Frankfurt, entry 2544, box 1.

Document Centers

The mass of archival materials and administrative records, the multitude of depositories, and the countless inquiries from their own governments were from the outset more than the intelligence officers and archivists accompanying the advancing armies could handle. The decision to establish so-called document centers was an important first step toward bringing the situation under control. At the document centers, document hunters from various government agencies and ministries could make microfilm copies of captured German records or analyze them on the spot in response to inquiries from their superiors. The British established a registry system for their centers to prevent records from disappearing and thereby made a move toward institutionalizing measures to protect archival collections.[157] The document centers thus played a double role: they made records available for use while also safeguarding them. They were not merely storage facilities where documents were simply stockpiled or held until being transferred elsewhere.

In July 1945, at the end of the SHAEF period, the centers were either closed in connection with troop redeployment or were turned over to the Control Commissions. The process of closing document centers could take a toll on the records. Time pressures, lack of manpower, or insufficient preparation for the future storage of records could tempt the personnel in charge to deal haphazardly with documents, even to go so far on occasion as to pulp them. At least until the end of 1946, German records of all types were constantly on the move as document and collection centers were set up, consolidated, and closed. It is impossible to reconstruct a complete list of the collection centers, and imprecise recordkeeping on the part of the Allies often makes it difficult to track particular record groups or to determine the quantities of documents seized.[158]

157 The clearest definition of the mission for the British Document Centers is found in the Intelligence Directive no. 7 of the British Intelligence Objectives Sub-Committee (BIOS), Handling of German Documents and Archives in the British Zone, Sept. 10, 1945, NA RG 260, FIAT Executive Office, box 43. The directive is based on the instructions from the German Document Panel in London and has been clearly influenced by Hilary Jenkinson. The mission of the Centers in the jurisdiction of the Rhine Army were "a) the protection of German documents and archives within their respective areas; b) the maintenance of a register showing the location and nature of German documents and archives within their area, or evacuated from it; c) the circulation of information contained in this register; d) the control and assistance of all exploiting agencies."

158 Unlike Wolfe, Short History, xxii, n. 2, I do not think it is possible "to trace in contemporary records the odyssey from German evacuation sites, through Allied document centers, to ultimate American depositories." This might work in certain, prominent cases like the records of the Auswärtiges Amt. But in contemporary record keeping, the assessment of quantities ("60 drawers," "5 truckloads," "small," and "4 large cases") and the naming of collections in either the German original or various English translations often undermine such efforts.

The most important British document centers were located in Herford, Minden, Bünde, and Düsseldorf. Each Corps District was to have at least one center of its own. Ad hoc collecting points were also set up, for example in Iserlohn, Nienburg, Bad Oeynhausen, and Hamburg. A collecting point in Delmenhorst specialized in records that were of interest to Canada and were to be sent there.[159] The British Control Commission for Austria gathered captured documents in Klagenfurt. The British also ran several smaller collection centers, often in locations where documents had been confiscated during the invasion. The U.S. Army established its most important document center in Austria in Linz. In Germany, the U.S. Third Army had its Document Center in Freising and the Seventh Army in Heidelberg. Both armies also had a number of temporary collection centers, often in places were documents had been found.[160] A handful of document centers were clustered around Frankfurt, where Eisenhower had his main headquarters: Griesheim, Oberursel, and Fechenheim. The center at Griesheim was used exclusively for assembling the records of IG Farben. Oberursel and Fechenheim focused on military records. Fechenheim served as the center for materials that were to be shipped to the United States. Oberursel functioned as part of the European Command's intelligence division.[161] Once procedures for handling captured documents were in place, the Oberursel center became responsible for the preservation, evaluation, and distribution of materials relevant to intelligence work.[162]

One of the most important document centers was the Ministerial Collection Center (MCC) in Fürstenhagen, southeast of Kassel. Documents from

159 Courtlandt Canby to Just Lunning, Information on British Document Centers, Aug. 21, 1945, NA RG 238, entry 52a, box 1.

160 This is based on a list of the 3rd Army Document Center, which the POLAD office forwarded to Washington. Enclosure to Dispatch no. 1418, Murphy to SecState, 3rd Army Accession List, Nov. 26, 1945, NA RG 84, entry 2531B, box 37. The list was drawn up shortly before the center in Freising was closed down, and it includes a list of the projected locations where the records were to be deposited. In addition, see the Periodic Report no. 1 of the Enemy Documents Unit, Main Headquarters CCG (BE) [in Bünde], Sept. 20, 1945, NA RG 260, OMGUS, FIAT, Executive Office, box 43. The report lists the document centers that existed at the time.

161 The full name was Document [Control] Section of the 7707th European Command Intelligence Center at Oberursel. The Center was under the command of Col. Lt. Gronich, who had already headed the document collection center in Algiers. See Capt. Courtlandt Canby to Lt. Just Lunning, Conversation with Capt. Ranis of USFET Documents Control Section, Aug. 11, 1945, NA RG 238, entry 52a, box 1.

162 "The Document Section at Oberursel is charged with receiving and screening all captured enemy documents when they are first discovered, and later on, after the documents have been utilized by all using agencies in the European Command, with the shipment of these documents to GMDS [German Military Document Section, Pentagon]. It is also the hub of all documents being shipped *to* the European Command *from* the States, and thus the distribution point of these documents." W. R. Rainford for the Deputy Director of Intelligence, HQ EUCOM, to Director of Intelligence, War Department, Mar. 30, 1948, NA RG 59, Lot File 78D441, Historical Office, box 23.

governmental ministries and institutions were gathered there, and former personnel of those bodies were held at the center to assist Allied officials in sorting through the captured materials. The MCC was a U.S. facility located in the American occupation zone; in practice, the Americans and British operated it jointly.[163] Under Operation Goldcup, the MCC was to take charge of documents that would be needed for the planned Four Power administration of Germany.[164] By August 10, 1945, the MCC was in possession of 1,420 tons of records and 52 tons of microfilm, and it had 1,300 former German government officials working for it.[165] In February 1946, the MCC began to transfer administrative records to German authorities in preparation for the creation of the Anglo-American Bizone – a quiet indicator that Four Power rule was failing. The remaining records and the German diplomatic files still stored in Marburg were transferred to the Ministerial Document Branch (MDB) in Berlin. Administratively, the MDB was part of the 6998th Berlin Document Center (BDC), which at that time was not yet a collecting point solely for materials related to the Nazi Party.[166] The situation had barely settled when the 1948 Berlin Blockade began to shake things up again. The Army considered the situation of the city so precarious that it briefly considered evacuating the entire BDC to western Germany. In the end, however, it decided in favor of a cheaper alternative and made preparations to destroy the collection of records should the Soviets invade. The water mains serving the BDC's building were enlarged so that the center could be flooded immediately in an

163 The "Founding Charter" of the MCC: USGCC, Goldcup Operations Staff, Ministerial Control Memorandum no. 15, Subject: Establishment of MCC Kassel, June 17, 1945, NA RG 242, BDC Directorate Files, box 10A. For a history of the MCC, see Born, "MCC." The sources use the names Ministerial *Control* Center or Ministerial *Collection* Center synonymously. Part of the MCC were the camps Hertzog, Esche, Foehren, Teichhof, and Camp Dentine, in which ministerial officials were brought together. It is unclear whether these stays were voluntary or due to "automatic arrest." At one point Born says: "The Germans we needed were brought along *if they cared to come.*" See State Dept., Memorandum of Conversation, Participants: Lester K. Born and Bernard Noble, June 21, 1946, NA RG 59, Lot File 78D441, Historical Office, box 23 (emphasis added). A British diplomat called it "a skeleton of German governmental departments which in due course will assist with administration of Germany." See Michael Creswell for the German Department, FO, Minutes, Sept. 17, 1945, PRO FO 370/1191 L3644.

164 Murphy, POLAD, to SecState, no. A-43, June 19, 1945, 740.00119 Control (Germany)/6–1945, FRUS 1945:3, 863f.; OMGUS, MCC: News Release, Nov. 23, 1945, NA RG 242, BDC History & Archives, box 16.

165 Ziemke, *U.S. Army,* 315. Because of the sources Ziemke uses, his figures appear to be more likely than those in FRUS 1945:3, 863, n. 84, where the figures for August 1945 are said to be 752 tons and 1,056 officials.

166 However, it received all of the party material that had been found in the Kassel MCC inventories and assigned it to its "NSDAP & Affiliated Records Branch" in Berlin-Zehlendorf. In October 1946, the center was renamed the 7771st Berlin Document Center. A branch depository of this center was the BDC Rear in Darmstadt. See Wolfe, "Short History."

emergency.[167] By special order, selected record groups, including two tons of files from the Reichssicherheitshauptamt (Reich Security Main Office) were flown to the United States or were transferred to a branch depository, the Berlin Document Center (Rear), in Darmstadt.[168] The Auswärtiges Amt records were flown out of Berlin in the cargo planes used for the Berlin Air Lift, the so-called candy bombers, on their return journeys west.[169]

Stolen Items, Goods, and "Souvenirs"

Of course, the naïve hunger of GIs, Tommies, Poilus, and Ivans for souvenirs impeded the collecting and screening work of the Allied agencies by no small degree. Long after the war was over, the trade with valuable Reich documents is said to have still flourished in America.[170]

The employment of Germans at the document centers caused the Americans headaches from the very start. All local personnel had to undergo a rigorous process of denazification. In the fear that German staff members might steal or tamper with the records, efforts were made to supervise them at all times. It soon became clear, however, that constant surveillance was too manpower-intensive.[171] Given the dependence of the commanding officers of the collection centers on the expertise of German archivists and librarians, close supervision threatened the work climate.[172] Strict controls were enforced, however, at the Offenbach Archival Depot (OAD), which

---

167 Col. Charles M. Adams, Deputy Director, Intelligence Division, HQ EUCOM, Jan. 18, 1951, NA RG 319, IRR Files, Impersonal Files, XE169191, box 22. See Col. Charles M. Adams, Deputy Director, Intelligence Division, HQ EUCOM, Memorandum for the Chief of Staff, July 12, 1951, ibid.

168 This is based on information in the list "Index of German Archives known or thought to have fallen into allied hands" submitted as an appendix by F. W. Marten, BritEmb Bonn, to Edward E. Tomkins, Western Dept., FO, no. 2015, June 8, 1960, PRO FO 371/154333 WG 2011/46. At the time, efforts were being made at the FO to determine what had happened to the records from the BDC. Under the rubric of "apparently shipped to the U.S.," the report listed small collections of files on medical experiments performed on concentration camp prisoners. Wolfe, "Short History," XVI, also mentions 2.5 tons from the Persönlicher Stab RFSS (Office of the Reichsführer-SS), 2.5 tons from SS-Oberabschnitte (SS regional offices), and a small number of records from the SS-Führungshauptamtes (SS-Head Operational Office).

169 See p. 94 below.

170 "Volk ohne gestern. Das Schicksal der deutschen Akten – Sammeln, ehe es zu spät ist!" *Christ und Welt*, Mar. 24, 1949, 12.

171 See PRO FO 370/1490 L1871: Security at Tempelhof.

172 In the fall of 1945, Lt. Col. Thomson spoke out against shipping the records of the Auswärtiges Amt abroad: "It would be a calamity to go anywhere without our German staff. We have no indexes to help us, and while it is true that we can gradually wade through the tons of material, it is almost impossible to find anything without the trained German assistance. I should not care to take our Germans to the US as semi-prisoners and expect them to give us good service." Thomson to Ivor T. Pink, CCG(BE), Oct. 24, 1945, PRO FO 370/1189 L3296.

collected Jewish books and sacral objects and sought to return them to their owners.[173] American officers more or less expected the local personnel to object to OAD's mission: "The German workers felt that all of this Nazi loot was their rightful booty; that the entire restitution operation was the undoing of work in which they still believed," an American librarian observed.[174] When a theft at the book depot of the Library of Congress Mission in Berlin was discovered, German workers were exonerated with the explanation that they were "more likely to steal the Tendenz material [i.e., Nazi literature] than scientific periodicals or monographs."[175] In fact, though, when German employees decided to risk jeopardizing the warm daily meal that came with a job with the U.S. Army, they were much more likely to pilfer movie and automobile magazines than literary relics of the Third Reich.[176] Theft of items at the OAD could not be attributed to the center's German employees. As the OAD's acting director wrote his superior in 1947, "any dwindling of the items . . . has not, to date, been traceable to German employees."[177] Certainly, more than a few of the German staff members were guilty of theft, but the results had to be worth the risk. It was, above all, goods that could be sold quickly and lucratively on the black market that disappeared. Judging by the reports of the OAD security guards, the most desirable items were electrical appliances, nails, and cigarettes. Once an entire motor was disassembled and carried past the guards. The comments of one OAD employee make clear the motivation behind such pilferage:

The controll at the main-entrance must be better. If somebody wants to steal something he can move it out of the plan[t] easily with a car. Who smoks the American Zigarettes? Who eats bread in a great quantity? I cannot do it with only 2 pounds the week and only a small salary.[178]

Governmental records and confidential official correspondence fell into German hands in a variety of ways, including theft. Those who thought they could cash in on their document finds by offering them for sale to American officials often did not get very far. One man, for example, asked an employee of the Library of Congress about the value of four packs of letters to Hitler;

173 Pomrenze, "Personal Reminiscences," 525.   174 Poste, "Books Go Home," 1704.
175 Verner W. Clapp, Director Acquisition, LoC, to Don C. Travis, Feb. 14, 1947, LoCM box 16.
176 Douwe Stuurman to Reuben Peiss, Summary of Munich Operations, June 1, 1946, LoCM box 8.
177 L. Wilkinson, Acting Director OAD, to General Lucius D. Clay, Memorandum, Unidentifiable Jewish books at the OAD, Apr. 29, 1947, NA RG 260, OMGUS Property Division, box 66.
178 Statement made by Kaspar Unger to Captain Bencovitz, Director, OAD, July 26, 1946, NA RG 260, OMGUS Property Division, box 250. The spelling and style are those of the original.

the letters were immediately confiscated.[179] The same thing happened to the person who tried to sell the so-called Kaltenbrunner reports for the exorbitant price of 200,000 Marks to the Institute for the Study of the National Socialist Era, the predecessor to the Institute of Contemporary History. The reports document the Gestapo's interrogation of individuals suspected of participating in the attempted assassination of Hitler on July 20, 1944. The papers were immediately confiscated by the U.S. Army and sent to Washington.[180] The British appear to have dealt with private offers in a less drastic manner. Royal Air Force officers in Berlin were accustomed to being offered documents for sale. Naturally they could have had such materials confiscated, as one officer explained, "but this would mean losing a source." Instead, they advocated "diplomacy": Venturing into the city's thriving black market for documents.

Many German documents . . . can be obtained on payment of money or goods (coffee, etc.) to their "owners." Only the "owners" know the whereabouts of the documents, some of which are buried in the Russian Zone. Some of the documents are periodically "hawked" around the four Sectors of BERLIN, and sold to the Power giving the best price. [Air Force Intelligence] suggests that many documents could be obtained if a sum of German marks were forthcoming.[181]

One problem that military authorities apparently found almost impossible to bring under control was the theft of important documents by members of the occupation forces themselves. While it was generally assumed that German employees would steal materials, the head of the Ministerial Collecting Center was astonished to learn that Americans, too, were susceptible to temptation.[182] "Souvenir hunting" and the "liberation" of documents were serious problems. Sargent B. Child complained in early 1946, "I have seen no evidence that the situation where the looting of books and archives,

---

179 Sargent B. Child, Archives Adviser, USGCC, to Luther Evans, Librarian of Congress, Sept. 21, 1945, LoCM box 34. See also Thomas R. Henry, "Hitler Considered a God Letter Collection Shows. Library of Congress Gathered Data in Ransacked Reichchancellery," *Evening Star*, Dec. 15, 1946, LoCM box 29.

180 John W. Wheeler-Bennett to P. H. Dean, German Political Dept., FO, June 11, 1948, PRO FO 370/1697 L5935; C. O'Neill, Office of Brit. POLAD, to P. H. Dean, Sept. 8, 1948, ibid., L5936. Wheeler-Bennett learned of this offer from his contacts to Dutch historians and had the information verified by the Americans through the Office of the High Commission. That office confirmed that an offer had been made to the Institute. However, the sources do not indicate how the Kaltenbrunner reports landed in the hands of the German seller and who that seller was.

181 D. J. Cooke, Flight Lt., Historical Records Section, HQ BAFO, to Air Ministry [London], attn. J. C. Nerney, Document Centers in British Zone and Berlin, June 17, 1949, PRO FO 370/1957 L3208.

182 Col. Henry C. Newton, Director, MCC, to Lt. Col. Hans Helm, Commanding Officer, BDC, Feb. 12, 1946: "It is conceivable that German clerks working in these Divisions might remove records, if they so desired. We have even had difficulty with US personnel attempting to remove records. I have no suggestion to offer in this matter." NA RG 260, FIAT, Executive Office, box 30.

which has been going on since the American occupation began, has lessened except for the fact [that] there are fewer today in our overseas army than there were two months ago."[183]

Such complaints give little evidence of the actual extent of theft, but Child undoubtedly touched on a sore spot.[184] With an eye toward lifting troop morale, President Roosevelt had issued a decree in late August 1944 permitting members of the armed forces to collect war trophies.[185] What was to be considered a trophy was precisely outlined. It appears that the decree gave retroactive sanction to an already existing practice, and it might also have further undermined discipline on this matter.[186] As early as the winter of 1945–1946, when the first wave of GIs returned home, the results of the souvenir hunt became evident in the United States. Librarians related incidents of receiving dubious offers of valuable manuscripts and books that obviously were not family heirlooms. Yet they did not dare report these to the police because they feared the sellers might then destroy the evidence.[187]

Souvenir hunting even affected documents in collections that had already been secured. The losses suffered at the Ministerial Document Branch in Berlin-Tempelhof serve as a case in point. Indeed, the center almost invited theft at first. When Clay ordered the transfer of the German diplomatic records from Marburg and the MCC in Fürstenhagen to Berlin, the buildings that were to house the records still lacked doors and windows.[188] Nor were there enough British and American personnel to supervise the German employees effectively, but that was the least of the center's difficulties.[189]

---

183 Sargent B. Child, Archives Adviser, OMGUS, Economic Div., Restitution Branch, to Chief, Restitution Branch, OMGUS, Mar. 14, 1946, NA RG 242, AGAR-S no. 508, box 1. On plundering, see also Nicholas, *Rape of Europa*, 342, 354–7.

184 References to "liberated" documents are frequently found in the literature, often in the form of anecdotes. For one example, see the discussion at a 1968 National Archives conference in Wolfe, *Captured German Records*, 109, 114; on the "liberation" of early Himmler diaries from his villa on Tegernsee, see Angress and Smith, "Diaries," 206.

185 War Department Circular 353, Aug. 31, 1944, quoted in Downey, "Captured Enemy Property," 500f.

186 During the 1990s, as the interest in the whereabouts of artwork increased, the issue was raised about plundering by American G.I.s, a behavior that until then had been chiefly attributed to Russian soldiers. Several cases are depicted in sensational manner by Alford, *Spoils of War*. See also the case study on the Quedlinburg treasures in Simpson, *Spoils of War*, 148–58; on the theft of jewels from the castle of the royal house of Hesse, see Petropolous, *Royals and the Reich*, 344–50; on a castle in Koblenz, see Weiß, "Ehrenbreitstein," 441–8.

187 "Priceless Loot," *Newsweek*, vol. 27, no. 2, Jan. 14, 1946, 18.

188 "The buildings into which the records were to go was [sic] not ready and all of the responsible officers knew that they could not be ready then. The move was ordered regardless . . . . The Political Division [i.e. Murphy; A.E.] had been notified about the condition of the buildings which were without doors and windows." State Department, Memorandum of Conversation, Major Lester K. Born and Bernard Noble, June 21, 1946, NA, RG 59, Lot File 78D441, Historical Office, box 23. Also, Born, "MCC," 255.

189 The British POLAD, Christopher Steele, complained about the conditions at Tempelhof: "I did not feel at all happy about the number of Germans who were working on the archives in the

More troublesome was the onslaught of visitors from various governmental agencies and ministries seeking access to the Auswärtiges Amt files. The State Department–Foreign Office team soon found itself in a situation "bordering on chaos."[190] The first document losses were soon discovered. Major T. H. Frame of the Foreign Office, who had already worked with the files of the Reich Chancellery at the Seventh Army's document center in Heidelberg, found upon looking through the papers again in Berlin "that at least one or two documents have been removed from the files, including the letter signed by the Kaiser accepting Bismarck's resignation, and the final draft of the letter of resignation." Several documents bearing Hitler's signature were also missing.[191]

Lt. Col. Thomson, who was in charge of the diplomatic records, was particularly irritated with the members of the chief prosecutor's office in Nuremberg. The staff had been given permission in September 1945 to remove documents from the captured Auswärtiges Amt files to prepare for the proceedings.[192] Thomson thought it was too risky to give the chief prosecutor's assistants free access to the files because "some of these Subsequent Proceedings people are more interested in scoops and souvenirs than in assembling evidence for trials."[193] The situation was soon out of control. "My American colleague and I are at one in suspecting that the motives of more than one research worker from Nuremberg are more influenced by private journalistic instincts than by a desire to further the cause of justice," Thomson observed in a memorandum.[194] One document that went

various storage rooms, and walking about the building carrying papers from one place to another, apparently under no Allied supervision of any kind." Steele to Donald Heath, Office of the American POLAD, Aug. 27, 1946, NA RG 84, entry 2531B, box 100.

190 Clifton P. English, Memorandum, Mission of EGA, and the difficulties encountered in carrying it out, Sept. 3, 1946, ibid. EGA stands for "Exploitation German Archives" and was the new name for the FO-SD team, although the Americans were the only ones to use it.

191 Major T. H. Frame, Foreign Office Investigator, to John T. Krumpelmann, Attaché, State Dept., July 30, 1946, NA RG 84, POLAD, entry 2531B, box 100.

192 W. D. Hohenthal, Chief, Intelligence Branch, POLAD, to W. H. Coogan, Office of the U. S. Chief of Counsel, Sept. 8, 1945, NA RG 238, entry 52a, box 1.

193 Thomson, Memorandum: Attachment of Liaison Officers to Visiting Delegations, Dec. 12, 1947, NA RG 59, Lot File 78D441, Historical Office, box 19. Apparently Thomson also had a problem with the fact that "the Nuremberg organisation are entirely American . . . and about half of them are Jews. I wish I could have the same confidence in their integrity as I have in the case of my own staff." Thomson, Admittance of Nuremberg Research Workers to Foreign Office/State Dept. Documents Center, June 16, 1947, ibid.

194 Thomson to John Krumpelmann, Oct. 5, 1946, NA RG 84, POLAD, entry 2531B, box 100. See further correspondence on the topic by Thomson and Clifton P. English in ibid. This coincides with the recollections of Kurt Rheindorf, a German who worked in Nuremberg during the trials: "During the so-called war criminal trials in Nuremberg and abroad, it happened often that, while compiling material for the defense, we ran into 'souvenir'-happy collectors from the 'other side' or were made aware of him (sic)." Rheindorf to Johannes Ullrich, director of the Political Archives, Dec. 16, 1959, PA/AA, B118, vol. 76.

missing as preparations for the prosecution of the surviving Nazi leaders were underway was the so-called Hoßbach Memorandum. Introduced as evidence document number PS-386, it played an important part in the major war crimes trial. It was presented, however, only in a notarized copy. Raymond Sontag, the chief American editor of *Documents on German Foreign Policy*, attempted in early 1947 to determine the fate of the original. Robert M. W. Kempner, the assistant chief U.S. counsel, remembered having seen the memorandum, "but in the movement of document centers it had disappeared," Sontag reported. "He believes it possible that some souvenir-hunter may have taken the original."[195] The office of the chief prosecutor had a bad reputation among the heads of the document centers. One observer described the way documents were managed in Nuremberg:

Some 27 different offices of OCC hold documents, and although there is a nominal central documents office, there is actually no such functioning office. . . . Impossible to name any one man as documents chief, although a Mr. Niebergall has been doing something like this job.[196]

In September 1946, the Ministerial Document Branch in Berlin decided not to lend any more original documents and to issue only copies of requested materials. By this point, over 1,000 originals had been "out on loan" for over a year, and the head of the American team thought it unlikely that they would ever reappear.[197]

THE ODYSSEY OF THE DIPLOMATIC RECORDS

The British and American preparations during World War II to seize the Auswärtiges Amt's files were an integral part of their planning for the occupation of Germany. Targeting the diplomatic archives of an enemy country was not without precedent. During World War I, warring nations in Europe had sought to gain possession of such records, assuming that they would hold the key to understanding the politics and aims of the adversary and

---

195 Raymond Sontag, Memorandum of Conversation, Jan. 24, 1947, NA G 59, Lot File 78D441, Historical Office, box 22. On the history of the memorandum's complicated trail, see Smith, "Überlieferung der Hossbach-Niederschrift;" Wright/Stafford, "Hitler, Britain and the Hoßbach Memorandum," 78–82, go into depth about the accusation that the memorandum could be fake.

196 G-2, War Department, Agencies Holding Documents in European Command, Oct. 27, 1947, NA RG 319, Records of Army Staff, entry 47B, box 496. In hindsight, Telford Taylor attributed more order to the way evidence was handled; see Wolfe, *Captured German Records*, 112.

197 Clifton P. English, EGA, Memorandum: Mission of EGA, and the difficulties encountered in carrying it out, Sept. 3, 1946, NA RG 84, entry 2531B, box 100.

could be exploited for political advantage.[198] The German themselves had
set the most recent example. Although officials in Washington and London
certainly hoped to seize as much of this kind of material as possible, the
success of their special units in capturing the lion's share of the Auswärtiges
Amt files exceeded all expectation. The captured files immediately became
a highly charged political issue. Although the British and the Americans
joined forces to safeguard their booty, they were often at odds on how to
handle it. One indicator of the tensions between the two allies was the frequency of document transfers. Materials were repeatedly packed, shipped,
unpacked, and then moved once again. Each move was prompted by a
clash of interest. The following section maps the odyssey of the diplomatic
records.

The Discovery of the Political Archives of the Auswärtiges Amt

We are left with an embarrassingly large quantity of documents (far more than we expected.)[199]

The joint document team from the State Department and the Foreign
Office was still stationed in Versailles when, on April 19, 1945, it received
news from the Counter Intelligence Corps (CIC) of a large stash of government records discovered in the Harz Mountains. On the trail of former
Foreign Minister Joachim von Ribbentrop, CIC agents had searched castles in Degenershausen and Meisdorf. At both castles, they found neatly
stacked piles of files arranged in order of the "mysterious numbers" they
bore.[200] The files turned out to be portions of the Political Archives of the
Auswärtiges Amt, which had been evacuated from Berlin in May 1943.[201]
After a roundabout journey, the records had ended up in the castles and
three other towns in the Harz Mountains. Until early April 1945, a courier
service maintained communication between Berlin and the branch repositories. Five days after receiving word of the discovery from the CIC, members

---

198 Zala, *Zensur*, 43f., 144–6; see also Posner, Historical Development of International Principles and
Practices Pertaining to Seized Enemy Records Through World War II, NA RG 59, Lot File
56D307, Files of the Ass't Legal Adviser for Germany, box 1.
199 Foreign Office, Notes for meeting to discuss 'finds' of German and Italian Documents, n.d. [June
14, 1945], PRO FO 371/46713 C3209/G.
200 History of the Counter Intelligence Corps, vol. 20: Germany Overrun – Part 1. (Baltimore, MD:
U.S. Intelligence Center Fort Holabird, March 1959), 65–7. The CIC's own depiction of events
has factual mistakes and a hagiographical touch and can only be used in conjunction with the
documentary evidence.
201 The decision to evacuate is documented in Kröger/Thimme, "Politisches Archiv," 251–7. See also
Philippi, "Politisches Archiv I," 148.

of the State Department-Foreign Office document team arrived on site. In Meisdorf, they met the archivist Heinrich Valentin and in Degenershausen, Witilo von Griesheim. Both offered extensive information about the records under their supervision.[202] Valentin had begun to burn secret files in early April on orders from Berlin; Griesheim said that he never received such orders.[203] Although they did not consider him trustworthy,[204] the British and Americans decided to take Valentin along with them to Marburg, where they transferred the entire archive.

The transfer was carried out in a rush because the British and Americans had no intention of sharing their find with the Russians, and the Harz castles were located in the territory designated for occupation by the Soviet Union.[205] With the help of former forced laborers, the British and Americans loaded roughly 400 tons of records onto trucks bound for Marburg. Ironically, the workers who helped the State Department-Foreign Office team snatch the records from the Soviet zone were themselves Russian.[206] On V-E Day, American troops also arrived to help with the loading. In the tumult of the victory celebrations, several bundles of documents were

202 Report on Visit by Representatives of Control Commission for Germany (British Element) and US Group Control Council to Ministerial Targets P67 and P69 – German Foreign Office and Propaganda Ministry – April 21st–28th 1945, Top Secret, Apr. 30, 1945, NA RG 59, CDF 1945–1949, 840.414/5–145; PRO FO 370/1490 L2706. See also, the report written by Valentin at the request Ralph S. Collins from the office of the Political Advisor, Brief Account of the Evacuation of the Files of the Political Archives of the Foreign Office in the years 1943–1945, July 25, 1945, NA RG 84, POLAD, entry 2531B, box 37.

203 During the first interrogation, Valentin admitted "only [!] to have destroyed about 1/3 of the secret files, consisting of the commercial policy files and others of relatively minor importance." Report on Visit, Apr. 30, 1945, NA RG 59, CDF 1945–1949, 840.414/5–145. The issue of the destruction of files is discussed in Kröger/Thimme, "Politisches Archiv," 257–61. The authors number the loss to be about 250 bundles. According to them, the destroyed files included not only those from the Handelspolitischen Abteilung (trade policy dept.) but also documents from the Paris embassy, the legal department, Pol. I. Military and others.

204 Valentin, born 1907, started his career at the Prussian Archvial Administration in 1937 and had worked as a Wissenschaftlicher Hilfsarbeiter (research assistant) at the Political Archives since 1940. He joined the NSDAP after the membership ban was lifted in May 1937. "Our impression was that Valentin is a highly strung, neurotic type whose health is far from good. While we do not consider him entirely trustworthy, he knows his job and is prepared to talk freely about the documents in his charge." Report on Visit, Apr. 30, 1945, NA RG 59, CDF 1945–1949, 840.414/5–145.

205 The decision was made by the political advisors Sir William Strang and Robert Murphy on April 27, 1945. See Report on Visit, ibid. The move is described extensively in Lt. Col. Robert C. Thomson to Ivor Pink, CCG(BE), May 23, 1945, PRO FO 371/46712 C2584/G. Blankenburg, although initially part of the British zone, landed in the Soviet zone after a local adjustment of the demarcation line. A map showing the American advances within Germany in May 1945 in relation to the previously agreed zonal borders is included in the appendix of Ziemke, *U.S. Army*.

206 "It is perhaps unfortunate that they should have used Russian labour to move the documents, as this will ensure that when the Soviet authorities move into the area, they will hear the whole story." Ivor Pink, CCG(BE), to Michael Vyvyan, German Department, FO, May 25, 1945, PRO FO 371/46712 C2584/G.

lost.[207] The removal of the Auswärtiges Amt files from the Harz Mountains was not the only incident of this kind. American troops transported archival materials, precious metals, and art treasures as quickly as possible from what was soon to become the Soviet zone westwards.[208] The head of the British team, Lt. Col. Robert C. Thomson, entrusted the evacuation of the Auswärtiges Amt's Political Archives to his American colleague Gardner C. Carpenter and left for Thuringia to investigate the rumors of a valuable cache of archival material in Mühlhausen.[209]

The Loesch Microfilms and the Schmidt Box. Thomson arrived in Mühlhausen on May 12. There he found more than three hundred staff members of the Auswärtiges Amt who had previously worked at the branch offices in Krummhübel but had been evacuated in February. Quite by accident, he ran into Ralph Collins from the State Department, who was on the same mission.[210] Together, they secured an additional fifteen truckloads of archival materials, which were also sent off to Marburg.[211] The news of Thomson and Collins's presence appears to have spread rapidly, for one of the German diplomats went to great effort to meet Thomson in person. The German asked him to deliver a letter addressed to Duncan Sandys, a prominent British conservative politician and also Churchill's son-in-law. As Thomson soon learned, the German was Karl von Loesch. He had worked with Paul Otto Schmidt, who, as Ribbentrop's interpreter and chief of staff, had been responsible for the security of the minister's secret files. Loesch's mother was English, and he himself had been born in London

---

207 "Confusion was caused by troops who were called in to help. On V.E. night they were in a hilarious condition, induced by potations and began to throw about bundles to celebrate the end of the war." Thomson to Ivor Pink, CCG(BE), May 23, 1945, PRO FO 371/46712 C2584/G.

208 Robert Murphy legitimized the apparently unprecedented evacuation of records from the former Reich ministries by arguing that there was no indication in international law that occupying troops had to leave records at the location where they were found. The records were to be transported to the U.S. zone "for safeguarding and convenient exploitation." See Murphy to Clay, June 19, 1945, NA RG 84, POLAD, entry 2531B, box 37. To date, the confiscations taking place during the military advances have been studied primarily with regard to art treasures and precious metals. See Goldmann, "Trojan Treasures," 201f.; Nicholas, *Rape of Europa,* 332–6; Plunder and Restitution, SR–98f.; Volkert, *Kunst- und Kulturraub,* 113–15.

209 Thomson to Ivor Pink, CCG(BE), May 23, 1945, PRO FO 371/46712 C2584/G.

210 The main source for the events is the report by Thomson, Discovery of Secret Archives of German Foreign Ministry, May 22, 1945, PRO FO 371/46712 C2548/G and NA RG 59, Lot File 78D441, Historical Office, box 6. The document is reprinted in the appendix of Zala, *Zensur,* 345–8; and paraphrased in König, "Deutsch-sowjetisches Vertragswerk," 434f. Less informative is the telegram from Murphy and Perkins to SecState, no. 2770, May 18, 1945, FRUS 1945:3, 1105f.

211 "Some items such as keys of safes and notes of lock combinations helped us to decide to take everything." Thomson also sent the former chancellor of the German embassy in London, Wilhelm Achilles, whom he had known for nearly twenty years, to accompany and look after the material. Apparently Thomson wanted to do Achilles the favor of getting him to the American zone. Thomson to Ivor Pink, CCG(BE), May 23, 1945, PRO FO 371/46712 C2584/G.

and had maintained his British citizenship. He had studied with Sandys at Oxford and wanted to reveal the secret hiding place of Ribbentrop's records to his prominent British acquaintance. Naturally, Loesch hoped to receive preferential treatment in exchange, ideally to be flown to Great Britain. The records in question were microfilm copies of the Auswärtiges Amt's most important and most confidential files from the years 1933 on, about 9,800 pages' worth of material.[212] The microfilms had been secretly produced by Ribbentrop's office at the end of 1943. When the office was evacuated, Loesch was given charge of both the original files and the microfilm copies. He repacked the films and placed them in a metal container. When the order came from Berlin to destroy the secret files, he burned the original documents as well as the cardboard cartons in which the microfilms had been packed. Then he buried the metal container at a country estate in the vicinity of Mühlhausen. "I would stress the fact," he wrote Sandys, "that this lot contains *only* the essential but also *all* the essential documents. There has never existed a similar collection in Germany." Loesch saw his future closely linked with these documents:

Personally, I would welcome an opportunity of being allowed to help as a historian, at least for the immediate future, in the examination and evaluation of the documents I have described to you. I honestly believe them to be the clue to the true history of our times when used as a complement to those in the possession of the British Government.[213]

Thomson and Collins decided to take Loesch at his word. Thomson was extremely careful, though, not to make any promises of special treatment. Instead, he entered into a type of gentlemen's agreement with Loesch: "I said that if he dealt honourably with me he could count on a like attitude on my part."[214] On May 14, Loesch led the two men to the place where the microfilms were hidden. The next day, Collins and Thomson took the find to Marburg. Loesch accompanied the convoy in his own car. The microfilms were immediately flown to London and developed at the Air Ministry. In the meantime, Loesch proved to be a useful partner. "He is making interesting disclosures and is quite willing to talk about his relations with Hitler and others," Thomson told his superiors. "The man might be an opportunist but he quite accepts the situation that he is in our power and

212 On the discovery of the so-called Loesch film, the most detailed account is in Zala, *Zensur*, 167–9; also Kent, "German Foreign Ministry Archives," 121f.; Kent, "Archives at Whaddon Hall," 44, n. 3; König, "Deutsch-sowjetisches Vertragswerk," 433–5.

213 The copy of the letter from von Loesch to Sandys in PRO FO 371/46712 C2548/G. Emphasis in the original. Thomson did indeed forward the original letter to Sandys.

214 Thomson, Discovery of Secret Archives of German Foreign Ministry, May 22, 1945, PRO FO 371/46712 C2548/G and NA RG 59, Lot File 78D441, Historical Office, box 6.

to my mind seems quite prepared to be useful to us in the interests of his own future."[215] In early June, Loesch let it be known that he had buried a second box of microfilmed documents at the same location. The fact that he only informed the British of the second cache a month after his initial overture to Thomson was probably part of his negotiating strategy. On June 12, Thomson retrieved the box, which contained copies of Schmidt's papers. Among the microfilmed documents discovered in the so-called Schmidt Box were the minutes of meetings Hitler and Rippentrop had conducted with politicians from nations collaborating with the Third Reich.[216] Of particular interest to the British were the files on the English writer P. G. Wodehouse, who, after having been detained as an enemy alien after the German invasion of France, had taped several radio broadcast programs for the Auswärtiges Amt.[217]

The Loesch microfilms and the Schmidt Box proved to be the most politically valuable and therefore the most potentially controversial finds of the Anglo-American document hunt. Foreign Office officials quickly realized the importance of the material. "I saw enough to convince me that they are dynamite," wrote one.[218] "It is obvious that there is red-hot propaganda material in this can of films," concluded another.[219] The microfilms contained the secret protocol of the Molotov-Ribbentrop Pact, a find perhaps second only to the minutes of the Wannsee Conference in impact on international politics. There were also documents dealing with trade negotiations with the Soviet Union in the winter of 1939–40, agreements between Hitler and Franco, Hitler's meeting with Pétain, and negotiations with the Japanese foreign minister in early 1941.[220] The British had the

215 Ibid.
216 J. I. Jones, FO, and Gardner C. Carpenter, State Dept., Discovery of Private Files of Dr. Paul Schmidt, Official Interpreter of German Foreign Office, June 13, 1945, PRO FO 371/46713 C3210/G and NA RG 59, Lot File 78D441, Historical Office, box 6; Thomson to John M. Troutbeck, Asst. UnderSecState FO, June 13, 1945, PRO FO 371/46713 C3210/G; Murphy, POLAD, to SecState, no. 3632, June 16, 1945, FRUS 1945:3, 1110. On the discovery of the "Schmidt Box," see Zala, *Zensur*, 169; also Kent, "German Foreign Ministry Archives," 121f.
217 Pelham Grenville Wodehouse (1881–1975) lived in Le Touquet, France, when the Wehrmacht occupied the country in June 1940. He was imprisoned and sent to Germany. Wodehouse taped five broadcasts in exchange for the return of his passport, limited freedom of movement, and reunion with his wife. After the war, he immediately presented himself to British military authorities. Unlike Ezra Pound and Knut Hamsun, Wodehouse's cooperation was apparently not politically motivated. Still, he remained controversial in Great Britain and the United States as a possible collaborator. See Bergmeier/Lotz, *Hitler's Airwaves*, 112–14.
218 Minutes of Geoffrey Harrison, May 23, 1945, PRO FO 371/46712 C2548/G. Before the war, Harrison had been Secretary at the British embassy in Berlin and by the end of the war he was one of the experts for Germany at the Central Department.
219 Minutes of John Michael Vyvyan, May 22, 1945, ibid.
220 E. Ralph Perkins to John M. Allison, AmEmb London, Memorandum: Microfilms of Secret Documents of the German Foreign Office, May 25, 1945, NA RG 59, Lot File 78D441, Historical

upper hand with the Loesch microfilms because the material had been sent immediately to London. Tensions subsequently developed between the British and their American allies on two levels. At the ministerial level, the question of who would receive copies of Ribbentrop's secret files was a source of discord. On the day-to-day working level at Marburg, British and American officials were divided on how to treat Loesch. The two disagreements deeply angered Robert Murphy and were to have a decisive impact on his later decisions regarding the diplomatic files.

Thomson had not in fact given his informant any reason to hope for privileged treatment.[221] Loesch was nonetheless transferred from the Soviet to the American zone, was granted permission to bring two other people with him, and was allowed to travel in his own car – concessions that were anything but trivial.[222] "I have treated him with civility," wrote Thomson, "but have avoided giving him the impression that we regard him as specially valuable."[223] In the same letter, however, Thomson admitted that "my services to him have been of a small nature, such as obtaining the release of two motor cycles used by the military." The American military government had imposed travel restrictions and evening curfews on the local populace. Germans living in the American zone were not free to travel more than a few kilometers from their homes unless they had special permits from the military government.[224] The U.S. Army had a monopoly on the fuel supply; as a result, gasoline was as desirable a commodity on the black market as coffee and cigarettes. With his "small services," Thomson helped Loesch circumvent the rules and regulations of the American military government and thereby duped his colleagues from the State Department.

The tensions over the treatment of Loesch escalated in August 1945. Gardner C. Carpenter, the American officer who had coordinated the evacuation of records from the Harz Mountains to Marburg, was bothered

Office, box 6; Winant, Ambassador, AmEmb London, to SecState, no. 5291, May 26, 1945, FRUS 1945:3, 1107–09; E. Llewellyn Woodward, FO, Second Report on the "Film Find," May 31, 1945, PRO FO 371/46712 C2957/G.

221 "I emphasized that he would be treated with consideration and would certainly not starve at Marburg, but that I was only empowered to make a promise covering the immediate future.... I am seeing that he is treated with courtesy and consideration but without tenderness, and needless to say he is under strict surveillance." Thomson, Discovery of Secret Archives of German Foreign Ministry, May 22, 1945, PRO FO 371/46712 C2548/G and NA RG 59, Lot File 78D441, Historical Office, box 6.

222 The two people were his secretary and his brother-in-law, Vice Consul Ruprecht Hopfen. See J. I. Jones, FO, and Gardner C. Carpenter, State Dept., Discovery of Private Files of Dr. Paul Schmidt, Official Interpreter of German Foreign Office, June 13, 1945, PRO FO 371/46713 C3210/G and NA RG 59, Lot File 78D441, Historical Office, box 6;

223 Thomson to John Troutbeck, June 13, 1945, PRO FO 371/46713 C3210/G.

224 Henke, *Amerikanische Besetzung*, 174f.

about the accommodating treatment being given to the former diplomat. Following his interrogation by William Cavendish-Bentinck, the British chief of the Joint Intelligence Committee, Loesch was suddenly granted a multitude of privileges. "He was given almost complete freedom of movement," Carpenter reported to Murphy, "He possessed an automobile, a motorcycle and a motor bicycle. He obtained in a mysterious fashion gasoline for trips to Kassel and other cities in the region." His gasoline ration was generous enough for him to take a trip to Munich, "from where he had the gall to telegraph that he was having a fine time."[225] So long as Loesch was Thomson's responsibility, there was little Carpenter could do. The situation changed suddenly in 1945.[226] One of the Americans working in Marburg had found evidence proving that Loesch had been an SS Untersturmführer. Under the directive on denazification issued on July 7, 1945, for the American zone, membership in the SS was grounds for automatic arrest.[227] Carpenter did what he had long wanted to do: "Yesterday, on orders of the Department of State, Loesch was arrested and placed in solitary confinement."[228] Loesch was later interrogated by the head of the American Counter Intelligence Corps in Marburg. As he reported to Murphy, Carpenter was informed by the interrogating officer that

(1) [American officials] had removed from von Loesch an authorization signed by a local Military Government officer entitling von Loesch, on recommendation of Col. Thomson, to American Army gasoline;
(2) that von Loesch had stated to [the interrogating officer] that when he had mentioned the subject of his membership in the SS to Col. Thomson, the latter had advised him to be very quiet about the matter and tell no one of it;
(3) that [the interrogating officer] had been given to believe that von Loesch was under the special protection of Col. Thomson and myself.

"I cannot but believe that with respect to von Loesch he [Thomson] is acting on instructions from above," Carpenter concluded.[229] These disclosures permanently ruined Carpenter's working relations with Thomson.

The Foreign Office briefly considered the idea of bringing Loesch to Great Britain. British officials appear to have concluded, however, that he had nothing more of value to offer. In his negotiations with the British,

225 Carpenter to Robert Murphy, POLAD, Aug. 18, 1945, NA RG 84, POLAD, entry 2531B, box 37.
226 "On my return to Frankfort following my leave, I was informed by Mr. Mason Drury that von Loesch had been placed 'in the custody of Vice Consul Gardner C. Carpenter.' By whom this had been done I could not find out . . . ." Ibid.
227 Rauh-Kühne, "Entnazifizierung," 39; Vollnhals, *Entnazifizierung*, 10f.
228 Carpenter to Murphy, Aug. 18, 1945, NA RG 84, POLAD, entry 2531B, box 37.
229 Ibid.

Loesch repeatedly mentioned his British citizenship, suggesting that it was grounds for him to be transferred to Britain. Cavendish-Bentinck suggested Loesch might be dissuaded with a reminder that, were he to arrive in Britain, he would be deemed a traitor and "a noose will be placed around his neck" – a turn of events that Loesch might agree would be "inconvenient."[230]

The Politics of File-Sharing. The Loesch episode created tension within the State Department-Foreign Office team and damaged working relations between the British and Americans in Marburg. It also provoked a tug-of-war over the distribution of copies of the microfilms. The problem began with the initial British evaluation of the films. The Foreign Office quickly dismissed the idea that the films might have been planted by the Germans to mislead the Allies. E. Llewellyn Woodward, an historical advisor to the Foreign Office, dispelled all doubt about the authenticity of the microfilms.[231] The material they contained was politically explosive, and that raised several complicated questions.

Officially, the joint document team was integrated within the CIOS structure. Therefore, the Loesch microfilms should have been shared with the governmental bodies accredited with CIOS. The British thought, however, that sharing the materials so widely was taking things much too far. It took the Foreign Office personnel a long time to convince E. Ralph Perkins, the head of the American team, to agree that the Loesch films were primarily of interest to the State Department and Foreign Office and therefore should not be shared with other ministries and agencies under the aegis of CIOS.[232] Moreover, the British had included a paragraph in their proposal for the European Advisory Commission's directive on archives that would prohibit the removal of documents from occupied territories.[233] Although the directive had not yet been adopted, the British themselves were undermining the principle behind it. Having won the race to secure the most desirable of the Auswärtiges Amt files, the British saw little advantage to be gained from pressing ahead with the directive. Foreign Secretary

230 "We have decided not to bring over to this country Karl von Loesch who provided us with these Microfilms. If he was landed in this country he could remain here and could apply for a writ of habeus [sic] corpus on the ground that he is a natural born British subject. We could counter this by warning him that in this case he is a traitor and that a noose will be placed round his neck, but it would be inconvenient and might give rise to publicity. He will be further questioned in Germany." Minutes of Cavendish-Bentinck, June 1, 1945, PRO FO 371/46712 C2957/G.
231 Woodward, Second Report on the "Film Find," May 31, 1945, PRO FO 371/46712 C2957/G.
232 Minutes of Harrison, May 23, 1945, PRO FO 371/46712 C2548/G. Perkins was finally recalled in July 1945. See also Kent, "German Foreign Ministry Archives," 122; Zala, *Zensur*, 176.
233 "7. . . . You will forbid the removal from Germany of any original records or archives." British Draft Directive on German Records and Archives, [July 13, 1944], FRUS 1944:1, 1490f.

Anthony Eden thus sought to put the brakes on it: "Sir W[illiam] Strang had better be warned to 'go slow' with this."[234] In the end, the transfer of the Loesch films to London was justified with the rather flimsy argument that microfilm copies, not paper originals, had been removed from Germany.[235]

Far more complex than the wrangling between the British and the Americans was their position toward the other Allies. The Loesch microfilms had been removed from the designated Soviet occupation zone, and the Allies were officially committed to establishing a Four Power government for Germany. One expert on Germany at the Foreign Office noted that "strictly the documents are, I suppose, the property of all Four Powers represented on the Control Machinery" and acknowledged that "both the French and more particularly the Russians have a particular interest in these documents." He argued in a memorandum that "we should let both the French and the Russian Governments have copies of the microfilm as soon as this can possibly be done."[236] Eden quickly squelched such suggestions: "No action of this kind without my specific approval, please."[237] Cavendish-Bentinck was also of the opinion that "we should hold hard as regards informing the French and Soviet Government of the discovery." He invoked the principle of reciprocity, which was later to be much belabored: "The Soviet Government have never informed us of any discovery that they have ever made and I do not see why we need show such zeal in informing them."[238]

The Foreign Office ultimately decided to send copies of the microfilms to the State Department in Washington but not to its representative in the occupation zone, Robert Murphy.[239] Murphy protested and took his complaint to Sir Ivone Kirkpatrick, Assistant Under-Secretary of State at the Foreign Office and Strang's Deputy Political Advisor in the British Control Commission. Murphy also had the American embassy in London inquire into the matter at the Foreign Office.[240] For its part, the Foreign Office enlisted the aid of the British ambassador in Washington to counter Murphy's efforts. Lord Halifax was instructed to raise the matter

---

234 Strang was the British delegate to the EAC. Marginal notes by Eden (signed "AE") in the Minutes of Harrison, May 23, 1945, PRO FO 371/46712 C2548/G.
235 "The documents were only removed from Germany because they were in microfilm instead of originals." Perkins to Frederick B. Lyon, Chief, Division of Foreign Activity Correlation, State Dept., May 28, 1945, NA RG 59, Lot File 78D441, Historical Office, box 6.
236 Minutes of Harrison, May 23, 1945, PRO FO 371/46712 C2548/G.
237 Ibid., marginal notes by Eden (signed "AE").
238 Minutes of William Cavendish-Bentinck, May 23, 1945, PRO FO 371/46712 C2548/G.
239 E. R. Perkins to John M. Allison, AmEmb London, Memorandum: Microfilms of Secret Documents of the German FO, May 25, 1945, NA RG 59, Lot File 78D441, Historical Office, box 6.
240 Minutes of Vyvyan, May 28, 1945, PRO FO 371/46712 C2548/G; Perkins to Lyon, May 28, 1945, NA RG 59, Lot File 78D441, Historical Office, box 6.

of the Loesch microfilms when he met Secretary of State Edward R. Stettinius in San Francisco at the founding meeting of the United Nations. He was to "discuss this problem personally with M. Stettinius" and do his "utmost to persuade him to instruct the United States Embassy not to press Mr. Murphy's request."[241] Stettinius was apparently persuaded; a day after meeting with Halifax, he ordered the embassy in London to drop Murphy's request.[242] Not until June 11, during a trip to London, did Murphy learn that the matter had been settled higher up.[243] Nonetheless, he continued to demand his own copy of the films.[244]

Murphy retaliated against the Foreign Office's maneuverings immediately: when the British wanted to fly the contents of the Schmidt Box out of Germany, he blocked the release of the documents from SHAEF headquarters.[245] Shortly afterward, the controversy on the treatment of Loesch escalated. There were also delays in developing the microfilms, a job for which the British Air Ministry was responsible. Murphy and the Americans in Marburg became increasingly impatient with their British counterparts. The smallest incident, such as the delay in supplying microfilm copies, prompted strong suspicions: "Conspiracy and a gross negligence or both are evident."[246] It is against this backdrop that we can understand the first move of a large amount of German diplomatic records from Marburg to the Ministerial Collecting Center in Kassel. For all intents and purposes, the move was completely unnecessary. But Murphy had the urgent need to demonstrate to the British who was the boss in the American zone.

241 FO to BritEmb Washington, no. 5566, Most Immediate, Top Secret, May 28, 1945, PRO FO 371/46712 C2548/G. The correspondence included the following instruction: "This telegram is of particular secrecy and should be retained by the authorised recipient and not passed on."

242 [Stettinius] SecState, San Francisco, to Acting SecState, Washington, May 29, 1945, FRUS 1945:3, 1109. The State Department sent the order to the embassy in London, no. 4344, on June 1, 1945. See also Halifax, BritEmb Washington to Foreign Office, no. 489, May 30, 1945, PRO FO 371/46712 C2607.

243 Murphy to H. Freeman Matthews, Director, Office of European Affairs, June 15, 1945, FRUS 1945:3, 1109f.

244 "When I was at SHAEF last week Mr. Murphy again complained to me with some vehemence that copies of the Top Secret German documents found by Lt. Col. Thomson were being withheld from him. I suspect that Mr. Murphy thought that I was responsible for this.... Mr. Murphy was not satisfied [by Bentinck's explanation] and maintained that he was entitled to a copy of these and any other documents found in Germany which he might desire. My impression of Mr. Murphy, to whom I took rather a dislike, was that if he could not find this grievance he would look for another." Minutes of Cavendish-Bentinck, June 22, 1945, PRO FO 371/46712 C2760/G.

245 FO to SHAEF Main (Kirkpatrick), no. 196, June 26, 1945, PRO FO 371/46713 C3210/G still announced that Carpenter would bring the "Schmidt Box" to London. E. Ralph Perkins describes Murphy's obstruction in his report Exploitation of German Political Archives for the Department of State, Aug. 20, 1945, NA RG 59, Lot File 789D441, Historical Office, box 6.

246 Murphy to SecState, no. 1336, Nov. 19, 1945, NA RG 84, POLAD, entry 2531B, box 37.

The Windsor File. The distribution of the Loesch film was not the only matter on which Halifax sought help from Stettinius while they were in San Francisco. He also brought up what, for London, could not have been a more delicate question: the location of the so-called Windsor File.[247] No other group of documents was pursued with so much determination and energy by the Foreign Office. The British obsession with the Windsor File and the demand that it be destroyed undermined the trust of the Americans directly involved with the Auswärtiges Amt records. The conduct of the British in this matter was another impediment to cooperation. A few years later, when Britain and the United States opened negotiations with West Germany on the return of the captured diplomatic documents, the Windsor File was the topic of greatest concern to the British cabinet, not least Prime Minister Winston Churchill.

King Edward VIII had caused a deep crisis for Britain's monarchy when he renounced his crown in 1936 to marry an American divorcée. Shortly after his abdication, Edward was created Duke of Windsor by George VI, his brother and successor, and soon retreated to the Continent. Before ascending to the throne, Edward had made no secret of his admiration for National Socialist Germany. A year after his abdication, he traveled to Germany, where he was received by Hitler and Göring. When the war began, the duke, then residing in southern France, became the focus of intense political maneuvering. Churchill could not call the former king back to Great Britain and place him in a position of responsibility, but he wanted urgently to shield the duke from German influence. In the eyes of Germany's foreign minister Joachim von Ribbentrop, Edward was the ideal candidate to take over the British throne once Germany had overpowered Great Britain. Churchill, hoping to get the duke off the Continent, tried to convince him in 1940 to accept the position of governor of the Bahamas. Edward had just moved from Spain to Lisbon, kept delaying his departure to the Bahamas, and was soon the target of intensive espionage. His comments about Great Britain and Germany were recorded and found their way into German intelligence reports. It was a copy of those reports formerly in the office of State Secretary Ernst von Weizsäcker that came to be known as

---

247 The Windsor File has attracted much attention in accounts about the duke and his alleged collaborationist tendencies. See Costello, *Ten Days*, 352–74. An account of the file's history and eventual publication in Sweet, "Einflußnahme;" see also Sweet, "Windsor File;" Kent, "Editing Diplomatic Documents," 473–6; based on State Department sources, Zala, *Zensur*, 179–81, 186, 195. Another episode that might have involved revealing correspondence between the duke and the Prince of Hesse in Petropolous, *Royals and the Reich*, 337–44.

the Windsor File after the war.[248] Edward's comments placed him "in a somewhat curious light," the historian Rohan Butler commented in July 1945 after an initial examination of the file.[249] To avert renewed debate on whether the duke had been inclined to collaborate with the Nazis, the Foreign Office attempted to pull the Windsor File out of circulation.

Copies of the file had, however, proliferated since its initial discovery. The original file was filmed in Marburg in the summer of 1945 in keeping with routine procedure for highly important political documents. Two copies of the film were made, one of which was sent to the Foreign Office and the other to the American embassy in London. The American copy later landed at the State Department.[250]

The Foreign Office addressed the issue of the Windsor File on several levels. Halifax pressed Stettinius in San Francisco either to destroy the American copy of the film or to hand it over to the Foreign Office.[251] The British embassy in Washington followed up with an aide-memoire to the State Department, and it attempted repeatedly to influence the department's position.[252] Later, British efforts focused on determining where the Marburg original would end up and ensuring that it and similarly sensitive documents did not fall into the hands of the prosecutors in Nuremberg. The British argued that the Windsor File was historically irrelevant, but the Americans disagreed. The only concession the American government made in the matter was to consent not to make or circulate any additional copies of the film. It did not intend, however, to give up possession of its

---

248 PA/AA, Büro StS, Akten betreffend deutsch-englische Beziehungen vom 19. Juni 1940 bis 31. Dezember 1940, vol. 3, R 29571; DGFP, Series D, vol. X, Verzeichnis der Dokumente, XXVI–XXVIII. The content of the Windsor File is summarized in Krumpelmann to Hohenthal, Request for Gist of Duke of Windsor Papers, Oct 30, 1945, NA RG 59, Lot File 78D441, Historical Office, box 24; in addition, Summary of Documents Relating to the Duke of Windsor, ibid., box 13.

249 Quote taken from Sweet, "Windsor File," 267. Like Woodword, Butler was brought in by the Foreign Office to be a historical advisor.

250 Krumpelmann to Hohenthal, Oct. 30, 1945, NA RG 59, Lot File 78D441, Historical Office, box 24.

251 ". . . an agreement made by former Secretary Stettinius and Lord Halifax in which it was agreed that neither government would make additional copies or otherwise reveal information on activities in Spain of a member of the Royal family." Memorandum [no author], Regulations on use of information from official German records exploited jointly by British Foreign Office and State Department investigators, May 20, 1946, NA RG 59, Lot File 78D441, Historical Office, box 13.

252 British aide-memoire, ref. G.240, Aug. 6, 1945, NA RG 59, CDF 1945–49, 862.414/8–645. The correspondence on the Windsor papers was always "top secret," which is no longer noted in the following. David Harris, a member of the division on Central European Affairs, called it a mistake to put the matter into writing because doing so was what really called attention to the matter. See David Harris, Stanford University, to Howard M. Smyth, July 25, 1959, NA RG 59, Lot File 78D441, Historical Office, box 11.

copy of the film or to destroy it.[253] James Byrnes, who succeeded Stettinius at the State Department in July 1945, instructed the chief U.S. prosecutor in Nuremberg not to use any documents as evidence to which his British counterpart objected. In practice, this order applied to only the Windsor File.[254]

The British were more successful with regard to the original file in Marburg. In early September 1945, Eisenhower ordered "the original documents dealing with relations between Great Britain and Germany between June and December 1940" to be sent from Marburg to his headquarters.[255] A courier picked up the file with an authorization signed by General Edward C. Betts.[256] What prompted Eisenhower to take action and what he wanted with the file remains unclear.[257] In September 1946, the members of the State Department-Foreign Office team decided that a loan period of one year was long enough even for a five star general and called for its return. Thomson was particularly adamant in insisting on its immediate return.[258] But the file was gone.[259] By the time Thomson sought its return, Eisenhower had already passed it on to the American ambassador in London, John Winant, who, in turn, passed it on to the Foreign Office

253 "The British Government is assured, however, that the Department of State will take all possible precautions to prevent any publicity with respect to the documents in its possession relative to the Duke of Windsor without prior consultation with the British Government." Aide-Memoire, State Dept., Oct 11, 1945, NA RG 59, Lot File 78D441, Historical Office, box 13. Further, Dean Acheson, UnderSecState, to John Balfour, BritEmb, Nov. 19, 1945, ibid. The Americans reacted to the case of the Windsor File much in the same way as they did to the political and personal wills of Adolf Hitler.

254 " . . . in view of concern expressed by BRIT GOVT over possible disclosure of captured material that might cause serious embarrassment, we also state . . . that we are requesting you [i.e. Jackson] not to use any documents to which your BRIT colleague makes objection without prior consultation with this DEPT." James Byrnes, SecState, to Murphy, POLAD, no. 686, Oct. 17, 1945, ibid. Murphy forwarded the news to Jackson on Oct. 18, 1945. The British were notified of this arrangement in the aide-memoire, State Dept., Oct. 11, 1945, ibid. The source makes it unequivocally clear that the arrangement only applied to the Windsor File.

255 Lt. Col. Thomson to Vyvyan, Sept. 7, 1945, PRO FO 371/46717 C5561.

256 The courier Hans F. Scheufele signed out the file binder on Sept. 5, 1945. The receipt is in NA RG 84, POLAD, entry 2531B, box 100. At the time, Brigadier General Betts was Deputy Director for War Crimes, Legal Division, USGCC/OMGUS.

257 Sweet, "Einflußnahme," 271, does not have a satisfactory explanation for this. He only notes that it was most likely Murphy who told Eisenhower about the file. If so, Murphy certainly did not tell him about it in order to encourage the General to stash away the file for himself, because a year later Murphy's office tried to have the file returned.

258 Donald R. Heath, Director, Political Affairs, OMGUS Berlin to Office of U.S. POLAD, Frankfurt, Sept. 4, 1946. "I should be glad if you would take immediate steps to recover a volume of documents entitled: 'Buero des Staatssekretär. Akten betreffend Deutsch-Englische Beziehungen vom 19. Juni bis 31. Dezember 1940'." Quote taken from Thomson to Krumpelmann, Nov. 18, 1946, both in NA RG 84, POLAD, entry 2531B, box 100.

259 W. A. Burress, Assistant Chief of Staff, G-2, HQ USFET to Donald R. Heath, Dec. 12, 1945, ibid.

in 1947.[260] With the original at the Foreign Office and one microfilmed copy at the State Department, the only other existing copy of the Windsor File was the microfilm in British possession. It was promptly destroyed.[261]

The Movement of Records

> *In general, there seems to be a tendency to take panic decisions and to snatch collections of archives away from the places where they are at present, with the idea that this will save them from the clutches of the Russians.*[262]

Considerable tension arose between the British and Americans during the initial months of their joint administration of German diplomatic records that went beyond the everyday disagreements that might be expected under the circumstances. The tension was a product of genuine mistrust that ran counter to the oft-proclaimed harmony of the Anglo-American partnership. Control of the records – the right to determine where they would be stored and who would have access to them – was a question of power. This power struggle occurred not only between the British and the Americans, but also between Robert Murphy and General Lucius D. Clay. The disputes over the Loesch microfilms and the Windsor File are indicative of the importance the contending parties attributed to the captured documents. The tension intensified during the summer of 1945 as the French and Soviets began to demand access to the well-guarded booty in Marburg.

From Marburg to Kassel. The Marburg Castle in the American zone was the ideal hiding place for the Auswärtiges Amt files. It was not easily accessible, had not been seriously vandalized in the final weeks of the war, and was not far from the American headquarters in Frankfurt.[263] Although Marburg was under American jurisdiction, Thomson was in charge of setting up the castle as a records facility. It was to be "operated for the purpose of installing, classifying, examining, and exploiting the A.A. [Auswärtiges Amt] material by a staff representing the Foreign Office and the Department of State."[264] The Americans initially had no objections to the arrangements Thomson made, but after the controversy over Loesch, they suddenly saw

---

260 Sweet, "Einflußnahme," 272. In July 1947, the file was returned to Berlin on the approval of George VI to be processed by the DGFP. See ibid, 278. Today the Windsor File is located at the Political Archives of the Auswärtiges Amt under the signature R 29571.
261 Sweet, "Einflußnahme," 277.
262 Minutes of Michael Creswell, FO, Nov. 20, 1945, PRO FO 370/1191 L3513.
263 Robert C. Thomson to Ivor Pink, CCG(BE), May 23, 1945, PRO FO 371/46712 C2584/G; Murphy to SecState, no. 545, June 30, 1945, FRUS 1945:3, 1113–16.
264 Initial Report on the Marburg/Lahn Document Center Covering the Period from its Inception [May 1945] to July 15 1945, NA RG 84, POLAD, Entry 2531B, box 37.

those arrangements working strongly to Britain's advantage. The British supplied the microfilming equipment, and the films were developed at the Air Ministry in London. The Royal Air Force personnel the Americans had initially regarded as helpful were now criticized for having "final word and complete control of all photographing and films and will brook no interference."[265] There was also an imbalance in manpower: Thomson's team had seven officers and eleven soldiers; the Americans had only five civilians.[266] As civilians, they had no authority to issue orders in a military operation.[267] The British also controlled logistics because the Americans did not have trucks and drivers of their own.[268] The head of the American team believed that Marburg was practically under British control.[269] To be in such a defensive position in their own zone was more than the American team could bear. "It is imperative," one of the American officers declared, "that we have at Marburg an administration by American forces so as to 'free' . . . the American element from British rule, I dare say, tyranny."[270]

For Robert Murphy, the complaints from the American document team came at just the right moment to help him take control of the Auswärtiges Amt files from the British, whom he thought had played him false in the Loesch affair. In September 1945, he received permission from the State Department to transfer the records from Marburg to the MCC in Fürstenhagen on the outskirts of Kassel.[271] The first groups of files were moved on September 12, "on personal initiative of Murphy."[272] The British were horrified. The MCC was the collecting center for administrative records for use in establishing a Four Power government and administrative

---

265 Krumpelmann to Col. W. D. Hohenthal, Director, Political Affairs, USGCC [i.e. Büro POLAD], n.d. [early October 1945], NA RG 84, POLAD entry 2531B, box 37.

266 Ibid.

267 " . . . the British with their military rank are bound to be able to get away with more than we Americans can with no rank." Krumpelmann to Hohenthal, Aug. 22, 1945, ibid.

268 "The Colonel uses the enlisted men as our auto drivers, thus making the transportation connected with our unit a British monopoly." Krumpelmann to Hohenthal, [early October 1945], ibid. See also G. Edward Reynolds to Murphy, Oct. 27, 1945, NA RG 59, Lot File 78D441, Historical Office, box 6.

269 Krumpelmann to Hohenthal, Aug. 22, 1945, NA RG 84, POLAD entry 2531B, box 37.

270 Krumpelmann to Hohenthal, [early October 1945], ibid. Further: "This should become an American set up under American control and the British be guests." Krumpelmann to Hohenthal, Aug. 22, 1945, ibid.

271 What prompted Murphy's action was a memorandum from G. Edward Reynolds, Sept. 5, 1945, NA RG 84, POLAD, entry 2531B, box 37. Reynolds "strongly recommended that this unit be put in charge of an American army officer whether or not the archives are to be moved to Kassel. It is further recommended that this be done without delay."

272 Michael Creswell, CCG(BE), [Report on] German Diplomatic and Political Archives, Oct. 3, 1945, PRO FO 370/1189 L3043.

apparatus for Germany. Did the Americans really want to put the diplomatic records into this pool? Still more problematic in the eyes of the British was the fact that the MCC was "full . . . of intelligent and inquisitive Germans," namely former ministerial officials and diplomats who had access to the records.[273] Sir William Strang attempted to prevent the transfer of the Auswärtiges Amt files. He argued that the ongoing work in Marburg would be needlessly interrupted. That was, however, hardly the Foreign Office's primary concern. The British were worried about losing control of the files, especially the Windsor File.[274] Murphy, replying in kind, voiced his concern about the lack of fire safety measures at Marburg castle. Nor did he pass up the opportunity to needle the British by informing his counterpart that the "possible embarrassment" arising from certain records was solely a British affair: "frankly, we do not have any anxiety on that score as far as American participation [in the project] is concerned."[275] The Foreign Office was well aware that this was a power ploy on Murphy's part. A member of the British Control Council considered his fire-safety argument "extremely flimsy" and no more than a pretext for a move that actually involved "a certain amount of American 'Empire building.'"[276]

The move to Kassel was never completed. On the same day that the first shipment of records left Marburg, Clay decided to grant the Soviets and the French access to the German ministerial records at the Kassel MCC. Moreover, he planned to have *all* of the records needed for the Four Power government of Germany shipped to Berlin. With this decision, Clay cut Murphy down to size. Murphy's attempt to wrestle control of the Auswärtiges Amt files from the British resulted only in chaos: the records

---

273 Lt. Col. Austin, JIC, Memorandum für Michael Creswell, Some Foreign Office Interests in Documents in Germany, Oct. 17, 1945, PRO FO 370/1191 L3644. Further, the minutes of Creswell for the German Department, Sept. 17, 1945, ibid.

274 "A further argument which occurs to me is derived from the case which I discussed with you the other day, and which I need not mention directly, in which we were anxious to secure the withdrawal from the German archives of a certain dossier. It seems to me, given the German talent for getting hold of the wrong end of the stick, that certain documents may well turn up which would be embarrassing to both or either of us, although representing a complete distortion of the facts." Strang to Murphy, Sept. 11, 1945, NA RG 84, POLAD, Entry 2531B, box 37. The "case" mentioned by Strang was naturally that of the Windsor File. The originals were no longer in Marburg, but had been sent on September 5 to Eisenhower's headquarters. Apparently Strang did not yet know this.

275 Murphy to Strang, Sept. 14, 1945, ibid.

276 "The move to KASSEL was (very hastily) undertaken on the personal initiative of Mr Murphy, who used the argument of fire-risks at MARBURG as a pretext. . . . There is, I think, a certain amount of American 'Empire building' about all this, as certain individual Americans seem anxious to get the whole thing under their own exclusive control." Michael Creswell, CCG(BE), [Report on] German Diplomatic and Political Archives, Oct. 3, 1945, PRO FO 370/1189 L3043.

were now split between two locations. By early October 1945, all records from the pre-1933 period were simply in dead storage at the MCC. The rest remained in Marburg, where they continued to be analyzed.[277]

The Other Allies. From the moment the Auswärtiges Amt files were discovered in the Harz castles, the Soviets were implicitly present in every Anglo-American decision. Earlier recommendations from senior officials that the Soviets be included in the administration and exploitation of the captured records were immediately rejected by the leadership at the Foreign Office and the State Department.[278] It was, however, clear to everyone that sooner or later the Soviets would begin to ask questions. The British also thought it would be appropriate to aid the French government in its prosecution of Philippe Pétain and Pierre Laval and the Norwegians in trying Vidkun Quisling by offering copies of documents as evidence.[279] But all involved realized that such a move would set off a chain reaction:

If we give the French this evidence, they may use it in court. If they use it in court they will have to establish its genuineness, i.e. they will have only photostatic copies, and it will be necessary to explain why they do not possess the original documents and why they can trust the copies. Thus the whole story of the 'find' will come out. We should then get a demand for the publication of other documents, and, incidentally, the Russians would ask why they had not been told about them."[280]

There was no time for long deliberations about whether or how the other Allies should be informed about the find. At the end of May 1945, two articles appeared in the British press reporting – inaccurately – that the records of the Auswärtiges Amt had been flown to Great Britain.[281] On June 20, the Foreign Office received an aide-memoire from Feodor Gusev, the Soviet ambassador and EAC representative in London. Gusev stated unequivocally that "the Soviet Government insists that Soviet experts be

277 J. D. Beam to Murphy, Oct. 2, 1945, NA RG 84, POLAD, entry 2531B, box 37; Strang to FO, no. 170, Oct. 4, 1945, PRO FO 370/1188 L3004/3004/402.

278 Minutes of Geoffrey Harrison, May 23, 1945, PRO FO 371/46712 C2548/G. In April 1945, a still somewhat disoriented member of Murphy's staff asked him whether the Soviets were to be informed about the discovery in Mühlhausen – meaning the Loesch film. Donald R. Heath to Murphy, Apr. 21, 1945, NA RG 84, entry 2531B, box 37.

279 Minutes of John M. Troutbeck, Asst. UnderSecState FO, June 13, 1945, PRO FO 371/46712 C3209/G. In preparation for an internal FO meeting the following day, Troutbeck wrote: "I do not see that we can avoid letting the French know very soon that we have documents bearing directly on the charges to be made against Pétain and Laval. Indeed it might be most inexpedient for us to hold evidence against Laval without producing it."

280 [Troutbeck], Notes for meeting to discuss 'finds' of German and Italian Documents, [June 14, 1945], ibid.

281 "Hitlers Secrets Sent to London," *Daily Express*, May 29, 1945; "Hitler's Private Files are Here," *Daily Herald*, May 31, 1945, copies in PRO FO 371/46712 C2761.

immediately allowed to study the German state archives captured by the Allied troops and, in particular, the archives of the German Foreign Office. For this purpose the Soviet Government intends to send several Soviet experts to London within the next few days."[282]

Gusev caught the Foreign Office off-guard. The Russian expert Sir Alexander Cadogan, who had not been fully briefed on the document issue, assured Gusev it was Britain's intention "to make the information afforded by these documents available to the Soviet Government."[283] His colleagues, however, intended nothing of the sort. Since Gusev based his demands on newspaper reports that were not accurate, one official suggested, why not simply deny everything?[284]

While the Foreign Office was still trying to decide how to handle the matter, the press once again intervened in the debate. The *Sunday Chronicle* published a report on the work done on the Loesch microfilms at the Air Ministry.[285] Publicizing this top-secret program bordered on betrayal of official secrets.[286] Thanks to this newspaper report, British diplomats could now be "quite certain that the Soviet Government will disbelieve a denial of the previous reports."[287] Gusev did indeed follow up on his demand, and it was no longer possible for the Foreign Office not to respond. The answer he received was, however, noncommittal. The Foreign Office denied the assertion that the Auswärtiges Amt files were in Great Britain and reported that they were still in Germany, buried "among the large mass of miscellaneous German archives located at different places in the area under SHAEF's control."[288] The British claimed that they did not have an

---

282 Aide-memoire, June 19, 1945, PRO FO 371/46713 C3351/G.

283 Minutes of Cadogan, June 20, 1945, ibid. Cadogan had already complained the week before to the Foreign Office that he did not have enough information about the German records. "I don't know what these documents *are* or what they contain. How *can* I express a useful opinion?" See diary entry for June 14, 1945, in Cadogan, *Diaries of Alexander Cadogan*, 752f.

284 Minutes of Vyvyan, June 22, 1945, FO 371/46713 C3210/G.

285 "Allies Record Nazi Secrets. Germany's Most Secret Documents are Safe in Allied Hands," *Sunday Chronicle*, June 24, 1945 (copy), PRO FO 371/46713 C3455/G.

286 The Air Ministry immediately initiated an investigation because, "this leakage is most disturbing from every point of view." The "mole" was never found. Minutes of the Air Ministry for Sir James Ross [who headed the filming project; A.E.], June 24, 1945; Sir James Ross to Permanent Undersecretary of State, FO, June 25, 1945, both in ibid.

287 Minutes of Vyvyan, June 25, 1945, in ibid.

288 Vyvyan to John M. Allison, June 28, 1945, NA RG 84, Entry 2600A, box 30. See also the minutes of Vyvyan, June 25, 1945, PRO FO 371/46713 C3455/G; Michael Vyvyan to John M. Allison, June 28, 1945, NA RG 84, entry 2600A, box 30; Winant, AmEmb, to SecState, no. 6519, June 28, 1945, FRUS 1945:3, 1112f. The answer that Gusev received from Sir Alexander Cadogan arrived on July 10, 1945, and stuck strictly to the version related here. It is documented in the Parliamentary Debates (House of Commons), Feb. 18, 1948, 1153–5, as part of questioning in which Foreign Minister Bevin had to inform Parliament exactly when the Soviets had demanded access to the captured documents.

overview of the collections and therefore that it was too early for the Soviet Union to send its experts. Eventually, a "reciprocal arrangement" would have to be reached. Gusev's reaction to this response is not known.

The adroit diplomatic explanations became untenable by September 1945, at the latest. Without prior warning, the U.S. military governor, General Lucius D. Clay, announced at a meeting in Berlin on September 12:

> that there were at Kassel the archives of a number of German Ministries and that he was sure he was speaking for the UK Delegation as well as for his own in proposing that the Soviet and French Delegations should have access to these archives and should be invited to appoint officers for that purpose. The French Delegation stated that they had already appointed such an officer.[289]

With this announcement, Clay caught everyone by surprise. Even Murphy had not been informed beforehand.[290] The general's actions caused a veritable crisis among the State Department and Foreign Office staff members[291] The British found themselves confronted once again with the possibility that the Windsor File might be copied and its contents disclosed.[292] Murphy, recognizing that his order to have the Auswärtiges Amt files transferred to Fürstenhagen inadvertently presented them to the Soviets on a silver platter, agreed to halt further transfers temporarily[293] and to leave the files dating from the Nazi period, "the 'cream' of the collection," in Marburg.[294] The material that had already arrived in Fürstenhagen remained packed in

289 Sir William Strang, POLAD Berlin, to FO, no. 79, Sept. 13, 1945, PRO FO 371/46717 C5673. Clay announced the decision at the meeting of the Coordinating Committee of the Control Council, in which the deputy governors of the military government in all four zones met. The committee was the heart of the entire control bureaucracy. See Mai, *Alliierter Kontrollrat*, 49f. Clay's invitation was prompted by a request from the Control Council for a report outlining which records were to be made available to the five departments designated at Potsdam to exist in each zone. See Memo for the Records, n.d. [Nov. 9, 1945], NA RG 165, War Department Special Staffs, entry 472, box 791.

290 Sir William Strang, POLAD Berlin, to FO, no. 79, Sept. 13, 1945, PRO FO 371/46717 C5673.

291 "I think crisis has arisen over General Clay's offering to disclose everything in the MCC to the Russians . . . ." Minutes of Michael Creswell, CCG(BE), to the German Department, FO, Sept. 17, 1945, PRO FO 370/1191 L3644.

292 "Finally, there is the question of witholding from the Russians and French certain special archives of particular interest to ourselves. Mr. Murphy told Sir William Strang that the Americans had nothing that they wished to withold, but he was prepared to arrange for the segregation of such archives as we might wish to withhold." Minutes of Troutbeck, Sept. 17, 1945, PRO FO 371/46717 C5673. The Windsor File had not been in Marburg since September 5. See Lt. Col. Thomson to Vyvyan, Sept. 7, 1945, PRO FO 371/46717 C5561.

293 After the visit of the Soviet delegation, he repeated his request to the State Department to complete the transfer of records from Marburg to Kassel. Murphy to SecState, no. 1012, Nov. 15, 1945, FRUS 1945:3, 1128f.

294 Michael Creswell, CCG(BE), [Report on] German Diplomatic and Political Archives, Oct. 3, 1945, PRO FO 370/1189 L3043. Likewise, the Minutes of Lt. Col. Thomson, Nov. 13, 1945, PRO FO 370/1190 L3466: Two thirds of the records were transferred to Kassel in September 1945 "but happily this includes all our junk and most of our lower-value documents."

crates.[295] The Foreign Office hoped that French and Soviet officials would overlook the crates when they visited, at least until British personnel had "an opportunity to extract anything of an embarrassing nature."[296] Because Clay had announced his invitation before a body of the Control Council, the State Department could do nothing to change the situation.[297]

Clay had yet another surprise for the captured documents team. On September 18, he announced that the MCC would be closed and all documents were to be transferred to Berlin by February 1, 1946. They were to be made accessible to the Four Power government for use in "the formation and operation of the Departments of the Central German Government," as agreed at the Potsdam Conference.[298] It was, in other words, no longer a matter of allowing French or Soviet delegations to visit Fürstenhagen but rather of giving all four occupying powers institutionalized access to German governmental records. As Truman, Churchill, and Stalin had tried to present a united front only weeks earlier at the Potsdam Conference, Foreign Office and State Department officials could hardly come out publicly against a measure intended to serve the Four Power government. Although the officials responsible for the captured documents affirmed their support for Four Power control in the extensive correspondence prompted by Clay's announcement, they tried to set conditions that would effectively deny the French and Russians access. They offered two basic counterarguments. First, the State Department and the Foreign Office insisted on the principle of reciprocity, and there was no basis for reciprocity with the French and Soviets because neither reported having had seized documents in its occupation zone.[299] Second, a new diplomatic service was not to

295　J. D. Beam to Murphy, Oct. 2, 1945, NA RG 84, POLAD, entry 2531B, box 37.
296　Foreign Office to Sir William Strang, POLAD, no. 64, PRO FO 371/46717 C5673.
297　The State Department unsuccessfully attempted to revise the decision. See Acting SecState to Murphy, no. 565, Sept. 28, 1945, FRUS 1945:3, 1118f.; H. Freeman Matthews, Director, Office of European Affairs, to General Hilldring, Director, Civil Affairs Division, War Department, Oct. 1, 1945, NA RG 59, CDF 1945–49, 840.414/9–2745; John Muccio, Office POLAD, to Office of the Director of Intelligence, Col. Henry C. Newton, Oct. 3, 1945, NA RG 84, POLAD, entry 2531B, box 37.
298　"Yesterday General Clay informed me that he wanted those records at the MCC which were needed for the formation and operation of the Departments of the Central German Government moved to Berlin as soon as possible. He stated a target date for the completion of this movement as some time in the month of February 1946." G. Bryan Conrad, Acting Director of Intelligence, USGCC (Germany), Memorandum for Political Adviser, attn. Col. Hohenthal, Sept. 19, 1945, NA RG 84, POLAD, entry 2531B, box 37. See also, Murphy to SecState, no. 575, Sept. 21, 1945, NA RG 59, CDF 1945–49, box 5702, 840.414/9–2145. The five administrative departments devised at the Potsdam Conference were transportation, finance, foreign trade, industry, and traffic.
299　"To date the Dept has no evidence of reciprocity in this matter on part of either the French or Russians." Acheson, Acting SecState, to Murphy, no. 564, Sept. 28, 1945, FRUS 1945:3, 1118f. Also, Foreign Office to Sir William Strang, no. 64, Sept. 19, 1945, PRO FO 371/46717 C5673. In the full conviction that they would be given access to documents in the future, the French had

be part of the government for Germany that the Allies had agreed upon at Potsdam, and thus there was no reason for Four Power access to the Auswärtiges Amt files.[300] The Foreign Office did consider the option of presenting copies of select documents to the French and Soviets but categorically rejected the idea of giving them equal access to the records in Marburg or anywhere else.[301] In late October 1945, René Massigli, the French ambassador to Britain, again demanded access to the Auswärtiges Amt records. The Foreign Office offered in response only to allow French officials to see copies in London, lest they come too close to the prized booty still held in Germany.[302]

Thomson did not agree with the evasive explanations and proposals the Foreign Office and State Department put forward. Obviously tired of the tug-of-war between the Allies, he gave a more realistic assessment:

Quite frankly, I feel that it is a mistaken policy to retreat elsewhere lest certain documents be seen by some parties who we have in mind. They know very well that we are here and what we are doing. . . . While it may be true that we should prefer that they do not come upon some papers, concealment will inflict a far more damaging effect on our relations. After all, let us remember that we are dealing with German archives and not with British or American documents, some of which would lead to considerable embarrassment if disclosed in certain quarters. I should really be quite glad if the Russians could see many of the papers. It would do us and the Americans no harm: rather the contrary. . . . We should reserve the exploitation (research, processing etc.) work to ourselves and the Americans, but why not invite the French and the Russians to send delegates . . . ? . . . To sum up, it is not too late to adopt a forthcoming attitude which would disarm suspicion and would probably yield little that would harm us.[303]

Thomson's views were not, however, to have any influence on British and American policy.

turned over to the Americans in May 1945 the legal department records from the Auswärtiges Amt that they had discovered in Ravensburg. See Martens, "Schicksal der deutschen Akten," xlv.

300 Byrnes, SecState, to Murphy, no. 763, Oct. 25, 1945, FRUS 1945:3, 1126; State Department Memorandum [transferred by John D. Hickerson, Deputy Director, Office of European Affairs, to Hilldring], Nov. 28, 1945, NA RG 165, War Department Special Staffs, entry 472, box 791; the same arguments are found in Acheson, Acting SecState, to Acting SecWar [Kenneth Royall], Jan. 21, 1946, FRUS 1945:3, 1134.

301 Michael Creswell, CCG(BE), German Diplomatic and Political Archives, Oct. 3, 1945, PRO FO 370/1189 L3043.

302 Foreign Office to BritEmb Washington, no. 12401, Dec. 11, 1945, PRO FO 370/1191 L3513; BritEmb Washington, Aide-memoire, Dec. 12, 1945, FRUS 1945:3, 1130f. The French were not content simply with copies. The situation is summarized by John Troutbeck in the Minutes, Nov. 10, 1945, PRO FO 370/1191 L3609: "In other words, they resented our apparent desire to keep the documents to ourselves and merely let the French see what we regarded as good for them."

303 Thomson to Ivor T. Pink, Oct. 24, 1945, PRO FO 370/1189 L3296.

The members of the Soviet delegation did not see any diplomatic documents during their first visit to Fürstenhagen. They arrived on October 3 and stayed for a week. The director of the MCC, Henry C. Newton, had assured Murphy beforehand that he could steer the visitors away from the diplomatic files.[304] But, he added, it would be impossible to keep the Auswärtiges Amt files hidden if the Soviets were to station a team at the MCC.[305] Hence, Newton urged Murphy to remove the files from Fürstenhagen altogether.[306] The Soviets had proven to be very well informed and had asked pointed questions daily about the location of the diplomatic documents.[307]

To Berlin. Clay listened to Murphy's and Strang's arguments, but his decisions were influenced by considerations far removed from theirs. With Germany and Japan defeated, the American military was redeploying and demobilizing personnel. The process reached a highpoint in November 1945, when 400,000 soldiers were sent back to the United States within a single month. The rotation of personnel to serve in the occupation of Germany did not function as planned, however, and the Army found itself short of 16,000 men in Germany at the close of 1945.[308] Moreover, troop morale had been sinking steadily since V-E Day.[309] Clay was forced to scale back the military government's administrative structures in Germany and find ways to make them operate more efficiently. At the same time, he had to comply with the policies agreed upon at the Potsdam Conference and with decisions of the Control Council, of which he was a member. Closing the MCC and transferring all captured records to Berlin was a pragmatic decision. That this order also applied to the Auswärtiges Amt files was Murphy's fault on account of his attempt to transfer the documents from Marburg to Kassel. In Clay's view, the British were the main source of tension on the issue of

---

304 J. D. Beam to Murphy, Oct. 2, 1945, NA RG 84, POLAD, entry 2531B, box 37.

305 A permanent delegation was never formed. Born, "MCC," 243, presents the events as if the Soviet government had wilfully undermined the chance to participate. "The Soviet Government was invited to participate in exploitation along with the other three powers, and in October sent a mission to report on MCC. It did not establish a resident staff or make use of the facilities available."

306 "It is obvious . . . that one hundred (100) percent security can only be obtained by either removing the records or by denying access to the French and the Russians." Newton to Office POLAD, attn. John J. Muccio, Oct. 15, 1945, RG 84, Entry 2531B, Office of POLAD, Box 37.

307 Newton to Office POLAD, attn. John J. Muccio, Oct. 15, 1945, ibid.; Murphy to SecState, no. 791, Oct. 16, 1945, NA RG 59, Lot File 78D441, Historical Office, box 21; Murphy to SecState, no. 823, Oct 21, 1945, FRUS 1945:3, 1122f.

308 Clay, *Decision in Germany*, 61f.; Henke, *Amerikanische Besetzung*, 970f.; Ziemke, *U.S. Army*, 422f.

309 Low morale affected the Document Center in Fürstenhagen, too. Born, "MCC," 245, reports in 1950: "No one who does not know at first hand the collapse of morale, efficiency, and control of our troops immediately after V-E Day can comprehend or even imagine some of the problems which faced both serviced and servicer in a condition such as that at MCC."

the captured documents even though the State Department objected just as strongly as the Foreign Office to giving the French and Soviets access.[310] Clay's position was clear: "The United States must insist upon running Germany on a four-party basis even though in some instances the British may be embarrassed."[311]

Clay's handling of the documents issue was consistent with his stance on Four Power government. He wanted to avoid a repeat of an embarrassing situation like the one that had occured during the Soviet visit to the MCC. Further, he had to consider the manpower shortage in the American zone. Finally, he sought to put an end to British protests and thus offered to have all the Auswärtiges Amt records simply transferred to the British zone.[312] His reasoning was simple, as Strang noted in a cable to London: "Since it was we rather than the Americans who were nervous about the Russians seeing possibly embarrassing documents, we had better have all Kassel and Marburg documents in our Zone, so that we rather than they could deal with Russian enquiries."[313] In other words, Clay wanted to push the problem to the other side of the zonal border so that "the British [will] be forced to accept full responsibility for refusal to participate in a quadripartite exploitation of [German] Foreign Office documents."[314] The Foreign Office was not sure how to respond to Clay's proposal. It was not necessarily eager to have the records in the British zone, and some staff members advocated shipping all the files to the United States.[315] For a brief time, there was even talk of giving up all responsibility for the files – an inversion of Clay's proposal.[316] The British Control Commission protested loudly against "the hasty proposal to move all the FO archives over the zonal frontier in a train and dump them in the British zone with the idea that they would be there less accessible to

310 "British representatives here immediately protested permitting representatives of the Soviet and French Governments to have access to German Foreign Office documents." OMGUS Berlin [General Clay] to War Department, CC-19233, Nov. 21, 1945, NA RG 165, War Department Special Staffs, entry 472, box 791.

311 James C. Davis, Chief, Economic and Supply Branch, Memorandum for the Director, Civil Affairs Division [Hilldring], Nov. 9, 1945, ibid.

312 He appears to have made the offer at a meeting on October 2 with General Robertson, his British counterpart. See Strang, POLAD, to FO, no. 170, Oct. 4, 1945, PRO FO 370/1188 L3004/3004/402.

313 Strang to FO, no. 231, Oct. 21, 1945, PRO FO 370/1189 L3191.

314 Murphy to SecState, no. 838, Oct. 25, 1945, FRUS 1945:3, 1124–1126, here 1125.

315 This proposal is found in the Minutes of E. Llewellyn Woodward, Oct. 12, 1945 and Oct. 13, 1945, PRO FO 370/1189 L3065. It is necessary to mention the British unease with Clay's proposal because the documents in FRUS 1945:3, 1124–7, 1129f., give the impression that the British were eagerly fighting to obtain possession of the diplomatic records.

316 "[W]e should get away from the tendency which we have shown of pretending that documents in the US zone are in some way a British responsibility. We have no responsibility but only a certain *privilege* on inspection and access deriving from the arrangement under CIOS. But need we take the lead?" Minutes of Vyvyan, Oct. 19, 1945, PRO FO 370/1189 L3043, emphasis in the original.

the Russians."[317] In the end, however, the Foreign Office accepted Clay's proposal to move the records to the British zone.[318]

Murphy was, once again, not kept informed and did not learn of Clay's offer to the British until Strang told him of it as preparations for the transfer of the files were already underway.[319] He immediately sounded the alarm at the State Department.[320] Murphy felt so strongly about this matter that he preferred to move the records to the American sector of Berlin and thus even closer to the Russians than to have the material in the British zone.[321] In Berlin, they could continue to be evaluated by the Anglo-American team but would be administered by the Americans alone. The British would no longer control the microfilming.[322] British officials argued vigorously against moving the captured documents to Berlin. The move, they contended, would attract too much attention and hinder the search for evidence needed in the Nuremberg trials.[323] The State Department leadership was not persuaded. Recalling the whole litany of complaints about British handling of the documents, the director of the Office of European Affairs advised the secretary of state against acceding to Foreign Office's request:

I personally do not believe in efforts to alter historical records by the destruction or permanent withholding of official documents. Quite frankly, conditions at Marburg are such that the British are, in the opinion of some of our people, enabled thereby to play fast and loose with the documents there. I feel sure they would not hesitate to remove any which showed appeasement policies of high British personalities in an unfavorable light. We have on occasion had difficulty obtaining micro-film copies of certain documents. The British, on one occasion, formally requested us to

---

317 Minutes of Creswell, CCG(BE), Nov. 20, 1945, PRO FO 370/1191 L3513.

318 FO, signed OTP, to Strang, Oct. 24, 1945, PRO FO 370/1189 L1391; BritEmb Washington, Aide-memoire, ref. G240/-/45, Oct. 26, 1945, FRUS 1945:3, 1126f.

319 "[Murphy] had no knowledge of the arrangement for immediate removal of the archives to the British Zone." Strang to FO, no. 231, Oct. 21, 1945, PRO FO 370/1189 L3191.

320 Murphy to SecState, no. 838, Oct. 25, 1945, FRUS 1945:3, 1124–6, here 1125.

321 Byrnes, SecState, to Murphy, no. 774, Oct. 31, 1945, FRUS 1945:3, 1127. At a conference in early November 1945 between Murphy, Clay and General Conrad, it was decided that the first step was not to undertake the move to the British zone. See Donald R. Heath, proxy for Murphy, to Clay, Nov. 5, 1945, NA RG 84, POLAD, entry 2531B, box 37. The decision for the move to Berlin is found in Murphy to SecState, no. 1236, Dec. 11, 1945, FRUS 1945:3, 1129f.

322 The details of the transfer were fought out between the State and War Department in December 1945. A review of the entire course of events is in Memorandum for the Director, Civil Affairs Division, Dec. 6, 1945, NA RG 165, War Department Specials Staffs, entry 472, box 791. The correspondence between the War and State Departments is found in FRUS 1945:3, 1132–5.

323 BritEmb Washington, Aide-memoire, Jan. 11, 1946, NA RG 59, Lot File 78D441, Historical Office, box 24. See also, Memorandum of Conversation, Ambassador Earl of Halifax to Under-SecState Dean Acheson, Jan. 3, 1946, NA RG 59, Lot File 78D441, Historical Office, box 24.

sanction the destruction of certain documents dealing with the Duke of Windsor's passage through Spain and Portugal in the summer of 1940.[324]

The transfer of the Auswärtiges Amt files from Kassel and Marburg to Berlin took place during the first week of February 1946. What had been the Ministerial Collecting Center in Kassel-Fürstenhagen now became the Ministerial Document Branch in Berlin-Tempelhof.[325]

The bickering over access to the Auswärtiges Amt files and the question of where they should be held cannot be attributed solely to British intransigence or interpreted exclusively as an early sign of the Cold War. For one, both the State Department and the Foreign Office attempted to wrestle away and retain full control over the diplomatic files not only from the military government (Clay) but also from the other Allies. The British were motivated by concern over the Windsor File. Murphy, by contrast, seems to have had more personal reasons for wanting to wrest control from the British. After the Foreign Office had initially declined to supply his office with copies of the Loesch microfilms, Murphy was convinced that the British were trying to withhold German documents from the Americans.[326] Once a portion of the files had been transferred from Marburg to Kassel, the situation developed a momentum of its own: the British, believing that the Americans had acted without consulting them, intensified their protests, which, in turn, reinforced Murphy's mistrust of them. Clay had very different interests: he was grappling with a personnel shortage. It remains open to question, however, how far he was truly trying to hold to the principle of Four Power government and to act on behalf of the Control Council.[327]

---

324 H. Freeman Matthews, Director, Office of European Affairs, Memorandum for the Secretary of State, Jan. 31, 1946, NA RG 59, CDF 1945–49, FW 840.414/1–2946. See also James W. Riddleberger, Chief, Division of Central European Affairs, Memorandum for Freeman Matthews and UnderSecState Acheson, Jan. 8, 1946, NA RG 59, Lot File 78D441, Historical Office, box 24.

325 Wolfe, "Short History," xii. The mission statement of the MDB held that the institution would "not in any manner be operated as a nucleus ministerial group. It will operate as a Documents Center where records, documents, [and] previously prepared studies will be available for reference and reading." Henry C. Newton, OMGUS, MCC, Mission of Ministerial Collecting Center in BERLIN, Jan. 19, 1946, NA RG 260, OMGUS, Records of the Executive Office FIAT, box 30.

326 Murphy could have ordered copies of the film from the State Department instead of requesting them only from the Foreign Office. See Sir Oliver Harvey, Private Secretary to Anthony Eden, to Sir Ivone Kirkpatrick, Political Division, CCG(BE), June 4, 1945, PRO FO 371/46712 C2760/G.

327 The historiography on the issue about who is to blame for the failure of Four Power control is presented in Mai, *Kontrollrat*, 1–15.

The Documents on German Foreign Policy *Project*

In June 1946, the State Department and Foreign Office agreed to publish a comprehensive selection of German diplomatic documents.[328] The publication was intended to make available a record of Germany's foreign policy between 1918 and 1939 before interest in the immediate past began to wane. The Foreign Office hoped to pull off a fait accompli in proposing an edition that adhered to strict scholarly standards. Having been bypassed in the decisions to move the captured documents to Kassel and Berlin, and worried that Clay might make them generally accessible, it wanted to bind the State Department to new rules on the handling of the documents.[329] This ploy was only partially successful. The State Department pursued an information policy in connection with the publication project that did not always take the British into consideration. Moreover, the project raised the issue of access anew in the form of the question whether the French and Soviets should be included in the project as co-publishers.

British Calculations and American Haste. The Auswärtiges Amt files offered a goldmine of material for public relations. Accordingly, the Foreign Office staff did not harbor great hopes about their chances of holding their American colleagues to joint, and thus simultaneous, publication of all German documents. "The State Department is extremely active and not always entirely free from 'local' political motives in publishing diplomatic material, and . . . this activity is not likely to be less when the documents concerned have a certain news value and do not raise any awkward questions for the United States Administration."[330] At the State Department, senior officials thought the captured documents were too valuable for shaping public opinion to be left to the historians alone. "Obviously the information contained in these documents has too great a significance on post-war U.S. foreign policies, and on American public opinion in relation to the Government's policies, to allow this information to lie inert in files because of lack of staff or lack of will to release it to the public."[331] The U.S. government had

---

328 Agreement of the United States, the United Kingdom, and France to Publish a Series of Volumes of Documents on German Foreign Policy, 1918–1945, FRUS 1946:5, 200f.

329 A similar line of argumentation in Zala, *Zensur*, 195f.

330 Foreign Office, Notes for meeting to discuss "finds" of German and Italian Documents, n. d. [June 14, 1945], PRO FO 371/46713 C3209/G. Just as pessimistic, the Minutes of Vyvyan, May 7, 1945, PRO FO 371/46712 C1652: "The Americans are, I believe, unlikely to be affected in their publication policy by respect for our views. . . . "

331 Rowena Rummel, Division of Public Liaison, to Francis Russell, Director, Office of Public Information, Apr. 15, 1946, NA RG 59, Lot File 78D441, Historical Office, box 6.

begun to adapt its information policy to its new role as a world power and was becoming increasingly involved in the competition for world opinion.

In mid-February 1946, the Foreign Office proposed that planning be started for a joint edition of German diplomatic records. It envisioned an "impartial and authoritative collection consisting of a selection from the German Foreign Office archives."[332] Such an edition, it believed, would have greater impact in the long run than piecemeal publication of choice documents for propaganda purposes.[333] The British soon learned, however, that the Americans thought there was indeed something to be gained from short-term publicity. That same month, the *Department of State Bulletin* published the first installment of a series that featured select German documents. The State Department made these documents available to squelch speculation in the press that material was being withheld for political reasons.[334] This action prompted the British to intensify their efforts to exercise more control over the captured documents. Although the Foreign Office suggested in its proposal that a Four Power edition would impressively demonstrate Allied unity to the world, it still preferred to conduct bilateral talks with the Americans first. Otherwise, it feared, the Soviets might demand full access to the documents.[335] The British proposal largely paralleled ideas under discussion at the State Department's Historical Office. The historians in both London and Washington wanted to preempt a repeat of the "war guilt" debate that had followed World War I.[336]

---

332 BritEmb Washington, Aide-memoire, Feb. 13, 1946, NA RG 59, Lot File 78D441, Historical Office, box 6.

333 "It is most desirable that the plums of this collection should not be allowed to leak out, or to be used piece meal for propaganda purposes. The effect of documents of this kind – as the Germans themselves showed in their publication of documents captured from the French – lies in their cumulative effect as a series, and not in the 'stunt' value of special items." E. Llewellyn Woodward, Second Report on the "Film Find" [i.e. Loesch film], May 31, 1945, PRO FO 371/46712 C2957/G.

334 Robert T. Miller to E. Wilder Spaulding, Dec. 13, 1945, NA RG 59, CDF 1945–49, 862.414/12–1345. The series began in the *Bulletin*, Feb. 24, 1946, 278–81, with an essay by Saxton Bradford on German foreign propaganda. See also Zala, *Zensur*, 179.

335 "... a publication derived from the combined efforts of all four Powers would be likely to make the deepest impression on world opinion. However, [...] although it would be desirable to include the Soviet Government in the scheme at an early stage in order to ensure their full cooperation [...], it is advisable and preferable to start informal discussions on an Anglo-American basis only. One reason for this view is that if the Soviet Government were invited to participate in the first informal discussion the Soviet Government might make a request to have access now to all these documents...." BritEmb Washington, Aide-memoire, Feb. 13, 1946, NA RG 59, Lot File 78D441, Historical Office, box 6.

336 "The production of an unbiased and authorative publication edited in this way should preclude the subsequent publication of a tendentious German collection such as was made after the last war." Ibid. Also, E. Wilder Spaulding, Historical Office, to Francis Russell, Director, Office of Public Affairs, Apr. 17, 1946, NA RG 59, Lot File 78D441, Historical Office, box 21. The reference

In the discussions about the transfer of the Auswärtiges Amt files from one location to another, the Americans had come to the conclusion that they need not fear compromising or incriminating revelations that might come to light from the captured documents.[337] The British proposal nonetheless prompted senior officials at the State Department to address a crucial question: "Is the Department prepared to support a policy of complete disclosure of German diplomatic documents even though some of them . . . may prove to be somewhat embarrassing to this Government?"[338] Deciding in favor of complete disclosure, the State Department agreed to start initial work on the project. The French and the Soviets were to be excluded from the initial planning, not least because the State Department believed there was reason to doubt that the objectivity of an edition could be guaranteed if it became a Four Power project.[339]

In June 1946, representatives of the State Department and the Foreign Office drafted a plan for the series *Documents on German Foreign Policy*.[340] The head of the State Department's Historical Office arrived in London with a well-developed proposal in hand, and the project followed the American proposal in large measure.[341] The project was to consist of approximately 20 volumes of 800–1,000 pages apiece. It would cover German foreign policy from 1918 to 1945 and would be divided into four chronologically organized series.[342] Each volume was to appear in English and German. The German edition, it was unanimously agreed, would be regarded as a cost of occupation; that is, German funds would be used to pay for it. As a matter of policy, the editors would not be government-employed historians.

making a connection between the DFGP and the German edition *Die Große Politik der europäischen Kabinette* will be discussed in chapter V in connection with historiography.

337 The Anglo-American team in Marburg had inspected the inventories one more time: "I have asked every member of the investigating teams individually and at a general meeting to mention any specific items so far read which might have unfortunate consequences if they were seen by other allies. No member of the British or American teams reports finding documents of a seriously compromising or incriminating nature which could be used against Britain or the United States." W. P. Cumming, Marburg, to Murphy, Oct. 23, 1945, NA RG 84, POLAD, entry 2531B, box 37.

338 Franics Russell, Director, Office of Public Affairs, to John D. Hickerson, Director, European Affairs, UnderSecState Acheson, William Benton, Ass't SecState, May 28, 1946, NA RG 59, CDF 1945–49, 862.414/5–2846. This source belongs in the context of the preparations for the edition *Nazi-Soviet Relations*. See Zala, *Zensur*, 213f.

339 Department of State, Aide-memoire, Mar. 7, 1946, NA RG 59, Lot File 78D441, Historical Office, box 6.

340 Extensively covered in Zala, *Zensur*, 195–7, 199–209.

341 Agenda for Meeting at London on Proposals to Publish German Diplomatic Papers, n. d. [June 1946], NA RG 59, Lot File 78D441, Historical Office, box 1. ". . . the final agreed proposals differ very little from the initial U.S. proposals which we presented at the first meeting and which, in the absence of any British paper, was used as the basis for the discussions." Howard Trivers to James Riddleberger, Director, Division of Central European Affairs, June 19, 1946, NA RG 59, CDF 1945–49, 862.414/6–1946 CSBM.

342 Series A (1918–1926), Series B (1926–1933), Series C (1933–1937), Series D (1937–1945).

Instead, they were to be "outstanding private scholars of high reputation" who would pursue their work "on the basis of highest scholarly objectivity" and, as was to be stated in the preface to the first volume of *Documents on German Foreign Policy*, "were to have complete independence in the selection and editing of the documents."[343] And if the editors were not able to agree whether particular documents should be included in *Documents on German Foreign Policy*, each government had the option of publishing those documents separately.

The British assumed that they had regained a large measure of control over access to the Auswärtiges Amt files in their agreement with the Americans on the *Documents on German Foreign Policy* project. The section on "Access" in the agreement read, "It is recommended that the German records to be used for this project should not be released for publication or other use by unofficial persons until the material involved has been approved for publication by the cooperating Powers."[344] This provision put the historians at the State Department at odds with the department's Office for Foreign Activity Correlation, which had been administering the Auswärtiges Amt files from the time they were discovered in the Harz Mountains. That office had repeatedly given individual documents to the press or members of Congress as background information. Withholding the more sensational documents from the press would be counterproductive, the office argued, because the reporters who were already accusing the State Department of excessive secretiveness were well informed about the extent of the captured records.[345] The Historical Office eventually agreed to interpret the access clause in a way that did not conflict with the State Department's public relations policy.[346] In other words, the State Department did not change its information policy but tried rather to improve its internal coordination.[347] Shortly after the agreement on *Documents on*

343 Proposals for Publishing German Official Papers agreed at Anglo-American Meetings held at Foreign Office, London, June 11–18, 1946, NA RG 84, POLAD, entry 2531B, box 100. See also, Kent, "Foreign Ministry Archives at Whaddon Hall," 46f.; Zala, *Zensur*, 205–8.
344 Proposals for Publishing German Official Papers agreed at Anglo-American Meetings held at Foreign Office, London, June 11–18, 1946, NA RG 84, POLAD, entry 2531B, box 100.
345 "It should be recalled that a number of newspapermen were employed by various intelligence agencies during the war and thoroughly acquainted with the nature and scope of these documents." Herbert Cummings to Ben C. O'Sullivan, July 3, 1946, NA RG 59, Lot File 78D441, Historical Office, box 6.
346 "Article 16 shall not be interpreted to interfere with the practice of releasing for publication selected documents for particular purposes in line with the policy of any of the cooperating powers." G. Bernard Noble, Historical Office, to James Riddleberger, Director, Central European Division, July 28, 1946, ibid.
347 Meeting in the Office of F. H. Russell, Acting Director, Office of Public Information, Aug. 6, 1946, ibid.

German Foreign Policy was signed, a State Department official nonchalantly informed a British colleague that there was "no binding commitment on [the Americans'] part for prior consultation with the British Government before publication of any German Foreign Office documents."[348] Once again, the British had failed to secure effective control over the Auswärtiges Amt files. The British embassy in Washington could do no more than try to contain the damage and requested that publication of documents outside the joint edition be kept to a minimum.[349]

Whatever suspicions the British might have had that they were being treated as less-than-equal partners must have been confirmed when the State Department issued a press release on October 3, 1946, announcing the publication project without mentioning British participation.[350] It was probably little consolation to the British that the American editor-in-chief, Raymond Sontag, had also not been informed of this announcement beforehand.[351] The British embassy registered a strong protest, and State Department officials were reportedly "rather taken aback by [its] vigour."[352] At the Foreign Office, it was feared that publicity about the planned edition of German documents would prompt probing inquiries by the House of Commons.[353] Furthermore, there was speculation that the Americans might be trying to annul the publication agreement by not mentioning the British.[354] By way of apology, the State Department explained that increasing pressure from the press made an immediate announcement necessary.[355] The feared columnist Drew Pearson had taken up the subject of the captured documents and, as the British embassy reported back to London, had

348 Memorandum of Conversation [between] Herbert M. Sichel, First Secretary BritEmb Washington, and Howard Trivers, Division of Central European Affairs, Aug. 28, 1946, ibid.
349 Ibid. The State Department once again underscored this point in an aide-memoire dated Sept. 13, 1946, PRO FO 370/1273 L4038.
350 Draft and final versions of press release no. 698, Oct. 3, 1946, NA RG 59, Lot File 78D441, Historical Office, box 6. Reprinted in *Department of State Bulletin*, 15: 380, Oct. 13, 1946, 690f.
351 "It would seem obvious that the chief of the project should have been consulted on the wording of the press release. I was not consulted." Sontag to Noble, Oct. 4, 1946, NA RG 59, Lot File 78D441, Historical Office, box 6. Noble informed Sontag that he had simply been overlooked.
352 Ambassador Lord Inverchapel, BritEmb, to FO, no. 5938, Oct. 5, 1946, PRO FO 370/1273 L4304.
353 "The Foreign Office fears that the publicity caused by the press release may bring about a question in the House of Commons in answer to which the Foreign Office would be obliged to state the facts." Memorandum of Conversation [between] Herbert M. Sichel, First Secretary BritEmb, Howard Trivers, Central European Division, Oct. 9, 1946, NA RG 59, CDF 1945–49, 840.414/10–946 CS/HH.
354 Ibid.
355 "One of the most vicious by-products of the Department's delay in sharing its captured material with the public has been the series of sharp criticisms appearing in the press and the attendant misrepresentation of the Department's motives. . . . Several columnists have joined the hue and cry." Saxton E. Bradford, Memorandum for Ass't Secretaries Francis Russell and William Benton, Status of Public Relations Exploitation of Captured Enemy Documents, Oct. 16, 1946, NA RG 59, Lot File 78D441, Historical Office, box 6.

reported in one column that the British government wanted to suppress certain documents in the hope of preventing the Soviets from releasing documents that linked important Englishmen to the Nazis.[356] The State Department corrected the one-sided picture of the publication project in another press release issued in January 1947.[357] The British must have realized that they were running the risk of being relegated to the role of junior partner when they proposed the project to the Americans. They would regain their equal status with the Americans only when the French joined the publication project.

The most important political question tied to the *Documents on German Foreign Policy* project – namely, the question of the participation of French and Soviet historians – had been set aside during the planning talks in London. Neither the British nor the Americans were in any hurry to include the other Allies.[358] At the State Department, it was assumed that the Soviets would join the project only to obstruct it, and opinion of the French was not much better.[359] During the London talks, the two sides agreed verbally not to issue an invitation to the other Allies and to wait for them to request to join the project.[360] This hurdle is one more indication that the British and the Americans did not attach great value to the possibility of participation by the other Allies.[361] There was, accordingly, little disappointment when it became clear that the Soviets were never going to ask to participate. The French, however, did join the project and signed the publication agreement in April 1947.[362]

The Initial Phase at Tempelhof. Work on *Documents on German Foreign Policy* began in Berlin in November 1946. The Foreign Office named John

356 Ambassador Lord Inverchapel, BritEmb, to FO, no. 5938, Oct. 5, 1946, PRO FO 370/1273 L4304.
357 Press Release no. 50, German War Documents Project (simultaneous release in London), Jan. 21, 1947, NA RG 59, Lot File 78D441, Historical Office, box 6.
358 Howard Trivers to James Riddleberger, Director, Division of Central European Affairs, June 19, 1946, NA RG 59, CDF 1945–49, 862.414/6–1946 CSBM.
359 "[W]e do have to protect ourselves against French and Russian recalcitrance. Collaboration involves such risks." Issues Involved in the Proposed Publication of German Official Documents, n.d. [May 28, 1946], NA RG 59, CDF 1945–49, FW-862.414/5–2846. "The British, I am sure, share our concern about Russian participation in the project, fearing that the Russians may enter it only in order to obstruct its conclusion." Howard Trivers to James Riddleberger, Director, Division of Central European Affairs, June 19, 1946, NA RG 59, CDF 1945–49, 862.414/6–1946 CSBM.
360 Trivers to Riddleberger, June 19, 1946, NA RG 59, CDF 1945–49, 862.414/6–1946 CSBM.
361 This assessment is derived not only from the procrastinating handling of the affair, but also from the language used in internal communication. See Office Memorandum Francis Russell, Public Affairs, to Asst. SecState William Benton, Oct. 21, 1946, NA RG 59, Lot File 78D441, Historical Office, box 6: "[T]he French and Russians . . . would be permitted to participate if they cared to do so on the basis agreed upon by us and the British."
362 French embassy in Washington, Aide-memoire, copy of the translation, Apr. 3, 1947, NA RG 59, CDF 1945–49, FW-862.414/4–347; State Department, Press Release no. 414, May 1, 1947, NA RG 59, Lot File 78D441, Historical Office, box 6.

W. Wheeler-Bennett as the British editor-in-chief. His American counterpart was Raymond Sontag of the University of California at Berkeley. The French appointed the diplomatic historian Pierre Renouvin, who resigned from the project in early 1948. His successor was Maurice Baumont.[363] The editors-in-chief were not based in Berlin and met only occasionally for editorial conferences. Staff members in Berlin, working with the actual documents, made preliminary selections, and the editors worked from microfilms.[364] The American work group in Berlin was made up of E. Malcolm Carroll of Duke University and the German émigré Fritz T. Epstein. The British team included Kenneth H. M. Duke, who had earlier worked with German records in connection with the Nuremberg Trials.

The historians arrived at Berlin-Tempelhof to find the team of intelligence officers from the Foreign Office and the State Department who had been responsible for the Auswärtiges Amt files since April 1945. As so often in the past, Murphy had not been informed of their coming, and his staff was not sure whether the historians were to be treated as reinforcements for the understaffed intelligence officers or as an independent team.[365] The fact that the historians had their own project and put an additional burden on the already weak infrastructure at Tempelhof hardly pleased the document center staff, who had to spend great amounts of time and energy tending to "visiting missions" from other countries and government agencies. Rarely did the intelligence staff find time to do the actual jobs they had been sent there to do.[366] Cooperation between the intelligence offers and the historians did not always run smoothly.[367] The problem was not solved until spring 1948, when the intelligence division at the State Department turned over responsibility for the captured records to the Historical Office.[368] Such administrative tension never arose among the British. Both intelligence and historical work were coordinated throughout by the Foreign Office Library.

Even among the historians, Anglo-American cooperation continued to be hampered by mistrust. Shortly after his arrival at Tempelhof, Sontag noticed a "surprising dearth of material on Anglo-German relations"

---

363 The editorial staff members are listed at the beginning of each volume of the DGFP.
364 For more on the work arrangements, see Kent, "Foreign Ministry Archives at Whaddon," 46–51.
365 Murphy to SecState, no. A-837, Oct. 14, 1946, NA RG 84, POLAD, entry 2531B, box 100.
366 John T. Krumpelmann to Murphy, Administration and control of depository containing documents and library of the former German Foreign Office, Aug. 21, 1947, ibid., box 176; John T. Krumpelmann to Jack D. Neal, Chief, Division of Foreign Activity Correlation, May 13, 1947, NA RG 59, Lot File 78D441, Historical Office, box 24.
367 Zala, *Zensur*, 200f., 228f.
368 State Department to POLAD Berlin, Mar. 8, 1948, NA RG 59, CDF 1945–49, 862.414/3–848.

during the late 1930s.[369] Once again, the Americans thought they were at a disadvantage vis-à-vis a better staffed British team.[370] Sontag feared *Documents on German Foreign Policy* might turn out to be a British product in the end.[371] The fact that documents were missing, notably those dealing with Britain's appeasement policy, could discredit the entire endeavor, Sontag feared, because "the British would be accused of suppressing the evidence."[372] He soon voiced his own suspicions along those lines when he informed the head of the Historical Office that he could not guarantee that the Loesch microfilms were intact: "Unfortunately, the films were taken to London after their capture, and the sceptic can argue that some parts of these films were suppressed by the British, who are the only ones who have had access to the original films. That is bad."[373] Sontag also complained that volumes 1 and 3 on Anglo-German relations were missing. Volume 3 contained the now famous Windsor File; the location of volume 1 remains a mystery to this day.[374] In 1947, the editors forced the return of the Windsor File from London by threatening to resign.[375] Other gaps in documentation were explained by transport accidents during the transfer of records and by the German destruction of records in 1945.[376]

Documents on German Foreign Policy was not the only project on which the American team of historians worked. In May 1947, leading officials at

369 Sontag voiced his "suspicion naturally raised by this gap." Sontag to Noble, Dec. 16, 1946, NA RG 59, Lot File 78D441, Historical Office, box 6.

370 "The British have a much firmer foundation for the systematic use of the German documents because . . . the Foreign Office had in mind the long-run utility of the documents." Sontag to Noble, Nov. 11, 1946. Sontag was even more explicit in his letter dated Jan. 2, 1947: "The British . . . showed from the outset that superb recognition of the long-range importance of history which they have developed over centuries. Long after the last Nazi and the last traitor have been punished, statesmen and nations will be formulating their policy upon the basis of what they think happened in the past. That the British recognized. . . . Therefore, . . . they have sought the largest possible participation in the shaping of the historical record." Both in NA RG 59, Lot File 78D441, Historical Office, box 6.

371 The State Department would "sponsor as a joint Anglo-American publication volumes which will in reality represent thoughtful selection only by the British." Sontag to Noble, Jan. 2, 1947, ibid. Using this pessimistic assessment, Sontag argued that his personnel be increased.

372 Sontag to Noble, Office Memorandum: Lack of Material on Anglo-German Relations in German Documents, Dec. 26, 1946, ibid.

373 Sontag to Noble, Jan. 2, 1947, ibid.

374 Ibid. Volume 2 starts in May 1939, so that volume 1 must have covered the period of the Munich Agreement. See also F. H. Russell, Office of Public Affairs, to Asst. SecState at the German Dept., Norman Armour, Mar. 22, 1948, ibid., vol. 13: "Volume I of this series, concerning the appeasement period, had disappeared by the time the American historians examined the Archives; how it disappeared has never been discovered."

375 Sweet, "Einflußnahme," 278.

376 In order to cover certain gaps in the record, interviews were again conducted with Heinrich Valentin, Karl von Loesch and Paul Schmidt. The interviews are in NA RG 59, Lot File 78D441, Historical Office, box 6. During the evacuation, a truck and trailer with secret files from 1920 to 1936 caught fire, leaving only charred remains. See also, Philippi, "Politisches Archiv I," 148.

the State Department discussed whether it would be beneficial to exclude the documents on the Molotov-Ribbentrop Pact from the joint Anglo-American edition and publish them in a separate publication, independent of the British. It was clear that such a step would have an adverse effect on Soviet-American relations.[377] During the summer of 1947, before a final decision had been made, Sontag and James Beddie began to prepare a selection of the most important documents on German-Soviet relations. In October, the State Department decided to move forward with a separate edition of the German-Soviet documents; Truman and his cabinet approved the decision in early November.[378] The collection was almost ready to go to press by that point, but its publication was put on hold pending the outcome of the Foreign Ministers Conference in London scheduled for December. Should the conference – contrary to all expectations – turn out to be a constructive exchange, publication of the collection could still be postponed.[379] On December 17, word came that the negotiations had proved fruitless, making any further consideration of Soviet sensitivities unnecessary. *Nazi-Soviet Relations, 1939–1941* thereupon went to press. Among the documents it presented was the Molotov-Ribbentrop Pact, including the secret protocol; this was the first publication of the text of the pact in full.[380]

The British embassy in Washington was not informed of the plans to publish *Nazi-Soviet Relations* until December 24. The Americans deliberately gave the British such short notice so that they would not have time to react.[381] The appearance of the book in January 1948 was an international sensation. Once again, the Americans had pushed the publication agreement with the British to the limit. The Foreign Office had to concede that

377 Francis H. Russell, Director, Public Affairs, to H. Freeman Matthews, European Division, May 19, 1947, NA RG 59, CDF 1945–49, 862.414/5–1947 CS/A; Charles E. Bohlen, Office of SecState, to Russell, May 28, 1947, NA RG 59, CDF 1945–49, 862.414/5–2847.

378 Memorandum of Conversation [of the] Ad Hoc Committee on Publication of Molotov-Ribbentrop Papers, Participants: Charles E. Saltzmann, John D. Hickerson, Llewellyn E. Thompson, Joseph C. Satterwaite, Dean Rusk, Fritz Oppenheimer, Francis Russell, C. V. Hulick, Oct. 2, 1947, NA RG 59, CDF 1945–49, 761.62/10–247; Memorandum for the Secretary [George C. Marshall], Nov. 6, 1947, ibid., box 6760, 862.414/5–2847.

379 C. H. Humelsine, Memorandum from the Office of SecState for [among others] Francis Russell, Nov. 15, 1947, NA RG 59, CDF 1945–49, box 6760.

380 Sontag/Beddie, *Nazi Soviet Relations 1939–1941. Documents from the Archives of the German Foreign Office.* Washington, D.C.: Department of State 1948. An extensive account of the creation of the edition is offered by Zala, *Zensur*, 210–26. Lipinsky, "Geheimes Zusatzprotokoll," features a convincing history of the impact of the Hitler-Stalin Pact on Eastern Europe until 1992, although he disregards the American edition of 1948 and gives the wrong impression that the "documents war" was, in this case, started by the Soviets.

381 Ambassador Lord Inverchapel, BritEmb, to FO, no. 7178, Dec. 24, 1947, PRO FO 370/1496 L7701.

the State Department remained "technically within its rights" in publishing the German-Soviet documents. Nonetheless, the State Department had yet again presented the British with a fait accompli. *Nazi-Soviet Relations* was, as Wheeler-Bennett noted, "an operation of political warfare."[382] That was precisely what it was meant to be. State Department officials patted themselves on the back for what they saw as a successful coup: "The Soviet Government was caught flat-footed in what was the first effective blow from our side in a clear-cut propaganda war."[383]

The Berlin Airlift in Reverse: The Move from Berlin to Great Britain. The odyssey of the Auswärtiges Amt files came to an end, or so it seemed, in the fall of 1948 with their transfer to Whaddon Hall, a country estate in Buckinghamshire between London and Oxford. This was the fifth time the documents had been relocated since they were discovered by Allied troops. Prior to the move to Great Britain, the entire publication project and 400 tons of material had been moved again within Berlin itself, namely, from Tempelhof to Berlin-Lichterfelde in the summer of 1947. Although the historians had settled in well, the intensifying Berlin crisis prompted them to reevaluate the situation. Bernard Noble, the head of the Historical Office at the State Department, visited the "front city" in April 1948 to get a first-hand impression. Local military authorities described the tensions with the Russians as extremely serious and convinced Noble that the captured documents should be flown out of the city immediately.[384] Destroying the documents in the event that the Russians tried to seize the western sectors of the city was deemed to be unfeasible. The staff on site responsible for the documents opposed moving them out of Berlin, viewing evacuation as a form of "desertion under fire."[385] British Political Advisor Christopher Steele believed an evacuation would send the wrong signal to the Berlin population; it could give the impression that the Western Allies were abandoning the city.[386] The transfer of the documents would thus have to take place in absolute secrecy. Whereas the British wanted to transport them to the Western occupation zones in Germany, Clay demanded that they not be left on the Continent. Stressing that the point of the operation was to

---

382 Minutes of Wheeler-Bennett for Sir Orme Sargent, Dec. 29, 1947, PRO FO 370/1493 L7701. Wheeler-Bennett seriously questioned the further purpose of the DGFP.
383 Humphrey, Historical Office, to Russell, Public Affairs, Nov. 10, 1948, NA RG 59, Lot File 78D441, Historical Office, box 24.
384 Noble, Report on Conference with the British and the French on German Documents Project, April 12–23, 1948, Apr. 26, 1948, ibid., box 6.
385 Humphrey to Noble, July 15, 1948, NA RG 59, CDF 1945–49, FW 840.414/7–1548.
386 Steele, Office of the POLAD, CCG(BE), to James Passant, Library, FO, Sept. 14, 1948, PRO FO 370/1697 L5545.

protect the captured documents from possible seizure by the Soviets, Clay argued that western Germany was ultimately no safer than Berlin: only in Great Britain would the documents be outside the Soviets' range.[387] In the end, the Auswärtiges Amt files left the city on the return flights of the cargo planes that kept Berlin supplied with food and fuel during the Soviet blockade of 1948–1949. The documents were flown to Hamburg and then transported by ship to Great Britain.

THE SITUATION ON THE EVE OF THE FIRST
GERMAN RESTITUTION DEMAND

The captured German documents were constantly on the move between 1945 and 1949. They had been evacuated during the war to protect them from air raids; removed by the British and Americans to protect them from being seized by the other Allies; flown out for intelligence exploitation; and moved from one administrative center to another. The chaos that accompanied the invasion of Germany came to a close with the end of SHAEF in July 1945. The establishment of zonal military governments brought about more structure in the management of the captured records, thus facilitating the ongoing inventory of the material.

British and American troops captured masses of records from all three branches of the German armed forces. The Luftwaffe, Germany's air force, had been the most effective at preventing the seizure of records by the enemy, burning between 50 and 60 tons of material.[388] All the Luftwaffe files that were captured were shared by the British and Americans.[389] The most comprehensive collection of records captured belonged to the German navy. The naval archives and materials from the Naval High Command were taken to Tambach castle near Coburg in 1944 for storage. The Germans had begun preparations to destroy these records but had not progressed very far before the invasion. The documents that British troops seized at Tambach were combined with additional naval documents captured in Flensburg and were shipped to London, where they were sorted and evaluated at the Admiralty. The U. S. Navy was given full access to these records and began to film them in August 1945 for its own use.[390] The lion's share of the records of the

---

387 Noble, AmEmb London, to State Dept., no. 1657, Apr. 21, 1948, NA RG 59, CDF 1945–49, 862.414/4–2148.

388 Endres, "Verbleib der Luftwaffenakten;" Henke, "Schicksal deutscher Quellen," 563.

389 See above, n. 40; Jackets, Air Ministry, to Acheson, Cabinet Office, Nov. 9, 1950, PRO CAB 103/458; as well as Fletcher, Use of Captured Records by Air Force.

390 Guides U-Boats and T-Boats, vii–ix; Ehrmann, "German Naval Archives;" Eller, "U.S. Navy Microfilm;" Heinsius, "Aktenmaterial der deutschen Kriegsmarine."

German army was shipped to the United States in the summer of 1945. The records were first under the jurisdiction of the G-2 division (Intelligence) of the War Department and stored at the German Military Document Section (GMDS) located at Camp Ritchie, Maryland. In the summer of 1947, the G-2 staff was relieved of the cost- and personnel-intensive administration of the records. The office of the U.S. Army's Adjutant General integrated GMDS into its Departmental Records Branch.[391] GMDS received more records in the summer of 1948, when all remaining military records in Berlin were flown out of the city during the Soviet blockade.[392] All captured documents transferred to the United States were classified at least as "confidential." This made them accessible only to accredited intelligence officers or official military historians. Under the terms of the Bissell-Sinclair Agreement, the Americans could not unilaterally change the security classification of the military records sent to Camp Ritchie, nor could they move them without consulting the British. The German military records, in sum, were terra incognita for outsiders in 1949. Aside from a limited number of British officials, no one outside of the Pentagon knew the full extent of the materials in the Americans' possession. The return of the military records to a German government was never discussed.

The records of the Auswärtiges Amt were stored at Whaddon Hall along with materials from other sources, notably the Reich Chancellery. A team of American, British, and French historians worked through the records, preparing them for a scholarly publication. The first volume of *Documents on German Foreign Policy* appeared in 1949 in English; the German edition followed a year later.[393] It became evident as early as 1949 that the original estimation of the time needed to complete the project had been "hopelessly optimistic."[394] By the time the Federal Republic of Germany was founded in 1949, the records had been in the hands of the Western Allies for four years. The various moves had repeatedly interrupted the archival processing of the captured documents and made systematic evaluation of them impossible. The Foreign Office and State Department intended that

---

391 Goldbeck, "GMDS," 32–5.
392 The trail of the records either cannot be reconstructed at all or only laboriously by using an array of lists and indices compiled at different times. For example, see the British "Index of German Archives known or thought to have fallen into allied hands," June 8, 1960, PRO FO 371/154333 WG2011/46.
393 *Documents on German Foreign Policy 1918–1945. From the Archives of the German Foreign Ministry.* Series D (1937–1945), vol. I: *From Neurath to Ribbentrop (September 1937-September 1938).* Washington, D.C., 1949.
394 Minutes of the German War Documents Conference, Oct. 5, 1949, NA RG 59, Lot File 78D441, Historical Office, box 18.

the Auswärtiges Amt files, unlike the military records, would eventually be returned to a new democratic German government, but only after the publication project had been completed.[395]

Most of the records of the Nazi party and its affiliated organizations captured by the Americans were housed at the NSDAP & Affiliated Records Branch of the Document Center in Berlin (BDC). The BDC was the head institution for a series of collecting points in Berlin, which included the Ministerial Document Branch (MDB). The MDB was the facility that had been established when the ministerial records were transferred to Berlin from Kassel-Fürstenhagen (MCC). In January 1947, the Americans began to turn over administrative records from German ministries and subordinate offices to the newly established West German bizonal offices. Only "unpolitical" records were transferred, that is, materials not classified as military, diplomatic, or party records.[396] Historical archives, which had been under the supervision of the military government to that point, were also placed back into German hands when the Anglo-American Bizone was established. These measures were part of the reconstruction of German governmental and administrative structures at the local level. During the Berlin blockade, 288 tons of records from various sources were flown out of the city to the United States or to the Berlin Document Center (Rear) in Darmstadt that had been created in response to the blockade.[397] It was at this time that the Auswärtiges Amt records were moved to Whaddon Hall as well. The number of records housed at the Berlin Document Center thus shrank steadily. By 1952, the NSDAP & Affiliated Records Branch in Berlin-Zehlendorf

---

395 "*Trusteeship.* It was the consensus of the conference that the British and United States Governments regard themselves as trustees of the German archives with the understanding that, on the completion of the work of the tripartite project, and as soon as a responsible political regime is established, the documentary collection will be returned to the German Government and people." Noble to Russell, London Conference on German Foreign Office Archives, January 24–February 2, 1949, Feb. 14, 1949, NA RG 59, Lot File 78D441, Historical Office, box 5. Raymond Sontag stated already in November 1946 his "purely private opinion that, when there was a satisfactory German government and our work was completed, the documents should be returned to the Germans. Mr. Passant and Mr. Wheeler-Bennett said that was their private opinion also but that their government had made no decision." Sontag to Noble, Nov. 12, 1946, ibid., box 6. Also on Trusteeship, see. State Department, Aide-memoire Mar. 16, 1949, NA RG 59, CDF 1945–49, 862.414/3–1649 CS/A.

396 The transfer shortly caused some concern at the State Department until it became clear that the records in question were only "routine material needed by the bizonal agencies in order to function." POLAD to SecState, no. A-91, Feb. 12, 1947, NA RG 59, Lot File 78D441, Historical Office, box 22. See also Born, MCC, 258.

397 The figures are taken from Wolfe, "Short History," XVI. The history of the BDC as institution is in Memorandum 7771 Document Center, Mar. 23, 1949, NA RG 319, IRR Impersonal Files, XE169191, BDC, box 22. Some of the records deposited in Darmstadt were denazification records created by the Americans – not records of German origin.

had reached the size it would maintain for years. The heart of the center, eventually known as simply the "BDC," was the NSDAP membership registry.[398]

398 See in general, Wolfe, "Short History;" and the catalogue *Holdings of the BDC*.

2

The First German Calls for Restitution

The British and Americans had the captured documents to themselves until the founding of the Federal Republic of Germany. Although some thought had been given to the long-term fate of certain holdings, it was only pressure from the West German government that spurred the Americans and British to consider concrete proposals for returning the documents to German possession. This chapter examines the first German calls for return of the documents and the beginning of negotiations. The account that follows focuses on the formulation of the West German demand for restitution and negotiating strategy. The first call for the return of the records came as early as 1946 from a group of German archivists who were closely watching the Allied confiscation and evacuation of documents in western Germany. Because the leading West German archives were the potential recipients of returning records, this chapter opens with a look at the German archival profession during the occupation and the early years of the Federal Republic.

ARCHIVISTS WITHOUT ARCHIVES

Scholars have only recently begun to tackle the role played by German archivists and archives during the National Socialist period.[1] The evidence suggests that the archival profession displayed a strong ideological affinity with Nazism and willingly embraced the new regime in 1933. Most German archivists had experienced the defeat of 1918 and the collapse of Imperial Germany as a national humiliation. Many of them never came to terms with the Weimar Republic and despised the democracy that had replaced the monarchy. They shared the widespread resentment against the Versailles

---

1 The latest scholarship in Kretzschmar, *Deutsches Archivwesen und Nationalsozialismus.* This section draws on research published in Eckert, "Managing their Own Past."

Treaty and actively contributed to efforts at changing the new postwar order in Europe.[2] Archivists were central players in the mushrooming network of institutes engaged in *Ostforschung*, the highly politicized study of Eastern Europe that served revisionist goals. The overriding purpose of *Ostforschung* was to prove that the territories Germany was forced to cede in the Versailles settlement were genuinely German – culturally, linguistically, historically, and ethnically.

Albert Brackmann, the director of Prussian Archival Administration, was among the radical advocates of the *Volkstumskampf*, the German "ethnic struggle." For him and like-minded officials, the issue was not to secure the Wilsonian right of self-determination, a notion they detested as "Western," for the ethnic Germans living in post-1919 Poland and Czechoslovakia. Rather, they insisted that Germany had claim to vast stretches of Eastern Europe on the basis of the centuries-long cultural contributions of Germans there. They contended that Germans were the natural elite entitled to rule over Eastern Europe because their *Kultur* had uplifted the non-German peoples of the region. *Ostforschung* was intended to provide proof for such claims. This scholarly discipline was aggressively anti-Polish and needed qualified academic personnel to feed into these propaganda efforts. At the Institute for Archival Science in Berlin-Dahlem, founded in 1930, Polish was, tellingly, a required language. The Prussian Archival Administration also sponsored research institutions specifically dedicated to *Ostforschung*, such as the Publikationsstelle Dahlem under the leadership of Johannes Papritz. Similar research efforts, somewhat less aggressive but just as politically motivated, focused on Germany's western borderlands (*Westforschung*).[3]

These research programs were firmly in place before 1933. There was little separating the proponents of *Ostforschung* and the Nazis in their views on the Versailles settlement or on German claims to territory in Eastern Europe.[4] The final demise of the Weimar Republic and the Nazi takeover in 1933 thus did not constitute a noticeable caesura for most German archivists. They did not need to reconsider their worldview. While there always remained space for individual disagreement with certain measures or

2 See Friedrich Kahlenberg's contribution to the panel discussion at 75th Archivtag in Kretzschmar, *Deutsches Archivwesen und Nationalsozialismus*, 498f.

3 Dietz/Gabel/Tidau, *Griff nach dem Westen.*

4 My interpretation of the symbiosis between *Ostforschung* and the Nazi regime is a composite based on numerous publications that appeared after the 1998 German historians' annual meeting in Frankfurt where the debate erupted. The number of publications on the topic has grown immensely. Some of the key titles on the issue are Burleigh, *Germany Turns Eastwards*; Fahlbusch, *Wissenschaft im Dienst*; Haar, *Historiker im Nationalsozialismus*; Melton, "Otto Brunner," 263–97; Piskorski/Hackmann/Jaworski, *Deutsche Ostforschung und polnische Westforschung*; Schöttler, *Geschichtsschreibung als Legitimationswissenschaft*; Schulze/Oexle, *Deutsche Historiker im Nationalsozialismus*; Mühle, *Hermann Aubin*.

policies, German archivists – as both archive professionals and civil servants – contributed to the functioning of the system throughout the period of Nazi rule. In 1933, at the annual meeting of German archivists in Königsberg, East Prussia, a local state archivist named Erich Weise declared,

The initial aversion of the German archivist against engaging in political matters has waned. As the keeper of the legal codes of the state and the nation, he has become the herald of the national cause. . . . Because Germandom [*Volkstum*] and the spirit of the state and the decisive will for ethnic [*völkisch*] survival have to be kept alive, the German archivists are fully behind the new Germany of January 30 [1933]. In the spirit of the Third Reich, they work with the *Volk* for the *Volk.*[5]

At the same venue, Brackmann called on his colleagues to embrace the National Socialist agenda:

The German archivists have to blend into the political developments of the times because as scholars of German history they are particularly connected to contemporary events. Hence, German archivists have followed the call of the great Führer of the new Germany and have put themselves fully at the disposal of the Fatherland. *Ostforschung* in particular is of prime importance for Germany.[6]

Leading archivists at the Prussian Archival Administration actively exploited the new political circumstances to further long-held goals, including expanding the Publikationsstelle, enlarging archival staffs, and heightening the visibility of their work. Most German archivists loyally served the Third Reich from Hitler's seizure of power to the country's surrender in 1945. Their engagement on behalf of the regime culminated in their wartime service in the occupied countries of Eastern and Western Europe. That service left many archivists deeply compromised at the war's end.

German archivists had much to answer for after 1945. They had, for instance, joined the Nazi party and its affiliated organizations in droves. In that regard, they differed little from other civil servants. After the Nazi Party lifted its moratorium on accepting new members in May 1937, 80 percent of all civil servants in Prussia and 63 percent in the Reich as a whole were party members.[7] The numbers were equally high among archivists: 80 percent became "party comrades" (*Parteigenossen*, or "Pg.s").[8] In some institutions, for example the Main State Archive of Saxony in Dresden, all archivists were party members.[9] Motives for joining varied, but

---

5 Musial, *Staatsarchive im Dritten Reich*, 29–31, 66–8, quote 31.
6 Ibid., 30, and Brockfeld, "Das Beispiel Eckhart Kehr," 278.
7 Rauh-Kühne, "Entnazifizierung," 40.
8 Musial, *Staatsarchive im Dritten Reich*, 33. In spring 1933, 25 percent of all archivists had already joined the party, the remainder followed once the party membership ban was lifted on May 1, 1937.
9 Ludwig, "Sächsisches Hauptstaatsarchiv Dresden," 52–68.

opportunism and conformism certainly played a role. Following a revision of the Reich Civil Service Act (*Reichsbeamtengesetz*) in 1937, membership in a Nazi Party organization, if not the party itself, became compulsory for a career in the civil service. This requirement increased the pressure on already employed archivists who had not yet fallen into line. Some of them tried to fulfill expectations by joining organizations such as the Mounted SA rather than the Nazi Party.[10] Although no one was formally obliged to join the party, the social pressure to do so was strong. Committed Nazis tried to coerce their less ideologically inclined colleagues into conformity. One archivist reminded another after the war, for instance, "how charmingly you once pointed out to me that I should not get myself into trouble by not using the Hitler salute and not wearing the party badge."[11] Despite such pressure, individuals did have some leeway, including the option of not joining the party. Although that decision might have affected one's chances of promotion, there is no known case of any archivist having been fired for not joining the NSDAP.[12] Still, in the words of historian Norbert Frei, "as the years passed, it was almost impossible for a German *Volksgenosse* not to be caught in some organizational way by the Nazi Party juggernaut."[13] Given the peculiar combination of coercion and consent that kept the Third Reich afloat, party membership is thus not necessarily a useful indicator of the degree of an individual's ideological commitment or support of Nazi policies. But for lack of a better indicator, the Allies used it after the war as a key criterion in denazification procedures, as, in fact, did the West Germans when they took over responsibility for denazification.

Apart from these individual decisions to associate with the new regime, German archivists also abetted the purge of their profession by removing individuals objectionable to the Nazi regime following the enactment of the "Law for the Restoration of the Professional Civil Service" (1933) and the so-called Nuremberg Laws (1935). The few Jews and Social Democrats employed as archivists were sacked. Some archives made their collections

---

10 Musial, *Staatsarchive im Dritten Reich*, 33. Musial estimates that ten percent of German archivists joined the SA, five percent joined the SS.
11 Wolfgang A. Mommsen, Nürnberg, to Wilhelm Rohr, Berlin, February 5, 1948, BArch, N1418, NL Rohr, vol. 9.
12 Johannes Ullrich of the Political Archives of the Foreign Office is a case in point. He repeatedly resisted exhortations to join the party and still became a legation councillor with civil service status in 1939. He was merely excluded from any further promotions. See Wiedergutmachungsbescheid, PA/AA, B100, Personalakte 2057; Hansen, "Ein wahrer Held," 95, 104–7. Individual space of maneuver during the war years is also emphasized by Lehr, "Archivpolitik im 'Generalgouvernement'"; Menk/Plantinga, "Bernhard Vollmer."
13 Frei, *The Führer State 1933–1945*, 88.

available for anti-Semitic propaganda purposes. The city archive of Cologne, for instance, contributed material to an exhibition entitled "The Eternal Jew."[14] After the Kristallnacht pogrom of November 1938, archivists participated in the confiscation of the records of Jewish institutions and organizations ostensibly to "secure" and "protect" archival material. This action, which yielded little material for public archives, was clearly anti-Semitic in motivation and intended to allow archives to profit from, as one archivist put it, "the last stages of the withdrawal of Jewry from the life of the German *Volk*."[15] Prominent among the archival profession's activities during the Nazi era was its part in genealogical research to prove "Aryan" descent, the so-called *Ariernachweis*. This service, more than any other activity, entangled the archival profession in the racist policies of the Nazi regime. Archival evidence, historian Wolfgang Ernst has noted, "became a matter of life and death," as it served as the basis for determining whether an individual would be subject to exclusion, deportation, and, ultimately, murder.[16] As the head of the Bavarian Archival Administration bragged in 1936, "there is no racial policy, there is no population genetics [*Erbbiologie*] without archives, without archivists."[17]

Through their service in the occupation regimes in Western and Eastern Europe, some German archivists participated in the violation of other countries' archival heritages. At least in the cases of France and the Netherlands, scholars have noted, German archivists were not directly involved in archival plunder.[18] That task fell, rather, to agencies such as the Einsatzstab Reichsleiter Rosenberg (ERR), the Gestapo, and the Sicherheitsdienst (SD). In neighboring Belgium, however, the very term "archival protection" (*Archivschutz*) became a euphemism.[19] In Eastern Europe – especially in Poland, the Baltic States, Ukraine, and the Balkans – matters were worse: German and Austrian archivists crossed the line into open exploitation and conscious neglect of these countries' archival and cultural heritages.[20]

---

14 Wisotzky, "Rheinische und westfälische Stadtarchive," 354–71.
15 Ludwig Clemm, State Archive Darmstadt, to Ernst Zipfel, Berlin, Dec. 7, 1938, quoted in Musial, *Staatsarchive im Dritten Reich*, 48. The attempts yielded few results because the Gestapo was the main competitor for these records and usually won the day. A case study on the archive of one Jewish community in Bönnen, "Schicksal des Wormser jüdischen Gemeindearchivs."
16 Ernst, "Archival Action," 22.
17 Josef Franz Knoepfler, quoted in Wisotzky, "Rheinische und westfälische Stadtarchive," 355 See also Fritzsche, "The Archive," 26–31; Herrmann, *Reichsarchiv*, 381–8; Musial, *Staatsarchive im Dritten Reich*, 44–6; Weiser, *Preußische Archivverwaltung*, 157, 167f.
18 Menk/Platinga, "Bernhard Vollmer," 217–71; Stein, "Georg Schnath," 175–94.
19 Herrebout, *De Duitse Archivschutz in Belgïe;* Herrebout, "Georg Sante."
20 Lehr, "Archivpolitik im 'Generalgouvernement'"; Lehr, *Vergessener "Osteinsatz";* Hutterer/Just, "Reichsarchivs Wien 1938–1945," 313–25; Grimsted, *Trophies of War and Empire.*

German Archives after World War II

Postwar Reckoning. After Germany's surrender in 1945, the German archival profession struggled with the devastating consequences of the war. The early postwar period was dominated by efforts to salvage archival collections, repair archive buildings, return relocated inventories to their original locations, and determine who survived the war. While trying to re-establish their profession, leading German archivists followed the Allied confiscation of German archives and official documents as closely as they could. They were the first to demand the return of the confiscated records. More than once, their interference injected a peculiar tension into the governmental negotiations on the return of the seized materials because the willingness of German archivists to speak out on this issue stood in sharp contrast to their reticence on their own wartime activities. They refused to see a connection between German archival policy during the war and the empty stacks at the Auswärtiges Amt's Political Archives and the newly founded federal archive, the Bundesarchiv, in Koblenz.

The most poignant aspect of the postwar reckoning was the fate of individual archivists. At least thirty-five archivists perished in the war, two were killed in air raids, and another seven died in captivity.[21] The postwar fates of archivists were sometimes random and not always related to their activities during the war. In early 1946, Karl G. Bruchmann found himself in an internment camp in Regensburg. As head of the NSDAP Gau archive in Upper Silesia, he had been considered a political functionary and thus fell under the American "automatic arrest" rule. His work as state archivist in Katowice, where he had cooperated with the Gestapo and SD in confiscating the holdings of Jewish publishing houses and libraries, does not appear to have been the reason for his internment: Allied authorities were not even aware of this work at that time.[22] Wilhelm Rohr, the right-hand man of archive functionary Ernst Zipfel, was forced to spend ten months in an American internment camp in Darmstadt. A minor party functionary at the neighborhood level in Berlin, Rohr was most likely arrested as a matter of course because he was employed at the Ministry of the Interior at the time of Germany's surrender. Once released and back in Berlin, he was prohibited from working as an archivist and ended up earning his living as a bricklayer. Wolfgang A. Mommsen, who worked for the Reichskommissariat Ostland in the Baltic States and on Soviet territory in the rear of

---

21 Musial, *Staatsarchive im Dritten Reich*, 175. The profession's journal, *Der Archivar*, for years featured a column with news on the wartime fates of archivists.
22 See Musial, *Staatsarchive im Dritten Reich*, 133f. Bruchmann, Internierungs- und Arbeitslager Regensburg, to Ernst Posner, Feb. 30, 1946, NA RG 200, Posner Papers, box 4.

the advancing German army, was sought by the Soviets as a war criminal. To evade arrest by the Americans and the risk of being handed over to the Russians, he lay low in rural Bavaria for a year. In May 1946, he presented himself to the American Counter Intelligence Corps and presumably offered to share his knowledge about the East.[23] At the time of his approach to the Americans, he was living at Schillingsfürst Castle, where he planned to sort through the house archive of Prince Hohenlohe until, as he put it, the whole "denazification circus" was over.[24]

Less fortunate was Martin Granzin, the former archivist of the city of Stade. From November 1941 until May 1943, he worked for the ERR task force, first in Ukraine and then in Ratibor, Upper Silesia. He was arrested in July 1945 by the Soviet secret police for reasons other than his association with cultural plunder, imprisoned for five years in Sachsenhausen, "sentenced within twenty minutes without witnesses and defense lawyer" in Waldheim in 1950, and not released until two years later.[25] Johannes Ullrich, head of the Political Archives of the Auswärtiges Amt disappeared into Soviet captivity the spring of 1945 and did not return until August 1955. It is possible that the Soviets had mistaken him for Hans Ullrich, an SS-Sturmbannführer in Breslau; it is also possible that he had simply been in the wrong place at the wrong time on April 28, 1945.[26] Finally, Georg Schnath, head of Gruppe Archivwesen, one of the German archive teams in France, found himself first interned by the Americans in Dachau and

23 Mommsen, Schloß Schillingsfürst, to Georg Winter, Sept. 14, 1947, BArch, N1333, NL Winter, vol. 31. Wolfgang A. Mommsen (1907–1986): PhD 1933, followed by training at the Institut für Archivwissenschaften (IfA); 1936 archival assistant at the Brandenburg House Archive Berlin; 1939 promotion to Staatsarchivrat at the Prussian Privy State Archive (GStA) Berlin; 1940 assigned to the German Archival Commission for Estonia and Latvia and sent to the Baltic together with Kurt Dülfer. Following a short return to the GStA in May 1941, he worked from October 1941 to April 1943 at the Reichskommissariat Ostland in Riga and for the Special Task Force for Archives (Sonderstab Archive) of the ERR in the rear area of Army Groups North; April 1943 drafted into military service; 1947 archivist at the State Archive Nürnberg; 1952 archivist at the Federal Archives in Koblenz; from 1967–1972 president of the Federal Archives in Koblenz.

24 Mommsen to Winter, Aug. 25, 1947, BArch, N1333, NL Winter, vol. 31; Mommsen to Wilhelm Rohr, Feb. 5, 1948, BArch, N1418, NL Rohr, vol. 9.

25 Granzin, Osterode/Hz., to Georg Winter, Sept. 21, 1954, BArch, N1333, NL Winter, vol. 2. At Waldheim he was accused of having pursued a "cultural policy" directed against the Soviet Union in his position as local cultural commissioner (Ortskulturwart). On German archival policy in the Ukraine, see Eichwede/Hartung, *NS-Kunstraub*, 41–7, 53–60; Heuss, *Kunst- und Kulturgutraub*, 164–7, 182–5; Lehr, *Vergessener "Osteinsatz."*

26 Hansen, "Ein wahrer Held," 95, 104–7; Ullrich to Eugen Meyer, Saarbrücken, Sept. 1, 1955, LA Saarbrücken, NL MeyerE 23; Ullrich to Posner, Oct. 10, 1956, NA RG 200, Posner Papers, box 6; on H. Ullrich from Breslau, see Rheindorf to Ullrich, Mar. 5, 1959, BArch, N1263, NL Rheindorf, vol. 408. Ullrich (1902–1965) graduated with a PhD in 1929 and completed archival training at the IfA (April 1930 to Sept. 1931). In June 1933, he accepted a position as research assistant (*Wissenschaftlicher Hilfsarbeiter*) in the Political Archives of the AA. He headed this archive from 1938 until 1945 and again from 1956 until 1965.

then held for six-and-a-half months in an unlighted and unheated French prison cell. The French charged him with "pillage en temps de guerre en complcité," but a French court acquitted him at the end of 1947.[27] Schnath, the only archivist to be tried in court, symbolically stood trial for all of his colleagues who had served in the occupation structures. He paid the price for the fact that the lines between archival protection and outright plunder had become suspiciously blurred.

Institutionally, the German archival profession reconstituted itself rather quickly. Control Council Proclamation no. 2, issued on September 20, 1945, permitted state and municipal archives to resume their activities.[28] The services that archivists could provide were too valuable for the occupation authorities to ignore. Initially, archival affairs fell under the jurisdiction of the Monuments, Fine Arts, and Archives (MFAA) division and were only gradually transferred to German hands.[29] This development was a step toward local German self-administration. German archivists regained control over lower-level archives, while the British and Americans retained their hold over material from the highest Reich authorities, the military, and the Nazi party.[30]

The most urgent task facing German archivists and Allied archival officers alike was to secure and return holdings that had been evacuated as a security measure against air raids.[31] Archive buildings were in urgent need of repair; in many cases, new construction was necessary.[32] The final tally of archival

27 Musial, *Staatsarchive im Dritten Reich*, 177; Schnath, "Drei Jahre Archivschutz," 343f.; Schnath to his wife, copy, Dec. 17, 1946; Schnath to Winter, Oct. 30, 1947, both in BArch, N1333, NL Winter, vol. 31.

28 Official Gazette of the Allied Control Council no. 1, Proclamation no. 2 (Certain additional requirements imposed on Germany), Sept. 20, 1945, sec. XII, para. 47. This was also followed by supplementary zonal directives. See Kahlenberg, *Archive in West und Ost*, 25f.

29 In the British zone, the archives were the responsibility of the MFAA from June 1945 until the establishment of the Bizone in January 1947. See Meekings, "Germany," 314. For the U.S. zone, see Poste, *Protection of Libraries and Archives*, 188.

30 Boberach, "Schriftgut der staatlichen Verwaltung," 139; Poste, *Protection of Libraries and Archives*, 186–9.

31 On wartime measures taken to protect archives within the Reich, see Henke, "Schicksal deutscher Quellen," 559–67; Herrmann, *Reichsarchiv*, 459–66; Herrmann, *Archiv(gut)schutz*, 174–6; Kröger/Thimme, "Politisches Archiv," 251–7; Musial, *Staatsarchive im Dritten Reich*, 96–107; Poste, *Protection of Libraries and Archives*, 171–5; Weiser, *Preußische Archivverwaltung*, 199–209; Weiß, "Ehrenbreitstein," 421–9, 432–7; the description of an evacuation depot is found in Schrenk, *Schatzkammer Salzbergwerk;* a general overview and the specific case of the Berlin Municipal Archives are included in Schroll, *Spurensicherung*, 97–144, esp. 97–113. A pertinent and often-cited essay by Rohr, "Archivschutzmaßnahmen," was commissioned by Ernst Zipfel as a postwar apologia and should be taken with a grain of salt.

32 On structural damage, see Born, "Archives and Libraries of Postwar Germany," 39–41; Musial, *Staatsarchive im Dritten Reich*, 175, 199; Poste, *Protection of Libraries and Archives*, 175–86; Schroll, *Spurensicherung*, 145–7. The overall situation was first described in 1948 by Vollmer, "Deutsches Archivwesen."

material lost during the war was devastating, even if far less extensive than the losses German libraries suffered. As the MFAA officers were surprised to discover time and again, the timely evacuation of archival material to salt mines or casemates had prevented even greater losses.[33] Nonetheless, evacuation, theft, confiscation, and destruction took a permanent toll on German archives and the archives of the countries Germany had occupied.[34]

In the Western zones, the archival profession reorganized itself on a decentralized basis. No trace remained of Zipfel's centralization efforts.[35] The Prussian Archival Administration, which had run seventeen state archives and the Berlin Archive School before 1945, was dismembered.[36] In June 1946, a *Zentralarchiv* (central archive) was established in Potsdam in the Soviet zone. The center of gravity of the archival profession nevertheless

33 The comparison to the fate of libraries is found in Poste, *Protection of Libraries and Archives;* also, Born, "Archives and Libraries of Postwar Germany," 35; Meekings, "Germany," 316. The archival advisor of the U.S. Control Authority, Sargent B. Child, concluded as early as May 1945 that the timely evacuation of historical archives had spared these from being damaged to the extent of the active office registries. See Child, USGCC, May 26, 1945, NA RG 260, OMGUS, FIAT Executive Office, box 30. See also Weiser, *Preußische Archivverwaltung,* 199, 207f., 217, who attributes much altruism to Ernst Zipfel's actions.

34 Benninghoven, "Reichs- und preußische Behördenüberlieferung"; Heinsius, "Aktenmaterial der deutschen Kriegsmarine"; Poll, "Schicksal der deutschen Heeresakten"; Rohr, "Schriftgut der obersten Reichsbehörden." The first attempt to summarize what was known as of 1969 is in Boberach, "Schriftgut der staatlichen Verwaltung"; and in 1977, Boberach, "Schriftliche Überlieferung." A case study on the fate of the Berlin Municipal Archive in Schroll, *Spurensicherung.* Several case studies focusing on archival plunder and counterplunder are offered by Grimsted, "Odyssee of the Smolensk Archive"; Grimsted, "Twice Plundered."

35 Ernst Zipfel (1891–1966) started work at the Reich Archives (RA) in 1920 although he had no archival training. Prior to this, he had pursed a military career as an officer in the Saxon army and had studied in Würzburg. In 1935 he was tasked with personnel and administrative matters at the RA; a year later he assumed the same duties in the Prussian Archival Administration. After the military archives were moved out of the RA and into the newly established Army Archives (Heeresarchiv), Zipfel became director in 1936 of the now civilian RA and at the same time acting director general of the Prussian State Archives. In September 1938 the latter appointment became permanent, which also meant heading the Institute for Archival Science at the Prussian Privy State Archives, the main training institution for Prussian state archivists. His political objective was to centralize the state archival administration under his command. In May 1940, he became the commissioner for archival protection for the western theater of operations, in April 1941 for the eastern theater, and finally in July 1942 for the entire Reich. This gave him the authority to issue directives to all civilian state archives for the first time. He consolidated this position by taking over the "Sonderreferat Archivwesen" (Special Department for Archives) in Rosenberg's ministry for the eastern territories (June 1942) as well as the subdivision for Archives and Documentation (Archiv- und Schriftgutwesen) at the interior ministry (January 1944). He filled key positions with archivists loyal to him. In April 1945, he had himself assigned to an operations staff of the interior ministry and sent to Lübeck, where he retired one day before Germany surrendered. Zipfel had joined the NSDAP in 1932, became chairperson of the association of Nazi civil servants in the Potsdam district in 1933, and applied for membership in the SS in 1939. His engagement in the party explains his rapid career after 1933. See Herrmann, *Reichsarchiv,* 287, 338–40, 444–6 passim; Leesch, *Deutsche Archivare,* 695; Lehr, *Vergessener "Osteinsatz,"* 53–6; Musial, *Staatsarchive im Dritten Reich,* 40f., 94–6 172f.; Pöhlmann, *Kriegsgeschichte,* 127; Rohr, "[Obituary] Zipfel"; Weiser, *Preußische Archivverwaltung,* 144–6 passim.

36 Kahlenberg, *Archive in West und Ost,* 26f; Weiser, *Preußische Archivverwaltung,* 211.

shifted from the Berlin region to the Western zones, where the first inter-regional cooperation among archivists took place. In December 1946, the Verein deutscher Archivare (VDA, Association of German Archivists) was founded along with the journal *Der Archivar*. Preparations were begun at that time to open a new archive school in Marburg; it enrolled its first class of students in 1949.[37]

German archivists attached new importance to establishing contact with British and American colleagues after the war and sought to improve the image of their profession abroad. They were sometimes surprised to discover how much Allied archival officers knew about German institutions and their personnel. Much of that information had been provided by the German émigré Ernst Posner during the war. Posner had prepared several studies of the German archival profession and had collected biographical data on seventy-two leading archivists, giving particular attention to classifying each of them politically.[38] Another source of information was the interrogation of archivists held by the Allies as prisoners of war.[39] The information they provided about wartime activities in the German occupied areas was at times unreliable, however.[40] The rapid reorganization of the archival profession would not have been possible without the expertise and cooperation of MFAA. Its officers proved to be indispensable in securing logistical support and building materials.

The Allied officers were also interested in how the German archivists reconstituted their profession. That was particularly evident when Ernst Posner returned to Germany as a "visiting expert" for the Cultural Affairs Branch of OMGUS in May and June 1949. Reporting on his visit, Posner

---

37 Kahlenberg, *Archive in West und Ost*, 34–41.
38 Posner, Biographical Data on 72 German Archivists Functioning in Germany, Austria and Various Occupied Countries, n.d. [presumably November 1944], PRO FO 1050/1406; Posner to Lt. Raymond Deston, Chief, Central Information Division, OSS, Nov. 30, 1944, NA RG 200, Posner Papers, box 4.
39 Hermann Schröter from the State Archive Osnabrück was captured by the British in September 1944. His information was partially inaccurate, but it added to existing knowledge especially on the wartime operations of archivists in the occupied territories. For example, Georg Winter was, according to Schröter, incorrectly identified as a NSDAP party member, but Schröter's information linking him to the Gruppe Archivwesen in France and later to the ERR was correct. See PW [Prisoner of War] Paper 30, CSDIC (UK) [Combined Services Detailed Interrogation Centre], German Archives, Oct. 23, 1944, NA RG 319, IRR XE01583, Impersonal Files, box 2.
40 A list compiled by MFAA in early 1945 named the leading German archival and museum experts and tried to establish their political leanings by grouping them in rough categories such as "party member," "reported unreliable politically," "doubtful," and "reported as looter." Incorrectly listed as party members were Georg Winter and Bernhard Vollmer. Named as "looters" were Winter, Erich Weise, Johannes Papritz, and Georg Schnath, while Heinrich Otto Meisner and Helmuth Rogge were featured as "100% Nazi." The list "Key to Personnel Reports," n.d. [probably early 1945], NA RG 331, entry 55b, MFAA Subject File, box 330.

painted an occasionally unflattering but essentially favorable picture of the profession in which he himself had trained. He attributed the nationalistic attitude prevalent among German archivists before the war to their traditional fixation on the state. Of the profession's two pillars – service to the state and service to scholarship – German archivists had always favored the state.[41] A career as an archivist in the upper ranks of the civil service required a doctoral degree, preferably in history. According to Posner, this requirement effectively excluded individuals of modest circumstances and kept the profession in the hands of the upper middle class. The aspiring archivist was trained at universities where, as Posner explained, "he was exposed to a preponderantly nationalistic interpretation of history."[42] This made for a highly competent, socially homogenous but elitist and self-referential archival service. Influences from other archival cultures did not penetrate this world. Precisely because the archival profession was so conservative and nationalistic in nature, Posner argued, it had been largely impervious to Nazi influence. Posner thought that National Socialism – personified among archivists by Ernst Zipfel – had been forced upon the profession from the outside.[43] This assessment reflects a large measure of wishful thinking, particularly in light of the fact that Posner himself had classified several archivists as "dangerous" in his biographical compendium of 1944 in the belief that they were convinced Nazis.[44] Reducing a complex

---

41 "Emphasis upon administration did not change when Ranke and his successors turned to the archives as the great repositories of historical source material. Glad though the archives were to serve the needs of the scholar, they did so with the feeling that they owed their first allegiance to the state and that . . . the *misera plebs* of genealogists and other non-competents should be kept away from the treasures of the past. . . . The fact remains, . . . that archives are state agencies rather than institutions, [and] that a great part of their service goes to the state rather than to the public. . . . And even accessibility of the archives to the scholar was understood with remarkable limitations." Posner, Report on the Public Archives of Germany, July 9, 1949, NA RG 242, AGAR-S no. 301, box 1.

42 Ibid. As early as 1947, American archive officers did indeed advocate dropping the requirement of a PhD for acceptance into higher levels of archival service. See Ulrich Wendland, director, Prussian Privy State Archives, memorandum [about a meeting with Lester K. Born], Apr. 24, 1947, GStA, HA I, Rep 178 B 1.3., vol. 1380.

43 "Under [Zipfel's] regime pressure on the rank and file of professional archivists increased markedly. Many of them were forced to join the party, and in the Archives School indoctrination with the Party ideology became part of the official program." Posner, Report on the Public Archives of Germany, July 9, 1949, NA RG 242, AGAR-S no. 301, box 1.

44 He classified Ludwig Bittner, Werner Frauendienst, Robert Lacroix, and Heinrich Otto Meisner as "cannot be trusted"; Karl Bruchmann, Wolfgang Kothe, Erich Randt, and Georg Tessin "should be closely watched"; Johannes Papritz was "too heavily compromised to be left in a leading position"; Helmuth Rogge, a member of the Mounted SS, was "probably one of the more dangerous persons in the rank of German archivist"; Wilhelm Rohr and Ernst Zipfel were "Nazi for ideological reasons." Posner, Biographical Data on 72 German Archivists Functioning in Germany, Austria and Various Occupied Countries, n.d. [presumably November 1944], PRO FO 1050/1406.

dynamic to an incursion of National Socialism into the archival profession, Posner concluded, erroneously, that

[i]t is doubtful . . . that [Zipfel's policy] resulted in any far reaching change in the outlook of German archivists. It is borne out by the fact that the record of German archivists during the occupation period from 1940 to 1945 is on the whole unblemished. On the other hand, it goes without saying that [after 1933] the nationalistic attitude already inherent in the profession became more outspoken than ever before.[45]

This assessment rested on the limited information Posner had in 1949 about archivists' wartime activities. Only three years later he would correct himself on this score and call attention to the fate of East European archives.[46]

In the "Purgatory of Denazification"

> *I cannot explain having joined the party for any reason other than conviction, but I do not think of myself therefore as a Nazi or a criminal and certainly do not find myself in bad company.*[47]

Archivists in Germany did anything but call attention to their services to the Nazi regime. Forced to confront their recent actions during denazification procedures, most of them depicted their work as unpolitical and claimed they had joined the Nazi Party under duress. Prominent archivists developed varying strategies to navigate through this period of political purges and position themselves as favorably as possible for the future. Those who had kept their distance from the regime – or claimed after the war to have done so – were in a position to provide affidavits to colleagues seeking to exonerate themselves. The period of denazification thus saw a transformation of power relationships within the archival profession as incriminated archivists put themselves in debt to colleagues who could attest to their political reliability.[48] In the end, most archivists who had held jobs during the Nazi era were employed again as archivists in the early days of the West German democracy.

45 Posner, Report on the Public Archives of Germany, July 9, 1949, NA RG 242, AGAR-S no. 301, box 1.
46 Namely in a memorandum for the State Department: Ernst Posner, A Study of the Historical Development of International Principles and Practices Pertaining to Seized Enemy Records Through World War II, January 1952, NA RG 59, Lot File 56D307, HICOG Policy Files, 1950–52, Files of the Assistant Legal Advisor, box 1. Here he examines the cooperation with the Gestapo and the SD, as well as the difference in the way archives in the West and East were treated. Poland and the Soviet Union, he contended, "saw the sternest measures in the matter of records seizure as well as in other respects."
47 Georg Schnath, Hanover, to Georg Winter, Mar. 6, 1948, BArch, N1333, NL Winter, vol. 87.
48 Ash, "Verordnete Umbrüche," 903–23; Rauh-Kühne, "Entnazifizierung"; Weisbrod, "Moratorium of the Mandarins."

Once postal communications were restored in Germany, archivists began to reach out to one another and exchanged news of their experiences during the war and its aftermath. In this private correspondence, they tacitly agreed upon a version of events that they hoped would hold up to Allied scrutiny. Those archivists who had served in Western Europe during the war seemed to have genuinely believed that their work had helped protect the cultural heritages of the occupied countries. Archivists assigned to Eastern European countries, by contrast, usually opted for silence about their wartime services.

Bernhard Vollmer, head of State Archive Düsseldorf and one of the leading figures in the postwar archival profession, had participated in the occupation of the Netherlands. Since that country was supposed to become an equal partner in Hitler's New Europe, it was treated in a relatively civil manner. Exchanges of archival material between the two states were carefully negotiated under Vollmer's guidance. After the war, he contended that "[German] 'archival protection' had grown out of the awareness of a pan-European responsibility for archival cultural goods across the continent."[49] Ludwig Clemm of the State Archive in Darmstadt claimed, "the works of the archival task force [in France] were really harmless, to the best of my knowledge no archival material was taken away, and the exchanges were deals based on reciprocity. For the West, this can well be proven."[50] Georg Schnath, who had headed that task force, maintained after the war that the French should even be grateful to the Germans: "What *we* achieved in and for France from 1940–44 is [now] being discreetly (or shamefully) hushed up."[51] In their defense of wartime archival policy, none of the archivists cared to take into account the inherently asymmetrical power relationship under conditions of military occupation. It was precisely that asymmetry that had prompted the Allies to issue the London Declaration of 1943. The Allies would regard all transfers of cultural goods – whether by sale, exchange, or outright expropriation – in occupied Europe as having taken place "under duress" and pledged to reverse such transfers after the war.[52]

---

49 Vollmer to Winter, April 17, 1946, BArch, N1333, NL Winter, vol. 31. Similarly Ernst Zipfel to Albert Brackmann, Feb. 23, 1947, HStA Han, Nds. 50, Acc 11/99 Nr 5: "We archivists responsibly preserved European cultural goods." On archival policies in the Netherlands see Musial, *Staatsarchive im Dritten Reich*, 155–7; Menk/Plantinga, "Bernhard Vollmer." Ernst Posner remarked about Vollmer: "It seems that he discharged his duties so tactfully that his relations with the Dutch archives were not permanently affected." Report on the Public Archives of Germany, July 9, 1949, NA RG 242, AGAR-S Nr. 301, box 1.

50 Clemm to Winter, May 7, 1946, BArch, N1333, NL Winter, vol. 88. See also Pfeil, "Archivraub und historische Deutungsmacht," 185.

51 Georg Schnath to Georg Winter, June 16, 1953, BArch, N1333, NL Winter, vol. 2.

52 Inter-Allied Declaration Against Acts of Dispossession Committed in Territories Under Enemy Occupation or Control (also known as "Declaration of London"), January 5, 1943, in Simpson, *Spoils of War*, 287.

That "duress" had played a major role in archival policy implemented in Eastern Europe and the Soviet Union was clear even to postwar archivists. They were therefore more careful with their comments in that regard. Wolfgang A. Mommsen self-servingly accused the Russians in 1947 of behaving worse than the Germans had during the war: "What is happening nowadays to the German cultural heritage is so outrageous that all our misdeeds towards cultural goods in the East pale in comparison."[53] More realistically, however, he acknowledged that some archivists still had to keep a low profile. "You know," he wrote Wilhelm Rohr, "the very specific reason why D[ülfer] in Marburg, W[inter] in Lüneburg, and I cannot live today in Berlin."[54] Winter shared this concern. In a 1947 letter to Schnath, who was then on trial in France, he voiced concern about archivists who, like himself, "had once been in the Baltic provinces and the Ukraine."[55] Writing another former colleague who had served in the Baltic, Winter speculated that Schnath would eventually be acquitted and, further, that the Soviets would likely deal more harshly with Germans accused of destroying cultural properties than the French would. Indeed, he found out that the Russians had placed everyone who had participated in German cultural policy in the East on a wanted list, claiming each person to be an "enemy of the people and war criminal."[56] Another reason for concern was the fact that a group of files documenting the work of ERR in the Baltic and Ukraine, where Winter had served, had fallen into Allied hands.[57] Winter thought German archivists should simply remain silent about their activities in the East. In the spring of 1947, however, Ernst Zipfel informed Winter of his intention to write an article for an American newsletter giving himself credit for having protected the cultural heritage of the occupied countries.[58] Winter immediately intervened. He chided Zipfel that it was "to put it mildly, inappropriate" to draw the slightest attention to the fact

53 Mommsen to Winter, September 14, 1947, ibid., vol. 31.
54 Mommsen to Rohr, July 15, 1948, Barch, N1418, NL Rohr, vol. 9. Kurt Dülfer (1908–1973) attended the IfA following completion of his doctoral studies in 1933 and started at the GStA Berlin in February 1935. By 1939 he had been promoted to archival assessor and in July 1941, to *Staatsarchivrat*. Like Wolfgang A. Mommsen, he was ordered to the Baltic in 1940, where he then remained, following a break in summer of 1941, from October 1941 until August/October 1944 at the Reichskommissariat Ostland and at the Special Task Force for Archives (Sonderstab Archive) of the ERR in the rear area of Army Group North. In 1946 he found a post at the State Archive Marburg and became the director of the archival school there in 1963. See Heuss, *Kunst- und Kulturgutraub*, 164–7; Leesch, *Deutsche Archivare*, 129; Musial, *Staatsarchive im Dritten Reich*, 139f., 163, 166, 195f.
55 Winter to Schnath, July 3, 1947, BArch, N1333, NL Winter, vol. 88.
56 Winter to Kurt Dülfer, June 29, 1947, HStA Hannover, Nds. 50, Acc 11/99 Nr. 7.
57 Lehr, *Vergessener "Osteinsatz,"* 328, 330.
58 Zipfel an Winter, March 14, 1947, BArch, N1333, NL Winter, vol. 29. Zipfel's earlier letters suggest that he credited himself for any archival material that survived the war. See Zipfel to Winter, November 20, 1945, ibid.

that archivists had been active in the Army rear, and to do so in "foreign publications" was even worse. He reminded Zipfel that archivists were drawn into activities that "foreigners" could easily misinterpret. "The security measures taken towards the end of the war in order to safeguard cultural goods from destruction will always be regarded differently by our adversaries; especially when they involved transferring such goods abroad, i.e. to Germany or into other occupied territories." Winter feared for the safety of the individuals Zipfel might mention since "foreigners" could still arrest them, even if only for further interrogation.[59] In the end, Zipfel refrained from writing the article, and the issue of German archival policy in occupied countries remained dormant until historians revisited the matter in the 1990s.

Bypassing the denazification process was not an option for most archivists. Clearance by Allied authorities or a German denazification board was the prerequisite for continuing or resuming government employment. The fact that many archivists had joined the party now came back to haunt them. In the American zone of occupation, everyone who had joined the party before May 1, 1937 – as 25 percent of archivists had – was automatically removed from office.[60] Georg Winter was a case in point. He had assumed the directorship of the Prussian State Archive, which was located in the American Sector of Berlin, in June 1945 after its previous director, Erich Randt, had been dismissed by the Soviet occupation authorities on account of his work in occupied Poland. Winter himself was summarily sacked the following month. Because of his membership in the ERR Special Task Force on Archives in Ukraine, he was barred from further work as an archivist and his financial assets were frozen.[61] He subsequently moved to the British zone, where he found employment in the State Archive in Hanover in the fall of 1946. Shortly thereafter, he became the director of the city archive in Lüneburg and brought in Ulrich Wendland, another Berlin archivist who had been fired for lying about his party membership.[62]

59 Winter to Zipfel, March 28, 1947, ibid.
60 Rauh-Kühne, "Entnazifizierung," 39. "Mandatory removal" means removal from employment and should not be confused with the "automatic arrest" rule for leading members of the SS, Gestapo, SD, SA, high functionaries of the party, and party organizations as well as leading civil servants in the occupied territories.
61 See the minutes of the archive's staff meetings during the summer of 1945, GStA PK Berlin Dahlem, HA I, Rep 178 B 1.3., Bd. 1417. The meeting of July 19, 1945, records the dismissal of Winter "until there is clarity about his job in the Ukraine." For Winter's mission in the Ukraine see Lehr, *Vergessener "Osteinsatz,"* 182–208, passim; Eichwede/Hartung, "Betr.:Sicherstellung, 41–7, 53–60; Heuss, *Kunst- und Kulturgutraub,* 164–7, 182–5; Musial, *Staatsarchive im Dritten Reich,* 161–7.
62 Winter to Joseph Gruser, Rome, February 3, 1951, BArch, N1333, NL Winter, vol. 30; Albert Brackmann to Winter, January 26, 1948, ibid.; Winter to Bernhard Vollmer, January 3, 1948, ibid., vol. 36; Gerhard Zimmermann, Berlin-Dahlem, to Winter, December 10, 1950, ibid., vol. 87. The

The sweeping denazification regulations and the opportunities for sub-
terfuge contributed greatly to the growing aversion to the purges.[63] The
Western Allies soon realized that they needed to hand over responsibility for
the denazification procedures to the Germans themselves if they wanted to
counter the increasing hostility.[64] The American Liberation Law of March
1946 was an important step in that direction. It instituted local civilian
courts under German authority (*Spruchkammern*) to review individual cases.
The *Spruchkammern* were authorized to hand down five possible verdicts,
ranging from "exonerated" to "main perpetrator," and to impose sentences
accordingly.[65]

The *Spruchkammern* operated on the presumption that the accused was
guilty and thereby put the burden of proof on the accused in clearing
his or her name. This obligation spurred production of so-called *Persilscheine* (named after the laundry detergent Persil), affidavits vouching for
the integrity of those who sought to exonerate themselves. Such affidavits
were solicited from people who were uncompromised and of high social
standing and authority. The need to obtain *Persilscheine* bred a defensive and
apologetic climate and closed off any remaining openness to reckon honestly
with the recent past – assuming such openness existed in the first place. It
led to pettiness since the procedure only asked for the justification of individual deeds, hence circumventing any inclination to ask larger questions
and engage National Socialism on moral grounds. Since Germans across
the board soon found themselves surprisingly united against denazification,
its ultimate outcome was a leveling of differences between perpetrators, fellow travelers, and true anti-Nazis. Many of them saw themselves as "those
damaged by denazification" and demanded redress for what the alleged
occupation injustice had done to them.[66] As one archivist lamented, "the
denazification orders" did not "take into consideration the still so justifiable
needs of the archives."[67]

State Archive in Hanover at times accomodated several compromised archivists from the former
Prussian Archival Administration, including Helmuth Rogge, Wilhelm Rohr and Erich Weise.

63 Rauh-Kühne, "Entnazifizierung," 40–2, 56f.; Vollnhals, *Entnazifizierung*, 55–64.
64 The French occupying power was the first to include Germans in the responsibility for denazification
    in fall of 1945. The Americans followed in March 1946 by issuing the Law for the Liberation
    from National Socialism and Militarism that turned denazification over to the Germans who set
    up local civilian courts (*Spruchkammern*). The British, meandering significantly in their policy,
    took until October 1947 to change their course. See Rauh-Kühne, "Entnazifizierung"; Wember,
    "Entnazifizierung nach 1945," 405–426; Vollnhals, *Entnazifizierung*, 262–72.
65 The categories were Major Perpetrators (I), Offenders (II), Less Incriminated (III), Fellow Travelers
    (IV), and Exonerated (V).
66 Quote in Frei, *Adenauer's Germany*, xii–xiii; see also Rauh-Kühne, "Entnazifizierung," 51f., 54, 63.
67 Sante, "Archive Großhessens," 7.

To supply someone with a *Persilschein* was to exert power. Among archivists, only those who were formally untainted or who could present resistance credentials were in a position to write affidavits that would carry weight with the *Spruchkammern*. The few non-party members among the archivists became sought-after character witnesses. Their letters could decide whether a colleague would remain in the profession. Writing affidavits was a complex process that transformed existing professional networks, leaving some people deeply indebted to others and thereby establishing subtle new hierarchies. That a postwar reputation for being free of Nazi taint was not necessarily based on fact is illustrated by the case of Albert Brackmann, the leading proponent of *Ostforschung* among the German archivists. When Brackmann reached the mandatory retirement age in 1936, he did not want to step down from his position as director general of the Prussian Archival Administration. His contract was not extended, however, as a result of an intrigue led by the historian Walter Frank, an ardent National Socialist with influential political connections. This setback did not put an end to Brackmann's professional activity. He devoted his retirement years entirely to *Ostforschung* and expanded his contacts to the SS. After the war, Brackmann successfully cited his involuntary retirement as evidence that he had been an opponent of the Nazi regime. With his newly acquired resistance credentials, Brackmann was in a position to provide his former colleagues with affidavits for denazification procedures.[68]

Georg Winter emerged as another important supplier of affidavits for archivists. He had not been a party member and could point to connections to the Confessing Church.[69] Winter helped clear at least nine colleagues, including such heavily compromised individuals as Ernst Zipfel and Zipfel's assistant Wilhelm Rohr.[70] Knowing full well just how compromised he was, Rohr hesitated for a long time to initiate denazification proceedings. In preparation for his hearing, he drafted an account of his own wartime

68 Burleigh, *Germany Turns Eastward*, 147–54, passim; Heiber, *Walter Frank*, 851–5; Musial, *Staatsarchive im Dritten Reich*, 40. See also the case of Erich Weise, who had joined the party in 1933, became a functionary in the civil service association (Reichsbund Deutscher Beamter), and was one of the German archivists in Warsaw during the war. At the Warsaw archives, he fired 50 percent of the staff (all "non-Aryans" and politically unwanted personnel) and oversaw the removal of records deemed of interest to the German state. For his denazification, he suppressed several facts about his career, lied about others, finally challenged the verdict, and, after revisions, emerged as a Nazi opponent. Lehr, *Vergessener "Osteinsatz,"* 109–12, 314–17.

69 Winter talks about his connection to the Confessing Church in his letters to Ernst Posner, June 6, 1946, NA RG 200, Posner Papers, box 6; and to Joseph Gruser, Rome, February 3, 1951, BArch, N1333, NL Winter, vol. 30. See also Rohr, [obituary] Georg Winter, 185. On Winter's quick denazification see also Lehr, *Vergessener "Osteinsatz,"* 313.

70 Winter, [Affidavit for Ernst Zipfel], June 11, 1946, BArch, N1333, NL Winter, vol. 29; Winter, Affidavit [for Rohr], June 8, 1948, ibid., vol. 31.

activities. He sent it to Winter, who returned it immediately. "Burn it," Winter advised, "it could damage you in many ways. Nobody asked you to confess your sins — that's between you and your God.... The most important thing is to obey the rule: not to say more than one is asked."[71] Thanks in part to new regulations that relaxed the denazification process, Rohr, to his surprise, was cleared of political taint in October 1948.[72] Zipfel completed the procedure a year later and informed his former colleagues that he had been classified as a "fellow traveler"; he did not advertise the fact that he had initially been deemed "incriminated" and had appealed that verdict.[73] From the perspective of the petitioner dependent on a *Persilschein*, preparing for the denazification process was humiliating. "It is actually quite embarrassing," complained Georg Schnath, "that you have to collect a bunch of praise and recommendations to prove that you were a Nazi but not a criminal!"[74]

The *Persilscheine* that Winter wrote deserve a closer look; they provide a good illustration of the semantic acrobatics used to sway *Spruchkammer* juries. As might be expected, Winter explained that other archivists had joined the Nazi party under coercion ("entered on the orders of Gauleiter Mutschmann"[75]), without their knowledge ("did not know how his name got on the Munich party list"[76]), or passively ("transferred from the SA to the Party"[77]). He gave their motives for membership a nonpolitical twist. One, an orphan, "longed to be independent"[78] and therefore joined the SA. Another joined the Mounted SA because, according to Winter, he "was devoted to various types of sport more than to politics."[79] Membership

71 Winter to Rohr, March 17, 1948, BArch, N1333, NL Winter, vol. 31.

72 Rohr benefited from the second revision of the Law for the Liberation from National Socialism and Militarism of March 25, 1948. From that point on, a summary procedure was used that issued occupational bans only to the main perpetrators and turned those labeled as offenders (Group II) into followers. See Vollnhals, *Entnazifizierung*, 23. The other information stems from Rohr's correspondence with Georg Winter on Mar. 17, 1948; May 23, 1948; Oct. 2, 1948; Dec. 19, 1948, BArch, N1333, NL Winter, vol. 31. In the letter dated June 13, 1948, his own prognosis: "I don't count on getting off very lightly, but also do not want to pass up a chance should it offer itself."

73 Zipfel to Rohr, May 29, 1949, BArch N1418, NL Rohr, vol. 84; Zipfel to Vollmer, June 3, 1949, HStA Dü. RWN 254–251. NL Vollmer, vol. 251; Lehr, *Vergessener "Osteinsatz,"* 314–17.

74 Georg Schnath an Winter, March 10, 1948, BArch, N1333, NL Winter, vol. 31.

75 Georg Winter, affidavit for Werner Ohnsorge, Feb. 20, 1947, ibid.

76 Albert Brackmann to Winter, Jan. 26, 1948, ibid., vol. 30. The subject of this letter is Ulrich Wendland, former director of the State Archive Danzig. The magistrate of Greater Berlin appointed him to be the successor of Gottfried Wentz as the head of the GStA. Wendland was dismissed summarily on Nov. 15, 1948, due to the falsification of his denazification questionnaire. He had not mentioned his party membership. See Winter to Vollmer, Jan. 3, 1948, BArch, N1333, NL Winter, vol. 36; Brackmann to Winter, Jan. 26, 1948, ibid., vol. 30; Gerhard Zimmermann, GStA, to Winter, Dec. 10, 1950, ibid., vol. 87.

77 Winter, affidavit for Wolfgang Kothe, June 1, 1947, ibid., vol. 30.

78 Winter, recommendation for Werner Ohnsorge, Fed. 20, 1947, ibid., vol. 31.

79 Winter, affidavit for Wolfgang Kothe, June 1, 1947, ibid., vol. 30.

in the Mounted SS was similarly explained by the fact that the person in question "was an enthusiastic horseman who had once owned a saddle horse."[80] Party membership was dismissed as camouflage of one's real sentiments ("no more than a veneer, as it were"[81]). And, in Winter's telling, having held a political office even a burden that deserved recognition ("grimly but silently [he] let himself also be burdened with the yoke of *Blockhelfer* [local organizer]").[82] Winter needed to put all his skills to work in writing on behalf of archivists who were known among their colleagues to have been dedicated Nazis. He described Zipfel, for example, as a "national idealist without extensive political insight and without any particular political-critical experience"[83] and maintained that Rohr's "social idealism that did not accurately comprehend the political realities"[84] had sent him down the "errant path"[85] of National Socialism. Even Rohr, he claimed, had been plagued "with reoccurring eruptions of doubt" about joining the Nazi party and had endured "bitter inner suffering" as a result of that decision.[86] Explaining away Zipfel's anti-Semitism was the hardest task of all. On his own initiative, Zipfel had secured the backing from the Reich Ministry of the Interior first to restrict and then to exclude Jews from using archives.[87] Winter nonetheless attested that "inwardly [Zipfel] rejected the party line against the Christian Church and the Jews."[88]

Even better than the word of a non-party member like Winter was a positive character reference from a Jew. It speaks for the utter desperation of some archivists, if not for their tact, that they sought affidavits from their onetime Jewish colleagues. Two Jewish archivists, Alex Bein and Hans Goldschmidt, had been employed at the Reichsarchiv in Potsdam at the

---

80 Winter to Ludwig Clemm, Darmstadt, July 24, 1950, ibid., vol. 88. The subject here is the senior archivist Helmuth Rogge from the Reich Archive. On Rogge, see the following section in this chapter.

81 Winter, affidavit for Joseph Benzing, Aug. 9, 1946, ibid., vol. 30.

82 Winter, affidavit [for Rohr], June 8, 1948, ibid., vol. 31.

83 Winter, [recommendation for Ernst Zipfel], June 11, 1946, ibid., vol. 29.

84 Winter, affidavit [for Rohr], June 8, 1948, ibid., vol. 31.

85 Winter to Rohr, Mar. 17, 1948, ibid., vol. 31.

86 Winter, affidavit [for Rohr], June 8, 1948, ibid., vol. 31.

87 Ernst, "Archival Action," 25f., 28f.; Herrmann, *Reichsarchiv*, 401–4; Musial, *Staatsarchive im Dritten Reich*, 44; Weiser, *Preußische Archivverwaltung*, 166f.; for Zipfel's request on Jan. 19, 1938, to enact the "Aryan paragraph" among archive users, see Weiser, 274–6. The letter reads: "If the Jew is being excluded from all other cultural life, then it is more important than ever to keep free of him in German historical research and depiction, this being the racial-ideological basis of our national existence." The letter was directed on several counts against Ernst Posner's private research work on the *Acta Borussica*, undertaken at the Privy State Archive in Berlin after his dismissal from archival service.

88 Winter, [Affidavit for Ernst Zipfel], June 11, 1946, in: BArch, N1333, NL Winter, vol. 29. Similarly, in the *Persilschein* for Rohr he writes: "[The party's] perfidous moves against the churches and against the Jewish people, among other things, deeply disgusted him."

time Hitler came to power. Bein emigrated from Germany to Palestine in 1933, and Goldschmidt was killed in a German air raid on London in 1940.[89] The Prussian Archival Administration had also employed Ludwig Dehio and Ernst Posner. Dehio suddenly found himself a "quarter Jew" under Nazi racial law but was able to survive by keeping a low profile. After the war, he was appointed the director of the State Archive in Marburg and headed the newly established archive school there. Approached by colleagues in need of character references, he quickly made it clear that he had no sympathy whatsoever for former party members.[90]

This left only Ernst Posner in Washington as a potential advocate, and his address in the United States was in high demand among German archivists. Merely having socialized with him before his last-minute escape from Nazi Germany in 1939 was enlisted as evidence by his former colleagues of their anti-Nazi attitude. Posner was asked by one, for example, "to confirm that we used to spent time together socially and went for a pleasant Sunday stroll in Grunewald with a coffee afterwards as late as 1938."[91] Although there is no confirmation from Posner's pen that his former colleagues had in fact attempted to rescue him from social death during the 1930s, his personal papers document the efforts some of them made to ingratiate themselves with him after the war. Held in an internment camp at Regensburg in February 1946, Karl G. Bruchmann asked Posner for an affidavit confirming "that I have always behaved correctly towards you as someone persecuted by National Socialism on racial grounds, that we corresponded after the 'assumption of power' [by Hitler] and that, as long as you still lived in Berlin, I supported your scholarly work on the *Acta Borussica* to the best of my abilities."[92]

The German archival profession managed the transition to democracy barely affected by Allied denazification efforts. British archive officer C. A. F. Meekings summed up the situation:

89 See Bein's memoirs "Hier kannst Du nicht jeden grüßen," 242ff.; Boberach, "Angehörige des Reichsarchivs," 17–19; Musial, *Staatsarchive im Dritten Reich*, 28f., 43f.

90 Dehio refused to consider a job applicant because that individual had joined a "criminal organization" and should be prepared to bear the consequences. See Hans Andres to Kurt Rheindorf, September 18, 1947, BArch, N1263, NL Rheindorf, vol. 488. See also Erich Weise to Bernhard Vollmer, Düsseldorf, October 16, 1945, HStA Dü, RWN 254–249, NL Vollmer, vol. 249.

91 Hermann Kleinau, Schöppenstedt near Wolfenbüttel, to Winter, Lüneburg, October 28, 1947, BArch, N1333, NL Winter, vol. 30. A similar approach was made by Wolfgang Müller who had moved into the position at the Privy State Archive that Posner was forced to vacate in 1933. He reminded Posner that he had called on him in 1935, after Posner's dismissal. See Müller to Posner, November 2, 1947, NA RG 200 Posner Papers, box 8.

92 Karl G. Bruchmann, Internment and Labor Camp Regensburg, to Posner, February 30, 1946, NA RG 200, Posner Papers, box 4.

For all but the blackest the regulations were interpreted with the well-being of the institution as a guide. No one was removed whilst he could be of service, and downgrading rather than removal was resorted to wherever possible. These measures for 'denazifiable' Archivists were all supported by their more innocent colleagues . . .[93]

Few archivists were unable to return to their posts.[94] The most prominent of those who were unable to continue their careers was Ernst Zipfel. During the Allied occupation, he peddled household products and tutored students.[95] He noticed that the archive directors who had previously answered to him did not exactly strain themselves to help him clear his name.[96] Oblivious to the new realities, he tried to promote himself as a candidate for the directorship of the State Archives of Lower Saxony and, later, of the yet to be established federal archive of the new West German state.[97] His former colleagues tacitly blocked his attempts to return to the profession.

Zipfel was the only person the German archival profession purged from its ranks. His former colleagues benefitted in a number of ways from expelling an avowed National Socialist. They would be able to point to the example of Zipfel as proof that the profession had indeed freed itself of Nazi taint. Thus mirroring larger trends in postwar German society, Zipfel was treated as if he had been the sole agent of Nazi influence in the archival profession, and removing him from the profession eased his former colleagues' transition to the new political order. Just as the majority of Germans were willing to ascribe responsibility for the crimes of the Third Reich to the small group of Nazi leaders who had been tried at Nuremberg, German archivists did not hesitate to make Zipfel the bearer of guilt for the profession as a whole. After his early retirement was secured, the archival profession could feel it had paid its dues and compensated for whatever objectionable things might have happened during the Nazi years. Archivists thereupon demanded an

---

93 Meekings, Germany [Archives 1939–1947], 315.

94 The archivist of the city archive in Frankfurt, Harry Gerber as well as the city archivists in Münster, Düsseldorf and Aachen were too compromised to return. Other archivists had to wait several years until they found themselves employed by an archive again. See Wisotzky, "Stadtarchive"; Schneider, "Stadtarchiv Frankfurt"; Manke, "Georg Tessin."

95 Zipfel to Bernhard Vollmer, Düsseldorf, June 3, 1949, HStA Dü, RWN 254–251, NL Vollmer, vol. 251.

96 The director of the state archive in Hanover, Rudolf Grieser, refused to write an affidavit for Zipfel and even demanded in an open letter that he would not return into the profession. See Zipfel to Vollmer, March 18, 1947, HStA Dü, RWN 254–251, NL Vollmer, vol. 251; Zipfel to Rohr, May 25, 1949, BArch, N1418, NL Rohr, vol. 84.

97 Zipfel to Rohr, March 31, 1949, BArch, N1418, NL Rohr, vol. 84; Zipfel to Rohr, September 17, 1949, ibid. For Zipfel's ambitions in Lower Saxony see Winter to Grieser, February 17, 1947, BArch, NL Winter, N1333, vol. 30; Brackmann to Winter, May 3, 1949, ibid.

end to the "snooping into the past"[98] and joined the chorus of voices calling
for a "general amnesty" and a *Schlußstrich*, a line under the Nazi past.[99] But
the past refused to go away. It unpleasantly merged with the present during
the founding of the Bundesarchiv in 1950–1952.

The Bundesarchiv

An Archive for the New West German State

> *What a difference to the founding of the Reich Archives more than thirty years ago! Back then,
> torrents of records for which it was hard to find room; today, a federal archive more or less without
> those old holdings.*[100]

The creation of Bundesarchiv in 1950 signaled and, in turn, helped consol-
idate the Federal Republic's status as a state in its own right. After the establishment of two German states in 1949, it was no longer realistic to think
that a national archive for Germany as a whole might still be possible.[101] The
Bundesarchiv was to receive records from the federal ministries; it was also
slated to receive the records of the zonal and bizonal administrations, the
holdings of the former Reich Archive and the Prussian Privy State Archive,
and the pre-1945 records of the highest Reich authorities and the German
military. None of these groups of materials was within its reach at the time
of its creation, however. The new federal ministries would not be ready
to transfer any records to the Bundesarchiv for some time to come. The
archival collections of the defunct German Reich, whose legal successor
the Federal Republic claimed to be, were in the hands of the Allies. The
Adenauer government was thus engaging in wishful thinking when it stipulated that the responsibilities of the Bundesarchiv would "include the care
of confiscated and [subsequently] restituted records as well as other records
from the jurisdiction of the Federal Republic and the former Reich. . . . "[102]
The Federal Republic's demands for the return of the captured documents

---

98 Rudolf Grieser, State Archive Hanover, to Winter, March 2, 1948, BArch, N1333, NL Winter,
    vol. 89.

99 Georg Schnath to Winter, March 10, 1948, ibid., vol. 31. See also Rohr to Winter, March 10,
    1948, ibid.; Zipfel to Vollmer, January 19, 1947, HStA Dü, RWN 254–251, NL Vollmer, vol. 251.
    For the mentality in postwar West Germany in regard to the winding up of denazification measures
    and undoing the Allied "denazification damage" see Frei, *Adenauer's Germany*.

100 Georg Winter to Ernst Posner, Washington, July 31, 1952, NA RG 200, Posner Papers, box 6.

101 The Central Archive for the Soviet occupation zone in Potsdam opened in June 1945. See Herr-
    mann, *Reichsarchiv*, 474–7; Kahlenberg, *Archive in West und Ost*, 31–3, 67–84.

102 The cabinet resolution of Mar. 24, 1950 quoted in Bruchmann, Bundesarchiv, 84. At the Dienst-
    stelle für Auswärtige Angelegenheiten (Office for Foreign Affairs) in the Chancellery, the attempt
    was made at the last minute to change the cabinet resolution and to add everywhere the phrase
    "with the exception of the archival material of the Foreign Office" in order to make sure that the
    new Federal Archives could not get its hands on diplomatic records. This attempt rekindled an old

were crucial to liberating the new central archive from its incongruous status as an archive without documents. Accordingly, the archive's leadership ardently supported the government's demands and repeatedly tried to spur the negotiations on the return of the captured records forward.

Word of the plans for a new central archive spread quickly among archivists. Those who had experienced trouble with denazification and were still looking for suitable positions were especially interested in the news.[103] Speculation centered on the questions of personnel, the location of the new archive, and its exact tasks. Many in the profession assumed the position of director would go either to Bernhard Vollmer, a driving force behind the creation of the Bundesarchiv, or Georg Winter, who had carefully promoted himself for the job since 1949.[104] Both Vollmer and Winter thought the Bundesarchiv should be located in the immediate vicinity of Bonn, the Federal Republic's seat of government. Hoping for the speedy return of the captured records, Winter recommended a location on the western bank of the Rhine; the Western Allies, he speculated, would have fewer reservations about restitution if the Bundsarchiv was located on the Rhine than if it were near "the zonal border" with East Germany.[105] In the end, the government decided to base the Bundesarchiv in Koblenz, about 35 miles south of Bonn on the Rhine. Winter, who was eventually appointed the archive's first director, was critical of that decision, thinking that the federal archives should be located at the seat of government.[106]

When Winter assumed his duties as director in March 1952, the Bundesarchiv did not have a building of its own, nor were there firm plans to provide it with one even though the first group of staff archivists was slated to start work in June.[107] Winter immediately tried to create a role for himself and the Bundesarchiv in the ongoing negotiations on the captured documents. By that time, the Bundestag had passed a resolution calling on the Western Allies to return all captured German records; Adenauer had

---

feud over the question whether the diplomats were allowed to maintain their own archive. See PA/AA, B118, vol. 28 and also below on the reestablishment of the Political Archives.

103 Wilhelm Rohr understood this better than he cared to admit: "Generally the impression must becoming more and more prevalent: whoever is still unemployed today must have been a really terrible Nazi." Rohr to Winter, Feb. 1, 1952, BArch, N1333, NL Winter, vol. 87. See also Frei, *Adenauer's Germany*, 56: "For this reason – and this was widely recognized – anyone still on the street because of his denazification notice . . . when the '131' law had taken effect, must have been quite strongly incriminated."

104 Booms, "Winters Weg zum Gründungsdirektor; Kahlenberg," *Archive in West und Ost*, 55–8.

105 Winter to Erich Wende, Interior Ministry, head of Department III (Culture), Aug. 3, 1950, BArch, N1333, NL Winter, 87.

106 Booms, "Winters Weg zum Gründungsdirektor," 258f., 263; Kahlenberg, *Archive in West und Ost*, 65f.; Müller, "Winter," 130; Winter, "Das Bundesarchiv," 106.

107 The first organizational plan from May 1952, BArch, N1418, NL Rohr, vol. 70.

raised the issue with the High Commission; and the Auswärtiges Amt had launched an effort to secure the return of its Political Archives. Preoccupied with its own records, the Auswärtiges Amt had not yet tried to determine the full extent of the non-diplomatic records confiscated by the Western Allies. That provided an opening for Winter. The Bundesarchiv initiated a survey and inquired at all federal agencies and institutions about materials from the period before 1945.[108] At the same time, archivists at the Bundesarchiv, resorting on occasion to unconventional methods, attempted to track down the location of German archival materials held abroad.[109] Wolfgang Mommsen, for example, scanned the footnotes of English-language publications for references to German documents.[110] Locating the confiscated German records became the central contribution of the Bundesarchiv in the return negotiations. The task proved hard to fulfill, however, and hampered the Germans' ability to request the return of specific documents on several occasions.[111] The appearance of the first *Guide to Captured Records* in 1952 and the irregular publication of the indices of captured records released by the National Archives and the Departmental Records Branch began to clarify the situation, at least on the American side.[112] On the British side, it was a deliberate policy not to release information about the materials in British possession.[113]

108 Ministry of the Interior, circular decree, Abgabe älteren Schriftguts an das Bundesarchiv, July 29, 1952, BArch, N1418, NL Rohr, vol. 70. Boberach, "Schriftliche Überlieferung," 54; Kahlenberg, *Archive in West und Ost*, 106; Müller, "Winter," 130f.

109 Winter to the Auswärtiges Amt, Rückgewinnung des in alliierter Hand befindlichen deutschen Schriftgutes, Dec. 2, 1954, BArch, N1418, NL Rohr, vol. 77. Winter submitted here the first lists of German material held in the Netherlands, Luxembourg, and Belgium.

110 Mommsen, "Deutsche Archivalien im Ausland;" auch Booms, "Bundesarchiv," 20; Kahlenberg, *Archive in West und Ost*, 106.

111 "The Germans said that they had found difficulty in preparing the memorandum [detailed restitution requests] as they did not know what archives were still in existence or where these were." JCC 47th Meeting, Apr. 2, 1952, PRO FO 370/2269 LS18/5. Also Rohr, Vermerk über die Besprechung im AA am 20. VIII. 1956, Aug. 25, 1956, BArch, B106, vol. 34724/4. Rohr advised against submitting a list of return requests to the Allies: "For the most part, the available material is not sufficiently complete for this purpose; the lists would therefore appear too sketchy and not include vital records."

112 1) Gerhard L. Weinberg, Fritz T. Epstein, Guide to Captured German Documents. War Documentation Project Study No. 1. (Maxwell Air Force Base, AL: USAF Air University 1952). 2) Preliminary Inventory of the German Records 1679–1945 in the World War II Collection of Seized Enemy Records. Compiled by Martin Rogin. Prelim. Inventory No. 24 (Washington, D.C.: GSA. The National Archives 1950). 3) Guide to Captured German Records in the Custody of Dept. of the Army Agencies in the United States. DRB Publication 51–10. Administrative Services Division. AGO. (Washington, D.C.: Juni 1951).

113 Wilhelm Rohr, BA, to the Ministry of Culture of North Rhine-Westphalia, May 14, 1958, HStA Dü, BR 2094–44. "Let us point out that absolute uncertainty exists concerning German archival material of non-military origin (also regarding the location of the depots), still in British hands today, because the English – contrary to the Americans – have kept silent about this to date."

Personnel Choices

> *Come now, surely in the whole of Germany you will be able to find archivists who are not tainted, right?*[114]

The Bundesarchiv was established by the Adenauer government in March 1950, but it did not begin to operate for another two years. The reason for this delay was the difficulty in recruiting qualified archivists who were fully beyond suspicion of having incriminated themselves during the Third Reich. Thanks to the intervention of the Bundestag representative Ludwig Bergsträßer, the network of former staff members of the Prussian Archival Administration did not completely dominate the choice of personnel for the Bundesarchiv. Bergsträßer, a historian known for his research on political parties, had worked at the Reich Archives in Potsdam from 1920 to 1935 and had launched his first foray into politics as a Reichstag delegate for the Deutsche Demokratische Partei (German Democratic Party) in 1924. He was suspended from his position as a senior archivist (*Oberarchivrat*) in 1933, having by then switched his political affiliation to the Social Democratic Party (SPD), and he was fired in 1935.[115] Being well-versed in archival matters, Bergsträßer closely followed the planning for the Bundesarchiv and paid special attention to the candidates for the leading positions. It was imperative, in his view, that "no man come to the Bundesarchiv either as the chief or as the head of a department who is not completely steadfast in his attitude against nationalist and militaristic impulses."[116] The choice of personnel must guarantee that "files that incriminate either the party or the Wehrmacht, of which there are presumably many, would not be locked away or possibly eliminated."[117] For Bergsträßer, professional competence could not offset a compromised past: an archivist was politically reliable only if he had "absolutely no connections to the party."[118] Bergsträßer thus raised the bar of acceptability to a height that archivists felt was insurmountable. Ludwig Clemm commented to Winter that it "will be difficult,

---

114 Quotation from Minister of the Interior Gustav Heinemann, reported by Winter to Grieser, State Archive Hanover, Oct. 14, 1950, BArch, N1333, NL Winter, vol. 87.

115 Zibell, "Ludwig Bergsträßer;" Pöhlmann, *Kriegsgeschichte*, 139, 148; Herrmann, *Reichsarchiv*, 290. Bergsträßer (1883–1960) worked from 1920 until 1928 usually in the research department of the Reich Archive in Potsdam, and was later transferred to the Frankfurt branch. He was a member of the Reichstag from 1924 to 1928.

116 Ludwig Clemm, StA Darmstadt, to Winter, Dec. 31, 1949, BArch, N1333, NL Winter, vol. 88.

117 Ibid. See also Bergsträßer's remark in the Bundestag, BT, 1. WP, Stenographische Berichte, 16. Sitzung, Nov. 10, 1949, 378: "What is needed is a scientifically trained management [of the Federal Archive] that – let me put it this way – ensures personnel choices that enable us to engage with the most recent past in critical ways."

118 Ludwig Clemm, StA Darmstadt, to Winter, Dec. 21, 1949, BArch, N1333, NL Winter, vol. 88.

if not impossible, to find that many 'unobjectionable' civil servants."[119] Nonetheless, Minister of the Interior Gustav Heinemann adhered to the strict standards Bergsträßer advocated. Already during his first interview for the post as director of the Bundesarchiv, Winter came under pressure to hire only archivists who had not been Nazi Party members: "Come now," Heinemann asked impatiently, "surely in the whole of Germany you will be able to find archivists who are not tainted, right?'"[120] But that was indeed Winter's problem.[121] "What will they say in Bonn," Winter lamented, "what will Herr Bergsträßer say when he learns that I couldn't think of any non-party member to recommend for the first staff of the Bundesarchiv?"[122]

Filling the top job at Bundesarchiv was an even greater challenge than finding uncompromised professionals to staff it. After Zipfel was thwarted early on by his colleagues, Winter began in 1949 to promote himself for the directorship.[123] Because he met the professional requirements and had steered clear of the party, it looked as if the position would indeed go to him. In July 1950, he began to negotiate details of the appointment with the head of the Ministry of the Interior's Cultural Department, Erich Wende.[124] Winter suddenly withdrew his name from consideration at the end of the year after a political denunciation he had written back in 1944 surfaced.[125] The incident undermined his reputation.[126]

At the Ministry of the Interior, the search began anew. Vollmer introduced Ernst Posner's name into the discussion. In October 1951, Hans Ritter von Lex, state secretary at the ministry, wrote to Posner in Washington to ask whether he might be interested in the directorship of

---

119 Clemm to Winter, Apr. 5, 1950, ibid.
120 Winter to Grieser, StA Hannover, Oct. 14, 1950, BArch, N1333, NL Winter, vol. 87. On the day of Winter's first visit to Bonn, Oct. 9, 1950, Gustav Heinemann resigned. He received the archivist a half an hour after his demission.
121 Winter to Diestelkamp, Oct. 24, 1950, BArch, N1333, NL Winter, vol. 87. "I . . . complained about the stipulation that only non-Pgs should be taken. But Heinemann did not really want to back down."
122 Winter to Clemm, July 24, 1950, BArch, N1333, NL Winter, vol. 88. In light of the complications involving his denazification, Wilhelm Rohr found "the attitude of the gentlemen – including that of the Minister, from whom I had gotten another impression – in the Pg. issue . . . disappointing." Rohr to Winter, Oct. 21, 1950, ibid., vol. 87.
123 Booms, "Winters Weg zum Gründungsdirektor."
124 Erich Wende (1884–1966), 1927–33 deputy director (Ministerialdirigent), later ministerial director at the Prussian Ministry of Culture, then regional court (Landgericht) director in Berlin, 1949 state secretary at the culture ministry of Lowery Saxony, 1950–53 head of Department III (culture) at the Federal Ministry of the Interior.
125 Winter to StS Hans Ritter von Lex, BMI, Dec. 31, 1950, BArch, N1333, NL Winter, vol. 87.
126 Booms, "Winters Weg zum Gründungsdirektor," 259–61. Winter had written a file memo in which he recorded that a certain student at the archive school in Dahlem had not returned the Nazi salute.

the Bundesarchiv.[127] Posner had strong memories of his encounters with German anti-Semitism and his narrow escape from the Third Reich.[128] Lex's letter did not, however, address any of the injustices Posner had suffered. Posner came to the conclusion that he could never "become a Ger[man] civil servant again without breaking my soul."[129] His decision was influenced by a letter from the émigré historian Hans Rothfels. Rothfels had returned to Germany in 1951 to take up a professorship in Tübingen. He warned Posner that, should he accept the offer, he would be "surrounded by injured ambitions and offended egos, not to speak of other resentments. The backlash is stronger than you can image based on the impressions of two years ago."[130] Much as Posner's former colleagues praised him, it is open to question just how warmly they would have welcomed his return. Awkward comments about an "American solution" to the Bundesarchiv's staffing problems cropped up in private correspondence. The offer to Posner was called a "concession" to the former occupying power, the Americans, and it was secretly hoped he would refuse. Nobody doubted Posner's qualifications, but questions were raised about the fact that the refugee "has been absent for over 15 years" – without, of course, ever considering why he left in the first place.[131]

In January of 1952, Georg Winter came under consideration once again. Nearly two years after the Adenauer government had created the Bundesarchiv, officials at the Ministry of the Interior were under great pressure to find a director. Winter, consequently, was in a stronger position than he had been back in 1950. His chances to implement his ideas about an ideal staff

---

127 Hans Ritter von Lex, StS BMI, to Posner, Oct. 28, 1951, NA RG 200, Posner Papers, box 2. Posner's rejection of the offer dated Nov. 29, 1951, ibid.

128 Posner was arrested on November 9, 1938, and taken to the concentration camp Sachsenhausen. He was released on December 16 after his wife had managed to secure emigration papers. Posner immigrated in January 1939 via Sweden to the United States. His American affidavits were provided by the historians Eugen Anderson and Merle Curti. See Giesecke, *Posner*, 12f.

129 The matter-of-factness of the letter appears to have put off Posner. This is revealed in a letter from Hans Rothfels, in which Posner had asked for advice on the matter. Rothfels to Posner, Nov. 20, 1951, NA RG 200, Posner Papers, box 2. On the clumsy and only semi-sincere efforts of German academic institutions to reinstate exiled scholars into their former rights see Krohn, "Unter Schwerhörigen?," 97–104, 110.

130 "Sie [würden] umringt sein von verletzten Ehrgeizen und beleidigten Leberwürsten, von anderen Ressentiments ganz zu schweigen. Der come back ist stärker als Sie Sich auf Grund der Eindrücke vor 2 Jahren denken können." Rothfels to Posner, Nov. 20, 1951, NA RG 200, Posner Papers, box 2.

131 Adolf Diestelkamp to Winter, December 19, 1951, BArch, N1333, NL Winter, vol. 87. Although it had been Vollmer who recommended Posner to the Ministry, he assured them that Posner would decline. "I emphasized from the start that Posner would turn it down. Besides, with all due respect to him, I felt the idea was amiss to call back a colleague who holds a reputable position abroad." See Bernhard Vollmer to Winter, February 12, 1952, ibid.

were enhanced by the fact that Gustav Heinemann had resigned as minister of the interior and nobody adhered strongly to Bergsträßer's criteria anymore. "Very advantageous," commented Bernhard Vollmer shortly after Heinemann's resignation in October 1950, "that [Robert] Lehr has become the successor of the naïve Heinemann, with whom no former Pg. would have had a chance."[132] Winter correctly assumed that a "simple membership in the party no longer plays a role now."[133] By 1952, Winter was in a position to fill posts as he saw fit. The first staff chart of the Bundesarchiv (May 1952) showed Adolf Diestelkamp, Wolfgang Kothe, Wolfgang A. Mommsen, Wilhelm Rohr, and Walther Vogel in the top-tier jobs. This list was incompatible with Bergsträßer's initial ideas about political acceptability.

The continuity in archival personnel between the Nazi era and the early Federal Republic had consequences for the general climate at the Bundesarchiv. Friedrich Kahlenberg points to a deficit in democratic thinking among this generation of archivists, who were firmly intent on preserving the Prussian archival tradition.[134] On a few occasions, the pasts of some archivists proved a hindrance in the negotiations for the return of the captured German documents and fueled mistrust among the Western Allies. A case in point was Wolfgang A. Mommsen's appointment as director of the Federal Archives in 1967. At that time, talks were underway about turning over the Berlin Document Center to the West Germans. Mommsen's career, particularly his wartime activities in the Baltic, was a point of concern for the responsible authorities at the State Department.[135] It was this concern about German officials' pasts – not unlike Bergsträßer's worries – that would prompt the Western Allies to demand from the German government a written guarantee of access to the records before they were willing to return them to the Federal Republic. Had Ludwig Bergsträßer completely failed

132 Vollmer to Winter, Oct. 19, 1950, BArch, N1333, NL Winter, vol. 87

133 Winter to Vollmer, Jan. 13, 1951, ibid.

134 Kahlenberg, *Archive in West und Ost*, 107: "Yet it would be wrong to overlook that a deliberate emphasis on maintaining continuity could constrain and hold in check the development of a new self-concept of archival work in a new societal environment as was expressed following the war, at least in the democratization of public life. If, at the end of the 1950s, a few representatives from the academic community (with an eye on the archivists at the Federal Archive) occasionally stated ironically that Prussia still survived in the Federal Republic in at least one institution, this certainly did not completely miss its mark . . ."

135 "The man who is scheduled to head the *Bundesarchiv* . . . where the Nazi Party and SS biographic files will eventually reside after their release from the Berlin Document Center, is Dr. Wolfgang Mommsen, acting director of the Bundesarchiv . . . Dr. Mommsen was in Estonia on a directed assignment for the Reichsfuehrer SS, Heinrich Himmler, who also served as *Reichskommissar fuer die Festigung deutschen Volkstums*. . . ." There might have been concerns on the part of State Department officials that Mommsen could be assailable from the GDR. See Morris, USBER Berlin to State Dept., no. A-535, Biographic Data on Dr. Wolfgang Mommsen, Candidate for Position as Director of the *Bundesarchiv*, May 18, 1957, NA RG 242, BDC Directorate Files, box 20.

to prevent the return of compromised archivists into leadership positions? Almost, perhaps – but he can be credited not only for the effort but also for disturbing the old-boy network at a crucial moment, as the following example illustrates.

The Rogge Case

"One has to train a bit the things that do not want to yield to us immediately."[136]

Winter considered it a curb on his authority as director designate that an outsider like Bergsträßer sought to influence the choice of personnel for Bundesarchiv. Winter had very specific ideas about the people with whom he wanted to work, and his thinking clearly did not coincide with Bergsträßer's on the question of the political backgrounds of civil servants. At the top of Winter's wish list stood Helmuth Rogge, whom he intended to hire as a department head. Rogge's past gave reason to question his commitment to the new democratic state. A onetime SS-Obersturmführer, he had acted as liaison officer for the SD and was no stranger to the art of political denunciation. Winter acted in full knowledge of Rogge's past and tried very hard to conceal it.

Helmuth Rogge, born in 1891, started his career as an archivist at the Reich Archives in Potsdam in 1921. He became head of the main department for nongovernmental archival materials and contemporary collections in 1938 and was promoted to the rank of senior archivist (*Oberarchivrat*) in 1941. In October 1933, Rogge was accepted into the Seventh SS Cavalry Unit Potsdam, a division of the Allgemeine SS, for which he served as training leader from November 1935 onward. In April 1940, he was promoted to Hauptsturmführer, the highest rank he would attain in the SS.[137] He joined the NSDAP after the lifting of the moratorium on accepting new members on May 1, 1937. Rogge was also a member of the NSV and, like the majority of civil servants, the Reich Federation of German Civil Servants. Beginning in 1937, he voluntarily served as an informer for the Security Service Head Office (SD-Hauptamt, SD II 211). The Security Service considered his reporting on colleagues so valuable that Franz Alfred Six recommended him for promotion in June 1939.[138] From that point

---

136 Winter to Rogge, Aug. 26, 1950, BArch, N1333, NL Winter, vol. 87.

137 SS membership number 132 590. In 1937, Rogge became Untersturmführer (Second Lieutenant), in June 1939 Obersturmführer (First Lieutenant) and in May 1940 Hauptsturmführer (Captain).

138 In the recommendation for a promotion by the SD-Hauptamt, II 211, Alfred Six, June 14, 1939, PA/AA, B118, vol. 740, it reads: "Realistically, [Rogge] is an irreplaceable colleague for the SD Head Office in so far as he is the most valuable expert in this area with regard to his attitude

on, SD-Inland (Amt III of the Reich Security Main Office, RSHA) availed itself of his expertise as an "expert for all questions and planning concerning the archival profession." In the assessment of the RSHA, Rogge displayed a "model National Socialist attitude."[139]

Rogge played a major role in drafting the 1938 German-Czechoslovak archive treaty. The treaty, exploiting the political situation following the Munich Agreement, required archives in Czechoslovakia to turn over archival materials the German negotiators considered to be of German origin. Although the occupation of Czechoslovakia rendered it superfluous, the treaty is worth noting here for the light it throws on Rogge's thinking. His demands showed no consideration for the other side. He advocated the pertinence principle over the provenance principle, which would have punched irreparable holes into Czechoslovak collections and violated professional archival standards, had it been applied fully.[140] Winter and Rogge had become acquainted with one another by the end of 1938 at the latest, when they were both involved in settling disputes over the distribution of Jewish archival materials seized in the wake of Kristallnacht.[141]

Winter's plan to offer Rogge a position at the Bundesarchiv met with immediate opposition from Bergsträßer.[142] In their correspondence, Ludwig Clemm warned Winter that Bergsträßer would "protest publicly in parliament" should Rogge be given serious consideration.[143] Winter thus knew from the outset that the planned appointment would meet with resistance and that he would have to find a way to downplay Rogge's past. When Winter presented his list of job candidates to the head of the culture department at the Ministry of the Interior for the first time, Rogge's name stood at the very top.[144] Winter assured the ministry that Rogge's membership in the Mounted SS was due solely to his passion for horses.[145] He

and competence within the entire German archival profession, in which very few SS men work. Through comprehensive memoranda he has enabled the Reich Führer SS [Himmler] to advance decisive initiatives for the National Socialist transformation of the archival landscape."

139 General biographical data in Herrmann, *Reichsarchiv*, 348, 569; Leesch, *Deutsche Archivare*, 496f. The data on party and SS careers stem from the answer to a query submitted to the BDC by the Auswärtiges Amt in 1960. Copies of Rogge's handwritten resume, promotion recommendations, etc., sent in response to this query are found in PA/AA, B118, vol. 740.

140 Herrmann, *Reichsarchiv*, 442; Musial, *Staatsarchive im Dritten Reich*, 73–5; Weiser, *Preußische Archivverwaltung*, 175f.

141 Herrmann, *Reichsarchiv*, 391f.; Musial, *Staatsarchive im Dritten Reich*, 47–9; Weiser, *Preußische Archivverwaltung*, 163f.

142 Rogge's name was introduced into the discussion by Bernhard Vollmer. See Clemm to Winter, Dec. 31, 1949, BArch, N1333, NL Winter, vol. 88. The letter also records Bergsträßer's strong reaction against Rogge.

143 Clemm to Winter, Feb. 23, 1950, ibid. See also Vollmer to Winter, Apr. 26, 1950, ibid., vol. 87.

144 Winter to Wende, Aug. 25, 1950, ibid.

145 See also Winter to Clemm, July 24, 1950, ibid., vol. 88.

maintained that he had not encountered "a particularly National Socialist attitude in Dr. Rogge." Winter went as far as to offer to vouch personally for Rogge if questions about his political beliefs were raised.[146]

Georg Winter's experience with whitewashing inconvenient biographical details might have been sufficient to achieve his aim in this instance had an incident from Rogge's past not come to light. Winter received a letter informing him that Rogge had denunciated a secondary school teacher for defeatist comments in 1944. The accused was said to have avoided trial in one of the special courts "by a hair." Brought instead before a disciplinary hearing headed by the minister for culture, he was reprimanded and transferred. "But those were very anxious weeks, and there were moments when I would not have bet a penny on his life," the man who brought the incident to Winter's attention wrote.[147] Winter discussed the case with a colleague who, like him, was well disposed toward Rogge. Neither had any illusions about the possible impact of this new information. "There is not doubt about the serious danger in which Rogge [!] would place himself should he again take on a public role – such as the proposed function at the [Bundesarchiv]," wrote Winter's correspondent. "Removal from office would certainly be the least of his problems."[148]

Upon learning that the denunciation had come to light, Rogge wanted to abandon the possibility of a position at the Bundesarchiv, but Winter was not yet willing to give up on him. "One has to 'train' a bit the things that do not want to yield to us immediately," Winter wrote him.[149] Toward that end, Winter even sounded out the man Rogge had denounced on whether he would speak out against Rogge's appointment.[150] Once he thought that possibility could be excluded,[151] Winter again proposed Rogge for a senior position at the Bundesarchiv in October 1950. Privately, he voiced doubts about his chances of prevailing against Bergsträßer.[152] In December 1950, Winter himself had to withdraw his application for the directorship of the Bundesarchiv after the denunciation he had made came to light. Rogge thus lost his avid supporter. Bergsträßer, who probably never learned about these behind-the-scenes efforts, continued to keep a close eye on plans for the Bundesarchiv. He intervened once again a few years later when

---

146 Winter to Wende, July 25, 1950, ibid., vol. 87.
147 F. Matthaesius, Gießen, to Winter, Oct. 19, 1948, ibid.
148 Grieser, Hannover, to Winter, Aug. 16, 1950, ibid.
149 Rogge to Winter, Aug. 24, 1950; Winter to Rogge, Aug. 26, 1950; both in ibid.
150 Winter to Matthaesius, Sept. 3, 1950; Matthaesius to Winter, Sept. 5, 1950; both in ibid.
151 Winter to Rogge, Sept. 5, 1950, ibid.
152 Winter to Wende, Oct. 29, 1950, ibid. See also Winter to Grieser, Oct. 24, 1950; Winter to Diestelkamp, Oct. 29, 1950; both in ibid.

he learned that Winter had granted Rogge privileged access to records.[153] Although Bergsträßer's efforts to prevent individuals with questionable pasts from being hired by the Bundesarchiv were ultimately not successful, he was able in the case of Rogge to disrupt the plans of Winter and his all-too comradely coterie.

After failing to land a post at the Bundesarchiv, Rogge became head of the archives at the federal government's Press and Information Office in May 1952. He retired from that position in 1956 as a high-ranking government official. In 1960, Rogge's career as an archive *user* came to an end when he was banned from the Political Archives of the Auswärtiges Amt on account of having made anti-Semitic comments in the reading room. He had complained about having to work in the same room "with Jews and Poles" and insisted on having a Polish professor moved elsewhere "so that he [Rogge] did not have to sit across from him and constantly see his face."[154] Rogge challenged the ban in court, and the case eventually landed in the Federal Administrative Court, the highest judicial instance for such matters, where he lost his battle in 1964. Strictly speaking, the court had to decide only whether the head of the archive was justified in expelling Rogge, but in its decision it also took a clear stance on Rogge's anti-Semitic comments. The remarks were "a provocation" and, given Rogge's past, displayed a "lack of discernment." His anti-Semitic comments represented "a direct assault on human dignity."[155]

The Political Archives of the Auswärtiges Amt

The Political Archives of the Auswärtiges Amt was the second archive to play a major role in the negotiations for the return of the captured records. Most of the ministry's files, whether in storage at the Political Archives or still in active use, had been seized by British and American troops in 1945. The Political Archives was re-established in 1951, and like the Bundesarchiv, it reopened with empty shelves. The return negotiations were just as vital for the archivists at the Political Archives as they were for their counterparts at the Bundesarchiv. The archivists at the Political Archives were able, however,

---

153 Bergsträßer to Winter, July 2, 1953; Winter to Bergsträßer, July 3, 1953; both in ibid., vol. 2.
154 Norbert Wagner, Verhandlung, Jan. 7, 1960; MinDir Hopmann, D1 [administrative head], via the State Secretary to Minister [Brentano], betr. Antisemitische Äusserungen eines Archivbenutzers; hier: ORR a. D. Dr. Rogge, VS, Jan. 8, 1960; both in PA/AA, B118, vol. 740.
155 Bundesverwaltungsgericht VII C 24.62, Urteil verkündet am 31. I. 1964; Verwaltungsstreitsache vor dem VII. Senat des Bundesverwaltungsgerichts, ibid. See also the correspondence between Ullrich and Eugen Meyer on this case, LArch Saarland, NL MeyerE 23.

to play a far more active role for the simple fact that the Auswärtiges Amt was representing the Federal Republic in the negotiations.

When the Federal Republic received the green light from the Allied High Commission (AHC) in 1951 to re-establish a foreign ministry, implementation was merely a matter of form. A shadow foreign service already existed and organizational plans for a foreign ministry had been drafted.[156] Several offices and institutions served as de facto precursors to the planned ministry, including the German Office for Peace Issues (Deutsches Büro für Friedensfragen) in Stuttgart, the liaison office to the AHC under Herbert Blankenhorn, and the Foreign Affairs Office (Dienststelle für Auswärtige Angelegenheiten) at the Federal Chancellery under Walter Hallstein. The fate of the Political Archives quickly became a matter of interest to these offices.[157] The German Office for Peace Issues felt it was being massively impaired in its planning for a future foreign ministry: "Without archives and libraries it is not possible right now to obtain an overview of the situation."[158] Reports by former staff members of the Political Archives and the Auswärtiges Amt soon provided these institutions with information about the evacuation of records from Berlin, their confiscation by the British and Americans, the transfers of the files within Germany and, in turn, to Britain.[159] The preface to the first volume of *Documents on German Foreign Policy*, which appeared in 1949, also shed light on the fate of the records.[160]

---

156 See Blasius, "Heißer Draht nach Washington"; Döscher, *Verschworene Gesellschaft*, 77–135; Maulucci, *Creation and Early History*; Müller, *Relaunching German Diplomacy*; Piontkowitz, *Anfänge westdeutscher Außenpolitik*; Ramscheid, *Blankenhorn*, 117–47; Wengst, *Staatsaufbau*, 183–9.

157 Botschaftsrat [a. D.] Forster, Deutsches Büro für Friedensfragen, to Hans Andres, Bad Grund/Hz., Aug. 6, 1947, PA/AA, B118, vol. 785

158 Deutsches Büro für Fiedensfragen, Die Regelung der auswärtigen Angelegenheiten bei der künftigen Bundesregierung, VS, May 1949. The memorandum was forwarded from the U.S. consulate in Stuttgart to the State Department. James R. Wilkinson, American Consul General, Stuttgart, to SecState, no. 247, May 26, 1949, NA RG 59, CDF 1945–49, 762.00/5–2649, box 4022.

159 File memo, Rücksprache mit Herrn von Griesheim am 10. 9. 48, Sept. 14, 1948, PA/AA, B118, vol. 785; Andres to Haack, Deutsches Büro für Friedensfragen, Mar. 29, 1950, ibid. Andres sent Haack his report "Die Akten des AA, ihre Evakuierung und ihr Verbleib nach der Kapitulation vom 8. Mai 1945"; Heinrich Valentin, Die Evakuierung der Akten des AA in den Jahren 1943–1945, notes, ibid.; Valentin to Hasso von Etzdorf, Dienststelle für Auswärtige Angelegenheiten, Chancellery, notes [on an interview with the former administrative assistant Wilhelm Nagorka], June 19, 1950, ibid., vol. 785; Rheindorf to Andres [with a copy of a report by Andres on the relocation depots for the Political Archives], Aug. 24, 1949, BArch, N1263, NL Rheindorf, vol. 148. See also Kröger/Thimme, "Politisches Archiv."

160 *Documents on German Foreign Policy 1918–1945. From the Archives of the Foreign Ministry.* Series D (1937–1945). Vol. I: From Neurath to Ribbentrop (September 1937-September 1938). London: HMSO 1949.

Re-Establishing the Archive. Established in 1920, the Political Archives was strictly a ministry archive. It received records from only the Auswärtiges Amt, and it was not subordinate to any governmental archival administration.[161] Those involved in the planning for the Auswärtiges Amt took it as a matter of course that the archive would be re-established and would operate independently as in the past.[162] Hans Andres and Heinrich Valentin, both members of the Political Archives' pre-1945 staff, were recalled by the Foreign Affairs Office in the summer of 1950 to work on rebuilding the archive. Hanns-Erich Haack was named director. His most urgent task was to regain possession of the confiscated records. "In the summer of 1950, when there were no records, the only question circulating was: When do we get our records back?"[163] When the re-established Auswärtiges Amt took up its responsibilities, the Political Department (Dept. II) was tasked with the negotiations on the return of the files of the Political Archives. After its efforts proved unsuccessful, Hallstein appointed the acting head of the Auswärtiges Amt's legal department, Wilhelm Grewe,[164] special envoy in 1955 and charged him with reviving the stalled negotiations.[165]

As an archive without documents, the Political Archives faced the same dilemma that would confront the Bundesarchiv. The empty stacks exerted great pressure on the institution to legitimize its existence. The creation of the Bundesarchiv exacerbated its problems. Andres predicted that a central federal archive would attempt to continue the efforts of the former Reich Archive to bring the Auswärtigs Amt's records under its control. He therefore asked Wilhelm Melchers at the Chancellery to nip any

161 The Political Archives had been using this name since February 1924; before, it had simply been called *Hauptarchiv*, or Main Archive. See Hans Andres, notes [on the history of the Pol. Archive, draft], May 21, 1951, PA/AA, B118, vol. 785. Also, Biewer, "Politisches Archiv;" Pretsch, "Politisches Archiv," 299f.; Philippi, "Politisches Archiv I."

162 File note, re: Auswärtiges Amt, unsigned, n.d. [May 1950], PA/AA, B118, vol. 785. "The rebuilding of the PA is a very large and important task. The attempt must be made to reassemble all records in some form since the German Bund."

163 Deutscher Bundestag, Stenographisches Protokoll über die 6. Sitzung des 47. [Untersuchungs-] Ausschusses, Vernehmung des Zeugen Haack, VS, Feb. 13, 1952. My thanks to Thomas W. Maulucci for this source. Further, Hans Andres, notes [on the history of the PA, draft], May 21, 1951, PA/AA, B118, vol. 785. Another function of the future PA, according to Andres, was "to check and monitor the publications prepared by the Allies of records from the former AA." Haack was replaced on June 1, 1951 by Hans Andres.

164 Wilhelm Grewe (1911–2000), 1947–55 professor of constitutional and international law at the University of Freiburg; 1951–52 head of the German delegation negotiating the end of Allied occupation; 1953–55 acting head of the Legal Department (Dept. V) at the AA; 1954 special envoy of the West German government to the Four Powers Conference in Berlin; 1955–58 head of the Political Department at the AA; 1958–62 German ambassador to the United States.

165 Löns, draft for StS Hallstein, Feb. 28, 1955, handwritten note: "not presented to StS," PA/AA, B118, vol. 489; Klassen, memo, Zuständigkeit für Aktenrückgabe Fragen, Mar. 28, 1955, ibid., vol. 28; Grewe to StS Hallstein, Mar 31, 1955, ibid., vol. 509.

such efforts in the bud.[166] Melchers therefore tried to modify the cabinet decision that established the Bundesarchiv with the proposal that the Auswärtiges Amt's records be explicitly excluded from the new institution's purview.[167] Although Melchers's efforts were fruitless, Haack declared unequivocally that diplomatic records would be administrated "as earlier" by the Auswärtiges Amt. "An accommodation at the future Federal Archives will not be taken into consideration."[168]

Staffing the Archive. The Political Archives returned to existence with new leadership. Johannes Ullrich, the wartime head of the archive, was still a POW in the Soviet Union when the re-established Auswärtiges Amt began work in 1951. Hanns-Erich Haack, its first postwar director, was not an archivist by training.[169] He was abruptly relieved of his post in June 1951 for reasons that remain unclear.[170] His successor was Hans Andres, who had been employed at the Political Archives until 1945 as a research assistant.[171] During his tenure as director, Andres repeatedly relied on the expertise of the historian Kurt Rheindorf, who was to be a key figure in the rebuilding

166 Andres to Melchers, Jan. 1. 1950, PA/AA, B118, vol. 785. Melchers was in charge of administrative affairs at the Office for Foreign Affairs (Dienststelle für auswärtige Angelegenheiten) at the Chancellery. See also Rheindorf to Andres, June 4, 1950, BArch, N1263, NL Rheindorf, vol. 148.
167 PA/AA, B118, vol. 28.
168 Haack, Bibliothek und Archiv, [note], Feb. 1, 1951; see also Haack to BMI, Mar. 16, 1951; both in ibid.
169 Haack held a doctoral degree in law and worked as a journalist for *Dresdner Neueste Nachrichten* before the war. He had his first assignment with the foreign service at the German Legation in Berne in 1939, followed by one at the economic department of the German Armistice Commission in Wiesbaden until 1942. In 1945, he worked for the Organization Todt and spent the postwar years as a freelance journalist until he was recalled to serve at the German Office for Peace Issues in January 1950. The BDC files show that Haack applied for membership in the NSDAP on September 27, 1939 and was listed as a member as of Jan. 1, 1938 (no. 5505498). Haack disputed vehemently that he ever was a dues-paying party member. See Personalbogen March 9, 1950; Haack, Mitteilungen des Document-Center zu meiner Person, June 7, 1950; Etzdorf, I Pers A, [Memo], May 23, 1952, both in PA/AA, PA Haack, no. 49179.
170 The journalist Michael Mansfeld speculated that Haack had acquainted himself with the AA personnel files returned in early 1951 and simply knew too much for his superiors' taste. See Michael Mansfeld, "'Ich sehe diese würd'gen Peers ...'... in der Personalpolitik des Auswärtigen Amtes," *Frankfurter Rundschau*, Nov. 16, 1951. Haack himself complained bitterly about his removal but did not explain the reasons for it. See Haack to Karl Wilde, Oct. 19, 1951, PA/AA, PA Haack, no. 49179. In his testimony for the parliamentary investigation (UA 47) in February 1952, he explained that he was relieved in order to prepare for an assignment in Chile. See BT, Stenographisches Protokoll über die 6. Sitzung des 47. [Untersuchungs-]Ausschusses, Vernehmung des Zeugen Haack, VS, Feb. 13, 1952, page 11.
171 Hans Andres (1901–1953) earned his doctoral degree in 1934 and worked from 1934 until 1938 at the Central Office for Postwar History, which was maintained by the Prussian Archival Administration. There he worked on the topic "Eastern European Policy of the Reich Government and the Army High Command" ("Die Ostpolitik der Reichsregierung und der Obersten Heeresleitung"). From 1938 to 1945, he was a research assistant (Wissenschaftlicher Hilfsarbeiter) at the Political Archives. He joined the NSDAP in 1940. On Sept. 28, 1944, he was promoted to legation counselor. On the Central Office, see Beer, "Landesstelle Schlesien," 122–8.

of the Political Archives even though he did not hold an official position.[172] Andres and Rheindorf had met when the latter worked at the Political Archives from 1941 to 1943. When Andres sought a job with the State Department team at Berlin-Tempelhof, Rheindorf provided him with a *Persilschein*.[173] Prior to the re-establishment of the Political Archives, the two men corresponded frequently, exchanging news about the fate of the captured files. A number of the official memos touching on the return of the captured documents and the *Documents on German Foreign Policy* project that Andres wrote as director of the Political Archives incorporated Rheindorf's views.[174] Peter Klassen, another former research assistant, was given a position at the Political Archives in March 1952. Immediately prior to that appointment, he had briefly served as the Auswärtiges Amt's liaison officer at Whaddon Hall. While in Britain, his wartime service as a "Jewish expert" at the German embassy in Paris came to light. The British thereupon refused to work further with him.[175] Andres prevented Klassen's dismissal and brought him to the Political Archives. Following Andres's death in November 1953, Klassen became head of the archive and was to hold the post until 1956.

172 Kurt Rheindorf (1897–1977) finished his habilitation in 1923 under Walter Platzhoff in Frankfurt and received in 1932 a non-tenured professorship (Medival and Modern History) at the university there. In 1933, he was dismissed from the university and taken into "protective custody" for a short time, sharing a cell with Kurt Riezler. The reason for his imprisonment was most likely an intrigue by faculty members who supported the NSDAP. Rheindorf blamed it on a denunciation by Mathias Gelzer, a Swiss historian for antiquity who was teaching in Frankfurt. See Rheindorf to Andres, June 7, 1946, BArch, N1263, NL Rheindorf, vol. 488. In 1939, he had to serve in the air force. A year later he was found guilty of "Wehrkraftzersetzung" (subversion and defeatism in the military). From 1941 until 1943, he worked in the Political Archives as a research assistant (Wissenschaftlicher Hilfsarbeiter), thanks to Johannes Ullrich. One of his tasks was to evaluate the Holstein papers. In 1941, he was sent for a short time on assignment with the foreign ministry's Archival Commission in France and then conscripted into the armed forces in March 1943. After the war he worked in Nuremberg in connection with the main war criminal trial. It is not even clear whether he worked for the prosecution or the defense. He subsequently served many times as an expert witness in various war criminal trials. From 1951 until the disappearance of Otto John in July 1954, Rheindorf worked as historical advisor to the Federal Office for the Protection of the Constitution (Bundesamt für Verfassungsschutz). Among other things, he conducted research in the BDC. The Auswärtiges Amt resorted to him in 1958–1959, to check the background of members of the AA there. Rheindorf maintained excellent contacts among historians and in diplomatic circles and was an expert for military and diplomatic archives. However, his correspondence should be used carefully; he tended to gossip and brag about himself, and was not always aboveboard to those people with whom he corresponded. For Rheindorf's Frankfurt years see Hammerstein, "Kurt Rheindorf und die Frankfurter Universität."

173 Andres to Rheindorf, July 3, 1946; Rheindorf to Andres, Jan. 24, 1947; Rheindorf, affidavit [for Hans Andres], Feb. 11, 1947, all in BArch, N1263, NL Rheindorf, vol. 488.

174 Rheindorf to Andres, Aug. 8, 1950, Aug. 17, 1950 [on diplomats' personal papers], Aug. 28, 1950 [on personal papers and the location of records abroad], all in BArch, N1263, NL Rheindorf, vol. 148; Rheindorf's assessment of the DGFP from Aug. 29, 1950, ibid., was incorporated verbatim in Valentin's report on the same topic from Sept. 18, 1950, PA/AA, B118, vol. 493.

175 See in this chapter, "The Klassen Incident."

Heinz Günter Sasse joined the staff of the Political Archives in 1953. He had worked in the Auswärtiges Amt's War Guilt Office (Kriegsschuldreferat) during the 1930s before moving to the Army Research Institute for Military History (Kriegsgeschichtliche Forschungsanstalt des Heeres) in Potsdam in 1938. After the outbreak of the war, Sasse was able to avoid conscription when the Auswärtiges Amt requested that he be assigned to its Archive Commission (AKO). From December 1940 to October 1941, he worked in Paris as an archivist for the AKO on the records of the French Foreign Ministry. While in Paris, he became acquainted with Peter Klassen, who was at the German embassy. In early 1953, Andres initiated the hiring of Sasse; when Klassen succeeded Andres, he secured a permanent position for Sasse.[176] From 1966 to 1971, Sasse served as head of the Political Archives.[177]

Johannes Ullrich returned home from captivity in the Soviet Union in 1955. He had headed the Political Archives from 1938 to 1945 and was reappointed to his former position in 1956. Ullrich was apparently not satisfied with the staff that had been assembled in his absence. He had already removed Klassen once from the Political Archives in late 1940.[178] He also distrusted Sasse because of an anti-English propaganda pamphlet that Sasse wrote in 1941. Ullrich had him transferred to a different department in 1959.[179]

The problem of continuity in personnel affected the negotiations on the return of the captured documents very concretely in the case of Peter Klassen. More generally, the Auswärtiges Amt was frequently held up as an example of how tainted Nazi-era elites were able to secure positions of authority in the Federal Republic. The British always proved more sensitive to this issue than the Americans during the negotiations on the captured

---

176 Andres, Beurteilung Sasses, Feb. 14, 1953; Klassen, Notiz betr. Dr. Heinz Günther Sasse, Dec. 2, 1953; Löns, head of Dept. I (Administration), Vorlage für StS Hallstein, Einberufung Dr. Heinz Günther Sasse, Jan. 9, 1954, all in PA/AA, B118, vol. 486.

177 Heinz Günther Sasse's work against the "war guilt lie" at the Zentralstelle für Erforschung der Kriegsursachen (central office for research into the causes of war), affiliated with the foreign ministry's War Guilt Office, probably predestined him to play a role in the Fischer controversy. In 1961, he published – under the rather uncreative pseudonym Heinz Günther – a piece on Polish border areas (Grenzstreifen). See Geiss, *Studien über Geschichte*, 115, 125; Herwig, "Self-Censorship," 99. For some postwar historians, Sasse was the embodiment of continuity from the Kriegsschuldreferat to the Political Archives.

178 Rheindorf to Epstein, Apr. 16, 1952, BArch, N1263, NL Rheindorf, vol. 154.

179 Heinz Günther Sasse, *England. Deutschlands Widerpart. Die deutsch-englischen Beziehungen von 1815–1940*. (Berlin, 1941). "I have," wrote Ullrich to Kurt Rheindorf on April 16, 1959, "never read the opus, only leafed through it and was shaken by the cheap loyalty to the cause for Ribbi's propaganda theses." BArch, N1263, NL Rheindorf, vol. 408. On Sasse's transfer, see Ullrich to Hopman, March 31, 1959; Hopman to Sasse, July 29, 1959, both in PA/AA, Personalakte Sasse, no. 56336.

documents, and they paid close attention to who was sitting on the other side of the negotiating table.

Throughout the period of the occupation, German archivists paid close attention to Western Allies' confiscations of records and relocations of seized materials. In October 1948, Bernhard Vollmer tried for the first time to direct the attention of the ministers of culture in the Bizone to the problem of confiscated records.[180] At the annual archivists' meeting in Wiesbaden in May 1949, German archivists called for the issue of captured records to be addressed in the anticipated peace treaty between Germany and the Allies.[181] But in Bonn, Vollmer was given to understand that he should stay out of the matter. The archivists' resolution was said to be "a private pronouncement, which the Federal Government does not intend to make its own by forwarding it." Vollmer was urged by the Auswärtiges Amt to show restraint in discussing this matter among other archivists, at least on the international stage.[182]

Historians in western Germany soon followed suit. In September 1949, at the first postwar meeting of their professional association, they passed a resolution critically noting that "the by far largest and most important portion of source material dating back to 1919, in some cases even to the Bismarck era, is found today outside of Germany and is practically inaccessible to German research." This situation was "alarming in both political and scholarly terms" and "intolerable" in the long run. Gerhard Ritter, the first postwar chairperson of the Verband Deutscher Historiker (Association of German Historians), added that the issue of the captured documents should not be put off until a peace treaty was signed, as it was still uncertain when that might take place. He also called for an end to the exclusion of German scholars from the work on *Documents on German Foreign Policy*.[183]

---

180 Minutes of the German Archive Committee (Deutscher Archivausschuß) in Düsseldorf, Oct. 6, 1948, BA/K, N1333, NL Winter, vol. 36. Henke, "Schicksal deutscher Quellen," 582f.; Kahlenberg, *Archive in West und Ost*, 55–7. See also Vollmer's preface to the first issue of *Der Archivar*, 1:1 (1947), 2f. The German archive committee was the extended board of directors of the German Archivists Association. Vollmer served as chairperson from 1947 until 1952.

181 *Der Archivar* 2:2 (1949), 48.

182 Dienststelle für Auswärtige Angelegenheiten im BkA to BMI, Ref. III.1 (Kultur, Archivwesen), Dr. Schaar, Sept. 5, 1950, PA/AA, B10, vol. 1701/1; Hanns-Erich Haack, Library and Archive, Memo, Sept. 13, 1950, PA/AA, B118, vol. 507.

183 Entschließung des deutschen Historikertages, *Historische Zeitschrift* 169 (1949), 669f.; also in *Der Archivar* 3 (1950), 40f.

Adenauer's office sent its first aide-memoire to the Allied High Commission in February 1950. The Bundestag debated the matter in May. Finally, in June 1950, Adenauer issued a categorical demand to the High Commission for the return of all documents confiscated in Germany. In Bonn, the legitimacy of this demand was considered self-evident. West German officials were therefore quite surprised when the Western Allies declined to comply with the demand at once. Only then did they realize that they faced tenacious negotiations on the matter. They had simply not counted on the Western Allies having a strong long-term interest in the captured documents. The Allies had, however, already demonstrated their interest by confiscating the records and then by publishing them. Challenged by the West German demands, they became all the more interested. In other words, the force with which the one side demanded the return of the files was matched by the other's tenacity in rejecting that demand.

Expectations

The information the West Germans gathered colored their expectations and led, in turn, to a miscalculation of the situation. In the summer of 1949, the former diplomat Werner von Schmieden reported that historians working on *Documents on German Foreign Policy* had assured him the files would be returned once a German government had been created. He had been told that the editors were working from microfilms and that the filming was as good as finished.[184] Similarly, the preface to the first volume of *Documents on German Foreign Policy* affirmed that the captured documents would remain in England only "until conditions in Germany become more stable."[185] In January 1950, Herbert Blankenhorn reported that the British High Commission had signaled that the Allies were willing to return political records from 1920 to 1930.[186] On the basis of the information available, archivist Heinrich Valentin came to the conclusion that "negotiations initiated by Germans concerning the return of records [would] not meet with very much Allied resistance" because the Allies themselves had emphasized that their possession of German records would be only temporary.[187]

---

184 Schmieden, memo, betr. Verbleib der Akten des AA, June 1, 1949, PA/AA, B118, vol. 785.
185 *Documents on German Foreign Policy 1918–1945. From the Archives of the Foreign Ministry*. Series D (1937–1945). Vol. I: From Neurath to Ribbentrop (September 1937-September 1938). London: HMSO 1949.
186 Haack, memo for Generalkonsul [Peter] Pfeiffer, Deutsches Büro für Fiedensfragen, Jan. 24, 1950, PA/AA, B118, vol. 785.
187 Valentin to Hasso von Etzdorf, Office for Foreign Affairs, Chancellery, memo, June 19, 1950, ibid.

It was with such positive expectations that the West German government first asked the Allied High Commission on February 23, 1950, when records would again be made available.[188] In response, the Western Allies voiced regret that they were not in a position to return records at that time because work on the *Documents on German Foreign Policy* project was still underway. The U.S. and British governments, as "custodians" of the papers, stated their intentions to return the records "period by period to the Federal Government as and when the historical scholars working on them have completed their task."[189] The Germans had good reason not to give too much weight to what was actually a negative answer because Great Britain began sending back forty tons of personnel, cashier, and budgetary records in December 1950. This shipment seemed to mark the beginning of the "period by period" return referred to by the Allies. Officials in Bonn counted on further shipments as a matter of course. Haack considered the matter to be no more than a problem of logistics and pondered in February 1951 just how to accommodate the rest of the records.[190] How could the West Germans have misjudged the situation so badly? What importance did the Allies attribute to Bonn's first demand for the return of captured documents?

The Return of Cashier and Personnel Files in 1950. The aide-memoire that Bonn sent in February 1950 and Blankenhorn's inquiry to the British High Commissioner, Sir Ivone Kirkpatrick, appear to have prompted the shipment of administrative records in December 1950. Kirkpatrick expressed understanding for the German argument that it was vital to have the pre-1945 personnel files on hand while setting up a new diplomatic service. He did not consider these records relevant to the *Documents on German Foreign Policy* project.[191] The British editor-in-chief, General Sir James Marshall-Cornwall, agreed with Kirkpatrick, but he also made clear that

---

188 Liaison Office to the AHC, Chancellery, aide-memoire, Feb. 23, 1950, PA/AA, B118, vol. 507. Hans Andres had already urged Wilhelm Melchers and Peter Pfeiffer at the German Office for Peace issues as well as Blankenhorn at the Chancellery to bring up the issue of restitution to the AHC. Both in PA/AA, B118, vol. 785.

189 "The three governments regret that they are at present unable to return any of the archives. But it is the intention of the United States and British governments, as custodians of these papers, to return them period by period to the Federal Government as and when the historical scholars working on them have completed their task." J. E. Slater, Secretary General, AHC, to MinDirg Blankenhorn, Verbindungsstelle, AGSEC(50)869, May 3, 1950, PA/AA, B118, vol. 507.

190 Hanns-Erich Haack, Library and Archive, [notes] betr. Akten des ehemaligen Auswärtigen Amtes, Feb. 1, 1951, PA/AA, B118, vol. 28.

191 Minutes Kirkpatrick for Passant, Apr. 4, 1950, PRO FO 370/2075 LS3/52. "These are of little value to scholars. But Adenauer wants them urgently in connexion with the appointment of consuls."

no further documents would be sent back to Germany before the project's completion.[192] Before transferring the personnel files to Bonn, the Foreign Office in London secured the consent of the Americans. The State Department redirected the shipment over Frankfurt so that the personnel files could be microfilmed before they were turned over to the West Germans.[193] Forty tons of material arrived in Bonn during December 1950 and January 1951.[194] Among the personnel records were questionnaires completed by all upper-level civil servants in active diplomatic service in 1944. They had to supply important dates in their careers and note their functions in the Nazi party, party organizations, and/or the SS. The questionnaires had become necessary after the wing of the foreign ministry housing the personnel department was destroyed during an air raid in November 1943.[195] These questionnaires were the most valuable materials in the shipment the Auswärtiges Amt received from the British in 1950–51.

Only gradually did the Auswärtiges Amt realize that there would be no further shipments in the foreseeable future. Haack was still confident in January 1951 that the return of the captured files was underway. A list of the transferred records was labeled "Delivery 1," as if a second would soon follow.[196] Before long, however, Haack was complaining that the British had not yet begun to send political records.[197] In their haste to respond to the West German request, the Allies had not obtained an official guarantee granting them access to the files in the future. The State Department criticized this omission three years later and insisted that the return of the remaining diplomatic records in 1956 would be handled differently.[198] The 1951 delivery was a tactical move. By feeding the West Germans forty tons

192 Minutes Passant to Kirkpatrick, Apr. 18. 1950, ibid.
193 Noble to Passant, May 5, 1950, ibid., LS3/65. This detour was decisive for later historical research on the Auswärtiges Amt during National Socialism. The microfilms arrived as T-120 rolls in the National Archives and compensated for the restrictive handling of personnel files in the Political Archives. Among those who benefited from this is Döscher, *Auswärtiges Amt im Dritten Reich*, 39f.
194 In all 4,400 sacks, of which 106 sacks were the personnel files of higher civil servants from 1867 to 1942, 200 sacks with personnel forms from 1943/44 and 36 sacks with name lists. See Chancery, Office of the UK High Commissioner to Passant, ref. 157/4/48/50, Aug. 24, 1950, PRO FO 370/2076 LS3/122.
195 BT, Stenographisches Protokoll über die 6. Sitzung des 47. [Untersuchungs]Ausschusses, Vernehmung des Zeugen Haack, VS, Feb. 13, 1952. The questionnaires of diplomats active before 1945 and returning into the foreign service since 1950/51 were not turned over to the Political Archives, but to the personnel department (Referat Pers A), and inserted into the active personnel files.
196 Haack, memo, Bericht über die Bibliothek und das Archiv, Jan. 30, 1951; Liste der zurückgegebenen Akten des ehem. PA (1. Sendung), n.d. [1951], both in PA/AA, B118, vol. 31.
197 Haack, memo, Jan. 12, 1951, PA/AA, B118, vol. 1; Haack, memo, Feb. 1, 1951, ibid., vol. 28.
198 Smith, Acting SecState, to HICOG Bonn, Feb. 19, 1954, NA RG 59, CDF 1950–54, 862.423/2–1954.

of mostly irrelevant records, the British and the Americans gained themselves some time while offering proof of their willingness to cooperate with Bonn on the issue of the captured documents. Bonn would not be able to accuse them of intransigence.

The Bundestag's Resolution on the Captured Documents

The demand for the return of the captured documents first landed on the agenda of the Bundestag in October 1949. The new West German parliament had convened for the first time only a month before. The fact that this issue would feature so prominently in the initial business of the new state cannot be explained solely by the administrative needs of the government ministries. Rather, it was the records' historical value that animated the Bundestag debate.

Although the motion for a resolution calling on the Western Allies to return German archives and registries was initially introduced by the National Right caucus,[199] it was subsequently appropriated by the SPD.[200] The Social Democratic deputies Ludwig Bergsträßer and Hermann Brill gave the resolution its final shape and tone.[201] Both were already deeply involved in efforts to enable the study of the recent past: the former in the discussions about establishing a federal archive, the latter in the founding of the German Institute for the History of the National Socialist Period (Deutsches Institut für Geschichte der nationalsozialistischen Zeit), which was later renamed the Institute for Contemporary History (Institut für Zeitgeschichte, IfZ). In light of the publications produced in the United States, Brill worried that Germany's historical research was gradually falling

---

199 The motion was submitted by the representatives Adolph von Thadden, Franz Richter alias Fritz Rößler, Herwart Mießner, Heinrich Leuchtgens, Heinz Frommhold and Franz Ott, who had been elected to the Bundestag via the lists of rightist parties in Lower Saxony, Hesse, and Bavaria. They had joined together to create the parliamentary group of the "National Right," which had evolved from the parliamentary group of the Deutsche Rechtspartei/Deutschen Reichspartei (DRP). On the maze of rightist parties in the early years of the Federal Republic and biographies on those mentioned above, see Jenke, *Verschwörung von rechts?*, 51f., 65–73, 236–40, passim.
200 BT, 1. WP 1949, Drucksache no. 149, Oct. 27, 1949. "It is moved that the Bundestag request the Federal Government to lodge a complaint immediately with the High Commissioners so that the German archives removed from Germany be returned to the Federal Republic of Germany posthaste." The committee approval in BT Parlamentsarchiv, 1. WP, 37. Ausschuß, Kurzprotokoll der 5. Sitzung des Ausschusses für Kulturpolitik am 25. Jan. 1950.
201 Hermann Brill (1895–1959) was a member of the Thuringian diet from 1919 until 1933 for the SPD (until 1922 for the USPD), and also in the Reichstag starting in 1932. He was arrested the first time in 1933, was sentenced to 12 years imprisonment in 1939, and incarcerated at Buchenwald concentration camp in 1943. In 1945, he was appointed minister president of Thuringia by the U.S. military government but went to Hessen when Thuringia became part of the Soviet occupation zone. From 1946 to 1949, he served there as undersecretary and chief-of-staff at the state chancellery in Hesse. He was elected to the first German Bundestag in 1949. See Overesch, *Brill*.

behind. He insisted that the resolution on the captured documents stipulate that the returned materials would be open to researchers.[202]

Why did West German politicians attach such importance to historical research? During the May 11 debate on the resolution, Hermann Brill gave a detailed account of what had happened to the captured German documents since 1945.[203] Although he referred to captured records in general, his primary concern was the material from the years 1933–45. The Bundestag Committee on Cultural Affairs explained to the Chancellery that the parliamentarians were specifically thinking of "archives of the former Reich ministries, the NSDAP, and the Wehrmacht."[204] Officials at the Chancellery did not consider it opportune, however, that the Bundestag was so brashly tackling such a sensitive topic and thought it "advisable . . . to withdraw the request for the return of the archives from the NSDAP and the Wehrmacht and to focus first on the archives necessary for the day-to-day work of the Federal Government."[205]

But the Bundestag deputies were not interested in this administrative argument. Brill considered the "study of historical truth" to be a "special German duty" that the Weimar Republic had neglected. The various research projects of the interwar years had not promoted a "historically accurate awareness of history." It was time to tell the "whole truth," Brill argued, "so that, after the tragedy of 1945, we experience a true catharsis in the best sense of Greek antiquity, a purification in the German awareness of history, one that . . . correctly depicts to the German people our position in the world and our mission at home."[206]

Brill's rhetoric, intended for Allied ears, sought to underscore the urgency of the matter. He stretched the point somewhat when he maintained that history had never before witnessed a situation in which "archival holdings

---

202 Kurzprotokoll der 15. Sitzung des Ausschusses für das Besatzungsstatut und Auswärtige Angelegenheiten, Apr. 20, 1950, Auswärtiger Ausschuß, 68f.
203 Brill relied on information provided by Bernhard Vollmer and Rudolf Holzhausen, who had offered their expertise to the foreign affairs committee. See Bernhard Vollmer, "Rückgabe deutscher Archive;" Rudolf Holzhausen, "Die Akten des Auswärtigen Amtes." Referate vom 24. Mar. 1950 gehalten . . . im Ausschuß für Auswärtige Angelegenheiten des Bundestags zu Bonn, both in BT Parlamentsarchiv, 1. WP, 7. Ausschuß, Anlage zum Protokoll der 12. Sitzung.
204 Wende, BMI, to the Verbindungsstelle zur AHK im Bundeskanzleramt, Jan. 31, 1950, PA/AA, B118, vol. 507.
205 Memo for Herbert Dittmann, Verbindungsstelle, about a telephone conversation with Wende, Jan. 31, 1951, PA/AA, B118, vol. 507.
206 BT, 1. WP, Stenographische Berichte 3, 63. Sitzung, May 11, 1950, 2312f. The only person in the Bundestag who dared to challenge this was the KPD member Heinz Renner. He said he could see "the old fascists from yesterday . . . holding the chairs at our universities." BT, 1. WP, Stenographische Berichte 3, 63. Sitzung, May 11, 1950, 2313f. His remarks met with laughter from the plenum.

have fallen completely into enemy hands and could be used at the enemy's discretion."[207] The quantity of records confiscated was daunting indeed, but the Allies had by no means seized the entirety of Germany's official archives. They had been very selective and did not touch, for example, state and or municipal archives, as Brill well knew. He thus acknowledged that – despite the confiscations – "a considerable amount" of material was still available for historical research within Germany.[208] By pointing to the available resources, Brill appears to have wanted to make sure that the Allied possession of the captured documents could not be used as an excuse to put off historical research on the Nazi years.

Brill advocated swift action because apologetic memoirs and sensationalist accounts of Nazism and the war were beginning to appear in quantity, especially in popular glossy magazines.[209] These depictions of the recent past were neither historically accurate nor politically acceptable to democrats like Brill and Bergsträßer. If such accounts were not countered by the facts, Brill feared, the next generation would have a "confused" or even thoroughly "poisoned" view of the Nazi era.[210] Echoing Brill's concerns, Hermann Mau, the first executive director of IfZ, lamented that "the German historical profession [has to] witness more or less passively how the history of National Socialism is currently being written with insufficient means and with the indeed questionable tendency to play down if not rehabilitate [the Nazi period] by journalists in the illustrated magazines."[211]

The proliferation of uncritical popular histories of the Nazi era and the war reflected a larger political dilemma that the Federal Republic faced in its early years. The new democracy derived its moral legitimacy from the delegitimization of the Nazi system, but its political parties were engaged in a "race for the votes of the fellow travelers."[212] In other words, the Federal Republic had to firmly reject everything National Socialism had stood for, but it could not disenfranchise the large number of its citizens who had embraced the previous regime. Even though National Socialism had been discredited in the eyes of many Germans at the moment of Germany's

---

207 BT, 1. WP, Stenographische Berichte 3, 63. Sitzung, May 11, 1950, 2310.
208 Ibid., 2312f.
209 On the high-circulation magazines *Stern* and *Quick* during the 1950s see Schornstheimer, *Bombenstimmung*, and the revised version, id., *Leuchtende Augen*. On the representation of the common soldier see Knoch, "Krieg des Landsers;" on memoirs by leading generals see Gerstenberger, "Strategische Erinnerungen;" Breit, *Staats- und Gesellschaftsbild deutscher Generale*, esp. 159–219.
210 BT, 1. WP, Stenographische Berichte 3, 63. Sitzung, May 11, 1950, 2312.
211 Hermann Mau, Director IfZ, to Bernard Noble, State Department, Historical Office, Apr. 16, 1951, IfZ Hausarchiv, ID 102/46.
212 Aretin, "Der Erfolgsdeutsche," 299. See also Frei, *Adenauer's Germany*, 310; Schildt, *Ankunft im Westen*, 116.

defeat, only a minority had truly accepted surrender and occupation as the prerequisites for a new beginning.[213] The postwar experience of Allied occupation was already overshadowing the Nazi dictatorship in many people's perceptions of the past. The material hardships and social upheavals of the postwar years were widely blamed on Allied occupation policies rather than understood as direct consequences of Nazism and the war, just as the war crimes trials and denazification procedures were interpreted as an accusation of collective guilt rather than as an attempt to hold individuals accountable for their actions. Memoirs, war trivia, and glossy history proved to be extremely popular because they served the needs of a large readership that blamed postwar hardships on the Allies. Unlike highbrow political and cultural journals, this material did not burden its readers with discussions about guilt and responsibility. The interest in such publications reflected an anti-Allied attitude that rapidly found expression after the Allied regulation of the press came to an end.[214]

There was an undercurrent of criticism of Allied policies in the demand for the return of the captured documents, too. Brill and other Bundestag deputies considered it necessary that "the history of recent times, especially that of the 'Thousand-Year Reich,' be evaluated by us Germans. Since foreigners and particularly the representatives of the three Western powers so often accuse us of not dealing enough with our most recent past, then they should give us the chance to do so."[215] The call for historical studies written by Germans contained an implicit dig at Allied re-education efforts.

Underlying the Bundestag debate on the captured documents was an inherent positivism and an unshakable belief in the power of historical truth as revealed in governmental records. As politics turned to history with a distinctly political need, the expectations West German politicians placed on historical scholarship might, in hindsight, seem unrealistic. These expectations were strongly tied to the tradition of German historicism. Historical truth, as Brill implied, was considered a singular, time-transcending truth free of the taint of subjectivity. The truth was buried in the records, waiting to be uncovered by the professionally trained historian. Only this process would yield the objective account of the past capable of stemming the tide of obfuscating, revisionist renderings of the Nazi years that might have an unwholesome impact on the fledgling West German democracy.

213 Lepsius, "Erbe des Nationalsozialismus," 229f.
214 The licensing requirement was repealed on Sept. 21, 1949 by Law no. 5, issued by the High Commissioners. See the regional study Frei, *Lizenzpolitik*, 83, 122f., 139–157; Frei, *Adenauer's Germany*, 107. A comparable development occurred in the book market.
215 Ludwig Bergsträßer (SPD), BT, 1. WP, Stenographische Berichte 1, 16. Sitzung, Nov. 10, 1949, 377.

The credibility and historical value of the documents lay in their provenance as official governmental records. The positivist attitude toward the
captured documents assumed a positivist view of the state, an attitude the
German archival profession had been steeped in for over a century. German archivists had long applied the principle of provenance in organizing
records in official archives, thereby replicating the state and its administrative
structures.[216] Historians drawing upon such archives approached the time-
transcending truth by methodically compiling the individual components
of a larger, lasting synthesis. Extracting the past from the records and weld-
ing it into a synthesis was thus a linear, almost mechanical and calculable
process. The executive director of the IfZ voiced his confidence in 1951,
for instance, that the history of National Socialism would be "wrapped
up" in thirty years.[217] Once the historical truth had been established, there
would not be much to add. Discussing the July 20, 1944, plot to assassi-
nate Hitler, for example, one leading historian maintained in 1954 that he
had "communicated everything that could be really important for historical
understanding."[218] Such a mindset explains the aversion of the German
historical profession to revisiting issues and topics deemed to have been
settled. Multiple interpretations would not yield greater insight and would
result only in an uneconomical repetition of work. Brill thus echoed the
thinking of most German historians when he advocated the "systematic"
(*planmäßig*) organization of historical research on the Nazi era during the
Bundestag debate on the captured documents.[219]

By a twist of logic, however, the positivist tenet that government records
were the avenue to historical insight did not lead to the conclusion that
whoever had possession of them had, consequently, direct access to the
historical truth. The participants in the Bundestag debate noted repeatedly
that German documents were in foreign hands and foreigners were using
them to write German history. During the negotiations for the return of
the captured documents, the Germans would return time and again to the
point that foreigners were not in a position to interpret German documents
correctly. The problem, in the Germans' view, was not that British and
American historians might have difficulties decoding initials and signatures

---

216 See the brilliant study by Vismann, *Akten*, here esp. 242–52.
217 "In etwa 30 Jahren," *Der Spiegel*, Apr. 25, 1951, 10f. At the time, the executive director was
Hermann Mau.
218 Gerhard Ritter to Paul Egon Hübinger, Head of Department III (Culture), Ministry of the Interior,
Nov. 2, 1954, BArch, B106, vol. 1209. Emphasis added. The book Ritter discussed here was his
Goerdeler biography.
219 BT, 1. WP., Stenographische Berichte 3, 63. Sitzung, May 11, 1950, 2312.

or understanding the particularities of Prussian record keeping.[220] Rather, the Germans held that only people who had lived through the Nazi dictatorship could truly understand its inner workings.[221] If, contrary to the tenets of positivist objectivism, personal experience was a prerequisite for historical understanding, only those who had lived through a particular period were capable of understanding its intricacies. Breaking with positivist objectivism, in other words, the Germans made personal experience a prerequisite for historical understanding of a particular period and thereby narrowed the pool of individuals capable of analyzing the recent past.[222] Indeed, the ability to truly understand, said historian Paul Kluke of the Institute for Contemporary History, "is perhaps granted only to those people who have had the dubious honor of personally living and suffering through the events, because a true understanding can only be purchased with the gravity of fate."[223] Thus, foreigners and German émigrés were by definition incapable of understanding life under National Socialism even if they possessed the records of the era. Kluke had in mind the Americans, who lived "in the completely different circumstances of a free people." They were therefore inherently unable to grasp "the utterly different preconditions of all decisions in National Socialist Germany."[224]

220 The American and British historians did indeed run into such mundane problems during their work on the *Documents on German Foreign Policy*. See James Joll, Oxford, to Erich Eyck, July 10, 1948, BArch, KLE 586F, microfilm 1: "I wonder if you know of anyone in this country who worked in the Auswärtiges Amt after 1933 and who is familiar with the methods of registration and circulation of documents in the office."

221 This line of reasoning seems to have emanated from the entourage of the defendants at the Nuremberg Trials, and here in particular from the trial against German diplomats (Ministries Trial, or Case 11). See the interview of Ernst von Weizsäcker, former State Secretary, with E. Malcolm Carroll and K. H. M. Duke, both members of the State Department-Foreign Office Team, Feb. 15, 1947, NA RG 84, entry 2531B, box 153. The interview took place before Weizsäcker was put on trial. In regard to the Allied publication, he stated that unless the German diplomatic "documents were accompanied by explanatory notes . . . uninformed readers would get an entirely false impression of the truth. These documents . . . were written in a style and spirit to make them acceptable to 'these madmen.'"

222 Conrad, *Verlorene Nation*, 245–55, was the first to emphasize the strong historicist legacy in early West German contemporary history. Especially the nineteenth century "Verstehensparadigma," the importance of empathic understanding of historical actors, saw a revival.

223 Kluke, "Aufgaben und Methoden," 7437. In 1955, Paul Kluke was director of the IfZ. In this article, he defended contemporary history against the claim that the close proximity in time to the events under consideration would make any assessment of them that used the classic methods of the historian impossible.

224 Kluke, ibid. Similarly, Hermann Aubin, Chairman, Association of German Historians, to Auswärtiges Amt, Political Department, May 14, 1956, PA/AA, B118, vol. 510; Ernst, "Blick auf Deutschland," 193, 207; Barthel, "Zur Problematik zeitgeschichtlichen Verstehens." Barthel's text is a review of Wheeler-Bennett's *Nemesis of Power* (1953). He was deeply dissatisfied with the book. The reason for its shortcomings lie, in Barthel's view, in the inability of the foreign author to penetrate the language of the Nazi years: "[Certain] sentences prove that Wh. B. was incapable of fully understanding the 'slave language' (E. Jünger) of dictatorships, this language of allusions and disguise, the subterranean communications, the codes in which words can mean the opposite."

Clearly, contemporary history in the early Federal Republic was anything but strictly an academic pursuit: it was highly political. Historians and political leaders alike sought to educate the public and saw professional historical scholarship as a means to delegitimize accounts of the past that glorified Nazism or obscured the regime's true character.[225] It was essential for the new West German state to establish the catastrophic record of the Nazi regime in order to launch a democratic new beginning and to legitimize the Federal Republic.[226] The scholarly study of the recent past was to play a major part in this process. Thus, it was no accident that the demand for the return of the captured documents occurred at the very beginning of the new parliamentary democracy. The restitution resolution belongs in the context of the wide-ranging effort to build a democratic political culture. Ideally, the return of the documents would facilitate the work of historians studying the Nazi era. The documents would not only supply information but, on account of their state provenance, would also establish the authority of accounts written on the basis of them. Using the returned records, it was hoped, West German historians would be able to produce an authoritative account of the Nazi era that, even if less entertaining than memoirs and popular histories, would in the long run become the standard interpretation of the recent past.

The Bundestag approved the resolution in May 1950; only the deputies of the Communist Party abstained.[227] Adenauer presented the Bundestag resolution to the High Commission in June 1950. Voicing his full support for the measure, he thereupon requested the return of all records from "former Reich authorities as well as the various military staffs and the highest party offices." The chancellor cited not only the government's administrative need for the documents but also the historical importance of the materials. An important task of the West German federal government, he argued, was to "enlighten the German people through scholarly work about what happened under National Socialist rule." The return of the captured records was the prerequisite for "impeccable research."[228]

Reactions to the German Demands

The British and Americans had certainly expected that a newly constituted West German government would request the return of official records,

---

225 Engstrom, "*Zeitgeschichte* as Disciplinary History," 415–17; Conrad, *Verlorene Nation*, 229f.
226 Lepsius, "Erbe des Nationalsozialismus," 232.
227 BT, 1. WP 1949, Drucksache no. 844, Apr. 20, 1950. The KPD motioned to change the petition so that the returned records would be turned over to an all-German trusteeship "until the reestablishment of national unity." See BT, 1. WP 1949, Drucksache no. 923, May 9, 1950.
228 Adenauer to the Chairman of the AHC, André François-Poncet, June 17, 1950, Adenauer, Briefe, nr. 257, 232f.

especially diplomatic records.[229] They had already held out the vague promise to return the diplomatic files at a point when "conditions in Germany [had] become more stable"[230] – a wording very reminiscent of the immediate postwar period and no longer thought to be in keeping with the times, at least by West Germans in 1950. The demand for the documents' return did not go unnoticed by the British and the Americans. They saw the increasing frequency of such requests in 1949 and 1950 as a concerted action, an interpretation that triggered several processes. In Britain, some historians adopted a rigidly defensive, unyielding attitude. At the State Department, officials realized that they had no clear idea which German records beyond the Auswärtiges Amt files had ended up in American custody. In light of their interest in integrating the Federal Republic into the West, the British and American governments had to respond to the German request. "After all," wrote a British diplomat, "it seems difficult to envisage any future German Government which is likely to prove a more trustworthy and deserving recipient of these documents than the one which we ourselves have created and endorsed."[231] Talks between the British and Americans led to a compromise offer made in a note dated July 6, 1951. That offer was, however, rejected by Bonn as an affront. The following section considers the first reactions of the British and Americans and describes the events leading up to the July 6 note.

The American Reaction. In Washington, the letter Adenauer sent to the High Commission on June 17, 1950, was interpreted as a categorical demand for the immediate return of all German records.[232] Work at the State Department since 1945 had focused solely on the diplomatic records. The

---

229 For example, see Passant, FO Library, minutes for Strang and Kirkpatrick, German Foreign Office Documents, July 9, 1949, PRO FO 370/1958 L3690: "It is also probable that, especially after publication of the first volume in the German edition and after the establishment of a West German Government, a demand may come from that Government for the return of the original archive." Also, Passant to Jamieson, BritEmb Washington, July 27, 1949, ibid.; Minutes of the German War Documents Conference, Oct. 5, 1949, NA RG 59, Lot File 78D441, Historical Office, box 18.

230 Preface to the *Documents of German Foreign Policy, vol. I (From Neurath to Ribbentrop)*. The preface was the result of an agreement produced by the DGFP editors' conference of January/February 1949, in which it was stated: "It was the consensus of three conferences that the British and United States Governments regard themselves as trustees of the German archives . . . with the understanding that, on the completion of the work of the tripartite project and the establishment of a responsible political regime in Germany, the documentary collection will be returned to the German Government and people." Quoted in [Memorandum], Department of State Holdings [of] Captured Enemy Documentation, n.d. [January 1950], NA RG 407, entry 360, box 3609. See also the U.S. aide-mémoire, Mar. 16, 1949, NA RG 59, CDF 1945–49, 862.414/3–1649, box 6760.

231 Minutes Gellately to Passant, FO Library, Jan. 17, 1950, PRO FO 370/2073 LS3/6.

232 That Adenauer was said to have demanded the "return of 'all categories' of German archives" can be read time and again in internal communications. For example, see Noble, State Dept., Historical Office, to Sherrod East, Director, Departmental Records Branch, Feb. 7, 1951, NA RG 407, entry 360, box 3609.

department's Historical Office had been supervising the *Documents on German Foreign Policy* project. No one at the State Department knew precisely which groups of documents were in the possession of the Army, Navy, Library of Congress, National Archives, Justice Department, trade bureaus, and other government agencies. Before Washington could respond to the West Germans, it had to determine the whereabouts of all the German documents in American hands. Bernard Noble, the head of the Historical Office, established an interdepartmental working group under his direction to compile this information.[233] In light of the German demands, Noble tried to broaden the working group's mandate: instead of just taking an inventory, he suggested, the group should also propose a position for the U.S. government on the issue of the captured documents.[234] At the time the working group was established, all federal departments and institutions except the National Archives were opposed to returning any documents.[235] Speaking on behalf of the Army, for example, the Departmental Records Branch declared that "the West German Government or any other former enemy government has no recognized right, moral or legal, in any captured military records and no general restitution of military records is now contemplated."[236]

As a result of resistance by the various government bodies in possession of captured records and a delay caused by the Korean War, the U.S. government was not able to assemble policy guidelines on the issue until October 1952.[237] Before then, the State Department had no policy to go by and could not make binding statements about the return except in connection with the Auswärtiges Amt files. The State Department had little choice but to resort to delaying tactics to gain time for coordinating among all of interested parties in Washington. One tactic was to reject the historical argument

---

233 The first meeting took place on Jan. 25, 1950. The protocol is found in NA RG 407, entry 360, box 3609. For a more extensive treatment of the work performed by the Interagency Conference on Captured Enemy Documentation, see the first section of Chapter 3. George Bernard Noble (born 1892) studied from 1910 to 1913 at the University of Washington in Seattle and spent the years 1913 to 1916 as a Rhodes Scholar in Oxford. His studies at Columbia University in New York were interrupted in 1916/17 when the United States entered WWI. In 1918–1919, he worked for the American peace delegation as a reporter on the state of the French public opinion. He incorporated these experiences in his dissertation thesis, completed in 1935, on the topic "Policies and Opinions at Paris, 1919." From 1953 to 1962, he headed the Historical Division at the State Department. His successor was William Franklin.

234 Acheson, SecState, to HICOG, no. A-2434, Feb. 3, 1951; Noble to East, Director, Departmental Records Branch (DRB), Feb 7, 1951, both in NA RG 407, entry 360, box 3609.

235 Wayne C. Grover, Archivist of the United States, to Maj. Gen. E. F. Witsell, The Adjutant General, Army Dept., Feb. 1, 1951, NA RG 407, entry 360, box 3609.

236 East to Noble, Feb. 27, 1951, NA RG 407, entry 360, box 3609.

237 Policy Regarding the Return of Seized German Documents, Oct. 24, 1952, NA RG 407, entry 360, box 3609. The policy is reproduced in Eckert, *Kampf um die Akten*, 480f.

presented by the Bundestag and Adenauer. The State Department pointed to the *Documents on German Foreign Policy* project to undermine Adenauer's claim that the captured records were needed in the Federal Republic for the "enlightenment" of the German people.[238] The stated goal of this project was to provide a comprehensive and readily accessible record of German foreign policy from 1918 through 1945. "The purpose of this publication . . . thus includes the purposes stated by the Chancellor," a draft reply noted.[239] Operating under constraint, the State Department initially provided Bonn with no more than provisional notification of the ongoing stock-taking of records.[240] In February 1951, Secretary of State Dean Acheson explicitly ordered the Office of the High Commissioner for Germany (HICOG) to drag its heels at the trilateral consultations held by the High Commission.[241]

American foreign policy makers were faced with a dilemma. In keeping with policy toward the Federal Republic generally, they wanted to show their willingness to accommodate Bonn's request. They were impeded, however, by other divisions of their own government.[242] The State Department therefore made a decision that would have far-reaching consequences: any upcoming negotiations with Bonn dealing with captured German records would be limited to the Auswärtiges Amt files. All other captured documents, most notably the military and Nazi party records, were to be excluded because the State Department had direct control, together with the Foreign Office, of only the diplomatic records. To initiate the

---

238 Adenauer to the Chairman of the AHC, André François-Poncet, June 17, 1950, Adenauer, Briefe, no. 257, 232f.

239 Draft Memorandum on Return of German Documents. Agreed upon by Mr. James Passant and Mr. John Wheeler-Bennett of the British Foreign Office and Mr. Noble, n.d. [March 1951], NA RG 59, Lot File 78D441, Historical Office, box 17. See also State Dept. to HICOG, no. 155, July 10, 1950, NA RG 59, CDF 1950–54, 862.423/7–150.

240 "I am to state that a survey of German archives under the control of the Occupying Powers is now in progress and that the Allied High Commission will not be in a position to give an answer until this survey has been completed." L. Handley-Derry, Secretary General, AHC, AGSEC(50)1552 POL, July 20, 1950, PA/AA, B118, vol. 507.

241 "It is . . . urged that discussion at HICOM level be postponed as long as possible pending receipt of further word on decisions reached. In no circumstances should it be implied that restoration of 'all categories' of captured documentation is a probability." Acheson, SecState, to HICOG, no. A-2434, Feb. 3, 1951, NA RG 59, CDF 1950–54, 862.423/1–2351. As a rule, the telegrams about return issues were written by Bernard Noble, Historical Office.

242 Walter J. Mueller, head of the BDC, summarized the problem: "The danger comes mostly from the attitude of Traditionalists, i.e. regular Foreign Service people who think in terms of 'normal relations' and who would, without knowing the value of our material to the U. S. Government, return the documents to the Germans as a sop." Mueller to Walter Kamprad, Division of Biographic Information, State Dept., Sept. 15, 1955, NA RG 242, BDC Directorate Files, box 1. See also Minutes Passant, Library, FO, to Kirkpatrick, High Commissioner, Jan. 31, 1950, PRO FO 370/2073 LS3/17: "Bernadotte Schmitt . . . said that some of the United States 'political boys' were beginning to talk of returning the documents as a gesture to the West German Government."

politically desired negotiations, it had to start with the Auswärtiges Amt files because all of the other records in American possession were out of its reach.[243] Officials at the Auswärtiges Amt were quite willing to accept this condition because their highest priority from the outset had been the retrieval of their own ministry's archive. This development fueled the suspicion at the Bundesarchiv that the Auswärtiges Amt was narrowly pursuing its own interests and was trying to exclude the Bundesarchiv from the negotiations.[244] Although the Auswärtiges Amt was not responsible for the limited scope of the negotiations, it did in fact concern itself with only its own records until 1952.

The British Reaction. The Foreign Office, too, closely followed the German discussion of the captured documents. It viewed the resolution adopted at the September 1949 meeting of the Association of German Historians as warning sign that pressure could be expected from Bonn.[245] The historians' resolution called for both the return of the captured records and the participation of German historians in the *Documents on German Foreign Policy* project.[246] The latter would directly affect the team of historians at Whaddon Hall, who were quick to reject unanimously any German participation.[247] James Marshall-Cornwell, the British editor-in-chief, stressed that "the Germans have admitted the ability and impartiality of the Editorial team. They have no justification (apart from national self-glorification) for demanding the return of the documents before the completion of the Project."[248] The head of the research section of the Foreign Office (Library), James Passant, supported this position.[249] In March 1950,

---

243 On this point, see the course of the first joint meeting of representatives from the High Commission and the AA on Oct. 31, 1952. The Allies opened the meeting with the announcement that they could only negotiate on the records of the former German foreign office. The protocols of the participants found in PA/AA, B118, vol. 507; PRO CAB 103/460; NA RG 59, CDF 1950–54, 862.423/11–552.

244 The head of the department for culture at the ministry of the interior, Paul Egon Hübinger, informed Peter Klassen from the Political Archives "that the opinion is widespread the AA is interested primarily in the return of its own records and neglects efforts for the return of the other records belonging to Germany." See Hübinger, memo, Apr. 30, 1955; further, Winter to BMI, Mar. 19, 1954 and June 12, 1955, all in BArch, B106, vol. 34723/3; StS Bleek, BMI, to StS Hallstein, AA, July 4, 1955, BArch, B198, vol. 1739.

245 Minutes and correspondence on the resolution passed at the historians' meeting found in PRO FO 370/2073, LS3/17.

246 Entschließung des deutschen Historikertages, *Historische Zeitschrift* 169 (1949), 669f.; "Entschließung des deutschen Historikertages," *Der Archivar* 3 (1950), 40f.

247 6th Editorial Conference, London, March 1950, PRO FO 370/2074 LS3/37.

248 Minutes Marshall-Cornwall, Feb. 9, 1950, PRO FO 370/2073 LS3/17.

249 E. James Passant was a medievalist by training. During the war, he left his position as a Fellow at Sidney Sussex College, Cambridge, and worked in the Naval Intelligence Division of the Admiralty. Under his direction, a four-volume handbook on Germany was produced, from which the historical

Sir Ivone Kirkpatrick, the British High Commissioner, proposed a compromise that addressed the concerns of the British historians while attempting to accommodate the Germans. If the Federal Republic were to request the return of the Auswärtiges Amt files, it would be informed that the Western Allies would not end the *Documents on German Foreign Policy* project prematurely. Whereas the diplomatic records would not be returned until the editors were finished with them, Kirkpatrick suggested that strictly administrative records from the Auswärtiges Amt archive could be turned over to Bonn.[250] The historians at Whaddon Hall accepted this proposal, which cleared the way for the return of the cashier and personnel records, but they objected to any further concessions to the Germans. They feared setting a precedent that might gradually undermine their position. In other words, even before the Bundestag resolution on the captured documents and Adenauer's first letter on the subject to the High Commission, many at the Foreign Office were resistant to the call for the return of the documents, and their resistance became all the stronger each time the Germans repeated that call.

London had given more thought to the remainder of the captured documents than Washington had. Already in 1947, an inter-ministerial committee called the Joint Consultative Committee (JCC) had been created under the direction of the historian John Wheeler-Bennett. It was the JCC rather than the Foreign Office that formulated what was to become official British policy on the German military and Nazi party records. In January 1950, the JCC presented the first British guidelines on document return, two years before the State Department produced a similar position paper.[251] The JCC refused to consider the return of any of the documents and blocked the efforts of the Foreign Office's German section and the British High Commission to press for a more conciliatory stance. The policy disagreement within the British government was sharper and more clear-cut than the divide in Washington. On one side stood the intransigent historians and the JCC; on the other the Foreign Office officials who dealt with Bonn

---

section "A Short History of Germany 1815–1945" was published in 1959 by Cambridge University Press. From 1945–46, Passant headed the German Section of the Foreign Office Research Division (FORD). In April 1946, he succeeded the historian Arnold Toynbee as head of FORD. When he retired in the spring of 1955, he was Director of Research and Librarian and Keeper of the Foreign Office Papers. His successors were Sir Archibold Duncan Wilson (until 1957) and Sir Cecil C. Parrott (until 1960).

250　The work group at Whaddon accepted Kirkpatrick's proposal at the sixth editorial conference in March 1950. Minutes Marshall-Cornwall, Feb. 9, 1950, PRO FO 370/2073 LS3/17. The text of the proposal is found in the letter from Noble to Passant, July 19, 1950, NA RG 59, CDF 1950–54, 862.423/7–1950.

251　For more information on the JCC, see the second part of Chapter 3.

on a daily basis and who sought to take a constructive approach toward relations with the Federal Republic. This rift was not a simple difference of opinion. More than once, the otherwise prudent and cautious Foreign Office officials lost their composure in the face of obstruction in their own camp. The muddled situation was ultimately resolved by a combination of pressure from the Americans and, more importantly, sheer fatigue among those on both sides of the British debate.

The Consequences for Documents on German Foreign Policy. Although the Foreign Office and State Department had control of the files of the pre-1945 Auswärtiges Amt, their agreement on the *Documents on German Foreign Policy* impeded the return of the files. There were two possibilities for accommodating the West German restitution demand. The first was to turn over all records irrelevant to the publication project. This explains the return of the personnel, cashier, and budgetary records in December 1950. The second was to reduce the scope of *Documents on German Foreign Policy*. The German requests were thus useful to the State Department, where doubts about the dimensions of the project had surfaced and support for scaling it back was growing.

Documents on German Foreign Policy had been designed as a four-part series covering the years from 1918 to 1945.[252] The State Department had initially reckoned that approximately twenty volumes would be published within three to four years.[253] The idea was to present the German documents to the world while the general public was still keenly interested in the war and its causes. Confronted with the task of selecting key items from more than 400 tons of documents, everyone involved with the project quickly realized that the original estimates for the time of completion were deeply unrealistic. The British and American editors clashed bitterly several times over the work pace. The British accused the Americans of "unscholarly speed" and of being more interested in publicizing sensational finds than in scholarship.[254] Raymond Sontag, on the other hand, harbored the suspicion "that the British government wished to delay, and not to facilitate, the publication of the documents."[255] By the

---

252 Proposal for Publishing German Official Papers, June 19, 1946, NA RG 84, POLAD, entry 2531B, box 100. See also Zala, *Zensur*, 205–7.

253 Raymond Sontag, German War Documents Project. Report for the Fiscal Year 1947, n.d. [July 1947], Langer Papers, Correspondence 1946–54, box 14; Noble to Charles Bohlen, June 19, 1947, NA RG 59, Lot File 78D441, Historical Office, box 21.

254 Sontag to Noble, John Wheeler-Bennett as Quintus Fabius Maximus, Feb. 27, 1948; Sontag to Noble, The "Tripartite" German War Documents Project, Dec. 20, 1948, both in NA RG 59, Lot File 78D441, Historical Office, box 6.

255 Sontag to Noble, Apr. 26, 1948, ibid.

summer of 1949, Sontag had come to consider the project a hindrance to historical research: "The project, if carried out as planned at present, will come to be regarded as an obstacle to historical research and as a means of withholding from scholars and from the public historical evidence of vital importance." It had been agreed at the project's inception that other historians would not have access to the records until the editors had completed their work. Sontag estimated in 1949 that the project would not be finished before 1960 and therefore recommended to Bernard Noble that it be limited to the planned Series D covering the years 1937–1945.[256] The American advisory committee on the project, which Noble had set up in 1947,[257] took Sontag's advice seriously after the German historians passed a resolution on the captured documents at their September 1949 meeting in Munich. In the interest of aiding historians in the Federal Republic, the committee noted, it might be "desirable to return to the Germans the documents prior to 1933 before it has been possible to publish Series A [1918–26] and B [1926–33]."[258] This proposal was in line with Noble's own concern that the project might get out of hand in terms of time and cost.[259]

Noble used the subsequent German calls for the return of the Auswärtiges Amt files as leverage against the Foreign Office when he proposed to reduce the *Documents on German Foreign Policy* project to the C and D series, i.e., to the years 1933–1945.[260] The advisory committee seconded the proposal and voiced its hope that the records from the Weimar Republic would soon be made available to all historians.[261] In October 1951, Noble announced to

256 Sontag to Noble, The Future of the German War Documents Project, July 25, 1949, ibid., box 5. In a similar tone, Hajo Holborn, Yale, to Noble, Jan. 17, 1952, ibid., box 4. See also Sontag to Noble, Nov. 18, 1949, ibid., box 5. Sontag's still optimistic calculation was: Series D (1937–1945), 13 or 14 vols., published 1949–1952; Series C (1933–1937), 7 vols., published 1952–1954; Series B (1926–1933), 6 vols., published 1954–1956; Series A (1918–1926), 13 vols., published 1956–1960.

257 The members of the first advisory committee were Sidney B. Fay, Guy Stanton Ford, Carlton J. Hayes, William L. Langer, Conyers Read, and Charles Seymour.

258 Opinions expressed by the Advisory Committee on the German War Documents Project at its Meeting, Nov. 25, 1949, Langer Papers, Correspondence 1946–54, box 14; also Sweet to Noble, Nov. 22, 1949, NA RG 59, Lot File 78D441, Historical Office, box 5.

259 Noble to Passant, Apr. 19, 1949; Passant to Noble, May 6, 1949, both in PRO FO 370/1956 L2419; Minutes of the German War Documents Conference, Oct. 5, 1949, NA RG 59, Lot File 78D441, Historical Office, box 18.

260 "I believe that we shall have to decide that Series A and B are infeasible and also that the records should therefore be thrown open [to private scholars]." Noble to Richard A. Humphrey, Oct. 12, 1951, NA RG 59, Lot File 78D441, Historical Office, box 4.

261 Summary Report of Meeting of the [U.S.] Advisory Committee of the German Foreign Office Archives Project, Nov. 16, 1951, PRO FO 370/2153 LS3/181; Noble to Langer, Nov. 28, 1951, Langer Papers, Correspondence 1946–54, box 13; [Noble], The German War Documents Project, Dec. 14, 1951, NA RG 59, Lot File 78D441, Historical Office, box 4.

James Passant at the Foreign Office that "the completion of the entire project as originally planned (covering 1918–1945 in English and German) is out of the question."[262] The British and French responded with incredulity. They balked, arguing that the study of Weimar-era diplomacy was a prerequisite for assessing the new West German government's reliability in matters of foreign policy. The Auswärtiges Amt files, they contended, thus served the needs of the Atlantic alliance.[263] Naturally, they were also aware that the return of the files would be delayed if *Documents in German Foreign Policy* was completed in the dimension originally planned. A compromise was reached in early 1952 whereby the years 1918 to 1933 would no longer be documented so thoroughly.[264] Ultimately, however, Noble in effect prevailed. In 1958, when the diplomatic files were turned over to Bonn, *Documents on German Foreign Policy* covered only the years 1933–1941.[265]

Noble's openness to every suggestion that might expedite the completion of *Documents on German Foreign Policy* reflected the American position on the project. He was by no means prepared to sacrifice the project on the altar of realpolitik.[266] But he supported the ideas of reducing the scope of the project and of bringing a German co-editor on board. At an editorial

262 Noble to Passant, Oct. 23, 1951, PRO FO 370/2152 LS3/158. Passant had to assume that the British High Commissioner Kirkpatrick would not be adverse to such plans. He had already considered something similar in early 1950. See Minutes Passant to Kirkpatrick, Feb. 2, 1950, PRO FO 370/2073 LS3/17.

263 "Such subjects as the degree to which the successive Weimar Governments were aware of the secret rearmament that went on in Germany, or the methods by which German diplomats played off the East against the West seem to us to deserve close examination, not only for historical reasons but as having a direct bearing on the present and future relations between the Governments of our two countries and that of Germany." Passant to Noble, Nov. 5, 1951, PRO FO 370/2152 LS3/158. See also Noble to Conyers Read, UPenn, Jan. 9, 1950; Noble, Memorandum of Conversation, Discussion of Future Program of German Foreign Office Archives Project, Jan. 14, 1952, both in NA RG 59, Lot File 78D441, Historical Office, box 4.

264 Record of a Meeting Held in Mr. Passant's Room, Mar. 3, 1952, NA RG 59, Lot File 78D441, Historical Office, box 4; Noble to Lewis, German Affairs, and Russell, Public Affairs, Report on Discussions in London and Bonn, Mar. 18, 1952, NA RG 59, CDF 1950–54, 862.423/3–1852. For this, Paul Sweet drew up a work plan: Sweet to Noble, A four-year program for the examination of the files on the Weimar Period, Mar. 1, 1952, PRO FO 370/2244 L3/38.

265 In July 1954, the British consented to shortening the edition by ending documentation with the year 1941 instead of 1945. See Minutes Passant for Frank Roberts and Kirkpatrick, July 29, 1954, PRO FO 370/2374 LS5/129. Noble had been pushing for this limitation since the autumn of 1951 because he thought developments in foreign policy would only be of great interest until the United States entered the war in 1941. See Noble to Passant, Nov. 30, 1951, PRO FO 370/2153 LS3/181. Margaret Lambert was incensed by the proposed limitation: "Could it perhaps be tactfully pointed out to our American colleagues that the British and French consider themselves to have been at war with Germany from September 3rd, 1939?" Minutes Lambert for Passant, Dec. 4, 1951, PRO FO 370/2153 LS3/181.

266 Noble emphasized repeatedly that the prestige of the State Department and the Foreign Office were linked through the document edition. The idea of transferring the records to Bonn, where the publication project would then be continued, was considered by Noble "only as [the] last

conference held in London in March 1951, he formulated the proposals that were subsequently incorporated in an Allied note to the Federal Republic on July 6, 1951.[267] Acting on the advice of Noble and the editors, the State Department instructed the High Commission to formulate a compromise that would serve the "legitimate needs of the German Federal Government" and make as many concessions as possible to Bonn but that would leave the diplomatic files firmly in Anglo-American control until work on *Documents on German Foreign Policy* project was complete.[268]

The Allied Offer of July 6, 1951

In a note sent on July 6 to the Adenauer government, the Allied High Commission (AHC) turned down the German request for the immediate return of *all* diplomatic records, citing the *Documents on German Foreign Policy* project as the reason for its decision.[269] As an interim solution, the AHC offered the immediate return of all political treaties, consulate and protocol documents, and the remaining cashier records. In early 1952, all records up to 1914 would follow. The Federal Republic would, moreover, be loaned a set of all microfilms made to date of records from 1919 to 1945. Bonn was also invited to assign a liaison officer to Whaddon Hall who would have full and free access to all documents. That officer could order copies and relay them along with information garnered from the files to the Auswärtiges Amt. With this offer, the AHC sought to counter the administrative argument put forward by Bonn that the records were essential for the government's day-to-day operations. Furthermore, the AHC invited Bonn to name a German historian to act as a co-editor of *Documents on German Foreign Policy* on equal footing with the American, British, and French editors. The note again confirmed the intention of the Allies to return all of the Auswärtigs Amt files upon completion of the publication project. No conditions were linked to this offer. The AHC wanted only

resort." Noble, Memorandum of Conversation with Mr. C. D. O'Neill, POLAD to the British High Commissioner, Mar. 15, 1951, PRO FO 370/2145 LS3/33.

267 Noble, Report on Trip to the United Kingdom and Germany, March 2–22, 1951, Mar. 24, 1951, NA RG 59, CDF 1950–54, entry 205K, 110.4-RE/3–2751; Draft Memorandum on Return of German Documents. Agreed upon by Mr. James Passant and Mr. John Wheeler-Bennett of the British Foreign Office and Mr. Noble, n.d. [March 1951], NA RG 59, Lot File 78D441, Historical Office, box 17; Noble, Memorandum of Conversation with Mr. C. D. O'Neill, POLAD to the British High Commissioner, Mar. 15, 1951, PRO FO 370/2145 LS3/33.

268 State Dept to HICOG, no. A-3554, Apr. 18, 1951, NA RG 59, CDF 1950–54, 862.423/4–1851.

269 J. G. Ward on behalf of Kirkpatrick, Chairman AHC, to Adenauer, AGSEC(51)1135, July 6, 1951, PA/AA, B118, Bd. 507. The full document is reproduced in Eckert, *Kampf um die Akten*, 478f.

assurance that the records would remain available to scholars of all nations for research after they had been turned over to the Federal Republic.

Bonn refused to consider the compromise the AHC proposed. In light of its categorical demand for the immediate return of all of the captured documents, the Adenauer government could only regard any interim solution as insufficient. In reality, the Auswärtiges Amt would have been overwhelmed by the materials the AHC was willing to turn over at once. The Political Archives did not possess sufficient stack space for just the pre-1945 administrative records, and most of the files would have had to be warehoused.[270] This situation hardly corresponded with the argument that the records were constantly needed for daily governmental business. The Adenauer government did not officially respond to the AHC's note until November 1952, and then only to reject it and repeat its categorical demand.[271] During the sixteen months between the AHC's note and Bonn's response, officials in London and Washington had more than once expressed amazement at Bonn's silence and interpreted it as a sign of lack of interest.[272] The Auswärtiges Amt thus maneuvered the talks on the return of the files into a dead end. In a rare moment of self-criticism, the head of the Political Archives admitted in early 1954: "To a great extent, we ourselves are the reasons for the failure so far."[273]

The Klassen Incident. Although Bonn took its time in issuing its official response to the July 6 note, the Auswärtiges Amt wanted to take immediate advantage of the invitation to send a liaison officer to Whaddon Hall. Once that officer had gained an overview of the situation, the Auswärtiges Amt could decide whether to name a German co-editor for the *Documents on German Foreign Policy* project. Hermann Mosler, head of the legal department, agreed with Bernard Noble in early March 1952 to dispatch at once Peter Klassen, a former research assistant at the Political Archives and wartime staff member of the German embassy in Paris who had not yet found a new position.[274]

---

270 In October 1952, it was estimated that the new building for the AA would be completed in February 1953, at the earliest. As it turned out, the building was not ready for use until 1954/55. See v. Haeften, Abt. V., memo, Oct. 27, 1952, PA/AA, B118, vol. 489.
271 Adenauer to the Chairman of the AHC, Ambassador Walter J. Donnelly, Nov. 22, 1952, PA/AA, B118, vol. 509.
272 Record of a Meeting held in Mr. Passant's Room, present: Noble, Dayet, Passant, Wheeler-Bennett, Mar. 4, 1952, PRO FO 370/2244 LS3/38.
273 Peter Klassen, Memo, Jan. 26, 1954, PA/AA, B118, vol. 489.
274 Mosler, Abt. V, memo, re. Rückgabe der Dokumente des Auswärtigen Amts, Mar. 1, 1952, PA/AA, B118, vol. 507.

The British and American historians working on *Documents on German Foreign Policy* were more than just a little surprised when Klassen unexpectedly arrived at Whaddon Hall. The West German consulate general in London had not officially announced his coming. James Passant and the project staff could only guess why Klassen was there. Passant estimated him to be forty years old and learned from Klassen himself that he had earned his doctoral degree in Kiel but that his chances for an academic career had been hindered after 1933. Klassen explained that he had worked at the Political Archives between 1939 and 1941, and he further reported that he had been in Berlin throughout the war and had been drafted as part of the Volkssturm at the end.[275] What struck Passant most upon first meeting Klassen was his "complete ignorance" of the *Documents on German Foreign Policy* project. "Indeed, he had clearly not even read the general Preface."[276] From the start, Passant made it clear that he viewed the sole purpose of Klassen's trip as exploratory and that he was not willing to negotiate any details of a possible German participation in the project with him.[277] Shortly after his arrival, Klassen announced that, in two weeks' time, he would be sending a report to Bonn; it was anything but clear to Passant what he intended to report upon. "[He] is fishing for any help we can give him. A good report will mean he can stay in London and find himself a job, which he hopes very much to be able to do." Several times Klassen asked whether records from the German embassy in Paris had landed in Allied hands.[278] "His main interest seemed to be to discover how complete was our holding and whether there were other diplomatic documents in the USA." His English was poor, his French distinctly better. After a few days, the situation became too bizarre for Passant, and he requested that the consulate general confirm Klassen's official status. His mistrust had grown so strong that he also asked the British High Commission in Wahnerheide to have Klassen investigated

---

275 [Memo for] Margaret Lambert, Dr. Peter Klassen at Whaddon with Dr. Noble, Mar. 6, 1952, PRO FO 370/2343 LS5/200.

276 Minutes Passant for W. D. Allen and Frank K. Roberts, Apr. 14, 1952, PRO FO 370/2244 LS3/38; at Whaddon, one was "inclined to suspect he had never seen the volumes before, but he tried valiantly to conceal this and frequently explained we must not be surprised if our work had not roused more interest in Germany; public opinion there was almost exclusively occupied with the daily round; even Hitler seemed completely forgotten, and if he were to return suddenly, like Napoleon from Elba, no one would notice him." [Memo for] Margaret Lambert, Dr. Peter Klassen at Whaddon with Dr. Noble, Mar. 6, 1952, PRO FO 370/2343 LS5/200.

277 Passant to O'Neill, Political Director and Head of Chancery, Wahnerheide, Mar. 19, 1952, PRO FO 370/2244 LS3/38.

278 [Memo for] Margaret Lambert, Dr. Peter Klassen at Whaddon with Dr. Noble, Mar. 6, 1952, PRO FO 370/2343 LS5/200; Ericson, Additional Note on Visit Klassen, Mar. 19, 1952, ibid. See also Noble's report on the Klassen visit, Mar. 10, 1952, NA RG 59, Lot File 78D441, Historical Office, box 4.

by the Federal Office for the Protection of the Constitution (Bundesamt für Verfassungsschutz, BfV),[279] the West German domestic intelligence agency. Once the High Commission looked into Klassen's background, the question of accreditation was moot. It was discovered that Klassen had worked from January 1941 to August 1944 in the information section (Informationsabteilung) of the Paris embassy and that he had last held the position of *Judenreferent* (Jewish expert) there. In the euphemistic terminology of the time, his responsibilities were described as "activities in the area of church propaganda to France."[280] Klassen headed the "Political Editorial Office" of the information section. From the fall of 1941 on, he devoted his time increasingly to anti-Semitic and anti-Masonic propaganda.[281] One of his projects was to launch the magazine *La Question Juive en France et dans le monde* in 1942 in cooperation with the ERR.[282] In April 1944, Klassen delivered a talk at a conference of so-called Jewish experts from German diplomatic missions across Europe, the "Arbeitstagung der Judenreferenten der Deutschen Missionen in Europe" in Krummhübel; among the topics discussed at the conference was the "physical elimination of Eastern European Jewry."[283] Klassen was certainly aware that this wartime record at the

279 Passant to O'Neill, Mar. 21, 1952, PRO FO 370/2244 LS3/44.

280 The deputy of Otto Abetz at the Paris Embassy and later head of the AA department for cultural policy in Berlin, Envoy First Class Rudolf Schleier, used this wording in September 1944, in order to prevent Klassen from being called up for military service. Conveyed in Andres, Aufzeichnung, Apr. 9, 1952, PA/AA, NL Andres, Paket 1. Schleier headed the information office XIV (anti-Jewish actions abroad), which had been set up on orders from Ribbentrop in early 1944. Its purpose was to coordinate all interested offices in order "to intensify and enhance anti-Jewish information abroad." For this purpose, every foreign mission was to appoint someone as the "Jewish expert" ("however, if possible, not the cultural aide"). Among other things, these "experts" worked closely with the "Aryanization advisers" of the RSHA. See Kriegsverbrecher-Prozesse, case no. 11, Weizsäcker (Wilhelmstraßen)-Prozeß, Document Book no. 63, 3319-PS, BArch, All. Proz. 1, Rep. 501, LVI B 80; also Hachmeister, *Gegnerforscher*, 246f. Klassen remained in the information department of the Paris embassy until September 1944 and then switched to the department for cultural policy at the AA in Berlin. The title "Jewish expert" (Judenreferent) is usually associated with Carltheo Zeitschel, who was responsible for "Jewish affairs" in the Political Department of the Paris embassy. See Fox, "German Bureaucrat," 179; Lambauer, *Otto Abetz*, 314f., 321–6, 422–8; Ray, *Annäherung an Frankreich*, 370–4.

281 Lambauer, *Otto Abetz*, 350–2, also 654.

282 Although the institute had a French director, it was actually run by the Paris Jewish desk of the Reich Security Main Office under SS-Hauptsturmführer Theodor Dannecker. The institute considered itself the precursor of an "Antisemitismus à l'allemande" and pacesetter for the tougher legislation of the Vichy government. See Ray, *Annäherung an Frankreich*, 368–70; Papen, "Schützenhilfe," 28f.

283 In his talk, he deplored the Catholic Church for having "supported the Jewish people largely in accordance with democratic ideology." He went on to say that several anti-Semitic films had not had the desired success among the French and that the film medium had to be used more extensively. "The information activities have to evolve from the French tradition and be conceived as a French affair." Useful approaches could be found among French fascists associated with Marcel Déat. A synopsis of the lecture is found in the Nuremberg document 3319-PS, see note 280. The sentence on "physical elimination" stems from the Krummhübel presentation by Alfred Six. See Hachmeister, *Gegnerforscher*, 266f., 283f.

Paris embassy under Ambassador Otto Abetz might cause problems for his mission on behalf of the Auswärtiges Amt. It was thus rather brazen of him to arrive at Whaddon Hall not knowing whether the British and Americans had documents about his service in Paris and, once in Britain, to ask about those documents.

The British were tipped off about Klassen by the historian Kurt Rheindorf. Rheindorf had been working as an advisor to the BfV since August 1951. The agency turned to Rheindorf on questions involving the historical and archival professions, and he reported directly to BfV head Otto John.[284] On the side, he earned a meager living with a series of minor jobs, one of which was to edit the English and German editions of Wheeler-Bennett's *Nemesis of Power*.[285] When Rheindorf and Wheeler-Bennett met in Cologne in March 1952 to work on Wheeler-Bennett's book, Rheindorf brought up the subject of Klassen. Always well informed, Rheindorf already knew about Klassen's dispatch to London. Klassen, Wheeler-Bennett reported to Passant, "was regarded unfavorably by the BfV." He was viewed as another example of the uncritical personnel policy of the Auswärtiges Amt – a policy that was under investigation by the Bundestag.[286] After hearing Rheindorf's assessment, Wheeler-Bennett predicted

If the German Government proposed to nominate a team consisting of the editor of Hitler's Tischgespräche [Gerhard Ritter] and a former member of Otto Abetz' staff[,] such a proposal would be coldly received by the existing editors who would find it difficult to believe that the Project was being taken either seriously or objectively.

The British High Commission asked Blankenhorn to replace Klassen immediately. Blankenhorn complied and ordered his removal, if only because Klassen had become an "optical burden."[287] Thanks to the intervention

284 Rheindorf's status with the BfV was based on a gentlemen's agreement that was hard to define. He considered himself "neither civil servant, nor employee," and ended his services abruptly when John disappeared in July 1954. He had met John during his university study in Frankfurt. See Rheindorf to Fritz T. Epstein, Sept. 24, 1954, BArch, N1263, NL Rheindorf, vol. 154.

285 Correspondence with Wheeler-Bennett, the proofs, etc. in BArch, N1263, NL Rheindorf, vol. 217.

286 This refers to the committee of inquiry (Untersuchungsausschuß) UA 47 of the Bundestages, which was established in 1951 following a series of articles that appeared in the *Frankfurter Rundschau* ("Ihr naht euch wieder . . . ," Sept. 1–6, 1951). The quotes by Wheeler-Bennett in Passant to O'Neill, Apr. 1, 1952, PRO FO 370/2244 LS3/53; see also Rheindorf to Epstein, Apr. 16, 1952, BArch, N1263, NL Rheindorf, vol. 154. On the UA, including a copy of the article series, see Döscher, *Verschworene Gesellschaft*, 151–245; Maulucci, *Creation and Early History*, 229–30, 258ff.

287 Frh. von Welck, I. Pers. A, Vermerk, Apr. 10, 1952, PA/AA, NL Andres, Paket 1. The dismissal from May 24, 1952 in ibid,

of Andres, Klassen was retained on the staff of the Political Archives.[288] Following Andres's death in 1953, Klassen took over the directorship of the archive.

Officials in both London and Bonn drew lessons from the Klassen incident. Most departments of the British government opposed the return of any of the captured documents.[289] The problematic liaison officer from Bonn and the publicity generated by a Bundestag inquiry on the Auswärtiges Amt's personnel policy increased British awareness of the issue. In May 1952, Alfred Wiener, the founder of the Wiener Library in London, submitted a report to the JCC on the personnel files that had been turned over to Bonn the previous year. Having learned that there were now "remarkable gaps" in the files, Wiener speculated that other records might also be tampered with "if they are not handed over to the right type of people."[290] Wiener's suspicions were shared by the Bundestag's fact-finding committee.[291] In correspondence among themselves, British officials and scholars increasingly cited these circumstances as an argument against the return of the captured records. The staff at the receiving institution, which included a number of pre-1945 employees, could hardly be trusted with records chronicling their actions during the Nazi period.[292]

The Germans, too, learned from the Klassen episode. In the future, all "optical burdens" and sensitive subjects were to be avoided. The archival activities of the Auswärtiges Amt during the war were one such topic. The ministry had dispatched its own archive teams to sift through or

288 Andres, Erklärung, Aug. 20, 1952 and Oct. 11, 1952, both in ibid. Andres certified that Klassen had belonged to a circle of colleagues who "shared a common, inner opposition to National Socialism." He had "never been an opponent of Jews;" in fact, "on the contrary, [he had] in innumerable conversations always sharply denounced the defamation of Jews in the former regime." His presence in Krummhübel was "purely coincidental," and the talk given there had contained "neither National Socialist catchwords nor any sort of anti-Jewish position." Klassen himself was attempting at the time to explain to the personnel department why he joined the party in 1933, membership number 2681767. See Anlage zum Personalbogen, Oct. 30, 1953, PA/AA, B118, vol. 486.

289 A more differentiated account of the positions within the British government follows in the second section of Chapter 3.

290 JCC 46th Meeting, May 7, 1952, PRO FO 370/2269 LS 18/6.

291 The committee chairperson requested the former president of the Higher Regional Court (Oberlandesgericht) Rudolf Schetter not to return the personnel files to the AA that had accrued during a preliminary investigation, "in order to avoid manipulation." See Döscher, *Verschworene Gesellschaft*, 180. Furthermore, the cross-examination of the archive's first directory, Haack, by the Bundestag deputy Hermann Brill (SPD), in BT, Stenographisches Protokoll über die 6. Sitzung des 47. [Untersuchungs-] Ausschusses, Vernehmung des Zeugen Haack, VS, Feb. 13, 1952.

292 For example, in Passant to Noble, June 8, 1953, PRO FO 370/2340 LS5/107. Passant argues here against the transfer of the publication project to Germany by saying "that a number of ex-Nazi officials are known to be working in the present Federal Ministry." The Adenauer quote in Stenographic Report of Untersuchungsausschuß 47 (UA 47), cited by Döscher, *Verschworene Gesellschaft*, 249.

confiscate diplomatic records of conquered countries. In May 1952, ministry officials learned that the historians Erwin Hölzle, Helmut Krausnick, and Ludwig Zimmermann were planning publications based on French records exploited during the war. The three men had been members of the Auswärtiges Amt's Archival Commission, which had copied, excerpted, and seized files from the French Foreign Ministry.[293] Word of the three historians' publication plans in 1952 drew a quick response from the Auswärtiges Amt. Its legal department was not worried about the possible legal repercussions of publishing documents copied during the war, but it did consider Hölzle, Krausnick, and Zimmermann's timing disadvantageous. The negotiations on the captured documents, the ministry's lawyers feared, could be "severely disrupted if materials from French records are published in Germany while [the negotiations] are taking place."[294] The Political Archives insisted, moreover, that the men had studied the papers in an official capacity, not as private individuals, and were thus not in a position to "decide on their own how to use the information acquired from the records at that time."[295] The Auswärtiges Amt decided to forestall trouble by trying to deprive Hölzle, Krausnick, and Zimmermann's projects of funding. The three had submitted grant applications to the German Research Foundation; the Auswärtigs Amt thus informed the foundation's president, Ludwig Raiser, of the possible complications that might arise from publication of their work. Raiser assured the ministry that he would cooperate to help prevent a "mishap."[296] The planned publications, none of which were near completion in 1952, did not appear until the 1970s.[297]

293 The Archival Commission of the AA (AKO) was only *one* of the groups in France interested in public and private archives. Another one was *Gruppe Archivwesen* under the military commander of France, the *Sonderkommando Künsberg*, as well as task forces dispatched by the Potsdam Army Archives (Heeresarchivs Potsdam). The AKO branch office in Paris was run first by Ludwig Zimmermann, then, from February 1943 onward, by Carl Heinrich Walther. In practice, it is hard to keep the members of the various groups apart, because there was a good deal of enmeshing, both of logistic and personnel resources. This becomes clear in Heuss, *Kunst- und Kulturgutraub*, 305–10; auch Kröger/Thimme, "Politisches Archiv," 248f.

294 VLR v. Haeften, Abt. V, Aufzeichnung für Abt. III [v. Nostitz], n.d. [May 1952], PA/AA, B118, vol. 75c.

295 Andres, PA/AA, Aufzeichnung für v. Nostitz und Kordt, May 27, 1952, ibid. Andres believed the historians were in a position to publish their work even without the DFG funds, so he demanded, with a nearly pathological control reflex, that there be a general requirement to first obtain approval for any publication from the AA.

296 Von Nostitz, Aufzeichnung für Abt. V, May 16, 1952, ibid.

297 From the personal papers of Ludwig Zimmermann, Walther Peter Fuchs published *Frankreichs Ruhrpolitik. Von Versailles bis zum Dawesplan* (Göttingen, 1971). The book by Erwin Hölzle appeared in 1975: *Die Selbstentmachtung Europas. Das Experiment des Friedens vor und nach dem Ersten Weltkrieg. Unter Verwertung unveröffentlichter, zum Teil verlorengegangener deutscher und französischer Dokumente* (Göttingen, 1975). In the prefaces of both books the authors mention the special circumstances surrounding the sources they used.

German Participation in Documents on German Foreign Policy. Among the questions the British and American note of July 6, 1951, posed for the Auswärtiges Amt was whether to accept the invitation to appoint "a German scholar" as a co-editor of *Documents on German Foreign Policy*. Officials at the Political Archives immediately fixed on the use of the singular. How could a single scholar master the flood of records without a staff? Andres raised this subject in July 1951 at a meeting with an American representative of the High Commission, who thereupon assured him that the July 6 note referred solely to the appointment of an editor and that it would be left fully to the discretion of the Federal Republic to decide how many research assistants should accompany the scholar appointed to that position.[298] Klassen also was told during his London visit that there would be a team of German assistants and that the German editor-in-chief would have a standing equal to his British and American counterparts.[299] The question was not as simple as the Americans would have the Germans believe, however. Whereas Noble thought it would be entirely reasonable for the German co-editor to have a staff of three assistants, Passant used the question of research assistants to postpone, if not entirely prevent, German participation. He argued for a literal reading of the July 6 note: *one* German scholar would be allowed to work on *Documents on German Foreign Policy*. He acted on the assumption that the Germans would find this unacceptable. Thinking along similar lines, the French representative backed Passant.[300] The Americans, British, and French resolved this dispute in March 1952, without having said a word about it to the Germans. Noble prevailed: the German editor would have a staff of assistants.[301]

Another issue linked to German participation arose in early 1952.[302] The project was experiencing financial difficulties. The personnel and printing costs of the German-language volumes of *Documents on German Foreign Policy* were covered from the funds the West Germans paid toward the costs of the Allied occupation.[303] That source would disappear once the

298 Andres, Aufzeichnung [on the AHC meeting of July 24], July 26, 1951, PA/AA, B118, vol. 489.

299 Klassen, Aufzeichnung, Mar. 24, 1952, PA/AA, B118, vol. 507.

300 Noble, Office Memorandum, Problems Relating to the German Foreign Office Archives Project, Mar. 31, 1952; [meeting protocol], Captured German documents in Allied hands outside Germany, Feb. 26, 1952: "Mr. Passant questioned the propriety of saying to any German authority that we wished to get an editorial team to join the project. The offer of 6th July was . . . for a single German scholar to co-operate with the Allied editors in chief. . . . M. Giraudet supported the U.K. point of view firmly." Both in NA RG 59, Lot File 78D441, Historical Office, box 4.

301 Record of a Meeting in Mr. Passant's Room, Mar. 3 and 4, 1952, both in PRO FO 370/2244 LS3/38.

302 Klassen, London, Aufzeichnung, Mar. 7, 1952, PA/AA, B118, vol. 489.

303 In return, the Allies each distributed 500 copies to public facilities in their zones, while the remaining copies were offered for sale.

Bonn Conventions went into force. With that in mind, Noble suggested early in the spring of 1952 that Bonn should be encouraged not only to accept the Allied offer of July 1951 but also to assume the costs of the German volumes.[304] Bonn would, in other words, remain the source of the funding on an ostensibly voluntary basis once the convention was enacted. The funding question grew more pressing at the beginning of 1953. The new administration of President Dwight D. Eisenhower announced the onset of an era of "less government" and budget-cutting. This new policy affected the budget of the State Department's Historical Office.[305] With the new Republican-controlled Congress critically examining all the ambitious projects initiated under the previous administration, it would have been unwise for the State Department to seek funding for the publication of the German edition of *Documents on German Foreign Policy*. Consequently, Noble informed his London colleague that the U.S. government could not assume the cost of the German edition, which would make Bonn's participation essential.[306] Meanwhile, time was running out for the West Germans. The longer they waited to respond to the July 6, 1951, note, the further the editors at Whaddon Hall progressed in selecting documents for the coming volumes, the less opportunity a German editor would have to influence editorial decisions.

That fear was voiced by Kurt Rheindorf in his correspondence with Hans Andres. He doubted that a German editor would still be able to influence the selection and scope of documents to be published. He also related the suspicion that the "German representative was to serve more as a potential scapegoat than as a true colleague."[307] As was often the case, Rheindorf's views found their way into the Political Archives' memos and became part of the ministry's internal discussion. Members of the legal department raised these concerns with Noble. In response, Noble suggested a reasonable solution: in each volume in which Germans participated, a statement could be added "that responsibility was not assumed for the volumes having appeared to date."[308] This suggestion was all but ignored, however, as the key decision-makers at the Auswärtiges Amt were firmer than ever in their opposition to accepting the Allied offer. Reflecting on

---

304 Noble to Lewis, German Affairs, and Russell, Public Affairs, Mar. 18, 1952, NA RG 59, CDF 1950–1954, 862.423/3–1852.
305 Even the office's own edition, *Foreign Relations of the United States* (FRUS), felt the budget cuts. See Zala, *Zensur*, 117.
306 Noble to Passant, Apr. 23, 1953, PRO FO 370/2339 LS5/80.
307 Rheindorf to Andres, Feb. 12, 1952, BArch, N1263, NL Rheindorf, vol. 148.
308 VLR v. Grolmann, Blomeyer, Abt. V, Aufzeichnung für Mosler [on a conversation with Noble], May 13, 1953, PA/AA, B118, vol. 508.

that opposition a few years later, Walter Hallstein presented the situation as if the Allies had actually demanded that the German editor endorse all the volumes already published. "Whether it would have been politically right and advantageous to the interest of German scholarship," Hallstein wrote to the minister of the interior, "to have a single German scholar retroactively associate his name with this enterprise, whose conception had already been planned, is highly doubtful." German acceptance of the terms of the July offer, he believed, would not have provided "free access to the records for German historical researchers." Whaddon Hall would not have opened its doors to German historians, and "recent German history would continue to be written in London and Washington without decisive German impact." He failed to add that regular British and American historians were not allowed at Whaddon Hall either unless they were part of the editorial team.[309]

The Refusal. By May 1952, officials at the Auswärtiges Amt had decided against the Allied invitation to name a German co-editor of *Documents on German Foreign Policy*. Instead, they planned to offer a counterproposal: the project as a whole should be moved from Whaddon Hall to Gymnich Castle outside Cologne.[310] Archivist Heinrich Valentin had been the first to suggest that the Allies should be persuaded to relocate the project. "The entire task could thus take on a different aura," he argued. "The German location alone would compel [the editorial staff] to become absorbed in the spirit and landscape of German history and German popular mentality [*Volksmentalität*] in a completely different way, and thereby to eliminate the anti-German prejudices that underlie the work and to arrive at an enhanced objectivity and an understanding that more closely approach reality."[311] The historians working on *Documents on German Foreign Policy* would undoubtedly have questioned whether direct exposure to the *Volksmentalität* of the 1950s would help them understand documents from the Nazi era and thus bring them closer to historical reality.

The idea to move the project was prompted by Klassen's report from Whaddon Hall in March 1952. After the project staff had explained the organization of the editorial work to him, Klassen estimated that, given the fact that only four volumes had appeared by that point, the full project – series A through D – would not be completed for another twenty to thirty years. He advised Bonn not to accept a "link between the question

---

309 Hallstein to Bleek, Apr. 19, 1955, PA/AA, B118, vol. 28.
310 See the second section of Chapter 4.
311 Valentin, Aufzeichnung, June [sic] 27, 1951, PA/AA, B118, vol 31.

of restitution and that of the publication of records."[312] During his stay at Whaddon Hall, Klassen still assumed that the Allied offer would be accepted, but in May 1952, the Auswärtiges Amt informed the Ministry of the Interior that the Allies had proposed an unacceptable deal linking the return of the captured documents to the publication project and recommended that the proposal be rejected. For its part, the Auswärtiges Amt had decided "to make the restitution of all its records now the prerequisite for participation in the Allied publication project."[313]

As resistance to the idea of participating in the *Documents on German Foreign Policy* project became firmer, so too did opposition to accepting the offer of microfilms and the immediate return of certain groups of records. The German historical profession, which Bonn claimed it wanted to help, was left empty-handed. Indeed, the Auswärtiges Amt appears to have worked against, not with, the historians. When individual scholars tried to obtain filmed documents from Whaddon, the Auswärtiges Amt intervened to block them. The Institute for Contemporary History (IfZ), for example, asked the head of the Culture Department at the Interior Ministry, Paul Egon Hübinger, to facilitate the purchase of a microfilm copy of Stresemann's personal papers. Officials at the Auswärtiges Amt deliberately misinterpreted the request and acted as if the IfZ had suggested that microfilms be accepted instead of the original records. The use of these microfilms in Germany, the Auswärtiges Amt maintained, would be equivalent to accepting the status quo, if not de facto, approval of the Allies' seizure and publication of German government documents.[314] The ministry's response to the IfZ did not mention the unequivocal assurances given beforehand by a British representative of the High Commission that the microfilms were regarded as only a temporary solution. "It was not the intention that they should replace the original archives . . . which it was the ultimate intention to return."[315]

312 Klassen, London, Aufzeichnung, Mar. 7 and Mar. 17, 1952, both in PA/AA, B118, vol. 489; quote is taken from Aufzeichnung, Mar. 21, 1952, PA/AA, B118, vol. 507.

313 Andres and Klassen, draft letter from AA to the ministry of interior, May 1952, PA/AA, B118, vol. 489.

314 Kluke, IfZ, to Hübinger, BMI, Leiter Abt. III (Kultur), July 23, 1954 and Stellungnahme Klassen, Aug. 25, 1954, both in PA/AA, B118, vol. 489; Blankenhorn to Hübinger, Nov. 6, 1954 and Vermerk Hübinger, July 27, 1954, both in BArch, B106, vol. 34723/3. The Auswärtiges Amt upheld its position on microfilms to the very end. Despite this, the IfZ did obtain microfilms by 1952, for example of the personal papers of Seeckt and Groener. See the draft letter to Bundespräsident Theodor Heuss, Dec. 1, 1952, IfZ Hausarchiv, ID1, vol. 5; Ullrich to Kluke, Feb. 8, 1957, ibid., ID103, vol. 1: "The AA does not intend to facilitate the purchase of microfilms produced by the Allies."

315 Dugald Malcolm, Chairman of Allied Delegation, Record of a Meeting of Representatives of the AHC and the Federal Government, Oct. 31, 1952, NA RG 59, CDF 1950–54, 862.423/11–552. In the German protocol for the same meeting, this claim of Malcolm's is not documented,

For once, the archivists at the Bundesarchiv agreed with their colleagues at the Political Archives. The purchase of microfilms was "politically imper-missible" because it would "mean for all practical purposes that Germany acknowledged the withholding and piratical exploitation of confiscated German records to the benefit of foreign researchers and institutes."[316] The microfilming of German documents was particularly aggravating to the archivists. It meant loss of control. Microfilms outside their custodianship made the elaborate requirements governing document access at an archive "invalid"; it would become "impossible to supervise the presentation of Auswärtiges Amt records to scholarly researchers."[317]

Not only did it refuse to facilitate the purchase of microfilmed docu-ments, but the Auswärtiges Amt also denied assistance to historians who wanted to travel to London to study captured German documents at the Public Record Office. When Werner Conze requested to have his applica-tion to use the London archive forwarded through diplomatic channels as required at that time, the Auswärtigs Amt refused. The ministry explained that the integration of German records into the holdings of British and American public archives and libraries could not be condoned and that supporting applications such as Conze's "would be tantamount to approval" of the Allies' actions.[318]

Bonn finally replied to the High Commission's offer of July 6, 1951, in November 1952 and firmly rejected the Allies' proposals. Adenauer acknowledged the offers to return some holdings immediately and to supply microfilm copies of others "with satisfaction" but nonetheless declined them and insisted instead "that the time has come to replace what was considered a provisional solution with a permanent agreement." The Allied offer, the chancellor maintained, should be revised accordingly. Adenauer repeated the demand for the immediate return of all diplomatic records of the pre-1945 Auswärtiges Amt, the possession of which by the Allies was "no longer justifiable" for legal and political reasons. He also acknowledged the Allied wish not to interrupt work on the *Document on German Foreign Policy* project, but was convinced that the transfer of the files to Germany could be conducted without hindering this work. As for the invitation to name a

---

tellingly, because it no longer fit into the picture in Bonn. Included are only the comments by Alois Tichy that films are not an acceptable substitute. The German protocol is found in PA/AA, B118, vol. 507.

316 Winter, BArch, to Hübinger, Dec. 2, 1954, BArch, B106, Bd. 34723/3.

317 Stellungnahme Klassen, Aug. 25, 1954, PA/AA, B118, vol. 489. On the topic of access to records and the loss of control, see the second part of chapter 5.

318 Conze to VLR von Graevenitz, Feb. 19, 1954, and Prill to Conze, Feb. 9, 1955, both in PA/AA, B118, vol. 487. Conze did end up working at the PRO years later. See Conze to Johannes Ullrich, Nov. 12, 1959, PA/AA, B118, vol. 237.

German scholar to serve as a co-editor, Adenauer said the Federal Republic would participate "in the scholarly evaluation of the records" and pay the costs of the German edition "following their restitution." In view of the recent Klassen debacle, Adenauer's response to the High Commission made no mention of the invitation to appoint a liaison officer.[319]

The Auswärtiges Amt's response to the High Commission's note of July 6, 1951, rested on what can be described only as a deliberate misreading. Having issued a categorical demand for the return of the diplomatic files, officials at the Auswärtiges Amt had no interest in trying to understand the Allied proposal. When the Social Democratic Bundestag deputy Fritz Erler asked in the spring of 1955 where things stood in regard to the return of the captured documents, the response he received from the Auswärtiges Amt reflected this skewed interpretation of the July 6 note. The Allies, Erler was told, had demanded that Bonn agree to the "retention of the records important to the work of the AA until the publication project was completed." "Only under this condition" would the Allies have turned over the older diplomatic records and allowed *one* German historian to participate in the project.[320]

319 Adenauer to Walter J. Donnelly, acting chairman of the AHC, Nov. 22, 1952, PA/AA, B118, vol. 509; English version in NA RG 59 CDF 1950–54, 862.423/12–452.

320 Löns, Abt. II, to Fritz Erler, April 14, 1955, PA/AA, B118, vol. 28; emphasis added.

3

The Positions of the United States and Britain

The number of American government agencies with an interest in the captured German records had by no means decreased since the end of the war. Those agencies that had participated in the seizure of records were drawn into the deliberations about the documents' future disposition. In January 1950, the State Department established an interdepartmental working group, the Interagency Conference on Captured Enemy Documentation. Its purpose was to compile an overview of the location of all German records held by U.S. government agencies and departments. The working group shifted its focus toward framing a return policy in 1951 after the British government announced a policy of its own in February of that year and as Bonn became more insistent in demanding the return of the captured documents. Before the creation of the Interagency Conference on Captured Enemy Documentation, only a few U.S. governmental agencies had inventoried the German documents in their possession or given thought to what should be done with them in the long term. Only the Library of Congress and the National Archives had already confronted the problem. It took the Interagency Conference two years to work out guidelines for a return policy. Interest in the German military records as an intelligence source revived with the outbreak of war in Korea; consequently, the talks about their return were suspended from the summer of 1950 until early 1951. It was not until October 1952 that the working group issued its policy guidelines on captured records. In the meantime, the State Department faced a dilemma: it had no policy yet to decide on the disposition of any captured documents but, for political reasons, sought to accommodate West German demands before such guidelines were issued. In the search for

169

a solution to this dilemma, State Department officials turned to the only documents under their immediate jurisdiction, the Auswärtiges Amt files, and tried to make concessions, against the wishes of the historians working at Whaddon Hall. They also tried repeatedly to fulfill German requests for specific groups of records. That resulted in a series of ad hoc returns. The Germans might have made more effective use of the State Department's willingness to facilitate the return of documents on an ad hoc basis had they not been so fixated on categorically insisting upon the restitution of all captured documents. The following section outlines the varying positions of U.S. government agencies on the issue of the captured documents. Those positions shifted as the war in Korea and the debate on German rearmament transformed the political context of the American policy debate on these records.

The First Attempt to Formulate a Return Policy

The Interagency Conference met for the first time on January 25, 1950, under the direction of Bernard Noble. Representatives of the Army, the Navy, and the Departments of Commerce, Justice, and State were in attendance along with officials from the National Archives. They were later joined by representatives of the Air Force, the CIA, the Joint Chiefs of Staff, and the Library of Congress.[1] At the first meeting, Noble asked the participants to describe their agencies' holdings of captured records, to explain the way the records had been used and were to be used in the future, and to report any existing agreements with other authorities or with the British. Noble went on to request that each agency develop a proposal for what should be done with the documents in its possession in the long run.[2] Although the agencies were quick to comply, the spectrum of opinion made it clear that the process to reach a consensus would be a long one.[3]

The discussion of the captured documents in the early 1950s rested on the assumption that, despite the Cold War, the four Allied powers and Germany would sign a peace treaty. The prohibition on German rearmament was still in force.[4] For the U.S. Army representatives, it was therefore

1 Minutes. Interagency Conference on Captured German Documents, Jan. 25, 1950 and Mar. 15, 1950, both in NA RG 407, entry 360, box 3609.
2 Interagency Conference, Agenda, Jan. 25, 1950, ibid.
3 Statements from the Central Air Documents Office, Navy, Department of Commerce, Library of Congress, National Archives, Office of Alien Property at the Justice Department, Department of the Army from February 1950, ibid.
4 See Schwengler, *Souveränität und Sicherheit*, 357. Deviating from this official Allied line, the planning staffs of the U.S. Army had been playing through the various constellations since December 1949, in which the participation of German troops was included. See Rupieper, *Besetzter Verbündeter*, 100.

clear that *no* military records would be returned to Germany. The confiscation of military material had always rested on the idea that "records are a weapon of war."[5] Consequently, retaining possession of German military records was considered a part of Allied demilitarization policy. The material was to be withheld from the German government permanently to prevent rearmament.[6] The files held at the German Military Documents Section at Camp Ritchie were handled accordingly. During processing for intelligence purposes, they were earmarked for "permanent custody."[7] The Army Department assumed "that it can impose anything it wants in the Peace Treaty, and one of the things that should be imposed is our rights in connection with captured records."[8] That view carried considerable weight because the Army was responsible for approximately 800 tons of captured military records administered by the Departmental Records Branch (DRB) of the Adjutant General's Office (AGO).[9]

The Army called attention to two further obstacles to the documents' return. The first was the Bissell-Sinclair Agreement with the British, which prohibited the U.S. Army from unilaterally deciding the fate of records confiscated during the phase of the joint high command (SHAEF). The second was the problem of security classification. The sheer volume of documents Allied troops had come upon made it impossible to undertake

5 "The military policy of protecting important captured enemy records from avoidable destruction, loss or damage is based on the sound knowledge that records are a weapon of war. There is great awareness of the value of records at SHAEF. . . . " Fred W. Shipman, Adviser on Archives to the War Department, and Wayne C. Grover, Chief, Records Management Branch, Adjutant General's Office, Memorandum: Captured German Enemy Records, Nov. 26, 1944, NA RG 242, AGAR-S no. 1101, box 2.

6 Control Council Directive no. 18 (Discharge and Dissolution of the German Armed Forces), Nov. 12, 1945, *Official Gazette of the Control Council for Germany*, 3, Jan. 31, 1946.

7 MIRS. History and Operations. London and Washington Branches, May 1, 1943–July 14, 1945, 5, 14f., NA RG 242, AGAR-S no. 1500, box 5.

8 Minutes, Interagency Conference, Mar. 15, 1950, NA RG 407, entry 360, box 3609.

9 Within the Army Department, the Adjutant General was responsible for records in the custody of the Army. The Departmental Records Branch functioned much like an interim archive. It stored the registries of the Army for a limited period, selected the material considered worth archiving, which was sent subsequently to the National Archives. The DRB maintained a Historical Branch, which supplied the official military historiography projects with records. The administration of captured records, especially in such massive dimensions as occurred after the Second World War, was unprecedented. In 1947, the Adjutant General assumed responsibility for the German Military Documents Section (GMDS) from G-2, Intelligence. In 1953, GMDS became the Captured Records Section (CRS) within the DRB. The director was Herman G. Goldbeck; the head of the DRB was Sherrod East. In 1958, the DRB was transferred in its entirety (personnel, records, and nearly all functions) to the National Archives (then known as the General Service Administration, GSA) and was established there as the World War II Records Division. On the work and administrative history of the DRB, see East, "Prototype"; Rohr, "Mikroverfilmung," 251f.; on the history of the GMDS itself, see Goldbeck, "GMDS"; the mission of the CRS is described in Memorandum: The Control and Servicing of Captured World War II Records Seized by the United States Army and Presently Deposited in DRB, AGO, January 1957, NA RG 242, AGAR-S no. 1575, box 6.

any sort of selection at the time of confiscation. All captured records were therefore given the blanket classification of "confidential."[10] Declassification could not proceed without British approval, military authorities noted, to say nothing of the personnel needed to carry out such a labor-intensive task.[11]

Other government agencies raised more specific problems. The first meetings of the Interagency Conference were devoted mainly to legal issues. Discussion centered on the status of German records under international law and the status of German property, which was deemed "enemy property" under American law.[12] The Justice Department's Office of Alien Property (OAP) had transferred copyrights and exploitation rights to the U.S. government within the framework of the Trading with the Enemy Act.[13] This process of "vesting" placed the legal title in the possession of the U.S. government[14] and thereby protected American users of German documents, patents, and literary works from possible damage claims by the former owners. During the Interagency Conference discussions, the OAP pointed out repeatedly that only a fraction of German documents had been subjected to the vesting process and that vesting more captured documents would be neither efficient nor useful.[15] Should it become politically expedient to return German records, a vesting order would be legally counterproductive because "no restitution of vested property . . . may be effected."[16] There

---

10 The Bissell-Sinclair Agreement is reprinted in Eckert, *Kampf um die Akten,* 466–72. The security classifications were "confidential," "restricted," "secret," and "top secret." See also Goldbeck, "GMDS," 33f.

11 Minutes, Interagency Conference, Jan. 25, 1950, NA RG 407, entry 360, box 3609.

12 The legal issues are dealt with in the first section of Chapter 4.

13 The Office of Alien Property at the Justice Department was the successor to the independent office of the Alien Property Custodian during the war. The director of the OAP held the rank of Assistant Attorney General. See Kreikamp, *Deutsches Vermögen,* 38; on the Trading with the Enemy Act, ibid., 20–7.

14 Unlike the procedure of "vesting" property, the legal step of "freezing assets" does not involve the transfer of legal ownership. Instead, ownership remains intact but the property is not accessible to the owner for a certain period of time. OAP was permitted to confiscate state property as well as private, literary, artistic, and scientific property through vesting. A vesting order could only be issued against a legally defined owner. On the jurisdiction and rights of the OAP, see Department of Justice, OAP: Summary Statement of the Jurisdiction and Policies of the OAP with Reference to Literary, Scientific and Artistic Works of Enemy Origin, Feb. 18, 1953, NA RG 64, Records of the National Archives, Planning and Control Cases, box PC-62. On American policy of confiscating German private property at the end of the war and later, see Kreikamp, *Deutsches Vermögen,* 24–43; on the vesting of copyrights, see Plunder and Restitution, SR 58–65.

15 Harold I. Baynton, Acting Director, OAP, Dept. of Justice, Memorandum to [the] Interagency Conference on Captured Enemy Documentation, Feb. 24, 1950; Revision of Statement of Justice [Dept.] as reported in the minutes of meeting March 15, 1950, Interagency Conference, n.d. [May 1950], both in NA RG 407, entry 360, box 3609.

16 "By virtue of section 39 of the Trading with the Enemy Act, as amended, no restitution of vested property to Germany or Japan, or nationals thereof, may be effected. . . . Therefore, in general, the

was no way to revoke a vesting order.[17] Governmental protection against possible claims from former owners of German patents, copyrights, and documents thus quickly became a central issue in the Interagency Conference's discussions of policy guidelines. This was particularly important for the Department of Commerce because it had made documents seized at German industrial and research facilities available to American companies.[18]

The only institutions that had considered the issue of restitution before the start of the Interagency Conference discussions were the National Archives and the Library of Congress. The U.S. Army had turned over materials seized from the Army Archive in Potsdam to the National Archives. These records included the personal papers of the generals Gneisenau, Scharnhorst, Seeckt, and Groener as well as a few "Hitler items," such as his private will and political testaments.[19] Wayne C. Grover, Archivist of the United States, wanted to return the historical documents sooner rather than later.[20] No professional archivist doubted that these papers belonged in a German archive. In a British review of the *Guide to Captured German Documents*,[21] Grover came under fire precisely because his institution possessed historical papers belonging to another archive.[22] But Grover had in fact attempted to turn those papers over to the Germans. When it became clear that the Interagency Conference would not settle on a return policy

rights in German and Japanese material subject to copyright which have been vested cannot be returned, and by the same token neither can the physical property which has been vested." Ibid.

17 When the son of Hitler's photographer Heinrich Hoffmann demanded the return in 1951 of the collection of his father's photos and other material from the period 1920 to 1944, which had landed in American hands, the Office of the Adjutant General prompted the OAP to issue a vesting order and thus blocked the threat posed by Hoffmann's claims. The documentation on the episode, including Vesting Order no. 17952 is found in NA RG 407, entry 369, box 3.

18 Department of Commerce, Office of Technical Services, Report on Holdings of Captured Enemy Documentation, February 1950, NA RG 407, entry 360, box 3906.

19 Preliminary Inventory of the German Records 1679–1945 in the World War II Collection of Seized Enemy Records. Compiled by Martin Rogin. (Prelim. Inventory Nr. 24). Washington, D. C.: The National Archives 1950, NA RG 242, AGAR-S no. 1205, box 2.

20 "As an archival agency the National Archives is strongly in favor of restitution to successor governments of those bodies of governmental archives that may be returned without violating military and political policies of this Government." Ibid.

21 *Guide to Captured German Documents.* (War Documentation Project. Study No. 1). Prepared by Gerhard L. Weinberg. Maxwell Air Force Base, Alabama: December 1952.

22 Elisabeth R. Poyser, "Review [of Guide to CGD]," *Journal of the Society of Archivists* [GB] 1 (1955–59), 53f.: "The question may be permitted whether the authorities of the National Archives propose to remain the perpetual custodian of what is listed (p. 61) under 'RG 242,' a composite unit of the Heeresarchiv Potsdam containing, i.a., not only documents regarding Schlieffen plan and Hans von Seeckt papers, but also appreciable accumulations of records of the 7-Years, Napoleonic and Franco-Prussian wars." Poyser also criticized the Library of Congress for holding several documents that she argued were clearly German cultural treasures. Among others, she named the 1774 charter for the Free Mason Grand Lodge of Germany, issued by Frederick II. This document was returned in September 1998. See also the mention made by Vollmer, "Deutsche Archivalien im Nationalarchiv Washington".

quickly, Grover requested special permission from the Adjutant General to return the materials from the German Army Archive immediately. He was instructed, however, to wait until an official policy was in place.[23]

The Library of Congress was yet another participant in the talks initiated by the State Department. The reason it was allowed to sit at the negotiation table in the first place was due to the holdings – primarily books, but also archival material and registries – it had received from the Army since 1945. In the autumn of 1945, the Library had sent a delegation to Germany with the aim of re-establishing lost relations to booksellers. The Library of Congress Mission was the only American library delegation recognized by the military government and exempted from the Trading with the Enemy Act. In association with 113 American research libraries, in what was known as the Cooperative Acquisition Project, the Mission was to buy books to fill the gaps in holdings for the years 1939 to 1945. At the same time, the Mission assisted the Army in formulating and implementing Order No. 4 of the Allied Control Council from May 1946. The order authorized retroactively the "denazification" of public libraries.[24] The Army soon viewed the library delegation as a suitable place to unload excess material, a view the Library of Congress was quite willing to encourage.[25] Even before the talks started in January 1950, the Library returned book holdings to Germany that had been falsely confiscated as Nazi literature.[26] At the start of the talks, it proposed the restitution of additional holdings.[27]

The willingness on the part of the National Archives and the Library of Congress to return captured German materials did little to help the State Department in its efforts to accommodate Bonn. A real breakthrough would not be possible without the collaboration of the Department of

---

23 Grover to Maj. Gen. E. F. Witsell, The Adjutant General, Army Dept., Feb. 1, 1951; Witsell to Grover, Mar. 14, 1951, both in NA RG 407, entry 360, box 3609.

24 Stieg, "Postwar Purge of German Public Libraries." On the Library of Congress Mission, there is to date only Gassert/Mattern, *Hitler Library*, 8–11; Waite, "Returning Jewish Cultural Property."

25 The holdings of the LoC at that time are in *Guide to Captured German Documents*, (War Documentation Project. Study No. 1). Prepared by Gerhard L. Weinberg. Maxwell Air Force Base, Alabama: December 1952, 30–60.

26 In 1948, 190 crates of books belonging to the *Weltkriegsbücherei* (World War Library) Stuttgart, the later *Bibliothek für Zeitgeschichte* (Library of Contemporary History), were given back, as were about 98,000 books and brochures from the library of the *Deutsche Arbeitsfront* (German Labour Front) that had originally been plundered from trade union libraries. In the fall of 1949, 28 crates with records from the *Reichspatentamt* (Reich Patent Office) were returned. See Report on Holdings of Captured Enemy Documentation. The Library of Congress, February 1950, NA RG 407, entry 360, box 3609.

27 Reference was being made to approximately 4,300 books that once belonged to the Japan Institute (est. 1926, Berlin) and were being reserved for the *Westdeutsche Bibliothek* in Marburg. Furthermore, the LoC also listed books that "could be returned" as the 3,383 books from the Hitler library, which however were never turned over, and the so-called "Eva Braun Collection" of 80 items. See ibid.

the Army, which was in possession of the overwhelming majority of the captured German files. With the onset of war in Korea in June 1950, the U.S. military suddenly viewed the German military records as a hot source of intelligence once again, namely on the Soviet Union and the Red Army. The interdepartmental talks on the captured files were interrupted for several months as result.

Korea. As early as 1946, many in the intelligence community in Washington assumed that there was nothing more to be learned from the German military records,[28] and some military and intelligence officials suggested that at least some of the material might be declassified and made available to historians and interested civilians.[29] At the opening of the Interagency Conference talks in 1950, Sherrod East, head of the Departmental Records Branch, declared, "Primarily, the Intelligence interest is gone in connection with the documents in question. As far as the Department of the Army and CIA are concerned, the interest has passed from Intelligence to Historical."[30]

The Korean War put an end to such talk. The use of the captured records for intelligence purposes increased rapidly.[31] Officials at the Departmental Records Branch now considered the German materials "one of the most valuable sources of intelligence information in matters pertaining to the USSR."[32] Before the first U-2 reconnaissance flights flew over Soviet territory in 1956, for example, the U.S. military relied heavily on the maps of the Soviet Union produced by the Wehrmacht.[33] The Army's intelligence division (G-2) drew upon the captured records in its studies on various

28 Oliver W. Holmes from the National Archives inspected the GMDS at Camp Ritchie in January 1946. The officer on duty explained "that the Intelligence research projects now in progress on the German records are scheduled for completion about June 1 [1946]. . . . He also said that the immediate objectives of G-2 [Intelligence] would then be served and they would be willing to relinquish their responsibility for the records. Obviously, the next important user of the records would be the Historical Division." Holmes, Report of Trip to Camp Ritchie, MD, to Inspect Captured German and Japanese Documents, Dec. 24. 1946, NA RG 242, AGAR-S no. 703, box 2.

29 This idea was supported especially by the Historical Division of the U.S. Army. See A. F. Clark, Deputy Chief, Historical Division, Disposition Form, to Director of Intelligence, Jan. 2, 1947; also JCS 950/20, May 21, 1948: Report by the Joint Intelligence Committee to the Joint Chiefs of Staff on Downgrading of Captured German Documents of Joint and Combined Interest, both in NA RG 319, entry 1018, box 1. See also Goldbeck, "GMDS," 33f.

30 [Minutes], Interagency Conference, Jan. 25, 1950, NA RG 407, entry 360, box 3609.

31 Herman Goldbeck, head of the Captured Records Section at the DRB, speaks in hindsight of an increase of use of about 300 percent. See his draft of an article from June 1956, NA RG 407, entry 371F, box 13. In addition, without figures, Goldbeck, "GMDS," 38.

32 East, Chief, DRB, Office Memorandum for the Chief of Military History, July 26, 1951, NA RG 407, entry 369, box 3.

33 Kahn, "Secrets of Nazi Archives," 53.

aspects of Soviet military strategy. A list of such studies compiled in 1955 reflects the general upswing in interest.[34] Of the sixty-six studies listed, twenty had been written in 1945–46 and forty-six in 1951–52. The impact of the war in Korea was evident in the topics addressed. Whereas the earlier reports dealt with aspects of German military organization, strategy, and technology (e.g., "German Permanent Fortifications," "German Training Methods," "German Army Mobilization"), those written in 1951–52, dealt solely with the Red Army (e.g., "Evolution of Soviet Tactics in WWII," "Soviet Army Group Operations Through Poland, the Balkans and East Germany," "The Soviet Army in Elastic Defense, Rostov Area").

Other research projects using German records were also initiated in the period between 1950 and 1952. One example is the War Documentation Project (WDP) at Columbia University, which had been commissioned by the U.S. Air Force.[35] The project was divided into two phases. During the first phase, a register of the captured records held by private research institutions and universities as well as by government agencies was prepared. In the search for documents, special attention was given to German and Soviet files that might yield information on the psychological warfare strategies used on the eastern front.[36] The Departmental Records Branch found this project very advantageous because about 40 percent of the military records in its custody had not yet been adequately evaluated as of the spring of 1951.[37] In the second phase of the WDP, which commenced in the spring of 1952, the project staff produced studies on topics such as the German military government, Russian collaboration, Russian tactics of resistance, and the strategy of the Germany army to combat partisan warfare on the eastern front.[38]

---

34 The list "Army Studies Based in Whole or in Part on Captured Records" was attached to a letter to Robert F. Kennedy, dated Apr. 1, 1955. Kennedy had asked about using captured records in his function as Chief Counsel for the Senate Permanent Subcommittee on Investigations at the Adjutant General's Office. The AGO used this list to justify the administrative expenses for the custody of German records. NA RG 407, entry 360, box 3609.

35 More specifically the study was commissioned by The Human Resources Research Institute (HRRI) of Air University, Maxwell Air Force Base, Alabama, and carried out by the Bureau of Applied Social Research, Columbia University. On the complicated administrative structure of the WDP, see Hans J. Epstein, Project Officer, Psychological Warfare Directorate, HRRI, Maxwell Air Base: Projected Organization of WDP Phase II, n.d. [early 1952], NA RG 407, entry 369, box 4.

36 Fritz T. Epstein, WDP Progress Report II, Apr. 30, 1952, NA RG 407, entry 369, box 4.

37 In the *Journal of Significant Events*, the daily journal of the DRB, the entry by Philipp Brower on Apr. 26, 1951, reads: "I mentioned [at a meeting] that about 40% of our captured records were not adequately cataloged."

38 F. O. Carroll, Director, HRRI, Maxwell Air Base, A Statement on the WDP, Phase II, May 15, 1952, NA RG 407, entry 369, box 4. Raul Hilberg, who worked on the project as a graduate student, wrote in his memoir *The Politics of Memory*, 72: "As I understood our mission, we were engaged in target research, not merely or even primarily physical targets but all the strengths and weaknesses of the USSR, including the morale of the Red Army and the civilian population. No

If the Korean War interrupted American efforts to formulate a policy on returning captured German military records, it also helped set the return of the records in motion. Even before the conflict in East Asia, the NATO member states had begun to contemplate the rearmament of West Germany.[39] The Korean War was the catalyst for the decision to have the Federal Republic contribute to the defense efforts of the Western alliance. That decision, in turn, had a direct impact on the issue of the captured documents, above all the military records. In early 1951, the Departmental Records Branch (DRB) prepared itself for a new situation:

The political milieu has changed. The total picture may well require the return to Germany of everything possible. For example, if the German Government insists, as one of its conditions prior to assigning German Troops to SHAPE, that to repair German honor and prestige properties and records taken from Germany be returned to it, Nazi-tainted or otherwise, there is little that foreign [policy] planners can do but accede. In other words, Germany now holds in Europe the balance between EAST and WEST and she will . . . use it for all it is worth. Records become an insignificant factor to us in such a situation.[40]

Although this assessment overestimates the strength of the German negotiating position, it does mark a change in policy on the captured records. The Army Department, represented by DRB head Sherrod East, became the driving force behind the formulation of interdepartmental policy guidelines. It strove to make the wording of the policy paper flexible enough to guarantee the United States full control over the return of records. The Federal Republic was to receive what it needed for its envisioned defense contribution. At the same time, no records were to be handed over that were still of interest to the United States for intelligence and military history purposes. In other words, Bonn would be served "as may become appropriate in furtherance of U.S. interests."[41]

objective, however, was clearly spelled out for us, and our aims remained murky." On adapting German techniques of countering partisan warfare, see Gerlach, *Kalkulierte Morde*, 1051f.

39 Planning on the American side, including the tension between the State and Defense Departments is studied by Rupieper, *Besetzter Verbündeter*, 98–139; the British perspective in Gossel, *Briten, Deutsche und Europa*, 47–64; and Dockrill, *Britain's Policy for West German Rearmament*; Köhler, *Adenauer*, 611–41, strongly emphasizes Adenauer's own initiative to have Germany contribute to a common defense.

40 SJP [Seymour J. Pomrenze], DRB, Office Memo, Mar. 7, 1951, NA RG 407, entry 360, box 3609. SHAPE = Supreme Headquarters Allied Powers Europe.

41 Memorandum by the Chief of Staff, U.S. Army, for the Joint Chiefs of Staff on Restitution or Other Disposition of Captured Enemy (i.e. German) Records, Mar. 30, 1951, Enclosure to JCS 1133/5, Apr. 4, 1951, NA RG 407, entry 360, box 3609.

The Second Attempt to Formulate a Return Policy, 1951. The Interagency Conference talks resumed in early 1951 under these new political circumstances. In preparation for a meeting of the conference scheduled for February 1951, Noble surveyed each of the participating agencies on its views on returning the captured documents. He himself was firmly convinced that records should be returned as soon as possible and focused his efforts on working out an "orderly and efficient program of restitution."[42] At the February meeting, he tried to persuade the other participants to divide their holdings into three categories: "1. Those [files] not subject to restitution, 2. those subject to restitution under certain specified circumstances and under certain safeguards, and 3. those available for restitution in the forseeable future without qualification."[43] Nobel's attempt to jump-start the return process sparked resistance among the other departments and particularly irritated the Library of Congress, which had been quite open in principle to the return of captured materials. "It seemed to be Noble's implicit assumption," noted librarian Dan Lacy, "that everything should be returned for which there was not some compelling reason to the contrary. The other agencies present, with the exception of the National Archives... were quite opposed to the return of any significant body of material."[44] The Army tried to dampen Noble's zeal by pointing out that the Federal Republic had "no recognized rights, moral or legal, in any captured military records and no general restitution of military records is now contemplated." Noble's proposal struck the other participants in the Interagency Conference as too crude. Documents would be returned to Germany, East later told Noble, only if restitution served "U.S. and NATO military and political objectives."[45] As long as the details of West German rearmament remained unclear, Noble's proposal to categorize documents according to need could not be implemented.[46] Noble was thus compelled to change his stance and from then on spoke of only a "selective transfer"

42 Noble to East, Feb. 7, 1951, NA RG 407, entry 360, box 3609.

43 Noble to East, Feb. 15, 1951, ibid; and the minutes of the meeting on Feb. 14, 1951, ibid.

44 Dan Lacy, Deputy Chief Assistant Librarian to The Librarian [Luther Evans], Feb. 15, 1951, LoC, Central File, box 398. The librarians were particularly upset because Noble did not appear willing to put himself into the shoes of the various other departments and offices and take their needs into consideration. "I have been unable to make Noble realize that the world does not end with the Foreign Office Archives and that there are other groups of material involved," Harry J. Krould, Chief, European Affairs Division, LoC, to Lacy, May 2, 1951, ibid.

45 East to Noble, Feb. 27, 1951, NA RG 407, entry 360, box 3609.

46 "A great deal of objection was raised to this procedure especially by the Army on the ground that the categories would be meaningless unless there had been some determination of United States policy as to whether German rearmament was to be permitted and to what extent." Dan Lacy, Deputy Chief Assistant Librarian to The Librarian [Luther Evans], Feb. 15, 1951, LoC, Central File, box 398.

of German documents instead of a restitution program.[47] Nonetheless, the State Department still aimed to fill the "legitimate needs of the Federal Republic of Germany."[48] It wanted the Interagency Conference to come up quickly with a policy that would allow as many records as possible to be returned to the Germans.

Following the February meeting, the military agencies began to coordinate their own efforts. On the initiative of the Adjutant General, the Joint Chiefs of Staff (JCS) dealt with the issue of the captured documents in light of "current political and military considerations" – in other words, with an eye toward the possible rearmament of West Germany.[49] The JCS considered it militarily necessary to return certain captured records: "However, it is neither desirable nor appropriate that all categories of captured enemy documents should be returned to ex-enemy countries." Furthermore, material on deciphering and intelligence matters, as well as "information likely to prejudice the national interest of the United States" should be retained.[50] The State Department and the Army Department clashed several times over the definition of "national interest." The Army insisted that the sentence declaring the United States' intention to return "the maximum possible amount of documentation" in the first draft of the Interagency Conference's policy paper be cut.[51] That insistence struck at the heart of the State Department's goals. The State Department, in turn, fought against the term "war booty," which the representatives of the military often used casually.[52] The State Department had always avoided using the term in diplomatic correspondence because of the implications it carried in international law, and under no condition did it want to see the term in the policy paper: the "'war booty' category ... appears to require retention," warned a memorandum.[53] In the end, the term was used in the policy paper but only in connection with documents confiscated before May 8, 1945, which thus fell under the 1907 Hague Regulations of Land Warfare.

47 Noble to East, Apr. 27, 1951 with attachment, NA RG 407, entry 360, box 3609.

48 Noble, Memorandum, Transfer to the Federal Republic of Germany of Captured German Documentation in Whole or in Part . . . , Apr. 26, 1951, ibid.

49 Edward F. Witsell, Adjutant General, Memorandum for the Chief of Staff, U.S. Army, Feb. 26, 1951, as an attachment to JCS 1133/5, Notes by the Secretaries to the Joint Chiefs of Staff on Restitution or other Disposition of Captured Enemy (i.e. German) Records, Apr. 4, 1951, NA RG 407, entry 360, box 3609.

50 Robert A. Lovett, Acting SecDefense, to SecState, June 8, 1951, ibid. Also, JCS 1133/6, June 4, 1951, ibid.

51 Draft statement of policy relating to restitution of captured German Documentation, Nov. 29, 1951, ibid.

52 [Minutes] Interagency Conference, May 17, 1950, ibid.; DRB Journal of Significant Events, Sept. 12, 1951, entry by Sherrod East, ibid., entry 375, box 1.

53 "The policy statement should nowhere require retention but rather set standards for permissive retention." Humphrey, Office Memorandum to Noble, Feb. 8, 1952, NA RG 59, CDF 1950–54, 862.423/2–852.

In the early phase of the interagency talks, reference was still made rather perfunctorily to the "restitution" of German records. However, both the librarians from the Library of Congress and the archivists from the National Archives opposed this term because, in their view, it implied that the American government sought to return unlawfully confiscated material. Because the confiscations had been sanctioned by Allied law and had served the aims of demilitarization and denazification, any suggestion of unlawful acquisition was not considered desirable.[54] Should it become politically expedient to turn over records to the Federal Republic, Lacy argued, the return should take the form of a "voluntary gift of materials."

A gift to which the United States has a clear and indefeasible title – a gift which is made not because there is any valid German claim, but because it suits the purposes of the United States, a gift, in other words, which is precisely analogous to transfers of munitions to the North Atlantic Treaty countries."[55]

The term "restitution" should be reserved for the return of cultural treasures plundered by the Germans during the war. The Library of Congress's insistence that the term "restitution" not be used in the Interagency Conference's policy paper reflected its sense of vulnerability. During the work of the Library of Congress Mission to Germany in 1946–47, the library was accused by the American Library Association of taking part in a purge of German public libraries, comparable to the Nazis' book burnings.[56] Some librarians at research libraries affiliated with the mission accused members of the mission of allowing themselves to become involved in plunder. The library's leaders thus took great pains to emphasize repeatedly the legal basis for the growing amount of material in the library's possession.[57] They would

54 "Under no circumstances should such materials be returned in such a manner that it would be construed as the restitution of German property now admitted to have been improperly or unlawfully seized." Lacy to Noble, Feb. 28, 1951, NA RG 407, entry 360, box 3609. See also Ernst Posner, A Study of the Historical Development of International Principles and Practices Pertaining to Seized Enemy Records Through World War II, January 1952, NA RG 59, Lot File 56D307, Assistant Legal Advisor for German Affairs, box 1: "We must strictly avoid giving the impression that we want to right a wrong that we have committed."
55 Dan Lacy, Deputy Chief Assistant Librarian to The Librarian [Luther Evans], Feb. 15, 1951, LoC, Central File, box 398. See also Evans to Richard A. Humphrey, Historical Division, State Department, Jan. 22, 1952, ibid.: "The return of any such material should be considered not as an act of restitution but as a gift to the Federal Republic . . . to assist it in the solution of its administrative problems and in the historical research projects which it sponsors."
56 The protest telegram of the ALA from May 14, 1946, in LoCM, box 7. The Control Council Directive no. 4 from May 20, 1946, became known as the "Book Burning Edict." See Public Information on the Occupation of Germany, June 25, 1946, NA RG 59, Lot File 55D371, Records of the Office of Western European Affairs, Subject Files, 1941–54, box 2. See also Michael Dobbs, "Nazi Loot May Line American Shelves," *Washington Post*, Jan. 5, 2000, C1.
57 Assistant Director, Processing Department, Memorandum for the Librarian, Enemy Publications Seized by Military Authorities in World War II, Feb. 7, 1951, LoCM box 27; Lacy to Noble, Feb. 28, 1951, NA RG 407, entry 360, box 3609.

not have agreed to any return labeled "restitution," which would imply the library had been involved in unlawful action. Whereas the first draft of the policy paper, dated November 1951, used the term "restitution," the second draft (February 1952) spoke instead of "return."[58] From that point on, "return" was employed in official correspondence. Only rarely did the phrase "to be donated to the Federal Republic" appear.[59]

The individual agencies raised a wide array of other issues and concerns that hindered progress in formulating a general policy on the return of the captured documents. The Justice Department considered the political situation in Central Europe to be volatile and feared that "an unfriendly German government might come into power or the territory of the present republic be overrun by the USSR."[60] It also suggested that German naval records be kept for at least fifty years until all claims for damages filed by American sailors against their own government were settled.[61] The Library of Congress, which had integrated numerous confiscated books into its collections and had passed several hundreds of thousands more on to other American research libraries, insisted on assurance that no one would be allowed to demand that those books be sorted out for return. Speaking for the State Department, Noble rejected formulations such as "return . . . as far as practicable" on the grounds that they opened the way for the refusal to return documents on account of the intensive labor required.[62] The CIA, by contrast, did not cause any problems. It was still evaluating German records and considered them "important and unique sources of intelligence information." The stipulation in the second draft of the policy paper that material would be retained if relevant to intelligence work gave the CIA all

58 Draft statement of policy relating to restitution of captured German Documentation (for interagency discussion within the United States Government), Nov. 29, 1951, NA RG 407, entry 360, box 3609; Policy on Return of Seized German Documentation, Feb. 14, 1952, NA RG 338, US Army Command, entry 33192, box 1.

59 Wolfe, "Sharing Records of Mutual Archival Concern," 296; Glenn, "Private Records Seized," 400f.; Wayne C. Grover, Archivist of the US, to Noble, Draft of General Records Schedule, July 10, 1953, NA RG 59, CDF 1950–54, 862.423/7–1053.

60 Joseph C. Duggan, Assistant Attorney General, Executive Adjudications Division, Department of Justice, to H. Freeman Matthews, Deputy UnderSecState, Aug. 15, 1952, NA RG 59, CDF 1950–54, 862.423/8–1552.

61 Apparently, a brisk lawsuit business had developed: sailors who had been captured and held as prisoners of war were suing the U.S. government "on grounds that the United States ship was negligently operated. Such a claim can be overcome only by a defense which can prove that the disaster was a result of the [German] U-boats' excellence rather than United States negligence." Conference on Policy Statement re. the Return of Seized German Documents, Sept. 18, 1952, NA RG 64, National Archives, Planning and Control Cases, box PC-62.

62 [Minutes], Return of German Documents, Sept. 10, 1952; Verner W. Clapp, Chief Assistant Librarian, Memorandum [for] The Librarian, Sept. 16, 1952, both in LoC, Central File, box 398.

the assurance it needed: it was willing to approve the July 1952 draft as it stood.[63]

Just as the talks on the policy guidelines finally appeared to be drawing to a successful and foreseeable close in the fall of 1952, the Army Department raised an issue that threatened to halt the process once again – namely, the issue of cost. The office of the Secretary of Defense proposed that the Federal Republic shoulder the costs of administering the captured documents until their return. In addition to the cost of shipping the files back to Germany, the West Germans would also be expected to pay for microfilming them before their return.[64] The imposition of that condition was the last thing the State Department wanted. "To insist upon reimbursement from the Germans for these expenses would largely counteract, or even nullify, the good political effect we hope to gain from the return of the documents."[65] The Army conceded the point in this instance because "the amount of money involved is not considered sufficient to warrant taking issue with the Department of State."[66]

The Pentagon did succeed, however, in holding up approval of the policy guidelines by calling attention to a legal obstacle to returning the captured documents to the Germans. In December 1952, Defense Secretary Robert A. Lovett put forward the novel argument that the German documents had become U.S. federal records through the act of confiscation.[67] The fate of federal records could be decided only with the approval of Congress. The State Department tried to refute this argument but, with the Interagency Conference under pressure to succeed, had to concede the point to the

63 Loftus E. Becker, Deputy Director, CIA, to H. Freeman Matthews, Deputy UnderSecState, July 21, 1952, NA RG 59, CDF 1950–54, 862.423/7–2152.

64 "It appears in the interest of the United States proper that the Federal Republic of Germany should be required to reimburse the United States for all the costs involved in the preparation of these documents for release, and in their release and transmittal." G. V. Underwood, Deputy Director, Executive Office, SecDefense, to H. Freeman Matthews, Deputy UnderSecState, Sept. 10, 1950, NA RG 59, CDF 1950–54, 862.423/9–1052.

65 "To insist upon reimbursement from the Germans for these expenses would largely counteract, or even nullify, the good political effect we hope to gain from the return of the documents." Matthews to Robert A. Lovett, SecDefense, Nov. 7, 1952; and Memorandum. Discussion on Policy Statement Regarding the Return of Seized German Documents, Sept. 23, 1952, both in NA RG 407, entry 360, box 3609.

66 W. E. Bergin, Adjutant General, Office Memorandum, Nov. 21, 1952. Approval of assuming the costs in William C. Foster, Deputy SecDefense to SecState, Dec. 29, 1952, both in ibid.

67 "OSD [Office SecDefense] was holding up approval of the policy statement on the grounds that the legal status of the records had to be resolved and that OSD legal staff was discussing the matter." Sherrod East, head of DRB, found the time-consuming development "unnecessary and unfortunate." DRB Journal of Significant Events, Dec. 9, 1952, entry by Sherrod East, NA RG 407, entry 375, box 1.

Defense Department.[68] In return, the Defense Department finally endorsed the policy paper at the end of December 1952, subject to clarification of the records' legal status.[69] The policy guidelines went into effect in April 1953 even though discussion of the legal issues and agreement with Congress on a "General Records Schedule" dragged on a while longer.[70]

The Policy Paper of October 24, 1952

The policy paper went through four drafts before taking on its final form.[71] It opened by citing the legal basis for the confiscation of German records, most notably the laws enacted by the Allied Control Council. Because the great majority of the documents had been confiscated during the period of occupation *after* Germany's surrender on May 8, 1945, the Hague Regulations on Land Warfare largely did not pertain. Under the heading "General Policy," the paper stated the willingness of the United States to return German records as part of the overall policy to effect the political and military integration of the Federal Republic into the Western alliance:

It is the announced policy of the United States to promote friendly relations with the Federal Republic of Germany on a normal basis, to bring about effective participation by the Federal Republic in the European Defense Community on a basis of equality, and to remove unnecessary obstacles to the attainment of these objectives. In view of this policy, the seized German documents will be returned to the Federal Republic.

More important than this declaration of general intent were the exceptions to the policy of return. Defining these exceptions – the British called them the "reserved" or "prohibited classes" of documents – had swallowed up a great deal of time in the Interagency Conference's talks. The definitions were intentionally vague in order to ensure sufficient leeway of interpretation.[72]

68 DRB Journal of Significant Events, Dec. 16, 1952, NA RG 407, entry 360, box 3906; Tetton P. Heffelfinger, Office of Counsel, Office Secretary Defense, Memorandum for the Record, Dec. 22, 1952, NA RG 59, CDF 1950–54, 862.423/12–2252 CS/B; on the time pressure, see Matthews to Robert A. Lovett, SecDefense, Nov. 7, 1952, ibid., FW 862.423/4–3053.

69 William C. Foster, Deputy SecDefense to SecState, Dec. 29, 1952, NA RG 407, entry 360, box 3609.

70 "The Statement of Policy . . . was issued on April 15, 1953, as rev. Oct. 24, 1952." Verner W. Clapp, Assistant Librarian of Congress, to Noble, May 28, 1954, LoC Central File, box 398.

71 The final version of Oct. 24, 1952 in NA RG 407, entry 360, box 3609; RG 59, CDF 1950–54, 862.423/9–1052; RG 64, National Archives, Planning and Control Cases, box PC-62. The policy paper is reprinted in Eckert, *Kampf um die Akten*, 480f.

72 James Passant and John Wheeler-Bennett from the Foreign Office, to whom Noble showed a draft of the return guidelines in March 1952, found the definition of the categories "rather over-generous

The following categories of material may be retained:

a. Such military, intelligence, cryptographic, technological, or other similar documents, as would, if returned, jeopardize the national security interests of the United States or its Allies.
b. Materials concerned primarily with German occupation of other states, the return of which would jeopardize the national security interests of the United States or its Allies. Such materials relating to the occupation of friendly countries may be returned to the respective friendly countries.
c. Documents tending to glorify the Nazi regime, or which are of inherent propaganda character, or which deal with the organization, personnel, and operation of Nazi Party institutions, except where such transfer would not jeopardize the democratic way of life in the Federal Republic.

The first category satisfied the intelligence community, which would not be noticeably affected by the return policy. It was also understandable that the Americans did not intend to return records to the Federal Republic that had belonged to countries occupied by Germany. The influence of the Cold War on the second category is much greater than first meets the eye, however. Records that had been confiscated by the Germans and had later fallen into American hands were to be returned only to "friendly countries." In 1952, this stipulation excluded all of the countries behind the Iron Curtain. Indeed, portions of the Smolensk party archives of the Communist Party of the Soviet Union were deposited in the U.S. National Archives until December 2002.[73] It was not until 1992 that Washington gave the Polish government Foreign Ministry records originally confiscated in Warsaw in 1939 by the Archive Commission of the Auswärtiges Amt.[74] They had been carefully locked away in the National Archives since 1949, and no reference to them was to be found in any finding aid.[75]

with regard to the willingness to return documents." Noble, Report on Discussions in London and Bonn, Mar. 18, 1952, NA RG 59, CDF 1950–54, 862.423/3–1852.

73 Grimsted, "Odyssey of the Smolensk Archive III," 143–151; Ken Ringle, "Soviet Records of Repression Returned to Moscow," *Washington Post*, Dec. 14, 2002, C1, C3; Celestine Bohlen, "A Stray Record of Stalinist Horror Finds Its Way Home," *New York Times*, Dec. 14, 2002, A21.

74 The Polish records were returned on April 21, 1992. The transfer treaty, signed by Vice President Dan Quayle and Polish Minister President Jan Olszewski, did not contain a clause obligating the Polish government to make the records accessible for research once they were again in Poland. The Polish government only waived all of its legal claims against the American government. The records were filmed before being sent back. The 56 rolls of film are available at the National Archives under the signature M1751. Information received from Dr. James Bradsher, National Archives, June 28, 2002; also, "Polish Records Returned in White House Ceremony," *Prologue* 24:3 (1992), 320.

75 The State Department turned over the records in 1949 to the Archives on the stipulation that "they shall be withheld from examination and consultation by officials, private individuals, or any other person.... The present policy of the Department [of State] is *not* to grant permission to examine or consult these records, except under most unusual circumstances. Therefore, it is requested that these records be omitted from any processed or printed guide, list, or statement made available to the public." The material in question comprised six crates with records from the years 1918–1940.

From the beginning of the interagency talks, all of the participating bodies had agreed on the third category of materials that would be excluded from the return policy, namely material "tending to glorify the Nazi regime." The pertinent paragraph of the policy paper was written under the assumption that the return of party papers and similar documents "might readily provoke or assist the development of a 'Hitler legend,' a neo-Nazi movement, or a revival of German militarism or totalitarianism."[76] For that reason, the State Department refused to consider even the possibility of turning the Berlin Document Center over to the Germans. The Justice Department also insisted that the NSDAP membership cards remain accessible for ongoing investigations into possible immigration violations.[77]

The return policy guidelines did not include a timetable. The initiative for returning records was left to the individual departments and agencies in possession of captured documents, and the guidelines gave them the framework they needed to respond to German requests. The Germans never learned of the policy paper. Not until October 1954 did the West German ambassador in Washington, Heinz Krekeler, hear for the first time about the Interagency Conference. When he inquired at the State Department, he was told that such a body did not exist. A more precise answer would have been that the conference no longer existed, as it had disbanded long before Krekeler received his answer in February 1954.[78] The *Vierteljahrshefte für Zeitgeschichte* could report only generally in 1953 that a "governmental committee had, after months of preparation, completed a draft of general guidelines for the use [sic] of confiscated German documents."[79] No one at the State Department intended to correct the Germans' misperceptions.[80]

Noble to Wayne C. Grover, Archivist of the United States, May 18, 1949, NA RG 59, Lot File 78D441, Historical Office, box 11. Original emphasis.

76 Noble, Memorandum [on a change in the policy paper], Apr. 19, 1957, as an attachment to a letter to Robert H. Bahmer, Deputy Archivist of the United States, May 20, 1957, NA RG 64, National Archives, Planning and Control Cases 050–104, box PC-62. This restriction was lifted in 1957 when the Army was preparing to return records, including party material. Apparently the political situation of the Federal Republic was considered to be sufficiently stable.

77 Joseph C. Duggan, Assistant Attorney General, Executive Adjudications Division, to Matthews, Aug. 15, 1952, NA RG 59, CDF 1950–54, 862.423/8–1552.

78 Krekeler, Botschafter, Washington, to AA, Oct. 29, 1953; id., Feb. 11, 1954, both in PA/AA, B118, vol. 508. Krekeler had his original information from a United Press correspondent.

79 "Deutsche Archive und Dokumente in Alliierter Verwahrung," *VfZ* 1:1 (1953), 95f. The information for this note came from Fritz T. Epstein.

80 "Dr. Noble stated that it was not proposed to show this [policy] document to the Germans." Verner W. Clapp, Chief Assistant Librarian, to The Librarian [Luther Evans], Sept. 16, 1952, LoC Central File, box 398. See also H. Freeman Matthews, Deptuty UnderSecState, to Wayne C. Grover, Archivist of the US, July 29, 1952, NA RG 59, CDF 1950–54, 862.423/7–2952: "This policy statement is not intended to be shown to the Federal Republic authorities."

Ad Hoc Returns

The State Department's willingness to return records opened the way to a series of ad hoc returns. Some resulted from German requests for particular groups of files; others occurred because American agencies sought to rid themselves of German material. The ad hoc returns were arranged bilaterally, which allowed the Americans to circumvent time-consuming consultations with the other Allies. That was particularly important for Washington: the State Department wanted quick results at least on "minor questions" because the tedious process of coordinating policy on the German diplomatic records with the British had come to a "standstill" by 1954.[81] Arranging returns at the level of the High Commission allowed the State Department to bypass the Foreign Office and the French Foreign Ministry.[82] An informal "Tripartite Working Group on Archives" handled the ad hoc returns. It was important to the State Department that HICOG acted in this matter not as part of the High Commission but as an autonomous representative of the U.S. government.[83] To inform the French of such returns was thought to be "a matter of courtesy" that did not grant them the right to raise objections.[84] This was all part of the effort to retain decision-making autonomy and to prevent the partners from "acquir[ing] either the right or the opportunity to subject each case to the requirement of tripartite approval, with the power on their part to outvote us."[85] However, for the negotiations over the documents from the Auswärtiges Amt and over the entire collection of military records, the Allies set great store on appearing outwardly in a unified and concerted manner.

American Offers. The completion of the Interagency Conference's position paper gave American governmental bodies the guidelines they needed in trying to dispose of confiscated German materials, particularly books and other printed works. The reasons for returning materials ranged from lack of space and the administrative expense to duplication of holdings. In all

81 Smith, Acting SecState, to HICOG Bonn, no. A-965, Feb. 16, 1954, NA RG 242, AGAR-S no. 2084, box 10.

82 "State prefers to deal with the British High Commission on restitution rather than with the British Foreign Office since State feels that the Foreign Office deliberately raises obstacles to restitution." Philipp Brower, Office memorandum for Sherrod East and Ken Munden, June 10, 1954, NA RG 407, entry 371, box 4.

83 "HICOG should continue to make it clear in Bonn that in return of seized documents HICOG is functioning as a US mission, not as an element of HICOM." Dulles, SecState, to HICOG Bonn, A-1308, May 6, 1954, NA RG 497, entry 371, box 4.

84 "It should be noted that notification of the French in such cases is a matter of courtesy, since the French (unlike the British) have no claim to any joint custodial rights over seized German documents now in American possession." Smith, Acting SecState, to HICOG Bonn, no. A-965, Feb. 16, 1954, NA RG 242, AGAR-S no. 2084, box 10.

85 Ibid.

instances, however, the materials returned were no longer of interest to American authorities. The alternative to restitution in many cases would have been to pulp the material. When such cases arose within the U.S. military, the Departmental Records Branch intervened and attempted to secure the documents.[86] The Intelligence Division of the European Command (EUCOM), for example, was prepared to destroy the German army service records and ID cards. As a result of the DRB's intervention, these materials were instead offered in 1953 to the Amt Blank, the predecessor of the Federal Republic's Ministry of Defense.[87] A similar situation occurred when the Berlin Document Center Rear in Darmstadt, the external branch of the BDC, was closed. The bulk of the files deposited there were denazification records, which were shipped to the United States in 1952.[88] There were, however, also about twenty tons of German documents.[89] A portion of the German materials was destroyed, and the rest was turned over to the Federal Republic. With little diplomatic ado, the Germans thereby received the personnel files of the Reich railroad, the Reichsnährstand, and the German Red Cross nursing corps, as well as the records of the Reichsarbeitsdienst and the Nazi Kraftfahrerkorps.[90] The West German authorities welcomed the receipt of these files because the materials were urgently needed to fulfill obligations set down in Article 131 of the Basic Law.[91]

86 In March 1950, the Adjutant General requested all military offices to report their captured record holdings and to turn these holdings over to the AGO once they were finished with them. The decree from March 31, 1950, Subject: Letter Report on Captured or Confiscated Records in Custody of Field Elements of the Department of the Army, ZI [Zone of the Interior, i.e. USA], NA RG 64, National Archives, Planning and Control Cases 050–104, box PC-62.

87 "Destruction of Personnel Records, even of those pertaining to enemy citizens, should be frowned upon. The alternative appears to be to recommend release to the German authorities for whatever disposition they care to make." Goldbeck, Acting Chief, GMDS, to Chief, DRB [East], Recommended Disposition of Wehrstammbuecher, Feb. 15, 1951, NA RG 242, Non-Record Material, box 107. Evidence that the material was released is derived from the List of Dispositions of Captured Records, n.d. [ca. 1960], ibid., box. 106.

88 Director of Intelligence, HICOG Frankfurt, to Dept State, no. 2310, Jan. 15, 1951, NA RG 59, CDF 1950–54, 862.423/1–1551; Charles M Adams, Jr., Acting Dir of Intelligence, HQ EUCOM, Memorandum, July 12, 1951; Bernard A Tormey, Commanding [Officer], to Director of Intelligence, USAREUR, Oct. 21, 1952, both in NA RG 319, IRR Case Files, box 22, XE 169 191. BDC.

89 Survey of Material still left at the 7771 Document Center, Rear, n.d. [1952], NA RG 338, US Army Command, entry 33192, box 1.

90 Adjutant General, HQ USAREUR, Disposition of German Records, 7771 Document Center (Rear), Aug. 22, 1952 and Oct. 28, 1952, NA RG 407, entry 360, box 3794; Wm. E. Bergin, Adjutant General, to Noble, May 28, 1953, ibid., box 3609; C. H. L. Venn, Berlin Government BOAR 1, to Passant, Library, FO, Analysis of the BDC Catalogue [as] Revised to 1st September 1951, Sept. 29, 1951, PRO FO 370/2152 LS3/160. For other examples of ad hoc returns, see Eckert, *Kampf um die Akten*, 225.

91 Trützschler, Abt. II, AA, to H. J. Joos, Secretary General of the AHC, Mar. 27, 1953, PA/AA, B10, vol. 1703/3; Steg, Abt. II, AA, to BMI, Sept. 19, 1952, BArch, B106, vol. 34723/2. Article 131 of Germany's Basic Law prescribed: "Federal law shall regulate the legal status of persons, including

The practice of ad hoc returns shows that ways could be found to return records if officials in Washington thought it was politically expedient to do so. Two examples illustrate this point particularly well. In January 1951, the biographical division of the CIA proposed that the personnel files of German army officers be microfilmed immediately "in *anticipation* of their *possible* restitution to the West German Government in the event that German military units are formed for the defense of Western Europe."[92] As a result, the U.S. Army began a filming program, budgeted at $16,000, even though the Germans had not yet requested the return of the files in question. The staff members of the Departmental Records Branch suspected that "restitution of these records will undoubtedly be used by the German Government as precedent in support of requests for return of other records."[93] It was not until a year later, in February 1952, that Adenauer requested the return of all Wehrmacht personnel records.[94] The return was held up until 1954, however, on account of the objections of the British, who feared they were being overridden by unilateral American concessions.[95]

The second example involved military training manuals (e.g., handbooks and instructional brochures) that the Amt Blank requested in the autumn of 1951.[96] The U.S. Army held duplicate copies and was therefore willing to comply with the German request. To avoid the delay that would ensue if the action were coordinated with the British, it was decided on the spot to *lend* the handbooks to the West Germans. "Restitution of captured documents is not involved nor contemplated, consequently the Bissell-Sinclair Agreement will not be compromised." It was assumed from the start, however, that the loan would be permanent.[97] By April 1952, the

---

refugees and expelled persons, who were public employees on 8 May 1945, left service for reasons other than regulations regarding public officials and salaries, and until now have not been reinstated, or have been reinstated in their earlier positions." A detailed look at the legal implementation of Art. 131 is found in Wengst, *Beamtentum zwischen Reform und Tradition*, 152–252; on the restorative dimension, Frei, *Adenauer's Germany*, 41–66.

92 Sherrod East, Memorandum thru Assistant Chiefs of Staff, G-1, G-2 for Chief of Staff, U.S. Army, Feb. 7, 1951, NA RG 407, entry 360, box 3609. The memorandum was not used, but summarizes the process. Emphasis added. The facts and circumstances of the case once again in Edward F. Witsell, Adjutant General, Memorandum for Chief of Staff, U.S. Army, Feb. 26, 1951, as an attachment to JCS 1133/5, Apr. 4, 1951, ibid.

93 Ibid.

94 Adenauer to the Chairman of the Allied High Commission, John J. McCloy, Feb. 19, 1952, PA/AA, B118, vol. 37.

95 Walter J. Donnelly, HICOG Bonn, to SecState, no. 1587, Oct. 8, 1952, NA RG 59, CDF 1950–54, 862.423/10–852. The return of Wehrmacht personnel files and the coordination with the British are handled in the third section of Chapter 4.

96 Urcel L. Bell for the Chief, Historical Division, HQ EUCOM, to Office of the Chief of Military History, Department of the Army, Sept. 10, 1951, NA RG 407, entry 360, box 3609.

97 "The desired procedure is to *loan* documents, as requested, to the Bonn government for a period of six months with option of extending the loan period if the project is not completed within

handbooks were on their way to Frankfurt.[98] Two years later, after the return policy was in place, this "loan" was re-labeled a "return."[99] The Army's actions in this instance were entirely in accord with Defense Department policy to support West German rearmament so far as possible.

German Requests. German requests for the return of specific groups of records reflected the advances being made in three areas: the establishment of governmental bureaucracy, the provision of social welfare benefits, and the expansion of sovereignty. For example, after the Germany Treaty was signed and the Federal Republic was allowed to resume civilian aviation, the Transport Ministry promptly requested the relevant records.[100] Requests for the records of agencies that had not performed an important political or military function during the Nazi era – e.g., the Reich Veterinary Office – were most likely to be fulfilled quickly and without complications.[101] Before the Auswärtiges Amt assumed responsibility for the issue of the captured documents, the Federal Ministry of the Interior acted on its own initiative and asked British and American authorities directly for the records it needed. In response to a request submitted in early 1950, the ministry received sixty-seven crates of administrative records from the BDC Rear later that year.[102]

The large gaps in government personnel records held a particular meaning in a newly founded state. In brief, the Federal Republic's new government ministries and agencies had to be staffed, and the most reliable indicator of an applicant's qualifications was previous civil service experience. Some of the gaps in governmental personnel files could presumably be filled by personal references and other documentation, notably denazification records. Federal officials also had to deal with an unprecedented number of claims to citizenship filed by Germans who had fled westwards or had been expelled from former German territories in the east. Proof of

that time." D. C. Turner, Asst. Adjutant General, for the Commander in Chief, HQ EUCOM, to Assistant Chief of Staff, G-2 (Intelligence), Department of the Army, Nov. 28, 1951, NA RG 407, entry 360, box 3609.

98 Adjutant General, Army Department, to Commander in Chief, EUCOM, attn. Intelligence Division, Apr. 18, 1952, ibid. Two further deliveries followed on June 16, 1952 and Dec. 15, 1953. The material was made up of leaflets about regulations on security classifications, troop transport, firing infantry artillery, training armored-tank troops, and similar items.

99 Adjutant General to Commander in Chief, U.S. Army, Europe (CINCUSAREUR), May 3, 1954, ibid.

100 The account in ibid. The German airline *Lufthansa* started service again on March 1, 1955.

101 The account in NA RG 59, CDF 1950–54, 862.423/8–1253. See also Georg Winter, Bundesarchiv, to the Interior Ministry, Betr. Akten aus dem Bereich der ehemaligen Reichsgesundheitsverwaltung, Dec. 4, 1953, BArch, N1418, NL Rohr, vol. 71.

102 The account in NA RG 59, CDF 1950–54, 862.423/2–1650.

citizenship was a prerequisite in filing for old age pensions and other social benefits. Compliance with Article 131 of the Basic Law, which required the federal government to reinstate former civil servants, was similarly dependent on access to personnel records. Article 131 also applied to career soldiers and was especially difficult to implement in this case because it was precisely the personnel records of all branches of the Wehrmacht that had been confiscated.[103]

The Americans advised the West Germans twice to pursue the path of ad hoc returns instead of categorically demanding the return of all the captured documents. For the State Department, the Germans' all-or-nothing approach meant having to involve the British and the French as long as there was no general agreement on the issue of document return.[104] The bilateral approach did not always work, however, as demonstrated by the example of the tug-of-war over the records of the Central Immigration Office in Łódź.

The Records of the Central Immigration Office Łódź. The Central Immigration Office (Einwandererzentrale) had been established in 1939 in the wake of Heinrich Himmler's appointment as Reich Commissioner for the Strengthening of Germandom (Reichskommissar für die Festigung des Deutschen Volkstums, RKF). The RKF was responsible for repatriating, naturalizing, and resettling ethnic Germans, so-called *Volksdeutsche*, in the Eastern European countries occupied by Germany. Its work was intended to serve the long-term goal of "Germanizing" the conquered eastern territories. In processing naturalization applications, RKF officials closely examined applicants' racial, ideological, and medical backgrounds.[105] The West German Interior Ministry first requested the return of the RKF naturalization records in July 1950. The racist motivation behind the records' origins notwithstanding, West German officials argued that they were crucial for clarifying the nationality of many postwar refugees residing in the

103 See Chapter 4, n. 220.
104 VLR v. Grolmann, Blomeyer, Abt. V (Rechtsabt.), AA, Memorandum [on a conversation with Noble] for Mosler, May 13, 1953, PA/AA, B118, vol. 508: "They [the Americans] are open to the idea of responding to detailed return requests but kindly ask not to place general demands." Even more explicit was the report of the German ambassador in Washington, Heinz Krekeler, dated Feb. 11, 1954, ibid.: "Cautiously, the American representative let it be known that, in his view, the Federal government was clinging too adamantly to its standpoint of 'all of nothing' in the matter of returning captured German records. In many cases, an agreement might have been possible had the German side insisted instead on the return of specific files, on the grounds that their return [filled] particular practical needs."
105 On the history and holdings of the Central Immigration Office files in the BDC, see the catalogue *Holdings of the Berlin Document Center*, 9–44; Heusterberg, "Personenbezogene Unterlagen," 157–61.

Federal Republic.[106] The request was turned down, however, and the West Germans filed at least another four requests for the records by the end of 1959. But although the State Department had no objections to their return, the RFK records remained in American possession.[107] The example of this group of records illustrates the bureaucratic and political vagaries that could complicate the return of captured documents. Such experiences helped make issues involving the return of records increasingly unpopular among both the Allies and the Germans by the mid-1950s.

At the time of the first German request, the RKF records were being used in the United States for immigration matters, especially for the Displaced Persons Program. The Americans offered, however, to provide the Germans with any information from the records they needed.[108] Two years later, the Interior Ministry tried anew. With the negotiations on the Germany Treaty drawing to a close, the time seemed opportune to the West Germans to bring up the Central Immigration Office files again. Officials at the Interior Ministry no longer wanted to be dependent on an American agency for information. The ministry was by then filing between 800 and 1,000 inquiries per month, and the BDC had announced its plans to charge processing fees for such services.[109] The U.S. office of the High Commission was receptive to the Interior Ministry's request. Because the Displaced Persons Program had ended by then, HICOG approved a partial return of the Central Immigration Office records.[110]

The timing of the request turned out to be less favorable than the Interior Ministry realized. In the autumn of 1952, the U.S. Army intelligence service

---

106 BMI to Dienststelle für Auswärtige Angelegenheiten im Bundeskanzleramt, June 22, 1950, PA/AA, B118, vol. 39. In 1955, the Federal Republic recognized the naturalizations undertaken by the RKF; this action also increased the urgency of the having access to the records of the Central Immigration Office as proof of citizenship in these cases. See Heusterberg, "Personenbezogene Unterlagen," 158.

107 In 1962, only 97 crates of Immigration Office records, so-called non-biographical material, arrived at the Federal Archives. See the draft letter from the BDC to Brian Melland, Cabinet Office, London, Apr. 17, 1963, NA RG 242, BDC Directorate Files, box 6.

108 J. E. Slater, Secretary General, AHC, to Herbert Dittmann, Dienststelle für auswärtige Angelegenheiten, AGSEC(50)1852 POL, Aug. 29, 1950, PA/AA, B118, vol. 39.

109 BMI to AA, Oct. 6, 1952, ibid.; Trützschler, Abt. II, AA, to AHC, Nov. 11, 1952, NA RG 59, CDF 1950–54, attachment to 862.423/1–1453. The BDC was financed by a mixture of funds from the budgets of the U.S. Army, the city of Berlin (occupation costs), and fees charged to institutional users of the BDC, with the exception of German offices, whose fees were covered by the occupation-cost payments. With the coming of the Germany Treaty, the Americans counted on losing the German financial contribution. In this connection, the idea was weighed to charge fees to German offices and institutions. Discussion on financing in NA RG 59, CDF 1950–54, 862.423/5–2353, 862.423/6–1953.

110 George L. West, Division of External German Affairs, Office of Political Affairs, HICOG, to State Department, no. 2007, Jan. 14, 1953, NA RG 242, BDC Directorate Files, box 3. The records recommended for this partial return are listed in the attachment to this document.

suddenly took an interest in the Central Immigration Office records. A senior intelligence officer argued that the records had been evaluated in the immediate postwar period with only the issue of denazification in mind. The document teams had been "unbriefed in the Communist problem," and consequently the files on "USSR nationals of German descent" now needed to be evaluated at once.[111] The German request, moreover, arrived in Washington as the Army and the State Department were locked in a tussle over responsibility for the BDC. The Army wanted to rid itself of the BDC for cost reasons, which was the exact reason why the State Department did not want to have it. The transfer of the BDC, the central repository of information on Nazi Party and SS members, to the Germans was still considered to be out of the question.[112] The U.S. Defense Department linked the issues of the BDC and the immigrations files, thereby ensuring neither came any closer to resolution.[113]

In July 1953, the Auswärtiges Amt raised the issue of the Central Immigration Office records once again at HICOG, where the case had come to be seen as "increasingly embarrassing."[114] The repeated back-and-forth over the files that had been requested consumed so much time[115] that, meanwhile, Congress passed the Refugee Relief Act (PL-203). The State Department informed the Office of the High Commissioner that the Central Immigration Office records were of "even greater value" for this immigration law than they had been for the displaced persons program. The records were now deemed to be the "greatest single source of information available to comply with the statutory security requirements . . . of the Act." The West Germans thus could not expect to receive the Central Immigration Office records until after the expiration of the Refugee Relief Act in July 1956.[116]

---

111 David Wagstaff, Chief, Plans, Policy & Training Branch, HQ USAREUR, Intelligence Division, to Commanding Officer, 66th CIC Detachment, Nov. 6, 1952, NA RG 319, IRR Impersonal Files, XE 169191, box 22. In March 1953, Wagstaff reported to G-2 (Intelligence) at the Army Department that "there is almost nothing of value to the U.S. in the current efforts against Communism contained in these records." Ibid.
112 Wolfe, "Short History," xix.
113 Dulles, SecState, to HICOG Bonn, no. 2010, Jan. 14, 1953, NA RG 59, CDF 1950–54, 862.423/1–1453; Memorandum of Conversation [between William Franklin, State Dept. and Philipp Brower, DRB], n.d., ibid., FW 862.423/1–1453.
114 George W. Renchard, Office of Political Affairs, HICOG, to State Dept., Aug. 12, 1953, ibid., 862.423/8–1253.
115 Dulles, SecState, to HICOG Bonn, no. A-499, Oct. 20, 1953, NA RG 59, CDF 1950–54, 862.423/8–1253; Hervé J. L'Heureux, Executive Director, HICOG Bonn, to State Dept., no. 2122, Feb. 12, 1954, ibid., 862.423/2–1254. HICOG again recommended the partial return, especially of "non-active" records.
116 Dulles, Sec State, to HICOG Bonn, no. A-13, July 6, 1954, ibid., 862.423/2–1254 CS/A; H. J. Joos, General Secretary AHC, to Ambassador Herbert Blankenhorn, Chancellery, AGSEC(54)601, Sept. 23, 1954, BArch, B106, vol. 1209.

In the meantime, most West German agencies were learning to live with the existing state of affairs, and no fault could be found with the information services provided by the BDC. Even the department responsible for matters of nationality at the Interior Ministry no longer considered possession of the Central Immigration Office records crucial.[117] Only the head of the Bundesarchiv regarded the matter as a question of principle, contending that "objection has to be raised to each Allied attempt to delay the return of German material."[118] In 1959, the Auswärtiges Amt undertook a last attempt to retrieve the Central Immigration Office files.[119] This time it was Isaac A. Stone, the director of the BDC, who spoke out against restitution. The BDC had already been obliged to turn over a quantity of "non-biographical material" as part of a series of returns. Had the BDC been forced to turn over the RKF records – in other words, biographical material – its very existence would have been undermined.[120] The Bundesarchiv did finally receive the Central Immigration Office files when the entire BDC was transferred to the Federal Republic in 1994.

POSITIONS WITHIN THE BRITISH GOVERNMENT

In London, much as in Washington, government ministries and agencies found themselves at odds on the return of the captured German documents. The differences of opinion within the British government were, however, much sharper than the divide between the State Department and the Army. The rift ran straight through the Foreign Office. The Central Department[121] and the British High Commission in Wahnerheide, in particular High Commissioner Sir Ivone Kirkpatrick, were in favor of showing good will and trying to accommodate Bonn's requests as far as possible. Their efforts centered on the Auswärtiges Amt files. The Foreign Office Library, which was responsible for *Documents on German Foreign Policy*, sided with the British historians at Whaddon Hall and took a firm line against returning the records. While the Foreign Office remained preoccupied with the future of the Auswärtiges Amt files, the guidelines for the other holdings, above

---

117 Frh. von Fritsch, Ref. IB5, Interior Ministry to Ref. III/2 [Hübinger, Culture Dept.], Feb. 2, 1955, BArch, B106, vol. 1209.
118 Winter to BMI, Jan. 12, 1955, ibid.
119 The AA pointed out the needs of the Berlin Landesausgleichsamt. Verbal note, Apr. 13, 1959, NA RG 242, BDC Directorate Files, box 3.
120 The memorandum on the Central Immigration Office written by the BDC staff and the official denial of Bonn's request are found in William R. Tyler, Counselor of Embassy, AmEmb Bonn, to State Department, no. 887, both in ibid.
121 The Central Department was headed by William D. Allen until May 1952. His successor was Patrick Francis Hancock. Until 1955, the Foreign Office also had its own German Political Department. It was incorporated into the Central (European) Department.

all the military records, were worked out in an interministerial committee, the Joint Consultative Committee (JCC). A close link between the JCC and the Foreign Office existed, however, in the person of John Wheeler-Bennett. Discussion of the diplomatic records was therefore never entirely divided from the deliberations on the other captured documents.

The Joint Consultative Committee (JCC)

The Foreign Office sacrificed some of its control over the captured documents by yielding decision-making authority over the German military records to the JCC.[122] Although the JCC acted under the auspices of the Foreign Office, the split within the ministry ensured that the JCC became a body that refused to approve the return of any records from the very beginning because only staff from the Library was represented on the committee. Officials who were inclined to support the return of documents could not exercise leadership in this committee, let alone issue orders. Ironically, the Central Department and the Office of the High Commission consequently found themselves at odds on the issue of the captured documents less often with Bonn than with their own colleagues and the representatives of other ministries in the JCC. The Central Department and the High Commission would have even welcomed a heavier barrage of demands from the Germans to help break through the obstructions to document return within the British government itself. However, demonstrating astounding inertia, the JCC made it as difficult as possible for British diplomats to grant even minimal concessions until the late 1950s, although the regular participants in the JCC's deliberations were not even ministers and agency heads but second- and third-tier civil servants. In close contact with one another, these bureaucrats were in a position to filter the information their superiors received and to shape policy decisions in the draft papers they prepared for them. Every time British diplomats in Bonn moved one step forward on the documents issue, the JCC members were able to use their positions to set matters two steps back. The JCC thus quickly came to embody the bureaucratic autonomy so feared by top-level officials.

The Origins and Responsibilities of the JCC. Shortly after accepting the post of British editor-in-chief of *Documents on German Foreign Policy* in 1946, John

---

122 There is no cohesive record collection on the JCC. However, by combining the files in FO 370 (Foreign Office, Library) and CAB 103 (Cabinet Office, Historical Section), supplemented by the personal papers of John Wheeler-Bennett at St. Antony's College, Oxford, a nearly complete reconstruction of developments can be achieved. Gaps caused by the irrational classification regulations for the FO holdings can be filled by CAB files.

Wheeler-Bennett realized that the diplomatic records held by the Allies were incomplete. Likewise, the historians preparing the official histories of the war for the Navy and Air Force were gradually becoming aware of the gaps in the military records in Allied possession. To gain an overview of which agencies possessed which records, Wheeler-Bennett invited the other government historians in the fall of 1947 to exchange information about the captured documents and word of new discoveries. The meeting proved fruitful: the Admiralty turned out to have *Führerbefehle* – orders issued by Hitler – that were of interest to the editors of *Documents on German Foreign Policy*.[123]

Inspired by the success of this interministerial consultation, Wheeler-Bennett extended the circle of participants and institutionalized the forum as the JCC, which met monthly under his chairmanship.[124] The purpose of the JCC was to gather information on all the captured German records, provide for reciprocal access to the records, and reach a consensus before German records were published. The Foreign Office was represented in the JCC by, in addition to Wheeler-Bennett, James Passant, the head of the Library, and the historian E. Llewellyn Woodward. Historians from the Admiralty and the Air Ministry also participated. The Cabinet Office played a major role in the JCC from the beginning because it coordinated the preparation of the official history of the Second World War. Other departments and divisions became involved as materials in their possession became the subject of discussions with the Germans.[125] It seemed self-evident to the participants in the JCC that, given the group's expertise, it would be involved in deciding upon a response to the first German request for the return of captured documents. In January 1950, Passant suggested to Sir William Strang that the JCC be recognized as an official governmental body.[126] As such, the committee would not only advise but also have a say in decisions on the captured documents. In February 1950, Wheeler-Bennett informed the American Joint Chiefs of Staff – not the State Department – of the establishment of the JCC as a decision-making body in the British government for matters pertaining to captured German records.[127]

---

123 Record of Informal Meeting of Joint Consultative Committee of Historians, Nov. 13, 1947, PRO FO 370/1493 L6876; Minutes Wheeler-Bennett for Passant, Jan. 2, 1950, PRO FO 370/2088 LS13/1.

124 2nd Formal Meeting of the Joint Official Historian's Consultative Committee, Dec. 11, 1947, PRO FO 370/1493, L7648.

125 For example, the Joint Intelligence Bureau of the Defense Ministry, the Public Record Office, as well as the Ministry of Supply, Department of Industrial and Scientific Research and the Board of Trade. The latter three oversaw the copies of technical papers from German firms.

126 Minutes Passant to Strang, Jan. 13, 1950, PRO FO 370/2088 LS13/1.

127 Wheeler-Bennett to Capt. T[racy] B. Kittredge, USNR, US Joint Chiefs of Staff, Feb. 2, 1950, PRO FO 370/2088 LS13/1.

Until the High Commission received Adenauer's letter requesting the return of all captured documents in June 1950, the JCC led a quiet existence.[128] It took note of the High Commission's decision to return the cashier's records and personnel files of the Auswärtiges Amt[129] but, taking its cue from the AHC, assumed that no other documents would be sent back to Germany in the immediate future.[130] The JCC had no objections to this first shipment of records to Bonn in 1950: the gradual return of documents to a democratic German government had been pledged in the preface to *Documents on German Foreign Policy*, and the financial and personnel records sent to Bonn were of no bearing to the publication project. The members of the JCC knew, moreover, that they could rely on the historians at Whaddon Hall to put up resistance, with Passant's backing, to any attempt to return diplomatic files while work on *Documents on German Foreign Policy* was still underway.[131] The committee's work generally focused on materials other than the diplomatic records, above all the captured military documents. Adenauer's June 1950 request for the return of *all* records prompted a knee-jerk reaction. Upon hearing that the chancellor had sent a note on the issue of the documents, several committee members were determined to reject the request it conveyed.[132]

Wheeler-Bennett coordinated the JCC's response. He did not reply to the British High Commission's request that the JCC compile a detailed register of all captured documents in British possession. He considered it "inadvisable to acquaint the Germans fully with the details."[133] The register had not been intended, however, for the West Germans – it was to be for the use of British officials. By insinuating that the register would be forwarded to the Germans, Wheeler-Bennett immediately gained the support of other ministries represented in the JCC. Even Passant was never able to persuade the JCC to compile such a register.[134] The British High

128 Adenauer to the Chairman of the AHC, André François-Poncet, June 17, 1950, Adenauer, *Briefe*, no. 257, 232f.

129 JCC 26th Meeting, July 6, 1950, PRO FO 370/2088 LS13/11.

130 "The three Governments regret that they are at present unable to return any of the archives." J. E. Slater, Secretary General, AHC, to MinDirg Herbert Blankenhorn, AGSEC (50) 869, May 3, 1950, PA/AA B118, vol. 507.

131 Minutes Acheson, CAB, to Sir Oscar Charles Morland, Undersecretary, CAB, and A. Johnston, Dec. 18, 1950, PRO CAB 103/458: "Although Mr. Passant is himself strongly opposed to the return of the documents, he has . . . some anxiety about the attitude which may be adopted by the [FO] department which deals with political relations with Western Germany."

132 For the Navy, Commander Saunders ascertained: "It would be highly undesirable that the naval records should ever be handed back to the Germans." JCC 26th Meeting, July 6, 1950, PRO FO 370/2088 LS13/11.

133 JCC 29th Meeting, Nov. 2, 1950, PRO FO 370/2088 LS13/15.

134 See Notes on Meeting held in Mr. Acheson's Room [CAB], Nov. 6, 1950, PRO CAB 103/458: "It came as a shock to hear Mr. Passant's suggestion that the Germans should be supplied with a complete survey of the holdings of documents in this country." Passant never suggested this.

Commission officials engaged in the negotiations with the West Germans on the captured documents were thus poorly prepared when the talks moved beyond the Auswärtiges Amt records. Bernard Noble, too, tried to wrestle a list of British documents holdings from the JCC for use in preparing a schedule for the documents' return. American governmental agencies and departments had willingly supplied such inventories.[135] The JCC had recognized early on, however, that by refusing to provide even a rough overview of the captured documents in British possession it could steer or at least drag out the discussion of the documents' return. Signals from Bonn confirmed the success of this strategy. The Germans found it difficult to formulate their demands with any precision "as they did not know what archives were still in existence or where these were."[136]

The Cabinet Office. The Cabinet Office was one of the departments with a strong interest in German military records. Its Historical Section, headed by Andrew Basil Acheson, was overseeing the preparation of the official history of British operations during World War II.[137] An Enemy Document Section (EDS) was added to the Historical Section in October 1948.[138] Under the direction of Brian Melland, who had worked in the German department of the military intelligence service MI 14 until 1945, the EDS supplied the authors of the official history with data and documents and was therefore dependent on access to German military records.[139] Because those records were in Washington, the EDS dispatched George W. S. Friedrichsen in August 1948 to serve as a liaison officer at the Departmental Records Branch as well as at the U.S. Army's historical division.[140] Like Melland, Friedrichsen was an MI 14 veteran. For Melland, he was an important and effective on-site informant, since Friedrichsen had a direct line to the

---

135 Acheson, Reflections on the Discussion with Dr. Noble, Dec. 8, 1953, PRO FO 370/2345 LS5/29; JCC 75th Meeting, Jan. 5, 1955, PRO 370/2426 LS5/13. Noble received a preliminary overview from his departments already in February 1940. See note 3.

136 JCC 47th Meeting, Apr. 2, 1952, PRO FO 370/2269 LS18/5. See also Wilhelm Rohr, BA, to Ministry of Culture, North-Rhine Westfalia, May 14, 1958, HStA BR 2094–44. "May we point out that complete uncertainty reigns concerning the German records of nonmilitary provenance still in British hands (and their location), because the British, unlike the Americans, have remained silent about this issue up to this point."

137 On the founding and early history of the Cabinet Office, see Naylor, "Establishment of Cabinet Secretariat"; on the Historical Section and the official histories, see Connell, "Official History"; Grunewald, "Travaux"; for the same subject covered by the participants, see Butler, "British Official Military History," and Frankland, *History at War.*

138 Brian Melland, EDS, Progress Report Oct. 1948-Oct. 1949, Oct. 14, 1949, PRO CAB 103/336.

139 Annan, *Changing Enemies,* 3, describes Melland (1904–1971) as a "theatrical character." During the war, Melland ran the department MI 14 (d), which dealt with German defense, the SD, and the Gestapo. The only biographical source on Melland is the obituary by Wheeler-Bennett in *The Times* (London), July 29, 1971, 20.

140 Friedrichsen to Melland, Mar. 29, 1950, PRO CAB 103/458.

Departmental Records Branch by way of his friendship with one of its employees, Philipp Brower.

Friedrichsen kept Melland informed on the meetings of the American Interagency Conference and tried to estimate the likelihood that the Americans would return documents in their possession. In January 1950, Friedrichsen reported that all parties concerned in Washington were united in opposition to restitution.[141] Eight months later, however, he identified the State Department as a possible weak link in the chain: "The State Department will...be a focus of political expedience-measures which might include the return of documents. These are the people who may create trouble, but not, assuredly the [Armed] Forces."[142] Melland used Friedrichsen not only to gather information but also to inform select American officials of the JCC's views. He wanted to be sure that people in Washington did not take the Foreign Office's official statements on the captured documents too seriously. Thus, he saw to it that General Klein at the Adjutant General's Office was informed "that we are not only sensitive but uneasy in London about the restitution question."[143] As Melland later reported, Klein assured Friedrichsen "that whatever the State Department was plotting, the U.S. Army was dead against giving back anything, and it was known [here at AGO] that the British were against sending *anything at all*."[144] The unofficial contact between the JCC and the Departmental Records Branch provided valuable information that did not appear in the minutes of the JCC meetings but nonetheless influenced its outlook. Melland must have been gratified to learn from Friedrichsen "that the German document 'experts' in the Department of the Army are inclined to share our views.... If large scale unilateral return of material to the Germans is undertaken, it is more likely to be the result of firm State Department pressure than of purely military decision." The Army, Friedrichsen told Melland, would have to follow the State Department line but would nonetheless still be able to deploy "stalemate tactics"[145] – tactics Melland himself was highly skilled in using.

141 Friedrichsen to Melland, Mar. 28, 1950, ibid. He quotes the staff member Ropshaw from the Germany section of the State Department as saying: "It would be politically inadvisable for mi[litary] records to be returned to Germany in view of our stated policy against any rearmament in Germany." At the Department of Commerce, the German records were said to be seen as "legitimate war booty."
142 Friedrichsen to Melland, Sept. 13, 1950, PRO FO 370/2088 LS13/10. The minutes of the JCC meeting on April 5, 1951, even speak of a "marked disposition on the part of the State Department towards appeasement" – a word that in the postwar English vocabulary was certainly not a compliment. See JCC 34th Meeting, Apr. 5, 1951, PRO CAB 103/458.
143 Minutes, Melland to Acheson, Jan. 17, 1955, PRO CAB 103/336.
144 Ibid., emphasis in original.
145 Ibid.

By the winter of 1955–56, the JCC members from the Cabinet Office had another concern. Like the editors of *Documents on German Foreign Policy*, the historians preparing the official history of the war were coming under criticism for working too slowly. The multivolume series *Victory in the West* and *The Mediterranean and Middle East* were still not complete at the end of 1955, and the authors were under growing pressure to wrap up their work on the remaining volumes. Had Washington acted to return the German military records quickly, the entire Enemy Documents Section would have been threatened. In the fall of 1955, Melland was required to give a cost accounting of the Enemy Documents Section's work.[146] The captured records not only provided the source material for historiography, they also provided jobs. Friedrichsen experienced this first-hand early in 1956 when he had to ward off efforts to reduce his position to a part-time one.[147] Apparently the personnel department believed that the yield from German sources no longer justified a full-time position in Washington.

In addition to Melland and Friedrichsen, another key figure in the years from 1949 to 1957 was Andrew B. Acheson, who headed the Historical Section at the Cabinet Office.[148] Like Melland, Acheson was an outspoken opponent of restitution and was always on the lookout for arguments to back his position. Acheson is a good example of the influence that administrative officials can exert on political decision-making within their departments. Although his superiors were prepared to grant the Germans' requests even if doing so would hinder work on the official history of the war, Acheson cleverly manipulated the flow of information in such a way that the Cabinet Office appeared to back the opponents of restitution in the British policy debate.[149]

The Admiralty and the Air Ministry. At the time the JCC was set up, the interests of the official historians stood in the foreground. Consequently, it was the historical departments of the Admiralty and the Air Ministry that became active in the work of the committee. Like the Cabinet Office, the Historical Section of the Admiralty had a Foreign Documents Section. Its head, Commander Malcolm Saunders, represented his ministry in

---

146 Melland, Functions and Personnel of the EDS, Nov. 16, 1955, PRO CAB 103/339.
147 Friedrichsen to Melland, Feb. 6, and Feb. 28, 1956, PRO CAB 103/339.
148 Acheson (1895–1959) began his career in the Colonial Office in 1920, where he rose to become Private Secretary to the Permanent Under-Secretary. In 1926 he became Full Principal and in 1938, Assistant Secretary. In 1948 he switched to the Cabinet Office, where he ran the Historical Section as Assistant Secretary until he retired in 1957. I would like to thank Richard Ponman, formerly at the Cabinet Office, London, for this biographical information.
149 For a detailed analysis of Acheson's tactics see Eckert, *Kampf um die Akten*, 239f.

the JCC.[150] The representative of the Air Ministry was Squadron Leader Jackets. Both men made it clear from the start that the return of the documents was not considered an option by their ministries. With only slight variation, the reasons they gave remained the same over the years. They argued that the authors of the official history of the war were not the only researchers dependent on the captured German documentation; the materials also served as the basis for "staff studies" used in training and were therefore needed for current defense planning. If official history projects no longer sufficed as justification for their position, military security provided another line of argument. The Admiralty argued, for example, that the German naval records, especially the materials on submarine warfare, might be highly useful in dealing with a "future aggressor, whether German or Russian. . . . If the original documents are returned to Germany we have no guarantee of their safe custody or their ultimate destination."[151] The evaluation of captured records was also said to be essential for current defense strategies because "the advent of the atomic age has not lessened the danger from enemy submarines."[152] Furthermore, both the Admiralty and the Air Ministry repeatedly pointed out that the records were being held in conjunction with the United States. No decision about the future of the documents could be made without consulting the Americans.[153] Even Acheson, no advocate of restitution, thought that Saunders held too uncompromising a position in the name of the Admiralty.[154]

The task of giving concise expression to the different ministerial reservations about the return of the captured documents fell to the JCC. As its members were drafting its first official position paper in November 1950, Acheson proposed that it should proceed on the assumption that "the documents were legitimate booty of war; they were as important as the material captured and logically should no more be returned after use than U-Boats

---

150 The head of the Historical Section was Rear Admiral Roger M. Bellairs. Among others, Walter Pfeiffer, the former archivist for the Kriegswissenschaftliche Abteilung (Military Science Section) of the German navy worked in Saunder's team at the Foreign Documents Section.

151 Rear Admiral Roger M. Bellairs, Chief, Historical Section, Admiralty, to Passant, July 31, 1950, PRO FO 370/2076 LS3/198. See also Bellairs to Acheson, Feb. 2, 1954, CAB 103/466.

152 [Admiralty], Exploitation of Captured German Naval Documents in the Admiralty, London, May 29, 1954, PRO CAB 103/462.

153 The agreements between the armed forces are found in Melland, EDS, Anglo-American Inter-Services Agreements relating to Captured German Military Archives, Nov. 7, 1950, PRO CAB 103/458. Between 1944 and 1947, the U.S. Navy filmed a great many of the naval records stored in London and maintained a team there until 1950. See Eller, "US Navy Microfilm"; Guides U-Boats and T-Boats, xi-xiv.

154 Attachment to minutes, Acheson to Morland, July 31, 1952, PRO CAB 103/459.

or captured armaments."[155] The Air Ministry had to back away from that position in part, however, when it found itself under political pressure to make the Luftwaffe personnel records accessible as the Federal Republic was establishing its new armed forces. Subsequently, the JCC had to try to prevent Bonn or the Foreign Office's German desk from turning this instance into a precedent. The British government, the JCC maintained, should never find itself in the uncomfortable position "where the retention of captured archives had to be justified to the Germans."[156]

Acheson's connections to the British Joint Intelligence Committee (JIC) of the Chiefs of Staff proved to be very helpful at this juncture because the JIC was one body that not even the Foreign Office could ignore.[157] In the course of planning for the European Defence Community (EDC), the JIC dealt many times with the subject of security and the trustworthiness of the West German officials who were slated to see confidential NATO materials. The British opinion of the potential secret bearers in Bonn was devastating: "Security in German official circles was virtually nonexistent."[158] An assessment in November 1952 was not very flattering:

> Generally speaking, Germans are psychologically unable to be as secure as, say, the British. Two principal reasons are –
> a) "Geltungsbeduerfnis" – the need to amount to something and to be somebody set apart from the mass, e.g., one who knows things that others do not know.
> b) Lack of an authority or individual who commands unquestioning loyalty, e.g., formerly the Kaiser, or Hitler.[159]

On top of these concerns about German psychology, the JIC was worried about structural security problems. West German federal ministries and agencies were said to have been in such a hurry to hire staff in 1949 that they often dispensed with background security checks. Party loyalties, the JIC feared, would outweigh the duty to be silent about military

---

155 Notes on a Meeting held in Mr. Acheson's Room, Question of Return of the Captured German Documents to the Federal German Government, Nov. 6, 1950; present: Acheson, Melland, Saunders, Jackets, PRO CAB 103/458.
156 JCC 48th Meeting, July 2, 1952, PRO CAB 103/459.
157 A comparison of Acheson's submission to Col. Gardiner, JIC, Ministry of Defense, Apr. 8, 1952, with the resulting report by the JIC, The Release of Captured German Documents to the Germans, JIC (52) 37, June 6, 1952, CAB 103/458 and 459 shows that the JIC report expresses the same concerns as Acheson, using his exact words. The JIC report deals with the differences between regulations in Washington and London governing the access to captured records.
158 Chiefs of Staff Committee. Joint Intelligence Committee. [Report on] German Security, JIC(52)73, Nov. 21, 1952, PRO CAB 103/460.
159 Joint Intelligence Committee (Germany), Security of Federal German Organisations, JIC(Germany)(52)95(Final), Nov. 5, 1952, as Appendix A to the JIC(52)73, Nov. 21, 1952, PRO CAB 103/460.

secrets.[160] High-level officials and, in particular, ministers "are presumed, or presume themselves to be, too important to be lectured on security," and every German official and politician had "the inevitable 'trusted friend'" somewhere. Moreover, low salaries made public officials susceptible to bribery. The JIC saw an especially grave security threat in the unchecked flow of classified information through networks of "old comrades."[161]

The JIC's lack of confidence in German security was soon confirmed by the so-called Naumann affair, which was a godsend for the JCC. In January 1953, the British military police arrested Werner Naumann, who had served under Goebbels as state secretary at Ministry of Propaganda and several other onetime Nazi officials. They were accused of planning to infiltrate West German political parties to advance neo-Nazi positions. In squelching this plot, the British were exercising their right as an occupation power.[162] When the JCC met in February 1953, several participants called attention to the statement in the preface *to Documents on German Foreign Policy* that the records would be returned as soon as "stable conditions" existed in Germany. The committee went on to conclude rather nonchalantly that "recent events in Germany had indicated that the pre-requisite, i.e. stable conditions in Germany laid down by the Custodian Powers for the restitution of documents, did not in fact exist."[163]

Economic and Commercial Interests. The British departments dealing with industry and commerce reaped the benefits of the work done by the Combined Intelligence Objectives Sub-Committee (CIOS) and the British successor organization, BIOS.[164] BIOS had always conceived of its work as a three-step process: the gathering of information on German research and industry, the evaluation of that information and dissemination of it to British firms, and the application of newly acquired knowledge.[165] Its

---

160 "Fights for personal advancement and party advantage foster the passage of information to unauthorised persons, who, despite obligations of position or statesmanship, do not report leakages (e.g., the SPD silence on the passage of duplicated material from the Chancellor's own office to the late Leader of the Opposition)." Ibid.

161 "Old loyalties frequently transcend present-day obligations. The Deputy Head of the B[undesamt] f[ür] V[erfassungsschutz] [Radke] is reliably reported as willing to supply certain BfV information to his former comrades in ex-soldiers' associations 'on an unofficial basis'.... Contacts existing between German ex-officers who are in Government offices and those ex-officers outside the Government must present a danger to security, particularly in respect to NATO information." Ibid.

162 On the Naumann affair, see Herbert, *Best*, 461–9; Frei, *Adenauer's Germany*, 277–302.

163 "It was agreed that the British Intelligence Authorities at Bonn should be notified. It was observed that the examination of the documents seized in connexion with the arrests [of Naumann et al., A. E.] might influence the whole question of the return of the captured documents in Germany." JCC 56th Meeting, Feb. 4, 1953, PRO CAB 103/460.

164 On CIOS, see Chapter 1.　　　　　　165 Farquharson, "Governed or Exploited?" 36f.

London office had collected 70,000 German patents by 1947. The Stationary Office published approximately 2,000 BIOS reports on German industrial facilities. British firms could order copies of captured German documents or send their own experts to the occupation zone, or later, the Bizone. British companies, especially mid-sized ones, and the armed forces took advantage of these opportunities extensively.[166] Most reports and documents were not classified as confidential material and were therefore available to anyone interested in them. The Commonwealth states (especially Australia), the United States, and even the former enemy Japan made good use of the available material.[167]

When Adenauer submitted the first request for the return of the captured documents in June 1950, most participants in the JCC believed that the German industrial documents held by the Board of Trade, the Ministry of Supply, and the Department for Industrial and Scientific Research (DSIR) could be kept out of consideration in the discussion. It was argued that the papers dealt chiefly with weapons research, which Germany was prohibited from undertaking.[168] The JCC feared that the British government would lose "irreplaceable information" should these papers be returned.[169] The patents and other research materials were therefore not even mentioned in the JCC's first policy paper (December 1950).[170] They became a topic of discussion, however, as the Foreign Office and the British High Commission pressed for at least a few small concessions to the West Germans as a gesture to acknowledge the new political atmosphere signaled by the pending expiration of the Occupation Statute.

166 Ibid., 34–8, including a quantification of demand. In the first nine months of 1952, the Department of Industrial and Scientific Research still registered 600 visitors, 600 written and 400 telephone inquiries, and sent off 400,000 pages of copied material. See Urquhart, Department of Scientific and Industrial Research (DSIR), to Acheson, CAB, Oct. 22, 1952, PRO CAB 103/460.

167 JCC 57th Meeting, Mar. 4, 1953, PRO CAB 103/460. Farquharson, "Governed or Exploited?" 39, maintains that German firms could also order reports and in this way were able to gain information about each of their competitors. However, an attempt appears to have been made to exclude German companies. This did not prove feasible: DSIR "had adopted a policy of discrimination against nationals of ex-enemy countries who applied for photocopies of documents held by the Department. In practice, this policy was unsatisfactory as such a national had only to employ a British agent in order to obtain the copies he requires. After discussion, it was agreed that the policy of discrimination should be dropped." JCC 69th Meeting, May 5, 1954, PRO CAB 103/461. Also, JCC 45th Meeting, Apr. 2, 1952, PRO CAB 146/141.

168 E. E. Haddon, Ministry of Supply to the UnderSecState, FO, Sept. 12, 1950, PRO CAB 103/458.

169 Ms. Johnston, JCC Secretary, to Acheson, Sept. 16, 1950, PRO CAB 103/458.

170 Request by the German Chancellor for the Return of Captured German Archives. Memorandum by the Joint Consultative Committee on Captured Enemy Documents, Dec. 15, 1950, PRO CAB 103/459. The memorandum is reprinted in Eckert, *Kampf um die Akten*, 472–477. The reason why industrial documents were not mentioned may have been because Wahnerheide wanted to avoid any reference to the economic exploitation of German sources by British industry in its official responses. See JCC 29th Meeting, Nov. 2, 1950, PRO FO 370/2088 LS13/15.

At first, Acheson questioned whether the industrial documents should still be retained in August 1952.[171] However, he was promptly requested by the affected departments and agencies to come up with wording acceptable to the Foreign Office that would, in the end, allow them to keep the documentation. The ensuing internal discussions of these materials took on distinctly nationalistic tones and revealed motives that were usually kept out of the JCC's correspondence and the minutes of its meetings. An official at the Ministry of Supply, for example, expressed the opinion that the loss of the industrial documentation was "a penalty for loosing [sic] a war. I am sure that if the position had been reversed, we should not get our classified research and development reports back."[172] The DSIR left no doubt that "German competition in the export market is now a serious factor, and it may be that the industrial documents we hold would enable British firms to meet this competition successfully."[173] Acheson was well attuned to the concerns of the ministries and agencies involved and echoed their insistence that they possessed primarily copies of German documents and only rarely originals. CIOS/BIOS agents, he maintained in a report to the Foreign Office, had been instructed at the time of the invasion and occupation of Germany to leave the originals at the German firms. How, then, could German firms claim that they had no access to their own papers?[174] Acheson did not get far with this line of argument, perhaps because Foreign Office staff remembered how CIOS actually operated. In fact, it was not unlikely that the copies found in Great Britain could indeed be the only surviving documentation.[175]

Acheson was forced to propose a compromise on the research and industrial documents to satisfy the Foreign Office, where officials were keenly aware that the Federal Republic would be allowed to undertake weapons research following its anticipated accession to the EDC and would therefore have grounds for demanding the return of industrial documents. The Ministry of Supply finally agreed in theory to approve the eventual return of

171 "If other considerations were not involved, we should see no reason why, so far as the UK is concerned, they should not be turned to Germany as and when they cease to be of value to British industries." Acheson, Report of the JCC: German Request for the Return of Captured German Archives, Aug. 22, 1952, PRO CAB 103/459.

172 L. J. H. Haylor, Ministry of Supply, to Acheson, CAB, Sept. 22, 1952, PRO CAB 103/466. Haylor cleared his letter with the Chief Scientist of the MoS beforehand.

173 D. J. Urquhart, DSIR, to Acheson, CAB, Sept. 6, 1952, PRO CAB 103/459.

174 Acheson, German Industrial Documents, Note of a discussion with DSIR, Oct. 9, 1952; Acheson to Passant, Oct. 10, 1952, both in PRO CAB 103/466.

175 E. J. Offord, Technical and Industrial Document Unit [at the] DSIR, to Passant, FO, Sept. 18, 1952, PRO FO 370/2249 LS3/113. It was reported that the unit had received a query from BMW about technical drawings of BMW motorcycles. Even though they had no originals, "it could well be that the ferro-print copies we hold are the only copies now available."

papers as soon as they were no longer in use – but only if the West German government explicitly requested them. Acheson also offered the ministry a loophole: "We could legitimately regard the documents as being in use, as long as it was felt necessary to retain them against the possibility that they might contain information of real value for our own research and development. . . No doubt this in practice would mean that the collection would have to be retained for many years."[176] Under the compromise Acheson brokered, German firms would be allowed to order copies of their own papers for a fee.

In his correspondence with Passant, Acheson speculated on the reasons behind Bonn's insistence on the return of industrial records. The materials were not governmental records, they could not be considered a part of the country's cultural heritage, and they were of no use for historical research.

National prestige seems to me in these cases a pretty thin argument. I daresay that German industrialists may retain a certain sense of humiliation at the knowledge that the fruits of German research and industry are still held and made available to industries in other countries against their will, and, as it were, by force. It is a reminder of their defeat, and no doubt their feelings may be shared in political circles in Germany.[177]

Acheson believed the real reason for the behavior of German firms lie in their "desire . . . to deprive their competitors . . . in this and other countries of the results of German research." He was mystified that the Foreign Office could even consider returning the papers "when we are straining every nerve to expand our own industrial production and exports."[178] Eventually, the Foreign Office accepted Acheson's proposal – which he himself apparently considered a remarkably generous concession to the Germans – more out of resignation than conviction.[179]

The Foreign Office. The Foreign Office played a key role in the matter of the captured German documents. It presented the official British position to both West Germany and the other Allies. It also shared responsibility for the administration of Auswärtiges Amt files with the State Department and supervised the preparation of *Documents on German Foreign Policy* at Whaddon Hall. Yet no other ministry was as divided over the document

---

176 Acheson, Memorandum, German Documents held by the Ministry of Supply, Oct. 10, 1952, PRO CAB 103/466.
177 Acheson to Passant, Oct. 10, 1952, PRO CAB 103/466; see also Acheson to Passant, Oct. 25, 1952, CAB 103/460.
178 Acheson to Passant, Oct. 10, 1952, PRO CAB 103/466.
179 Gellately, FO, to Acheson, Nov. 12, 1952, PRO CAB 103/460.

issue as the Foreign Office. The senior officials responsible for policy on Germany at the Central Department and the High Commission collided time and again with Passant.[180] Whereas the Central Department considered the return issue secondary to far more pressing matters, Passant sided with the historians at Whaddon Hall. Passant's views against restitution were close to those of Wheeler-Bennett.[181] But he had to represent the views and voice the concerns of the Foreign Office policy-makers at meetings of the JCC to avoid marginalizing himself at the ministry. Passant thus found himself caught in the crossfire several times at JCC meetings when he defended the positions of senior Foreign Office staff, even though he did not share them.

After the resolution adopted by German historians at the 1949 meeting of the Association of German Historians, it was clear to Foreign Office Library officials that the captured documents would soon become a political issue. Passant anticipated Bonn's argument that the records from the old Auswärtiges Amt would be needed in establishing the new one. "It may be fairly suggested," he wrote, "that a completely new start in German methods of conducting foreign policy would be the best thing."[182] At first, British High Commissioner Sir Ivone Kirkpatrick agreed with Passant that it would be impossible to interrupt work on *Documents on German Foreign Policy* and that the Germans would just have to wait until the project was completed. Once Adenauer's note was presented to the High Commission, however, Kirkpatrick changed his mind and recommended the adoption of a "policy of minor concessions." Political circumstances, he believed, would make continued British possession of the Auswärtiges Amt files difficult if not impossible. Hoping to persuade Kirkpatrick to change his mind once again, Passant sent him the JCC's December 1950 policy paper and emphasized that all governmental departments and agencies concerned were against an early return of the captured documents.[183] The Central Department nonetheless refused to endorse the JCC's position. It argued that the JCC paper ignored the German arguments – arguments the Central Department considered entirely justified in light of the new Allied policy. The JCC was reminded, moreover, that it was the Allies themselves who had decided to allow the Federal Republic to re-establish a diplomatic

---

180 For a biography of E. James Passant, see Chapter 2, n. 249.

181 Minutes, Acheson for Morland and A. Johnston, Dec. 18, 1950, PRO CAB 103/458.

182 Minutes, Passant for Sir Ivone Kirkpatrick, Jan. 31, 1950 and Feb. 2, 1950, both in PRO FO 370/2073 LS3/17. The resolution is printed in *Historische Zeitschrift* 169 (1949), 669f.

183 Minutes, Passant for Sir Donald St. Clair Gainer, Permanent Under-Secretary of State, German Political Department, Jan. 4, 1951, PRO CAB 103/458.

service: continued custody of the records would not be consistent with the new policy of allowing Bonn considerable freedom of action in setting up its new foreign ministry. Although work on *Documents on German Foreign Policy* was not to be stopped, the Central Department deemed it necessary that the Foreign Office be "as liberal as we can" on the issue of the captured documents.[184] Passant and Wheeler-Bennett even traveled to Wahnerheide to present the JCC standpoint in person, but they could not persuade the High Commission to abandon its conciliatory stance toward West Germany. Commission officials were already engaged with the issue of German rearmament and argued that "if German assistance was wanted on big issues, minor concessions must be made."[185] Already in 1950, Kirkpatrick thought that it was not enough simply to argue that the records were still necessary for historical research in England. He therefore suggested that materials of secondary importance should be sent back to Germany immediately to gain time. Proceeding in stages was his only concession toward the JCC's position. As Acheson accurately noted, "the question of the return of German archives [was] a matter of comparatively minor importance" for the High Commissioner.[186]

Passant's position within the JCC became difficult after Adenauer introduced the issue of the captured documents into the negotiations on the Germany treaty. In April 1952, the chancellor demanded that the High Commissioners issue a strong declaration affirming that the archives and registries held by the Allies were German property and would be returned. With a great deal of effort, Kirkpatrick was able to convince Adenauer to exclude this topic from the ongoing negotiations and to handle it separately. Kirkpatrick did not expect, however, that the Germans would relent on this point. He predicted that the High Commissioners would not be able to avoid the issue after the summer break and therefore promised Bonn negotiations on the return of the documents.[187] The JCC felt it had been completely overridden and accused Kirkpatrick of overstepping his authority and "capitulating" to Adenauer.

It then became Passant's task to justify the actions of the High Commissioner to the JCC – to defend, in other words, a position at odds with his own views. He explained that, politically, Kirkpatrick had no choice but to hold out the prospect of negotiations. The High Commissioner could not

184 Minute, W. D. Allen, proxy for St. Clair Gainer, to Passant, Dec. 27, 1950, ibid.
185 JCC 29th Meeting, Nov. 2, 1950, PRO FO370/2088 LS13/15.
186 Minutes, Acheson for Morland and A. Johnston, Dec. 18, 1950, PRO CAB 103/458.
187 *Adenauer und die Hohen Kommissare 1952* (II), no. 41, Apr. 9, 1952, 71. Kirkpatrick, Wahnerheide, to FO, no. 476, Apr. 10, 1952, PRO FO 370/2244; and Aug. 13, 1952, PRO CAB 103/459.

have simply ignored Adenauer's explicit demand. "Negotiation, however, does not mean wholesale surrender," Passant argued. The Foreign Office was prepared to consider realistic concessions but would not recognize the demand for immediate return of the documents as a legitimate claim. Passant appealed to the JCC on Kirkpatrick's behalf to reconsider its stance. The High Commissioner feared that British intransigence on the documents could set off a "'political row' in Germany" that "might seriously affect the prospect of ratification of the Contractual Arrangement by the Federal Parliament at Bonn."[188] That scenario was, of course, an exaggeration. The issue of the captured records was important to only a small, elite group, the Bundestag debate of May 1950 on the matter notwithstanding. It received little attention in the German press, and there was never a chance that it might have bearing on a decisive political matter such as participation in the EDC.

The other members of the JCC were not persuaded by Passant's arguments. As Achson observed, "They did not regard the changed relationship with Western Germany as a reason in itself for making concessions over the documents."[189] Still, the JCC condescended to revise its policy paper of December 1950 under Acheson's direction. The revised paper, finished in August 1952, presented the position of the Foreign Office accurately. At the same time, however, so many restrictions and reservations had been added that officials at the Central Department quickly realized that no real progress had been achieved.[190] For example, the JCC acknowledged the "general principle that the captured archives . . . should ultimately be returned," but then added that it would not be possible to draw up a timetable. In other words, the JCC's acceptance of returning the documents in principle amounted to little in practice. The JCC also placed a great deal of importance on consultations with the Americans. Acheson's worst nightmare was that the British and Americans would not present a concerted front to the Germans, who would then, in his words, "be in a position to play us off against one another."[191] The bottom line was that the concessions the JCC could envision gave their colleagues at the British High Commission in Wahnerheide nothing to work with. The Central Department was therefore forced to bring in heavier artillery and sent Sir Frank Roberts, the undersecretary of state at the Foreign Office, to address the JCC at its next meeting. Although Roberts started out by trying to communicate

188 JCC 49th Meeting, Aug. 14, 1952, PRO FO 370/2269 LS18/11.
189 Minutes, Acheson for Morland, CAB, Aug. 20, 1952, PRO CAB 103/459.
190 Acheson, Report of the JCC [on the] German Request for the Return of Captured German Archives, draft, Aug. 22, 1952, PRO CAB 103/459.
191 Minutes, Acheson for Morland, Aug. 20, 1952, PRO CAB 103/459.

the new political situation to the committee in a conciliatory way, he soon stopped mincing his words: "There was a good deal of misgivings at the Headquarters of the United Kingdom High Commission in Germany regarding the Committee's attitude toward the forthcoming negotiations with the Germans."[192] Despite Roberts's intervention, the JCC stuck to a restrictive position and would consider negotiation only on records that were relevant to West German rearmament in the context of the EDC.

From the perspective of the Central Department and the Office of the High Commissioner, the JCC continued to be an obstacle to their efforts to move forward on the issue of the captured documents. The talks between the JCC and the foreign policy officials stalled in 1952 as each side held tenaciously to a position all too familiar to the other. In November 1953, following the West German government's proposal to transfer the *Documents on German Foreign Policy* project to Germany, Kit Barclay of the High Commission once again attempted to communicate as clearly as possible the central concern of British diplomats in Bonn:

Our own day-to-day business of Anglo-German relations is more and more with the Federal Ministry for Foreign Affairs, who are the very people who feel most strongly about the Archives. They feel that the present German offer is a good one. If we turn it down or fail to produce a reasonable alternative we risk injecting a little poison into all our dealings with them at a time when we are trying to build up our contacts with them.[193]

Although British officials remained at loggerheads, the Western Allies and Bonn were eventually able to come to terms on the return of the captured documents. In March 1956 the governments finally agreed on the terms of the return of the Auswärtiges Amt files; that agreement, in turn, paved the way for negotiations on the return of the military records. On the British side, compromise on the captured documents was made possible by a series of changes, including increased American pressure on the British and less categorical overtones by the Germans in the negotiations. Looking ahead for a moment, we see that it was not until 1958, at the start of talks on non-diplomatic records, that the Foreign Office finally won the upper hand over the JCC. Francis Hancock, the head of the Central Department, was one of those involved who no longer wanted to exert his diplomatic energies on internal negotiations:

I used to sit on the JCC myself and I know how frightfully difficult and obstructive some of its members are. In those days we thought we had done quite well when

192 JCC 53rd Meeting, Nov. 5, 1952, PRO FO 370/2269 LS18/15.
193 Kit Barclay, Office of the High Commissioner, Memorandum: German Foreign Office Archives – Arguments, n.d. [November 1953], PRO FO 370/2344 LS5/248.

we got agreement to return the veterinary archives, and the archives relating to the history of Heligoland! But nowadays we have got further than this in our political relations with Germany and it does not seem worthwhile annoying the Germans just to satisfy one or two old dug-outs in the Admiralty.[194]

The new director of the Library, Cecil Parrott, could only agree and announced a new policy toward the JCC.[195] Apparently the officials at the Foreign Office had simply had enough.

The Development of the JCC Policy Papers

The JCC issued four policy papers between 1950 and 1958. The following section presents a diachronic comparison of these policies. Although the JCC discussed only military archival material, the progress made in the negotiations on the diplomatic records had an impact on the military documents, too. To the degree that a solution for the diplomatic records appeared imminent, the JCC came under pressure to make concessions on the other papers.

The first policy paper was completed in December 1950. It was the immediate reaction to the Bundestag debate of May 1950 and to the subsequent petition for restitution that Adenauer sent to the High Commission. This paper was a secret internal memorandum and was sent to the Americans to serve as a basis for a joint communiqué; it was not made available to the West Germans. As noted above, the JCC was firmly opposed to complying with Bonn's request. The JCC maintained

(1) that it is essential that the United States Government should be consulted before any instructions on this matter are sent to the United Kingdom High Commissioner;
(2) that it would be dangerous to security and defence to comply with the German request;
(3) that such a step would give offence in former allied countries;
(4) that it would severely hamper the preparation of the official Histories of the War.[196]

While these conclusions appear quite harmless, the instructions spelling out the actual meaning of each of them were tough. They left the Central

---

194 Minutes, Hancock, May 27, 1958, PRO FO 370/2548 LS5/42.
195 "The Committee could not be more obstructive. They just sit there and think up reasons why they should hold on to documents which no one here needs. Any reasonable action by a German today becomes at once the object of their gravest suspicions and they waste hours of my time dissecting German motives." Minutes, Parrott, May 30, 1958, ibid.
196 Request by the German Chancellor for the Return of Captured German Archives. Memorandum by the Joint Consultative Committee on Captured Enemy Documents, Dec. 15, 1950, PRO CAB 103/459. The memorandum was unanimously approved at the 30th meeting on Dec. 7, 1950, and accepted by the Chiefs of Staff in January 1951. It was signed by John Wheeler-Bennett. The memorandum is reprinted in Eckert, *Kampf um die Akten*, 472–7.

Department and the High Commission no latitude for negotiations with the West Germans.

The oft-repeated reference to the necessity of consultations with the U.S. government retroactively increased the importance of the agreements the two countries' armies had concluded at the end of war.[197] Originally prompted by the practical considerations of dividing up captured documents and guaranteeing reciprocal access to them, the agreements were now wielded by the JCC as shields to fend off the threat of the records' return – a topic that had not come up for discussion when the agreements were being worked out.[198] The JCC argued that the arrangements were still binding and, consequently, that any unilateral action would constitute a "breach of agreement." Knowing that consultations with Washington would likely be time-consuming and would stall negotiations with the Germans, the JCC invoked the agreements with the Americans as a delaying tactic against those officials at the Foreign Office eager to accommodate Bonn. At the same time, the demand also camouflaged the actual powerlessness of the JCC: the German military records were in American hands, not British. By urging the British government not to act without the Americans, the JCC was trying to ensure that it would be included in any discussion of the documents' return.

The most potent argument the JCC could deploy against the documents' return was military security. The 1950 policy paper defined two broad categories of documents that were not to be turned over to third parties – the West Germans above all – without the approval of both governments. These "prohibited classes" were

(a) Documents of special interest to the Armed Forces, namely documents dealing with the following subjects:
　　(i) British, United States or Allied clandestine or secret intelligence activities.
　　(ii) Cryptographic matters of any shape or kind.
　　(iii) Soviet clandestine or intelligence services.
　　(iv) Interrogations by the Germans of Allied personnel.
　　(v) The existence or activities of, or intelligence obtained by, German agents in Allied or Allied occupied territory.

(b) Documents the disclosure of which might prejudicially affect the national interest of the United States or the United Kingdom with respect to relations with other foreign Governments.

197 On the various agreements among the armed services, see Chapter 1, n. 40.
198 To support its interpretation, the JCC could use the following sentence in the Bissell-Sinclair Agreement of May 1945: "Such military archives and documents [as captured jointly] shall be disposed of as mutually agreed."

Because sheer quantity had thus far made it impossible to process all of the records in Allied possession, the JCC argued, fulfilling Adenauer's request for the immediate return of the documents meant that many would be returned sight unseen. Such a move was considered thoroughly unacceptable, if for no other reason than the danger that the material could fall into Russian hands in Germany. The JCC also noted that the military records were being used intensively for defense studies and constituted the only source of reliable information on the Red Army.

The policy paper also cited the need to keep the government historians supplied with research materials. "Various books have been published since the war based on conversations with German officers and other enemy sources; it is by no means certain that these give a true picture of the facts, and it is highly desirable that they should, if necessary, be corrected by a study of contemporary documents."[199] The Cabinet Office had inserted this language into the memorandum and was, to a certain degree, conceding the dilemma facing it: its official histories were ponderous enterprises. While the project moved slowly ahead, other publications threatened to sate interest in the subject. Winston Churchill was the first to deliver his version of the war years, a six-volume account that was published between 1948 and 1953. The authors of the official history had no choice but to respond to Churchill's authoritative but highly partisan and selective account of events.[200] The memorandum's reference to books already published appears, though, to have been a direct jab at the British military historian Basil H. Liddell Hart. Liddell Hart was already persona non grata at the Cabinet Office as a result of his criticism of Churchill's strategic decisions during the war. Furthermore, he advanced the view in his writings that Hitler had seduced and abused the leadership of the Wehrmacht – an explanation many West Germans warmly welcomed.[201] The allusion to Liddell Hart – the mention of "conversations with German officers" would have tipped off everyone familiar at that time with the burgeoning historical literature on the war – would bolster the argument presented in the JCC memorandum should it

199 Memorandum by the Joint Consultative Committee on Captured Enemy Documents, Dec. 15, 1950, PRO CAB 103/459.
200 See Connell, "Official History," 332: "The official histories of World War II...have all been...corrections and amplifications of the Churchill version." On Churchill's overwhelming influence on the depiction of the Second World War, see Reynolds, "Churchill's Writing of History"; Reynolds, *In Command of History*.
201 In 1948, Liddell Hart published a book that was based on interviews with German generals and admirals. In Britain, the title of the book was *The Other Side of the Hill;* in the United States it appeared as *The German Generals Talk*. On the historical interpretations of Liddell Hart, see Searle, "Jetzt dürfen sie reden"; Searle, "A Very Special Relationship".

ever be presented to the Cabinet and thus to Churchill himself, who had just been re-elected Prime Minister. [202]

The JCC's 1950 policy paper included a rather hypocritical argument for denying the West German request for the return of the captured documents. The return, the JCC maintained, would compromise the interests of Britain's wartime allies. Those Allies would have been quite surprised to learn that they suddenly played such an important role in the documents issue. Up to that point, the Americans and British had been rather restrictive, or at least dilatory, in granting representatives of other governments access to German records, and they had made available, at most, only carefully pre-selected materials. As the members of the JCC knew very well, document access was power.

The 1950 policy paper did take account of political developments in the Federal Republic. One paragraph took note of the debate on German rearmament. The JCC conceded that, given the plans for West German participation in the EDC, Britain could no longer retain the Luftwaffe personnel records. At the close of the paper, the committee rejected Bonn's argument that the records were urgently needed in Germany for scholarly research on the Nazi period: "If this means enlightenment regarding the evils of Nazi political theory and practice, ample material is already available for the study of this subject, including the large collection of German documentary records of the Nuremberg Trials."[203]

The British embassy in Washington presented the JCC memorandum to the State Department in February 1951 and asked for an American statement on Adenauer's request for restitution.[204] The memorandum landed in the Historical Division on the desk of Bernard Noble, who was in the middle of drafting the Interagency Committee's guidelines on the return of captured German documents. The British could thus not expect a quick response.[205] Progress was achieved only on the Auswärtiges Amt files. On July 6, 1951, the Allies sent a note in response to Adenauer's request; in May 1952, they announced their intention to open talks on the return of the

---

202 The JCC policy paper is dated December 15, 1950, the elections took place on October 25, 1950, and Churchill was commissioned to form a government the following evening.

203 Memorandum by the Joint Consultative Committee on Captured Enemy Documents, Dec. 15, 1950, PRO CAB 103/459.

204 BritEmb Washington, Aide-Memoire no. 101, Ref. 2011/11/51, Feb. 20, 1951, NA RG 407, entry 360, box 3609.

205 Noble informed the members of the Interagency Conference of the fact that the British policy paper had arrived, but did not forward its contents for another eight months. Sherrod East, head of the Departmental Records Branch, did not receive the JCC paper until October 1951. See cover letter, Noble to East, Oct. 2, 1951, ibid.

Auswärtiges Amt files.[206] The Central Department wanted the negotiations to commence immediately because it had been the British High Commissioner who had convinced Adenauer in the spring of 1952 to keep the issue of the captured documents out of the negotiations on the Germany Treaty. In return, Kirkpatrick wanted to make it possible for Adenauer "to say publicly in Germany" – before the Bundestag debate on ratification of the Germany Treaty – "that the talks about the return of the captured German documents have begun."[207] In light of the opposition of all other government agencies to the negotiations, Foreign Secretary Anthony Eden felt it necessary to bring the matter before the Cabinet.

That was the occasion for the JCC's second policy paper, which was issued in August 1952.[208] Once again, close collaboration with the Americans was held up as the "cardinal principle" of policy on the captured documents. Moreover, a common policy had to be developed not only with the Americans but also with the French before the start of negotiations with the Germans. The only concession the JCC was willing to make to the Germans was to agree in principle that the records would be returned at some unspecified time. For reasons of security, however, certain holdings would be excluded. The JCC added two more categories of "prohibited classes" to those listed in the first policy paper, namely, "intelligence material relating to Allied countries" and "documents removed by the Germans from other countries." Once again, the JCC refused to commit itself to a return schedule. The Germans should be informed of the *intention* to return records but should not be given a binding timetable. The Chiefs of Staff approved the paper and called for a cabinet decision on the matter of captured records.[209]

Eden thus informed the Cabinet about the German diplomatic and military files on October 10, 1952. Holding to longstanding practice, he treated the two groups of materials as separate issues. He recommended that negotiations on the Auswärtiges Amt files be opened on the basis of the July 6 note. As for the military records, he did not hide the fact that the ministries involved would prefer to make no concessions whatsoever to the Germans. Eden, however, thought all but the most sensitive documents should be returned and adopted the German argument about the lessons of history

---

206 Adenauer to McCloy, Chairman of the AHC, May 24, 1952 and McCloy to Adenauer, May 27, 1952, PA/AA, B118, vols. 507 and 508.

207 Minutes, Acheson for Morland, Sept. 24, 1952, PRO CAB 103/459.

208 Report of the JCC. German Request for the Return of Captured German Archives, Aug. 22, 1952, PRO CAB 103/459. The five-page paper had been drafted by Andrew B. Acheson.

209 The Chiefs of Staff accepted the second JCC policy paper on Apr. 9, 1952. See C.O.S. (52)484, 125th Meeting, Sept. 4, 1952, PRO CAB 103/459.

as his own: "Such records contain the basic history of the country's past and ... without them its history cannot be written."[210] He proposed the start of preliminary talks with the Americans and the French. The categories of military records to be retained had to be worked out jointly; but once those were defined, the return of the remaining papers could begin. The Cabinet adopted only some of his proposals. It authorized the Foreign Office to begin talks in Bonn on the Auswärtiges Amt records as stipulated in the note of July 6, 1951. The Cabinet was of the opinion "that there need be no obligation to return all the German military documents." The defense minister received the authority to define the "prohibited categories" in consultation with the Chiefs of Staff. The Cabinet also approved the proposal to start talks with the American and French governments on a common policy on the issue of the military records.[211]

The Cabinet's decisions cleared the way for the British High Commission to arrange the first meeting in Bonn on the matter of diplomatic records, which took place without delay two weeks later.[212] At the same time, the JCC was commissioned to come up with proposals in line with the Cabinet's approval of the return of certain categories of military documents. The JCC put forward its proposals in its third policy paper, issued in March 1954.[213] For the very first time, the JCC named categories of records that "can be released" to the Germans. Much more attention was given to the reasons for retaining other categories of material, however. Therein lay a decisive change. Much as the JCC had feared, the victorious powers now found themselves in the position of having to justify their possession of documents seized from a vanquished foe.[214]

The records listed for return were the naval records until 1914 and air force records prior to 1933. This concession was dwarfed, however, by the size of the categories that were to remain in Allied custody for a variety of reasons. Among the records to be kept were all papers from the High Command of the Wehrmacht; the High Commands of the army, navy, and air force; naval records from the period after 1914; air force records after 1933; and sources documenting the economic impact of the air war. The

---

210 German Request for the Return of their Captured Archives. Memorandum by the Secretary of State for Foreign Affairs, C(52)329, Oct. 10, 1952, PRO CAB 103/466.
211 CC(52) 85th Cabinet Conclusions, Oct. 14, 1952, PRO CAB 128/25.
212 The meeting of representatives from the Auswärtiges Amt and the High Commission took place on October 31, 1955, in Bonn. The minutes of the meeting are found in PA/AA, B118, vol. 507 and PRO CAB 103/460.
213 JCC. Report by Working Party, German Documents (Excluding Diplomatic Documents), Mar. 16, 1954, PRO FO 370/2340 LS5/97. The report was approved by the Chiefs of Staff on April 27, 1954.
214 See JCC 48th Meeting, July 2, 1952, PRO CAB 103/459.

JCC once again produced a list of "prohibited classes." This list echoed the reservations set out in the American policy paper but was much more detailed and specific.[215] To forestall laborious consultations on particulars, the JCC tried to simplify matters by suggesting that "the simplest method of safeguarding documents in these classes may be for all German 'intelligence' documents to be retained." The reasons given for retaining records were the same provided in the first two JCC policy papers: the needs of the official history projects, the value of the records to potential aggressors, the lack of security measures in Bonn, and the Cold War, particularly "the unsettled political conditions and outlook in Europe." With regard to West Germany's participation in the EDC, the JCC had already accepted that the Amt Blank would need certain records. Bonn was not, however, to be allowed to define what it needed, as the Americans had proposed. "We fear that such an approach . . . may encourage [the West Germans], for political reasons, to make comprehensive requests which would have to be resisted." Instead, the Americans and the British should continue to retain initiative and control.

The JCC's fourth policy paper, issued in March 1958, signaled the committee's retreat in the face of changing circumstances. The issue of the Auswärtiges Amt files had been settled by that point, and most of those files had already been sent to Bonn.[216] Passant had left the Foreign Office Library in 1955. Responsibility for the issue of the captured documents now lay with the new head of the Library, Cecil C. Parrott, and his deputy, Charles Henry Fone. The JCC lost another of its most vocal supporters when Acheson retired from the Cabinet Office. The antagonism between the diplomats and the members of the JCC – "Melland & Co." as Fone referred to them derogatorily[217] – had come to a head. The diplomats refused to spend a minute more than was absolutely necessary on the document issue. "This vexed question," asserted Ambassador Christopher Steel, "should finally be disposed of and removed as a potential irritant in our relations with Germany."[218] By willfully ignoring the changing

215 "(1) British, United States or Allied clandestine or secret intelligence activities. (2) Cryptographic matters of any kind. (3) Soviet clandestine or intelligence services. (4) Interrogations by the Germans of Allied personnel. (5) The existence or activities of, or intelligence obtained by, German agents in Allied or Allied occupied territory. (6) German intelligence material relating to Allied countries. (7) Documents captured by the Germans from other countries. (These should eventually be returned to their original owners). (8) U-boat records of both World Wars."

216 See Chapter 4 below; Philippi, "Politisches Archiv I," 139–41.

217 Minutes Fone for Parrott, June 5, 1958, PRO FO 370/2548 LS5/42.

218 Christopher Steel to Sir Frederick Hoyer Millar, no. 2015, June 23, 1958, PRO FO 370/2548 LS5/44; and as attachment to the JCC 110th Meeting, July 2, 1958, PRO FO 370/2556 LS20/8.

relationship between West Germany and the Western Allies, as well as the ongoing integration of the Federal Republic within the Atlantic alliance, the JCC had marginalized itself. According to Fone, "the atmosphere in which the Committee deliberates is that of 1945."[219] Consequently, the Foreign Office was no longer willing to work on the basis of the 1954 policy paper. "The report is inevitably out of date and several of its conclusions derive from consideration of Germany as an ex-enemy country rather than as a partner and ally in NATO." The JCC would have to revise its policy yet again. With this, the committee surrendered to a situation in which the best it could hope for was to save face, because in Washington preparations were well underway for the return of military documentation. The U.S. Army was declassifying and filming records and setting a concrete schedule for their return. The development was irreversible. All that the members of the JCC could do was to try to retain a fraction of input or, if even this did not succeed, at least to pretend they still had such influence.

The policy paper of March 1958 systematically revised each point of the 1954 paper in response to the new political realities. The JCC acknowledged that it was necessary to undertake "certain radical departures" from its previous policy.[220] All records from the period up to 1933 could be returned by the end of 1960, the committee concluded. Records from after 1933 could be returned in the three years after 1960, "as and when they are no longer required for research." Apparently, the effort to provide loopholes had not disappeared. But the records from the High Command of the Wehrmacht and each of the armed forces were no longer excluded per se from restitution. Naturally, the JCC remained true to its conviction that "security reasons" precluded the return of certain groups of records. Yet by then the JCC had lost the power to push through any such exceptions. The impact of the new policy paper, so much is clear, was limited to the records in British custody. For the very first time, the Admiralty and the Air Ministry deigned to produce the long denied rough overview of the German records in their possession.[221] Indeed, the return

219 "The Chairman has explained to me that some of its members have personal reasons for feeling bitter and I understand that, but a lot of time is wasted by their tendency to dissect and seek an ulterior motive in every German approach or act, and to think up obstacles." Minutes, Fone, June 27, 1958, PRO FO 370/2548 LS5/44.

220 Joint Consultative Committee on Captured Enemy Archives. Report by Working Party. German Documents in the United Kingdom (excluding Diplomatic Archives), Mar. 24, 1958, PRO FO 370/2548 LS5/42.

221 Akten des früheren deutschen Marinearchivs. Zur Zeit in London gelagert [compiled by Amtsrat Walter Pfeiffer], October 1958, PRO FO 2549 LS5/65; the reference to a similar list by the Air Ministry is found in Fone to P. A. Wilkinson, BritEmb Bonn, Nov. 26, 1958, PRO FO 370/2550 LS5/68.

of naval records began in March 1959[222] and was completed in the late 1970s.[223]

222 Johannes Ullrich to Federal Ministry of Defense, Jan. 27, 1959, PA/AA, B118, vol. 125. The first 20 tons arrived in Germany on March 3, 1959, and were sent on to the West German Research Institute for Military History in Freiburg, much to the irritation of the Federal Archives. See also Sasse, London, to Ullrich, Jan. 21, 1959, ibid.
223 Boberach, "Schriftliche Überlieferung," 57; Henke, "Schicksal deutscher Quellen," 598f.; Sand-hofer, "Rückführung"; Werner, "Rückführung."

4

Negotiation Marathon

In big league politics, the question of returning records is a minute matter.[1]

The issue of the captured documents continued to be an unwieldy, much resented "war-related burden" for all involved through the 1950s. It developed into one of those problems that everyone said they wanted to see resolved, but for which no solution was forthcoming. If the search for a solution was already hampered by disagreements within both the British and the American governments, the matter became even more complex when the West German government brought the interests of its various ministries and agencies to the negotiating table. Once the negotiations officially opened, the British and Americans could no longer exclude the French. The negotiations thus became a quadripartite concern. This chapter focuses on the negotiations between these four governments. The diplomatic and military records were the subject of separate negotiations and will thus be discussed separately here. Before turning to the negotiations, however, this chapter will consider the legal debate on the status of the captured documents.

DEFINING THE LEGAL STATUS OF THE CAPTURED RECORDS

The records of the former German embassy in Madrid were turned over to the West German government in March 1952. This gesture by the British government was warmly welcomed because Bonn needed the papers as it prepared to establish diplomatic relations with Spain. In transferring the records, the Allies made a statement that Bonn found highly offensive, however. The secretary of the British embassy in Madrid informed Bonn that the approval given by the United States, Great Britain, and France for

---

1 Wilhelm Rohr, memorandum [minutes of meeting on Dec. 7, 1955, with Hübinger], Jan. 2, 1956, BArch, B198, vol. 1739. The sentence was put forward by Peter Klassen of the Political Archives.

219

the transfer of the embassy records was "an act of grace" that could not "be interpreted as recognizing any claim of the Federal German Government to be regarded as the owner of such German State property."[2] The Political Department of the Auswärtiges Amt objected immediately. It rejected the implications of the wording "act of grace" and argued that this formulation implicitly denied the Federal Republic's rights of ownership to these records. In no previous communication regarding embassy or consulate records, Bonn protested, had anyone on the Allied side implied "that the records had become Allied property." Bonn emphatically restated its view that the Madrid embassy records "were and are property of the Federal Republic, like all other records from the former German Reich."[3] The High Commission, in turn, was unequivocal in its response: it found itself "unable to agree with [the German] views regarding the legal status of German archives seized by the Three Powers. The Allied High Commission must reaffirm in this connection that it lies exclusively within the competence of the Three Powers to decide on the disposal of any such archives held in their possession."[4]

The Madrid embassy records brought the long-simmering question of the ownership of the documents to the fore. The contradictory use of the terms "ownership" and "property" helped to obscure the issue. The legal department at the Auswärtiges Amt and leading West German archivists invoked international customary law and the Hague Regulations of Land Warfare of 1907 in defending Bonn's claim to the captured documents.[5] The British and Americans quickly refused to discuss the issue further because it was obvious that the Allied and West German positions were irreconcilable. Indeed, the ownership issue was never resolved, and it is not the aim here to try to determine after the fact which side was right and in fact the legal owner of the captured documents.[6] It is more important to show, instead,

---

2 J. R. Cotton, BritEmb Madrid, to Oskar Schlitter, West German Representation Madrid, Dec. 13, 1952, PA/AA, B10, vol. 1703/3.

3 Trützschler, Abt. II, AA, to John Golay, Secretary General AHC, Feb. 14, 1953, ibid. See also Andres, PA/AA, Vorschläge für die Ablöseverhandlungen über die Rückgabe der von den westl. Besatzungsmächten beschlagnahmten Akten, Mar. 11, 1952, PA/AA, B118, vol. 489.

4 Golay to MinDir Blankenhorn, Chancellery, AGSEC (53)478, May 30, 1953, PA/AA, B10, vol. 1703/3.

5 Anlage zum Abkommen betreffend die Gesetze und Gebräuche des Landkrieges vom 18. October 1907, *Reichsgesetzblatt* 1910, 107–51, esp. here 147–51.

6 The legal situation in regard to the international protection of cultural property has been discussed much in the course of the restitution debates of the 1990s. The focus, however, was more on movable art objects, and less so on archival material. See Kaye, "Laws in Force"; Fiedler, *Internationaler Kulturgüterschutz*, on archives, esp. 82–4, 142–9; Fiedler, *Kulturgüter als Kriegsbeute;* Fiedler, "Safeguarding of Cultural Property"; Prott/O'Keefe, *Law and the Cultural Heritage* III, esp. chap. 15 (Restitution and Return of Cultural Objects). Fitschen, *Rechtliches Schicksal von Akten*, examines specifically the fate of archives under changes of rule and territory.

how this irresolvable issue was finally circumvented in order to move the negotiations past stalemate.

Embassy and Consulate Registries

Upon the outbreak of war, it is customary for combatants to expel the diplomatic corps of their opponents. Hastily abandoned diplomatic real estate and property, including archives and registries, are not lost but transferred to the custody of a so-called protecting power. This protecting power is a neutral country that mediates between the opposing sides in the absence of ongoing diplomatic ties with one another. In World War II, for example, Switzerland looked after American interests vis-à-vis the German Reich and in the countries occupied by Germany, just as it represented the interests of Germany in the United States and a number of other countries. Switzerland kept the records of the German embassy in Washington after Germany declared war on the United States.[7] A protecting power usually steps in after a belligerent has been defeated and performs diplomatic and other services on its behalf. Hence, Switzerland should have taken custody of German archives in neutral countries after May 8, 1945. This generally did not happen, however, because the Allies were of the opinion that Germany's unconditional surrender made the functions of the protecting powers superfluous. As the supreme authority in occupied Germany, the Allied powers terminated German diplomatic relations with other nations and recalled the now-abolished Third Reich's representatives from abroad.[8] They also demanded that the protecting powers turn over German embassy properties, registries, and archives to them.

The State Department moved quickly in 1945 to arrange for the transfer of German diplomatic archives in neutral countries to American custody.[9] On March 31, 1945, it instructed its embassies to contact the foreign ministries of their host countries immediately following Germany's capitulation and to demand entry to the German embassy buildings.[10] Although the instructions spoke of taking possession of the embassy archives in the interest of *all* powers at war against Germany, the Americans had not informed the British of this step.[11] Indeed, speed was of the essence because the British

---

7 On the role of Switzerland as a protecting power for Germany with regard to diplomatic records, see Zala, "Dreierlei Büchsen der Pandora."

8 Control Council, Proclamation no. 2, Section III, 7a-c (Sept. 20, 1945), *Official Gazette*, no. 1 (Oct. 29, 1945), p. 8. See also FRUS 1945:3, 475–7.

9 See FRUS 1945:3, 1136–48.

10 Circular Telegram to all Diplomatic Missions, Mar. 31, 1945, FRUS 1945:3, 1136f.

11 State Department, Division of European Affairs, unused memorandum for H. Freedman Matthews, Seizure of German Embassies, Consulates and Other Offices in Neutral Countries, Apr. 20, 1945,

had learned of the Auswärtiges Amt's instructions to German diplomatic personnel to destroy embassy records upon the fall of Berlin at the very latest. This order put the Allies in a dilemma. The legal prerequisite for confiscation of German embassy property – a declaration of surrender – did not yet exist. But waiting for the surrender would mean giving German diplomats time to destroy embassy archives.[12] During May 1945, both before and after Germany's surrender on the 8th, representatives of the Allied powers entered German embassies and consulates and confiscated documents. Each protecting power was requested to withdraw from that function and to serve as a trustee on behalf of the Allied Control Commission.[13] American officials confiscated specific documents and sent them to Washington. The great majority of the German embassy and consular records, especially consular materials such as birth and marriage records, were stored in the countries in which they were seized. None of the documents were sent to Whaddon Hall – a fact that was to be of great importance in the subsequent course of events –nor were they considered in the negotiations on the Auswärtiges Amt files in British possession.[14]

The State Department never systematically addressed the question of the legal status of the embassy and consular records, dealing with it instead on a case-by-case basis. When the Federal Republic began to build its foreign service, it received the records of the Washington embassy and New York consulate in 1950 without any ado.[15] The State Department could easily turn embassy records over to the West Germans if the records were in sole American custody. It would instruct the American embassy in the country in question to inspect the German records once more for materials that might be of interest to the intelligence agencies and then to hand them over to West German diplomats.[16]

The British took an entirely different approach to the embassy and consular records. The Foreign Office considered archives and registries part

RG 59, CDF 1945–49, box 4130, 800.414. The situation was cleared up with the British ambassador about a week later. See Memorandum of Conversation, Apr. 26, 1945, FRUS 1945:3, 1139f.

12 BritEmb to State Department, Aide Memoire: German Official Property in Neutral Countries, May 1, 1945, FRUS 1945:3, 1140f.

13 On the various reactions of the host countries and their willingness to cooperate with the Allies, see the synopsis in FRUS 1945:3, 1148. A case study is depicted in Weidemann, "Akten der Deutschen Gesandtschaft Kabul." Several South American countries linked their cooperation with certain conditions; specifically, they were guaranteed the right to inspect German records first.

14 Culbertson, AmEmb Madrid, to State Dept, no. 308, July 2, 1947, NA RG 84, POLAD, entry 2531B, box 176.

15 Andres, PA/AA, to Trützschler, Abt. II, Oct. 9, 1952, PA/AA, B10, vol. 1701/1.

16 This is what happened with the records of the German consulate general in Lourenço Marques, Mozambique. See State Dept to AmEmb Cairo, no. A-319, Mar. 25, 1953, NA RG 59, CDF 1950–54, 862.423/3–1153.

of Germany's "foreign assets." Those assets were to be confiscated, liquidated, and divided up among Germany's wartime enemies according to criteria worked out at a conference on reparations held in Paris in late 1945.[17] For years, the Federal Republic fought against the sale of onetime embassy buildings and other property; the loss of such facilities made the re-establishment of a diplomatic infrastructure an expensive undertaking.[18] The British treatment of embassy records as foreign assets accounted for the use of the phrase "act of grace." It also played a role during the return of the diplomatic records that had been stored at Whaddon Hall. The Political Archives of the Auswärtiges Amt included many embassy and consulate records, and embassy records were among the first materials the West Germans received following the exchange of diplomatic notes in March 1956 that settled the issue of the return of the Auswärtiges Amt files. The Foreign Office was adamant, however, that the 1956 agreement applied only to embassy and consular records that had been incorporated into the Political Archives by 1945 and not to documents seized at German embassies and consulates at the end of the war.[19]

London and Washington addressed their differing views on the embassy archives in early 1953 as they prepared to turn the German records from Bangkok over to Bonn. The British once again spoke of the transfer as an "act of grace" on the part of the Allies. The State Department disapproved of that wording and indicated that it preferred to see the transfer as a "matter of mutual convenience."[20] In response to an inquiry from the British, the State Department affirmed that the United States did not consider embassy records to be foreign assets. "We distinguish between documents and other types of state property, as e.g., embassy [buildings] etc. – property which might be subject to sale – which documents would not."[21] This response was less the product of proverbial American pragmatism than a consequence

---

17 The legal basis for this interpretation was Proclamation no. 2, (see note 8), which ordered German authorities to cooperate in compiling inventories of foreign assets. The Control Council law no. 5 (October 30, 1945) subjected all German property abroad to the authority of the victors. See Kreikamp, *Deutsches Vermögen*, 365f.

18 Bundestag, 1. Wahlperiode 1949, Drucksache no. 3969, Nov. 17, 1952. In the attachment, Walter Hallstein: "Denkschrift über die Wegnahme der bundeseigenen, im Ausland gelegenen Dienstgebäude des ehemaligen Auswärtigen Amtes." Here the relevant Allied decrees, orders, and laws are again listed.

19 Minutes F. M. Young, Oct. 4, 1955: "We should make it clear that we are returning only those consular archives which came into our possession with the German Foreign Office Archives. Other consular archives which remained at the resp. German embassies and consulates were taken over at the end of the war and treated as German external assets." PRO FO 370/2432 LS5/102.

20 State Dept. to AmEmb Bangkok, no. 2026, Apr. 28, 1953, NA RG 59, CDF 1950–54, 862.423/4–2853.

21 File note, May 20, 1953, ibid., no decimal number, MF C0040, roll 22, frame 873.

of an interdepartmental dispute in Washington. At the time Bonn requested the Bangkok records, the State Department was still working out the official American policy on the captured German documents with the other departments and agencies involved, notably the Army. A conflict had arisen because the Army maintained that, upon confiscation, the documents had become U.S. federal records and could therefore be returned to the Germans only with Congressional approval. The State Department, traditionally eager to operate with as little interference from other governmental bodies as possible, adopted the position that the American government held "no legal title" to these records.[22] According to this interpretation, the captured documents were not federal records and, consequently, the State Department could dispose of them as it saw fit and use them as a bargaining chip in negotiations with Bonn. The Army's view on the documents' status was very close to the Foreign Office's, and for that reason the State Department could not accept the British position without implicitly conceding the point to the Army.[23]

The differences in their views notwithstanding, the British and Americans faced the task of responding to German objections to the phrase "act of grace." The Foreign Office wanted to see the view that the Federal Republic did not have "title" to archives become firmly established. The British did not want to see their position on the other captured documents compromised by casual treatment of the embassy records.[24] The American High Commission agreed. Even if the U.S. government was about to adopt a policy of returning German records "in order to promote friendly relations," the German view of the legal status of the records could not remain uncontested. HICOG therefore asked the State Department "to refute without delay the German claim that these documents are the property of the Federal Republic."[25] The State Department chose, however, to approach the matter more carefully, if for no other reason than to avoid aggravating the internal conflict with the Army. The aim was to return the

---

22 Adjutant General's Office, Dept. Records Branch, Journal of Significant Events, entry from Dec. 16, 1952, NA, RG 407, entry 375, box 1.

23 Dulles, StateDept to HICOG Bonn, no. A-1335, Mar. 18, 1953, NA RG 59, CDF 1950–54, 862.423/2–2653. The property rights aspect was said to be "a technical legal point of considerable difficulty which has been subject of interdepartmental discussion in Washington for some time. Point has been raised that if US has title there may be serious question whether the records can be disposed of without Congressional approval. Department has argued that at most we have right of disposition until there has been an affirmative act to take title."

24 Gifford, AmEmb London, to SecState, no. 2885, Nov. 20, 1952, NA RG 59, CDF 1950–54, 862.423/11–2052.

25 George W. Renchard, Office of Political Affairs, HICOG, to State Dept., no. 2562, Federal Republic Claims Title to Former German Archives, Feb. 26, 1953, NA RG 59, CDF 1950–54, 862.423/2–2653.

uncontroversial records to the Germans as soon as possible and to treat the issue as a logistical, not legal, matter. Therefore, the only possible answer was a pragmatic one: "Germans will never concede that Allies have title, and we cannot concede they have title. [The] issue should never have been raised and must now be disposed of in a practical way," Dulles instructed HICOG.[26] From this point on, representatives of the Allied High Commission refused to engage, either verbally or in writing, in discussion of the legal aspects of the matter with the Germans.

Despite their evasiveness on the documents' legal status, the British and Americans continued to turn over embassy records to the West Germans.[27] Hans Andres, the head of the Political Archives, was the first to understand that the Allies sought to avoid taking a legal standpoint but were willing to return records on a case-by-case basis. Andres came to the conclusion that it would be advantageous "not to discuss the basic question of legal title to the records any further."[28] The head of the Political Department, Herbert Blankenhorn, acted on Andres's assessment and proposed to the High Commission that "basic legal issues" not be discussed in the future.[29] Two briefs commissioned by the Auswärtiges Amt's legal department reached the same conclusion: "Because the German legal situation is, after all, unclear, it might be prudent *not* to put the *legal aspects* in the foreground during the forthcoming negotiations on the return of the archive."[30] The German legal advisors considered the case of the active embassy records within the context of German foreign assets, as did the British, but came to the same conclusion as the Americans, namely that these records were *res extra commercium* and therefore could not be liquidated – unlike real estate or furnishings – and used for purposes of reparation. The only value that such archival material had was derived from their link to the state. As that link was "essentially indivisible," the German lawyers argued, the records were of value only to the "owner state," not the occupying state. The confiscation of government records was therefore "an act of barbarism."[31] Both legal briefs focused primarily on the Hague Regulations of Land Warfare

---

26 Dulles, SecState, to HICOG Bonn, no. A-1335, Mar. 18, 1953, NA RG 59, CDF 1950–54, 862.423/2–2653.

27 In August 1954, they received the records of the Paris embassy; in March 1955, those of the consulates in Innsbruck, Graz, Klagenfurt, Linz, and Salzburg.

28 Andres, PA/AA, Memorandum for Löns, Pfeiffer, Steg, June 19, 1953, PA/AA, B10, vol. 1703/3.

29 Blankenhorn to the Secretary General of the AHC, Eric G. Gration, Aug. 21, 1953, PA/AA, B10, vol. 1703/3 and B118, vol. 489.

30 VLR Mühlenhöver, Abt. V [Legal Dept.], to Ref. 117, PA/AA, Feststellung der Rechtslage in Bezug auf die beschlagnahmten Akten des früheren AA, Dec. 23, 1954, PA/AA, B118, vol. 28, original emphasis.

31 Janz, Abt. V [Legal Dept.], to Abt. II [Political Dept.], Frage des Eigentums an im Besitz der Drei Mächte befindl. deutschen staatlichen Archive und Akten, July 31, 1953, PA/AA, B118, vol. 28.

of 1907 as a possible legal basis for Allied actions and cited interpretations of international law from the turn of the century. Allied decrees issued after May 1945 were ignored.[32] Nonetheless, the legal briefs referred extensively to the correspondence with the High Commission, as if every letter or every remark by a High Commissioner were a legally binding statement.[33] British officials commented upon this habit acerbically: "The Germans do not hesitate to interpret any statement in the way which suits them wherever German external assets are concerned."[34]

The German legal arguments point to a fundamentally different under-standing of the nature of the occupation than that of the Western Allies. The backdrop for this difference of perspective was the so-called continuity debate, the question of whether the German Reich had ceased to exist as an entity in international law when it surrendered unconditionally.[35] As legal historian Bernhard Diestelkamp points out, this was first and fore-most a political, not a legal, question. If it was assumed that the German Reich continued to exist within the framework of international law, then the Allies had only taken custody of the country's sovereignty when the Reich became powerless to act. Under that circumstance, the occupiers were bound by the general rules governing international customary law, the Hague Regulations of Land Warfare, and the Geneva Conventions. If, however, it was assumed that the German Reich no longer existed and the Allies were acknowledged as the "highest authority," then they could impose whatever measures on the Germans they were allowed to impose on their own people.[36] Not surprisingly, the idea that the German state was only temporarily powerless was very popular among German legal schol-ars. The continuity argument lent itself to critiques of Allied policies, and

---

32 Janz, ibid., even maintains that "the Allies had also not yet not provided any special stipulations for archives and documents in their legislation." He thus ignores various laws, directives, and orders issued by the Allied Control Council and the implementation regulations issued in each of the zones. He only discusses AHC Law no. 63, from Sept. 5, 1951, which addresses issues of reparation and restitution.

33 This is particularly clear in Mühlenhöver's evaluation, VLR Mühlenhöver, Abt. V, to Ref. 117, PA/AA, Feststellung der Rechtslage in Bezug auf die beschlagnahmten Akten des früheren AA, Dec. 23, 1954, PA/AA, B118, vol. 28.

34 Minutes F. M. Young for Fone, Oct. 8, 1955, PRO FO 370/2432 LS5/102.

35 A review of the topic with the relevant literature is found in Majer, "Grundlagen des Besatzungsrechts."

36 Diestelkamp, "Rechtsgeschichte als Zeitgeschichte," 184, cites the Potsdam Conference as an exam-ple: If the German Reich was only incapacitated in August 1945, then it was not bound by the decisions of the Big Three regarding the territories east of the Oder and Neisse rivers, because the victors were not allowed to exert such authority over foreign territory. However, if the German Reich no longer existed as a state at the time of the conference, then the Allies did represent the highest existing authority and their decisions were indeed binding.

German legal scholars readily embraced it in the early postwar years to challenge the legitimacy of the occupation.[37]

The Auswärtiges Amt eventually realized that nothing could be gained from a protracted argument on the legal status of the captured documents. It repeatedly instructed the Ministry of the Interior accordingly.[38] The question of the documents' status resurfaced when talks on the return of non-diplomatic records began in January 1958. The German lead negotiator tried to get the Western representatives to agree that the Federal Republic was "the only rightful owner of the archives." Although he was chiefly interested in substantiating the West German claim of being the only legitimate representative of the German people – a claim directed against East Germany – the British and Americans refused to be drawn into discussion of the issue again.[39] Their stance made it possible to focus the negotiations on the logistics of restitution.

Legal Regulations in the United States and Great Britain

Beyond wrangling with the Germans' sometimes self-serving legal arguments, officials in the United States and Great Britain also had to take into consideration their own domestic legal contexts. In Great Britain, the fundamental legal premise was that "all booty captured from a hostile nation, whether on sea or land, belongs to the Crown."[40] The Admiralty was adamant in maintaining that the German navy records were war booty and therefore no longer German property. In the United States, the right of disposal over war booty was a question of national, not international, law. It was the responsibility of Congress to pass the required legislation on a case-by-case basis.[41] American treatment of the documents from the time they

---

37 Ibid., esp. 187, 192, 196, 200, 205.

38 Klassen, memorandum, Mar. 1, 1955, PA/AA, B118, vol. 39; Wilhelm Grewe, Head of Political Dept., to Minister of the Interior, Rückgabe deutscher Akten aus alliiertem Gewahrsam, Jan. 7, 1957, ibid., vol. 511.

39 Peter Wilkinson, BritEmb Bonn, to Parrott, Library, FO, Feb. 6, 1958, PRO FO 370/2547 LS5/6. Wilkinson suggested rejecting the German claim on the basis of Art. 43 of the Hague Regulations and was promptly muzzled by the legal department: "In the course of the years the Germans have many times accused us with breaches of the Hague Regulations, and we have with equal frequency replied that those Regulations could not and did not apply after May 8, 1945. . . . I suggest that it ought to be communicated to [BritEmb] Bonn in suitable language that they would be putting their feet in it, if they invoked the Hague Regulations, just because, on this occasion, it might suit us to do so."

40 Downey, "Captured Enemy Property," 500.

41 Downey, "Captured Enemy Property," 499: "The ultimate disposition of captured enemy property is not a question for international but for domestic law. The United States Constitution provides that the Congress shall make rules concerning captures on land and water." He refers here to Art. I,

were seized onward was guided, however, more by political considerations than by consistent application of the law.[42]

The State Department had to decide on a legal framework for handling the captured documents for the first time in connection with the Windsor File. At the San Francisco Conference in June 1945, Lord Halifax, British ambassador to Washington, asked Secretary of State Edward Stettinius either to destroy the microfilm copy of the Windsor File or to turn it over to the British. Stettinius assured Halifax that the United States would safeguard British interests, but Halifax nonetheless repeated his request in writing. Once in writing, the matter was sent on its way through government channels.[43] The Europe specialists at the State Department rejected the British argument that the Windsor File was of no serious historical interest. The U.S. government, they argued, was morally obliged to preserve the papers of another government. Moreover, they noted, federal law prohibited the removal or destruction of the papers of a federal agency without Congressional approval.[44] The Federal Records Disposal Act of 1943 applied to records "made or received by any agency of the United States Government . . . in connection with the transaction of public business."[45] Only the Archivist of the United States was authorized to determine whether such records could be destroyed or otherwise disposed of. The archivist's determination then had to be approved by a Congressional committee.[46] Stettinus relayed these historical and legal arguments when he informed Halifax in October 1945 that the State Department would not destroy or turn over its microfilm copy of the Windsor File.[47]

Useful as the Federal Records Disposal Act had been in dealing with the Windsor File, the State Department would have preferred to ignore it

section 8, clause 11: "[The Congress shall have power] to declare War, grant Letters of Marque and Reprisal, and *make Rules concerning Captures on Land and Water*" (emphasis added).

42 Glenn, "Private Records Seized," 405.

43 David Harris to Howard M. Smyth, Historical Division, State Department, July 25, 1959, NA RG 59, Lot File 78D441, Historical Office, box 11.

44 Memorandum, H. Freeman Matthews, Director, Office of European Affairs to UnderSecState Dean Acheson, Sept. 10, 1945, ibid., box 13.

45 Records Disposal Act as approved July 7, 1943 (PL 78–115), United States Statutes at Large, vol. 57, pt. 1, 380–3, here: 380.

46 The committee in question was the Joint Committee on the Disposition of Executive Papers. The Federal Records Act itself did not spell out the consequences for violation of the law, but criminal statutes provided drastic sanctions for such cases. The Criminal Code stipulates in 18 USC Sec. 234 and 235 that the offending official will be dismissed, "forever afterwards disqualified from holding any office," and must face a fine of $2,000 and a prison sentence of as much as three years. See Herbert S. Marks to UnderSecState Dean Acheson, Laws Applying to Disposal of Public Records, Oct. 10, 1945, NA RG 59, Lot File 78D441, Historical Office, box 13.

47 Aide Mémoire, SecState to Lord Halifax, BritAmb, Oct. 11, 1945, FRUS 1945:3, 1120f.

during the interdepartmental deliberations on policy guidelines for return-ing captured documents. Just as the Interagency Conference was on the verge of agreeing on a draft policy paper in December 1952, the office of Defense Secretary Robert A. Lovett expressed concerns over the legal status of the German records. The American government, the Defense Depart-ment maintained, had attained "some property interest" in the German documents through the act of confiscation; consequently, the documents fell under the Federal Records Disposal Act. The term "war booty" also surfaced again during the last stages of the interagency policy delibera-tions. The State Department had always carefully avoided using this term in diplomatic correspondence because of its implications under international law. But under pressure to bring the policy discussion to a close, it finally conceded the point to the Defense Department.[48] In keeping with the pro-visions of the Federal Records Disposal Act, Wayne Grover, the Archivist of the United States, was thereupon commissioned to prepare a schedule for the return of the captured records. Congress passed this plan on August 1, 1953. Acting on the advice of Ernst Posner, Grover emphasized in the plan he submitted to Congress that the act of returning documents to the Germans in no way implied that the documents had been illegally confis-cated; the documents, Grover explained, were "to be donated to the Federal Republic."[49] The detour via the legislative branch imposed by the Defense Department added another eight months to the time it took to ratify the return policy.

As the Departments of State and Defense wrangled over the legal status of the captured documents, the National Archives was left to grapple with another thorny legal problem: the question of copyright. This was a critical issue if the archive was going to fulfill its task of making records available for research. Among the captured German documents held by the National Archives in 1950 were the personal papers of several Prussian military figures

---

48 Adjutant General's Office, DRB, Journal of Significant Events, entries for Dec. 9 and 16, 1952, NA RG 407, entry 375, box 1; quote from Tetton P. Heffelfinger, Office of Counsel, Office Secretary Defense, Memorandum for the Record, Dec. 22, 1952, NA RG 59, CDF 1950–54, 862.423/12–2252 CS/B; on the time pressure, see Matthews to Robert A. Lovett, SecDefense, Nov. 7, 1952, NA RG 59, CDF 1950–54, FW 862.423/4–3053. Not even Sherrod East, head of the DRB, thought the objection raised by the Defense Secretary was justified. East argued that captured records were not covered by the federal laws.

49 Wolfe, "Sharing Records of Mutual Archival Concern," 296; Glenn, "Private Records Seized," 400f.; Wayne C. Grover, Archivist of the U.S., to Noble, State Department, Historical Office, Draft of General Records Schedule, July 10, 1953, NA RG 59, CDF 1950–54, 862.423/7–1053; State Dept to HICOG, Bonn, no. A-180, July 29, 1953, NA RG 59, CDF 1950–54, 862.423/7–653. The policy paper dated Oct. 24, 1952, is reproduced in Eckert, *Kampf um die Akten*, 480f.

from the collection of Heeresarchiv (Army Archives) in Potsdam.[50] The position of the National Archives was clear: it wanted to return these historical materials to a successor German government. Grover still assumed that the matter of the captured documents would be settled in a peace treaty with Germany. But while Grover was waiting for a diplomatic resolution to the issue, researchers were using the materials from the Heeresachiv in the National Archives' reading room. Grover needed to protect the archive, its staff, and the users against the possibility of German claims of copyright violation. He thus had an article drafted for inclusion in the anticipated peace treaty. Germany, it was stipulated, was to abandon all such claims, both governmental and private, of copyright infringement. The most important paragraph was "pretty sweeping,"[51] as a senior official at the National Archives acknowledged, and would have obliged the Germans not only to forgo claims for copyright infringements but also to renounce claims to return of the documents altogether. Germany, the draft treaty article read, would abandon

all claims for the return to Germany or nationals thereof of any publications, documents, manuscripts, literary or artistic works, or records which are or were the property of Germany or nationals thereof and which were removed from Germany or territories occupied by Germany by authorized representatives of any or the Allied or Associated Powers.[52]

Grover also sought to provide legal protection against potential copyright infringement claims in connection with works published before the expected ratification of a peace treaty. He turned to the Justice Department's Office of Alien Property and requested to have copyrights transferred to his agency for the interim period.[53] However, a general vesting order for the German records located at the National Archives would have been a catastrophe for the restitution efforts of the Federal Republic. The Trading with the Enemy Act, the legal basis for transferring property rights, did not

---

50 These included the papers of Field Marshalls von Boyen, von Gneisenau, von Moltke, and von Roon, and Generals von Seeckt and Groener. See *Preliminary Inventory of the German Records 1679–1945 in the World War II Collection of Seized Enemy Records.* Compiled by Martin Rogin. (Prelim. Inventory Nr. 24). Washington, D.C.: GSA. The National Archives 1950: "As an archival agency the National Archives is strongly in favor of restitution to successor governments of those bodies of governmental archives that may be returned without violating military and political policies of this Government." See also *Guide to Captured German Documents,* 61–3.

51 Memo from E. G. Campbell, Chief, Records Scheduling Branch, May 19, 1950, NA RG 64, National Archives, Planning and Control Cases, box PC-62.

52 Suggested Language for Future Peace Treaties with Germany and Japan. Renunciation of Claims by Germany, n.d. [May 1950], and the attached memo from Campbell, ibid.

53 Grover to Jess Larson, Administrator, General Services Administration (GSA), May 29, 1950, ibid. At the time, the National Archives were part of the GSA, which made Larson Grover's boss and the man through whom correspondence with the Justice Department had to be conducted.

provide for the return of property once it had been transferred to U.S. government ownership. The only exception was the property of Nazi victims.[54] The Office of Alien Property turned down Grover's request, arguing that the State Department had already declared restitution a political objective and that a vesting order would be an obstacle to that goal.[55]

Because the prospects of a peace treaty continued to remain unclear, Grover tried to have at least a protective clause for the National Archives inserted into the policy paper the Interagency Conference was preparing.[56] He was not successful, however, and consequently the National Archives took the radical step in 1952 of denying nongovernmental users access to the German records until further notice.[57] Grover did not share the State Department's view that the archive users were sufficiently protected by the 1952 Settlement Convention.[58] Finally, he assigned one of his own legal specialists to work on the problem. The counsel mistakenly assumed that Grover was asking about copyrights held by private German citizens, even though in most cases government records were involved. As a result of this misunderstanding, the reply from the GSA was very discouraging: the use of original and filmed German records would constitute a violation of copyright for which the archive user would be legally liable. "Use" in this context meant the citation of the records in a book or article, not the act of reading them.[59] The confiscation of records, the counsel contended, had not ipso facto "dispossessed" the owner. Only the microfilms that the State Department had produced for its own use – such as for the *Documents on German Foreign Policy* series – had become federal records over which the government had the right of disposal. This view of the documents'

54 On the jurisdiction of OAP, see Department of Justice, OAP: Summary Statement of the Jurisdiction and Policies of the OAP with Reference to Literary, Scientific and Artistic Works of Enemy Origin, Feb. 18, 1953, NA RG 64, National Archives, Planning, and Control Cases, box PC-62. On the Trading with the Enemy Act, see Kreikamp, *Deutsches Auslandsvermögen*, 20–7; on the procedure of "vesting" copyrights, etc., by the OAP, see Plunder and Restitution, SR 58–65.

55 Paul V. Myron, Deputy Director, OAP to Russell Forbes, Acting Administrator, GSA, Aug. 16, 1950, NA RG 64, National Archives, Planning and Control Cases, box PC-62.

56 Grover to H. Freeman Matthews, Deputy UnderSecState, July 29, 1952: "The National Archives is particularly interested in obtaining a waiver of claims based on literary property rights or analogous rights that might result from use or reproduction of the seized German documents." See also, Conference on Policy Statement, re. The Return of Seized German Documents, Sept. 18, 1952, both in ibid.

57 Conference on Policy Statement, re. The Return of Seized German Documents, Oct. 22, 1952, ibid.

58 Matthews to Grover, Nov. 7, 1952, ibid.

59 "Use of information secured from such records and stated in speeches, written articles, etc., by way of conclusions or contrast with appropriate citation or footnote reference definitely constitutes infringement of the literary property rights of the true owners, even though the quotation, in whole or in part, is not included. Attributable source carries liability." General Counsel, GSA, to Archivist of the United States, Apr. 30, 1953, ibid.

legal status was at odds with the position the State Department adopted in response to the West Germans' attempts to invoke the Hague Regulations on Land Warfare. Grover had to choose between withholding the records and microfilms from researchers or having researchers assume liability for possible copyright violations. He chose the latter option. From that point on, the National Archives informed researchers in a two-line statement about the copyright problem with the hope – but without the certainty – that no user would have to fight a court battle over the matter.[60]

The British faced a similar problem. The legal staff of the British High Commission feared that once the Germany Treaty came into force "it will be open to the Federal Government to challenge our interpretation of Occupation legislation before the Arbitration Tribunal."[61] To protect against compensation claims, Parliament expanded the existing Enemy Property Act in October 1953[62] to shield specifically against alleged copyright violations in connection with the German records and documents. The law ended the legal efficacy of the German copyright but did not transfer copyright to the Crown. It applied to all documents that had been brought to the United Kingdom by representatives of the British government before July 1951 and for which a copyright existed before March 1949.[63] Legal experts, including the Foreign Office's lawyers, were not certain this approach would work, however, once national laws were enacted in conjunction with the Settlement Convention.

The copyright question was put on the agenda by the impending publication of the Holstein papers. At Whaddon Hall, the historians Norman Rich and M. E. Fisher had edited the memoirs of Friedrich von Holstein, a key

---

60 "Some of the papers may have been of private origin, but the fact of their seizure is not believed to divest their original owners of any literary property rights in them. Anyone, therefore, who publishes them in whole or in part without permission may be held liable for infringement of property rights." Quote taken from Wolfe, *Captured German Records*, 267. This statement also appears at the front of all *Guides to German Records Microfilmed at Alexandria*.

61 M. F. P. Herchenroder, Retention of German Archives, Mar. 7, 1952, PRO FO 370/2244 LS3/44.

62 The Settlement Convention was one of the supplementary agreements of the Germany Treaty. See Kreikamp, *Deutsches Auslandsvermögen*, 48–57, esp. 52f. On the enemy property legislation in Great Britain, see Foreign Office, *British Policy Towards Enemy Property*. Specifically, the topic here is the Enemy Property Act of Oct. 29, 1953, Part II (Special Provisions as respects Germany), Section 6 (Infringements of copyright). Bob Dixon, German Research Department, Foreign & Commonwealth Office, was kind enough to provide me with this text.

63 So the interpretation of the legal department at the Foreign Office: Minutes J. L. Simpson, May 7, 1953 and July 6, 1953, PRO FO 370/2339 LS5/90 and FO 370/2341 LS5/146. "The effect of Clause 6 of the Enemy Property Bill will be to extinguish any subsisting German copyright or any German enemy interest in copyright." Further: "The effect of the Enemy Property Bill, as I understand it, will be to extinguish the German copyright and to vest the property in the documents in the Crown."

figure at the Auswärtiges Amt during the imperial era, in their spare time and informed descendents of Holstein living in Great Britain of the project.[64] Cambridge University Press contracted the book and asked the Foreign Office to obtain the approval of the West German government. James Passant was concerned that such a request "might even raise questions about the right of the Allies to publish the German Foreign Ministry Archives in the *Documents on German Foreign Policy* series."[65] The legal department of the Foreign Office shared these concerns: "We cannot approach the German Federal Government for 'consent' or an acknowledgement of no objection . . . without in some sense admitting that the Federal Government might have a right to object."[66] The question of copyright in this instance was complicated, moveover, by the question of ownership: it was open to debate whether the Holstein papers were government or private property at the time of their confiscation in 1945.[67]

The Foreign Office decided to let sleeping dogs lie in the belief that the issue could not be definitively resolved. It did not send an official request to the West German government. The British High Commissioner merely informed Blankenhorn in September 1953 that an edition of the Holstein papers was in the works. Blankenhorn never brought up the matter again, and the Foreign Office took his silence as a sign that the Auswärtiges Amt had no objections. Bonn did in fact tender a note of protest two years later, but, because Kirkpatrick believed the protest was simply "for the record," the matter went no further.[68] Although it apparently recognized the tenuousness of the British position, the Foreign Office's legal department expected that Bonn would pursue its goals through diplomacy rather than legal action. The West Germans' sole aim was to gain possession of the Auswärtigs Amt files, and, much as the British legal experts expected, they opted for negotiation, not litigation.[69]

---

64 *The Holstein Papers. Vol. I: Memoirs and Political Observations.* Ed. by Norman Rich and M. E. Fisher, Cambridge 1955. In the preface, xvi–xxiii, the editors reiterate what they know about the provenance of the records.

65 Minutes Passant, July 3, 1953, PRO FO 370/2341 LS5/146.

66 Minutes Simpson, July 6, 1953, ibid.

67 The German embassy in London issued a note of protest against the publication. It was argued that the Holstein papers were official documents to which West Germany was rightfully entitled due to its status as the legal successor of the Reich. The fact that Privy Councilor von Holstein had not handed over the papers to the Political Archives at the time was in itself an infraction, because the papers had been generated in the course of his tenure in office. See Aide Mémoire, Jan. 17, 1955, PRO FO 370/2440 LS17/1.

68 Minutes Kirkpatrick, Jan. 24, 1955, ibid.

69 Minutes Simpson, July 6, 1953, PRO FO 370/2341 LS5/146.

THE DIPLOMATIC RECORDS, 1952–1958

The German Course of Negotiation

The Chancellor Intervenes. On March 1, 1952 – after the West German government had decided to reject the proposals the Allies offered in their note of July 6, 1951, but before it had informed the Allies of that decision – State Secretary Walter Hallstein announced that Bonn wanted to address the issue of the captured documents in the negotiations on the so-called Bonn Convention, the agreement that would end the Allied occupation of the Federal Republic.[70] The Allies had not expected the West German government to make the return of the captured documents a top priority.[71] They tried to skirt the issue by asking Hallstein for a list of the materials in question.[72] Because the Germans did not know what records the Allies had or where they were held, compiling a list would take time.[73] The British hoped this hurdle would eliminate the problem for good,[74] but in early April 1952, Hallstein submitted a very general list.[75] A few days later, Adenauer raised the topic in a meeting with the High Commissioners. The chancellor demanded an "agreement in principle" that "the German archives held in Allied custody were German property and would be returned."[76] The British High Commissioner, Sir Ivone Kirkpatrick, indicated that his government was willing in principle and suggested that the issue would be better addressed outside the negotiations on ending the occupation.[77]

---

70 Hallstein made this announcement on March 1, 1952, at the meeting of the General Committee, the body working on the issue of ending Germany's occupation status. Reference was being made to *all* of the records confiscated in Germany, not specifically the diplomatic ones.

71 The news of Hallstein's announcement arrived in London during an editorial conference of the DGFP. "This news startled us a little bit," wrote Noble to George L. West, Deputy Chief of Internal Political and Governmental Affairs Division, HICOG, Mar. 5, 1952, NA RG 59, Lot File 78D441, Historical Office, box 4.

72 John M. Raymond, Legal Division, German Affairs, to Noble, Mar. 13. 1952, ibid.

73 "The Germans said that they had found difficulty in preparing the memorandum as they did not know what archives were still in existence or where these were." JCC 45th Meeting, Apr. 2, 1952, PRO FO 370/2269 LS18/5. Once Hallstein did present a list, he added that the list was not to be considered final, but would continue to be amended. State Secretary Hallstein to Chairman of the Allied Delegation for matters concerning Replacement of the Occupation Statute, Apr. 4, 1952, NA RG 338, U.S. Army Command, entry 33192, box 1.

74 Con O'Neill, Head of the Political Office at the British High Commission, to Passant, Mar. 19, 1952, PRO FO 370/2244 LS3/44. The Germans had not yet submitted the list, wrote O'Neill, "and it suits us best to leave the matter dormant.... there is nothing to be gained on our side by covering the matter in the Contract. The longer the Germans leave the question the easier it will be for us to refuse to insert a new subject into the agreements and for the moment all appears to be well."

75 Hallstein to Chairman, Apr. 4, 1952, NA RG 338, U.S. Army Command, entry 33192, box 1, with the attached "List of German Files, Archives and Libraries at present in Allied hands."

76 Meeting no. 41, Apr. 9, 1952, *Adenauer und die Hohen Kommissare 1952*, 71.

77 Ibid. As well as Kirkpatrick to FO, no. 476, Apr. 10, 1952, PRO FO 370/2244 LS3/59.

Adenauer might well have come away with the impression that the Allies would not resist his demands.

Hermann Mosler, the head of the legal department at the Auswärtiges Amt, wanted written confirmation of the British position.[78] Therefore, Adenauer brought up the matter again at a meeting on April 28. This time, Allied resistance was obvious. André François-Poncet, the French High Commissioner, declared that the records were war booty and thus no longer German property. With unusual bluntness, he stated that his government would not even consider returning the materials in its possession.[79] Adenauer and François-Poncet rapidly became so tied up over the ownership question that Kirkpatrick's proposal to hold separate talks on the matter became all the more urgent if further negotiations on the Bonn Convention were not to be blocked by the restitution demand. Portentously, François-Poncet insisted on France's victor's rights even though very few German documents were in French possession.[80] Adenauer eventually agreed to address the matter in writing.[81] He thus wrote U.S. High Commissioner John J. McCloy, the AHC chair at the time, in May 1952, to propose consultations.[82]

The Germans, unaware that the British had insisted on preliminary discussion among the Allies, had to remind the High Commission of their desire for talks on the Auswärtiges Amt files.[83] Moreover, the British

---

78 Mosler wanted the following passage included in chapter nine of the Settlement Convention, Certain Claims against Foreign Nations and Nationals: "The Three Powers will return to the Federal Republic the public or privately owned German records, archives, and libraries that are still in the possession of the Three Powers." Mosler to Wilhelm Grewe, Apr. 8, 1952, PA/AA, B118, vol. 507.

79 Meeting no. 45 on Apr. 28, 1952, *Adenauer und die Hohen Kommissare 1952*, 143f.; Kirkpatrick to FO, no. 562, Apr. 29, 1952, PRO FO 370/2244 LS3/62.

80 A decision by the Allied Control Council gave the French the responsibility for running the Wehrmacht Information Office (WASt) in Berlin-Wittenau. From the Americans they received the records of the Armistice Commission, the Military Commander for France, and, as also ordered by the Control Council, the records of the People's Court that pertained to French citizens. Martens, "Schicksal der deutschen Akten," L, LIIIf. The stance taken by François-Poncet on the records issue corresponded with his general performance within the AHC: when France held the chairmanship of the Commission, the cards were stacked against the interests of the Germans. François-Poncet tended to guard the victor's rights zealously. Köhler, *Adenauer*, 668; further, Rupieper, *Besetzte Verbündete*, 57.

81 Meeting no. 45 on Apr. 28, 1952, *Adenauer und die Hohen Kommissare 1952*, 143f.; Extract from Minutes of the 47th Meeting of the Special [Steering] Committee, Apr. 30, 1952, PA/AA, B10, vol. 1702/2.

82 Adenauer to John J. McCloy, Chairman of the AHC, May 24, 1954, PA/AA, B118, vols. 507, 508. McCloy's approval on May 27, 1952, was not delivered until July 25, 1952. See Trützschler, Aufzeichnung [über den] Stand der Verhandlungen, July 6, 1953, PA/AA, B118, vol. 508.

83 A summary of the correspondence is found in George W. Renchard, Division of External German Affairs, Office of Political Affairs, HICOG, to State Dept., German Political Affairs, no. 909, Oct. 1, 1952, NA RG 59, CDF 1950–54, 862.423/10–152. On the British desire for a tripartite meeting see Roger Dow, US Member, Working Group on the Return of German Archives, HICOG, no. 815, Sept. 23, 1952, ibid., 862.423/9–2352.

Cabinet still had to approve that such a meeting with the Germans take place.[84] Not until October 31, 1952, a good six months after Adenauer's heated exchange with François-Poncet, did representatives of the four countries sit down together for the first time to discuss the return of the captured documents. The Allies intended to focus the discussion on the proposals set out in the note of July 6, 1951; in other words, they planned to restrict the talks to the Auswärtiges Amt archives.[85] The Americans wanted to leave with an agreement on German participation in *Documents on German Foreign Policy* that would spread the costs of the project. The Germans' objective, as they had already made clear, was to negotiate the return of all the captured documents. They saw the possible participation of German historians in the publication project as a bargaining chip: German participation and financial support were to be traded for the return of the records.[86]

Given the participants' conflicting objectives, the talks were doomed from the outset. The West Germans were not willing to accept the immediate return of only the pre-1914 records as proposed in the July note, and the Allies were not willing to offer more than that. The *Documents on German Foreign Policy* project was still sacrosanct to the Allies, the Americans' concerns about its cost notwithstanding. The German offer to finance the project if it were relocated to the Federal Republic did not help advance the talks. That proposal, the French representative insisted, could not be trusted.[87] Following the unproductive meeting, the Auswärtiges Amt finally decided to respond in writing to the July note. Adenauer rejected the note's proposals and announced that the time had come "to replace what had been conceived as a provisional solution with a definitive settlement." He demanded once again the return of all seized records, without

84 German Request for the Return of Their Captured Archives, Memorandum by the Secretary of State for Foreign Affairs [Anthony Eden], C(52)329, Oct. 10, 1952, PRO CAB 103/466. The cabinet authorized talks on the basis of the Allied note of July 6, 1951, meaning that they were to be limited to diplomatic records. See CC(52), 85th Cabinet Conclusions, Oct. 14, 1952, PRO CAB 128/25.
85 Record of a Meeting of Representatives of the Allied High Commission and the Federal Government held at Mehlemer Aue on Friday, October 31, 1952, to discuss the proposals contained in AGSEC(51)1135 [Note of July 6, 1951] concerning the return of the Federal Republic of public and private archives, NA RG 59, CDF 1950–54, 862.423/11–552 and PRO CAB 103/460. The German version: Niederschrift über die 1. Besprechung betreffend Rückgabe der deutschen Archive, Bibliotheken und Akten in Mehlem am 31. Oktober 1952, Nov. 4, 1952, PA/AA, B118, vol. 507.
86 Brückner, Political Dept., report [for the State Secretary], Oct. 27, 1952, PA/AA, B118, vol. 507.
87 "The French representative was further of the opinion that once the archives had been returned to Germany it would become increasingly difficult for the staffs of the editors-in-chief to obtain access to the documents despite any assurances that the Germans on their part might be willing to give." George L. West, Chief, Division of External German Affairs, Office of Political Affairs, HICOG, to State Dept., no. 1225, Nov. 5, 1952, NA RG 59, CDF 1950–54, 862.423/11–552.

exception, and asked for "the most rapid possible setting of a new date for negotiations."[88]

In proposing to move the publication project to Germany and promising its uninterrupted continuation, the German diplomats had overlooked some practical limitations. For one, the Auswärtiges Amt did not have the facilities to store the documents. Hans Andres, the head of the Political Archives, pointed out in early 1953 that the ministry was not equipped to accommodate even the first group of materials the Allies proposed to return, the pre-1914 files. Completion of new archival stacks was not expected before the spring of 1954.[89] Nonetheless, Heinz von Trützschler, the Political Division official responsible for the negotiations, considered it "completely out of the question" that a logistical problem should undermine Bonn's call for the documents' return. The problem of storage could be immediately solved by renting space or, if all else failed, by storing the files temporarily at the Bundesarchiv in Koblenz.[90] Mere mention of Koblenz in this context was a red flag to Andres. He had expended much energy in fending off possible claims to the diplomatic records by the Bundesarchiv even before the Political Archives had been re-established.[91] He now acted quickly. He petitioned for the necessary funds to transport and store the records so that work on *Documents on German Foreign Policy* could be continued with German participation.[92] To house the publication project, the Auswärtiges Amt looked into the possibility of renting Gymnich Castle, which was located only a short distance from Bonn.[93] The Bundestag allotted more than a half million Deutschmarks for the project, a considerable sum for the recently established state.[94] In May 1953, the Allies were informed of the state of preparations; in October, Bonn again formally proposed the transfer of the project to the Federal Republic.[95] The offer did not, however,

---

88 Adenauer to the Chairman of the AHC, Ambassador Walter J. Donnelly, Nov. 28, 1952, copy in PA/AA, B118, vol. 509, draft in ibid., vol. 489.

89 Andres to Brückner, Political Dept., Jan. 24, 1953, PA/AA, B118, vol. 544. The memorandum includes the handwritten comment by Löns, Abt. II., Jan. 27, 1953: "The return of records is of utmost importance. We must be prepared to accept at any time what we can get. The question of space is not allowed to delay restitution."

90 Brückner, Political Dept., to Andres, Feb. 9, 1953, PA/AA, B118, vol. 544.

91 Trützschler, Abt. II A, to Andres, Feb. 12, 1953, PA/AA, B118, vol. 544.

92 Andres to MinDir Peter Pfeiffer, Mar. 4, 1953, ibid. and vol. 508.

93 Andres to Brückner, May 5, 1953, PA/AA, B118, vol. 489.

94 The sum of DM 559,300 is mentioned in ibid. The Bundestag approved these funds on July 1, 1953. As a comparison, the first budget of the Bundesarchiv in 1952 was DM 632,900 and that of the IfZ for 1951, DM 251,848. The figures in Booms, "Bundesarchiv," 18; Möller, "Institut für Zeitgeschichte," 26.

95 Aide Mémoire über die Rückgabe der Akten des ehemaligen Auswärtigen Amtes, May 6, 1953, PA/AA, B118, vol. 508; Adenauer to the Chairman of the AHC, Oct. 19, 1953, ibid.; draft in ibid., vol. 489.

draw an immediate response. Officials in Bonn had to decide their next move. The lease for Gymnich Castle was ready to be signed. "We must act practically as if we already have received the approval of the AHC to get the records."[96] Indeed, the Adenauer government and the Bundestag had gone to great lengths to secure return of the captured documents. The Americans were alone in giving Bonn's proposal serious consideration. The offer of financial support to ensure the completion of *Documents on German Foreign Policy* received immediate notice at the State Department Historical Office.[97] Bernard Noble saw the proposal as the solution to the financial problems caused by Congressional budget cuts and therefore increased pressure on his British partners to accept the offer. The HICOG staff likewise supported the German proposal as best they could. "HICOG is impressed by the apparently sincere efforts of the Federal Government to make acceptable the Chancellor's proposal," a staff member reported to the State Department.[98] The documents issue, he also warned, "could conceivably become an unfortunate election issue" in the upcoming 1953 Bundestag campaign.[99]

That election was of crucial importance to the Allies. Their initial difficulties with Adenauer notwithstanding, the British and Americans had come to consider the "Old Man from Rhöndorf" as the political leader most likely to keep the Federal Republic on a pro-Western course. Accordingly, three weeks before the Bundestag election, James B. Conant, McCloy's successor as U.S. High Commissioner, urged the Allies to help the chancellor by allowing him to inform the voters that the three Western Allies had "agreed in principle to return former German Foreign Office archives."[100] Conant's staff went so far as to inspect Gymnich Castle.[101] They also intervened on behalf of the Germans when, at one point, Noble became fed up with the standstill in negotiations and adopted a "take-it-or-leave-it" attitude. The days were over when such a lordly approach was possible, they explained to him. "Since the Fed[eral] Rep[ublic] has been offered equality in contributing to the defense of the Western European Community, it is

---

96 Brückner, memorandum, May 7, 1953, ibid.
97 Bruce, Acting SecState, to HICOG Bonn, no. 2178, Nov. 5, 1952, NA RG 59, CDF 1945–49, 862.423/10–3152.
98 George W. Renchard, Office of Political Affairs, HICOG, to State Dept., no. 3532, May 8, 1953, NA RG 59, CDF 1950–54, 862.423/5–853.
99 Ibid.
100 "Adenauer can conceivably reap political advantage from announcement during elections campaign that three powers have agreed in principle to return former German Foreign Office archives." Conant to SecState, no. 653, Aug. 14, 1953, NA RG 59, CDF 1950–54, 862.423/8–1453. The Bundestag election was held on September 6, 1953.
101 Renchard to Noble, Sept. 5, 1953, NA RG 59, CDF 1950–54, 862.423/9–253.

not realistic to continue to deny the early return of most seized German documents in our possession."[102]

German diplomats learned through informal channels about the help they were receiving within the U.S. High Commissioner's office. That information made the fruitlessness of their efforts all the more discouraging. The Auswärtiges Amt gradually became aware of the lines of division in London and Washington. The slow progress of the negotiations, the Germans realized, was a sign that more was happening behind the scenes than the carefully worded notes from the Allies might suggest. At a meeting in August 1952 with representatives of HICOG, Hans-Bernd von Haeften of the Legal Division heard for the first time that the British and Americans were required by wartime agreements to come to a joint decision regarding seized documents.[103] This explained why they placed so much importance on concerting their positions. In the summer of 1953, Hardo Brückner of the Political Division hypothesized about the real reason for British resistance. Officially, the hindrance was said to be the *Documents on German Foreign Policy* project. Brücker believed the more important factor was an engrained mistrust of the Auswärtiges Amt and its staff. British officials and scholars thought, he reported, "it was possible that we could conceal documents if not have them disappear altogether."[104] The mistrust Brückner detected stemmed from experiences connected to the establishment of the new Auswärtiges Amt, the uncertain fate of the personnel records, and the bad aftertaste left by Klassen's unsuccessful mission to London.

Bonn never made a serious attempt to find out whom it was dealing with on the Allied side or to research the background of the historians who so determinedly torpedoed their efforts for the return of the documents.[105] Nor did it try to gather information on the publication project's Historical Advisory Committee, which the British deemed so important.[106] "I consider it completely absurd," protested Peter Klassen of the Political Archives,

---

102 Dulles, SecState [written by Noble], to HICOG Bonn, no. 4732, Mar. 27, 1953, NA RG 59, CDF 1945–49, 862.423/3–2453; George W. Renchard, Office of Political Affairs, HICOG, to Noble, Apr. 22, 1953, ibid., 862.423/4–2253.

103 [Minutes of meeting] VLR v. Haeften, Aug. 28, 1952, PA/AA, B118, vol. 507: "The meeting revealed that an Allied agreement exists which precludes any unilateral move by a custodian power to return documents in its possession to Germany."

104 Brückner, Abt. II, memorandum [for MinDir Herbert Blankenhorn], *Englischer Widerstand gegen die Rückführung der von den Alliierten beschlagnahmten deutschen Noten*, July 30, 1953, PA/AA, B118, vol. 508.

105 In his reports from London, Klassen had listed the names of the three main editors, including that of Margaret Lambert. Naturally, these names could also be found in the imprint of the DGFP volumes. Klassen to AA, Mar. 17, 1952, PA/AA, B118, vol. 489.

106 The members of the board were John W. Wheeler-Bennett, Lewis Namier, E. Llewellyn Woodward (for a while), Rohan Butler, and W. N. Meddlicott.

"that the Foreign Office lets itself be hindered in making a political decision by a commission of scholars that it set up itself."[107] Over the course
of 1954, German officials detected signs that senior figures at the Foreign
Office were in favor of returning the documents. Frank Roberts, Under-
secretary of State at the Foreign Office, was "very favorably disposed,"
Klassen reported.[108] Francis Hancock, head of the Central Department,
also signaled to Bonn's ambassador that his department was not the source
of trouble on the documents question.[109] The Germans were not aware of
the full scope of the division within the Foreign Office, however.

Pulling Out the Stops

*The language of the Chancellor's letter is in places unjustifiably strong and indeed reminiscent
of some of the Nazi documents which he now wishes to recover.*[110]

Adenauer's renewed offer to house the *Documents on German Foreign Policy*
project at Gymnich Castle in October 1953 touched off a round of negotiations between the Allies that the Germans were not informed about. From
the German point of view, the year 1954 seemed to be passing without
any obvious developments. Unbeknownst to them, disagreement among
the Allies on the return of the Auswärtiges Amt files reached a new high
point. The Americans threatened to pull out of the *Documents on German
Foreign Policy* project entirely if the British failed to approve the move to
Gymnich Castle. Senior officials at the Foreign Office were also in favor of
accepting Bonn's offer, but the British historians associated with the project
were able to muster powerful political allies in blocking the move to West
Germany.[111]

The Allies responded to the Gymnich proposal in October 1954 with a
counterproposal. The records from the Weimar Republic were just being
prepared for filming at Whaddon Hall, the Allies explained; moving the
project at this point "would disrupt the existing professional and technical
staffs and cause the loss of some of the most experienced and valuable
members."[112] The West German government was thus once again invited
to send a team of German historians to join the *Documents on German Foreign
Policy* project on equal footing with the American, British, and French

---

107 Klassen, memorandum, Feb. 26, 1954, PA/AA, B118, vol. 508.
108 Klassen, report, "Frage der Aktenrückgabe," Sept. 24, 1954, PA/AA, B118, vol. 489.
109 Botschaftsrat Schlitter, German Mission in London, to AA, Jan. 16, 1954, ibid.
110 Roger Allen on behalf of British High Commissioner Sir Frederick Robert Hoyer Millar to
     Anthony Eden, Jan. 18, 1955, PRO FO 370/2426 LS5/7.
111 Sweet, "Einflußnahme."
112 Roger Allen, Executive Chairman, AHC, to Chancellor, AGSEC(54)644, Oct. 22, 1954, PA/AA,
     B118, vol. 508 and PRO FO 370/2426 LS5/7.

editors. The German scholars would, in addition, be given responsibility for the German edition of the project. The Allies' counterproposal did not list specific, chronologically defined groups of files for immediate return, as had the note of July 6, 1951. Internal Foreign Office and State Department memos make clear, however, that the Allies once again had the pre-1914 records in mind; the political materials from the period 1936–1945, which Bonn eagerly sought, would follow only later.[113]

The Auswärtiges Amt took the Allied response as a complete rejection of Adenauer's proposal. Frustrated by the long silence, by the decision to keep the project in Great Britain, and by the rejection of their demand for the immediate return of all the captured documents, the Germans replied harshly.[114] Adenauer declared the existing state of affairs "unacceptable." The "stable conditions" cited in the preface to *Documents on German Foreign Policy* as the prerequisite for restitution had clearly been achieved with the establishment of the Federal Republic. Therefore, he could "see no legal reason, nor any other reasons that could justify further delay in returning the records." Much of the material in the Allies' possession was not needed for the publication project, the chancellor charged, and several crates of files had not even been unpacked. In light of the pace with which work on *Documents on German Foreign Policy* was progressing, he continued, "it is thoroughly improbable that the document publication 'is approaching its final stage.'"

Nearly nine years after the declaration by the Three Powers[115] that they considered the state of war with Germany to be over, at a moment in which the Allied powers are on the verge of reinstituting full sovereignty to the Federal Republic, the Federal Government is being denied crucial records needed to properly run the business of its ministries, to clarify the legal situation of many citizens of the Federal Republic, and to establish objectively the truth in German historical research.[116]

Bonn was pulling out all the stops. The Auswärtiges Amt instructed diplomats in Paris, Washington, and London to demand no-strings-attached

---

113 This becomes evident in the memorandum Return of the German Foreign Ministry Files, January 1955, PRO FO 370/2426 LS5/7 and the instructions of the State Department to HICOG, no. CA-6355, Mar. 24, 1955, NA RG 59, Lot File 78D441, Historical Office, box 3.

114 Adenauer to the Chairman of the AHC, André François-Poncet, Dec. 29, 1954, PA/AA, B118, vol. 28. Translation: NA RG 59, Lot File 78D441, Historical Office, box 3; PRO FO 370/2426 LS5/3. The document is reprinted in Eckert, *Kampf um die Akten*, 484–7.

115 The wording "declaration by the Three Powers" is Bonn's attempt to avoid using the expression "unconditional surrender." On ending the state of war under international law in 1951, see Schwengler, "Souveränität und Sicherheit," 235–7.

116 Adenauer to the Chairman of the AHC, André François-Poncet, Dec. 29, 1954, PA/AA, B118, vol. 28. Translation: NA RG 59, Lot File 78D441, Historical Office, box 3; PRO FO 370/2426 LS5/3.

return of the captured documents.[117] Government officials discussed the issue for the first time with the press and provided information on the stalled negotiations.[118] Finally, the Auswärtiges Amt arranged for a query in the Bundestag that would give Hallstein the opportunity to call public attention to the "unacceptable" situation.[119]

Adenauer could not have picked a worse time to intervene. Senior officials at the Foreign Office, tired of the internal debate on the documents, were exasperated. "The language of the Chancellor's letter," the deputy of the British High Commissioner wrote in a letter addressed directly to Foreign Secretary Eden, "is in places unjustifiable strong and indeed reminiscent of some of the Nazi documents which he now wishes to recover."[120] James Passant, too, considered the "tone and temper" of Adenauer's response objectionable.[121]

British officials seized upon Adenauer's mention of the "stable conditions" prevailing in Germany. The reference to "stable conditions" in the preface to the first volume of *Documents on German Foreign*, they maintained, referred to Germany as a whole. "Conditions in Germany as a whole are clearly still far from stable; at least any West German politician, including Dr. Adenauer, who attributed stability to the present partition of Germany, would be signing his own political death warrant," Roger Allen observed to Eden.[122] James B. Conant, U.S. High Commissioner and soon-to-be U.S. ambassador to the Federal Republic, became increasingly concerned about his British colleagues' rapidly diminishing willingness to compromise on the captured documents, adding that they were "thoroughly fed up with this problem."[123] The British, he reported, were no longer willing to negotiate and wanted instead to dump the records that were no longer needed at Whaddon on Bonn's doorstep. "[They] wish [to] return unneeded documents immediately and just let [the] Germans wait for rest until we [are]

117 The circular decree of Feb. 5, 1955, is not available but summarized in [Johannes Ullrich,] Aufzeichnung über die Etappen der Verhandlungen zwischen der Bundesregierung und den Drei Mächten, n.d. [1956], PA/AA, B118, vol. 29.

118 Löns, Memo for State Secretary, Mar. 12. 1955, PA/AA, B118, vol. 28.

119 Bundestag, 2. WP, 79. Sitzung, Stenographische Berichte, May 4, 1955, Query of Deputy Arnholz (SPD). The parliamentary question had already been conceived in October 1954. See Klassen, [minutes of meeting], Oct. 1, 1954, PA/AA, B118, vol. 508. The point that this motion was devised at Auswärtiges Amt and not by the deputy himself was not lost on the Americans. See Elim O'Shaughnessy, Director, Office of Political Affairs, AmEmb Bonn, to State Dept., no. 2537, May 31, 1955, NA RG 59, CDF 1955–59, 862.423/5–3155.

120 Allen to Eden, Jan. 18, 1955, PRO FO 370/2426 LS5/7.

121 Minutes Passant, Jan. 21, 1955, PRO FO 370/2426 LS5/7. Also Minutes Lambert, Jan. 13, 1955, ibid., LS5/3.

122 Allen to Eden, Jan. 18, 1955, PRO FO 370/2426 LS5/7.

123 Conant to SecState, no. 3000, Apr. 13, 1955, NA RG 59, CDF 1955–59, 862.423/4–1355.

ready to give them back."[124] For their part, British diplomats in Bonn laid blame for the failure of the negotiations on the Auswärtiges Amt and its "'all-or-nothing' attitude."[125] "The Allies, if they wished, could be equally stiff-necked and claim the right to retain all German government archives as booty, but are evidently unlikely to do so."[126] In the consultations between the Allies on drafting a reply to the chancellor's letter, the British categorically ruled out another invitation to Bonn to send a team of German historians to participate in the preparation of *Documents on German Foreign Policy*.[127]

Despite their pique, British officials eventually agreed with their American counterparts that the Germans must have misinterpreted the October 22 note.[128] The Americans sought to renew the offer so that the Germans would clearly understand what they were turning down.[129] The note with the renewed offer, sent in May 1955, criticized the "tone and content" of the chancellor's letter of December 1954 before going on to present the Allied offer point-by-point to clear up "basic misinterpretations." The work process at Whaddon Hall was explained in great detail. Only the records on the Weimar Republic, which were in the process of being filmed, could not be given back immediately. Everything else, the Allies said, could be returned: all records from 1867 to 1914; all records from the period of World War I; all but a few protocol documents and consulate records; all materials from 1936 to 1945; and all embassy records except for those dating

---

124 Ibid. and Allen to Eden, Jan. 18, 1955, PRO FO 370/2426 LS5/7.
125 "That so far no large measure of agreement has been reached is largely due to failure on the German side to discuss any of the sets of Allied proposals made to them." George Bell, on behalf of the Head of Information Department, BritEmb Bonn, n.d. [June 1955], PRO FO 370/2430 LS5/69.
126 Ibid.
127 "It is interesting to note that throughout the protracted discussions concerning this note [of May 31, 1955] the British attempted to eliminate all encouragement for the participation of German historians at Whaddon Hall." O'Shaughnessy, May 31, 1955, NA RG 59, CDF 1955–59, 862.423/5–3155.
128 They had the Americans to thank for this benefit of the doubt. In an early evaluation of the Chancellor's letter, the question was posed at the State Department whether "the Federal Republic [has] misunderstood our proposals because it wants to misunderstand them in order more easily to reject them in the hope of getting better terms, or is a genuine misinterpretation involved here?" Dulles, SecState, to HICOG Bonn, CA-6355, Instructions containing suggestions for a reply to [Adenauer letter], Mar. 24, 1955, NA RG 59, Lot File 78D441, Historical Office, box 3. See also O'Shaughnessy, May 31, 1955, NA RG 59, CDF 1955–59, 862.423/5–3155: "Informal soundings in the Foreign Office have indicated that the Chancellor's rejection of the October 22nd offer may well have been based on an honest misunderstanding of that proposal."
129 "We believe [it] highly desirable [to] renew October offer in perfectly clear form so we can be certain Ger[man]s know what [they are] rejecting." Conant to SecState, no. 3000, Apr. 13, 1955, NA RG 59, CDF 1955–59, 862.423/4–1355. "Door should be left open for them to accept offer but without pressing them to do so." Dulles, SecState, to HICOG Bonn, no. 2851, Apr. 18, 1955, NA RG 59, CDF 1955–59, 862.423/4–1355.

from the Weimar Republic.[130] The Allies' May 1955 offer differed from their October 1954 offer in presentation but not in substance. Whereas the earlier offer proposed the return of everything except for Weimar, the later replaced that apparently confusing wording with a detailed chronological list of the groups of documents to be returned.

The British-American note of May 1955 prompted officials at the Auswärtiges Amt to pat themselves on the back. Although the offers of October 1954 and May 1955 were essentially the same, the Auswärtiges Amt celebrated the fact that the "custody powers" had finally "dropped the claim to make the full return of the records dependent on the completion of the publication."[131] The Allies, according to Wilhelm Grewe, who had headed the negotiations since March 1955, had at last abandoned the "condition" that German historians had to participate in the publication project. That the Allies were intent on reducing German historians to scholarly peonage was pure invention on the part of the Auswärtiges Amt, which did not want to abandon its all-or-nothing demand. Initially, the Auswärtiges Amt had welcomed the Allied offer to include German experts in the preparation of the documents publication as "real progress." Grewe still thought that the Allied offer of May would make it difficult to get the three governments "to abandon their positions." He thus proposed negotiations so that Bonn might secure "at least the return in the near future ... of the documents mentioned."[132] The minimum Grewe hoped to achieve was in fact what the Allies had been offering since July 1951.[133] Taking stock a year later, Johannes Ullrich, recently released from a Soviet POW camp and reinstalled as the head of the Auswärtiges Amt's Political Archives, came to what, in hindsight, seems the most judicious assessment of dispute over the Auswärtiges Amt files:

During the four years of negotiation, the Allies have barely moved from their standpoint. Had the Germans seized the opportunity at once, they could already have been as far in 1952 as they are in 1956. The only [Allied] concession [since July 1951] has been to turn over the records from 1936–45, which came only as a result of the completion of the publication on this period; the concession therefore

130 The offer was sent to the Auswärtigen Amt in identically worded notes from the three Allied embassies on May 31, 1955. The American copy is found in NA RG 59, Lot File 78D441, Historical Office, box 11 and in PA/AA, B118, vol. 509.
131 Wilhelm Grewe, report [for State Secretary], June 7, 1955, PA/AA, B118, vol. 28.
132 Grewe to State Secretary, June 7, 1955, PA/AA, B118, vol. 28.
133 "Anticipating an early return, in 1951, we actually repacked some of these files and have kept them ready ever since. These archives could therefore have been in Bonn long since, had they been required there." Minutes Lambert, Jan. 13, 1955, PRO FO 370/2426 LS5/3. The July 6 note did yet not include the political records for the years 1936–1945, but all of the other records groups listed also in May 1955. The document is reprinted in Eckert, *Kampf um die Akten*, 478f.

corresponds with the original formulation 'return period by period.'. . . . The Allies have not issued an official statement to the effect that they intend to withhold the Pol[itical] Arch[ives] from the Federal Government. From the beginning, the Allies considered themselves to be custodians, whereby, however, custody was interpreted liberally, as demonstrated . . . for example by the sale of microfilms.[134]

No Sovereignty Without Records. For the West Germans, control of the records of the Federal Republic's precursors was an integral element of national sovereignty. As early as May 1951, two months after Bonn was given responsibility for its foreign relations, Hallstein asserted that the Allies' retention of the German diplomatic archives was not compatible with the "degree of sovereignty" the Federal Republic had attained.[135] The negotiations on the Germany Treaty offered the West Germans an opportunity to push the limits of the country's sovereignty. The attempt the following year to settle the documents issue in the context of the Germany Treaty – the treaty that was to end the Allied occupation of the Federal Republic – was a pragmatic move that also carried much symbolic value. As an unsolicited letter to Adenauer put it, "if, by way of the Germany Treaty, we as a nation are to receive more than 'a slice of sovereignty,' then we as a people have to have our archives again."[136] The pending ratification of the Germany Treaty appeared to be an advantageous moment to bring up the documents issue yet again.[137] But even the legal experts at Auswärtiges Amt did not think that the ratification of the Germany Treaty (together with the treaties known as the Paris Agreements) in May 1955 would bolster the Federal Republic's claim to the records under international law.[138] However, the growing web of agreements between the Federal Republic and Western allies found expression in the Germans' demeanor. With the chancellor's note of December 1954 in his hands, James Passant commented: "The

---

134 Aufzeichnung über die Etappen der Verhandlungen zwischen der Bundesregierung und den Drei Mächten, n.d. [summer 1956], PA/AA, B118, vol. 29. Emphasis added. The date of the note coincides with Johannes Ullrich's return to office as head of the Political Archives, hence the assumption of his authorship

135 Hallstein to Wende, Interior Ministry, May 17, 1951, PA/AA, B118, vol. 507. Schwengler, "Souveränität und Sicherheit," 225–7, 237–9.

136 Albert M., Hanover, May 5, 1952, PA/AA, B118, vol. 507.

137 "The London [nine-power] Conference and the forthcoming conferral of sovereignty to the Federal Republic should be taken advantage of." Klassen, Gesprächsprotokoll, Rückgabe der Akten des Auswärtigen Amts, Oct. 1, 1954, PA/AA, B118, vol. 508.

138 "In the opinion of [the Legal] Department, the possible ratification of the Paris Treaty has no legal consequences for the restitution claim, although politically, the recognition of sovereignty of the Federal Republic could have a beneficial effect on it." VLR Mühlenhöver, Legal. Dept., to Political Archives, Feststellung der Rechtslage in Bezug auf die beschlagnahmten Akten des früheren Auswärtigen Amts, Dec. 23, 1954, PA/AA, B118, vol. 28, and B10, vol. 1703/3.

nearer the Federal Republic comes to attaining full sovereignty the more peremptory its demand for the return of its documents becomes."[139]

The West German government's failure to secure the return of the captured documents was a sore point that the East German government was able to exploit for propaganda purposes. In June 1955, the Soviets sent a shipment of German archival materials to the government of the German Democratic Republic.[140] In turn, the East Germans loudly welcomed the "magnanimous decisions by the Council of Ministers of the USSR." This "new proof of trust" between the socialist allies stood in sharp contrast, East Berlin contended, to the "shameful fact" that Britain and the United States had not displayed comparable trust in Bonn.[141] The timing of the Soviet initiative was no accident: coming soon after the triumphant ratification of the Paris Agreements, the Soviet gesture toward East Berlin was a deliberate ploy to make the West German government's talk of sovereignty and its claims to be the legal successor of earlier German governments look ridiculous.[142] The message came across loud and clear. *Der Spiegel*, for example, wrote:

The actual state of our sovereignty is proven by the fate of the German archives, which are still in Allied hands. The current owners only want to return them once a major portion of the documents have been published. . . . Quite cleverly, the East has exploited this incomprehensible behavior of our new allies for propaganda purposes in recent weeks: the press office of the GDR announced that the Soviet Union has returned a major portion of the captured German records.[143]

Archivists at the Bundesarchiv considered the Soviets' return of ministerial records to the Central Archive in Potsdam – their East German competitor – an affront, and they were angered by the Western Allies' refusal to counterbalance it:

It is not compatible with the sovereignty reinstated to Germany that its archives and records continue to be retained. Every free civilized people is entitled from a moral,

139 Minutes Passant, Jan. 21, 1955, PRO FO 370/2426 LS5/7.
140 The shipment of returned archival material comprised about 140,000 pieces, that is, only a fraction of what was actually held by the Soviet Union. See Henke, "Schicksal deutscher Quellen," 581; Lötzke, "Übergabe deutscher Archivbestände"; Lötzke, "Bedeutung"; Grahn/Lötzke/Weiser, "Unterstützung der UdSSR," esp. 51; Schroll, *Spurensicherung*, 176f.
141 "UdSSR übergab DDR wichtige Archive. Übergabeprotokoll in Moskau unterzeichnet. Neuer Vertrauensbeweis der UdSSR," *Neues Deutschland*, July 1, 1955.
142 "Sensationelle Dokumentensammlung. Wertvolle Materialien zur deutschen Geschichte aus der UdSSR. Wann folgen die USA?," *Berliner Zeitung*, Oct. 1, 1955. West German journalists were invited to Potsdam and reported from there that the archivists of the Central Archive left no doubt "that a truly German historiography of the last 50 years is not possible without the material from the holdings of the former Reich ministries still being retained in the United States and Great Britain." "Pankow verwaltet 140.000 AA-Akten. Lagerung in Potsdam," *Die Welt*, Oct. 1, 1955.
143 Paul Rathje, "Souveränität," *Der Spiegel*, June 1, 1955, 4.

non-material standpoint to safeguard and scientifically evaluate the testimony of its past. To disregard this fundamental national right would be to defame the German people before themselves and the rest of the world and would permanently impair the German relationship with the Allies. Soviet Russia has pre-empted the Allies by announcing that all seized German material will be returned straightaway. The attempt to outdo the Western Allies thereby is obvious and will not fail to have an impact on the whole of Germany.[144]

Speaking on behalf of the West German historical profession, Hermann Aubin warned officials in Bonn that

In the future, a group within the German historical profession, namely those living in the Soviet-occupied zone, will be again in a position to conduct original research on German history of the previous century on a broad scale, whereas [source] materials will still be kept from historians in the Federal Republic by the powers with whom we are allied.[145]

Although the Allies paid close attention to West German responses to the Soviets' return of captured documents to the GDR, they did not change their stance on the documents issue.[146]

The Adenauer government, determined to end the Federal Republic's subordination to foreign powers, came to view progress in the negotiations on the captured documents as a measure of progress in establishing the country's sovereignty. Bringing the occupation to an end and erasing its consequences was a major goal shared by all the political parties in Bonn during the first five years of the Federal Republic's existence.[147] The documents issue was so incendiary, not on account of the practical problems their absence caused but rather on account of the documents' symbolic importance. The struggle for the files was also a struggle for the power to interpret German history.

Behind the Scenes

At the same time that internal policy debates were unfolding in Washington and London, the American and British governments were trying to settle

---

144 Draft notes for a letter to Prof. Grewe at AA by Wilhelm Rohr, Bundesarchiv, n.d., BArch, B198, vol. 1739. From this resulted the letter written by Georg Winter to Wilhelm Grewe, June 21, 1955, BArch, B106, vol. 34724/4.

145 Hermann Aubin, Vorsitzender, Verband der Historiker Deutschlands, to the Politische Abt. des AA, Oct. 21, 1955, PA/AA, B118, vol. 509.

146 David Henry, Chief, Eastern Affairs Division, U.S. Mission Berlin, to State Dept., no. 9, July 6, 1955, NA RG 59, CDF 1954–59, 862.423/7–655; Elim O'Shaughnessy, Counselor of Embassy, AmEmb Bonn, to State Dept., Aug. 25, 1955, ibid., 862.423/8–2555; as well as the minutes in PRO FO 370/2429 LS5/57 and LS5/59.

147 Frei, *Adenauer's Germany.*

on a joint response to the West German government's demand for the return of the captured documents. Their aim was always to present a united front to the Germans. The British were particularly adamant not to give the West Germans an opportunity to play one of the Allies off against the other.[148] Coordinating policy was often difficult, however, on account of the deep disagreement within the ranks of the British government. For reasons of cost, the State Department's Historical Office wanted to accept the German offer to transfer the *Documents on German Foreign Policy* project to Gymnich Castle. The British historians involved were fiercely opposed to that proposal. This section examines how the historians were able to become so influential that British diplomats ended up acting against their own better judgment.

Safeguards. Bonn's offer to transfer *Documents on German Foreign Policy* to Germany was rather vague about particulars when it was first mentioned in October 1952. The British editor-in-chief, Margaret Lambert, and the chairman of the JCC, John W. Wheeler-Bennett, objected immediately nonetheless. A move would inevitably interrupt work on the project, they contended, and several of the historians involved could not imagine living and working in West Germany. The more important question for Wheeler-Bennett and Lambert was, however, whether the project could be carried out "on the necessary basis of scholarly impartiality and objectivity" on German soil.[149] Their doubts rested on the evaluation of *Die Große Politik der europäischen Kabinette*, a multi-volume collection of documents published in the 1920s under the aegis of the Auswärtiges Amt, that was being conducted at the time at Whaddon Hall. In this evaluation, original documents had been compared with those published in the edition. It was discovered that Friedrich Thimme, the chief editor, had occasionally subjected the selection of documents to patriotic self-censorship.[150] In view of these findings, Ivone Kirkpatrick proposed to the High Commission that, instead of relocating the teams of scholars compiling *Documents on German Foreign Policy*, the size of the staff at Whaddon Hall be increased, thereby accelerating the speed of the project, so that the records could be sent back sooner.[151]

---

148 Foreign Office, Aide Mémoire, Sept. 28, 1953, NA RG 59, Lot File 78D441, Historical Office, box 19.
149 Minutes Wheeler-Bennett, Margaret Lambert, Dec. 12, 1952, PRO FO 370/2341 LS5/136.
150 On the examination of *Große Politik* see chapter 5.
151 Holmes, AmEmb London, to SecState, no. 4568, Feb. 17, 1953, NA RG 59, CDF 1950–54, 862.423/2–1753; Hooker, FirstSec AmEmb London, Mar. 24, 1953, ibid., 862.423/3–2453; Botschafter Aldrich, AmEmb London, to SecState, no. 5239, Mar. 24, 1953, NA RG 407, entry 360, box 3609.

Yet the more specific German proposal presented in May 1953 was simply too attractive to the Americans to be ignored out of courtesy to the British.[152] They felt that the Germans had "met our previous objections about the transfer of the Historical Project to Germany and that it ought therefore be accepted."[153] Bernard Noble still thought that German participation was essential if *Documents on German Foreign Policy* was to be completed. To put more pressure on his London colleagues, he even entertained the idea of stopping work at Whaddon Hall completely.[154] In the hope of making the proposed relocation acceptable to the British, Noble compiled a list of safeguards the Germans would be required to uphold.[155] Francis Hancock, the head of the Foreign Office's Central Department, was not averse to Noble's proposal. The Office of the High Commissioner at Wahnerheide and the Undersecretary of State Frank Roberts also recognized the pragmatic advantages of the move. Roberts presented Noble's proposal of a transfer with safeguards to Sir William Strang and voiced his support for it. Strang, however, effectively killed the proposal on July 8, 1953: "For reasons which I have explained to Mr. Hancock, and of which Passant is fully aware," he wrote cryptically in the margins of the minutes of a meeting, "consideration of this paper [on the proposed safeguards] had better be deferred for a while."[156]

---

152 At no point did State Department officials share the British concern that the objectivity of the publication would suffer in Germany or that the move would represent an unacceptable interruption. Still, they did agree to the British rejection of the proposal for a short while, only to disagree once Bonn made the offer of Gymnich Castle. See Minutes Hancock, Apr. 2, 1953, PRO FO 370/2338 LS5/60; Dulles, SecState, to AmEmb London, no. A-1492, May 5, 1953, NA RG 59, CDF 1950–54, 862.423/3–2453.

153 Minutes Hancock to Frank Roberts, May 15, 1953, PRO FO 370/2340 LS5/103.

154 Noble to Passant, May 26, 1953, PRO FO 370/2340 LS5/106. The British took Noble's consideration of an American pull-out from the DGFP project very seriously. See I.F. Porter, BritEmb, to W. D. Allen, Central Department, FO, May 27, 1953, PRO FO 370/2340 LS5/119; Minutes Hancock, May 30, 1953, ibid., LS5/110: "If the Americans did withdraw, I hardly see how we could go on with the project in this country."

155 These safeguards held that the staff in Cologne had to be acceptable to the Allies; that no original document would be removed from the publication offices until the project was completed; that the Whaddon records would not be combined with the holdings already existing in Bonn; that historians would have unhindered access to the stacks; that the West German government would have to guarantee the unimpaired continuation of work; that the administration of the project as well as the supervision of the transfer and renewed shelving of records would fall to a group of representatives from the four participating governments. See U.S. Aide Mémoire, May 21, 1953, PRO FO 370/2340 LS5/110; U.S. Aide Mémoire, May 26, 1953, ibid., LS5/113; Memorandum [on conditions essential to any agreement to transfer the Tripartite Project to the Federal Republic], May 27, 1953, NA RG 59, CDF 1950–54, 862.423/5–2753; Smith, Acting SecState to AmEmb London, no. 7651, May 29, 1953, ibid., 862.423/5–2753; the conditions are also listed in the minutes Hancock for Passant, June 17, 1953, PRO FO 370/2341 LS5/137.

156 Handwritten note by Strang on the minutes by Roberts, July 8, 1953, PRO FO 370/2341 LS5/136. At the time, Strang was Permanent Under-Secretary of State for Foreign Affairs, that is the highest ranking civil servant at the Foreign Office.

The Windsor File was back. Not only Bonn's offer to house the *Documents on German Foreign Policy* project but also "the suppression of a particular file" was now at issue.[157] At the same time that the Americans were pressuring their British colleagues to accept the offer, the editors were deciding on the selection of documents that would be published in volume 10 (Series D). That volume was the responsibility of the American team and covered the year 1940. The Windsor File had already been chosen for publication, and the volume was to be sent to the printer in mid-1954.[158] In delaying consideration of Bonn's offer, Strang was acting on instructions from above. The American ambassador in London could only speculate about the pressures that had suddenly come to bear upon his British partner. Secretly, he was given to understand, however, "that this was the sort of thing that Churchill would feel strongly about."[159] The prime minister had assumed responsibility for foreign affairs in April when Foreign Minister Anthony took a six-month medical leave. As Paul Sweet has shown, Churchill made the Windsor File a top priority and attended to it personally despite his health problems (he suffered a stroke in late June 1953).[160] He set off a veritable firework of activity to prevent its planned publication. President Dwight D. Eisenhower, who had become familiar with the matter back in 1945, received a letter from Churchill requesting help in what the British considered an extremely delicate situation. Foreign Minister George Bidault of France was also asked to support the effort to block plans to include the Windsor File in *Documents on German Foreign Policy.*[161]

Churchill raised the matter with his cabinet on August 25, 1953. The prime minister seemed convinced that the Windsor File was not of historical interest and therefore did not need to be published, at least not during the Duke of Windsor's lifetime. Churchill would have liked simply to forbid its publication. He realized, however, "that, if this story was likely to be published in any event, it would be even more embarrassing if it could be said that the United Kingdom Government had attempted to prevent its publication." Nonetheless, he still wanted the file suppressed. Lord Salisbury

---

157 Minutes Hancock for Geoffrey Harrison, Sept. 11, 1953, PRO FO 370/2343 LS5/193. The unmentionable file was also refered to as "the special file" or "the particular difficulty" or simply "these papers." The minutes in which the matter of the Windsor File was discussed – unlike those dealing simply with other matters having to do with the transfer – were classified as "secret" or "top secret."

158 Sweet, "Einflußnahme," 279.

159 Ambassador Winthrop Aldrich, AmEmb London, to SecState, no. 661, Aug. 17, 1953, NA RG 59, CDF 1950–54, 862.423/8–1753.

160 Eden returned to work on Oct. 5, 1953. Sweet, "Einflußnahme," 282f.

161 These events are depicted in detail in Sweet, "Einflußnahme"; Sweet, "Windsor File"; see also Kent, "Editing Diplomatic Documents," 473–6; Thimme, "Politisches Archiv," 346–8; as well as Zala, *Zensur*, 291–3, 302f.

did not find the papers as explosive as the prime minister did. He reported that Margaret Lambert had already signaled her willingness to cooperate. Although she would not tolerate outside interference or other infringement of her editorial independence, she might be receptive to Churchill's plan to delay publication of the Windsor File substantially. It was thus decided at the Cabinet meeting that Lambert would do all she could to slow the publication process down.[162] As soon as publication was imminent, the duke would be forewarned and an official statement agreed upon.[163] Churchill continued to follow the matter with close interest right up to the publication of the Windsor File in 1957, two years after he had left office.[164]

Churchill's interest had direct bearing on the delicate balance between supporters and opponents of the proposal to move the *Documents on German Foreign Policy* project to West Germany. Times became bad for the diplomats who advocated the transfer of the publication project to West Germany. The chances were bleak for arranging a conference with the Americans and French even to discuss the safeguards necessary for such a move, let alone decide in favor of the transfer. Owing to Churchill's direct intervention, the British historians had gained even greater momentum. Just knowing Churchill's wishes in the matter was enough to force the diplomats to take the concerns and opinions of the scholars into greater consideration than they would have otherwise.

To Publish or Not to Publish? On September 16, 1953, Margaret Lambert met with the prime minister.[165] Immediately after the meeting at Downing Street, Lambert announced to the American and French editors, Paul Sweet and Maurice Baumont, that she was willing to support a radical

---

162 Salisbury "said that he had seen the British historian, Miss Lambert, and he believed that she might be more accommodating than had been suggested earlier in the discussion. Certainly she would not welcome an attempt by one of the three Governments to limit the discretion which they had previously accorded to the historians to decide on objective historical grounds which documents should be published. But she had *herself* made the suggestion that publication of this correspondence might be delayed if the documents of the Weimar Republic were published in advance of the volume [10] at present planned for publication." Confidential Record of Cabinet Discussion on 25th August 1953, C.C.(53) 50th Conclusion, Top Secret, No Circulation Record, Aug. 28, 1953. Emphasis added. It could not be determined exactly when the Salisbury-Lambert meeting took place that led to the remarks by Lambert quoted here.

163 Confidential Record of Cabinet Discussion on 25th August 1953, C.C.(53) 50th Conclusion, Top Secret, No Circulation Record, Aug. 28, 1953. The document is reprinted in Eckert, *Kampf um die Akten*, 482–4.

164 Churchill to Sir Norman Brook, n.d. [Dec. 15, 1954], PRO CAB 21/3776: "I am relying upon you to watch with the utmost vigilance from month to month the development of this affair in order that the Government of the day shall be enabled to make any simultaneous statement they may think proper."

165 Lord Salisbury and the Minister of Labour, Sir Walter Monckton, also attended the Lambert-Churchill meeting. See Sweet, "Einflußnahme," 284.

change in the work and publication schedule of *Documents on German Foreign Policy*. Work on the Series D (1937–1945), which included the nearly completed volume 10, should be stopped immediately, she proposed, so that attention could be focused on completing Series C (1933–1938). The stated objective was to delay the publication of the Windsor File for several years.[166] In describing her meeting with Churchill to Sweet, Lambert made it sound as if she had adamantly fought against suppressing the Windsor File. Although Sweet expressed his admiration for her efforts, he could not support an abrupt shift of focus from Series D to Series C because it made neither scholarly nor organizational sense.[167] Lambert was nevertheless quite adamant about the new course of action. In response to Sweet's concern that the nonappearance of a volume in an ongoing series might raise suspicions, she argued that "no one will particularly miss volume X" as long as volumes from the other series continued to appear. Should Sweet feel empty-handed without volume 10, she added, he could take over the editing of one of the volumes assigned to the British.[168] To deprive Sweet of the opportunity to raise objections to the change in the publication schedule, Lambert arranged that he not receive an invitation to the talks on safeguards planned for November. "If [Sweet] comes before he has been converted . . . I anticipate that he and Dr. Noble will merely raise fresh difficulties along the lines they have already, and Dr. Sweet will find it harder to retreat from his position." In the same tone, she continued:

It seems essential that Dr. Noble be now told firmly what the position is, and that he should have accepted it before he comes over here. For this reason, no final date for his arrival should be fixed until he has faced the facts. The plan will fail of its purpose unless it is applied promptly and further work on volume X stopped at once. This must be our immediate objective and will evidently require shock tactics.[169]

James Passant informed Noble that Lambert enjoyed strong support in London. He did not hesitate to speculate that she might possibly resign if the Americans did not accept her plan. It would then be unclear who should decide about the safeguards for the transfer of the project to West Germany.[170] Lambert's threat to resign, in sum, was not a protest against the

---

166 Sweet to Lambert, Oct. 16, 1953, PRO FO 370/2343 LS 5/220. Here he also reported Lambert's suggestions from Oct. 8, 1953. See also Sweet, "Einflußnahme," 284f.
167 "Naturally I am relieved to learn that your judgment as a historian has been accepted that volume X should not appear in print without the documents in question." Sweet to Lambert, Oct. 16, 1953, ibid. Further, Sweet, "Einflußnahme," 282f., 286f.
168 Minutes Lambert for Passant, Oct. 21, 1953, PRO FO 370/2343 LS5/220.
169 Minutes Lambert, Oct. 24, 1953, ibid., LS5/221.
170 Passant to Noble, Oct. 28, 1953, ibid.

possible suppression of the Windsor File. With Passant's help, Lambert used the threat to compel the Americans to accept a change in the publication schedule that would delay the appearance of the Windsor File. Passant, in turn, used Lambert's threat in his attempt to block the relocation of *Documents on German Foreign Policy* to West Germany.

To give Lambert additional support and provide scholarly backing for her demands, Lord Salisbury approved the establishment of a historical advisory committee. Lambert had requested the creation of such a body in August 1953, noting that Sweet had one on which he could depend.[171] The newly established committee consisted of John Wheeler-Bennett, E. Llewellyn Woodward, Lewis Namier, J. R. M. Butler, and W. M. Meddlicott – the most formidable group of opponents to the documents' return imaginable.[172] Indeed, the advisory committee proved to be of one mind with Lambert at its first meeting on October 15, 1953, and approved the immediate halt to work on Series D.[173] Lambert also knew the committee could be counted on to offer stiff resistance to pressure to relocate *Documents on German Foreign Policy* from Whaddon Hall to Gymnich Castle, and that was precisely why the advisory committee had the full support of Lord Salisbury.[174] It was also the reason why Francis Hancock, who was still attempting to start talks on safeguards, knew he was in for trouble. As negotiations with the Americans approached, he tried to circumvent the advisory committee. "I have always felt that in this connection the Advisory Committee would be a millstone round our necks," he complained to Passant.[175]

Lambert succeeded at first in pushing through her plan against American opposition. Upon returning from London in November 1953, Noble told Sweet that he had little recourse but to approve the stoppage of work on Series D.[176] Sweet nonetheless continued to work on the series in the hope that the Windsor File would cease to be an issue once Churchill

---

171 Lambert to Passant, Aug. 30, 1953; Minutes Passant for Roberts, Strang, Hancock, both in PRO FO 370/2342 LS5/184. Members of the first American advisory committee were Sidney B. Fay, Guy Stanton Ford, Carlton J. Hayes, William L. Langer, Conyers Read, and Charles Seymour.

172 Minutes Passant for Strang, Sept. 3, 1953, PRO FO 370/2343 LS5/202/G.

173 *"The Committee unanimously recommended* that publication of a series of documents on the Weimar and early Hitler periods should be started as soon as possible, and that Series D should be held back to allow the earlier series to come out more rapidly." Minutes of Meeting of the Historical Advisory Committee held at the Foreign Office Library, on October 15, 1953 at 3p.m., PRO FO 370/2343 LS5/220. Original emphasis.

174 "This seems an excellent plan + I approve the membership of the new committee." Minutes Salisbury, Sept. 9, 1953, regarding the Minutes Strang to SecState [Salisbury], Sept. 8, 1953, PRO FO 370/2343 LS5/202/G.

175 Minutes Hancock for Passant, Sept. 30, 1953, PRO FO 370/2343 LS5/201.

176 Sweet, "Einflußnahme," 289.

left Downing Street. At the editors' meeting in July 1954, Sweet, backed by Baumont, demanded that Series D be continued.[177] The British position became untenable. The alternatives that Passant proposed would have created an even bigger scandal than publication of the Windsor File.[178] Volume 10 finally appeared on August 1, 1957. Inserted in the volume was a statement by the British government that consequently directed even more attention to the "particular file." The Duke of Windsor himself had insisted on such a démenti and tasked Walter Monckton with writing one.[179] The Cabinet Office also briefed the royal family before the appearance of the much dreaded volume 10.[180]

"A stink in our nostrils." The determination of Churchill and his cabinet to suppress the Windsor File was a major setback to Foreign Office officials who were open to compromise with Bonn. With Eden still in convalescence, they had to deal with Lord Salisbury, who had been brought in as acting foreign secretary. Salisbury, encountering the documents issue for the first time, considered the debate on return premature. Why, he asked, should anything be returned before a peace treaty was signed and ratified? Salisbury in effect turned back the clock and reverted to the assumptions of 1950, assumptions that diplomats at the Central Department had worked so hard to change. When approached by Frank Roberts, the head of the Central Department, Salisbury did not want to approve even the proposal that the British enter into talks with the other Western Allies on the safeguards

177 Minutes Lambert, July 29, 1954, PRO FO 370/2374 LS5/129. Here she alleges that Sweet agreed to skip over volume X. What he actually said in October 1953 was that the volume could anyway not appear until May 1955. Sweet to Lambert, Oct. 16, 1953, PRO FO 370/2343 LS5/220. Further, Minutes Passant, Aug. 11, 1954, Minutes Frank Roberts, Aug. 12, 1954, both in PRO FO 370/2374 LS5/131. The most incisive reference: Minutes Passant, Sept. 8, 1954, ibid., LS5/143: "There can be no doubt that the main agreement between the PM and Miss Lambert was that she would do her best to induce her US and French colleagues to 'switch' their activities to the Weimar period. She had every reason to suppose that she had been successful until the recent Editorial Conference in July, when both Dr. Sweet and Prof. Baumont expressed a strong preference for continuing the publication of Series D. It is very clear that, if such a programme is now adopted, the documents in dispute will be published in 1956, unless the whole project collapses before then. This would be directly contrary to the views of the PM and the Cabinet who, on 28th [*sic*, 25th] August, 'agreed that it was very desirable that these docs should not be published during the Duke's lifetime.'"

178 Minutes Passant, Sept. 20, 1954, PRO FO 370/2374 LS5/143.

179 "I regard it as essential . . . that the FO 'démenti' should be entirely general in character and should ignore all specifically alleged anti-British statements attributed to me, as a pack of lies. . . . And with regard to . . . your persuasive powers . . . , it would be only fair to emphasise that I needed no persuasion, whatsoever, firstly, not to return to Spain, nor secondly, to sail for the Bahamas on August 1st, the date stipulated by Winston and to which I agreed." Excerpt from a letter by the Duke of Windsor to Sir Walter Monckton, Jan. 18, 1955, PRO CAB 21/3776.

180 Norman Brook, Cabinet Secretary, to Sir Michael Adeane, Private Secretary Buckingham Palace, July 10, 1957; Adeane to Brook, July 20, 1957, both in ibid.

to be imposed as a condition for the transfer of the *Documents on German Foreign Policy* project to Germany. He considered the issue a matter for Churchill to decide.[181] Roberts did not get much further with the Permanent Under Secretary, Sir William Strang, who was willing to approve plans for a tripartite meeting only in exchange for a guarantee that an agreement on the safeguards would not be seen as a commitment to proceed with the transfer. Strang was driven by concern about the Windsor File. If, after coming to terms on the safeguards, Britain found itself "morally committed to agree to the transfer, then it would be more honest to tell the Americans and French here and now that whatever the ultimate decision reached, we are not going to let this particular file of papers out of our hands," Strang bluntly acknowledged to Roberts. "Can you," he then asked, "confirm that we shall be in no way committed even morally?"[182]

Britain would thus discuss the safeguards that would be a prerequisite for the project's transfer but would exclude the transfer itself from consideration.[183] Strictly speaking, the British did not have much to negotiate. On October 8, they nonetheless informed the Americans that they were willing to discuss safeguards "without prejudice to the question whether the archives are to be transferred to Germany or not."[184] The first meeting, scheduled for October 26, fell through because the French did not indicate whether they would attend.[185] In the meantime, Adenauer had repeated the offer of Gymnich Castle. The State Department's attempts to set up a tripartite meeting now coincided with Margaret Lambert's efforts to stop work on Series D. Knowing full well how urgently the State Department wanted to start talks in light of Adenauer's renewed offer, James Passant exploited the situation to advance Lambert's objectives. "It now seems necessary," he advised Strang, "to bring further pressure to bear on Dr. Noble who has been discussing the situation [i.e., the proposed suspension of Series D] with Dr. Sweet. In this connection it would be well to defer a definite reply to the Americans on fixing a date for the [tripartite] discussions on

181 Minutes Salisbury for Strang, Sept. 7, 1953, PRO FO 370/2343 LS5/193. Salisbury took the occasion to express his opinion that it was anyway far too early to publish documents from the war period and that the project at Whaddon Hall should be stopped.

182 Minute Strang for Roberts, Aug. 21, 1953, ibid.

183 "No decision is at present being sought on the question of transferring the Historical Project to Germany. We are only seeking authority to embark on an examination with the Americans and the French of the necessary safeguards *if* it were transferred to Germany. These talks would be carried out without any commitment as to transfer, on which the position of Ministers would be specifically reserved." Minutes Harrison for Sir Pierson Dixon [Strang's representative], Sept. 12, 1953, ibid. Also Minutes Hancock, Sept. 21, 1953, ibid.

184 Brit. Aide Mémoire, Oct. 8, 1953, NA RG 59, CDF 1950–54, 862.423/10–853. Also Dillon, AmEmb London, to SecState, no. 1374, Oct. 6, 1953, ibid., 862.423/10–653.

185 Botschafter Aldrich, AmEmb, to SecState, no. 1738, Oct. 22, 1953, ibid., 862.423/10–2253.

safeguards."[186] By the end of October, officials in Washington had figured out that something was afoot in London.[187]

A conference on the documents issue finally convened on November 25, 1953, in London. Noble arrived with a draft response accepting Adenauer's proposal to move the Auswärtiges Amt files and publication project to Gymnich Castle. To his disappointment, the draft was not needed.[188] The British and French tried to impose safeguards the Americans considered needlessly strict, impractical, and too likely to meet with German opposition. Margaret Lambert demanded, for example, that Gymnich be declared extraterritorial.[189] But even that step, she warned, would not prevent German staff members from suppressing documents that might embarrass leaders in Bonn. "She mentioned specifically Chancellor Adenauer's connection with Rhineland separatists in the 1920s."[190] Given the differences in the Allies' positions, the fact that the tripartite meeting did in the end produce a consensus on safeguards must have been seen by all participants as a breakthrough. The British and French successfully pushed for the condition that all the Weimar-era records be filmed before the proposed move take place. The decision on the move itself was to be left to the leadership of the three governments.[191]

Back at his desk in London after the conference, Francis Hancock began to prepare for the final step: cabinet approval for the move. He drafted a bill for the foreign secretary, who was quite preoccupied with other matters at the 1954 Foreign Ministers Conference in Berlin.[192] Together with Frank Roberts, Hancock openly challenged the historians. He believed that the *Documents on German Foreign Policy* project was doomed and would not survive to completion.[193] While drafting the cabinet bill, he made it clear to Passant that "we ought quite frankly and brutally to bring out the

186 Minutes Passant for Strang, Oct. 26, 1953, PRO FO 370/2343 LS5/221.
187 "Request London advise whether in its judgement this [tripartite] discussion really desired by British, and explain reasons for delay." Smith, Acting SecState, to AmEmb London, no. 2447, Oct. 22, 1953, NA RG 59, CDF 1950–54, 862.423/10–2253.
188 Draft, part of Peter Rutter, Second Sec of AmEmb London, to State Dept., no. 2041, Dec. 7, 1953, ibid., 862.423/12–753.
189 "The opinion of the Legal Adviser was so firmly against such a concept that even the determined Miss Lambert had to give up the point." Ibid.
190 Ibid.
191 The conference report written by Passant and dated Dec. 2, 1953, contains in the attachments the "Proposal for Quadripartite Publication of German Foreign Office and Related Papers, 1918–1945," PRO FO 370/2344 LS5/249. Further, see Rutter to State Dept, no. 2041, Dec. 7, 1953, ibid., 862.423/12–753; Dulles, SecState, to AmEmb London, no. 3305, Dec. 22, 1953, NA RG 59, CDF 1950–54, 862.423/12–2253.
192 The (seventh) Berlin Conference of Foreign Ministers took place from Jan. 25 to Feb. 18, 1954.
193 "The publication project is doomed anyway sooner or later." Minutes Hancock for Passant and Pat Dean, Jan. 28, 1954, PRO FO 370/2371 LS5/29.

implications of what we are proposing, viz. the probable demise of the historical project."[194] If the project was moved to Germany, the British historians would certainly resign, Hancock reckoned. But if it remained at Whaddon, the Americans might possibly back out. At the same time, political circumstances made it imperative to accommodate Bonn. Hancock thought it preferable to act while Britain could still set conditions for returning the documents rather than waiting until the Federal Republic was in a position to exert pressure to achieve its goals.[195] Accepting the likely collapse of the project, Passant countered, would be a major embarrassment to the American, British, and French governments.[196] Passant, a firm supporter of the historians, was subsequently placed in the uncomfortable position of having to draft a formulation of Hancock's proposal for the foreign secretary's approval.[197]

The proposal that Anthony Eden was to submit to the cabinet accepted the German offer: the publication project would be moved to the Federal Republic. However, because the British historians would then certainly resign – a risk the Foreign Office took for granted – only the documents would be relocated to Gymnich Castle. One of two courses of action would be pursued with the Windsor File: either it would be pulled before the records were returned or its fate would be decided "on an 'old boy basis,'" as Roberts had long envisioned.[198] Eden presented the issue to the Cabinet at the end of March and simplified matters by proposing to "return the documents and abandon the publication project."[199] The Cabinet agreed on the condition that the documents be filmed beforehand.[200] As the American

194 Minutes Hancock for Passant, Feb. 11, 1954, ibid.

195 "I think that at the rate the Germans are advancing towards the resumption of sovereignty and the probability that she will soon become the most powerful country on the Continent, pressure upon us to release these documents to the Germans will increase rapidly. Unless we are prepared to hazard a first-class row we shall have to give way." Minutes Hancock, Jan. 28, 1954, PRO FO 370/2371 LS5/29.

196 "Your solution involves a considerable loss of 'face' on the part of the three Governments now engaged in the Project." Minutes Passant for Hancock, Jan. 29, 1954, ibid.

197 The drafts and other minutes on this topic are found in PRO FO 370/2371 LS5/29. Passant's dilemma is clearly presented in Minutes Hancock, Feb. 2, 1954, ibid.: "Mr. Passant has agreed with the text of the draft, [although] he does not himself support the proposals made in it."

198 Ivone Kirkpatrick, Submission to SecState, The Archives of the Former German Foreign Ministry, Feb. 15, 1954, PRO FO 370/2371 LS5/29; Kirkpatrick to Frank Roberts, Berlin, Feb. 15, 1954, ibid.; Minutes Roberts for SecState [Eden] and Parliamentary UnderSecState [Anthony Nutting], Feb. 22, 1954, ibid., LS5/38. Quote is found in Minutes Roberts, Sept. 5, 1953, PRO FO370/2342 LS5/192.

199 Norman Brook, Cabinet secretary, [Submission to the] Prime Minister, Captured German Archives, C.(54)109, Mar. 23, 1954, PRO CAB 103/461. See also Frank Roberts, German Diplomatic Archives, Brief for Cabinet on March 24, Mar. 23, 1954, PRO FO 370/2371 LS5/46/G.

200 "The Cabinet – Agreed that the German diplomatic documents which had fallen into Allied hands at the end of the war might be returned to the custody of the German Federal Government..., provided that steps could first be taken to make microfilm records, not only of the principal

embassy reported to Washington, this decision was "taken against strong opposition of all historians."[201]

As Allied policy-makers weighed Adenauer's offer, the British historians loudly registered their opposition to the proposed move. In view of the safeguards conference, Lambert's Historical Advisory Committee had unequivocally stated its position: moving the project would be interpreted everywhere as "an act of restitution and even expiation, and, by implication, [would] cast doubts on the impartiality of Allied editorship of the volumes so far published." The Allied historians would be in an intolerable situation once they were on German soil. They would not be able to trust the Auswärtiges Amt officials and archivists, and the German historians would grudgingly look upon them as "unwanted partners." It would become increasingly difficult to administer the project "since the Germans will feel such controls to be offensive to them and *ehrenrührig* (touching their honour)." In short, the committee declared, "we should profoundly deplore the loss to historical truth which such developments might well entail."[202] Interestingly, evidence of the dispute that ensued is not to be found in Foreign Office records but in reports the U.S. embassy in London sent to Washington. On this topic, British officials abandoned all diplomatic discretion in informing their American colleagues of the ongoing conflict. With growing astonishment, the U.S. embassy officials cabled reports on the intensifying British infighting, which gave Washington an idea of how intense the dispute had become over an issue so peripheral to world politics. In early February 1954, the embassy reported, the Foreign Office was "'up a gum tree' on this question."[203] In mid-March, one British official told American colleagues "confidentially and with singular candor" that "the British historians are a stink in our nostrils."[204] The same official reportedly went into a "tirade against the British historians for their obstructiveness" three months later when telling his American colleagues about the interaction between the Foreign Office and the historians after the Cabinet had

documents of the Weimar period, but of all the main documents which had not already been published in the selection of Documents on German Foreign Policy." CC(54)24th Conclusions, Mar. 31, 1954, PRO CAB 128/27.

201 Ambassador Aldrich, AmEmb London, to SecState, Apr. 13, 1954, NA RG 59, CDF 1950–54, 862.423/4–1354.

202 Statement agreed by the members of the Historical Advisory Committee at a meeting held on December 5, 1953, PRO FO 370/2371 LS5/38. The paper is signed by Butler, Wheeler-Bennett, Medlicott, and Namier. At the time, Woodward was a visiting professor at Princeton.

203 Benjamin M. Hulley, FirstSec of Embassy, AmEmb London, to State Dept., no. 2663, Feb. 4, 1954, NA RG 59, CDF 1950–54, 862.423/2–454.

204 Peter Rutter, SecondSec of Embassy, AmEmb London, to State Dept., no. 3123, Mar. 16, 1954, ibid., 862.423/3–1654.

decided against the latter and the details of implementing the decision had to be arranged.[205]

The Cabinet decision represented a breakthrough for the complicated British situation, at least on paper. Because the Cabinet had stipulated the microfilming of the captured records as a condition for their return, there was no way to wind up the matter quickly. At the safeguards conference in November 1953, participants estimated that filming the Weimar records would take six months. In March 1954, Passant talked of needing a year for the work, and by July, the estimate had grown to three to four years.[206] Bernard Noble, who seldom lost his temper, accused Passant of pursing a "policy of delay and indecision."[207]

Following further rounds of unpleasant consultations, the Allies finally agreed on an answer to Adenauer's offer to transfer the *Documents on German Foreign Policy* project to Germany. The Allies' note of October 22, 1954, gave no hint of the nerve-wracking disputes that had taken place behind the scenes. Because the Allies did not explicitly accept Adenauer's offer but proposed to return all records except those pertaining to Weimar, the Germans interpreted the note as a total rejection of their proposal. This prompted Adenauer's aforementioned harsh response of December 29, 1954. Only against the backdrop of the Anglo-American struggles and the rebellion of the British historians is it understandable why officials at the British High Commission, who had fought so hard on Bonn's behalf, regarded Adenauer's response as a slap in the face.

The Agreement

As insignificant as it may seem to millions of newspaper readers, this event can be called a nearly epochal one for German archival history.[208]

After several years of difficult negotiations, everyone involved with the captured Auswärtiges Amt files was relieved when attention could be shifted to the logistical details of sending the documents back to Germany. But much to the alarm of the Allied representatives, a discussion with the West Germans on August 11, 1955, opened in much the same manner as previous meetings had ended. The head of the German delegation, Hardo

---

205 Rutter to State Dept., no. 4015, June 11, 1954, ibid., 862.423/6–1154. It is unclear who each of the British officials were. Only once, namely in 1959, did Margaret Lambert publish an article on the subject of German records in Allied custody. At no point in this article did she even hint to a dispute. See Lambert, "Source Materials," esp. 191–3.

206 Minutes Passant for Roberts and Kirkpatrick, July 29, 1954, PRO FO 370/2374 LS5/129.

207 Noble to Passant, Mar. 15, 1954, PRO FO 370/2371 LS5/42.

208 Philippi, "Politisches Archiv I," 139.

Brückner, categorically demanded the return of *all* German records; the Allies responded, as usual, that they could only confer on the diplomatic records. Brückner thereupon called attention to the Soviets' recent transfer of captured documents to the German Democratic Republic. "The Federal Republic," he stated, "appears defenseless before questions raised as to why its sovereignty should not be as complete as that of the GDR, which at least is getting the semblance of treatment as an equal from the Soviet Union."[209] The British refused to be ruffled any longer by the Germans' categorical demand. "Fortunately," the new head of the Foreign Office Library commented, "we can take that hurdle when we come to it, but speaking personally I am sure that there is not the remotest possibility of their wishes being gratified."[210] The Allied condition that the records be made accessible to researchers from around the world following their return to Germany proved to be uncontroversial. The West German government had already consented to this condition. The negotiators agreed that their governments would formally settle the matter of the diplomatic records through an exchange of notes rather than by treaty. Bonn was to submit a draft. With a solution to this "wretched subject" in sight, the negotiators were able to create a far friendlier atmosphere at the following meetings than had existed at earlier ones.[211]

The exchange of notes on March 14, 1956, initiated the return of the diplomatic records.[212] The first 100 tons of records arrived in Bonn that autumn.[213] The transfer was to be completed by March 31, 1958. Brückner had insisted on setting a specific date so that the West German government could announce it to the public.[214] The head of the Political Archives sent the archivist Hans Philippi to England to help with the preparations. Philippi

209 The German minutes of the meeting on Aug. 11, 1955, are found in PA/AA, B118, vol. 509; the reports from the British and American embassies, in PRO FO 370/2431 LS5/88 and NA RG 59, CDF 1954–59, 862.423/8–2555. Quote cited in the latter.
210 Charles Henry Fone, Library, FO, to Kit Barclay, Aug. 26, 1955, PRO FO 370/2431 LS5/88.
211 Elim O'Shaughnessy, Counselor of AmEmb Bonn, to State Dept., no. 886, Oct. 28, 1955, NA RG 59, Lot File 78D441, Historical Office, box 3.
212 Hallstein to the Ambassadors of the USA, France and Great Britain [identical text], Mar. 14, 1956, PA/AA, B118, vol. 510. Also in PRO FO 370/2472 LS5/31. Published in US Department of State, U.S. Treaties and Other International Agreements Series, vol. 7:2, #3631 (Washington, D.C.: GPO 1956), 2119–24; Exchange of Letters between the Government of the UK of GB and Northern Ireland and the Government of the Federal Republic of Germany concerning the transfer to the Federal Republic of Archives of the former German Foreign Office, March 14, April 12, 1956. HMSO, Germany no. 1 (1957). Excerpts also reprinted in Henke, "Schicksal deutscher Quellen," 594f.; facsimile in the illustration section of Wolfe, "Captured German Records".
213 Philippi, "Politisches Archiv I," 139. A description of the way these records were organized is found in Philippi, "Politisches Archiv II".
214 Klassen, Suggestions for a Press Release, Apr. 20, 1956; Press Release no. 431/56, Apr. 20, 1956, both in PA/AA, B118, vol. 510. *Bulletin des Presse- und Informationsamtes der Bundesregierung* no. 77, Apr. 24, 1956, 711; "Die Aktenlücke," *Frankfurter Allgemeine Zeitung*, Apr. 24, 1956.

confessed to being "not a little surprised at the colossal mass of records" that his archive was to receive and asked how "we in Bonn are supposed to cope with the situation."[215] While the return process was still underway, the re-established Political Archives opened its reading room. Scholars could consult materials there beginning on April 1, 1957.[216] By this point, the *Documents on German Foreign Policy* consisted of nine published volumes of Series D in English and seven in German. The preparations for further volumes were, in part, well underway. Editorial work on the project came to an end in March 1959, and the final volume, the thirteenth in all, was published in 1961.[217]

The agreement on the Auswärtiges Amt files brought no respite for the Allies and West Germans. They had barely come to terms on the diplomatic records before the Auswärtiges Amt, under pressure from the Bundesarchiv, requested the start of talks on the return of the captured military records. Georg Winter, the director of the Bundesarchiv, was very interested in commencing talks on "the other" records because his institution had barely benefited from the breakthrough on the diplomatic records.[218] The lion's share of the documents Great Britain returned went to the Auswärtiges Amt. On October 16, 1956, West German diplomats sent identically worded notes to the Allied embassies, urging the start of negotiations on the return of the archival materials still in Allied custody.[219]

THE MILITARY RECORDS, 1951–1958

The negotiations on the military records and the records of Nazi party organizations did not begin until January 1958. Once again, the talks had been preceded by a flurry of behind-the-scenes consultations between the Allies. Starting in the early 1950s, a set of complicated talks, independent of those on diplomatic records, took place on coordinating a policy among the Allies for these other records. By the time they sat down at the negotiating table with the West Germans in 1958, a series of preliminary decisions had already been made without the Germans' input. The driving force behind the return of these materials was the U.S. Army. Its initiatives prodded the

215 Philippi to Ullrich, Aug. 27, 1956, PA/AA, B118, vol. 510.
216 *Bulletin des Presse- und Informationsamtes der Bundesregierung* no. 175, Sept. 20, 1957, 1620. On the problem of access, see Chapter 5, Section 2.
217 F. Bouffanais, FranzEmb London, to Duncan Wilson, Libary, FO, Jan. 19, 1956, PRO FO 370/2471 LS5/10; Noble to Wilson, Feb. 15, 1956, ibid., LS5/18; Annex to Meeting of the Historical Advisory Committee held at FO Library, Mar. 6, 1956, PRO FO 370/2472 LS5/37.
218 Minutes, Discussion on the return of captured German Records, [at the request of the Bundesarchiv director], Feb. 10, 1956, PA/AA, B10, vol. 1699.
219 Verbal note, Oct. 16, 1956, PA/AA, B118, vol. 510.

British along. The JCC's obstructive tactics continued to put a brake on the internal decision-making process within the British government, however. That situation was not evident to the Germans, who, meanwhile, were preoccupied with disputes over the distribution of documents that had not yet been returned. One special case was that of the Wehrmacht personnel records. They had been requested by the West German chancellery in 1952. Adenauer could justify this request in a way that neither the Americans nor the British could abrade because, in the end, the Anglo-American side was just as interested in the West German defense contribution as was the chancellor.

The Wehrmacht Personnel Records and Pension Claims

During the summer of 1951, the West German consulate in London was bombarded with questions from former Luftwaffe officers who needed documentation to support their claims to veterans' benefits under the provisions of Article 131 of the Federal Republic's constitution. Knowing that the Luftwaffe personnel records were held by the British Air Ministry, the Consul General asked the Foreign Office in August how information could be retrieved from those files.[220] The British found themselves involuntarily caught up in the red tape of German social welfare policy. Former servicemen's rank, length of service, and decorations all had bearing on pension and benefit claims.[221] The Air Ministry had no objections to disclosing such information, but it also had little interest in getting involved helping veteran bomber pilots with their pension claims.[222] "Any approach by individuals should be strongly resisted," the JIC advised.[223] The British could resist as strongly as they liked, but individual German veterans still sent their inquires

---

220 General Consulate of the Federal Republic London, to Foreign Office, Aug. 23, 1951, PRO FO 370/2150 LS3/130.

221 Frei, *Adenauer's Germany*, 49. Some of these inquiries were handled by the Central Record Office of the Bundesarchiv in Kornelimünster near Aachen. Since 1954, this office had been collecting all the personnel records of former Wehrmacht members. See Bruchmann, "Bundesarchiv," 88f.; Dillgard, "Zentralnachweisstelle." Georg Winter criticized the inadequacy of the material collected in Korneliemünster; see Winter to German Embassy, Washington, D. C., June 29, 1955, PA/AA, B118, vol. 37. In addition, there was also self-help literature, i.e., from the Verband Deutscher Soldaten/Bund der Berufssoldaten (ed.), *Wenn die Beweispapiere fehlen*, arranged by Wolf Keilig (Munich 1954).

222 C. V. Mears, Group Captain, Deputy Director of Intelligence, Air Ministry, to Secretary, Joint Intelligence Committee, Oct. 24, 1951, PRO CAB 103/458.

223 Joint Intelligence Committee, JIC(51)116th Meeting, Nov. 2, 1951, PRO CAB 103/458. Only official inquiries by the Federal Government were to be processed at the government's expense.

directly to Allied offices – in droves.[224] The Allies found themselves sitting involuntarily in the same boat as the West German government. Officials at the U.S. High Commission found it intolerable that the U.S. government was "paying the administrative costs of what is essentially a legitimate German Government operation."[225] The British passed the problem back to the German consulate, which received five to ten requests for help with claims applications daily. One lone consulate official had to handle 700 requests between September 1954 and March 1955.[226] Veterans' frustration over the inaccessibility of their service records resulted in a series of administrative lawsuits against the West German government and, as the Minister of the Interior noted, prompted "public discussion detrimental to the reputation of legislative bodies."[227] The social-benefit claims drew attention for the first time to the absence of the Wehrmacht personnel records. Under pressure to act, the Adenauer government tried to link the return of the military personnel files to the issue of rearmament. Yet even this potent linkage did not bring about a quick solution to the problem. It was not until four years after the Consulate's inquiry at the Foreign Office that the files were placed in West German hands.

Rearmament. Adenauer sent a request for the return of military personnel records to High Commissioner McCloy in February 1952. Setting his sights on the proposed European Defence Community treaty, the chancellor argued that the records were crucial to the process of making the "correct selection [of personnel] in the political and professional sense" as Germany went about re-establishing its armed forces.[228] By referring to the "correct selection" in the "political sense," the chancellor had pressed the right buttons. It was, of course, in the Allies' interest to ensure that the new Bundeswehr not be staffed with individuals who might later be revealed to

224 Fred W. Shipman, Records Officer, State Department to Ollon D. McCool, AGO, Apr. 24, 1951, NA RG 407, entry 360, box 3609; S. H. Gellately, FO Library, to Noble, May 28, 1954, NA RG 59, CDF 1950–54, 862.423/5–2854; D. M. Spottiswoode, Office of the British High Commissioner, to AA, Oct. 21, 1954, PA/AA, B118, vol. 492.

225 Guy A. Lee, HICOG Bonn, to State Department, no. 2707, Apr. 9, 1954, NA RG 59, CDF 1950–54, 862.423/4–954.

226 Schlange-Schöningen, Diplomatic Representation of the Federal Republic in London, to AA, Mar. 22, 1955, PA/AA, B10, vol. 1699.

227 MinDirg Anders, Interior Ministry, to AA, Betr. Nachweis von Tapferkeitsbeförderungen gemäß . . . Art. 131 GG, Jan. 8, 1954, PA/AA, B118, vol. 492. In connection with this, the West German government once again requested on Mar. 29, 1954, to have the Wehrmacht personnel records returned. The letter from Hardo Brückner, Political Dept., to AHC in PRO CAB 103/461; draft in PA/AA B118, vol. 492.

228 Adenauer to McCloy, Feb. 19, 1952, PA/AA, B118, vol. 37. The draft by Wolfgang Holtz, Theodor Blank's deputy at Office Blank, from Jan. 28, 1952, ibid. and BArch, B136, vol. 6840/1.

have been war criminals; such publicity would only intensify the controversy over German armament in the Federal Republic and abroad.[229] The
request was also sent to the British because the Luftwaffe personnel records
were in British possession. The French, too, were asked to return the personnel records they held, namely naval records stored at the Wehrmacht
Information Office in Berlin-Wittenau.[230] The British and the Americans
did not learn until several months after the fact that the chancellor had
included the French in this matter. It would prove to be a hindrance.[231]

The Americans agreed quite quickly to return the German army records
held at the Departmental Records Branch.[232] Adenauer's request had been
anticipated as early as January 1951. Although guidelines on restitution were
not yet in place, officials at the Defense Department were willing to view
the personnel records as a special case and to ship them immediately to
Germany. Pentagon officials were aware, however, that, under the terms
of the Bissell-Sinclair Agreement, the State Department was required to
consult with the Foreign Office before the records could be turned over
to the Germans.[233] By June 1952, the personnel files of 70,000 army officers and 825 Waffen-SS troops and officers were ready for transfer, along
with the files on civilian employees of the Wehrmacht, military service

---

229 The problem is most accessible in the 1954 debate on the acceptability of former members of the
Waffen SS for the new West German armed forces, the Bundeswehr. Documented in PRO FO
371/109640. See Meyer, "Einstellung ehemaliger Angehöriger der Waffen-SS in die Bundeswehr."

230 The Deutsche Dienststelle für die Benachrichtigung der nächsten Angehörigen von Gefallenen
der ehemaligen deutschen Wehrmacht (German Office for the Notification of Relatives of Fallen
Members of the former German Wehrmaht) had previously been called the "Wehrmachtsaus-
kunftsstelle für Kriegsgefangene und Kriegsverluste" (Wehrmacht Information Office), abbreviated
as WASt, which I use in the following. The WASt functioned as a German agency under the
supervision of the French Control Commission. In 1948, the WASt had received a portion of
the naval records from the British, papers that were no longer of use upon the completion of the
denazification process. Some were even destroyed. On the history of the records, see Wilhelm
Rohr, Bundesarchiv, Aktenvermerk über den Besuch der 'Deutschen Dienststelle' (WASt) in
Berlin-Wittenau am 12. und 15. September 1952, Sept. 22, 1952, BArch, N1418, NL Rohr, vol.
70; 47th JCC Meeting, June 9, 1952, PRO FO 370/2269 LS18/9; Heinsius, "Aktenmaterial der
deutschen Kriegsmarine," 201; Overmans, *Militärische Verluste*, 100–3, 157f.

231 The problems posed by the lack of personnel records has not yet been studied. Indications of these
are found in Krüger, *Amt Blank;* Meyer, "Situation der deutschen militärischen Führungsschicht";
Meyer, "Fragen der personellen Auswahl"; Stumpf, "Wiederverwendung."

232 The internal coordination at the Department of the Army is documented in NA RG 407, entry
370, box 3609. Only the department G-2 (Intelligence) expressed concerns, because the American
return guidelines were not yet available.

233 "In the interest of accelerating the build-up of German armed forces to the full extent contemplated,
the Department of Defense is considering treating these documents as a special case. . . . That
is, . . . it is proposed that this particular set of documents be made available for release prior to
the establishment of overall and long-term policies and procedures to cover the restitution of
documents in general." Marshall S. Carter, Director, Executive Office, SecDefense, Memorandum
for the SecArmy, May 22, 1952, NA RG 242, AGAR-S no. 1001, box 2. And Carter to SecState,
June 4, 1952, NA RG 407, entry 371F, box 11.

records (*Wehrstammbücher*), pay books, and index cards recording individual Wehrmacht officers' deployments and promotions.[234] These preparations and, in particular, the speed with which they were carried out are another example of the assistance the Defense Department was willing to provide the West Germans – assistance that was not mentioned to the other Allies.[235]

Experience suggested that the State Department would not have an easy time securing British approval for the transfer of the Wehrmacht personnel records. Adenauer's request had divided opinion in London along predictable lines. British High Commissioner Kirkpatrick was open to complying with the request and could count on the full support of higher ranking officials at the Foreign Office.[236] The JCC and the Joint Intelligence Committee (JIC), by contrast, were opposed and tried to block return of the personnel files. The JCC demanded intensive, time-consuming consultations with the Americans. Dependent on the JCC for information, the JIC always adopted the same view as the JCC.[237] The most generous solution Air Ministry officials could imagine was to let German officers work on the records under supervision.[238] Once again, Kirkpatrick was left empty-handed. He blamed the historians and their backers for giving "the Germans ground for suspecting that our reason for retaining the files is that we wish to collect intelligence against the German air contingent to the European Defence Force."[239] Because British consent to the transfer of personnel records did not appear to be forthcoming, the U.S. Army found a pragmatic solution that adhered to the terms of the Bissell-Sinclair Agreement but nonetheless circumvented the British. An official from the Amt Blank, the precursor to West Germany's Defense Ministry, was sent to Washington in October 1952. At the Departmental Records Branch, former Lt. Col. Max Schwerdtfeger worked through the personnel records

234 List of Captured German Personnel Records Requested by the Federal Republic of Germany, n.d. [March 1952], NA RG 407, entry 371F, box 11; Carter to SecState, June 4, 1952, NA RG 407, entry 371F, box 11. The files on foreigners who had served in the Waffen-SS and of Austrian officers who had served in the Wehrmacht after 1938 were not included in the records earmarked for immediate return.

235 McCloy, HICOG Bonn, to SecState, no. 738, Secret, Eyes only for Byroade, Apr. 16, 1951, NA RG 407, entry 370, box 3609.

236 Kirkpatrick to Sir Frank Roberts, FO, Mar. 22, 1952; D. P. Reilly, FO, to the Secretary of the Joint Intelligence Committee, Apr. 4, 1951, both in PRO CAB 103/458.

237 The JIC discussed the case of the personnel records in connection with a draft drawn up by Andrew B. Acheson that thus represented the JCC positions. Acheson to Col. Gardiner, JIC, Ministry of Defense, Apr. 8, 1952, PRO CAB 103/458.

238 Minute of JIC (52) 46th Meeting, Apr. 25, 1952, PRO CAB 146/141.

239 C. E. King, FO, to F. J. Fressenges, Air Vice Marshall, Air Ministry, June 23, 1952, PRO CAB 103/459.

of the higher-ranking German officers.[240] The British and French were not informed of his visit beforehand.[241]

Contrary to expectations, the British made a decision relatively quickly. In late September 1952, the American embassy in London reported that the British government would return the Luftwaffe personnel records to Bonn. The handover was to take place without publicity.[242] Just how the Foreign Office had overcome the resistance of the JCC was not clear, and it was a fragile truce.[243] Pleased with this breakthrough, the Departmental Records Branch prepared to ship the personnel files Schwerdtfeger had selected to Bonn. This smooth start came to a rapid halt after the French unexpectedly imposed obstacles to the transfer of the documents. When the British and Americans informed the French – pro forma, they thought – that the transfer of Wehrmacht personnel records was imminent, the French High Commissioner produced Adenauer's March 1952 letter requesting the return of military personnel files in French possession.[244] Unwittingly, the chancellor had placed veto power in French hands. The French High Commissioner, determined to assert France's equal standing, insisted that the Allies coordinate their actions.[245] Coordination among the Allies thus began all over again.

Faced with this new obstacle, Kirkpatrick's thin basis of support for the planned transfer collapsed. The British Air Ministry retreated to the position that the records might just as well be made available to West German officials in London. According to an American report, officials in London were increasingly inclined to think that it would be best to wait until after the Federal Republic ratified the EDC treaty to return the personnel records.[246] The British and French governments both had to contend with considerable domestic opposition to German rearmament. The Quai

240 Theodor Blank, Chancellery, to AA, Sept. 10, 1952, PA/AA, B118, vol. 37; DRB Journal of Significant Events, Oct. 31, 1952, NA RG 407, entry 375, box 1.
241 Bruce, Acting SecState, to AmEmb London, no. 3373, Nov. 17, 1952, NA RG 59, CDF 1950–54, 862.423/11–1752.
242 Ambassador Walter S. Gifford, AmEmb London, to SecState, no. 1835, Sept. 29, 1952, NA RG 59, CDF 1950–54, 862.423/9–2952; Ambassador Walter S. Gifford, AmEmb London, no. 1555, Sept. 30, 1952, ibid., 862.423/9–3052.
243 Brian Melland warned that, in light of the success, the Germans would "certainly try to exploit every loophole and may well seek to retrieve all kinds of documents on the plea of the EDC contribution." Minutes Melland to Acheson, Oct. 22, 1952, PRO CAB 103/103.
244 Adenauer to the French High Commissioner, André François-Poncet, Mar. 17, 1952, PA/AA, B118, vol. 37.
245 H. B. MacKenzie Johnston on behalf of P. J. E. Male, Chancery, Office of the High Commissioner, Wahnerheide, to Passant, Dec. 20, 1952, PRO CAB 103/460. Samuel Reber, HICOG Bonn, to SecState, no. 2851, Dec. 19, 1952, NA RG 59, CDF 1950–54, 862.423/12–1952.
246 See Auchincloss, German Political Affairs, State Dept., Draft Telegram to HICOG Bonn, Dec. 8, 1952, NA RG 407, entry 371F, box 11.

d'Orsay supported the British position because the transfer of the military personnel records would result in a public outcry "that [the] Germans are 'already reconstituting [the] Wehrmacht.'"[247] Outside of Whitehall, the topic remained emotionally laden, too. The naval correspondent of the *Daily Telegraph* claimed to have learned from "Continental sources" that the West German government had demanded the return of the records. He dwelt on the documents most likely to strike a nerve with the British, namely the records concerning the U-boat campaigns, and painted a bleak picture should they be returned: "If they got into the hands of a Power planning in terms of World War III, the consequences for Britain and her Allies might be grim indeed."[248] A commentary in the *Telegraph* the next day pushed this argument even further. The German demand "does not deserve a moment's consideration."[249] There should be limits to the accommodation of the Federal Republic, the paper insisted. "No further appeasement of the filthy Hun!" one outraged citizen wrote the Foreign Office, and other letters echoed that sentiment.[250] The newspaper article prompted the former Labour minister Hugh Dalton, a declared opponent of rearmament, to bring up the question in the House of Commons. Dalton pressured Undersecretary of State Anthony Nutting with his inquiries on the U-boat records, asking him to state whether the German request had been denied.[251] This was a warning to British diplomats that the document issue could become very explosive indeed.

In Washington, officials were desperately seeking a solution that would give the West Germans access to but not possession of the records. The idea was to ship them to an American military base located on German soil; the Germans could use the records there but they would be administered by the Americans.[252] The Americans stuck to this plan and refused to be deterred by British objections.[253] They argued that such a move was

---

247 Ambassador Dunn, AmEmb Paris, to SecState, no. 4104, Jan 23, 1953, NA RG 59, CDF 1950–54, 862.423/1–2353.
248 Nowell Hall, "Germans Seek Return of Naval Archives. U-Boat Record of Operations," *Daily Telegraph*, Oct. 3, 1952, PRO CAB 103/460. From the Cabinet Office, Acheson appears to have suspected deliberate indiscretion and inquired at the Admiralty about the origins of the article, because: "It has an 'inspired' ring to it."
249 "Bonn Request being Studied," *Daily Telegraph*, Oct. 4, 1952, ibid.
250 Letter of Peter Buxbaum to FO, Oct. 5, 1952, PRO FO 370/2249 LS3/131.
251 AmEmb London to State Dept, no. 1948, Oct. 24, 1952, NA RG 59, CDF 1950–54, 862.423/10–2452. The debate in the House of Commons took place on October 22.
252 Conant, HICOG Bonn, to SecState, no. 3803, Feb. 13, 1953, NA RG 59, CDF 1950–54, 862.423/2–1353.
253 "Once the archives are in Germany," went the British objection, "the Federal authorities will be all the more desirous to obtain their custody." FO Memorandum for AmEmb, London, Mar. 20, 1953, PRO FO 370/2338 LS5/58.

strictly an American administrative matter and did not constitute a return of records.[254] In the fall of 1953, the German army personnel records arrived at Camp King in Oberursel near the Frankfurt headquarters of the U.S. Army (USAREUR).[255] Staff members from the Amt Blank were able to work with the records there starting in April 1954.[256] The Luftwaffe records had been made available to German officials in London in September 1953.[257] The French did not follow suit until December 1954.[258] In the end, it was the French parliament's rejection of the EDC treaty in late 1954 that cleared the way for the transfer of the military personnel records to Federal Republic's newly established Defense Ministry the following year.[259]

The Timetable for Return

The U.S. Army learned an important lesson from the JCC's attempt to prevent the transfer of the Wermacht personnel records. The Bissell-Sinclair Agreement obliged the Army to coordinate its actions with the British, which made returning documents a cumbersome process. Military officials wanted to have a freer hand in the future and to avoid time-consuming negotiations at all costs. When possible, the Army simply presented the British with a fait accompli that did not violate the letter of the Bissell-Sinclair Agreement. Without input from the British, the Departmental Records Branch worked out a timetable for returning documents, and the Department of the Army was determined to hold to that timetable. For its part, the JCC envisioned a new Bissell-Sinclair Agreement. Its members wanted to work out a common Allied policy paper before the initial talks with the West Germans. The JCC, too, had learned something from the case of military personnel records, namely, that bringing in the French

---

254 Dulles, SecState, to AmEmb London, no. 6453, Mar. 27, 1953, NA RG 59, CDF 1950–54, 862.423/3–2453; Minutes Hancock, Apr. 2, 1953, PRO FO 370/2340 LS5/118.

255 The personnel files were not, as Wolfram Wette assumes, delivered to the Historical Division in Karlsruhe. No evidence has been found either to confirm or discount the idea that the German officers employed there had a chance to clean up their own personnel files. Wette, "Neue Form, alter Geist," *Die Zeit*, Mar. 18, 1999.

256 Zinn Garrett, Civil-Military Relations Officer, HICOG, to Blank, Apr. 7, 1954, PA/AA, B118, vol. 492. The Germans still had some complaints about the arrangement. See Elmar Brandstetter to MinRat Kuhbier, Interior Ministry, Sept. 30, 1954, PA/AA, B118, vol. 492.

257 J. G. Ward, Acting UK High Commissioner, to Adenauer, Sept. 1, 1953, PA/AA, B118, vol. 37.

258 Henry Bayle, French High Commission, to Amt Blank, Dec. 28, 1954, PA/AA, B10, vol. 1699.

259 The Americans informed the West German government of returns in January, the British followed suit in July of 1955. The French set up a lending service for the naval personnel records in October 1955. Records were flown from Berlin to Bonn, but were required to be returned to the WASt after a six-week period. The reason for this was that the WASt had been placed under French administrative control by way of a Control Council decision in 1946 and no one wanted to touch the arrangement because it would have involved the Soviets.

complicated matters even further. Including the French in future deliberations thus became one of the JCC's main objectives.

Review, Microfilm, Transfer. Following the conclusion of negotiations on
German diplomatic records in October 1956, the West German government requested talks on the remaining materials, particularly the military
records.[260] The U.S. Army had already begun to plan for the transfer of
the military records even before Bonn made its request: "In anticipation
of such action, the Department of the Army has developed a program for
the orderly disposition of seized German documents now in the custody
of the Departmental Records Branch," a senior officer informed Noble
in the early spring of 1957.[261] The Army envisioned a three-step program
of "review, microfilm, and transfer." The security classifications of all the
documents were to be reviewed; important files would be microfilmed; and
the files would then be transferred to West Germany in batches between
1958 and 1962. There were several reasons why the DRB was so well
prepared. First, by the mid-1950s, it was evident to Pentagon officials that
Bonn would sooner or later ask for the return of all remaining military files.
The West German government's frequent inquiries about specific holdings
made it clear to the Americans that the documents issue would not simply
disappear with time. The Army thus faced the choice of either waiting to
see what the Germans would ask for next or taking the initiative and drafting a timetable for return that best served its own interests. The officials
responsible decided in favor of the latter.[262] Second, the legal questions
concerning the right of Congress to decide the fate of seized records had
been clarified within the context of the initial ad hoc returns in 1953–54.[263]
Third, a group of historians had approached the Army in 1955. They
concerned that the captured documents would be returned to the Federal
Republic before American scholars had an opportunity to study them or
to make copies for future research. The historians' concerns prompted the
Army to start a comprehensive program of declassification.[264] The Army's
timetable for the return of the military records benefited several parties in
the long run: the Germans got back their records, the American historians

260 Verbal note, Oct. 16, 1956, PA/AA, B118, vol. 510.
261 Herbert M. Jones, Adjutant General, to Noble, Mar. 26, 1957, NA RG 407, entry 371F, box 14.
262 See the situational analysis by Seymour J. Pomrenze, Disposition of Captured Records in the
   Custody of the Department of Defense, n.d. [ca. Feb. 1956], NA RG 407, entry 371, box 4; and
   an unsigned Memo for Record from the office of the Assistant Chief of Staff, Intelligence from
   June 1956, ibid.
263 On the implementation of the Federal Records Disposal Act, see Chapter 4, n. 45.
264 The group of historians, the American Committee for the Study of War Documents, is discussed
   in Chapter 5.

secured access to the records beforehand, and the Army rid itself of a costly and personnel-intensive administrative responsibility.

The three-step program of review, microfilm, and transfer was an ambitious project. It was based on the sorting and ordering that had been started at the German Military Documents Section (GMDS) at Camp Ritchie. In the course of the work, archivists had created a series of record groups that facilitated the appraisal of the material.[265] As defined in the policy paper drafted by the Interagency Conference, documents touching upon the national security interests of the United States were excluded from return. Beyond that, however, Departmental Records Branch officials were no longer willing to be constrained by the official guidelines. Even the paragraph excluding the return of material from the NSDAP, its affiliated organizations and offices, and Nazi propaganda materials was not exempt.[266] In light of the rapid integration of the Federal Republic into the Western community, this paragraph appeared to be no longer relevant. To clear the way for the return of Nazi Party records and related materials, the Departmental Records Branch arranged to have Bernard Noble negotiate with the other departments involved on revoking the paragraph.[267] It was eventually agreed that developments over the previous five years had shown no reason to fear that the return of Nazi Party records would destabilize democracy in West Germany. This agreement accorded the Departmental Records Branch more leeway, and the decision to retain or return such records could now be made on a case-to-case basis with "the basic presumption . . . being in favor of return."[268] The quantity of documents in the "prohibited classes" was thereby reduced from roughly 20,000 linear feet in 1952 to 6,000 linear feet in 1957.[269] Several types of records were designated for indefinite retention

---

265 Goldbeck, "GMDS"; Rohr, "Mikroverfilmung," 253f. The record groups resulted from applying the principles of both pertinence and provenance and were indeed the best possible arrangement for the confusing, chaotic mass of files (and partial files) that landed in the hands of the army starting in 1945.

266 "Documents tending to glorify the Nazi regime, or which are of inherent propaganda character, or which deal with the organization, personnel, and operation of Nazi Party institutions, except where such transfer would not jeopardize the democratic way of life in the Federal Republic." The return policy is reprinted in Eckert, *Kampf um die Akten*, 481f.

267 Seymour J. Pomrenze, DRB, Memorandum for Mr. O[llon] D. McCool, Chief, Records Administrative Branch, AGO, Apr. 12, 1957, NA RG 407, entry 371, box 4.

268 "The Department [of State] therefore feels that each group of records comprising the general category described in para. 4(c) of the policy statement should be examined on its own merits with regard to its suitability for return to the Federal Republic, the basic presumption, however, being in favor of return." Noble, Memorandum [on changing the policy paper], Apr. 19, 1957, as the enclosure to a letter to Robert H. Bahmer, Deputy Archivist of the United States, May 20, 1957, NA RG 64, National Archives, Planning and Control Cases, box PC-62.

269 Sherrod East, Report of the Chief [of] DRB for the Fiscal Year Ending 30 June 1957. Summary of Major Events and Problems, NA RG 242, AGAR-S no. 1206, box 2; Pomrenze, Memorandum for McCool, Apr. 12, 1957, NA RG 407, entry 371, box 4.

in the timetable drafted in February 1958:[270] Russian and German military maps;[271] portions of the archive of Hitler's official photographer, Heinrich Hoffmann;[272] and transcripts of the interrogations of American and British prisoners of war.[273] Among the documents to be retained temporarily were the files of the Luftwaffe headquarters, SS leader Heinrich Himmler's office, the Reich Ministry for the Occupied Eastern Territories, the deputy for the war economy in Serbia, and the Reich Commissariat Ostland. The retention of the latter group of materials was in keeping with the policy that documents linked to Germany's occupation of other countries would be turned over to the countries affected.[274]

The first delivery was shipped as planned in March 1958. That same year, the Departmental Records Branch became part of the National Archives, which took over the schedule for the documents' return. This administrative restructuring may have been a reason why the Americans were not able to adhere to their ambitious schedule. It was not until 1968 that the DRB's return program came to a preliminary close.[275]

The British Skeptics. The activity in Washington was watched suspiciously by the JCC. In declassifying documents so quickly and putting forward a timetable for returning them, the Americans seemed to have effectively revoked the British say on how the documents would be handled. The British opponents of restitution had already sensed trouble in the first American statement in 1953 that outlined ideas for the return procedure. The Americans had explained that they wanted to make the process as simple as possible. There should be a general understanding on the types of materials that would be returned, the Americans thought, but "it would not seem practicable to require that every document, or category of documents, be the subject of a separate decision by the two Governments."

---

270 Herman Goldbeck, Chief, Captured Records Section, to the Acting Assistant Branch Chief, Military Records Branch, Disposition Plan – Captured German Records, Feb. 24, 1958, NA RG 242, AGAR-S no. 1564, box 6.

271 RG 1043, German and Russian Map Collection, 1175 linear feet. In early 2002, the Americans turned over military situation maps to the Federal Archives – Military Archives in Freiburg once the maps had gone through an elaborate reproduction process. See Gießler, "Archivalienrückführungen aus den USA".

272 RG 1040, Private German Enterprises, 350 linear feet. The Hoffmann Collection is kept still today at the National Archives. See Herz, *Hoffmann & Hitler*, 18f.

273 RG 1033, German Air Force Commands – Reports covering American and British POWs.

274 Sherrod East, Chief, DRB, Request for Restoration of Classification on Certain German Records, Apr. 22, 1957, NA RG 407, entry 371F, box 14. See also paragraph 4(b) of the policy paper.

275 Boberach, "Schriftliche Überlieferung," 56f.; Henke, "Schicksal deutscher Quellen," 597f. In 1964, Bruchmann, "Bundesarchiv," 90, estimated the amount of records having arrived until then from Alexandria to equal 5,800 running meters.

Instead, the Americans contended, each government should decide the fate of the records in its custody and inform the other "not always for a specific decision or concurrence on the part of the latter, but in order to provide an opportunity for comment . . . ." This minimalist approach also dispensed with negotiations with the Germans. Instead, meetings between the two sides were to be of an informative nature, and the West German government would be told what records it could expect to receive.[276]

The JCC, painfully aware of its weak position, realized it could do little to influence the Americans' actions. The bulk of records were located in the United States, and their transfer across the Atlantic had been approved by the British army at the end of the war. Allowing each government to decide on its own about the documents in its possession would mean a very real loss of power for the British. The JCC thus remained adamant about the arrangement set down in the Bissell-Sinclair Agreement and repeatedly attempted to at least slow down the preparations underway in Washington.

The JCC especially distrusted the release of records by the DRB. In 1953, the DRB published a general list of records that would be available for historical research.[277] Melland interpreted this step as a violation of the Bissell-Sinclair Agreement. "As we have long expected," he complained, "the Americans are 'going at it alone' . . . irrespective of joint ownership or any previous joint consultation."[278] For Melland and his colleagues in the JCC, a matter of principle was at stake. "This move towards full-blooded restitution has been organised without any reference to the British."[279] Melland and the other critics of American policy nonetheless had to admit, somewhat grudgingly, that British national security interests had not been damaged by the release of records at the end of 1953 or by the first ad hoc returns in 1954. However, they argued, damage could have occurred, to say nothing of the possible consequences of future unilateral action by the Americans.[280]

276 "Any agreement with the Germans should be confined to specific matters, such as practical arrangements for returning records. Our approach should be . . . to inform them what records we prepared to return and discuss with them how this can most conveniently and satisfactorily be handled." Department of State, Aide Mémoire, May 5, 1953, PRO FO 370/2340 LS5/97. The U.S. policy paper was presented as an attachment to the aide-memoire.

277 DRB, General List of Seized Records Available for Unofficial Research, Reference Aid no. 15 (DRB Publication 54–1), February 1954, is located, among other places, in BArch, N1188, NL Schieder, vol. 651.

278 Minutes Melland to Acheson, Feb. 17, 1954, PRO CAB 103/461.

279 Melland to Friedrichsen, May 13, 1954, PRO CAB 103/462.

280 "Actually, from the practical angle, none of the . . . groups of documents . . . concerns our every-day requirements. But what is going to happen next? . . . The Americans have already declassified and 'made available to the general public' certain files . . . which we would not be prepared, so far, to treat so liberally. Which are the next candidates for release and restitution?" Ibid. "Nothing in the OKW and OKH collections of an operational or intelligence nature has been declassified." Minutes

Although the JCC could not find "sufficient grounds at present for a protest,"[281] it felt the need to remind Washington very clearly of British interests. The JCC thus turned to the British Joint Services Mission (BJSM) and asked it to establish a direct line of communication with the Army. The members of the JCC wanted to bypass the diplomatic channels because they suspected that the State Department was misinforming the American military about British objections since it supported the return of the captured documents to West Germany for political reasons.[282] The JCC hoped the U.S. Army would be open to a more restrictive policy. Officials at the DRB were not receptive, however. The British military attaché acting on behalf of the JCC was told by the DRB that "it was proper for the State Department to handle restitution."[283] One meeting took a particularly unfavorable turn for the JCC: the DRB representative, Seymour J. Pomrenze, insisted that the DRB could only undertake the type of detailed consultation demanded by the British if the British provided a comprehensive listing of the record groups in their possession.[284] It was the JCC's policy, however, not to produce inventories of their captured documents, lest such inventories arouse covetousness if placed in the wrong hands.[285]

It was clear to the JCC after this encounter that the Americans did not want to formulate a joint Anglo-American policy and did not want to have to clear every document slated for return with the British. The Americans maintained, rather, that British and American positions were so similar that it was no longer necessary to coordinate their plans and that the time had come to take action. Confronted by the prospect of unilateral action on the part of the Americans, the JCC hit on the idea of turning to

Melland to Acheson, Feb. 17, 1954, PRO CAB 103/461. The British Joint Services Mission in Washington was also informed: ". . . although there is no reason to suppose that any harm has yet been done, we do not know how far the process of declassification will be carried." Sir Harold Parker, Ministry of Defence, to Major-General C. R. Price, June 8, 1954, PRO CAB 103/462.

281 JCC 70th Meeting, June 2, 1954, PRO CAB 103/462.

282 ". . . we should not be surprised to learn that their [the American; A.E.] Service Departments have never been informed in any detail of the representations the Foreign Office have made to the State Department. . . . such indications as have reached us suggest that the State Department have been ineffective in bringing the views which the Foreign Office have conveyed to them to the notice of the appropriate Divisions in the Service Departments which handle German documents. We hope that this will be remedied by transferring the negotiations to the Service channel." Ibid.

283 DRB, Journal of Significant Events, Oct. 21, 1954, Entry by Philipp P. Brower, NA RG 242, AGAR-S 1976, box 8.

284 Wing Commander J. Wallace, BJSM, Washington, to Chiefs of Staff Committee, [minutes of meeting on Nov. 17, 1954], Dec. 3, 1954, PRO CAB 103/462.

285 Accordingly, it was stated in the British aide-memoire dated Feb. 18, 1955, which summarized the Washington talks of the BJSM, that the departments were not in a position to compile such an index. However, the U.S. government was free to create one for its own holdings. PRO FO 370/2428 LS5/45.

the French.[286] During negotiations on the diplomatic records, the French representatives had always supported the JCC's position – that is, they, too, sought to impede the return of the captured documents. The French had also noticeably slowed down developments in the case of the Wehrmacht personnel records. The French, JCC members reasoned, should therefore be informed of British and Americans plans to concede to German demands for restitution, with the reassurance that the interests of the Allies were being protected by the retention of several "prohibited classes" of materials.[287] The question of whether or how to include the French occupied the British and Americans for a solid year. Officials at the Department Records Branch feared that keeping the French abreast of plans to return particular groups of records would give them a de facto veto: "Suddenly to confront them [the French] with a statement of policy without any precise event to hang it on to might only cause them to prick up their ears and start making awkward suggestions and comments."[288] Washington was little impressed by the fact that the French had also been an occupation power and had participated in the negotiations on the diplomatic records.[289] Instead of a formal diplomatic note, as the British envisioned, Bernard Noble informed the French by way of a short memo. The British embassy secretary, Frederick Leishman, advised London strongly against interfering with the U.S. approach.[290] He recognized the purpose of the note and understood the reasons behind his American counterparts' ambiguity: "They wish to retain the maximum of flexibility, and claim that we are working very happily together on the basis of our own separate policy statements, and the area of broad agreement which these imply."[291]

Having failed to get the French involved as planned, the British made one last attempt to slow the Americans' return of documents by invoking the terms of the Bissell–Sinclair Agreement. In December 1956, George Friedrichsen reported to the Cabinet Office that a major declassification

---

286 Memorandum Acheson, Jan. 26, 1955, PRO FO 370/2426 LS5/13.

287 BritEmb Washington, Aide-memoire, Feb. 18. 1955, PRO FO 370/2428 LS5/45. The British draft for an aide-memoire to the French was attached.

288 Leishmann, BritEmb Washington, to Fone, Library, FO, May 17, 1955, PRO FO 370/2429 LS5/52; quote in Leishman to Duncan Wilson, Director Library, FO, Feb. 14, 1956, as attachment to JCC 85th Meeting, Mar. 7, 1956, PRO FO 370/2481 LS20/3.

289 The most obvious clash is reported in Leishman to Wilson, Jan. 17, 1956, as attachment to JCC 84th Meeting, Feb. 1, 1956, PRO FO 370/2481 LS20/2.

290 "If you regard this American draft as hopelessly inadequate and wish to insist on major revisions, we will have to produce new and more telling arguments, and also probably take the matter up at a much higher level if there is to be any chance of settling this long problem without a great deal of further delay." Leishman to FO, Feb. 27, 1956, as attachment to JCC 85th Meeting, Mar. 7, 1956, PRO FO 370/2481 LS20/3.

291 Ibid.

process was about to begin at the Departmental Records Branch's storage facility in Alexandria, Virgina. "From the security point of view," Basil Acheson observed after hearing the news, "there is little difference between returning documents to Germany and placing them at the disposal of the general public."[292] As the British correctly concluded, the main objective of the Departmental Records Branch's review process was no longer to make the records stored in Alexandria available to researchers; declassification, as Melland noted, "was tantamount to a decision to restore the documents to the Germans."[293] Leishman thus had to travel to Washington once again to inform Noble of the JCC's objections. He reminded the State Department that documents in the prohibited categories could not be turned over to the Germans without prior consultation with the British.[294] The DRB staff surmised from Leishman's intervention that things would not calm down until they cleared up some basic misunderstandings about the criteria for declassifying and returning documents.[295] No one in Washington intended, however, to include the British in the declassification process.[296] This was also the impression Leishman received, particularly when Noble told him frankly that the "Defence Department were inclined to take the view that they were entitled to declassify or reclassify any documents held by them without reference to anyone."[297]

Tensions eased as soon as Army officials explained the timetable for return in detail.[298] The British apparently needed reassurance that documents in

292 Acheson, Memorandum [on] Security of Captured German Official Records, Dec. 31, 1956. Also Wilson to Leishman, Jan. 30, 1957, as attachment to JCC 95th Meeting, Feb. 6, 1957, both in PRO CAB 103/463.

293 Melland to Fone, Feb. 27, 1958, PRO FO 370/2547 LS5/16.

294 Wilson to Leishman, Jan. 30, 1957, as attachment to JCC 95th Meeting, Feb. 6, 1957, PRO CAB 103/463; Leishman to Wilson, Feb. 8, 1957, as attachment to JCC 96th Meeting, Mar. 6, 1957, ibid.

295 "It was generally agreed that there has been a failure of communication between the US and British governments with respect to restitution policy and more specifically with respect to security classification of and access to captured records." Sherrod East, Security Review of Captured Records, Feb. 8, 1957, NA RG 407, entry 371, box 4.

296 Philipp Brower, DRB, Memo Slip, Feb. 21, 1957, NA RG 407, entry 371, box 4. Brower "didn't think it was anybody's intention to clear the declassification with the British."

297 "I immediately pointed out that this would make a complete nonsense of all our work together over the past three years. These captured German documents were the subject of inter-governmental understandings to which the Defence Department was just as much a party as the State Department." Leishman to Wilson, Mar. 22, 1957, as attachment to JCC 97th Meeting, Apr. 3, 1957, PRO CAB 103/463.

298 Leishman to Wilson, Mar. 29, 1957, ibid.; DRB Journal of Significant Events, Declassification, Microfilming and Restitution of German Records, Apr. 8, 1957, entry by Philipp P. Brower, NA RG 407, entry 375, box 5; Paper read by Ollon McCool [at a meeting attended by Ballentine, Pomrenze, East, Brower and Goldbeck], Apr. 8, 1957, NA RG 407, entry 371F, box 14. This presentation was included in an aide-memoire to the British, dated Aug. 30, 1957. Note in PRO CAB 103/464.

prohibited categories would not be declassified. Moreover, they received a ninety-day period in which to lodge objections to the planned declassification and return of specific materials. The JCC eventually came to the conclusion that the review procedure in Alexandria was "very constructive" and the situation "reasonably under control."[299] In 1960, even Brian Melland acknowledged in hindsight:

I am impressed by the apparent thoroughness with which the U.S. personnel concerned have withheld dubious files – almost all of them intelligence material – from the declassification programme.... Not only have the Americans covered their own interests but they appear also to be fully alive to British and other Allied interests (e.g. the French, the Belgians).[300]

Once the JCC had been pacified, the Americans could focus their efforts on getting rid of the recently introduced ninety-day objection period. In February 1958, they proposed issuing a "blanket approval" for the declassification, microfilming, and return of records.[301] Allied consultation was thus reduced to mere archival accounting. Although the JCC raised objections about the Americans' implementation of their review and return plans, those objections did not affect the DRB's timetable. Moreover, the JCC was never able to bring about the close collaboration it sought with the Americans. It was reduced to rubber-stamping Washington's plans for transferring documents to the Germans. At the same time, the JCC was losing ground within the British government. By the time the first shipment of records from Alexandria left port in 1958, the JCC had outlived its function. The Foreign Office gained the upper hand, which meant the British holdings too would soon be on their way to Germany.

Getting a Share of the Pie: Interarchival Rivalries

In light of the agreement reached on returning diplomatic records, the Auswärtiges Amt called on the Allies in October 1956 to broaden the scope of the talks to include the remaining archival material.[302] A new round of negotiations finally began in January 1958. In the interim, the Allies made a few important decisions independently of the Germans. Consequently,

299 JCC 102nd Meeting, Nov. 2, 1957; Melland to Burke Trend, CAB, Oct. 9, 1957, both in PRO CAB 103/464.
300 Melland to Friedrichsen, Mar. 14, 1960, NA RG 242, Non-Record Material, box 112.
301 State Department, Aide-memoire, Feb. 11, 1958, PRO FO 370/2547 LS5/12. Commented on extensively by Melland to Fone, FO, Feb. 27, 1958, PRO FO 370/2547 LS5/16.
302 Verbal notes to the ambassadors of the United State, Great Britain, and France, Oct. 16, 1956, PA/AA, B118, vol. 510. The identically worded British and French answers, Dec. 19, 1956, the American on Jan. 2, 1957, in ibid.

the Americans thought there was little left to discuss. Their timetable for return had been in place for a while, and the first shipment from Alexandria was ready to go. For the Germans, the period between 1956 and 1958 was also eventful with regard to the document issue. The Bundesarchiv intensified its efforts to intervene in the way negotiations were conducted but encountered resistance from the Auswärtiges Amt and the Defense Ministry. At times, the coordination of German interests degenerated into an open fight between the competing governmental bodies for a share of the returning records.

Officials at the Bundesarchiv and its parent agency, the Ministry of the Interior, had long thought that the diplomats in Bonn conducted negotiations far too ineffectually. It was particularly galling to the Bundesarchiv that the Auswärtiges Amt, in focusing on the diplomatic records, was acting solely in its own interest – and was not doing a good job of it.[303] In March 1956, when the exchange of diplomatic notes seemed to hold out the possibility of completing the first round of negotiations, the Bundesarchiv saw its chance. By the mid-1950s, the archivists in Koblenz had successfully disassociated the Allied confiscation of German archives at the war's end from German archival policies in occupied Europe. Refusing to acknowledge that the German archival profession had participated in the violation of the rights of other peoples, leading Bundesarchiv staff members insisted that Germany's rights be respected. Bundesarchiv director Georg Winter, citing the Hague Regulations of Land Warfare, called the "abduction of records" a "culturally harmful action."[304] Wilhelm Rohr, Winter's trusted aid, maintained that "every free civilized people" had a "fundamental national right" to the written legacy of its past.[305] Both men repeatedly invoked the Nuremberg verdict against Alfred Rosenberg, in which the "seizure and removal of cultural treasures [was] denounced and punished as a crime," but did not mention the participation of some archivists, including Winter himself, in the work of the Einsatzstab Reichsleiter Rosenberg (ERR).[306] Nor did they see fit to call attention to the fundamental differences – in scale, motivation, and consequences – between the ERR's

---

303 Klassen, report [on a conversation with MR Osterloh, Interior Ministry] for Löns, Aug. 15, 1953, PA/AA, B118, vol. 489; RegDir Scheidemann, Interior Ministry, memorandum, July 4, 1955, BArch, B106, vol. 34724/4.
304 Winter to Scheidemann, Interior Ministry, June 10, 1955, BArch, N1418, NL Rohr, vol. 77.
305 Rohr, Draft notes for a letter to Prof. Grewe at AA, June 21, 1955, BArch, B198, vol. 1739.
306 Ibid. See Heuss, *Kunst- und Kulturraub*, 164–7, 182–5, 197f.; Musial, *Staatsarchive im Dritten Reich*, 125–38, 161–7; Freitag/Grenzer, *NS-Kunstraub*, 41–60, esp. 41–5, 55–7; Grimsted, *Trophies of War and Empire*, 177–213, esp. 198, estimates that more Ukrainian archive material was destroyed by the Red Army itself in the face of the German military advance than was plundered on the part of the Germans.

plundering of cultural properties and the Western Allies' confiscation of archival records.

Bundesarchiv officials faced a tremendous challenge in trying to cast doubt on the legality of the Allies' confiscation of documents without opening the way for a discussion of Germany's wartime treatment of other countries' archives. In a letter to Auswärtiges Amt, Winter denounced the Allied confiscations as "booty-taking" and asserted that the occupiers could not claim that the Germans had behaved in the same way during the war.[307] On other occasions, he conceded that the Auswärtiges Amt might have engaged in "some record abduction" from the archive of the Quai d'Orsay and the Potsdam army archivists from the French Ministry of War, which did indeed set a "poor example." As for the legality of those actions, all Winter had to say was that they "had, after all, been actions taken during the war."[308] Clearly, when it came to discussing the wartime record, some German archivists were simply blind to their own transgressions. But as archivist Josef Henke observed in 1982, the question of whether Germany had the right to demand the return of all archival material was not only a legal but also a moral issue.[309]

In his crusading spirit, Georg Winter pushed for an uninterrupted continuation of the talks. He had very peculiar ideas about the best way to achieve this goal. Everything, he thought, needed to proceed more quickly. "We cannot allow the previous [slow] pace at which the negotiations on the records of the Auswärtiges Amt were conducted to be forced upon us again."[310] It was simply not acceptable that Germany should beg for the records "morsel for morsel."[311] More vigorously than the diplomats, Winter wanted to "chip away relentlessly at the opposing front."[312] He advised Johannes Ullrich on how this could best be done: "The leading premise of the Bundesarchiv is: start extensive negotiations – first with the comprehensive claim – but then move forward in negotiations by attempting to divide the 'enemy.'"[313] Winter intended to build support for this strategy

307 Winter to the AA regarding a conversation with Wilhelm Grewe, June 21, 1955, BArch, B106, vol. 34724/4.
308 Winter to Scheidemann, Interior Ministry, June 10, 1955, BArch, N1418, NL Rohr, vol. 77.
309 Henke, "Schicksal deutscher Quellen," 601.
310 Winter to Brückner, Abt. II., AA, Feb. 13, 1956, PA/AA, B118, vol. 510 and BArch, B106, vol. 34725.
311 Winter to Interior Ministry, Nov. 27, 1956, BArch, B106, vol. 34723/3.
312 Winter to Scheidemann, Interior Ministry, June 10, 1955, BArch, B106, vol. 34723. The quote was the advice that Winter gave Peter Klassen from the Political Archives at a meeting that same day.
313 Ullrich, memorandum, Aug. 20, 1956, PA/AA, B118, vol. 747.

by whipping up a "storm in the international press."[314] In his opinion, the Germans had international law on their side and, consequently, "publicizing our objectives [would] lead the opinion of broad, law-abiding circles also in the Allied countries to support us and weaken the resistance of the brutally egoistic enemy."[315] Aware of Winter's lack of diplomatic finesse, officials at the Auswärtiges Amt tried to rein in his fighting spirit already in 1953. A decree issued in July of that year prohibited him from directly interfering in the negotiations, which meant he was not allowed to contact Allied offices himself. Nor was Winter able to secure funds in the Bundesarchiv's 1954 budget for an official trip to the United States.[316] The diplomats jealously guarded their monopoly on negotiations. When Winter turned to the Federal Republic's embassy in Washington in June 1955 to inquire about the location of German army personnel records, the Auswärtiges Amt shot off a strong reprimand to the Ministry of the Interior.[317]

Winter's attempts to influence the negotiations exacerbated the long-running dispute on whether the Auswärtiges Amt should be permitted to maintain its own archives or, like other federal ministries, be required to turn its inactive registries over to the central national archive. The battle between the two head archivists made its way up the bureaucratic ladder all the way to the ministerial level.[318] The Auswärtiges Amt claimed it needed all diplomatic records for its daily business. The Bundesarchiv countered with the argument that two world wars and the constitutional rupture of 1933–45/49 had rendered the pre-1945 materials obsolete and thus appropriate for transfer to the Bundesarchiv. The real issue behind this interdepartmental struggle was the question of which archive would house the diplomatic records upon their return to Germany. The Bundesarchiv wanted all records up to 1918; the Political Archives wanted all of them.[319] The dispute – already being called a "feud" at the Bundesarchiv[320] – escalated in 1956. The positions of the two agencies were irreconcilable.

314 Rohr, memorandum [on a meeting with MinDir Hübinger], Jan. 2, 1956, BArch, B198, vol. 1739.
315 Winter to AA, June 21, 1955, BArch, B106, vol. 34724/4 and PA/AA, B118, vol. 28.
316 Winter to Interior Ministry (reported by Rohr), Mar. 19, 1954, BArch, B198, vol. 1739.
317 Winter to German Embassy in Washington, D.C., June 29, 1955; Hübinger, Abt. III (Kultur), Interior Ministry, to AA, Sept. 6, 1955, both in PA/AA, B118, vol. 37. The army personnel records had already been turned over to the West German government at the beginning of the year, something the Auswärtiges Amt had not told the Interior Ministry.
318 The correspondence on this subject is bundled in PA/AA, B118, vol. 163.
319 Winter to AA, June 21, 1955, PA/AA, B118, vol. 28; State Secretary Bleek, Interior Ministry, to State Secretary Hallstein, AA, July 4, 1955, BArch, B198, vol. 1739; Winter to the Minister of the Interior, Oct. 29, 1955, BArch, B106, vol. 34724/4; Foreign Minister Brentano to Minister of the Interior Schröder, Apr. 26, 1956, BArch, B106, vol. 34724/4.
320 Rohr to Scheidemann, Interior Ministry, Aug. 25, 1955, BArch, B106 vol. 34724/4.

Officials at the Bundesarchiv considered involving the cabinet and prominent public figures, including the federal president, in the dispute.[321] "The fundamental retention of diplomatic records would affect the nerve center of the Bundesarchiv; as a resource for scholarship, it would remain forever a torso."[322] At the Political Archives, officials rose to the challenge and attempted to exclude their opponents in Koblenz from all negotiations concerning the Auswärtiges Amt files. The archivists at the Political Archives were angered to learn that Winter succeeded in becoming a member of the negotiating delegation headed by Wilhelm Grewe. His inclusion in this delegation was caused merely by a slip in the wording of a letter to the undersecretary at the Ministry of the Interior.[323] Relations between the two institutions were strained, to put it mildly, and the tension between them affected the shaping of the West German negotiating position.[324]

Because the Bundesarchiv hardly benefitted from the return of the diplomatic records,[325] the second round of negotiations became absolutely essential for Georg Winter and his institution. He urged Johannes Ullrich, his contact at the Auswärtiges Amt, to force the Allies to agree in principle to the return of all captured documents. The German negotiators had been anything but successful with categorical demands up to that point, however. They therefore intended to try a new approach and work on the basis of more specific requests. Winter was against this strategy. The carefully worded note of October 1956 that was intended to restart negotiations was not strong enough for him. He continued to demand "negotiations on the bulk of the alienated [*entfremdet*] holdings of German archival material or

321 Rohr on behalf of Winter, to Interior Ministry, Apr. 26, 1956, ibid. The letter comments on a letter from Foreign Minister Heinrich von Brentano to Interior Minister Gerhard Schröder. See also, Scheidemann, Interior Ministry, to Bundesarchiv, Aug. 3, 1956, ibid.

322 "I will never give my consent to the autonomy of the so-called Political Archives as demanded by the Auswärtiges Amt." Winter to the Minister of the Interior, Oct. 29, 1955, BArch, B106, vol. 34724/4.

323 State Secretary Hallstein, AA, to State Secretary Bleek, Interior Ministry, Apr. 19, 1955, PA/AA, B118, vol. 509. After discovering the mistake, Peter Klassen of the Political Archives stated in a memo dated July 20, 1955, (PA/AA, B118, vol. 28) that the original intention had been "to prevent the Federal Ministry of the Interior from being brought into the negotiations on the return of Auswärtiges Amt records and thereby, as had been long expected, would lay claim to these records through the Federal Archives. In the submitted version of the letter . . . the draft had been . . . altered at the spot to read exactly the opposite. . . . The consequence was that the director of the Federal Archives was appointed to the German delegation to the negotiations."

324 On the rivalry, although not impartial, see Kahlenberg, *Archive in West und Ost*, 114–19.

325 From the shipments sent by Whaddon Hall in the autumn of 1958, the Federal Archives received 17 tons of records from the old and new Reich Chancellery, as well as three tons of records from the Office of the Presidential Chancellery, the Vice-Chancellor, the Adjutant Office of the Führer, the Reichsstatthalter (Reich Lieutenant) von Epp, Gouvernor General Frank, Reich Minister Speer and several party offices.

at least on certain large collections."[326] For practical reasons, he thought it reasonable first to have the Allies turn over the collections still located on German soil. These included the collections of the Wehrmacht Information Office (WASt), the Overseas Branch of the U.S. Justice Department in Munich, the Berlin Document Center (BDC), and the BDC branch office in Darmstadt.[327] Ullrich tried, in vain, to explain that the BDC was the institution the Allies would be least likely to turn over to the Federal Republic. It would not be wise, he counseled, to start negotiations on the "precarious topic of the return of the [Nazi] party records."[328] Such an approach would lead only "to a refusal and thus to a dead end."[329] Winter saw no need to take Allied sensitivities into consideration. The issue of the captured documents was already such a source of ill feeling, Winter maintained, it would not matter where the German negotiators tried to apply pressure.[330] Indeed, he counted on Allied opposition to the requests he proposed, having noted a

strongly felt reluctance in certain circles to give up the trophies of the last war, which – in the ecstasy of total victory – they thought was their rightful booty to dispose of with unchecked arbitrariness. And this reluctance grows; it seeks justification through reference to the incredible crimes of National Socialism, and to National Socialistic, military, and imperialistic traits of the German people, which seem to manifest themselves so crassly in the captured documents. There exists an unmistakably sincere fear that the return of these documents to the vanquished could reawaken certain tendencies now perhaps simply dormant. We have to break through this wall of defense.[331]

326 Winter to Ullrich, Nov. 24, 1956, BArch, B198, vol. 1740. The demand to have all records returned appears in nearly all of his letters. The note of Oct. 16, 1956, PA/AA, B118, vol. 510, had called upon the Allies to negotiate on "additional archival holdings," which were necessary for administrative purposes.

327 Winter to AA, Feb. 13, 1956, PA/AA, B118, vol. 510. In 1952, the Interior Ministry had attempted for the first time, in conjunction with the Federal Office for the Protection of the Constitution, to take the BDC under its wing. Winter to Interior Ministry, Nov. 10, 1952, BArch, B106, vol. 34723/2; Interior Ministry to the President of the Federal Office for the Protection of the Constitution, Nov. 25, 1952, ibid. and PA/AA, B118, vol. 37. At the time, the BDC was in the process of being transferred from the Army to the HICOG.

328 Ullrich, report [on the meeting on Aug. 20, 1956], Aug. 20, 1956, PA/AA, B118, vol. 747; Rohr, "Vermerk über die Besprechung im Auswärtigen Amt am 20. VIII. 1956," BArch, B106, vol. 34724/4. See also Grewe to Minister of the Interior, Jan. 7, 1957, PA/AA, B118, vol. 511.

329 Ullrich to Dirk Oncken, Political Dept., Mar. 23, 1957, PA/AA, B118, vol. 747.

330 "When it comes to restitution demands, the Federal Archives argues that one would always, without fail, be confronted with resentment on the part of the Allies, which in some way or another could only be nipped in the bud by a total demand of all records. It would be a mistake to bow [to the Allies] in the sense of relinquishing demands at first for party records and records from the highest, most prominent Reich authorities, which ran under the headings of 'Imperialism,' 'Nazism,' and 'Racism,' as has been suggested by the Political Archives." Ullrich, report, Aug. 20, 1956, PA/AA, B118, vol. 747.

331 Winter to Minister of the Interior, Feb. 20, 1957, PA/AA, B118, vol. 747.

In preparation for the negotiations, the Bundesarchiv was asked to draw up a wish list. The Berlin Document Center stood atop the Bundesachiv's list and would continue to do so in later rounds of negotiations.[332]

The confrontational course pursued by Georg Winter caused German diplomats many a headache. Because Winter would be present at the talks with embassy representatives, officials at the Auswärtiges Amt thought it "imperative" to remind the Ministry of the Interior that the Political Department of the Auswärtiges Amt would be setting the wording of the German negotiating position in the talks.[333] When Paul Kluke, the executive director of the Institute for Contemporary History, asked to be included in internal talks held prior to the new round of negotiations, Johannes Ullrich refused. Kluke, like Winter, was primarily interested in the Nazi Party records. In Ulrich's view, Kluke's "participation – even if only in the internal negotiations – could lead especially to a reinforcement of the Bundesarchiv's position, which is not beneficial to the interests of the [Auswärtiges Amt]."[334] An article in the *Frankfurter Allgemeine Zeitung* written at the Interior Ministry's instigation made the ministerial feud public by complaining about the "departmental egoism" the Auswärtiges Amt was displaying in its handling of the documents issue. The article also mentioned the Bundesarchiv's interest in securing the return of the materials held at the Berlin Document Center.[335] In the wake of the publication of this conspicuously well-informed article, Foreign Minister Heinrich von Brentano wrote his cabinet colleague Interior Minister Gerhard Schröder to demand that Winter "be replaced by another suitable gentleman" from the ministry.[336] It was thus not at all self-evident that Winter would participate in the talks with the embassy representative in January 1958.

The Arrival of Ad Hoc Returns from the United States, 1954–1958. While Winter was fighting with the Auswärtiges Amt over the disposition of the documents the Federal Republic hoped to regain, the first group of records the United States returned on an ad hoc basis arrived in West Germany. Records from the Reichsnährstand went to the Federal Ministry of Food,

332 The first copy of the wish list is included as an attachment to Oncken, report, Feb. 24, 1958, PA/AA, B118, vol. 30; a more specific copy as attachment to the verbal note to the U.S. embassy, dated Mar. 3, 1958, BArch, B106, vol. 34724 and PA/AA, B118, vol. 747.
333 Ullrich to Dg11 and D 1 (MinDir Löns), Dec. 19, 1956, PA/AA, B118, vol. 29.
334 Ibid.
335 Karl Korn, Co-Editor of *Frankfurter Allgemeine Zeitung*, to Hübinger, July 17, 1956, BArch, B106, vol. 34713/3; Hansjakob Stehle, "Geschichte zwischen Staub und Akten. Schleppende Rückgabe deutscher Dokumente an das Bundesarchiv," *Frankfurter Allgemeine Zeitung*, Sept. 10, 1957.
336 Brentano to Schröder, Sept. 30, 1957, BArch, B106, vol. 34724/4; Winter's justification to State Secretary Anders at the Interior Ministry, Nov. 5, 1957, ibid.

Agriculture, and Forestry; the personnel records of the old transportation ministry went to the new one. Those from the army were sent from Oberursel to the Ministry of Defense without the Bundesarchiv ever being informed of their arrival. Much to Winter's frustration, the Bundesarchiv had neither been informed of or involved in these and other document transfers from the United States, "to say nothing of the fact," he added, "that not a single sheet of paper has landed in the Bundesarchiv."[337] In his protests, Winter always referred to the Bundesarchiv's founding charter. The cabinet decision of March 1950 designated one of the tasks of the Bundesarchiv to be the "supervision of the confiscated and subsequently returned records."[338]

The situation took on a new dimension during the planning for a "document center" at the Defense Ministry. The military document center, which had been conceived at Amt Blank in collaboration with the Institute for Contemporary History (IfZ),[339] was placed under the direction of Lieutenant Colonel Hans Meier-Welcker, a former member of the General Staff. The center claimed to be the legitimate collection point for all military records in the Federal Republic, a claim that put it on a direct collision course with the Bundesarchiv. The Bundesarchiv feared that it would have to contend with the "departmental egoism" not only of the Auswärtiges Amt but also of the planned Defense Ministry. The dispute eventually reached the cabinet, which decided that the military document center would not be permitted to call itself an archive and would serve as an intermediary repository for military archival materials awaiting evaluation by the Bundeswehr. The Bundesarchiv, in turn, established a military archive in 1955 that was to receive records from the military document center.[340] Not surprisingly, the cabinet decision had solved the problem in theory but not in practice. Long before the first crate from Alexandria arrived at Bremerhaven, a fierce dispute broke out between the Bundesarchiv and the military document center.

The dispute was triggered by the return of the personal papers of several generals. These materials, spanning three centuries of German history, were

337 Winter to Bundesminister des Innern, Apr. 14, 1956, BArch, B106, vol. 34724/4.
338 The wording of the cabinet decision of March 24, 1950, is found in Bruchmann, "Bundesarchiv," 84.
339 On the establishment and early history of the Document Center, see Forwick, "Militärarchiv und Bundeswehr," 126f.; Kehrig, "Entwicklung des militärischen Archivwesens"; Wiggershaus, "Amtliche Militärgeschichtsforschung," 115–17.
340 Winter to Interior Ministry, Nov. 26, 1955, BArch, N1333, NL Winter, vol. 33. Kehrig, "Entwicklung des militärischen Archivwesens," 401–4. Finally, in 1968, the Bundesarchiv integrated the Document Center into its military archive.

returned by the U.S. National Archives in April 1954.[341] Unbeknownst to the Bundesarchiv, the papers went directly to the military document center. When the Bundesarchiv subsequently demanded that the papers be turned over to its military archive on the grounds that they were clearly not relevant to current military planning, Meier-Welcker did not comply.[342] Similarly, maps from the Franco-Prussian War of 1870–71 and World War I were also transferred to the document center rather than to the Bundesarchiv.[343] When it became clear that the Auswärtiges Amt bore primary responsibility for sending these materials directly to the military document center, Winter turned to the Ministry of the Interior. He accused officials at the Auswärtiges Amt of systematically usurping the Bundesarchiv's responsibilities. "This line of action taken by the Auswärtiges Amt can only be interpreted as the intentional and radical elimination of the Bundesarchiv."[344] To Winter's great dismay, Johannes Ullrich invited a representative from the document center to the internal preparatory meetings prior to the new round of talks with the Allies, thereby granting Meier-Welcker precisely the privilege he had denied Paul Kluke. Winter also learned that the Defense Ministry had presented its own wish list, thus paralleling Winter's own efforts.[345] In light of the tensions between the Bundesarchiv and the Auswärtiges Amt, Winter had to back down. The Bundesarchiv's defeat was again made evident when the first shipment of naval records arrived from London in the spring of 1959. The Koblenz archivists learned almost by accident that the material had arrived – at the military document center.[346]

The first captured documents turned over to the Bundesarchiv arrived in 1958 in line with the timetable established by the Army's Departmental Records Branch. This shipment included files from several governmental ministries and other organizations, notably the Organization Todt; the office of the Reich Commissioner for the Strengthening of Germandom; the

341 These were the papers of the generals von Roon, Scharnhorst, Winterfeldt, Gneisenau, Moltke, Mertz von Quirnheim, Groener, Ludendorff, Seeckt, and others. See Preliminary Inventory of the German Records 1679–1945 in the World War II Collection of Seized Enemy Records. Compiled by Martin Rogin. (Preliminary Inventory no. 24) Washington, D.C.: General Services Administration. The National Archives 1950.
342 Wolfgang A. Mommsen to Minister of Defense, Jan. 10, 1956; Meier-Welcker to Bundesarchiv, Feb. 27, 1956, both as copies in BArch, N1333, NL Winter, vol. 33.
343 Klassen to Ministry of Defense, Feb. 11, 1956, PA/AA, B118, vol. 45.
344 Winter to Minister of Interior, Apr. 14, 1956, BArch, B106, vol. 34724/4.
345 Winter, Memo on a meeting at AA on August 20, Aug. 25, 1956, BArch, B106, vol. 34724/4. Winter protested against involving the Defense Ministry.
346 Johannes Ullrich had arranged the transfer there. See Ullrich to BMVtg, Jan. 27, 1959, PA/AA, B118, vol. 125; Erich Murawski, copy of memorandum, BA-MA, Apr. 14, 1959, BArch, N1418, NL Rohr, vol. 77; Rohr, memorandum, Apr. 20, 1959, BArch, B198, vol. 916; Rohr to Bundesinnenminister, Apr. 23, 1959, BArch, B106, vol. 34724/4.

Reich Ministry for Weapons, Munitions, and Armament; and the German Academy of Munich.[347] Brian Melland of the British Cabinet Office, who was usually concerned that the Germans might receive too much, was reassured by this first shipment: "If this is all the Americans intend to return in 1958, I shall not be surprised if there is a violent reaction by the [German] Federal Government."[348] A year later, material also arrived from the prized Berlin Document Center, namely, some "non-biographical holdings" that had been standing unused in the stacks for years.[349] By and large of little political interest, the records came from institutions such as the Reich Postal Ministry, the Nazi Party's buildings department, and the Tegernsee district heating plant.[350] The staff at the Bundesarchiv had certainly envisioned something else when talking about the return of documents, the director of the Berlin Document Center speculated. "Dr. Winter, the head of the Bundesarchiv, more than agrees with this judgment. In fact, he is sorry to have accepted most of it because of the space and labor problem."[351] The trend was clear: Washington was sending the least important records first.

The Start of the Second Round of Negotiations. The new round of negotiations started on January 13, 1958. The talks took place in an atmosphere quite different from that of the tense discussions on the diplomatic records. The Auswärtiges Amt did not attribute as much importance to these talks as it had to those dealing with its own records. Consequently, it replaced Grewe as the lead negotiator with a lower-ranking official, Johannes Ullrich.[352]

347 Herman Goldbeck, Chief, Captured Records Section, to the Acting Assistant Branch Chief, Military Records Branch, Disposition Plan – Captured German Records, Feb. 24, 1958, NA RG 242, AGAR-S no. 1564, box 6; verbal note to the U.S. embassy, Feb. 3, 1958, PA/AA, B118, vol. 747

348 Minutes Melland, Mar. 27, 1958, PRO FO 370/2547 LS5/9.

349 Brian Melland, CAB, Historical Section, to Fone, Library, FO, Dec. 18, 1958, PRO FO 370/2550, LS5/82. "Friedrichsen . . . now informs me that the intended restitution affects only those documents which are stored at Darmstadt [BDC Rear, A.E.], i.e. dormant documents which have been lying there for years."

350 All told, there were 350 crates of records. See Isaac A. Stone, Director, BDC via U.S. Mission Berlin, to State Dept, no. 577, Feb. 17, 1959, NA RG 242, BDC Directorate Files, box 2.

351 Stone, BDC, to Melland, London, Sept. 10, 1959, NA RG 242, BDC Directorate Files, box 6. Stone was also partially responsible for the "worthlessness" of the delivery. In a letter to the historian Oron J. Hale, University of Virginia, he explained that he had withheld the records of the SA and the Main Office for Communal Policy (Hauptamt für Kommunalpolitik) because he did not want them to leave his hands without prior microfilming. Stone to Hale, Mar. 17, 1959, Hale Papers, box 9.

352 The British were relieved to learn that the Germans "are now anxious to keep the talks at working level." Michael Williams, BritEmb Bonn to Cecil C. Parrott, FO Library, no. 2015, Mar. 27, 1958, PRO FO 370/2547 LS5/21. At the Foreign Office, there had been concern that the records issue could still be lingering at the undersecretarial or minister level. "We want to avoid giving the

The American representative proceeded as if there was nothing to negotiate and focused on the DRB's timetable for reviewing, filming, and returning documents. According to the report of the British representative, the German participants seemed not to have understood the Americans' explanation and grasped only that the filming would not be completed until 1960: "The date obviously shook the Germans."[353] From then on, they considered the microfilm project to be the main hindrance to restitution.[354] Not until the German embassy in Washington reported in greater detail on the three-step program did it become somewhat clearer that the U.S. Army was going about the matter of returning records methodically.[355] It took time for officials at the Auswärtiges Amt and the Ministry of Defense to accept the program. They attempted several times to have the timetable changed so that particular materials – for example the papers of the Army High Command – could be returned immediately.[356] The answer to such requests was always the same: any deviation from the scheduled timetable would throw the entire project into chaos.[357] Sherrod East urged Noble to explain to the Germans once and for all that the timetable could not be changed without British approval. In any case, East added, it was not based "on mere caprice as [the Germans] seem to imply."[358] Less tactfully, Noble offered to sell microfilm copies of the requested records to the Germans. Defense Ministry officials bitterly sneered at that offer.[359] Noble tried to iron out the glitch by turning over the microfilms as a gift.[360] In

Germans any excuse to raise the question of return of the archives as a matter of principle at a high level." Parrot to Williams, Mar. 14, 1958, ibid., LS5/17.

353 Williams to Parrot, Feb. 6, 1958, PRO FO 370/2547 LS5/6.

354 Bruce, AmEmb Bonn to Sec State, no. 2243, Jan. 22, 1958, NA RG 407, entry 371, box 4. The telegram makes it clear that the American diplomat had spoken about the microfilming as well as the return timetable. From the German minutes of the meeting, however, it is obvious that the German representatives only registered the information on the microfilming. See Ullrich, Protokoll über die Besprechung . . . am 13. Januar 1958, Jan. 13, 1958, PA/AA, B118, vol. 30; Oncken, Referat 200, report, Jan. 14, 1958, ibid., vol. 747; [Bundesarchiv version of minutes], Verhandlungen mit den Vertretern der drei Westmächte im Auswärtigen Amt am 13. Januar 1958, Jan. 17, 1958, BArch, N1418, NL Rohr, vol. 77.

355 German Embassy in Washington to AA, May 5, 1958, PA/AA, B118, vol. 30.

356 Major Stahl, Fü B III 4 [i.e. the German Federal Armed Forces Command], Defense Ministry, to AA, Oct. 10, 1958, ibid.

357 Ibid.; German Embassy in Washington to AA, Mar. 23, 1959, ibid.

358 NND Journal, Apr. 25, 1960, entry by Sherrod East, NA RG 242, Non-Record Material, box 107.

359 Since the records sought by the Germans were scheduled for return toward the end of the timetable, "they now generously offer to *sell* us the microfilms. What is more, anyone in a position to pay can pursue this 'path of acquisition.' Well, no one can stop this inflation of sources. That this leads to new aspects for analyzing German records from the period before 1945 must be accepted as the consequence of war, meaning the victor's claim to war booty, even if this will make the archivists' hair stand on end." Hptm. Seitz, Fü B III 4 [Bundeswehr Command], Defense Ministry, to Politisches Archiv, Feb. 18, 1960, PA/AA, B118, vol. 125. Original emphasis.

360 Alice W. Clement, 2nd Secretary, AmEmb Bonn, to Ullrich, May 4, 1960, ibid.

September 1960, Johannes Ullrich finally asked for a copy of the return timetable, which greatly enhanced German understanding of the American project.[361]

The Americans sent the first shipment of materials in the Army's possession to the Federal Republic in March 1958. Occurring so shortly after the commencement of the renewed negotiations, this shipment gave the Germans the impression that things were moving quickly.[362] It would, however, have taken place even without the meetings in Bonn. The Americans' action put the British in a difficult position. It was easier for the Americans to begin returning documents en masse because they held large quantities of unimportant material. The records in British possession, by contrast, were exclusively "service material... of real value" in the judgment of the JCC.[363] Still, the British did not want to appear less generous than their American partners. "They are in a better position to make gestures of this kind," admitted British ambassador Christopher Steel, "but it is psychologically important that we should not appear to be lagging behind."[364]

Although the second round of negotiations did bring noticeable change in British and American return policies to the benefit of the Germans, there was still no happy end in sight. The technicalities involved in returning the naval records alone proved to be a tough undertaking. The Foreign Office finally succeeded in extracting a list of the German naval records under the care of Commander Malcolm Saunders, the head of the Foreign Documents Section at the Admiralty.[365] Yet after providing the list, Saunders tried to prevent the Foreign Office from forwarding it to the Germans.[366] Following an interagency skirmish,[367] the British embassy representative was finally in

---

361 German Embassy in Washington, verbal note, Sept. 26, 1960, PA/AA, B118, vol. 123. The embassy received the plan on Oct. 18, 1960.

362 [Winter or Rohr], memorandum, Mar. 3, 1958, BArch, N1418, NL Rohr, vol. 77; verbal note to the U.S. embassy, Mar. 3, 1958, PA/AA, B118, vol. 747.

363 Parrott to Williams, BritEmb Bonn, Mar. 14, 1958, PRO FO 2547 LS5/17.

364 Williams for Sir Christopher Steel to Sir Frederick Hoyer Millar, no. 2015, June 23, 1958, PRO FO 370/2548 LS5/44.

365 [Amtsrat Walter Pfeiffer], Akten des früheren deutschen Marinearchivs. Zur Zeit in London gelagert, October 1958, PRO FO 370/2549 LS5/65.

366 In Saunders' interest, Melland managed to have the list "truncated" and stripped of any references to post-1933 material. Melland to Fone, Nov. 11, 1958, PRO FO 370/2550 LS5/68.

367 Saunders reacted to a letter from Parrott from the Foreign Office Library "in which you imply that there is a reluctance to meet the German request for the return of the documents, I am unaware of any obstruction or lack of goodwill in the Admiralty. Indeed, we are anxious to return as soon as possible all the records to which, by the terms of the [JCC] working party report, the Germans are entitled. Yet the magnitude of the task of returning this large collection in an orderly fashion may not be fully appreciated in the Foreign Office.... To suggest that we are 'sitting on documents for the sake of retaining them' is entirely irrelevant." Saunders to Parrott, no. 86, Nov. 25, 1958, PRO FO 370/2550 LS5/73.

a position to announce at the Bonn meeting of October 10, 1958, that the naval records from 1867 to 1933 would be returned by 1960 in three installments.[368] The West German naval attaché in London was nonetheless unable to shake off the feeling "that Saunders, whose job is linked as closely as possible to the German naval archive, tries by every possible means at least to delay its return."[369] At the Defense Ministry, impatience was growing the longer army records remained unavailable. In the fall of 1959, Inspector General Adolf Heusinger got the military attaché in Washington involved and broached the subject himself during a visit there.[370] In the five years since the founding of Bundeswehr, military officials argued, recruitment and training in the new army had been hampered by its inability to draw on "the treasure of experience from the Reichswehr and the Wehrmacht."[371] Not until it was announced that a shipment of strictly military records would arrive in November 1960 did the situation settle down for a while.[372] The Defense Ministry continued, however, to fight with the Bundesarchiv and Washington over military records for many years.

What Remained Behind? No treaty or exchange of diplomatic notes on the return of military records ever materialized. The British and Americans never promised the West Germans that they would return all of the captured documents in their possession. At the opening of the second round of negotiations, Georg Winter had the feeling "that the Western powers [did] not intend to return one hundred percent" of the files.[373] The army attaché posted at the Federal Republic's embassy in Washington had the same impression.[374] The Americans and British did indeed want to reserve the option to retain records belonging to the prohibited categories in keeping with the positions set out in their respective policy papers. Those materials had, accordingly, been excluded from the Departmental Records Branch's timetable for reviewing and returning documents. The British were not so

---

368 Ullrich, Protokoll über die Besprechung mit den Vertretern der Drei Mächte . . . , Oct. 10, 1958, PA/AA, B118, vol. 30; Peter A. Wilkinson, BritEmb Bonn, to Fone, no. 2015, Oct. 13, 1958, PRO FO 370/2550 LS5/68; Ullrich to Defense Ministry, Jan. 27, 1959, PA/AA, B118, vol. 125.

369 A. Zimmermann, Naval Attaché at the German Embassy to Defense Ministry, July 21, 1959. Embassy counselor Ritter shared Zimmermann's assessment. Ritter to AA, Aug. 25, 1959, both in PA/AA, B118, vol. 125.

370 Heusinger to Military Attaché Frhr. von Schleinitz, Oct. 15, 1959, ibid.

371 Stahl, Fü B III 4 [Bundeswehr Command], Defense Ministry, to Ullrich, Mar. 21, 1960, PA/AA, B118, vol. 125.

372 Ullrich, memorandum, Nov. 21, 1960, PA/AA, B118, vol. 123. Among the records announced to be in the shipment were those of the OKW, OKH, OKL, Luftgaukommando and the Waffen SS.

373 Winter (Berichterstatter: Rohr), memorandum, Jan. 21, 1958, BArch, B106, vol. 34724/5.

374 Oberstlt. Paulsen, Army Attaché at the German Embassy, memorandum, Mar. 15, 1960, PA/AA, B118, vol. 123.

well prepared. During the negotiations, they were still deciding how strictly to apply the categories set out in the JCC paper. The matter was indeed delicate. By 1958, it was difficult to justify the retention of German documents on the grounds of security. The British embassy in Bonn reminded the Foreign Office that the Germans "are now allies in the closest sense of the word and participate in all the most secret planning at SHAPE. They will be hard put to it to believe we are justified on security grounds in withholding from them documents of which some are already more than twenty years old."[375] That year, the British secretary of defense put an end to the JCC's attempts at obstruction. He closed the last possible loopholes and ordered "a very strict standard in deciding which documents must be withheld on security grounds." To exclude any possible misunderstanding, his order stipulated that "security must not be used as an excuse for wholesale retention. Much of the material must now be so old as to have no real security interest."[376]

The Germans probably expected never to receive all of the military records. In an interview with the *National Observer* in 1966, historians from the Military History Research Office in Freiburg expressed their discontent. "We know," one of them was quoted as having said, "that both the British and American governments have extracted from those documents which have been returned to us papers which, if they came into the public domain, would embarrass them seriously."[377] At the State Department and the National Archives, this assertion was seen as an unfounded attack.[378] Although the official policy paper on restitution had stipulated three categories from which material could be retained, these had been phased out step by step. The head of the Historical Office at the State Department, Bill Franklin, summed up: "The only type of documentation that we have not returned as a matter of principle is that pertaining to intelligence, and counter-intelligence, cryptography, and certain technological-military subjects considered important to the security of the United States."[379] Franklin

---

375 Michael Williams, BritEmb Bonn, to Parrott, Sept. 25, 1958, PRO FO 370/2549 LS5/60. See also Parrot to Williams, Mar. 14. 1958, PRO FO 370/2547 LS5/17: "We do not want to give them the impression that they cannot be trusted with material of defence significance at a time when they are allied with us in Nato."

376 SecDefense to Foreign Sec, Aug. 12, 1958, PRO FO 370/2549/ LS5/54.

377 "A New German History, Rumors of Betrayals, A Question of Defeat," *The National Observer* 5:40, Oct. 3, 1966, 1, 23.

378 Robert H. Bahmer, Archivist of the United States, to William M. Franklin, Director, Historical Office, State Dept., Oct. 13, 1966, NA RG 64, National Archives, Planning and Control Cases, box PC-62.

379 Franklin to Bernadotte Schmitt, Nov. 14, 1966, NA RG 59, Lot File 78D441, Historical Office, box 1. Franklin's description reiterates paragraph 4(a) of the policy paper.

could not see what should be "embarrassing" about this for the British or American governments.

Which records did the Allies retain? This question still tantalizes many researchers. Unfortunately, the existing sources do not provide a satisfactory answer; we can only venture an educated guess.[380] The reference to the prohibited categories in the British and American return guidelines is, taken on its own, misleading: as explained above, those categories did not remain fixed.[381] A number of German documents became "federal records" when they were incorporated within American government files – for example, as evidence in war crimes prosecutions – and were thus retained. Such records can be found in Record Groups at the National Archives, such as RG 238 (Office of the Chief of Counsel for War Crimes), RG 243 (U.S. Strategic Bombing Survey), and RG 226 (OSS). Records originating from countries occupied by Germany were slated to be returned to the countries of origin, not the Federal Republic.[382] Cold War politics interfered with those plans, however, and some materials were not returned until well after 1990.[383] A series of Hitler portraits are still stored in a U.S. Army facility.[384] The so-called Hoffmann Photo Collection also remains in the United States.[385] In 1998, the Library of Congress parted with a charter issued by Frederick the Great in 1774 allowing the establishment of a Masonic lodge.[386] The British sent unorganized fragments from the collection Pers. Z – instructions on deciphering coded messages – to the Political Archives in 1999.[387] A number of military situation maps of the western and eastern fronts used by

---

380 For France, see the index of the French national archive *La France et la Belgique sous l'occupation allemande 1940–1944.*

381 Zala, *Zensur*, 244–6, reads them that way.

382 "We are also not returning those papers of non-German origin which were seized by the Nazis and found in German files. Papers of the latter sort have been returned to the country of origin, but in all cases of consequence we have made photocopies and have inserted them into the German files at the appropriate point." Franklin to Bernadotte Schmitt, Oct. 20, 1966, NA RG 59, Lot File 78D441, Historical Office, box 1.

383 In 1992, the Polish government received about 50,000 pages from the Polish foreign ministry. The return of records from the Smolensk Archive of the CPSU followed in December 2002. See Ken Ringle, "Soviet Records of Repression Returned to Moscow. Russia's Collective History," *Washington Post*, Dec. 14, 2002. The French government, which, after all, had been on the "right" side of the Iron Curtain, also had to wait until 1955 to receive microfilms that the Archival Commission of the Auswärtiges Amt had made of the archival holdings of the Quai d'Orsay. More films were returned in 1966. The films had been "forgotten" in the secret vault of the State Department at the National Archives.

384 Information from Prof. Gerhard L. Weinberg, Efland, NC, May 26–28, 2000.

385 See note 272.

386 This was the founding charter for the Grand Lodge of Germany from 1774. Exactly how the document landed in the Library of Congress can no longer be reconstructed with certainty. It had been kept at the library since 1952 "for safe-keeping."

387 Information received from the Political Archives, July 13, 2000.

the German general staff arrived at the German Military Archive in 2002. The American military had consulted these maps throughout the 1950s and returned them only once they could be satisfactorily reproduced.[388]

The Clinton administration's liberal declassification policy, embodied in Executive Order No. 12958 of April 17, 1995, and the Nazi War Crime Disclosure Act of 1998 (PL 105–246), resulted in the uncovering of still more captured German documents.[389] Implementation of that order turned up an unexpected cache of documents held by the National Security Agency (NSA).[390] Under paragraph 4(a) of the return guidelines, the documents could have been categorized as "cryptographic materials" and thus retained. It appears more likely, however, that they had never been in the purview of the Departmental Records Branch or the National Archives. Franklin's reaction to the 1966 *Observer* article thus corresponded with his information at the time. No official either at the State Department or the National Archives could have known what material had already disappeared in the channels of the intelligence and secret service agencies during the phase when the policy paper was being worked out. The NSA, founded by President Truman in late 1952 as one of his last official acts, did not participate in the formulation of the policy paper at all and was thus never put into

388 See note 271.
389 EO 12958 ordered the release of records that are more than twenty-five years old, as long as there are no convincing grounds against doing so. Should the authorities not be able to substantiate these grounds clearly, the records are to be "automatically declassified whether or not the records have been reviewed." Thus, EO 12958 turned the existing release policy on its head. Until it was issued in 1995, records were reviewed in order to decide which could possibly be declassified. Now they had to be reviewed to determine whether they need to remain closed. The Disclosure Act accelerated the impact of EO 12958, in that it was aimed specifically at documentation concerning contacts of American offices with Nazi perpetrators. The Washington bureaucracy, especially the intelligence services, were therefore compelled to go through their secret vaults to find anything having to do with Nazi Germany. See Eckert, "Nazi War Crime Disclosure Act"; Breitman/Goda/Naftali/Wolfe, *U.S. Intelligence and the Nazis*, 4. The Bush Administration used the attacks of September 11, 2001, as an opportunity to return to more restrictive archival policy. This was apparent, among other measures, in manipulations of the Presidential Records Act, a post-Watergate measure meant to increase transparency of government business and activity. It also manifested itself in a comprehensive "reclassification program," which enabled the security agencies to reclose records already open to the public for reasons of national security interests. These steps have been documented and challenged by the American Historical Association, the National Coalition for History, the National Security Archive, and other organizations. For an introduction to the issues, see the coverage in the *New York Times*, the *Washington Post*, the columns by Bruce Craig for the National Coalition for History at http://www.h-net.org/~nch/ and the website of the National Security Archive at http://www.gwu.edu/~nsarchiv/news/20011128/ (accessed Nov., 2010).
390 Part of this is now in NA RG 457: Records of the National Security Agency/Central Security Service. Historic Cryptographic Collection, Pre-World War I through World War II. In April 1996, the NSA released 1.3 million pages in 1,440 archive boxes in answer to a FOIA inquiry by Richard Breitman, American University. German material was also among these records. See Breitman, *Official Secrets*, 235–46.

the position of having to disclose any holdings. Just how the NSA came to possess German records is open to question.

Unlike the NSA, the CIA did participate in the deliberations on a return policy in the early 1950s. In fact, the CIA was one of the first government agencies to approve the policy guidelines and did not cause any problems during this process because the policy paper did not affect its work in any way, thanks to paragraph 4(a).[391] None of the files pulled by either the CIA or the NSA figured in the Departmental Records Branch's return schedule or were included in the American Committee for the Study of German Documents' microfilming project. The microfilms, in other words, reflect not only the organizational status of the captured documents in the 1950s but also the extent of knowledge about their existence.[392] We cannot preclude the possibility that additional German documents will resurface, especially in the United States. They may appear in private collections, such as the papers of the late Robert M. W. Kempner, a former prosecutor at the Nuremberg Trials.[393] Or they may still sit in the vaults of the CIA, which fanned such suspicion through its obstructive attitude toward the Nazi War Crime Disclosure Act.[394] Such archival fragments will be eloquent testimony to the many fissures along the fault line of World War II that continue to pose challenges to archivists and historians even today.

391 Loftus E. Becker, Deputy Director, CIA, to H. Freeman Matthews, Deputy UnderSecState, July 21, 1952, NA RG 59, CDF 1950–54, 862.423/7–2152.
392 Even single pages taken from war diaries (*Kriegstagebücher*) are found in RG 457. These must have been of interest to intelligence agencies in the late 1940s and were therefore pulled. See various pages from the wartime diary of the Submarine Commander (Befehlshabers der Unterseeboote, BdU) from February and August 1943 and March 1944, NA RG 457, Records of the National Security Agency/Central Security Service. Historic Cryptographic Collection, Pre-World War I through World War II, box 1279. The KTB itself was filmed with the gaps that thus existed, and the pages were considered to be lost from that point on. The full extent of the resulting problems has not (yet) been estimated.
393 Kempner, who died in 1993, donated the papers to the Holocaust Museum. However, the museum had to fight a court trial with a junk dealer over parts of this collection. The case was decided in favor of the junk dealer, who intended to sell particular pages on the autograph market. See Ralph Vigoda, "Nazi Papers in Custody Fight," *Philadelphia Inquirer*, Mar. 25, 2003; Joseph A. Slobodzian, "Battle over Nazi Papers Settled," *Philadelphia Inquirer*, Nov. 7, 2003; Axel Frohn, "Dokumente im Müllsack," *Der Spiegel*, Nov. 3, 2003.
394 Douglas Jehl, "C.I.A. Said to Rebuff Congress on Nazi Files, *New York Times*, Jan. 30, 2005; Rep. Carolyn B. Maloney (Dem.), "Letter to the Editor: The CIA's Files about the Nazis," *New York Times*, Feb. 6, 2005.

5

Ad Fontes: The Captured Documents and the Writing of History

The issue of the captured German documents and archives created a situation among American, British, and West German historians that was as unusual as it was tension-laden. In the view of West German scholars, important source materials on World War II, the National Socialist era, the Weimar Republic, and earlier periods of German history were being withheld from the legitimate interpreters of the German past. "Certainly it is not only an unnatural but also a politically dangerous situation," complained the Freiburg historian Gerhard Ritter, "that we Germans are no longer in a position today to write the history of our own misfortune from our own sources."[1] German historians were, however, anything but in agreement about what exactly that "misfortune" was. Was it the end of the Weimar Republic and Hitler's rise to power? The invasion of Poland in 1939 and the war? Or simply the fact that Germany had lost the war? Did the country's misfortune begin with Allied policy at Versailles in 1919? Or had Germany's national development taken an aberrant turn with Bismarck – or perhaps even earlier – that led to Hitler?

After 1945, the "German question" was by no means a question for the Germans alone. The horrific toll in human life taken by the Nazis' war of aggression and genocidal policies made Germany's past a subject of more than national interest. The German occupation of much of Europe made National Socialism a chapter in the histories of several other nations, and the Allied struggle to defeat the Third Reich added still more countries to the list of those whose histories had become entangled with Germany's.

---

1 Gerhard Ritter, Denkschrift betreffend planmässige Neuorganisation wissenschaftlicher Studien zur Geschichte der neuesten Zeit, n.d. [January 1949], Hausarchiv IfZ, ID1, vol. 1. Similarly, Ritter, "Gegenwärtige Lage," 11: "The way things stand today, according to one . . . estimate, 80% of the sources for our most recent history . . . are located abroad and . . . we cannot even write the history of our own misfortune without foreign help."

The scholarly study of the recent German past thus could not be an exclusively German pursuit. Historians outside of Germany, especially in Great Britain and the United States, had taken up the Nazi era as soon as the war ended. Although popular histories of National Socialism and the war were rapidly proliferating, professional historians had only just begun to work on the period. The master narrative and main lines of interpretation were still taking shape. And the conditions for this effort could not have been better: the trove of the captured German records seemed to hold promise of an unprecedented experiment in historical scholarship. As the Harvard historian William L. Langer put it: "The historian could not ordinarily expect to have access to such records in less than fifty or a hundred years, and only the fortunes of war have brought this mine of information to our shores."[2]

Although the captured documents were under American and British control, British and American historians had less access to them than their West German counterparts assumed. The diplomatic files held at Whaddon Hall were open only to researchers affiliated with the *Documents on German Foreign Policy* project. Access to the military records in Washington was extremely restricted as well. Access to the captured documents, in other words, was a problem for British, American, and German historians alike. Within the German historical profession, Gerhard Ritter was particularly outspoken on the issue of access to the diplomatic records. The Munich-based Institute of Contemporary History sought to locate important Nazi Party materials in Allied possession as a first step toward eventually working with these papers. In the United States, a committee established in the mid-1950s lobbied to have the German military records microfilmed before they were returned to West Germany in order to ensure that they would be available to American researchers. Restricting, not expanding, access was the goal of the politically well-connected British historians who wanted to see the captured documents remain in Allied possession. The issue of access was, at heart, a question of power, above all the power to interpret German history. The struggle for this power unfolded at a time when West German historians were attempting to find their way back into the international scholarly community and to regain their foreign colleagues' trust.

DOCUMENTS ON GERMAN FOREIGN POLICY

The *Documents on German Foreign Policy* series was the most visible result of the confiscation of German records. The fact that the Allies began

2 William L. Langer, Harvard, to Boyd C. Shafer, AHA, Apr. 30, 1958, Langer Papers, box 1.

publishing German diplomatic records shocked German observers and was perceived by many Germans as part of the Allies' resented "re-education" program. The connection between *Documents on German Foreign Policy* and the German edition of diplomatic records published in the wake of World War I, *Die große Politik der europäischen Kabinette*, was too obvious for the informed observer to overlook. From the start, *Documents on German Foreign Policy* was intended to forestall a repeat of the "war guilt" debate that had followed World War I. The Allied governments had a strong political interest in this attempt to steer historical interpretation, and they backed their public affirmations of support by committing the necessary funds for the project. They thereby underscored the political and cultural importance of the diplomatic records, as did the West Germans with their adamant demands for the documents' return.

German Reactions to Documents on German Foreign Policy: *The Press*

In the summer of 1950, a columnist for a newspaper in Hanover asked whether the German public had given any thought to the fact that the archival record of Germany's foreign policy since 1867 had fallen into "enemy hands." These documents, the columnist reminded his readers, recalled the "fateful path of the German people" from the establishment of the North German Federation to the "national catastrophe." The impact of the seizure of the diplomatic records on German political life and scholarship, he contended, was comparable to economic impact of the confiscation of German patents. The absence of the records was causing the "temporary paralysis of the nerve fibers of our national historical memory."[3] The *Hannoversche Allgemeine* was one of the few newspapers that tried to start a public discussion on the issue of captured records. Although Bundesarchiv director Georg Winter wanted to whip up a "storm in the world press,"[4] the Auswärtiges Amt itself repeatedly attempted to deter journalists from taking up the issue of the diplomatic files in Allied possession. Uncontrolled publicity was considered to be troublesome.[5] Nevertheless, the statements that appeared in the press allow for a spot check of editorial opinion.

3 Adolf Halfeld, "Die Wilhelmstraße," *Hannoversche Allgemeine Zeitung*, July 15, 1950.
4 Wilhelm Rohr, BA, memo [on a meeting at Interior Ministry], Jan. 2, 1956, BArch, B198, vol. 1739. See also Winter to AA, June 21, 1955, PA/AA, B118, vol. 28.
5 Winter, memo [on the meeting with Brückner, Klassen and Rohr at the AA], Feb. 10, 1956, BArch, B198, vol. 1740. Not until 1955 did the Auswärtiges Amt want somewhat more publicity about the deadlocked negotiations. See Peter Klassen, ref. 117, to Dg. 11 [Löns], Mar. 9, 1955 and Löns to State Secretary, Mar. 12, 1955, PA/AA, B118, vol. 28.

The newspaper articles on the subject were unambiguous. The confiscation and publication of German governmental records was considered one of the "most humiliating chapters" in the history of the German people. "If its archives are taken away, a nation is stripped of its history and is robbed not only of the sources of its history but also of the possibility to write its own history. It must then see its own history through the eyes of the outside world, even those of its former enemies."[6] In another article, the confiscation of the records even stood as "one of the most serious humiliations, for which we have Hitler to thank."[7] The Allies had "captured and taken away a piece of German history," namely the diplomatic records that all nations treat as their "most important historical sources." Such records, the article maintained, "are protected better than others and become available to research only after a waiting period and in due consideration of the interests of the state. Whoever captures them can look deep into the most intimate facets of a nation." Moreover, they contain "the future historical interpretation of [the nation's] foreign relations and its place in the world." The loss of diplomatic records meant that "the control over the writing of history is placed in foreign hands. One then has to take the victors' portrayal of the past as one's own."[8] A West German reviewer of the Holstein memoirs, which were first published in Britain in 1955, read the book "not without bitter feelings and in the renewed awareness of the depth of our fall."[9] Another paper lamented the "demolition of our history." The seized records were "for the state and its people what genealogical charts, property title deeds, and household account books are to families. If the material is destroyed, historical identity ends." Along with the other war losses caused by bombings and expulsion, the columnist continued, Germans were now forced to suffer the "dismantling [*Abrüstung*] of German history by the victors."[10]

The rejection of historical interpretation from abroad, the fear of being deprived of the nation's history, and the sense of injured national pride

6 "Die Rückkehr der Akten," *Rheinzeitung* (Koblenz), Apr. 25, 1956. In a similar vein, Paul Sethe, "Unrecht schlägt den eigenen Herrn," *Frankfurter Allgemeine Zeitung*, Dec. 28, 1951: with the appearance of the first volume of the Allied edition, Sethe calls the absence of diplomatic records one of the "most humiliating side effects of our unconditional surrender."
7 "Geschichtsquellen als Kriegsbeute. Die Akten des Auswärtigen Amts kehren zurück." This article is found in the business records of the Bundesarchiv, without source citation, but stamped as received on May 7, 1956. BArch, B198, vol. 132.
8 Ibid.
9 Wilhelm Schüßler, "Vergiftete Luft. Die Holstein-Memoiren," *Frankfurter Allgemeine Zeitung*, June 18, 1955.
10 Dr. K., "Die Demontage unserer Geschichte. Unersetzliche Archive wurden zerstört, entführt oder dem Osten ausgeliefert," *Hamburger Freie Presse*, Oct. 20, 1950.

were the central themes of these articles.[11] For Germans willing to distance themselves from the Nazi era, the Hitler years stood like a barrier of guilt that marked a fundamental break in the course of German history.[12] The more distant past, however, seemed to hold still untainted sites of memory that offered a reassuring vision of German history. If there was no choice but to accept the fact that Germany had been discredited by the most recent chapter of its history, preserving such sites of memory became crucial. But because the source materials for Germany's pre-1933 history had been lost, some contemporary observers believed that the ability to interpret history had been lost as well. The physical removal of governmental records, press commentators argued, was akin to a stroke that threatened to erase Germany's national historical memory.[13] Having stolen German history, the victors were now in a position to use the "advantage of first impressions to influence our picture in a way that satisfied their interests."[14]

German history, as written by foreigners using documents in Allied possession, was thus perceived as an illegitimate re-import, another facet of the Allies' program to "re-educate" the Germans. Defensive responses were not long in coming. Commentators in the press reminded readers that the decision to publish *Documents on German Foreign Policy* had been made at a time when the collective guilt of the Germans, indeed of the whole of German history was taken as given by the Allies. By the time work on it began, however, the project had become tainted by the "atmosphere of Nuremberg, which even many British and Americans now consider discredited."[15] One commentator could see no reason anymore to put up with the "triumph of the overzealous 're-educators' who [had construed] in one bold stride a long 'false path' of German history" from Luther to Hitler. He likened the case of the captured documents to that of war criminals and argued that it was time to "close the book on a chapter . . . that in the history of the occidental world represents a disgraceful and ignoble novelty."[16] Critics of *Documents on German Foreign Policy* did not, of course, care to note that the publication was not an interpretive narrative history but

---

11 Wolfrum, *Geschichtspolitik in der Bundesrepublik*, passim, on the general lament over the loss of history, 222–38.

12 Wolfrum, ibid., 225; Berg, *Westdeutsche Historiker*, 261f.

13 Halfeld, "Die Wilhelmstraße."

14 "Geschichtsquellen als Kriegsbeute," BArch, B198, vol. 132.

15 Both quotes from Halfeld, "Die Wilhelmstraße."

16 Naturally, reference to the plundering of archives under German occupation was not conducive to this type of rhetoric and was conveniently ignored. Both quotes from: Walter Görlitz, "Aktenlager in der alten Torpedofabrik. Jüngste deutsche Geschichte kann noch nicht geschrieben werden: Dokumente in alle Welt zerstreut," *Die Welt*, Mar. 31, 1955.

a collection of documents. Those who did acknowledge that point found reason to question the selection of documents:

Without raising doubts about the will of these foreign scholars to be objective, we must still, time and again, place their work . . . in question. . . . Even with the best intention to be as unbiased as possible, we always have to assume that the selection made by our former enemies is different from that which German historians or even a mixed German-Allied commission would have made.[17]

German commentators considered it tactless on the part of the Allies not to have included German historians in the editorial team responsible for *Documents on German Foreign Policy*. The *Frankfurter Allgemeine Zeitung*, for example, wrote, "As ungrudgingly as we welcome these scholarly efforts – as conscientious research is fruitful for all nations regardless of the researcher's own nationality – it is regrettable, even disturbing, that German historians were excluded from this publication."[18]

Documents on German Foreign Policy was to remain a thorn in the side of the West Germans. The closer the Federal Republic came to attaining sovereignty, the louder the press complained about the publication project.[19] The *Süddeutsche Zeitung* had noted already in 1950 that "the speed of restitution" would function as a "barometer of the termination of the state of war and of [the Allies'] illegal actions."[20] In 1955, *Der Spiegel* pointed to the issue of captured documents as an indicator of "how sovereign we actually are."[21] Applying that standard, other publications suggested that the Federal Republic was apparently less sovereign than the GDR, which had received large quantities of captured documents from the Soviet Union.[22]

17 "Wo bleiben unsere Akten?" *Rheinzeitung* (Koblenz), May 21, 1953. In a similar vein, Halfeld, "Die Wilhelmstraße": "Not because we harbor any sort of doubt about the objectivity, the unconditional search for truth of those Allied scholars, but we would have been glad to see German historians involved, simply as a matter of principle and for the sake of appearance . . . " As well as "Akten der Wilhelmstraße wieder nach Deutschland," *Süddeutsche Zeitung*, Weihnachten 1950: "Foreign eyes have seen other things as being important in the selection . . . than we would have had to do."
18 "Die Aktenlücke" [editorial], *Frankfurter Allgemeine Zeitung*, Apr. 24, 1956. Written just as cautiously, the editorial "Holsteins Briefe," *Frankfurter Allgemeine Zeitung*, May 17, 1955: "It is a good thing if German history is also being written abroad. However, it is not a good thing if German history, especially the most recent period, can only be written by foreigners."
19 For example, see the article "Noch immer konfisziert," *Rheinzeitung* (Koblenz), Jan. 29/30, 1955, that denounced the "export" of sources on Weimar and the Nazi period: "And [this is being done], even though it was felt that we Germans have needed to be prompted repeatedly since the years of re-education to take stock of ourselves and maintain a critical self-awareness. Or could the real reason for the still outstanding restitution of German archival holdings be that the current custodian countries are not interested in establishing a reliable depiction of history because they fear that otherwise they will held co-responsible for the political catastrophes of that period?"
20 "Akten der Wilhelmstraße wieder nach Deutschland," *Süddeutsche Zeitung*, Weihnachten 1950.
21 Paul Rathje, "Souveränität," *Der Spiegel*, June 1, 1955: 4.
22 "Moskau gibt Akten zurück," *Frankfurter Allgemeine Zeitung*, May 23, 1955; "Das Archivmaterial unterwegs," *Frankfurter Allgemeine Zeitung*, July 2, 1955; "Pankow verwaltet 140 000 AA-Akten.

East Berlin did not pass up the chance to exploit this event as a propaganda coup over Bonn.[23]

Reactions in Academia. West German researchers and scholars responded more evenhandedly to *Documents on German Foreign Policy* than did commentators in the press. Reviewers did, however, take their time in publishing assessments of the project. The first review by a professional historian – written by Paul Kluge for *Historische Zeitschrift* – did not appear until 1953. Consequently, the prevailing impression in the United States was that German historians intended to ignore the Allied edition.[24] In the fall of 1952, Paul Sweet complained to Fritz T. Epstein that their German colleagues ranted about the publication in long letters, "but, so far, the *Historische Zeitschrift* has given no notice of its existence."[25] In fact, the first German review of the publication, written by the former diplomat Rudolf Holzhausen, appeared in the journal *Europa-Archiv* in 1949.[26] The editor's prefatory comment accompanying Holzhausen's review sounded a very different note than the nationalistic commentaries that would follow in the press. Noting the oddity of accessing German records through a foreign publication, the journal's editor went on to emphasize "that this is the only possible way. As long as the archives were in the custody of the rulers of the Third Reich, they remained closed to any review. Right now, an evaluation of the material in today's Germany would be faced with

Lagerung in Potsdam," *Die Welt*, Oct. 1, 1955. See also Lötzke, Übergabe deutscher Archivbestände; Lötzke, "Bedeutung"; Grahn/Lötzke/Weiser, "Unterstützung der UdSSR," esp. 51.

23 "Sensationelle Dokumentensammlung. Wertvolle Materialien zur deutschen Geschichte aus der UdSSR. Wann folgen die USA?," *Berliner Zeitung*, Oct. 1, 1955; "UdSSR übergab DDR wichtige Archive. Übergabeprotokoll in Moskau unterzeichnet. Neuer Vertrauensbeweis der UdSSR," *Neues Deutschland*, July 1, 1955.

24 See also the note by Peter Klassen, Politisches Archiv, June 14, 1952, PA/AA, B118, vol. 507: "By the way, it is a conspicuous fact that, so far, German historians have not taken any notice of the publication of our records. We are not aware here of any reviews of the published volumes of documents in German historical journals."

25 Sweet continues: "Instead, the HZ published a long review of the Seidl publication and not only ignored *Deutschland und die Sowjetunion 1939–41*, but stated that these documents, apparently through some well-laid plot on our part, blieben so gut wie unbekannt to the German public. I can't help wondering if you have taken any steps to inform Dehio of the facts about this publication, with which you were so intimately connected." Sweet to Epstein, Oct. 22, 1952, BArch, N1102, NL Epstein, box 61. Alfred Seidl was the defense layer for Hans Frank and Rudolf Hess at the first Nuremberg trial. From the official U.S. publication on German-Soviet relations (1948), he extracted material for his book *Die Beziehungen zwischen Deutschland und der Sowjetunion 1939–1941. Dokumente des Auswärtigen Amtes* (Tübingen: Laupp'sche Buchhandlung 1949).

26 Even though the reviewer did not yet have the first volume of Series D *Von Neurath zu Ribbentrop* in his hands, he relied on the extensive review of the English version by A. J. P. Taylor. See Rudolf Holzhausen, "Die Quellen zur Erforschung der Geschichte des 'Dritten Reiches' von 1938 bis 1945," *Europa-Archiv* 4:21 (Nov. 5, 1949): 2585–90. A. J. P. Taylor, "Foreign Office Archives. Publishing the German Documents," *Manchester Guardian Weekly*, July 21, 1949.

nearly insurmountable practical obstacles." The chief obstacle was the new state's meager financial resources; the editor did not, however, reflect on the question whether the political atmosphere would have been conducive to a rigorous assessment of the documentary record of the Third Reich. Still, the editor offered what was to be the only clear endorsement of *Documents on German Foreign Policy* by a German. He found it "satisfying" that "at least in Western circles, one seems to be aware of the responsibility that accompanies the confiscation of Reich archives."[27]

Two of the earliest German reviews of *Documents on German Foreign Policy* emphasized the circumstances in which the project had been conceived.[28] Historian Karl-Dietrich Erdmann called the publication a "useful research tool" but disputed the claim that the project was a truly international endeavor.[29] As long as other researchers did not have free access to the originals of the published documents and no German historian acted as a co-editor, Erdmann held, *Documents on German Foreign Policy* did not fulfill the basic requirement of the scholarly principle of verifiability. Paul Kluke, writing in *Historische Zeitschrift*, made a virtue out of necessity. It was not to be expected, he suggested, that the "former wartime enemies" would show much sympathy toward the German position. But, at the same time, the fact that the documents were eventually to be turned over to the Germans meant that the British and American editors could not make special allowance on issues potentially embarrassing to their own governments. None of the nations involved, in other words, would be able to draw political advantage from the documents, to the clear gain of historical scholarship. *Documents on German Foreign Policy*, Kluke concluded, provided "extensive exposure of the most confidential material . . . to a degree unmatched by hardly any other collection."[30] Neither Erdmann nor Kluke expressed any criticism of the publication's editorial techniques. The volumes, each said, were factual and professional.

Documents on German Foreign Policy was of course of tremendous interest to the Auswärtiges Amt. In 1950, Heinrich Valentin, an archivist at the Political Archives, produced a report on the volumes published up to that

---

27 Introduction by "H.V." to Holzhausen, "Die Quellen zur Erforschung."

28 Erdmann, "Aktenpublikationen zur Neuesten Geschichte," *Geschichte in Wissenschaft und Unterricht* 3 (1952): 507–11; Kluke, "Die englischen und deutschen diplomatischen Akten," *Historische Zeitschrift* 175 (1953): 527–41.

29 Erdmann, "Aktenpublikationen zur Neuesten Geschichte," *Geschichte in Wissenschaft und Unterricht* 3 (1952): 507–11

30 Kluke, "Die englischen und deutschen diplomatischen Akten," *Historische Zeitschrift* 175 (1953): 527–41.

point.[31] He stressed that the editors-in-chief bore the full responsibility for the project and were staking their own reputations on its scholarly integrity. Valentin contended, however, that all claims about editorial objectivity were compromised by the political objectives of the project, the lack of opportunity for other scholars to verify the records, and the exclusion of German historians from the project. Moreover, Valentin insinuated that the British were suppressing documents and maintained that, on the orders of Robert Thompson, "certain documents" had been removed and sent to Britain in 1946. Finally, Valentin felt that the chapter titles were "not always free from value judgments." All in all, he concluded, *Documents on German Foreign Policy* was "by no means an undertaking free from political taint."[32]

No one else at the Auswärtiges Amt, it is interesting to note, shared Valentin's opinion. His colleague Peter Klassen criticized "small language inaccuracies" that identified the editors as non-native speakers. On the whole, however, "it cannot be said that the selection and order of records exhibit a distinct bias. The reader is offered an abundance of documents that do indeed permit a different assessment of the entire political complex." The introductions, appendices, and footnotes, Klassen found, adhered to accepted editorial standards. "When one considers how many chances the footnotes alone could have offered for biased interpretations, then it can be said that this publication does not adopt a stance anywhere that is unnecessarily unfavorable to us."[33] The former diplomat Wibert von Blücher went so far as to send the British editor Margaret Lambert a letter praising volume eight, which, in covering the opening months of the war, touched upon his activities as the German envoy in Helsinki during the Russian-Finnish war. The selection of documents displayed scholarly objectivity, he wrote, and "no German scholar could have done it better."[34] Observers in

---

31 Valentin to Consular Department [Steg], Sept. 18, 1950, PA/AA, B118, vol. 493. The task of producing a review of the publications that had appeared up to that point was assigned the Political Archives while it was in the process of being re-established. Overburdened with work, archive director Hans Andres asked his friend Kurt Rheindorf for an evaluation of the Allied publication. Rheindorf's commentary was incorporated into Valentin's letter, often verbatim, proving once again that Rheindorf was the éminence grise of the Political Archives during its early history. See Rheindorf to Andres, Aug. 29, 1950, BArch, N1263, NL Rheindorf, vol. 148.

32 The document publication, particularly the English edition, was certainly anything but holy scripture. On factual errors in the translations, glossarys, and the identifications of individuals, see Weinberg, "Critical Note;" see also the letters Rheindorf wrote to Epstein during 1950 in: BArch, N1263, NL Rheindorf, vol. 154.

33 Klassen, Bemerkungen zu den Ausführungen von Herrn Prof. Mosler [legal dept.], June 14, 1952, PA/AA, B118, vol. 507

34 From Blücher to Lambert, Jan. 22, 1955, PA/AA, B2, vol. 100; see also, Blücher to Hallstein, Dec. 22, 1954, PA/AA, B118, vol. 75b: "In my case, the editors have truly done their work 'on the basis of highest scholarly objectivity.'"

the Auswärtiges Amt, in short, did not find any scholarly defects in *Documents on German Foreign Policy* that would bolster German demands for the records' return. The only remaining complaint was the simple fact of the publication's existence.

A German Co-Editor?

The Allied note of July 6, 1951, included the offer to the West Germans to name a German co-editor to the *Documents on German Foreign Policy* project. Until the Allied proposals were finally rejected by the Adenauer government, there was much speculation on all sides about which German scholar might or should be offered the editorship. The Auswärtiges Amt claimed the right to fill the position. German historians quickly joined the discussion. Officials at the historical departments at both the State Department and the British Foreign Office also deliberated about acceptable German candidates. Each ministry asked leading historians in its own country for recommendations. Their suggestions offer an interesting snapshot of the often sketchy information British and American historians had about their German colleagues.

Re-Establishing Contact. The Allied occupation forces were accompanied by a number of historians, including several German emigrants who had been forced to flee the country in the 1930s. They were interested in finding out how German historians were trying to explain National Socialism. The political activities and attitudes of German scholars were also of great interest. Walter L. Dorn of Columbia University was General Clay's advisor on denazification matters and was, consequently, extremely well informed on the denazification process. Most likely out of professional interest, he paid close attention to scholars who had been able to continue their careers after 1933.[35] Fritz T. Epstein, who had to flee Germany before finishing his *Habilitation* thesis at the University of Frankfurt, returned to the country for the first time in 1947. In connection with his research for the publication "Nazi-Soviet Relations," he studied the Auswärtiges Amt files the Americans were holding at Berlin-Tempelhof.[36] One of the historians he

---

35 On denazification, see Schulze, *Deutsche Geschichtswissenschaft*, 121–30; Conrad, *Verlorene Nation*, 141f., 145. Dorn, *Inspektionsreise*, 105, reports on his meeting with Ludwig Dehio in Marburg in April 1947.

36 *Das nationalsozialistische Deutschland und die Soujetunion 1939–1941. Akten aus dem Archiv des Deutschen Auswärtigen Amts.* German edition edited by Dr. E. Malcolm Carroll and Dr. Fritz T. Epstein. (Washington, D.C.: Department of State/Druckhaus Tempelhof, 1948). This was the German edition of *Nazi-Soviet Relations*.

met at Tempelhof was Paul Kluke, who was employed by the U.S. Army as an archivist.[37] Francis L. Carsten, a legal scholar and historian of Prussia who had immigrated to Britain, gave lectures throughout the British zone as part of the re-education program in the early phase of the occupation.[38] Other historians – including George W. Hallgarten, Felix Gilbert, Harold Deutsch, and Oron J. Hale – were sent to Germany as intelligence officers or as members of special missions. Little is known about their contacts with German historians during the occupation, however.[39]

By 1947, German historians had begun to renew their international contacts through the mail. Within a short time after the end of the war, Gerhard Ritter had established a wide-ranging network of correspondents.[40] He was still quite well remembered abroad for his appearance at the 1938 International Congress of Historical Sciences in Zurich, where he argued against attempts to make a *völkisch* hero of Martin Luther. Moreover, his association with the conservative opposition circle around Carl Friedrich Goerdeler and imprisonment after the July 20, 1944, assassination attempt stood as evidence of his anti-Nazi credentials.[41] The undisputed doyen of the German historical profession was Friedrich Meinecke. Many historians who had emigrated from Germany and gone to the United States had been his students, and a number of them sought to re-establish contact with him, their scholarly, political, and professional differences in some instances

37 Kluke worked at the Ministerial Document Branch from 1946 to 1948, handling diplomatic records. In the 1950s, when Kluke was at the IfZ, his acquaintance with Epstein became an important conveyer for information regarding problems connected to restitution. See Kluke to Ernst Posner, Dec. 3, 1947, NA RG 200, Papers of Ernst Posner, box 8.

38 Berghahn/Cohn, "Francis Carsten," 10. See also the report by Bing, "Study and Teaching of History."

39 Gilbert and Deutsch were part of the DeWitt C. Poole Mission, who questioned staff members from the Auswärtigen Amtes for the State Department. Gilbert had been transferred to the Mission from the OSS for this work. Gilbert, *A European Past*, 205–10, describes visits to the universities of Heidelberg and Freiburg and mentions a conversation with Gerhard Ritter. In the summer of 1945, Hale was part of the Shuster Commission, whose members interrogated the main war criminals in the Luxembourg detention camp *Ashcan*. The archivist Ernst Posner also returned to Germany. In 1949, the military government requested him to act as an expert for German archival matters.

40 Those with whom he corresponded are found in Ritter, *Historiker in seinen Briefen*. His first letters to William L. Langer at Harvard are dated 1947. The correspondence is found in Langer Papers, box 13. That same year he also contacted (again) Roland Bainton (Yale) and the British historian George P. Gooch. Cornelißen, *Ritter*, 437, 457f., emphasizes that Ritter did not create his international network of contacts until after the war.

41 In Zurich, Ritter became embroiled in an argument with the Kiel historian Otto Scheel. See Cornelißen, *Ritter*, 246, 253–9, who points out that Ritter's Zurich protest "cannot be interpreted primarily as an act of political opposition and certainly not as the articulation of a fundamentally democratic way of thinking." The conventional view of Ritter's Zurich appearance is in Erdmann, *Ökumene der Historiker*, 235f. Further, Ritter to Hermann Witte, Sept. 7, 1938; Ritter to Otto Scheel, Sept. 10, 1938, and Sept. 25, 1938, all in Ritter, *Historiker in seinen Briefen*, 332–6. On Ritter's imprisonment, see ibid. 9–11, 391f., n. 1.

notwithstanding.[42] An important contact for many British historians was the Göttingen medievalist Percy Ernst Schramm. For the Americans, Ernst Posner and Kurt Rheindorf were important sources of information about German historians.[43] The importance of informal channels and personal contacts should not be underestimated at a time when German scholars had few opportunities to correspond with foreign colleagues or to publish abroad.

British and American historians did not ask probing questions about the role of the German historical profession during the National Socialist period or about the actions of individual historians. William L. Langer of Harvard, for example, stopped short of outright criticism when he wrote Gerhard Ritter in 1947: "It was a matter of particular grief to us to realize that a good number of our German colleagues . . . should have accepted, and even furthered, doctrines and interpretations which struck us as not only a negation of the finest German traditions, but also of most of the things that western civilization has stood for." Qualifying himself, Langer added that "those of us who have made history our profession have an obligation to try to understand rather than simply to condemn." The order of the day, Langer thought, was to reconstruct Germany, both intellectually and materially.[44] What little Langer and other foreign scholars knew about their German colleagues' views before 1945 rested mainly on what the Germans were willing to tell them. They largely accepted their German colleagues' explanations of their actions during the Nazi period and did not put pressure on them to re-examine their conduct.[45] British and American historians were less interested in asking what their German colleagues had

42 Walther, "Emigrierte deutsche Historiker," 46; Schulin, "Deutsche und · Amerikanische Geschichtswissenschaft," 183. Several of Meinecke's postwar contacts are documented in Meinecke, *Ausgewählter Briefwechsel;* Ritter, Meinecke. *Akademischer Lehrer und emigrierte Schüler.*

43 Rheindorf corresponded with Fritz T. Epstein and John Wheeler-Bennett, Posner with Ludwig Dehio, Eugen Meyer, and Paul Kluke, among others. The connections can be reconstructed through the personal papers of Epstein, Posner, and Rheindorf. Less fruitful is the study of the Wheeler-Bennett papers.

44 Langer to Ritter, Dec. 18, 1947, Langer Papers, Corr. 1946–54, box 13. Langer turned his words into deeds soon thereafter by supplying Ritter, or more specifically the Freiburg University library, with American journals and books. Similarly, Hajo Holborn ensured that the German journal *Historischen Zeitschrift* receive copies of American reviews. Likewise, Ernst Poser also made special efforts to see that *American Archivist* and other journals were available to German archivists.

45 See the rather placid assessment of German historiography up to 1945 by Gilbert, "German Historiography" (1948). There is no evidence that American historians took any note of the book by Max Weinreich, *Hitler's Professors* (1946). Among others, Weinreich pointed to the role of historians in *Ostforschung,* "Eastern studies," which was given an important role in planning National Socialist population policy. Weinreich also reported on activities outside university circles in openly anti-Semitic "research" facitilities. Weinreich's book was only rediscovered after 1998 during the debate on Eastern studies and republished in 1999. See also Remy, *Heidelberg Myth,* 3; Schöttler, *Legitimationswissenschaft,* 12. Further, Barkin, "German Emigré Historians," 149, who describes an

done between 1933 and 1945 than in finding out how they intended to explain National Socialism and what lessons they would draw from that disastrous chapter of German history.

As more senior German historians sought to re-establish their prewar foreign contacts, a new generation of historians took advantage of the revival of international scholarly life to meet their British and American colleagues.[46] The Hamburg historians Fritz Fischer and Johann Albrecht von Rantzau made strong impressions on the British participants at a gathering of British and German historians held in Oxford in March 1950. Writing later to Bernard Noble at the State Department, James Passant of the Foreign Office called attention to Rantzau's "aloofness from any kind of nationalism, and a supra-national conception of history which is exceptional among German historians."[47] At the time of the conference, Rantzau had just failed to place an article in *Historische Zeitschrift;* editor Ludwig Dehio rejected it because it contained criticism of Gerhard Ritter. The article appeared instead in the journal *Die Sammlung* and strengthened Rantzau's anti-establishment reputation.[48] The positive impression Rantzau and Fischer made on their foreign colleagues at the Oxford conference was reinforced by the "remarkable rudeness" of the "Ritter faction" toward the two.[49] Such impressions could become quite important to the careers of rookie scholars. American historians in particular were eager to support German scholars whom they thought might challenge exculpatory interpretations of National Socialism's

incident in the 1960s illustrating the reverence of emigrant historians for their German academic mentors.

46 I adopt the generational definition among German historians offered by Schulin, "Weltkriegserfahrung."

47 Passant to Noble, June 8, 1951, NA RG 59, Lot File 78D441, Historical Office, box 4. On the conference, see Rantzau's article: "Zur Tagung deutscher und englischer Historiker in Oxford," *Die Zeit,* Apr. 20, 1950. From Germany came Fritz Ernst, Fritz Fischer, Herbert Grundmann, Hermann Heimpel, Richard Nürnberger (Bonn), Fritz Wagner (Marburg), Helmut Roehr (Marburg), and Otto Voßler (Frankfurt). Among the British participants were A. J. P. Taylor, Geoffrey Barraclough, James Joll and the Labour MP, R. H. S. Crossman.

48 "Individualitätsprinzip, Staatsverherrlichung und deutsche Geschichtsschreibung," *Die Sammlung* 5 (1950), 284–99. See also Gerald S. Graham, a student of Ritter, to William L. Langer, Harvard, May 16, 1950, Langer Papers, Personal Correspondence, box 10: "[Ritter] also tells me that Rantzow's [sic] manuscript which Barraclough recommends to the British public was previously sent to the Hist. Zeitschrift, and turned down with Meinecke's approval 'nicht wegen seines kritischen Inhalts, sondern wegen der Gehaessigkeit des Tones und der oberflaechlichen Begrundung [sic] der Anklagen gegen unsere Historiker seit 1945.' I believe the words are those of the editor Dehio." Also, Schulze, *Deutsche Geschichtswissenschaft,* 105. Rantzau became a titulatory professor associated with the Technical University of Berlin in 1951 and tenured professor there in 1954.

49 "[Fischer's] analysis of the social theories of Lutheranism and their effect caused great indignation with Ritter and his followers. . . . It was an admirable product of learning and political insight. The representatives of the Ritter faction reacted with remarkable rudeness." Passant to Noble, June 8, 1951, NA RG 59, Lot File 78D441, Historical Office, box 4. See also Fritz Fischer's travel journal, entries of March 24 and 31, 1950, BArch, N1422, NL Fischer, vol. 90.

place in German history. It was no accident that Fischer, Rantzau, Hans Herzfeld, Paul Kluke, and Fritz Wagner were awarded grants to American universities in 1952.[50] Rantzau was also one of the historians featured in a volume edited by Hans Kohn of the City College of New York. An émigré himself, Kohn traveled to West Germany in 1951 and again in 1952 to get a sense of the country's intellectual landscape. The trips resulted in a collection of studies by German historians whose voices Kohn thought should be heard abroad.[51] In his introduction to the collection, Kohn briefly outlined the position these historians opposed:

Some German publicists and historians expound the thesis that National Socialism was not primarily a German movement but the result of general trends common to all Western peoples. Hitlerism is presented as something which could have happened anywhere and which happened in Germany only as a result of some tragic circumstances for which the Germans are in no way responsible.[52]

A revision of historical interpretations, Kohn held, was "not a question of new facts or documents but of a new perspective, of a different frame of values."[53] Such a view did not square well with the resolution passed at the first postwar meeting of historians in Munich in 1949, which called for the return of all records.[54] However, an observer for the British Foreign Office who kept an eye on unfolding developments within the historical profession in Germany came to the same conclusion as Kohn: "The problem is not so much the availability of German documents concerning recent history as the readiness or reluctance of German historians to deal with recent German history."[55]

Recommendations. By 1950, the State Department was seeking ways to lower the costs of publishing *Documents on German Foreign Policy* and to accelerate the pace of the project. One possibility that occurred to officials in

---

50 Fischer's trip to the United States was financed by the Governmental Affairs Institute in Washington, D.C. Fritz Ernst had already been at Princeton in 1950 with a research fellowship and taught as a guest professor at the University of Wisconsin in 1955. That same year, Fischer taught at the University of Notre Dame, Indiana. This information can be derived from correspondence found in the personal papers of Fritz Fischer and William L. Langer.

51 Among these were Karl Buchheim, Franz Schnabel, Alfred von Martin, Hans Herzfeld, Ludwig Dehio, Friedrich Meinecke, Johann Albrecht von Rantzau, Ellinor von Puttkamer and, almost as outsiders in this volume, Walther Hofer and Hajo Holborn. Hans Kohn (ed.), *German History. Some New German Views* (Boston, 1954).

52 Ibid., Introduction, 14; a direct attack against Ritter is found in his essay "Rethinking Recent German History" in ibid., 27f., 30.

53 Ibid., 26.

54 "Entschließungen des deutschen Historikertages," *Historische Zeitschrift* 169 (1949), 669f.

55 Dietrich Mende to James Passant, Library, Foreign Office, Feb. 1, 1950, PRO FO 370/2073 LS3/17.

Washington was to have a German editor and German researchers join the project. As explained in the previous chapter, nothing came of that idea. At an editors' conference in London in March 1950, the British, French, and American historians involved in the project unanimously rejected the idea of German participation. Bernadotte Schmitte, the American editor-in-chief, said he would immediately resign should the decision go the other way. Maurice Baumont also expressed his lack of enthusiasm.[56] Undeterred, Bernard Noble, the chief advocate of inviting the Germans to join the project, did not give up. He arranged to have James Passant at the Foreign Office gather recommendations of possible candidates for the position of German co-editor.

The Foreign Office's main source of information on West German historians was Dietrich Mende, a former Prussian civil servant employed at the Foreign Office Research Department.[57] He kept track of the German historical profession's meetings and congresses and studied the course catalogs of the leading West German universities to get an impression of what was being taught. He detected a "conspicuous escapism from contemporary history."[58] The only offering on the recent past he came across was a lecture course on the period 1918–1933 at the University of Tübingen.[59] Based on his conversations with German scholars, he concluded that there were two explanations for this avoidance of the recent past. Under the watchful eye of the Allied military authorities, professors shied away from the most recent past out of the fear of saying the wrong thing. They also felt that their students would reject a probing analysis of this period. Mende was sharply critical in his assessment of these explanations: "The first explanation indicates nationalistic views, the second indicates timidity in the face of nationalistic views."[60] One general trend within the historical profession that Mende observed was the perseverance of the *kleindeutsche* or Borussian

---

56 6th Editorial Conference, London, First Session, Mar. 20, 1950, PRO FO 370/2074 LS3/37; Minutes Passant to Kirkpatrick, Apr. 18, 1950, PRO FO 370/2075 LS3/52.

57 Dr. Dietrich Mende quit his civil service job as a finance administrator (*Oberfinanzrat*) at the Berliner Bau- und Finanzdirektion in 1935, and emigrated in April 1937 from Germany to England. From 1945 until the summer of 1951, he worked at the Foreign Office Research Department (FORD). See Reusch, *Londoner Institutionen*, 333, n. 27.

58 Mende to Passant, Feb. 1, 1950, PRO FO 370/2073 LS3/17. See this source also for the following quotes by Mende.

59 Mende's impression of the coursework in the early years after the war is confirmed by Schulze, *Deutsche Geschichtswissenschaft*, 112–16. However, Mende overlooked a lecture course on the history of National Socialism that Gerhard Ritter wrote in 1946 and held during the Winter Semester 1946/47 in Freiburg. See Cornelißen, "Institutionalisierung der Zeitgeschichte," 343.

60 Francis L. Carsten experienced first hand what could happen if one did not back away from nationalist views. At one of his lectures on a tour through the British Zone in 1947, people in the audience called him a "bolshevist" for his interpretation of German history. See Berghahn/Cohn, "Francis Carsten," 10.

school, both in terms of personnel and interpretation, as was shown by the Bismarck debate at the 1949 congress of German historians. For Mende, the subject of Bismarck served as a litmus test to gauge German historians' willingness to challenge prewar interpretative orthodoxies.[61] He found little reason for encouragement at Munich. Hans Rothfels, for example, took the opportunity to reassert the established view of Bismarck and did not try to use an analysis of Bismarck's policies to spur a more general debate on the course of German history.[62] Mende was disappointed that the new Bismarck biography by the emigrant Erich Eyck was received negatively and that even the Catholic historian Franz Schnabel did not oppose the orthodox interpretation of Bismarck.[63] Mende concluded that leading German historians, still fixated on "national interest," continued to regard raison d'état as "the supreme criterion of policy." Such navel-gazing did not bode well for German participation in *Documents on German Foreign Policy*, Mende concluded, and "the prospect of an impartial edition of documents seems to be small."[64]

Mende's observations carried considerable weight with decision-makers at the Foreign Office.[65] Gerhard Ritter, he thought, was unacceptable for the post of co-editor of *Documents on German Foreign Policy*. Although Ritter's "anti-Nazi record is as clean as anybody's can be," he remained a Prussian conservative with a "surprising lack of understanding of international affairs."[66] Mende called attention to a lecture Ritter delivered in London in October 1949 that was critical of the failure of British politicians to render assistance to the conspirators behind the July 20, 1944, assassination attempt upon Hitler.[67] Among those in attendance at the lecture was John Wheeler-Bennett, who held a more critical and skeptical view

61 Schulze, *Deutsche Geschichtswissenschaft*, 174f., 224f. On the various post-1945 interpretations of Bismarck see Conrad, *Verlorene Nation*, 62–88. The spectrum of relevant contributions on Bismarck is included in Gall, *Bismarck-Problem*.

62 Hans Rothfels, "Bismarck und das 19. Jahrhundert," Gall, *Bismarck-Problem*, 84–96; on Ritter's invitation of Rothfels, see Berg, *Westdeutsche Historiker*, 179–82; an overview of Bismarck historiography in Jefferies, *Contesting the German Empire*, 49, 69–79.

63 "All of them – even Schnabel, endorsed the orthodox conception of Bismarck's policy." Mende to Passant, Feb. 1, 1950, in PRO FO 370/2073 LS3/17.

64 Ibid. The German words "nationale Interesse" appear in the original correspondence.

65 In October 1951, Mende presented his views to the editors-in-chief of the DGFP. In a letter to Noble, Passant called Mende a person "upon whose judgement of personalities I place great reliance." Passant to Noble, June 8, 1951, NA RG 59, Lot File 78D441, Historical Office, box 4.

66 Mende to Passant, Feb. 1, 1950, PRO FO 370/2073 LS3/17.

67 Ritter traveled to England at the invitation of the British organization German Educational Reconstruction. See Berghahn, "Deutschlandbilder 1945–1965," 241. The visit left a lasting, insipid aftertaste among the British. In a letter to Hermann Heimpel in May 1951, Geoffrey Barraclough admitted that his dislike of Ritter "was formed, in common with that of most of my English colleagues, at the time when he visited England, for reasons which it is unnecessary to specify." Quote taken from Schumann, "Gerhard Ritter," 399.

of the German resistance.[68] As historical advisor to the Foreign Office and chairman of the JCC, Wheeler-Bennett was in constant contact with James Passant and likely informed him of Ritter's views.

The first choice of the British for a German co-editor was the Heidelberg medievalist Fritz Ernst.[69] He had never been a member of the Nazi party, a de facto prerequisite for the position. Indeed, Ernst had ignored several calls to join the party; at his denazification hearing in 1946, his refusal to join was taken as an act of resistance. The fact that he had joined the SA in December 1933 while he was a student in Tübingen did not make a significant difference in his denazification trial, nor were officials in London aware of it. They were struck above all by his part in rebuilding the University of Heidelberg even if he was not one of the more progressive faculty members.[70] In taking Ernst as their candidate of choice, officials at the Foreign Office focused largely on formal criteria and did not grapple with the ambiguities of his career. Another scholar under discussion in London was Fritz Fischer. James Joll of New College, Oxford, had met him at a conference in Oxford in early 1950 and recommended him to the Foreign Office.[71] Fischer was not, however, among the candidates the Foreign Office settled upon. Ernst topped the list James Passant relayed to Washington, followed by Percy Ernst Schramm, "despite his short connection with the Nazi party."[72] Passant also quickly summarized London's objections to other scholars whose names had come up for discussion: "Bergstraesser seems too old, Rothfels too nationalistic, Rantzau too controversial, Fis[c]her is described as a teacher rather than a scholar, Wagner is not very distinguished yet."[73]

---

68 In his memoirs from 1975, Wheeler-Bennett summarized his views on the resistance one last time: "I had always emphasized that we should never make promises to the German Resistance." Germany had to be thoroughly defeated, and "in the long run it was a good thing that the coup had failed." Quote taken from Bullock, [obituary] "John Wheeler-Bennett," 817f. On the context of British views of the July 20 assassination plot, see Kettenacker, "Haltung der Westalliierten," esp. 30f.

69 Proposal to appoint a German Historian to Collaborate with the Editors-in-Chief in the German War Documents Project, Oct. 16, 1951, PRO FO 370/2150 LS3/127.

70 Remy, *Heidelberg Myth*, 69f., 113f., 118–21, 185–7, 210–13. The fact that Ernst spoke fluent English may also have been a reason why he was recommended. See Fritz Fischer's note about this in his travel journal, entry Mar. 21, 1950, BArch, N1422, NL Fischer, vol. 90.

71 Joll to Passant, Jan. 23, 1951, PRO FO 370/2145 LS3/21. Dietrich Mende had also mentioned Fischer in a positive vein.

72 Schramm joined the SA in May 1934 and the NSDAP in 1937 after the ban on membership was lifted. He was responsible for the war diary at the Wehrmacht High Command (OKW) starting in 1943 and published it after the war. Until 1932 he supported the German People's Party (DVP). It is reported that, during the 1930s, he also wore the uniform of the Mounted SA at the University of Göttingen. See Ericksen, "Kontinuitäten," 220, 232.

73 Passant to Noble, Nov. 6, 1951, PRO FO 370/2150 LS3/127. He is referring here to Ludwig Bergsträßer and Fritz Wagner, Marburg.

The State Department, too, was considering potential German editors. Bernard Noble asked several historians for recommendations[74] and interviewed Hermann Mau, the director of the Institute for Contemporary History (IfZ), during a trip to West Germany in early 1951. The American historians were generally tactful but could on occasion be very blunt in their assessments of their German colleagues. For example, Walter L. Dorn warned emphatically against Ulrich Noack of the University of Würzburg, who actively and "with a definitely anti-American edge" advocated neutrality for the Federal Republic.[75] Carl Hinrichs was unacceptable to Dorn on account of his "evident Nazi sympathies." Dorn also found it suspicious that Hinrichs had been able to hold on to his position at the University of Halle, which suggested that he was acceptable to the Soviets. Wilhelm Mommsen, Günther Franz, and Percy Ernst Schramm were, in Dorn's view, "Nazi[s]."[76] Dorn's assessment of Günther Franz was based on Franz's appearance at the 1937 historians' congress in his SS uniform, and his disapproval might have been even more adamant had he known about Franz's work with the Security Service (SD) and with the Reich Security Main Office (Office VII).[77] Unlike their British colleagues, the Americans were not willing to ignore either Schramm's membership in the Nazi party and the SA or his wartime service on the staff of the Wehrmacht High Command. Hajo Holborn advised steering clear of Siegfried Kaehler of Göttingen, "a staunch Bismarckian nationalist" who, in Holborn's view, was professionally competent but difficult to deal with.[78] The Americans ruled out medievalists on the grounds that their expertise lay elsewhere, but, like the British, they were willing to consider making an exception in the case of Fritz Ernst. Here, Noble could concur with the recommendations from London. He also found Otto Becker, Heinz Holldack, and Egmont Zechlin acceptable, even though Zechlin was said to have leaned "pretty far toward Nazism." Ludwig Dehio, Fritz Hartung, and Franz Schnabel were

---

74 Noble asked Hajo Holborn (Yale), Walter L. Dorn (Columbia), Felix Gilbert (Bryn Mawr) and Theodor Mommsen (Princeton). NA RG 59, Lot File 78D441, Historical Office, box 4.

75 Dorn to Noble, Aug. 23, 1951; Holborn to Noble, Aug. 26, 1951, both in NA RG 59, Lot File 78D441, Historical Office, box 4. For more on Noack, see Schulze, *Deutsche Geschichtswissenschaft*, 116.

76 Noble to Passant, Oct. 21, 1951, PRO FO 370/2153 LS3/176. The suggestions of the historians Sidney B. Fay (Harvard) and Felix Gilbert (Bryn Mawr) were included in the list sent with this letter.

77 Behringer, "Bauern-Franz und Rasse-Günther."

78 Holborn to Noble, Aug. 26, 1951, NA RG 59, Lot File 78D441, Historical Office, box 4. During the Weimar period, Kaehler had not been able to bring himself to recognize the Republic; he would have preferred a "Prussia without Wilhelm II." These views were not compatible with those of the democrat Holborn. See Kaehler, *Kaehler*, 51.

also discussed but could not be considered for the post of co-editor because of their other commitments.[79]

The remaining question for the Americans was what to do about Gerhard Ritter. Dorn could not imagine anyone who would be "more suitable" for the German editor's position. Moreover, Dorn was one of the few scholars to praise the edition of Hitler's table talks that Ritter published in 1951, declaring it "a courageous work of a clearly anti-Nazi historian."[80] Holborn was much more guarded. Ritter was admittedly West Germany's leading historian, Holborn noted, and he could hardly be rejected if Bonn proposed him. The editors of *Documents on German Foreign Policy* would, however, find Ritter "not easy to work with."[81] The State Department thus settled on the position that Ritter would be accepted for the editor's post only if Bonn insisted on nominating him. Meanwhile, American and British officials worked through informal channels to forestall Ritter's nomination. The Foreign Office frankly informed Herbert Blankenhorn that Ritter was not wanted.[82]

Foreign historians and officials were, generally speaking, not rigorous in their scrutiny of German historians and often lenient in their assessments of even compromised individuals. For the scholars working on *Documents on German Foreign Policy*, the most essential requirement for the potential German editor was political acceptability. The American historians, particularly the émigrés, searched among their German colleagues for scholars who might bring new perspectives to the study of German history. What was needed, according to Hans Kohn, were not new facts or sources, but new questions and interpretative frameworks. Above all, American historians hoped for a weakening of the German fixation on the state and the decoupling of nationalism and historical scholarship. Herein lies the significance of the support American and British historians gave Fritz Fischer during the controversy over his book *Germany's Aims in the First World War*

---

79 Dehio was said to be "one of the most scrupulously honest, able, and finest spirits of all German historians. Democrat, politically impeccable"; Hartung was "scrupulously honest, scholarly, and politically altogether unobjectionable"; and Schnabel was a "scholar of high rank and a convinced liberal; highly respected in France, Great Britain and [the] U.S.; reputation spotlessly clean." The list was an attachment to the letter Noble to Passant, Nov. 21, 1951, PRO FO 370/2153 LS3/176.

80 Dorn to Noble, Aug. 23, 1951, NA RG 59, Lot File 78D441, Historical Office, box 4.

81 Holborn to Noble, Aug. 26, 1951, NA RG 59, Lot File 78D441, Historical Office, box 4.

82 Dugald Malcolm, Wahnerheide, to Passant, May 5, 1952, PRO FO 370/2245 LS3/66; Mosler, report, Mar. 1, 1952, PA/AA, B118, vol. 507: "As far as the Americans are concerned . . . it has been transmitted through private channels for quite a while that Prof. Gerhard Ritter . . . would not be the man one would like to see the Germans proposing." In a letter to the AA, Hans Rothfels also came out against Ritter and proposed instead that the IfZ lead the German participation on the publication project. Rothfels to Theo Kordt, May 7, 1953, PA/AA, B10, vol. 1699.

in the early 1960s. They were not supporting methodological innovation – Fischer's book was rather traditional in conception – nor were they necessarily fully persuaded by his argument. Above all, they supported him for the simple fact that he was a German who was offering a new reading of the German past.

Gerhard Ritter. Word of the State Department and Foreign Office's reservations about Gerhard Ritter was favorably received at the Auswärtiges Amt. At the Political Archives, the preferred candidate was Kurt Rheindorf, an expert on the pre-1945 records. He lacked, however, the international standing the British and Americans expected of a German co-editor. Hans Andres, the director of the archive, introduced the idea of nominating Rheindorf. Rheindorf had helped Andres with the latter's denazification process; Andres's recommendation may well have been prompted by private considerations.[83] Officials at the Auswärtiges Amt also briefly considered the idea of establishing a commission of historians in which all political views and religious backgrounds would be represented. The head of the legal department, Hermann Mosler, had Gerhard Ritter, Franz Schnabel, and Karl Dietrich Erdmann in mind. Erdmann, a Protestant and member of the younger generation of historians, was seen as a counterbalance to Ritter, from whom Mosler expected "difficulties." Schnabel was Catholic. All that was missing from this line-up, Mosler acknowledged, was a "leftist oriented historian." Given the make-up of the German historical profession, it was not surprising that Mosler had a hard time coming up with a name.[84] The proposal for such a commission was not pursued any further.

The question of German participation on the *Documents on German Foreign Policy* project was also discussed among West German historians. Hermann Mau of the IfZ welcomed Noble's suggestion that German scholars be included on the project.[85] However, the board of trustees and the advisory board of his institute in Munich did not share his enthusiasm. They feared that German cooperation "could be interpreted as a silent acceptance of the current status of the records of the Auswärtiges Amt"[86] – a view that was also gaining ground in Bonn. Mau was disappointed by the vote against participation. In his view, the Auswärtiges Amt's insistence on

---

83 See Chapter 2, n. 172, for biographical information on Rheindorf. The recommendation of Rheindorf through Andres is found, e.g., in Report Andres, July 30, 1951, PA/AA, B118, vol. 507. Fritz T. Epstein also mentioned Rheindorf in his contact with the State Department. Epstein to Noble, Sept. 28, 1951, BArch, N1102, NL Epstein, box 61.
84 Mosler to Hallstein, Nov. 12, 1951, PA/AA, B118, vol. 493.
85 File notes Mau, Mar. 14, 1951, IfZ Hausarchiv, ID102, vol. 46.
86 Mau to Noble, Nov. 7, 1951, ibid.; Mau to AA, Nov. 7, 1951, PA/AA, B118, vol. 489.

the immediate return of all the diplomatic files did not serve the institute's research interests.

Many German historians were interested in the idea of German participation on *Documents on German Foreign Policy*, but none pursued the matter as energetically as Gerhard Ritter. The resolution passed at the 1949 historians' congress in Munich was chiefly a result of his efforts, and he was not one to pass up any opportunity to publicize his demands.[87] Ritter considered himself the legitimate spokesperson for the German historical profession, a claim that could perhaps be justified until 1953 by his position as chairman of the Association of German Historians but also rested on a very generous self-assessment. It would have been inconceivable to Ritter that neither the British and Americans nor the Auswärtiges Amt wanted the editor position to fall to him. At a meeting at the Ministry of the Interior in May 1953, he concluded his remarks by declaring that the German team should be headed by a "representative, internationally renowned scholar" and, in turn, he was prepared to "make the sacrifice of leading the German historian commission for a while."[88] Ritter's extensive network of contacts within the government facilitated his lobbying efforts on his own behalf. Ritter also maintained contacts with leading historians in Great Britain and the United States, and he repeatedly brought up the subject of the captured documents in his correspondence with them.[89] During a trip to the United States in early 1953, Ritter met with Bernard Noble and Paul R. Sweet. He reported on these meetings to his contacts at various ministries in Bonn. The heads of the Interior Ministry's cultural affairs department clearly drew on information supplied by Ritter and echoed his opinions in their correspondence with the Auswärtiges Amt on the documents issue. Ritter's efforts culminated in the resolution adopted at the 1953 congress of German historians. On Gerhard Ritter's initiative, the assembled historians voiced their "urgent wish" to see the West German government do everything possible to ensure that German participation in the *Documents on German Foreign Policy* project "can indeed begin in the near future and not be delayed by the negotiations on restitution, irrespective of the legal German claim."[90] Archivists at the Political Archives

---

87 "Entschließung des deutschen Historikertages," *Historische Zeitschrift* 169 (1949), 669f. Further, Ritter, "Ist das deutsche Volk politisch 'unreif'?" *Neue Zeitung*, Jan. 6, 1949.

88 Winter to Ministry of the Interior, June 1, 1953, BArch, B106, vol. 34723/2.

89 Among these people were William L. Langer, Walter L. Dorn, Hans Rothfels (professor in Chicago until 1956; also in Tübingen starting in 1951), Fritz T. Epstein, George Peabody Gooch, and Guy Stanton Ford.

90 Ritter to Löns, AA, Sept. 30, 1953, PA/AA, B118, vol. 493; the text is also found in Minutes Lambert to Passant, Jan. 6, 1954, PRO FO 370/2344 LS5/249.

did not appreciate Ritter's politicking. Klassen considered his efforts as part of an

apparently well-planned campaign of American scholars, acting on a governmental mission, who want to convince the AA, by way of German professors, to accept the offer to participate in the Allied publications of our records, in order thereby to avoid having to RETURN THE RECORDS soon . . . We should ignore this attempt to exert pressure on us through representatives of German academia and not enter into a discussion with the German historians who have been approached by the Americans for this purpose.[91]

Hans Andres considered the Bremen resolution to be "disturbing" and an "unwanted intervention in the negotiations."[92]

Ritter's intense activity invites closer scrutiny. Without a doubt, his interest in this issue of the captured documents was genuine.[93] He was, however, concerned primarily with his own work and only secondarily with the research needs of the colleagues on whose behalf he claimed to speak. To the ministries, he lamented the absence of the particular groups of records that he wanted for his own research. In 1953, for example, he needed source material for his biography of Carl Goerdeler.[94] While working on *Staatskunst und Kriegshandwerk* (translated as *The Sword and the Scepter*) in 1954, he wanted to study the records of the Army High Command and other papers from the period of 1914–1918.[95] A year later, he was preparing a study on the Schlieffen Plan and sought access to Schlieffen's personal papers.[96] By 1955, Ritter was complaining bitterly about the situation to the Auswärtiges Amt. The Allies' "refusal" to return records from the period 1914–1918 was the result, he charged, of "nothing more . . . than the egoistic wish of certain British historians to benefit from these holdings." The English used the records for publications of a "strictly private kind." There was, moreover, reason to suspect that "private interests are prevailing

---

91 Klassen, file notes, May 21, 1953, PA/AA, B10, vol. 1699, original emphasis.
92 Andres, Memo for Trützschler, Oct. 22, 1953, PA/AA, B118, vol. 493. Andres appeared to be particularly incensed that the civil servant at the Interior Ministry in charge for science and scholarship, Mr. Kipp, identified with the resolution.
93 In the fall of 1950, he traveled to Berlin just to investigate the archival situation there. See Ritter, Ergebnis meiner Archivreise nach Berlin, Oct. 11–18, 1950, Dec. 1, 1950, BArch, B106, vol. 34723/1; Ritter, "Ergebnis Archivreise."
94 In April 1953 Ritter was permitted to see the so-called Kaltenbrunner Reports at the Departmental Records Branch in Washington; afterward, he used them in his Goerdeler biography. The Kaltenbrunner Reports were written in the course of the Gestapo interrogations of individuals suspected of belonging to the July 20 conspiracy.
95 Ritter to Trützschler, Nov. 22, 1954, PA/AA, B10, vol. 1703/3.
96 Ritter to Trützschler, May 17, 1955; Ritter to Klassen, Nov. 19, 1955, both in BArch, N1166, NL Ritter, vol. 286.

over German interests." Curiously, "German interests" appear to have been identical with Ritter's own: the "retention of the most valuable source material," Ritter noted, "hits me personally the hardest."[97] It was not lost on Ritter's correspondents that his support for German participation in *Documents on German Foreign Policy* was not entirely disinterested.[98]

Ritter's attempt to influence the Auswärtiges Amt received a major setback in October 1955. Hermann Aubin, Ritter's successor as chair of the Association of German Historians, announced to the Auswärtiges Amt that German scholars were no longer seeking to participate in *Documents on German Foreign Policy* and thus formally retracted the association's 1953 resolution.[99] At the same time, he called for an intensification of negotiations on the return of the captured documents so that German historians might be freed from the "extremely embarrassing situation" of having to rely on foreign publications in discussing new interpretations of German source materials.[100]

Die große Politik der europäischen Kabinette *in the 1950s*

The German documents publication *Die Große Politik der europäischen Kabinette* hovered in the background while *Documents on German Foreign Policy* was in the planning stage. The British and the Americans took on the task of publishing German diplomatic documents themselves in order "to forestall the development of a 'revisionist' interpretation of the origins of the war, such as happened after World War I."[101] *Die Große Politik* had played an important part in the interwar debate on war guilt, in the work

---

97 Ritter to Hardo Brückner, Politische Abt. AA, Nov. 22, 1955, PA/AA B118, vol. 509. If it was not possible to get these records returned, then Ritter suggested "that at least I be granted direct access to the originals."

98 Winter, Bundesarchiv, to Scheidemann, Interior Ministry, June 10, 1955, BArch, N1418, NL Rohr, vol. 77. At a meeting held at the Auswärtigen Amt, it turned out that Ritter was the only one present who approved of participation. "But the only thing that really interests him is to study the records himself as quickly as possible." See also Hübinger, Interior Ministry, Culture Dept., memo, Sept. 18, 1956, BArch, B106, vol. 34725: Hübinger reports that Ritter organized a session on the records issue at the 23rd Historians Congress in Ulm: "Under his [Ritter's] direction, the session focused extensively on matters reflecting strictly personal interests, which are of secondary importance within the scope of the problem overall. Prof. Rothfels pointed this out during the meeting."

99 Likewise, Paul Kluke, IfZ, to Fritz T. Epstein, July 23, 1955: "The work with the diplomatic records has progressed too far to have us still participate:" IfZ Hausarchiv, ID102, vol. 37.

100 Aubin to Politische Abteilung, AA, Oct. 21, 1955; Löns to Aubin, Nov. 3, 1955, both in PA/AA, B118, vol. 509.

101 Noble to Charles Bohlen, June 19, 1947; also, E. Wilder Spaulding to Russell, Apr. 17, 1946, both in NA RG 59, Lot File 78D441, Historical Office, box 21. See also Zala, *Zensur*, 201f.

of the Auswärtiges Amt's "war-guilt department" (*Kriegschuldreferat*) during the Weimar Republic, and in scholarship outside of Germany.[102] It
was also to play a role in the 1950s far different from that envisioned by
those who had conceived the project. The historians working at Whaddon
Hall saw in *Die Große Politik* a potential argument against transferring their
own project to Germany: evidence of politically motivated omissions or
censorship might serve as reason not to give the Germans a leading role
in preparing *Documents on German Foreign Policy*.[103] The historian H. C.
Watt has characterized the debate about *Die Große Politik* in the 1950s as a
continuation of the interwar "world war of documents."[104]

Checking Die Große Politik. Prior to the German demand for restitution,
no one was interested in the records of Wilhelmine Germany. Until January
1951, they were still stored in the very same postal sacks in which they
had been flown out of Berlin to Great Britain in 1948. There had been
doubts outside of Germany about the accuracy of *Die Große Politik* since
the 1920s, and Allied officials raised the possibility on a few occasions
of checking the printed texts of documents against the originals in their
possession.[105] Academic historians, however, initially showed little interest
in such an examination. Bernadotte Schmitt, who had played a prominent
role in the American debate during the 1930s on the origins of World War
I,[106] held that "the pre-1914 period was a 'dead duck,' and that no one was
much interested."[107] It was only the possibility that evidence of bias in *Die
Große Politik* could be used as an argument against German participation
in *Documents on German Foreign Policy* or even against the return of the
captured records that sparked interest in the Imperial-era materials. "If the
unreliability of the *Große Politik* could be proved," John Wheeler-Bennett

102 Evans/Baylen, "History as Propaganda;" Heinemann, *Verdrängte Niederlage;* Herwig, "Clio
    Deceived;" Jäger, *Historische Forschung,* chaps. 1 and 2; Thimme, *Friedrich Thimme;* Wittgens,
    "Senator Owen;" Zala, *Zensur,* 57–77.
103 The link between the cross-check of *Große Politik* and restitution has also been noted by Watt,
    "British Historians;" Zala, *Zensur,* 68f.
104 Watt, "British Historians."
105 "From the historical point of view . . . there is the interesting question . . . how far, if at all, the
    Germans falsified or rendered tendentious by judicious omissions the picture of Germany [sic]
    foreign policy presented in *Die grosse Politik.*" Minutes Passant to Sir Orme Sargent, Feb. 18, 1949,
    PRO FO 370/1953 L605. See also, Sweet to Noble, Nov. 22, 1949, NA RG 59, Lot File 78D441,
    Historical Office, box 5.
106 In the revisionism debate, American historians discussed the degree of responsibility that Germany
    had in causing the First World War.
107 Minutes of the German War Documents Conference, Oct. 5, 1949, PRO FO 370/2073 LS3/14.

suggested in the spring of 1950, "it would be an irrefutable argument for not admitting German historians to the Project."[108]

It was the younger historians at Whaddon Hall who were most interested in carrying out a textual examination of *Die Große Politik*. At the sixth editors' conference (March 1950), M. H. Fisher and Norman Rich, who were collaborating on an edition of Holstein's memoirs, presented proposals for an examination of *Die Große Politik*.[109] In their work with the Holstein papers, they had come across office records of the war-guilt department in the files of the Political Archives. Their initial assessment of the records led them to suspect "that the editors of the '*Große Politik*' were guided by considerations of political expedience rather than by a strict regard for historical integrity. Whole documents or parts of them have been suppressed because of political repercussions which their publication might have produced." Fisher and Rich were themselves not immune from the temptation to employ scholarship for political ends, however: "Proof that the '*Große Politik*' is not a historically objective publication would be of value as a counter-argument to any German demands for the return of the Archives now held by the Allied Governments."[110] At the same time, however, the proposed examination of *Die Große Politik* could have had political repercussions that the Foreign Office and State Department sought to avoid. The Federal Republic of Germany was preparing to rebuild its diplomatic service. Should the German policy of instrumentalizing history during the interwar period be exposed at such a sensitive moment? In light of the political situation, James Passant ordered the examination to be conducted with the "strictest secrecy" possible to avoid offending Bonn – at least until evidence supporting the allegations had been found.[111]

The examination of *Die Große Politik* did not begin until 1951, when the British, French, and American historians working on *Documents on German Foreign Policy* came under increased political pressure to make concessions

---

108 6th Editorial Conference, London, Mar. 20, 1950, PRO FO 370/2074 LS3/37.
109 M. H. Fisher, Proposal for a Review of The Grosse Politik, Mar. 8, 1950; Norman Rich, Examination of the Holstein Nachlass [and] Examination of the files 'Politisches Archiv P.A. 26', n.d. [Mar. 8, 1950], PRO FO 370/2074 LS3/35. M. H. (Fredy) Fis[c]her fled Germany for Australia, where he was first detained before he enlisted in the British army. Following the work at Whaddon Hall, he became an editor of the Financial Times. I thank Prof. Norman Rich for the biographical information.
110 Fisher, Proposal, ibid. See also [Minutes of a] Meeting held at Whaddon Hall, Mar. 24, 1950, PRO FO 370/2074 LS3/37.
111 6th Editorial Conference, London, Mar. 20, 1950, PRO FO 370/2074 LS3/37. For political reasons, Maurice Baumont also considered it "imprudent at the present juncture," to attack publicly *Die Große Politik*. The results of a cross-check should only be used internally. See also, Minutes Passant to Kirkpatrick, Apr. 18, 1950, PRO FO 370/2075 LS3/52.

to Bonn. Because the historians at Whaddon held government jobs, they did not have the freedom to make use of the documents as they desired. The decision to check the accuracy of *Die Große Politik* lay with the foreign ministries. While the French and British supported the proposal, Bernard Noble opposed it for several reasons. It was not simply concern about the political consequences for Bonn that spurred his opposition. He was also struggling with a shortage of manpower. In the autumn of 1951, the State Department had only two men working at Whaddon Hall, Paul Sweet and Norman Rich. Although Rich definitely wanted to start work on the Imperial era records, Noble could not afford to reassign him to that task. The *Documents on German Foreign Policy* project had long been criticized for its slow progress. Rather than reassign Rich, Noble attempted to secure outside funding to have another American historian sent to Britain to work on the check of *Die Große Politik*.[112] American historians did not display much interest in the project, however. The members of an American Historical Association committee dealing with the issue of access to World War II records thought an examination of *Die Große Politik* "not very much worthwhile," Noble informed Sweet. "They did not doubt that there were distortions, but . . . it is a field which is much less important to historians than the later period." Even worse, they expressed "rather harsh criticism of the idea that we were proposing to send in a historian who would have special privileges and enjoy advantage over other historians."[113]

In fact, Fisher and Rich, too, had recognized that the examination of *Die Große Politik* would not only be relevant to historical scholarship but would also be advantageous "in the competition for academic preferment to be able to present oneself as an expert on the archives for the period 1870–1914, as well as on those for the later period."[114] There was indeed a generational impetus behind the interest in *Die Große Politik*. It coincided with the emergence of a new generation of specialists on German history

---

112 Sinclair W. Armstrong of Brown University was being considered for the job. See Noble to Passant, Sept. 21, 1951, PRO FO 370/2151 LS3/143; Noble to Armstrong, Sept. 10, 1951; Noble to Sweet, Oct. 1, 1951; Sweet to Noble, Oct. 9, 1951, all in NA RG 59, Lot File 78D441, Historical Office, box 4.

113 Noble to Sweet, Oct. 12, 1951, NA RG 59, Lot File 78D441, Historical Office, box 4. The American Historical Association's Committee on the Historian and the Federal Government was established in 1949 to examine the analysis of World War II inside and outside of the government. The question of access to source materials was one of its chief concerns, and it also considered the tension between official mission and scholarly integrity faced by historians serving in the government. The committee was chaired by Conyers Read; the other members included Gordon A. Craig, Kent Roberts Greenfield, Hajo Holborn, Dexter Perkins, and, as corresponding members, Raymond Sontag and Oron J. Hale. The two chief opponents to an examination of *Die Große Politik* were Craig and Holborn.

114 Sweet to Noble, Oct. 22, 1951, NA RG 59, Lot File 78D441, Historical Office, box 4.

who were embarking on their academic careers. The work of this up-and-coming generation, which included Hans Gatzke, George O. Kent, Otto Pflanze, Norman Rich, and Gerhard L. Weinberg, was greatly influenced by access to German records.[115] They entered the academic job market in the early 1950s, along with many other young historians who were completing their university educations with the help of the GI Bill. To be able to work in proximity to German records, either in Whaddon or Alexandria, was hardly the worst option open to them because it allowed them to gain a foothold in the profession and to obtain fresh research material.[116]

After several attempts to persuade Noble to change his mind,[117] the examination of *Die Große Politik* began without direct American participation.[118] In March 1952, James Joll of Oxford presented a preliminary report based on comparison of the published versions of a number of documents dealing with key events against the originals. The report was evenhanded in its general assessment:

While there is much material of interest that is not published in the *Grosse Politik*, it is difficult, given the date and circumstances of publication, to blame the Editors for these omissions, or to impugn their good faith, especially as they were under constant pressure and supervision by politicians . . . while on occasions, they even seem to have been definitely mis-led. . . . Thus there does not seem any ground at present for whole-sale attack on the *Grosse Politik* and its Editors. Omissions and

115 Weinberg was not involved with diplomatic records, but with military ones in Alexandria, Virginia. As for the British, it is noteworthy that Ernest K. Bramsted and D. C. Watt were employed at Whaddon. Working on the Washington War Documentation Project under the direction of Fritz T. Epstein as of 1951 were Raul Hilberg and Henry Friedlander, who both became known Holocaust historians, as well as Earl Ziemke, John Armstrong, and Alexander Dallin. Among those entering the ranks of the historical profession at the end of the 1940s and in early 1950s were Gordon Craig, Peter Gay, Leonard Krieger, George L. Mosse, Carl Schorske, and Fritz Stern, none of whom were associated with the records issues as were those mentioned above.

116 This does not at mean that the historians working at Whaddon Hall would have been able to publish German records simply as they saw fit. The Holstein Papers volume put out in 1955 by Rich and Fisher was preceded by several years of preparation, in which matters such as copyright issues had to be addressed. Many research projects, if granted permission in the first place, had to be pursued outside regular working hours.

117 Bernadotte Schmitt to Noble, Oct. 2, 1951; E. Llewellyn Woodward, Princeton, to Noble, Jan. 6, 1952, both in NA RG 59, Lot File 78D441, Historical Office, box 4. Woodward feared that the return of diplomatic records without a cross-check of *Die Große Politik* would be interpreted by the Germans as approval of this edition.

118 At the editors conference of Oct. 2, 1951, the editors all agreed to a resolution which read: "The Editors-in-Chief, in the course of their researches into the post-1918 documents of the German Foreign Ministry, have found evidence which has given them reason to doubt whether the selection and presentation of the documents published in Die Grosse Politik . . . have been consistently carried out in accordance with strict historical objectivity. They have therefore authorised a probe of certain of the original material used in Die Grosse Politik. It is the strong view of the Editors-in-Chief that the results of the probe whether positive or negative should be published, together with the evidence." PRO FO 370/2152 LS3/161. Such a publication never appeared.

perhaps occasional distortions are not in my opinion sufficient to prove the whole publication unreliable.[119]

Joll proposed that a portion of the newly available material be published to spur scholarly discussion of the documents' content. "This would undoubtedly be of more use than a sterile controversy about the motives and methods of the Editors of the *Grosse Politik*," he believed. Joll was alone in this opinion, however. His French colleague, Jacques Grunwald, a staff member at Whaddon Hall, thought *Die Große Politik* was open to challenge: "The sampling carried out so far provides a solid foundation for challenging the impartiality of the *Große Politik*."[120] Margaret Lambert also thought Joll's assessment was too lenient. In her opinion, the German editors had let themselves be guided by politically motivated decisions more often than they were willing to admit. "I remain unconvinced," Lambert wrote, "that this is entirely for reasons of space or owing to different interpretations as to what is historically important."[121]

The results of the examination of *Die Große Politik* provided opponents of returning the captured documents with yet another argument. It appeared for the first time in official correspondence when the Foreign Office informed the State Department of its position on Adenauer's proposal to relocate the *Documents on German Foreign Policy* project to West Germany. German sponsorship of the project, the Foreign Office maintained, would jeopardize its reputation for scholarly independence.[122] The results of the examination circulated quickly among British and American historians.[123] In late 1952, papers pertinent to the history of *Die Große Politik* became generally accessible when the Foreign Office and the State

119 James Joll, Report on the pre-1914 Archives of the German Foreign Ministry, Mar. 1, 1952, PRO FO 370/2244 LS3/47. The key events were the first and second Marocco crises of 1905/06 and 1911, respectively, as well as the Hohenzollern candidature for the Spanish throne. In 1957, Georges Bonnin, a member of the French DGFP team, published a collection of documents related to this particular set of events. See, Bonnin, *Bismarck and the Hohenzollern Candidature*.

120 Jacques Grunwald, Note sur les sondages effectués dans la *Grosse Politik* au sujet de la crise marocaine de 1911, Februar 1952, in PRO FO 370/2244 LS3/47.

121 Minutes Lambert to Passant, Mar. 17, 1952, ibid.

122 Robert G. Hooker, First Sec. of USEmb London, to State Dept., no. 4510, Mar. 24, 1953, NA RG 59, CDF 1950–54, 862.423/3–2453. The fact that the answer actually did refer to the cross-check of *Große Politik* becomes clear in a letter from Passant to Noble, June 8, 1953, PRO FO 370/2340 LS5/107: "Our fear that the reputation of the Series [DGFP] for impartiality and completeness would suffer in the event of transfer to Germany is quite simply based on the fact that, in the past, the Germans have deliberately suppressed documents which they regarded as compromising."

123 Lynn M. Case, chair of the Committee for the Study of War Documents, to Howard Ehrmann, University of Michigan, Mar. 9, 1957: "After the revelations in the London *TLS* (1953) we all became aware of the deliberate suppression of documents by Thimme, which the Whaddon Hall material could rectify. It was one of the talking points in our requests for money to be used in the pre-1918 material." Hale Papers, box 8, folder 5.

Department deposited microfilm copies of the papers of Gustav Stresemann at the Public Records Office and the National Archives.[124]

The Debate in the Times Literary Supplement. It was not long before the discussion of *Die Große Politik* moved into a public forum. In late July 1953, the *Times Literary Supplement* (*TLS*) published a review of the fifth volume of *Documents on German Foreign Policy*. The review – unsigned, in keeping with the paper's policy at the time – concluded:

So long as these German archives are in the hands of the Western Allies there need be no fear of manipulations of the texts such as those which have been discovered to have taken place in Germany after the other war. It will be a depressing day for historians if and when the German claim to the return of their Foreign Office documents is recognized.[125]

A letter to the editor quickly followed. A. J. P. Taylor of Magdalen College, Oxford, called for evidence of the alleged "manipulations" in *Die Große Politik*. "I have long wanted to pin some dishonesty or fraud on the editor of the *Grosse Politik*," Taylor added, "but I have never found evidence of any."[126] Taylor also took a jab at the editors of *Documents on German Foreign Policy* for the project's slow progress, especially in comparison to the five years it took to complete *Die Große Politik*. Taylor's letter was the opening salvo in a sometimes polemical series of exchanges. Agnes Headlam-Morley, an Oxford professor, weighed in on Taylor's side. She defended *Die Große Politik* and attacked the editors of the *Documents on German Foreign Policy* series for denying German scholars access to the diplomatic records. Without the Imperial and Weimar era records, she argued, the West German government was not in a position to take a stance on the allegations about *Die Große Politik*. Moreover, the editors' slowness was preventing other historians from using the records of the Weimar years. She demanded the general release of records "so that historians can judge for themselves whether in fact political considerations influenced the selection

---

124 Gatzke, "Stresemann Papers." There is no proof that the Stresemann papers were declassified in order to prompt a public debate on the *Große Politik*. More likely, this step was a concession to the American advisory committee of the DGFP, which was always pressing for the declassification of sources from the Weimar period. See Noble, Memorandum of Conversation, Discussion of Future Program of German FO Archives Project, Jan. 14, 1952; Holborn to Noble, Jan. 17, 1952; Record of a Meeting Held in Mr. Passant's Room, Mar. 3, 1952, all in NA RG 59, Lot File 78D441, Historical Office, box 4; Passant to Noble, June 8, 1953, PRO FO 370/2340 LS5/107.
125 "Hitler and the Smaller Powers," *TLS*, no. 2687, July 31, 1953: 490.
126 A. J. P. Taylor, "German Diplomatic Documents," *TLS*, no. 2688, Aug. 7, 1953: 507. A. J. P. Taylor, who had read each of the *Große Politik* volumes in 1933–1934, distrusted the work. See Burk, *Troublemaker*, 139, 275.

of documents. Until this is done it would be wiser and more courteous to avoid unsubstantiated innuendoes."[127]

The first reply to Taylor came from E. Llewellyn Woodward and Rohan Butler, both editors of the Foreign Office's series *Documents on British Foreign Policy, 1919–1939,* and members of the advisory committee on *Documents on German Foreign Policy.* They said that they had seen convincing evidence in the materials now in Allied possession that the editors of *Die Große Politik* had been denied important records and that Thimme had omitted passages of certain documents for political reasons.[128] They did not address the question of Thimme's independence; as the editors of the Foreign Office's documents series, they must have been aware of the tension between editorial independence and the official mission of publishing governmental records.[129] It was not without irony that they had cleared their reply to Taylor with the Foreign Office before submitting it to the *TLS.*[130] The *TLS* reviewer also responded and directed criticism at the Political Archives. During the interwar period, the reviewer contended, the Political Archives had misled researchers by removing certain documents from the files. Given the "crypto-Nazi feelings and methods in the Foreign Office in Bonn to-day," the reviewer was not optimistic about what might happen to the captured documents once they were returned.[131]

The debate became less polemical with the publication of letters from James Joll and Isabella M. Massey. Each offered evidence of distortions in *Die Große Politik* drawn from the Stresemann papers.[132] Although the evidence he offered was damaging, Joll tried to be fair to Thimme and his staff. The British document series on the outbreak of the war comprised eleven volumes, he noted, as compared to the forty of *Die Große Politik,* and British records from 1902 on were still not open to researchers. So

---

127 Agnes Headlam-Morley, "German Diplomatic Documents," *TLS,* no. 2689, Aug. 14, 1953: 521. Among her colleagues, Headlam-Morley was considered a Germanophile. See Trevor-Roper to Kluke, Nov. 1, 1955, IfZ Hausarchiv, ID102, vol. 43. Although Herbert Butterfield, Cambridge (Peterhouse), did not intervene in the debate, he had already published a critical assessment of government historians and their privileged access to records two years earlier. See Butterfield, "Official History."

128 Woodward and Butler, "German Diplomatic Documents," *TLS,* nr. 2690, Aug. 21, 1953: 535.

129 A. J. P. Taylor attacked Woodward and Butler as the editors of *Documents on British Foreign Policy* for having "to subordinate their independence to a Government department." See Burk, *Troublemaker,* 271f. On the tension between "objectivity" and the government's *raison d'état,* Zala, *Zensur.*

130 Minutes Passant to Frank Roberts, Aug. 15, including the full text of the editors' letter, Aug. 17, 1953, PRO FO 370/2342 LS5/182.

131 Your Reviewer, *TLS* no. 2690, Aug. 21, 1953: 535. See also HERWIG, "Clio Deceived," 98f.; and the introduction by Georges Bonnin, *Bismarck and the Hohenzollern Candidature,* where other censorship practices are documented.

132 Massey, *TLS,* no. 2693, Sept. 11, 1953, and *TLS,* no. 2698, Oct. 16, 1953.

long as those records were not available, *Die Große Politik* would remain indispensible.[133] German historians followed the debate with astonishment. "If that which is presented in the letters is all that compilers have to show for months of drawn-out discussion [even though] the entire material has been available to them for a long time," Fritz Ernst commented, "then it is not very much." British criticism of *Die Große Politik*, he concluded, was not adequate justification for refusing to return the documents.[134] Hans Andres simply commented that "poor Thimme [had] made the irredeemable mistake of not publishing the entire Political Archives."[135]

The timing of the *TLS* review of volume 5 of *Documents on German Foreign Policy* was almost certainly no accident. Developments in the negotiations with West Germany on returning documents had often prompted the British historians associated with the project to threaten to resign and take their case to the public.[136] They were confident of having the complete support of James Passant, who had repeatedly presented their position to Patrick J. Hancock at the Foreign Office. The *TLS* review and the resulting controversy came precisely at a point when things were looking very bleak for the historians: having secured Gymnich Castle, the Auswärtiges Amt had prepared the way for the transfer of the project to Germany. Officials at the State Department wanted to accept the offer and thus increased pressure on the Foreign Office. Senior British officials were indeed willing to go along. Opposition from John Wheeler-Bennett, Margaret Lambert, and James Passant did not prevent the Central Department from opening talks with the Auswärtiges Amt on the details of a transfer and the guarantee of access. The only way to throw a wrench in the works was to go public. The timing of the *TLS* review (July 31, 1953) and the apparent insider-knowledge it displays suggests that the anonymous reviewer either was associated with or had close ties to the Foreign Office Library or the *Documents on German Foreign Policy* project.

---

133 Joll, "German Diplomatic Documents," *TLS*, no. 2695, Sept. 25, 1953: 613: "And even if more cases of Thimme's deliberate suppression of documents come to light, the *Grosse Politik* will remain one of the most important and valuable publications of its kind.... So we are in fact far better served with German material than with British, for there are only 11 volumes of published British documents as compared with 40 of the *Grosse Politik*.... When our own archives are available up to 1918 to the extent to which the German records have become through force of circumstances, we shall then be in a stronger position to criticize German editorial methods."

134 Ernst, "Londoner Diskussion." Ernst could not have known that the cross-check of *Die Große Politik* never took place on the scale desired by the British and French since the Americans opposed the idea. Therefore, the months had not really been used for the work.

135 Andres to Paul Kluke, Nov. 6, 1953, PA/AA, B118, vol. 487.

136 Gifford, AmEmb London, to Sec State, no. 3433, Dec. 19, 1952, NA RG 59, CDF 1950–54, 862.423/12-1952.

The debate in the columns of the *TLS* corroborated the view widespread among its readers that the Weimar government had contributed to the falsification of history, and that charge was frequently repeated in the ensuing public discussion of the captured documents. The publisher of the *Daily Mail* echoed it when he protested to Foreign Secretary Harold Macmillan in 1955 about the return of records from Whaddon Hall: "The Germans told the most appalling lies about their share in the affairs leading up to 1914. . . . They quite unscrupulously altered and suppressed documents to suit their theme, which was of course that Germany was in no way to blame for the war."[137] Similarly, Lewis Namier made reference to *Die Große Politik* in voicing concern about the early volumes of the Auswärtiges Amt's series *Akten zur deutschen auswärtigen Politik (ADAP)*, the continuation of *Documents on German Foreign Policy*. In 1959, he advised the British not to participate in this four-country, German-led project. "In the end, the Allied historians would have to cover with their names and authority manipulations undertaken by the Germans in selecting documents for publication."[138] Such strong words were out of step with the times, however, and did not go unchallenged.[139] Nevertheless, the accusation of German editorial tampering continued to be heard on occasion.[140]

The Continuation of the "World War of Documents"? The *TLS* episode throws the fissured relationship between some British and German historians into sharp relief and tells us something about mutual perceptions among these scholars. The historian D. C. Watt was the first to point out that the British historians opposed to returning the captured German documents always linked their opposition to the war-guilt debate and the alleged misrepresentations in *Die Große Politik*. Watt sees a "ferocious hostility towards Germany inherent in [this] generation of senior [British] historians" who had

---

137 Arthur Gore to Harold Macmillan, June 27, 1955, PRO FO 370/2430 LS5/67.

138 Lewis Namier to Cecil Parrott, Library, FO, May 14, 1959, PRO FO 370/2569 LS5/28. In a similar vein, the negative statement by Rohan Butler, May 13, 1959, ibid., LS5/27: "The Germans would doubtless like to combine the best of both worlds, namely, control of their own archives with an ex-allied rubber stamp of respectability."

139 "I came away unconvinced by Namier, owing to a perhaps unworthy suspicion that his distrust of all Germans amounts to prejudice." Sir James Butler, Cabinet Office, to Parrott, June 17, 1959, PRO FO 370/2569 LS5/40.

140 In 1964, Raymond Sontag asked about the exact procedure for selecting documents for the ADAP and about guarantees "against the possibility of the German editors' hiding or concealing documents of critical importance." Summary Minutes [of the] Meeting of the [US] Advisory Committee on Documents on German Foreign Policy, Dec. 30, 1964, Hale Papers, box 10, folder 14. Gatzke, "Quadripartite Project," 333, called the microfilms of German records stored in London and Washington "added insurance." See also, "Historical Truth," *Manchester Guardian*, May 28, 1956, including the letter to the editor dated June 5, 1956.

apparently not forgiven the Germans for their scholarly coup in publishing the pre-1914 diplomatic documents.[141] This argument suggests a reading of the debate on *Die Große Politik* as a continuation of the interwar battle over war guilt – a continuation, as it were, of the "world war of documents" made possible and spurred on by the shift in control of the source materials in which the *Documents on German Foreign Policy* project becomes a direct response to *Die Große Politik*. But as much as the resentment of some British historians towards their German colleagues was rooted in the interwar years, World War II had fundamentally changed the stakes in the debate on the origins of World War I.

The involvement of British scholars with the war effort dates from its outbreak in August 1914 when British historians participated in war propaganda. They took up the question of responsibility for the war almost at once, and they reflected common opinion by ascribing responsibility to the German and Austro-Hungarian empires.[142] The growing criticism of the Versailles peace settlement sparked a re-evaluation of the war-guilt question, however. George P. Gooch was the most prominent historian to question the consensus on the issue. He argued that the secret diplomacy conducted by all of the nations involved was responsible for the war: the "sole guilt" of Germany gave way to the "common guilt" of the main actors. Gooch adapted Lloyd George's comment in his memoirs in which he stated Europe was sliding into a war as a result of a web of fateful entanglements and not the intentional actions of certain politicians or military leaders.[143] Relieving Germany of sole responsibility for the war served the interests of British foreign policy. It allowed Britain to support the Weimar Republic on the international stage and to groom it as a counterbalance to France in the League of Nations. The revisionist interpretations also ended up playing an important role in justifying British appeasement policy toward Hitler. Historian Harold Temperly called the annexation of Austria unavoidable and the Munich Agreement a type of compensation for Versailles. Even after

---

141 See the key sentences in Watt, "British Historians," 179: "Proposals to return the archives to Germany ran into the bitter opposition of . . . senior British historians. . . . The memoranda they submitted to [E. J. Passant] . . . both illustrate and, in part, explain the ferocious hostility towards Germany inherent in their generation of senior historians. They demonstrate in addition that this hostility was rooted, not in any ideological hostility towards Nazism, but in the continuation of attitudes formed by the War Guilt controversy over the origins of the First World War, and the damage they believe to have been caused to British interests by the willingness of American historians of European diplomacy (and of 'informed' American opinion) to accept the German case."

142 Hadsel, "Gooch," 271f.; Pogge von Strandmann, "Mobilizing Public Opinion"; Pogge von Strandmann, "Britische Historiker," 929–33; Sharp, "Some Relevant Historians"; Urbach, "Zeitgeist," 173.

143 Jäger, *Historische Forschung*, 110f.; Pogge von Strandmann, "Britische Historiker," 934–6.

the start of the Second World War, Gooch still defended the legitimacy of appeasement politics.[144]

The political divide between supporters and opponents of appeasement among British diplomatic historians persisted after 1945. Assessments of the causes of World War I were closely bound up with views on British politics in the years 1938–39 and the outbreak of World War II. The historians united in trying to prevent the return of the captured documents shared common views on the recent past and the political debates of the late 1930s. Lewis Namier, John Wheeler-Bennett, Rohan Butler, and E. Llewellyn Woodward, for example, adhered to the view espoused in Allied wartime propaganda that National Socialism was the logical, almost predetermined consequence of developments that began with Luther, or, at the very latest, Bismarck.[145] Butler and Namier had each put forward this reading of German history. During the war, Namier was still vehemently attacking G. P. Gooch for his evaluation of the origins of the 1914 conflict. His criticism conflated Gooch's positions on World War I with his stance on Britain's policy toward Germany in the late 1930s: "[In 1914] Britain was threatened, and appeasement at any price would have been no less dangerous in the years before 1914 than it proved 25 years later. From that we were saved by the statesmen who made the Triple Entente – apparently to Dr. Gooch's lasting regret."[146] E. Llewellyn Woodward, one observer later recalled, was even "obsessed by the idea that somewhere in the German records before 1914 there must be a contemporary equivalent to the Hossbach memorandum."[147] At the end of the 1930s, John Wheeler-Bennett joined the ranks of Tory dissidents associated with Churchill and became a strong opponent of appeasement.[148] Like Namier, his scholarly mentor, Wheeler-Bennett took an uncompromising stance concerning the German conservative resistance to Hitler. His views on Stauffenberg and his fellow conspirators changed little in the years after July 20, 1944. Hitler's would-be assassins, he thought, were exponents of Prussian-German militarism

---

144 Cline, "British Historians"; Pogge von Strandmann, "Britische Historiker," 935; Steiner, "Historian and the Foreign Office," 50.

145 Along those lines see Rohan Butler, *Roots of National Socialism* (London, 1941). This depiction of German history as a linear progression "from Luther to Hitler" is often labeled "Vansittartism" (named after the British diplomat Lord Vansittart). A review of the various positions on Germany in the United States and Great Britain is found in Eckert, *Feindbilder im Wandel*, 41–54; Goldman, "Controversy over 'Vansittartism'"; Hönicke, "'Know Your Enemy'"; Später, *Vansittart*, 125–64, 246–9.

146 Namier's review of Gooch's *Studies in Diplomacy* (1942), quote taken from Rose, *Lewis Namier and Zionism*, 137. See also Später, *Vansittart*, 217–230; Urbach, "Zeitgeist," 173f.

147 Letter from D. C. Watt to author, Aug. 22, 2001, 5.

148 Bullock, [obituary] "Wheeler-Bennett," 813f.

who were prepared to abandon the Third Reich not because they were disgusted by it but because it was heading toward defeat. Wheeler-Bennett's book *Nemesis of Power* (1954) on the Machiavellian politics of the German army in the years from 1918 to 1945 arrived in British bookshops just in time to influence the debate on West German rearmament.[149] Wheeler-Bennett and like-minded historians continued in the 1950s to promote Churchill's condemnation of Neville Chamberlain's foreign policy in the 1930s.[150] The historical-political agenda pursued by these historians went far beyond simply revisiting the war-guilt question in the 1950s. The resistance to the return of the German diplomatic records was a consequence of this agenda. The results from cross-checking *Große Politik* with the original documents provided the rationale for the bitter resistance to the return of the files. Yet it had been precisely for this purpose that these results had been sought after in the first place.

The *scholarly* reasons for a re-examination of *Die Große Politik*, which did indeed exist, were lost in the political fray. From the time of the collection's publication, many foreign scholars had suspected that its editors had manipulated the source materials for political purposes.[151] Even if the results of the spot check of documents in *Die Große Politik* had not come in so handy for the fight against returning the captured records, the prominence of *Die Große Politik* would have justified the check of the published texts against the original documents. In its scope and the timing of its appearance (1922–1927), this edition represented the most important source for the study of the origins of World War I. It played a dominant role not only in research but also in teaching. "And indeed," wrote A. J. P. Taylor in 1949, "English and American universities are still teaching a German version of events or at best teaching within a German pattern."[152] That Taylor did not cite the collection in his *The Struggle for Mastery in Europe* (1954) was

---

149 Kettenacker, "Haltung der Westalliierten," 22f., 30f.; Schlie, "Das Ausland und die deutsche Opposition," 162; Watt, "Perceptions of German History," 153. See also the review of *Nemesis of Power* by Barthel, "Problematik zeitgeschichtlichen Verstehens," 611, 614, 618–24.

150 The intransigence exhibited by Wheeler-Bennett in his evaluation of the conservative resistance was something Churchill himself could not afford as a supporter of West German rearmament. On Churchill's views of history, see Reynolds, *In Command of History*. An example for the wrangling over the assessment of appeasement in the 1950s is in Beck, "Politicians versus Historians." A discussion on Namier's publications after 1945 is in Watt, "Namier and Contemporary European History."

151 Bourgeois, "Les Archives d'État" (1927); Woodward, *Short Journey*, 238 (1942). Also, Heinemann, *Verdrängte Niederlage*, 85; Thimme, *Friedrich Thimme – Briefe*, 44f.; Zala, *Zensur*, 70–2.

152 A. J. P. Taylor, Foreign Office Archives. "Publishing German Documents," *Manchester Guardian*, July 21, 1949: 5. See also Woodward to Margaret Lambert, Dec. 11, 1952, in Watt, "British Historians," 183.

deemed noteworthy by at least one reviewer.[153] If the long-standing suspicions about *Die Große Politik* could be substantiated, an American historian thought, "then the very foundations of study of that period are shaken, if not demolished and a great deal of modern history will have to be revised in the light of all the relevant German source material."[154]

The suspicions about *Die Große Politik* were only one facet of the reservations many British historians had about their German colleagues during the 1950s. As early as 1942, E. Llewellyn Woodward was pessimistic about the future of historical scholarship in Germany:

Within a decade . . . Germans will try once again the plan which succeeded so well during the interval between the two wars. Once again they will try to 'organize sympathy.' They will ignore the background of diplomatic documents; they will scrape the archives and scratch at every small morsel of evidence which can be twisted into an apology for German guilt in causing the present war. . . . I can guess the main line of German apology. Hitler and a small minority of German national socialists were responsible for the war. The victors of 1918 were responsible for Hitler and national socialism; therefore the victors of 1918 are the real 'war criminals.'[155]

In light of such predictions, it is not surprising that British historians were extremely sensitive to any hint of self-exculpation in German discussions of National Socialism and the war. They took note of the Ranke revival in the late 1940s[156] as well as the efforts of German historians to "export" responsibility for National Socialism by emphasizing its European roots. In explaining the rise of Nazism, they pointed to the Jacobin phase of the French Revolution as a starting point for overzealous nationalism in Europe, and introduction of the masses into politics by way of the Industrial Revolution was seen as a prerequisite for the emergence of fascist movements. National Socialism thus became a product of modernity rather than the outcome of a specifically German course of development.[157] Elements of this interpretation figure prominently in Ritter's *Europa und die deutsche*

---

153 About A. J. P. Taylor's *Struggle for Mastery in Europe 1848–1918* (1954), Asa Briggs writes that "[o]ne of the most interesting features of this book is its refusal to take German interpretations of recent history on trust or to lean too heavily on the massive supports of *Die Grosse Politik*." Quote from Burk, *Troublemaker*, 275.
154 Conyers Read to Bernadotte Schmitt, Oct. 6, 1951, PRO FO 370/2343 LS5/200.
155 Woodward, *Short Journey*, 236–9, 243.
156 Conrad, *Verlorene Nation*, 156. The anonymous reviewer of a volume of Ranke letters, appearing in *TLS*, no. 2519, May 12, 1950, 285f., interpreted the new German interest in Ranke not as a "publishing accident," but "one attempt among many to find normality and self-confidence among their own kind." At the same time, it was an attempt "to evade the responsibilities of the day, as Ranke evaded them."
157 Conrad, *Verlorene Nation*, 171–4, 256–8, 267f.; Iggers, *Deutsche Geschichtswissenschaft*, 341f.; Jäger, *Historische Forschung*, 112; Schulze, *Deutsche Geschichtswissenschaft*, 78, 226f.

Frage (1948), which immediately drew fire from Geoffrey Barraclough of the University of Liverpool. Barraclough called the book a "shameless piece of propaganda" and accused Ritter of writing a state-authorized history.[158] Ritter was not very receptive to such criticism. He considered all British historians – with the exceptions of George P. Gooch and Herbert Butterfield – to be hostile to Germany and Germans.[159] He suspected that Namier was the driving force behind the "basic anti-German attitude" of the *Times Literary Supplement*.[160] He may well have taken all criticism of German historical scholarship from abroad as "summary condemnation,"[161] but his own statements contributed more than a little to his British colleagues' mistrust of German historians.

In fact, Ritter and most other West German historians showed no interest after 1945 in resuming the battle over the origins of World War I. They thought this battle had already been decided in the German historical profession's favor. At the 1949 congress of German historians, Ritter declared that "the fight over the so-called 'war-guilt question' has . . . finally led to the worldwide success of the central German arguments."[162] Lloyd George's concept of Europe 'sliding into war' emerged as the consensus opinion among German historians.[163] That interpretation of events was subsequently endorsed at a bilateral Franco-German conference on schoolbooks in 1951, thereby removing a long-standing bone of contention.[164] Clearly, West German historians considered the issue of responsibility for World War I a closed case. "As irrefutable and self-evident as the 1939 question of guilt was," Wolfgang Benz noted of this consensus, "so adamantly

---

158 Ritter, *Historiker in seinen Briefen*, 460–3, quote in note 2. In this context, see once again the introduction by Kohn, *German History. Some New Views*, esp. 14f., 25f. Barraclough was also critical of the first postwar issue of *Historische Zeitschrift;* one article, he thought, attempted to blame the Western powers for Hitler's rise to power and to make them responsible for the war. See Barraclough's letter to the editor in *Der Monat* 2:17 (February 1950), 535–8. See also Barraclough, "What is the Future of Germany?" Further, Berghahn, "Deutschlandbilder 1945–1961," 242f.; Cornelißen, *Ritter*, 464–8, 490–6; Schulze, *Deutsche Geschichtswissenschaft*, 105f.

159 Carsten, "From Revolutionary Socialism to German History," 37: "I had to explain to Gerhard Ritter, who was firmly convinced that *the* British historians were anti-German, that they had many, very different opinions on the subject of Germany; but Ritter remained unconvinced." See also Cornelißen, *Ritter*, 458, 468f. including n. 225.

160 Ritter to von Trützschler, AA, May 17, 1955, BArch, N1166, NL Ritter, vol. 286

161 Ritter, "Gegenwärtige Lage," 15f.   162 Ibid., 16.

163 Jäger, *Historische Forschung*, 109–14.

164 "Deutsch-französische Vereinbarung über strittige Fragen europäischer Geschichte," *Geschichte in Wissenschaft und Unterricht* 3 (1952), 293: "The documents do not support the imputation that any government or people harbored in 1914 the deliberate will to wage a European war. Mutual mistrust had reached the most intense degree possible, and the belief prevailed in leading circles that war was unavoidable; every side was convinced the other intended to attack, every side accepted the danger of war, and a guarantee for security was seen only to exist in a system of alliances and constant military buildup" On this agreement, see also Cornelißen, *Ritter*, 470–6.

was the taboo of the 1914 question of guilt defended."[165] In this context, *Die Große Politik* suddenly stood as a monument of German historical scholarship. As Ritter observed at the 1949 congress,

Following the collapse of 1918, the German historical profession produced over a course of five years no less than 54 formidable volumes of political records on the historical period leading up to the First World War, in a well-wrought arrangement and carefully annotated. This act, which so astounded the world, and the simultaneously commencement of so-called war-guilt research, which succeeded in asserting its ideas and arguments in all civilized countries, brought forth proof that German historical research does not need to be ponderous to retain its thoroughness and conscientiousness.[166]

Pace Ritter, it was not the "ponderousness" of *Die Große Politik* but rather the editors' arrangement and annotation of documents that had come under criticism. Ritter's remarks are indicative of a change in attitude among German historians toward *Die Große Politik*. Political and scholarly developments in the aftermath of World War II made it opportune for the German historical profession to celebrate *Die Große Politik* as one of its proudest achievements. When the collection was in preparation during the 1920s, however, it was held in little esteem within the profession. Annelise Thimme correctly points out that the leading German professors of history at the time had all turned down the editorship. Although several historians supported by the Auswärtiges Amt's War Guilt Office were awarded honorary degrees for their efforts, the editors *of Die Große Politik* received no such recognition. Moreover, nationalist historians had rejected the republican government's editorial project out of hand.[167]

The new-found respect for *Die Große Politik* after 1945 explains German historians' sensitivity to the findings discussed in the *TLS*. Calling the accuracy and objectivity of *Die Große Politik* into question would undermine its original purpose, namely to refute the claim that Germany bore responsibility for starting World War I. Reopening the debate on the origins of

165 Benz, "Etablierung der Zeitgeschichte," 15. See also the biographical text by Annelise Thimme, "Geprägt von der Geschichte," 206f., in which she paraphrases Hans Rothfels: "Now . . . that the Allies had their hands full with the Second World War, one couldn't roll out the guilt issue of the First World War once again."

166 Gerhard Ritter, Denkschrift betr. planmässige Neuorganisation wissenschaftlicher Studien zur Geschichte der neuesten Zeit, n.d. [Jan. 1949], Hausarchiv IfZ, ID1, vol. 1. Ritter sent the memo, dated Oct. 1, 1949, to the West German Ministry of the Interior. It is found in Ritter, *Politischer Historiker*, 456–9, albeit without the passage quoted here.

167 Thimme, *Friedrich Thimme – Briefe*, 44–6. Jäger, *Historische Forschung*, 106, suspects that decidedly anti-republican historians distanced themselves from projects supported by the Auswärtiges Amt because they did not see a link being made between the fight against the Allied theory of war guilt and the stab-in-the-back legend. In other words, the Auswärtiges Amt was not radical enough for them.

World War I would, in turn, jeopardize the post-1945 consensus among West German historians on the place of National Socialism in German history. Most had responded to the urgent task of explaining the origins of Nazism by arguing that the Nazi period was a historical aberration. That interpretation left earlier eras free of taint and stood in defiant opposition to the equally ahistorical "Luther to Hitler" argument of Allied wartime propaganda.[168]

If the post-1945 consensus on the "slide-into-war" argument broke down, the main burden of responsibility for World War I would again fall to Germany and, as a consequence, the interpretation of National Socialism as a break with German tradition would be fatally undermined. Foreign criticism of *Die Große Politik* threatened to do just that. And the West Germans could not simply shrug off criticism from scholars in Great Britain or the United States as "agitation," as they could the views of East German historians, not least because the allegations of British and American historians rested on evidence from German records, the relevance of which West German historians themselves had confirmed with their repeated demands for their return.

It was still possible for West German historians to forestall a revival of the war-guilt debate, but doing so required substantial effort and energy. Shortly before the 1955 International Congress of Historical Sciences in Rome, Hermann Aubin, then chairman of the Association of German Historians, gave his colleague Theodor Schieder some instructions. Schieder was slated to chair a panel that was to include a presentation on reopening the war-guilt question. Warning that "difficulties" might arise from that presentation, Aubin encouraged Schieder to intervene as chairperson if need be. Schieder could cut off "derailments that distracted from the scholarly level." In a real emergency, he could take the floor himself; moreover, Schieder could count on Aubin to take steps to ensure "that in all sections, where a political derailment appears possible, several of us are present to be able to take the floor."[169] In light of such strategic choreography for a conference, it becomes possible to see why Fritz Fischer's *Griff nach der Weltmacht* (1961) immediately took on the dimensions of a "national

168 For this much discussed issue, see Benz, "Etablierung der Zeitgeschichte"; Iggers, "Deutsche Geschichtswissenschaft," 338–47, 349; Kwiet, "NS-Zeit in der westdeutschen Forschung"; Conrad, *Verlorene Nation*, 231f., points out the symbolism evident in establishing the IfZ outside the institutional framework of a university: by doing so, the "Third Reich" was being extracted from university research, just as it was thought to exist "outside" of German national history.

169 Aubin, on the letterhead of the historians association, to Schieder, Aug. 8, 1955, BArch N1188, NL Schieder, vol. 448. According to Erdmann, *Ökumene der Historiker*, 300, n. 3, the title of the section was "Liberalism and Structural Changes in modern society from the 19th to the 20th century." The book does not offer any additional information on the actual section proceedings.

catastrophe" for national-conservative historians.[170] Aubin was clearly of the opinion "that it is indeed to the credit of our contemporary historical research that it mastered the war-guilt question after 1919. It must do so again, if necessary, or if similar questions arise for the Second World War."[171] And was that not precisely the reason why the Allies had initiated the *Documents on German Foreign Policy* project?

CONTEMPORARY HISTORY

In a programmatic essay published in 1953, Hans Rothfels defined contemporary history as the study of "the era of those living and its scholarly treatment."[172] As he identified the contemporary era with his own lifetime, Rothfels, as other scholars have noted, effectively delineated contemporary history's research subjects.[173] By taking the historian's present as the point of reference, contemporary history received a generational component which opened up the discipline to continuous rejuvenation, reconstituting the scope and content of contemporary history with each respective generations of scholars.[174]

Establishing contemporary history as a field of research after 1945 took more than merely defining its scope, however. The emerging subdiscipline was not necessarily welcomed by specialists in other, more venerable branches of the discipline. The main charge against it was that of "presentism." Contemporary history, it was held, confronted researchers with the epistemological challenge of transcending their own memories and experiences of the period they were studying. Historians dealing with more chronologically remote periods called contemporary history a "contradiction in terms" and reminded their colleagues that it was the ideal of "objectivity" that united the profession.[175]

170 Büro Staatsekretär, Schönfeld, memo to be presented to the State Secretary, Dec. 6. 1961: The director of the Political Archives, Johannes Ullrich, reported to "have received a call from Prof. Schieder, Cologne, who brought up the Fischer book on the issue of war guilt for the First World War and called this work a 'national catastrophe.'" PA/AA, B 2, Ref. 117, vol. 72 (fiche 157). Theodor Schieder later emphatically denied having made this call during the debate on the authenticity of the Riezler diaries. See his letter to the editor in *Die Zeit*, Aug. 12, 1983: 27.
171 Aubin to Schieder, Aug. 8, 1955, BArch N1188, NL Schieder, vol. 448.
172 Rothfels, "Zeitgeschichte als Aufgabe," 2. The essay appeared in the first issue of *Vierteljahrshefte für Zeitgeschichte*.
173 Conrad, *Verlorene Nation*, 225.
174 Koselleck, "Stetigkeit und Wandel aller Zeitgeschichten," 246, 257; Hockerts, "Zeitgeschichte in Deutschland," 19; on Bracher's definition, see ibid., 6. Schwarz, "Neueste Zeitgeschichte," 8. Further, Geyer, "Im Schatten der NS-Zeit," 26f.
175 For contemporary skepticism on the claim of objectivity, see Reichmann, "Study of Contemporary History as Moral Duty," in *On the Track of Tyranny*, 191f. A broader discussion of the criticism of contemporary history in Eckert, "Transnational Beginnings."

West German contemporary historians of the 1950s sought to deflect the charge of presentism by remaining conservative in their methodology. Rothfels warned them not to deviate from established historical methods and to strive for objectivity. He advocated a historicist "mental discipline" to create distance to the object of study, and insisted that the source materials of contemporary history be subjected to "that rigorous examination of authenticity and trustworthiness, the principles of which have been fully developed during the last 150 years."[176] At the same time, he argued that the overlap between the contemporary historian's period of research and own lifetime was by no means a disadvantage. Chronological proximity to one's period of study gave the contemporary historian "unique leverage" because he did not need first to immerse himself in the "spirit of the times." It was much easier for contemporaries to put themselves into the shoes of both those who acted and those who suffered than it was for historians who approached their research topic "from a distance" and through "historical intuition."[177] Reliving the past, Munich historian Paul Kluke agreed, "becomes even more intense, vivid, [and] convincing the closer we are to the era we want to portray."[178]

This line of argument in response to critics of contemporary history within the German historical profession also provided a means to determine who could speak authoritatively about it. If the epistemological prerequisites for understanding were tied to personal experience, historical truth, particularly with regard to National Socialism, was revealed primarily to "those people who have had the dubious honor of personally living and suffering through the events, because a true understanding can only be purchased with the gravity of fate." Foreigners and emigrants were thus excluded by definition from ever understanding life under National Socialism, and this applied specifically to Americans, who lived "in the completely different circumstances of a free people." They were therefore inherently unable to grasp "the utterly different preconditions of all decisions in National Socialist Germany."[179]

The charge of presentism was also bound up with the problem of the unavailability of source material. To enter the canon of serious historical scholarship, research had to be based on primary sources, which in other

---

176 Rothfels, "Zeitgeschichte als Aufgabe," 4. Conrad, *Verlorene Nation*, 239–47, rightfully points to the strong elements of historicism that made a (re-)appearance in postwar West German contemporary history.

177 Rothfels, "Zeitgeschichte als Aufgabe," 6.   178 Kluke, "Aufgaben und Methoden," 7432.

179 Kluke, "Aufgaben und Methoden," 7437; similarly, Fritz Ernst, "Blick auf Deutschland," 193, 207; Hermann Aubin, Chairman, Association of German Historians, to Auswärtiges Amt, Political Department, May 14, 1956, PA/AA, B118, vol. 510.

historical disciplines usually meant official state records. If such sources were not available for a particular period, that period could obviously not be the subject of historical scholarship.[180] This second criticism of contemporary history touched directly on the problem of the captured documents. These records had been produced by ministries, governmental agencies, and other official bodies. If such materials were to become available, specialists in contemporary history would be in a position to employ methods similar to those of their colleagues studying more remote periods of history. They could, in other words, effectively counter the charge of presentism, at least as far as the scarcity of sources was concerned. Practitioners of contemporary history therefore entered the fray over access to the captured German records.

The Institute of Contemporary History and the Problem of Sources

The founding of the Institute . . . is one of those duties of the state, which, if not fulfilled, calls into question the purpose of the entire apparatus of the state.[181]

The establishment of the Deutsches Institut für Geschichte der natio-nalsozialistischen Zeit (German Institute for the History of the National Socialist Period), as the IfZ was originally called, was a protracted project. Given the conflicts over financing, scholarly focus, and views on how to deal with the Nazi past, it was anything but certain that the institute would ever open its doors, much less establish itself firmly on the West German academic landscape – as it, in fact, managed to do within a matter of years. An effort to found such an institute was launched in 1947. Plans for financing the project were undermined, however, by the currency reform of 1948. With the exception of Bavaria, the state governments were reluctant to make firm commitments to funding research on the Nazi era.[182] The institute was formally established on September 11, 1950. The constitutive meeting failed, however, to resolve several key questions about the institute's mission and work. What did it mean to account for Germany's Nazi

180 In 1960, historian Peter Rassow of the University of Cologne put it this way: "Historical eras in the scholarly sense are those for which the historian has unhindered access to the unprinted sources as well." Quoted in Conrad, *Verlorene Nation,* 227, 220–3, 227–9.
181 Hermann L. Brill, Head of the State Chancery in Hesse, to Staatsminister Anton Pfeiffer, Head of the State Chancery in Bavaria, July 7, 1948, IfZ Hausarchiv, ID1, vol. 1.
182 On the history of establishing the institute, see Auerbach, "Gründung des Instituts"; Benz, "Etablierung der Zeitgeschichte," 18–24; Conrad, *Verlorene Nation,* 229–32; Cornelißen, *Ritter,* 534–9; Cornelißen, "Institutionalisierung der Zeitgeschichte," 350–4; Gimbel, "Origins of the Institut"; Möller, "Institut für Zeitgeschichte," 7–27, passim; Schulze, *Deutsche Geschichtswissenschaft,* 229–39.

past? How did scholarly research and *Volkspädagogik* (educating the public) relate to one another? Would the institute, although state funded, be able to establish its scholarly independence? Would the institute eventually become a "Mecca for researchers of contemporary history" or the "Vatican of re-education"?[183] Not surprisingly, the tensions over the objectives and character of the institute re-emerged during the selection of personnel. Following a fierce dispute, the board of trustees and the advisory board agreed on a compromise candidate for the post of secretary general: Hermann Mau, a medievalist from Leipzig. Mau headed the institute from February 1951 until his death in October 1952.[184] Helmut Krausnick then served as interim director until Paul Kluke was appointed to the post in 1953.[185]

---

183 The phrases are found in Röder/Weiß/Lankheit, "Archiv des Instituts," 109.

184 Hermann Mau (1913–1952) earned his PhD in 1941 in Leipzig; his doctoral adviser was Hermann Heimpel. From 1940–1941, he was *Assistent* at the History Seminar, University of Leipzig; in May 1941, he followed Heimpel to the Reich University at Strasbourg. In 1944, he earned his habilitation at Strasbourg with the thesis "Das Reich und Cluny" (The Reich and Cluny), which evolved, in his words, "by scrutinizing the excessive National Socialist interpretation of the concept of the Reich." His formal relationship to the NSDAP amounted to a membership in the National Socialist University Lecturers League. Mau writes: "My fundamental opposition to National Socialism became clear to me back in 1931 during the altercation with my older brother, who went the opposite direction and later became a small party functionary. Nothing ever changed about this opposition. However, I was not part of the German resistance. I survived the years rather unscathed by assuming the role in 1933 of the unpolitical individual." After the war, he received a temporary teaching post for medieval history in 1946 in Leipzig. He joined the CDU-East and became involved in establishing a CDU group at the Leipzig university. For these political activities, he was imprisoned for a month. After his release, he fled to the West in 1948 and established a student and worker dormitory in Munich that he ran. In 1950, he received his venia legendi, the right to teach, for modern history at the University of Munich. On February 1, 1951, he became the director of the IfZ. He was, as Karl Buchheim recalls, the ideal compromise candidate in such a highly politicized position. Mau died on October 25, 1952, in an automobile accident. See the detailed CV of Hermann Mau, n.d. [1950], in IfZ Hausarchiv, ID1, vol. 5; H. Buchheim, "Hermann Mau"; K. Buchheim, "Sächsische Lebensgeschichte," 258f.; Möller, "Institut für Zeitgeschichte," 23f.; Schulze, *Deutsche Geschichtswissenschaft*, 237f.

185 Paul Kluke (1908–1990) earned his PhD in 1931 from the University of Berlin with the thesis "Heeresaufbau und Heerespolitik Englands vom Burenkrieg zum Weltkrieg" (Army Structure and Policy in England from the Boer War to the World War) and also passed his state examinations to teach history and English in 1932. Following a short period as an *Assistent* to Hermann Oncken, he switched to the Central Office for Postwar History in Postdam, which was administered by the Prussian Archival Administration under Albert Brackmann. Between October 1939 and September 1940, he evaluated captured Polish records in Berlin. Because his wife was Jewish, he was not permitted to publish any scholarly work. In the fall of 1944, he was arrested and sent to a forced labor camp. After the war, he taught school for a short while, then changed jobs to work in the Ministerial Document Branch of the Berliner Document Center, where, as the head archivist for the State Department-Foreign Office team, he coordinated the work done by German employees on organizing diplomatic records. In Winter Semester 1949/50, he earned his habilitation degree in modern history at the Free University Berlin with a thesis on "Die Rheinische Autonomiebewegung 1918-1919" (The Rhenish Autonomy Movement, 1918–1919). The work was never published "in light of the actuality of the topic for foreign policy [in the early 1950s], for the study of which Adenauer's working files were also used." From 1953 to 1959, Kluke was the director of the IfZ, from 1975 to 1977 the founding director of the German Historical Institute in

The initial plans for the institute were shaped by the fact that the records of the NSDAP party offices were stored in Munich, albeit in American custody. Tapping into that repository seemed an obvious move,[186] and officials from the Bavarian State Chancellery blithely approached the issue as if a simple letter addressed to the Munich Collecting Point would be all that was needed to get the papers they sought.[187] When matters turned out to be a bit more complicated, the founders of the institute shifted their focus. The institute was not being founded in order to study an existing collection of documents; its first task, rather, would be to collect source materials.[188] Gerhard Kroll, a Bavarian politician who briefly served as interim director of the institute, went as far as to emphasize that, "Not the writing of history but its documentation is our prime concern."[189] However, the beginnings of an archive for contemporary history – the ultimate goal of the original idea – did not go unchallenged. Archivists protested that the institute threatened to intrude upon the prerogative of state archives. A compromise was reached in 1950 whereby the institute was designated a *Zentralnachweisstelle*, a central documentation office. It would collect copies of official documents, not originals, as well as the private papers of individuals, eyewitness reports, and transcripts of documents. It would also be responsible for determining the whereabouts of Nazi-era records worldwide.[190] In a card catalog designed for this purpose, archivist Anton Hoch compiled all available information on Nazi records, the majority of which were not yet accessible to researchers.[191] The institute enjoyed the full backing of U.S. High Commissioner John J. McCloy in this pursuit. He ordered that "all possible assistance be extended [to] the German Institute for the History of the National Socialist Period . . . to enable it to gain access to the materials

London. Quote in Paul Kluke, Curriculum Vitae, December 1954, BArch, N1213, NL Rothfels, vol. 1; further, Seier, [obituary] "Kluke."

186 Auerbach, "Gründung des Instituts," 529.

187 Officials requested that "all document material relevant to the intended purpose" of the institute yet to be established be "submitted, in as far as it is no longer needed by American agencies. The material would be held in trust here and turned over to the institute as soon as it comes to life." Fritz Baer, State Chancery of Bavaria, to Collecting Point München, Arcisstraße, Oct. 7, 1948, IfZ Hausarchiv ID1, vol. 1.

188 The task of collecting research materials was pushed energetically, particularly by the representatives of Hesse, Hermann L. Brill und Culture Minister Erwin Stein. See Cornelißen, *Ritter*, 534f., n. 49. Gerhard Ritter had hoped the institute would analyze the Nuremberg records, a task that – in his opinion – should have been the main purpose of the institute. Ritter to IfZ, June 16, 1953, IfZ Hausarchiv, ID102, vol. 16.

189 Kroll to Werner Hilpert, Finance Minister of Hessian, July 28, 1949, IfZ Hausarchiv, ID1, vol. 1.

190 Auerbach, "Gründung des Instituts," 539; Röder/Weiß/Lankheit, "Archiv des IfZ," 106f.; Schulze, *Deutsche Geschichtswissenschaft*, 235f. See also the Minutes of the 28th Annual Meeting of German Archivists in Wiesbaden, May 31, 1949, Point IV, "Archivalische Quellen zur jüngsten deutschen Vergangenheit", GStA, HA I, Rep. 178 B 1.3., vol. 1380; see also *Archivar* 2:2 (1949), 47f.

191 This card catalogue no longer exists. Information from the IfZ archives, Sept. 15, 2000.

it requires."[192] From the High Commission's reference library, the institute received a collection of Nazi brochures and books. The Americans also supplied copies of the proceedings of the Nuremberg trials.[193]

Although its collections grew continuously, the institute was not able to gain access to certain important groups of materials. The appearance of the first volume of *Documents on German Foreign Policy* in 1949 and the footnotes in several articles by American and British historians painfully reminded German historians that the most important sources on Germany's recent past were still off-limits to them.[194] The demand for equal access to the records became intertwined with the argument that those who had experienced National Socialism firsthand could most authoritatively analyze life and politics under Hitler. "Someone who has lived in a dictatorship knows what resistance means there," wrote Fritz Ernst in a review of American publications on Germany's recent history, adding that "someone who has never lived in a dictatorship will find this hard to understand."[195] Pointing to international interest in contemporary history, Gerhard Ritter noted that, "Today all countries publish their records very quickly." He critically added, however,

we were not even asked whether we also want to do this or not. What we do not publish is published and interpreted by foreigners, who also seized our archives. But even with best intention to present the truth, no foreigner will understand German things from within as well as we do ourselves, and he will never be able to fend off the suspicion or prejudice that he is not telling the whole truth; at least among those who do not want to hear.[196]

Ritter was not alone in thinking the German public might not be open to accounts of the German past written outside of Germany. Many German historians argued that interpretations from abroad were likely to be condemned as re-education measures. Such worries about the popular reception of foreign scholarship went hand-in-hand with doubts about the value of the documentation assembled for the Nuremberg trials as a source for contemporary history. Such doubts were not prompted by the methodological

---

192 Glenn C. Wolfe, Director, Office of Administration, HICOG, Staff Announcement no. 199, June 5, 1951, LoC Central File, box 398. Hermann Mau only learned of McCloy's order during his trip to the United States in the summer of 1951. See Journal Mau, entry 48, July 13, 1951, IfZ Hausarchiv, ID101, vol. 4.

193 Auerbach, "Gründung des Instituts," 540. Cornelißen, *Ritter*, 523.

194 Ernst, "Blick auf Deutschland," 208–11; Mommsen, "Deutsche Archivalien im Ausland." German observers were not yet aware that Anglo-American researchers too had only limited access to the records.

195 Ernst, "Blick auf Deutschland," 211.

196 Ritter, [memo] Über die Notwendigkeit der beschleunigten Errichtung eines zentralen Instituts für die Geschichte der jüngsten Vergangenheit, IfZ Hausarchiv, ID1, vol. 1.

challenges in using court records, but by a general suspicion of a body of material compiled by the victors. Hermann Mau thought that these records were better than nothing but warned,

Only when [the German historical profession] itself can undertake the inspection and selection of documents will it be able to rise above the suspicion that it has been limited in its depiction of the history of National Socialism to sources that were selected by non-German bodies using something other than strictly scholarly criteria. Such a suspicion would, from the start, negate the results of all efforts at writing the history of the National Socialist period from having any impact on the German public.[197]

Whereas Ritter often took a nationalistic tone in arguing that the right of interpreting the recent German past should be reserved for Germans – or, better yet, himself – Mau, Kluke, and the other IfZ historians assumed a more conciliatory tone toward their foreign colleagues. Rather than question the ability of British and American scholars to understand the German past, they focused on gaining access to Nazi-era records, wherever they might be held. This more pragmatic attitude was evident, for example, in a letter Karl Buchheim wrote to Fritz T. Epstein:

Neither do I wish to represent the view of those mocking voices who say that the Germans will more likely be allowed to deploy 100 divisions again before they ever get their records back, nor do I think that the speedy return of records is the unconditional prerequisite for German history writing. However, I am firmly convinced that it would be advantageous if [German historiography] would be accommodated in some appreciative way.[198]

In the hope of gaining access to the documents in American possession, the institute sought potential supporters in the High Commission and tried to find funding for research trips to the United States. When Bernard Noble was visiting Germany in March 1951, Mau used the opportunity to secure an invitation to the United States for himself.[199] Backed by Shepard Stone, the director of the public affairs division at HICOG, Mau traveled for seven weeks throughout the United States in the summer of 1951.[200]

Hermann Mau's Trip to the United States in 1951. Noble had invited Mau without first consulting the other government agencies involved with the

197 Hermann Mau, [memorandum for Bernard Noble], Washington, D.C., June 12, 1951, NA RG 59, CDF 1950–54, box 5176.
198 Buchheim to Epstein, Oct. 18, 1950, IfZ Hausarchiv, ID102, vol. 37.
199 Memo Mau, Mar. 14, 1951; Mau to Noble, Apr. 16, 1951, both in: IfZ Hausarchiv ID102, vol. 46.
200 Stone financed the trip from his budget. McCloy [Stone] to SecState, no. 8136, Apr. 9, 1951; Acheson to HICOG, no. 6950, Apr. 16, 1951, both in NA RG 59, CDF 1950–54, 862.423/4–951. The trip lasted from June 6 to July 25, 1951.

captured German records, and the trip would for that reason likely have been canceled if Mau had not had McCloy's support. Neither the Library of Congress nor the Departmental Records Branch (DRB) wanted to play host to such a visitor while the policy paper on the documents was still in the works. Officials at the DRB warned Noble that, without previous consultation with the British, they could not allow Mau to see classified holdings.[201] Noble could not, however, postpone Mau's visit, if for no other reason than McCloy's insistence. Mau, according to the High Commissioner, had been tasked by Adenauer to look for records documenting the German persecution of Jews. If Mau's trip did not take place, the Americans would be forfeiting an important opportunity to enlighten the Germans.[202]

Mau arrived in Washington in early June 1951. He made the situation easier for his hosts by carefully avoiding the issue of the documents' return. Mau emphasized that his institution was interested above all in access and would be happy with copies of source materials. Domestic political matters, particularly the history of the Nazi party, were the IfZ's main concern; foreign policy, the Wehrmacht, and the war were, Mau explained, of only secondary interest to the institute. Accordingly, he was most interested in the records of the Ministries of the Interior, Justice, and Propaganda, the Reich Security Main Office, the Reich Chancellery, and the national leadership of the NSDAP and the party's affiliated organizations.[203] Mau's host arranged a visit to the Library of Congress, where he was given free access to the stacks. He also had the opportunity to work in the National Archives and to visit the Hoover Institution in California, but he was not permitted to visit the DRB because confirmation of British consent had not yet arrived.[204]

While Mau was in the United States, the IfZ issued its first publication, *Hitlers Tischgespräche im Führerhauptquartier 1941–1942*, an edition of Hitler's table talk as recorded by two mid-level officials stationed at his

201 Harry J. Krould, Chief, European Affairs Division, to Dan Lacy, Deputy Chief Assistant Librarian, May 2, 1951, LoC Central File, box 398; Noble to Kellermann, May 25, 1951, NA RG 59, CDF 1950–54, 862.423/5–2551; DRB Journal of Significant Events, May 31, 1951, entry by Philipp P. Brower, NA RG 407, entry 375, box 1.
202 Acheson, SecState, to HICOG, no. 8123, May 31, 1951, NA RG 59, CDF 1950–54, 862.423/5–2851; McCloy to State, no. 9744, NA RG 59, CDF 1950–54, 862.423/6–351. Both letters are quoted in Brochhagen, *Nach Nürnberg*, 56, albeit in incorrect sequence, therefore presented in the wrong context. See also Hermann Mau, [memorandum for Bernard Noble], Washington, D.C., June 12, 1951, NA RG 59, CDF 1950–54, box 5176: He writes that the West German government had commissioned him "to look out for documents that are characteristic for the inhumane character of the National Socialist regime and are suitable for early publication in Germany."
203 Hermann Mau, [memorandum for Bernard Noble], Washington, D.C., June 12, 1951, NA RG 59, CDF 1950–54, box 5176.
204 See the travel journal that Mau kept during the trip in IfZ Hausarchiv, ID101, vol. 4; DRB Journal of Significant Events, July 23, 1951, entries by Philipp P. Brower and Sherrod East, NA RG 407, entry 375, box 1.

headquarters.[205] Ritter had persuaded the institute to publish the book to reveal to the public the "grotesqueness of this leadership." He wrote the introduction but did not provide critical analysis of the context in which the monologues had taken place. Instead, he let the text stand on its own without commentary in the belief that Hitler would "unmask" himself.[206] Ritter also thought this publication would help make the IfZ known to the public at large. He was certainly correct on that point. Sensational excerpts were serialized in the popular magazine *Quick* – without Ritter's knowledge or approval, he claimed.[207] *Hitlers Tischgespräche* became a major scandal. One of the first critics to speak out was Hannah Arendt, who accused Ritter of offering "Hitler's propaganda" camouflaged as scholarship, of doing a sloppy job in editing the text, and of not providing a commentary to guide readers. Bavarian Minister President Hans Ehard reprimanded Ritter publicly in the state parliament; Adenauer let Ritter know of his displeasure. Moreover, the Office for the Protection of the Constitution decided in response to the scandal to conduct background checks on several members of the institute.[208] Ritter wanted to sit out the crisis and to hold on to his seat on the IfZ's advisory board, but he was forced to resign in late 1951.[209] Despite Ritter's resignation, Mau noted in dismay, the IfZ remained "married" to the "questionable publication."[210]

The damage to the IfZ's reputation and to Mau's mission in the United States was immense. The Foreign Office, which was informed about the

---

205 Henry Picker, *Hitlers Tischgespräche im Führerhauptquartier 1941–1942*, commissioned by Deutschen Instituts für Geschichte der nationalsozialistischen Zeit, compiled, introduced, and published by Gerhard Ritter, Bonn, 1951.

206 Cornelißen, *Ritter*, 538–45, quote 540, 543; Conrad, *Verlorene Nation*, 247–9; Möller, "Institut für Zeitgeschichte," 35–39; Ritter, *Politischer Historiker*, 475–9; Schulze, *Deutsche Geschichtswissenschaft*, 239f.

207 Cornelißen, *Ritter*, 542. In June 1951, Ritter wrote to his "Fellow Historians" ("die Herren Fachkollegen") that the preview of *Hitler's Tischgespräche*, which appeared in *Quick*, "was initiated by the publishing house, without my previously obtained consent and very much against my wishes." BArch, N1188, NL Schieder, vol. 372.

208 Traces of this background check are found in BArch, N1263, NL Rheindorf, vol. 204. Rheindorf reviewed the institute's work program and ran a background check at the BDC on some employees. He had not been at all receptive to the idea of the institute from the very beginning and reacted strongly to the publication of *Table Talks*. See Rheindorf to Epstein, Sept. 28, 1951 and Jan. 17, 1952, both in ibid., vol. 154. It is very well possible that the investigation by the BfV occurred on Rheindorf's initiative. Rheindorf was particularly alarmed by the employment of Dr. Max Werner, a former member of the Free Corps Epp, who joined the party already in 1923, became a member of the SS in February 1934, rose to become a *Hauptsturmführer* and editor of the the "Black Corps" ["Schwarzes Korps"], an SS newspaper, from 1934–39. In 1952, Krausnick was forced to justify to Bundestag member Walter Menzel why Werner of all people had been assigned the job of analyzing records on the "Röhm Putsch" of 1934. Krausnick tried to defuse the situation by answering that Werner was only there to assemble material. The correspondence between Menzel and Krausnick is found in IfZ Hausarchiv, ID34, vol. 75.

209 Cornelißen, *Ritter*, 542–4.

210 Mau to Rheindorf, Nov. 2, 1951, BArch, N1263, NL Rheindorf, vol. 204.

Washington visit, sent a note to Bernard Noble at Wheeler-Bennett's prompting that expressed great irritation over the book. Noble agreed with his colleagues in London that the publication of *Hitlers Tischgespräche* did not "seem to be a very appropriate beginning for this Institute which presumably aims to do some so-called 'debunking' of the Hitler and Nazi myths."[211] Even before the book was published, the State Department had reservations about the presence of Gerhard Ritter on the institute's board: "[He] is a strong nationalist and also quite anti-British and perhaps somewhat less anti-American."[212] Noble asked his counterpart at the Foreign Office's Library, James Passant, how London assessed the institute's staff and its debut publication, confiding that "our people here regret the appearance of that book . . . We expressed our surprise and embarrassment to Mau, and he himself regretted the episode."[213] Passant assigned the British High Commissioner's office the task of investigating the matter. The report that followed cast the institute in a very bad light. Hermann Mau was accused – unjustly – of harboring "strong Nazi sympathies." Objection was also raised to the employment of a former Wehrmacht general.[214] *Hitlers Tisch-gespräche* was, according to the report, an "unsuitable work of practically no scientific value which tends to excite morbid interest in the Hitler regime instead of enlightening the German public about the historical background to Nazism."[215] On the basis of the report, Passant concluded "that the object of the Institute is rather to stimulate a revival of public interest in Hitler and his regime than to supply impartial information about National Socialism."[216] The blow *Hitlers Tischgespräche* dealt to the newly founded IfZ's standing had important practical consequences. Mau's attempt to secure access to the Berlin Document Center for his IfZ colleagues was now blocked by the previously supportive Shepard Stone. "Don't make any commitments to him about anything," Stone advised Kurt Rosenow, the BDC director. "We have helped him, as you know, but until the Institute is cleaned up we wish to make no promises."[217]

---

211 Noble to Peter Ericsson, Whaddon Hall, July 11, 1951, NA RG 59, Lot File 78D441, Historical Office, box 4.
212 Noble to Kellermann, Division of German Information and Reorientation Affairs, May 25, 1951, NA RG 59, CDF 1950–54, 862.423/5–2551 CS/E.
213 Noble to Passant, July 25, 1951, PRO FO 370/2150 LS37120.
214 On the cooperation with ex-General Hermann Foertsch, see Conrad, *Verlorene Nation*, 251–4.
215 Con O'Neill, Wahnerheide, to Passant, Nov. 3, 1951, PRO FO 370/2153 LS3/164.
216 Passant to Noble, Nov. 15, 1951, ibid. Meanwhile, in West Germany, the nickname "institute for the advancement of National Socialism" ("*Institut zur Förderung des NS*") was circulating; see Rheindorf to Epstein, Sept. 28, 1951, BArch, N1263, NL Rheindorf, vol. 154.
217 Stone to Rosenow, Jan. 7, 1952, NA RG 242, BDC Directorate Files, box 7. See also, Mau to Rheindorf, Oct. 5, 1951 and Nov. 2, 1951, BArch, N1263, NL Rheindorf, vol. 204. Mau mentions that "certain irritations" caused by *Tischgespräche* had hurt his negotiations with HICOG.

The situation did not improve for Mau – and by extension the IfZ – after he returned to Munich and prepared a report on his trip to the United States. From what he had learned about the content of the position paper on the captured documents being drafted in Washington, Mau correctly assumed that the return of documents was not being ruled out as a matter of principle and preparations were in fact underway to facilitate their return in the future. He had certainly not expected such a development and noted the "surprisingly gratifying turn of events" in his travel journal.[218] In his report, which he distributed widely, he related that, on his own initiative, Noble had "officially" informed Mau that he, Mau, need no longer focus on gaining access to the captured documents because all signs were pointing to their return. The *Frankfurter Allgemeine Zeitung* and the *Süddeutsche Zeitung* publicized Mau's report.[219] Mau's report began to circulate just as the final round of consultations on the American policy paper were underway in Washington. Other agencies had long accused the State Department of proceeding too quickly on the issue of the documents' return. That Noble might have made the comments Mau reported corroborated that opinion. The DRB announced that Mau's views were basically wrong. "The Army has records under quite adequate control for purposes of current exploitation."[220] In London, the JCC complained of the "reckless character" of Mau's report.[221] Noble complained to Mau, who then revised the passage at issue and sent the report out again.[222] To one recipient of the revised report, Mau maintained "that I am still convinced I rendered the content of the conversation accurately."[223]

218 Journal Mau, entry 48, July 13, 1951, IfZ Hausarchiv, ID101, vol. 4.

219 The sentence in question reads: "After I had been received in the State Department on my arrival with an expression of satisfaction that I had only raised the question of access, and not that of return, Dr. Noble surprised me at a certain stage in the conversations with the *official* communication that the Americans were ready in principle to return the documents." Webb, Acting SecState, to HICOG [Noble to Shepard Stone], no. A-947, Sept. 19, 1951, NA RG 59, CDF 1950–54, 862.423/9–1951. "Rückgabe der deutschen Archive?," *Frankfurter Allgemeine Zeitung*, Aug. 13, 1951; Ernst Müller-Meiningen, Jr., "Das Dritte Reich in der Retorte," *Süddeutsche Zeitung*, Aug. 18/19, 1951.

220 The Army's standpoint is paraphrased in telegram no. A-947, Sept. 19, 1951, NA RG 59, CDF 1950–54, 862.423/9–1951.

221 JCC 38th Meeting, Sept. 6, 1951, PRO CAB 103/458; Passant to Noble, Sept. 13, 1951, PRO FO 370/2151 LS3/139, quote in Passant to Noble, Sept. 27, 1951, PRO FO 370/2151 LS3/145.

222 A copy with the new page 9 is in BArch, B198, vol. 113. On Mau's distribution list were at least Kurt Rheindorf, Fritz T. Epstein, the Auswärtige Amt and the Interior Ministry. A short version of the report can be found in the 1951 journal *Geschichte in Wissenschaft und Unterricht*. See Mau, "Deutsche Archive und Dokumente."

223 Mau to Legationsrat Strohm, Political Department, Sept. 25, 1951, PA/AA, B10, vol. 1702/2. It is wrong to interpret Mau's trip as if he conducted return negotiations in the United States and attained a review of the issue, as in Möller, "Institut für Zeitgeschichte," 25f. The work on the return policy had started before his trip and was not influenced by it. Even the assumption that Mau

From that point on, Bernard Noble was reluctant to receive German visitors, as the IfZ realized when it tried to send another historian to work in the Library of Congress and the Hoover Institution in 1952.[224] The visit did not take place until 1954.[225] That same year, Kluke, who had in the meantime succeeded Mau as the institute's director, complained bitterly:

We still have to make do with the crumbs that fall from English and American tables. . . . We beg for a few microfilms of declassified records while the local scholars can access at least part of the files. . . . We know that the historical study and thus the intellectual mastering of this time period need to be an international undertaking, but we finally want the opportunity to work together as equals at least on our own records.[226]

From the German perspective, the prospects of gaining access to captured documents seemed only to diminish. In 1955, a group of American historians, startled by the news that the military records might be returned to Germany, formed the American Committee for the Study of War Documents. The committee sought to raise the funds necessary to finance the microfilming of all of the files before they were returned and to make the microfilms available for research. The existence of filmed copies, it was thought, would also pre-empt any attempt by the Germans to classify or destroy the original files upon their return, thus serving the interests of both American and German scholars in the long run. The benevolence of the committee's aims was not self-evident to the Germans, however. German historians protested against the filming project, which they feared might postpone the return of the records indefinitely.

Into the Future: The American Microfilming Project

"Scholars Fear U.S. Will Return Nazi Archives Before Full Study" – an article in the *New York Times* on March 6, 1955, reminded American historians that a vast trove of source material on the recent German past was stored in their own backyard.[227] That material was, however, closed to so-called private research, that is, to researchers who were not affiliated with

---

had given negotiations a "strong impulse," as Graml/Woller, "Vierteljahrshefte," 53, maintain, is not tenable. On the contrary, the opposite – a setback – nearly occurred.

224 Kenneth J. MacCormac, Chief, Exchange Staff, American Consulate General, Munich, to Mau, Aug. 6, 1952; Mau to MacCormac, Oct. 9, 1952, both in IfZ Hausarchiv, ID102, vol. 39.

225 Guy A. Lee, HICOG, to State, Apr. 8, 1954, NA RG 59, CDF 1950–54, 862.423/4–854.

226 Kluke to Francis Carsten, London, Nov. 5, 1954, IfZ Hausarchiv, ID102, vol. 39.

227 Anthony Leviero, "Scholars Fear U.S. Will Return Nazi Archives Before Full Study," *New York Times*, Mar 7, 1955. Further coverage of the issue: "Going To Bonn? Hitler File here Stirs New Interest," *Washington Post and Herald*, Mar. 23, 1955; "Concern at Possible Return to Germany of Nazi Documents," *Daily News Bulletin* no. 162, issued by the Jewish Telegraphic Agency, Apr.

the U.S. government or military. Early attempts by scholars to gain access to the German documents in American possession collided with the onset of the Korean War in 1950; the needs of wartime intelligence precluded scholarly use of the German military records. The historians, in other words, had started their lobbying too soon.[228] Not until 1953 did the U.S. Army release files for scholarly research for the first time.[229] Two years later, with the Paris Treaty in sight, it looked as if the records might be returned quite rapidly, without American historians having had a chance to benefit from their presence in the United States.[230] The article in the *New York Times* spurred several historians to action. A group of specialists in German and Central European history joined forces to ensure that the records would be microfilmed before they were returned.

The American Committee for the Study of War Documents could point to an impressive list of members and supporters when it met for the first time on October 29, 1955.[231] Hans Kohn and George W. Hallgarten independently of one another had both had the idea of creating such a committee.[232] Reginald H. Phelps (Harvard), who published a study on the membership structure of the NSDAP, served as its first chair. The other members included Harold D. Lasswell (Yale), Carl J. Friedrich (Harvard), Koppel Pinson (Queens College, NYC), Raymond J. Sontag (University of California), Boyd C. Shafer from the American Historical Association, Fritz T. Epstein (Library of Congress), and Walter L. Dorn (Ohio State University,

---

4, 1955; "Tragödie für den Geheimdienst," *Frankfurter Allgemeine Zeitung*, Mar. 9, 1955; Walter Görlitz, "Aktenlager in der alten Torpedofabrik," *Die Welt*, Mar. 31, 1955.

228 One such attempt was initiated by the American Historical Association. See Conyers Read to William L. Langer, Mar. 16, 1950, Langer Papers, box 13; Robert Livingston Schuyler, President, AHA, to Dean Acheson, SecState, Nov. 7, 1951, NA RG 59, CDF 1950–54, 862.423/11–751; Bernard Noble to Schuyler, Nov. 28, 1951, NA RG 59, CDF 1950–54, 862.423/11–2851. Another attempt was undertaken by the Carnegie Foundation. The episode in Langer Papers, box 14.

229 DRB, General List of Seized Records Available for Unofficial Research, Reference Aid no. 15 (DRB Publication 54–1), February 1954, BArch, N1188, NL Schieder, vol. 651; Weinberg to Rothfels, Oct. 20, 1953, IfZ Hausarchiv, ID102, vol. 43. Goldbeck, "GMDS," 50–2; Weinberg, "German Records Microfilmed," 199.

230 "Some ten years have passed since the material was acquired. The full processing, recording, and utilization of the material for the broad historical purposes that it can be expected to serve, are yet to be achieved." Memorandum on the Organisation and Purposes of the American Committee for the Study of War Documents, September 1955, Hale Papers, box 8.

231 Documentation on the initial meeting in ibid. The sources concerning the history of the Committee are found in the papers of Oron J. Hale at the University of Virginia. Hale was the third and last chairman of the Committee and had received the papers of his two predecessors Reginald Phelps (Harvard) and Lynn Case (Philadelphia). In late 1956, the Committee was incorporated into the American Historical Association (AHA) so that important sources also lie among the AHA papers located in the Manuscript Division of the Library of Congress.

232 Hans Kohn to Oron J. Hale, July 14, 1955; George W. Hallgarten, memorandum for E. Malcolm Carroll, Oron J Hale, Guy Stanton Ford, Hans Gatzke, Gordon Craig, Reginald H. Phelps, both in Hale Papers, box 8.

later Columbia). The committee fully realized that it would need contacts in the political and business communities for its lobbying and fund-raising to succeed. Here, the committee could count on help from Shepard Stone, who, after leaving the High Commission, had become the director of the Ford Foundation's European program. This foundation financed the initial phase of the microfilming project. Other supporters included the former High Commissioner John J. McCloy and a number of philanthropists and foundation presidents. The committee established a direct line of contact to Congress through its secretary general, Sidney Wallach. Wallach headed the office of Representative Arthur G. Klein and was successful in persuading the congressman to take active interest in the committee's efforts.[233] Officials at the DRB quickly realized that Klein, largely at Wallach's prompting, was the only member of the legislative branch keeping a close eye on the project.[234]

The initial challenge for the committee was to obtain the cooperation of the Army. Prior to the committee's first meeting, George Hallgarten explained its plans to the head of the DRB, Sherrod East. "If Dr. Hallgarten's enthusiasm is only partially realized," East noted, "DRB can look forward to considerable research activity in captured records including pressure for downgrading and microcopying."[235] The committee's representative reassured DRB officials that they were not interested in the political aspects of the return issue and had no intention of "telling the U.S. Government how to go about restituting records or what records to restitute." The committee was, however, "strongly interested" in ensuring that declassified records were made available to "everybody," including German scholars, and "continually in some form."[236]

Declassification proved to be the pivotal issue. All the German records had received a blanket security classification, and only the Army's Intelligence section (G-2) had the authority to re- or declassify them. The Department of the Army was thus being asked not only to approve the microfilming project per se but also to reconsider the issue of declassification. Reviewing materials for declassification would require a great deal of manpower and

---

233 On March 7, the day the article appeared in the *New York Times*, Klein submitted an inquiry to the House of Representatives and had the article printed in the Congressional Record, Proceedings and Debates of the 84th Congress, First Session. He argued that it would weaken the United States in its fight against totalitarianism to return the records. Further Rep. Arthur G. Klein to John Foster Dulles, SecState, May 17, 1955, NA RG 59, CDF 1955–59, 862.423/5–1755.

234 DRB Journal of Significant Events, Mar. 28, 1955, entry by Ken Munden, NA RG 407, entry 375, box 3.

235 Ibid., Aug. 29, 1955.

236 DRB Journal, entry by Philipp P. Brower, Sept. 29, 1955, ibid.

consultation with the British.[237] Oron J. Hale, who had been an intelligence officer at G-2 during the war, negotiated with the Army on behalf of the committee. In early 1956, he felt that prospects were bleak. The committee's goals seemed too ambitious, he reported to a colleague, and the Army's plans for the captured German records too vague.[238]

Several developments at the Department of the Army worked to the committee's advantage. Army officials had realized during the preparation of the interagency policy paper that the status of the German military records would eventually have to be reconsidered. The Army had already decided to supply the West German military with materials such as training manuals and personnel records.[239] Consequently, it would have to address the issue of declassification at some point. The committee's requests prompted the establishment of a multi-year program for dealing with the captured German records. The three-step process of "review, microfilm, transfer" was devised with the committee's concerns and objectives in mind.[240] Army intelligence officials realized they were about to be swamped with work and looked for help. In autumn 1956, they handed over the job of making the preliminary decisions on declassification to the DRB archivists, a step that accelerated the review process.[241] The review did not necessarily lead to the automatic declassification of records, however. At times, it seemed that more documents were being withheld than released. By late 1959, "the volume of records remaining classified was out of all proportion to the amount that might reasonably be expected to be in that category." Files relating to Waffen-SS units active on the Eastern front, for example, were immediately reclassified without review.[242]

---

237 Army Statement Before the American Committee for the Study of War Documents, Oct. 29, 1955, ibid.; Classification of Captured German Records in D[epartment of the] A[rmy] Custody, DRB Journal, Jan. 24, 1956, ibid.; Policy Statement on Captured Records, transmitted by Col. Scott-Smith, n.d. [May 1956], Hale Papers, box 8.

238 Hale to Phelps, n.d. [March 1956], Hale Papers, box 8; Hale to Epstein, Apr. 26, 1956, ibid.

239 See Chapter 3, n. 98.

240 "It was decided that it was incumbent upon Army to draft immediately a plan for the disposition of the captured records. The plan will cover proposed filming, declassifying, and the restitution or continued Army retention of the captured records." [minutes of meeting DRB and G-2], Plan for Disposition of Captured Records, Nov. 1, 1955, DRB Journal of Significant Events, NA RG 407, entry 375, box 3.

241 The general in charge at G-2 had an internal report done on "how Intelligence can best discharge its declassification responsibilities." DRB Journal, Mar. 29, 1956, entry by Sherrod East, ibid. The directive is explained in Memo for Record, n.d. [Oct. 2, 1956], NA RG 242, AGAR-S no. 1560, box 6; and in Weinberg to Hale, Oct. 19, 1956, Hale Papers, Box 8. Until then, G-2 had proven to be the bottleneck in declassifying records. One reason for this was that the G-2 staff was not as familiar with the records as the DRB archivists were. With the change in procedure, the DRB archivists could now make specific suggestions for declassification.

242 Weinberg to Hale, Nov. 15, 1959, Hale Papers, box 10. See also Weinberg, "German Records Microfilmed," 200f.

On July 2, 1956, the historians' committee received the go-ahead to begin the microfilming.[243] Work began a month later at the former Navy torpedo factory in Alexandria, Virginia, where the German records were stored.[244] Gerhard L. Weinberg supervised the operation. He had completed his doctorate at the University of Chicago as a student of Hans Rothfels. From his participation in the War Documentation Project under Fritz T. Epstein, Weinberg was already familiar with the captured material.[245] Upon completion, the microfilms were sent to the National Archives, where they were made available to researchers. Weinberg reported in September that twenty-two rolls of film had been transferred to the National Archives during the project's first three months of operation; by December, the figure had grown to over 1,000.[246] The documents were usually filmed in bulk, which Weinberg argued was not only less expensive and faster than selecting individual documents for filming but also made it easier to maintain consensus on the filming process.[247] Although arranged in record groups, the documents were not necessarily organized in a meaningful fashion. The use of the documents for intelligence purposes had played havoc with the organization of the files, and the microfilming process was forced inevitably to set this status quo into stone.[248] A register was compiled as the files were filmed. The resulting guides offered a summary of the content and are still indispensable today for the use of the films.[249] Two rules were to be observed in filming the documents. First, if a still-classified file accidentally turned up among declassified materials, it would be filmed and its existence noted

---

243 John A. Klein, The Adjutant General, to Boyd C. Shafer, Executive Secretary, AHA, July 2, 1956; General Robert A. Schow, G-2 Intelligence, to Hale, Oct. 15, 1956, both in Hale Papers, box 8.

244 The Committee sponsored another microfilming project with funds from the Ford Foundation. In 1956, Howard M. Ehrmann (University of Michigan) filmed pre-1914 records held at Whaddon Hall that were slated to be turned over to Bonn later that year. See Ehrmann to Phelps, Oct. 11, 1956; and A Report to the Ford Foundation on the Projects of the American Comittee for the Study of War Documents at Whaddon Hall, England, both in Hale Papers, box 8.

245 Out of the work by the WDP grew the *Guide to Captured German Documents*. (War Documentation Project. Study no. 1). Prepared by Gerhard L. Weinberg. Maxwell Air Force Base, Alabama: December 1952. The guide indexed all declassified and thus usable German holdings located in facilities other than governmental ones and the Library of Congress.

246 Weinberg, Quarterly Report, Sept. 14, 1956, Hale Papers, box 8; DRB Journal, AHA Convention 1956, Jan. 7, 1956, entry by Sherrod East, DRB Journal of Significant Events, NA RG 407, entry 375, box 3.

247 The suggestion of the less expensive version of "bulk filming" came from Sherrod East. See DRB Journal, June 15, 1956, entry by Philipp P. Brower, ibid. The procedure differed from that at Whaddon Hall, where only a select number of records were microfilmed. Weinberg had always been a vocal critic of the procedure in England. See Kent, "Foreign Ministry Archives at Whaddon," 53; Sontag, "German Diplomatic Papers," 65; Weinberg, "German Records Microfilmed," 202.

248 Rohr, "Mikroverfilmung," 253f.; Weinberg, "German Records Microfilmed," 201.

249 The Guides are described extensively and dismissed as unwieldy in Rohr, "Mikroverfilmung," 254–8; further AHA, Supplement to the Guide to Captured German Records, 1–3; Perman, "Microfilming," 442; Weinberg, "Akten in den Vereinigten Staaten."

in the register. The microfilm copy would not, however, be turned over to the National Archives. Second, the copies of records containing protected information about individuals or dealing with matters that fell outside the purview of the agreement on the return of documents were designated "R[estricted] Reels." These reels contained information that fell under the protection of personal privacy or were related to materials excluded from return to Germany. The National Archives was not permitted to sell copies of the R-Reels, and researchers needed special permission to use them.[250]

The historians in Alexandria worked under great time pressure. The influence of the Cold War on West German–American relations made the return of the captured German records increasingly likely. The Army continued to send documents to the Federal Republic on an ad hoc basis in order to cut storage costs or to satisfy a particular West German request. Picking up on that practice, Weinberg began to realize what had already escaped his cameras. Although the committee had permission to film all records before their return, it was up to the committee to raise the money to cover the costs of the filming: "If we do not have the money, too bad," as Weinberg bluntly summarized.[251] Financing the microfilming operation at Alexandria remained a headache. The Ford Foundation provided $69,000 in seed money; securing additional funding proved difficult. The committee's board decided in late 1956 to move under the umbrella of the American Historical Association in the hope of increasing its chances for fundraising.[252] In June 1957, Hale reported "the near collapse of our War Documents project," and the situation remained precarious.[253] The committee survived from grant to grant until the Department of the Army rid itself of the DRB in 1958.[254] The captured documents section, including staff, was turned over to the National Archives, which thereupon worked

250 Permits were issued by the Office of the Adjutant General. Today the films are accessible. The categories for the R-Reels were: "1. Interrogations of allied personnel. 2. Strictly personal affairs of nationals of U.S and allied countries. 3. Personal name files of any national of any country. 4. Strictly personal information, about any national of any country, which should be withheld because of humanitarian considerations. 5. Materials which would adversely affect U.S. or its allies in current international affairs. 6. Unclassified but non-restitutable (i.e. Nazi Party records)." Weinberg, "Quarterly Report," Hale Papers, box 8. See also DRB Journal, AHA Captured Records Filming Project, Mar. 26, 1957, entry Sherrod East, DRB Journal of Significant Events, NA RG 407, entry 375, box 3.

251 Weinberg to Case, May 7, 1957, LoC, AHA Collection, box 480.

252 Lynn M. Case, Chairman, American Committee for the Study of War Documents, to the Executive Board of the Committee, n.d. [early 1957]; Shafer, AHA, to Case, Jan. 9, 1957; Guy Stanton Ford to Case, Feb. 27, 1957; Lynn M. Case to the members of the Committee, Feb. 28, 1957, all in Hale Papers, box 8.

253 Hale to George N. Shuster, President, Hunter College NY, June 17, 1957, Hale Papers, box 8.

254 Financial support came from the Ford Foundation, the Old Dominion Foundation, the Lilly Foundation as well as Frank Altschul.

with the committee to continue the project. The committee assumed the jobs of reviewing and indexing the materials; the Archives took over the technical process of microfilming.[255]

The committee was not simply a footnote in the story of the American historical profession. Institutionally, it was the precursor of the Conference Group for Central European History within the American Historical Association.[256] More importantly, the committee made a lasting contribution to research on contemporary history by its scholarly and organizational achievements in mastering the microfilming and rough indexing of a mountain of records. Before the committee took action, contemporary history had not been an uncontroversial subfield within the American historical profession. The idea of studying the "era of those living" with established scholarly methods ran up against criticism in the United States similar to that expressed in Great Britain and Germany: historians had neither the sources nor the distance necessary to treat the present as history.[257] With the microfilming project, the committee effectively refuted the criticism that official source materials for the recent past were not available. The microfilming project delivered source material at a decisive moment in the development of the American historical profession. A new generation of specialists on Europe entered the profession in the early 1950s. Their interest in the recent past often had biographical roots. Many of them had escaped Germany or Austria as youths in the 1930s.[258] Historians of Central Europe could count on a continuing interest in their field inside and outside academia because scholarly attempts to explain National Socialism and its crimes had barely begun and because divided Germany remained a political hot spot during the Cold War. The influence of the Cold War on the boom in research on contemporary Europe in the United States can hardly be overestimated. Research on totalitarianism in the 1950s presupposed that studying National Socialist Germany would offer insight into the Soviet Union – that knowledge about one dictatorship would help illuminate another. The committee repeatedly played this card in its numerous grant

---

255 Perman, "Microfilming," 438; Weinberg, "Microfilming German Records," 205.

256 After the Committee had been incorporated into the AHA, several members formed the Conference Group in 1957, which published the journal *Central European History*. On the beginnings of this group, see Oron J. Hale to Hans Kohn and Walter L. Dorn, Nov. 15, 1957; call to establish the group, dated Nov. 26, 1957; Oron J. Hale, The Conference Group for Central European History: Its Organisation and First Two Years, 1957–1959, n.d., all in Hale Papers, box 11.

257 See Eckert, "Transnational Beginnings."

258 Such scholars included Werner T. Angress, Henry Friedlander, Hans Gatzke, Peter Gay, Raul Hilberg, Georg G. Iggers, George O. Kent, Klemens von Klemperer, Peter Loewenberg, George L. Mosse, Fritz Stern, and Gerhard L. Weinberg. See Epstein, *A Past Renewed*, 13. On the development of the special academic field of German history at American universities, see also Jarausch, "Provokation des 'Anderen,'" 435–7.

applications: the German records in Alexandria were, it argued, "the fullest records of a twentieth century totalitarian regime available to students and scholars; they are worthy of study and we are not likely to have such a body of records available for any other dictatorship."[259]

Microfilming as Deliberate Obstruction?

> *The Americans had the essential material . . . in their hands and kept it to analyze themselves. Before their publications appeared, no one else was to be let near it.*[260]

Word of the committee's plans reached West German historians and archivists in the summer of 1955 just after the British, American, and West German governments had come to an agreement on the return of the German diplomatic records.[261] Although the negotiations had not addressed the captured military records, officials at the Bundesarchiv hoped that negotiations would resume immediately and produce results quickly. Bundesarchiv director Georg Winter thus could not help but see the microfilming project as a deliberate attempt at obstruction devised to postpone the return of the captured records and to put German historians at a disadvantage. Just as the British historians at Whaddon Hall had tried to sabotage the return of the diplomatic records, so, too, in Winter's reckoning, were the Americans now attempting to prevent the return of the military records. The microfilming project amounted to "the same thing on the part of American historians," he complained.[262]

It is well known that the American historical profession eagerly took possession of the confiscated records after the war. Modern German history and German contemporary history today are to a disproportionately large degree written in the United States. It is understandable but also lamentable that they take advantage of these circumstances and do not intend to part with the records any time soon.[263]

The idea that all members of the American historical profession had been able to make use of the German records in the United States since the end of the war was, of course, incorrect. Researchers who were not affiliated with the official war history projects or *Documents on German Foreign Policy* had

---

259 Project proposal for the Old Dominion Foundation, March 1958, Hale Papers, box 9.
260 Auerbach, "Gründung des IfZ," 535.
261 Fritz T. Epstein informed Hans Herzfeld, Paul Kluke, Hans Rothfels, and Theodor Schieder. See Epstein to Schieder, Aug. 14, 1955, BArch, N1188, NL Schieder, vol. 651.
262 "At the negotiations in the AA on August 11 of this year, it became quite clear that it is not so much the Allied governments but the Allied historians who opposed and continue to oppose an immediate return of the AA records." Winter to Interior Ministry, Aug. 16, 1955, BArch, B106, vol. 34725.
263 Ibid. See also Winter to Posner, Feb. 21, 1956, NA RG 200, Posner Papers, box 6.

access only to materials held by private research institutions.[264] Historians who were not involved in government-backed projects benefited from the DRB's first release of declassified files in 1953, material sufficient, as Weinberg wrote to Rothfels, "to keep a lot of graduate students busy for a long time to come."[265] They could use the personal papers of several Prussian generals at the National Archives.[266] They also had access to the microfilms from Whaddon Hall that had been deposited at the National Archives and the Public Record Office. The teams at Whaddon had, however, filmed comparatively little material. Up until 1956, Bernard Noble complained repeatedly to James Passant, sometimes in quite harsh terms, about the limited quantity of Weimar-era documents that had been released on film.[267] In short, American historians unaffiliated with official publishing projects did have access to some materials that their German colleagues could not easily use, but the bulk of the captured German records were off-limits to them. That was precisely the reason why the committee had been formed in the first place.

Moreover, the microfilm project was not directed against West German historians. The committee's original idea was, in fact, to cooperate with them. Fritz T. Epstein anticipated an unfavorable German reaction to the microfilming project and warned his American colleges early on that "the impression could easily be gained that the project is only a smokescreen to further postpone the return of the documents."[268] Hans Kohn also anticipated German objections. In his proposal to form a committee, Kohn wrote that the group's objectives would be, first, to microfilm the material and, second, "to encourage, thereafter, its early return to Germany."[269] At the committee's founding meeting in October 1955, Epstein drew attention to German sensitivities:

---

264 *Guide to Captured German Documents.* (War Documentation Project. Study no. 1). Prepared by Gerhard L. Weinberg. Maxwell Air Force Base, Alabama: December 1952.

265 Weinberg to Rothfels, Oct. 20, 1953, IfZ Hausarchiv, ID102, vol. 43.

266 Preliminary Inventory of the German Records 1679–1945 in the World War II Collection of Seized Enemy Records. Compiled by Martin Rogin. (Preliminary Inventory no. 24) Washington, D.C.: General Services Administration. The National Archives, 1950. Included in this were the papers of von Seeckt and Groener. In 1952, the National Archives halted public use of these holding because copyright issues could not be clarified.

267 Starting in 1952, the American advisory committee for the DGFP demanded the release of Weimar records, because it was foreseeable that the editors would not be able to cover this period in the near future. Not until March 1956 did the British advisory committee concede, when it was already clear that work in Whaddon would end in March 1959. See Statement of Views, Annex to Meeting of the Historical Advisory Committee held at Foreign Office Library, Mar. 6, 1956, PRO FO 370/2472 LS5/37.

268 Epstein to Rothfels, July 5, 1955, BArch, B186, vol. 1739.

269 Kohn to Hale, July 14, 1955, Hale Papers, box 8.

We must realize that the question of restitution has long become a matter of prestige for the Germans. Among those concerned about the return of documents . . . it is generally felt that their former archives – whatever their content, good or bad from the point of view of a nation's pride and honor – are an undeniable and inalienable part of Germany's past; that to regain custody of them is a natural right of the German people . . . .[270]

Although all agreed that there should indeed be cooperation between U.S. and West German historians, it remained unclear what form such cooperation would take. For a time, the committee considered setting up a parallel work group in Germany[271] and donating a complete set of the microfilms to the Institute for Contemporary History.[272] In any case, the committee acted in the belief that its work "would also be welcome to the German and other European historians who might especially share our interest in obtaining microfilms of the documents."[273]

For all the talk about cooperation and openness, however, there was no way to gloss over the fact that the microfilming project had been initiated in part because American historians did not trust the assurances of West German government officials, archivists, and historians that the files would be open for research after their return to Germany. The IfZ's publication of *Hitlers Tischgespräche* had raised serious doubts about the direction that German contemporary history was headed. This book, the president of the American Historical Association feared, "may be the beginning of . . . a dangerous myth if it is not promptly corrected by a revelation of the facts as disclosed in the German records themselves."[274] The launch of the IfZ's journal *Vierteljahrshefte für Zeitgeschichte* was an important step toward assuaging such concerns but did not dispel them entirely.[275] Many members of the committee were diplomatic historians and had been closely following the debate on the accuracy of *Die Große Politik* in the *Times*

---

270 Excerpts from the Address by Dr. Fritz Epstein at Meeting on October 29, for Circulation to Members of the Committee Only, [Oct. 29, 1955], ibid.
271 "Dr. Hallgarten brought out that the Committee will set up a similar committee in West Germany to find out what documents German scholars would be interested in having reproduced." DRB Journal, Sept. 21, 1955, entry by Philipp P. Brower, DRB Journal of Significant Events, NA RG 407, entry 375, box 3.
272 "A second positive film was also being considered. This was to be given to Germany, possibly to the Institute für Zeitgeschichte." DRB Journal, Jan. 7, 1957, entry by Herman Goldbeck, NA RG 407, entry 375, box 3.
273 George F. Hallgarten, memorandum, n.d. [June 29, 1955], Hale Papers, box 8.
274 Robert Livingston Schuyler, President, AHA, to Dean Acheson, SecState, Nov. 7, 1951, NA RG 59, CDF 1950–54, 862.423/11–751.
275 Department, University of Oregon-Eugene, May 11, 1953, Dorn Papers, box 1; Dorn to Rothfels, Oct. 5, 1953, BArch, N1213, NL Rothfels, vol. 1; Langer to Rothfels, June 5, 1953, Langer Papers, box 13. On the history of the journal, see Graml/Woller, "Vierteljahrshefte."

Literary Supplement.[276] That exchange did little to dispel the mistrust prevalent among American historians. The planning for microfilming thus began on the premise that "there is no reason to believe that the documents, once returned, will be fully available to the scholarly world."[277] The first experiences that American historians had as users of West German archives in the 1950s did not improve the situation. Reginald Phelps, for example, was apparently not able to consult the files of the Bavarian state police after they had been returned to Munich in August 1954 although he had already once worked with them at the DRB.[278] A number of readers reported similar experiences in 1956, which prompted Weinberg to draw the conclusion that restitution was "the scholastic equivalent of destroying the documents."[279] These experiences and perceptions became well entrenched as negative stereotypes that survived well into the 1990s.[280]

Given the suspicions that prevailed on both sides of the Atlantic, it is not surprising that discussions between German and American scholars about the microfilming project were anything but tension-free. At the Tenth International Congress of the Historical Sciences in Rome in September 1955, the participating West German and American historians talked right past one another.

Returning to the International Stage: Rome 1955. The Rome meeting of 1955 was the first international congress of historians to reflect the new postwar world order. The 1950 congress in Paris had been no more than a gathering of scholars from the Western nations.[281] In 1955, by contrast, a delegation

---

276 The "revelations" in the *TLS* offered a reason to invest in the microfilming of pre-1914 diplomatic records.

277 American Committee for the Study of War Documents, Executive Committee Meeting, Dec. 10, 1955, Harold D. Lasswell Papers, box 5. See also the comments of Rep. Arthur G. Klein to John Foster Dulles, SecState, May 17, 1955, NA RG 59, CDF 1955–59, 862.423/5–1755: "Such material . . . must not be jeopardized or lost to us by its casual return to a country where its nationalist forces may be disposed to destroy the full record or to conceal it forever from the scrutiny of the civilized world."

278 "Some of these records . . . were not filmed before shipment and are now gone. Dean Phelps came here to use one of these groups – Bayerische Landespolizei – was informed they had been returned; tried to get at them when he was in Germany; was refused." Weinberg to Case, May 7, 1957, LoC, AHA Collection, box 480. See also Weinberg to Case, Oct. 25, 1957, Hale Papers, box 8.

279 Gerhard L. Weinberg to Hans Rothfels, Nov. 14, 1956, IfZ Hausarchiv, ID102, vol. 47.

280 See the article on the Berlin Document Center by Gerald Posner, "Secrets of the Files," *New Yorker* 70:4, Mar. 14, 1994: 39–47, as well as Hearing before the Subcommittee on International Security, International Organizations and Human Rights of the Committee on Foreign Affairs, House of Representatives, 103rd Congress, 2nd Session, Apr. 28, 1994.

281 Cornelißen, *Ritter*, 446–9; Erdmann, *Ökumene der Historiker*, 264, 277f.; Konferenzbericht bei Heimpel, "Internationaler Historikertag in Paris;" Ritter, "Der X. Internationale Historikerkongreß in Rom."

from the Soviet Union participated.[282] There was also a group from East Germany determined to gain recognition as a delegation in its own right and eager to emphasize the achievements of the "historiography of the working class."[283] The West Germans were admitted as full participants for the first time since the end of the war; five years earlier, they had been allowed to send only an unofficial delegation to Paris, and it had been relegated to the sidelines.[284] The West German delegation did not want to "sit demurely in the corner" in Rome and sought to play "a prominent role."[285] Prior to the conference, both sides of the German divide prepared a detailed choreography of their appearance, hand-picked their speakers, and fixed their positions.[286] The *Frankfurter Allgemeine Zeitung* celebrated Rome as the resurrection of German as a conference language: "All of the 'Eastern peoples' . . . and sometimes even the Poles and not the least the Soviet Russians spoke German. . . . There was a feeling as if an axle was sliding once again into its old box."[287] Buoyed by the Paris treaties, conservative West German historians were prepared to meet any challenge posed by outsiders on questions of their national history.

Hans Kohn used the Rome congress as an opportunity to convene a meeting to inform European historians about the microfilming project.[288] The Americans attending were Bernadotte Schmitt, Boyd C. Shafer of the AHA, and Howard M. Smyth, the American editor of *Documents on German Foreign Policy*. Margaret Lambert, the British editor, joined them. The only West German historians to attend were Paul Kluke and Hans Herzfeld. Kohn outlined the committee's preliminary plans. It was envisioned that two junior scholars would work directly with the files and that a supervisory board would make decisions about publications. The committee's most important goal, Kohn stressed, was to secure the release of the documents for scholarly research. Kluke suggested that Kohn did not have a full grasp of

282 A noted event at the Congress was a quarrel over the Hitler-Stalin Pact. See Erdmann, *Ökumene der Historiker*, 319f.
283 Sabrow, "Ökumene als Bedrohung," 185f.; Sabrow, *Diktatur des Konsenses*, 263–5. The East German historians did not present any papers because the decision to take part in the congress was made too late to have any contributions of theirs considered.
284 The institutional break between West and East German historians occurred at the historians meeting in Trier and led to the founding of an East German association in 1958. See Cornelißen, *Ritter*, 451f.; Sabrow, "Ökumene als Bedrohung," 190–5; Schumann, "Gerhard Ritter," 405–8.
285 Gerhard Ritter to his siblings, Dec. 21, 1953, quoted in Cornelißen, *Ritter*, 449f.
286 Ibid.
287 Josef Schmitz, "Auferstehung einer Sprache," *Frankfurter Allgemeine Zeitung*, Sept. 24, 1955. Other reports on the congress: E. F. Jacob, "Homage to History from 1,500 Scholars," *The Times* (London), Sept. 10, 1955; Gerhard Ritter, "Begegnung der Nationen. Vom X. Weltkongreß der Historiker in Rom," *Süddeutsche Zeitung*, Sept. 24/25, 1955.
288 Epstein to Schieder, Aug. 14, 1955, BArch, N1188, NL Schieder, vol. 651. Paul Kluke, memo, Sept. 30, 1955, BArch, B106, vol. 34725. The meeting was held on Sept. 9, 1955.

the quantity of material at issue, reminding him that the team of historians at Whaddon Hall had been at work for a decade and was still sifting through the 400 tons of diplomatic records in British possession. Leaving the military records in the United States for the purpose of filming would effectively exclude German scholars on account of the prohibitive costs of travel, Kluge argued, and employing one German historian in Washington hardly constituted full cooperation. The records should instead be transferred to Germany, he insisted, where they could also be microfilmed. The Federal Ministry of the Interior guaranteed scholarly access on German soil but opposed the possibility "that the planned microfilming would further delay the ultimately necessary return." Schmitt retorted that the Americans could choose to consider the files trophies of war because Berlin, where most of the material originated, had been a war theater. Kluke, usually moderate in tone but in this instance obviously agitated, snapped back that Berlin had not been an American theater of operations and that, by Schmitt's logic, one might as well turn the documents over to the Russians. Hans Kohn closed the meeting with the comment that the return of the captured documents without prior microfilming was out of the question and that he would "raise hell" if the Germans pressed for their immediate return.[289]

The full extent of the discord that arose in Rome soon became evident. Epstein dispatched frosty letters to Kluke and Theodor Schieder, claiming that the encounter had seriously undermined American willingness to cooperate with the Germans. Although Epstein himself had not been present in Rome, he nonetheless felt that Kluke had not given adequate consideration to the American concerns.[290] He advised him to restrain himself in pressing for the documents' return: "Your efforts and demands, e.g. in Rome, were, as I regret to have to tell you rather bluntly, directed to the wrong address. They had the opposite effect of what you intended to achieve with your suggestion or urging."[291] The return of the records, Epstein continued, was a political question on which American historians had no influence.[292] Instead of demanding the return of all the military records, Kluke would be better off paying attention to the material that had

---

289 The meeting was only documented by Kluke in his memo [for the Interior Ministry], Sept. 30, 1955, BArch, B106, vol. 34725; quote from Kluke to Epstein, Sept. 27, 1955, IfZ Hausarchiv, ID102, vol. 37.
290 Epstein to Schieder, Oct. 30, 1955, BArch, N1188, NL Schieder, vol. 651.
291 Epstein to Kluke, Nov. 11, 1955, IfZ Hausarchiv, ID102, vol. 37 and BArch, B106, vol. 34725.
292 Epstein thought Kluke had been in the United States long enough to know that the question of restitution was an "extremely complicated, controversial, and above all, *political* issue." Epstein could only shake his head at the idea that someone who should know better seriously believed "that it would only take a suggestion or even a demand by American historians to prevent the State Department or other offices here, having custody of German record holdings, to implement

already been returned to Germany, such as the holdings of the former army archive and the records of the Bavarian state police.[293]

As Kluke tried to patch things up with Epstein,[294] the Ministry of the Interior, the Bundesarchiv, the Auswärtiges Amt, and a group of historians coordinated the next steps to be taken in the matter. The question at hand was whether German historians should cooperate in the microfilming project, which, from the perspective of German officials, appeared irreconcilable with the concurrent demand by the West German government for the return of the records. George Winter took an undiplomatically radical stance: "Are we partners of the Allies or a colonial people?" he exclaimed. With such rhetoric, he was continually tripping up Kluke's efforts to pursue a more compromise-oriented approach.[295] Kluke was, in fact, the only one to understand the dilemma faced by the American historians, whose own government had not given them access to the captured documents. He urged the German officials and his fellow historians not to assume malicious intentions on the part of the Americans.[296] In talks with his officials in Bonn, he supported the Americans' position by saying that their worries about a reclassification of the records once the material was back in German hands had to be taken very seriously: "We don't have anything left to hide in our most recent history since the crimes of that period have long been evident, but [we] can still benefit from impartial scholarship."[297]

Theodor Schieder, a historian at the University of Cologne, had formed a different impression in Rome. He was convinced that the American microfilming project was intentionally geared toward preventing the return of the records.[298] He expressed that view during a meeting on the captured documents at the Ministry of the Interior in early December 1955 and found most of the other participants in agreement with him. For Schieder, the issue was an existential question for the German historical profession. In

measures that have *political* motives." Epstein to Schieder, Oct. 30, 1955, BArch, N1188, NL Schieder, vol. 651, original emphasis.

293 Epstein to Kluke, Nov. 11, 1955, IfZ Hausarchiv, ID102, vol. 37 and BArch, B106, vol. 34725.

294 "Mr. Herzfeld also got the same impression as I, that the conversation did not lead to a burning of bridges or that my behavior did much damage in the china shop." Kluke to Epstein, Dec. 12, 1955, and Nov. 28, 1955, both in ibid.

295 Wilhelm Rohr, memo [minutes of meeting on Dec. 7, 1955, with Hübinger], Jan. 2, 1956, BArch, B198, vol. 1739.

296 Kluke to Hübinger, BMI, Leiter, Abt. III (Kultur), Jan. 21, 1956, BArch, B106, vol. 34725.

297 "Yet it remains very noteworthy that part of the rationale for the American project is the fear that the files will be reclassified after their return to Germany. In my view, we cannot take this motive seriously enough." Kluke to Hübinger, July 19, 1955, ibid.

298 Schieder to Ritter, Dec. 6, 1955, BArch, N1166, NL Ritter, vol. 286 and N1188, NL Schieder, vol. 372.

his view, the microfilming project threatened to exclude German historians entirely from primary source research.[299] Kluke tried to salvage the idea of German cooperation in Washington but was chided by Winter. Winter claimed that the IfZ's policy of buying microfilms from Washington had already weakened the German position because it implied consent to the retention and filming of the records. Cooperation would further damage the German cause: "The more we participate and thereby afford the [filming] project the semblance of legitimacy, the less there is pressure on the opposing side to return the records."[300] An agreement was reached to work toward a "normalization" of relations. In the context of this meeting, however, "normal" could only mean the return of the German records.[301] The Association of German Historians was "officially authorized" to represent this position.[302] Kluke lamented that "a hardening of positions has occurred on our side which does not get us anywhere . . . If, in the meantime, we push our refusal to the point where we do not participate but wait for the Auswärtiges Amt to be successful [in the negotiations], then for all scholarly purposes we cut ourselves out of the picture."[303]

The Germans did not in the end participate in the microfilming project in Alexandria, and, as Kluke predicted, West German historians were left empty-handed. In the 1950s, scholars could not simply arrange on their own to visit foreign archives and had to work through diplomatic channels. The Auswärtiges Amt often facilitated such research trips and expected the recipients of its assistance to report on their scholarly activities upon their return. Similarly, the Bundesarchiv and the Auswärtiges Amt's Political Archives viewed visits by foreign researchers as a facet of West German cultural diplomacy. In short, German and American scholars could not simply organize transnational cooperation as they saw fit. Such initiatives became unavoidably entangled in governmental policy. Although this did not mean the government could steer historical scholarship in any direction it liked, it could exert control over the conditions affecting historical research – by way of access to records.

299 Wilhelm Rohr, memo [minutes of meeting on Dec. 7, 1955 with Hübinger], Jan 2, 1956, BArch, B198, vol. 1739. See also Hermann Aubin, Chairman of Association of German Historians, to AA., May 14, 1956.
300 Wilhelm Rohr, memo [minutes of meeting on Dec. 7, 1955, with Hübinger], Jan. 2, 1956, BArch, B198, vol. 1739.
301 MinRat Scheidemann, Interior Ministry, Abt. III (Kultur), memo, Dec. 21, 1955, BArch, B106, vol. 34725, PA/AA, B118, vol. 510 and BArch, N1188, NL Schieder, vol. 651.
302 Speech Hübinger, memo Rohr, Jan. 2, 1955, BArch B198, vol. 1739.
303 Ibid.

Granting Access

*The Federal Republic would like to take this opportunity to renew once again its repeatedly
issued statement that it will store returned records in a proper archival manner and allow domestic
and foreign scholars access to the records.*[304]

The Federal Republic of Germany committed itself in an exchange of diplomatic notes with the governments of Britain, the United States, and France
to guaranteeing scholars, both German and foreign, access to the returned
records at all times. From then on, the German diplomatic records until
1945 were to open for historical research. The Allied confiscation of German governmental records and Bonn's urgent wish to have them returned
created a situation that opened wide the gates to previously inaccessible
or well-guarded collections. A similar situation arose again in 1989–1990
when, for a short time, the political upheaval following the fall of the Berlin
Wall unexpectedly gave open access to the vast store of information compiled by the East German government, most notably by the Stasi.[305] As
inviting as the analogy between 1945–1949 and 1989–1990 may seem, the
two cases are very different. The Stasi records were turned over directly
to the Stasi's victims and are today administered by an agency that has no
institutional ties to the one that created the files. By contrast, the diplomatic
records the Allies had seized were turned over to a state that claimed to be
the sole legal successor to the German Reich that had collapsed in 1945.
Upon their return, these records were stored in a ministry that stood out
among the institutions of the early Federal Republic for its continuity of
personnel.[306] The records returned to the place of their origin, sometimes
into the very same hands that had created them.

This section examines how the West German government came to make
the not quite voluntary concession to give broader access to archival records
than many other governments did, Britain and the United States included.
It will also look at the way the rules governing access were actually applied
at the Bundesarchiv and at the Political Archives of the Foreign Office.
Although the body of source material on reading room practices at the two
institutions is not satisfactory, it still offers some insight into the way they
handled the loss of control over their holdings resulting from, above all, the
British and American microfilming projects.

---

304 Hallstein to the Ambassadors of the United States, France and Great Britain, [identical text], Mar.
    14, 1956, PA/AA, B118, vol. 510.
305 Henke, *Wann bricht schon mal ein Staat zusammen?*; Weber, "Gefahr der Aktenvernichtung." Kleß-
    mann, *Zeitgeschichte in Deutschland*, 11f., compares 1989/90 with 1945 and establishes, as I do in
    the following, important differences between the situations.
306 Döscher, *Verschworene Gesellschaft*, 303–12, passim.

The 1956 Terms of Use at the Political Archives. The stipulation that the records being returned to West Germany would have to be made available to scholars of all nations for research first appeared in the Allied note of July 6, 1951.[307] The head of the Political Archives, Hans Andres, did not view this provision as a problem. The records of the Imperial era up until 1914 had been open to researchers before the start of the war in 1939. Andres acknowledged, however, that "certain restrictions on use" had applied in instances in which granting access to particular materials might not serve the interests of German foreign policy. Archival use by foreigners was based on reciprocity. Only users from countries "that maintained a particularly hostile position toward the German Reich (such as Poland at the time)," Andres explained, were not granted access.[308] In offering this rosy account of prewar policies, Andres neglected to mention the once common practice of removing documents from folders before they were delivered to archive users, nor did he elaborate upon German achives' anti-Polish policies.[309] He also did not appear to understand fully that the West German government was hardly in a position in 1951 to decide whether to be accommodating, let alone to demand reciprocity. He suggested that Bonn respond to the Allies by accepting the stipulation to open records up to 1914 for foreign researchers "under the same conditions of use that German researchers are subject to."[310] Those "conditions of use" had not yet been decided, however, as Political Archives' shelves were still largely empty in the summer of 1951.

In its draft response to the Allied note of July 6, the Auswärtiges Amt's Political Department offered a guarantee of access that went too far for Andres. The draft, Andres noted, pledged that Bonn would "conform fully" to the Allied governments' wish that foreign scholars be given "unhindered access" to the diplomatic files after their return.[311] Even the Allies, he complained, did not expect such a concession. Andres thus proposed an alternative wording intended to safeguard the West German government's initiative. Instead of offering "unhindered access," the Political Archives would "place these records at the disposal of foreign scholars for purposes

307 J. G. Ward for Ivone Kirkpatrick, Chairman AHC, July 6, 1951, AGSEC(51)1135, PA/AA, B118, vol. 507: "In this connection [i.e. return of pre-1914 files] the Allied High Commission would welcome confirmation that these files will thereafter be available for research by scholars of all nations."
308 Andres, "Stellungnahme zur Note vom 6. Juli 1951," July 20, 1951, PA/AA, B118, vol. 489.
309 Hallgarten, *Imperialismus vor 1914*, n. viiif.; Haar, *Historiker im NS*, 107–10; Musial, *Staatsarchive im Dritten Reich*, 22f., 54.
310 Andres, "Stellungnahme zur Note vom 6. Juli 1951," July 20, 1951, PA/AA, B118, vol. 489.
311 Andres to Brückner, Political Department, Nov. 11, 1952, PA/AA, B118, vol. 507.

of scholarly research."[312] In addition, the Auswärtiges Amt reaffirmed that foreign users who wished to use the archive would have to notify the Auswärtiges Amt in advance through their home countries' embassies.[313]

Officials at the High Commission were not certain how much access to the diplomatic files they could demand. The head of the chancellery of the British High Commissioner, Con O'Neill, questioned London's proposal to demand full and permanent access. "A condition of this sort is something we certainly cannot expect to secure German acceptance of, save in exceptional circumstances."[314] The Allied High Commission was initially even more circumspect and insisted only that scholars working on *Documents on German Foreign Policy* be guaranteed free access to the diplomatic records.[315] This insistence was, interestingly, more modest than the offer the Germans had already made. Not until the summer of 1955 did the acting director of the Foreign Office Library, Charles Henry Fone, instruct the British embassy to press to have the records fully open for research and to specify that "German and foreign scholars means all *bona fide* scholars and not just members of the [*Documents on German Foreign Policy*] project."[316] Since the British actually edited the final draft of the note on the return of the diplomatic records for their colleagues at the Auswärtiges Amt,[317] the British ideas were fully implemented. The West German government would guarantee access to the records at all times to domestic and foreign scholars.[318] The

---

312 "The Federal Government will readily comply with the wish expressed by the Allied governments in this context, to place these records at the disposal of foreign scholars for the purpose of scholarly research." Ibid. This wording was then included in Adenauer's note to the Chairman of the AHC, Ambassador Walter J. Donnelly, Nov. 22, 1952, PA/AA, B118, vol. 509.

313 [Osterloh], memo, Interior Ministry, [Culture dept.], Aug. 12, 1953, BArch, B106, vol. 1209: "The AA wishes to reintroduce the former rule that foreigners can only visit and use archives in Germany if they have received AA permission to do so through diplomatic channels."

314 O'Neill, Political Director and Head of Chancery, Wahnerheide, to Passant, Library, FO, Sept. 26, 1952, PRO FO 370/2249 LS3/122.

315 AHC to the Chancellor, Oct. 22, 1954, PA/AA, B118, vol. 508: "The Government of the Federal Republic should permit, upon request, the historians of all the Governments engaged in the project to do the necessary checking of the originals after the transfer of the documents to Germany."

316 Fone, Library, FO, to Kit Barclay, BritEmb Bonn, Sept. 30, 1955, PRO FO 370/2432 LS5/102. See also [British] Comments on German draft of proposed exchange of notes, n.d. [early October 1955], PA/AA, B118, vol. 509.

317 The note was "set in writing, word for word, with the representatives of the three embassies and [had] already been approved by the three governments in this revised version, as each of the three representatives verbally confirmed." PA/AA, B118, vol. 510.

318 Walter Hallstein, on behalf of the foreign minister [Heinrich von Brentano], to James B. Conant, U.S. Ambassador, Mar. 14, 1956, PA/AA, B118, vol. 510. Published in U.S. Treaties and Other International Agreement Series, vol. 7:2, no. 3613, 2119–24; Exchange of Letters between the Government of the UK of Great Britain and Northern Ireland and the Government of the Federal Republic of Germany concerning the transfer to the Federal Republic of Archives of the former German Foreign Office (March 14), April 12, 1956. Her Majesty's Stationary Office, Germany no. 1 (1957); Henke, "Schicksal deutscher Quellen," 594f.

German diplomatic service was instructed accordingly once the transfer of the documents was completed.[319]

The exchange of notes and the guarantee of access created an international precedent[320] and had an impact on the next issue on the agenda, namely, the return of military materials. With the agreement on the diplomatic records in place, the West German government tried to get negotiations started on military records. In a preliminary communication with the Allied governments, Bonn declared itself prepared to sign a treaty with the three Western Allies "that guarantees the unlimited, free access to the archives to be reacquired by designees of each of the three governments and by free scholarly research."[321] The phrase "free scholarly research" was deliberately chosen to create a loophole for excluding historians from East Germany and the other Soviet bloc countries. For their part, the Allies assumed that all other document-return agreements with the Federal Republic would include access guarantees.[322] The State Department did think it necessary, however, to address the issue of access explicitly when non-biographical materials from the Berlin Document Center were transferred in 1961.[323]

The precedent of guaranteeing access to German governmental records had an unintended side effect. Inadvertently, it generated pressure on the British and American governments to supplement the German record with

319 Ministerialdirektor Georg von Broich-Oppert, Runderlaß 1. An alle Arbeitseinheiten, 2. An sämtliche diplomatischen und konsularischen Vertretungen der Bundesrepublik, Offenlegung der Akten des AA aus der Zeit bis 1945 vor der internationalen Wissenschaft, July 8, 1959, PA/AA, B2, vol. 72.

320 Following the peace treaty of San Francisco in 1951, again in 1958, and in the early 1960s, Japan received diplomatic records and business papers, among other material, which American agencies had confiscated for intelligence purposes and as evidence for the Tokyo war crimes trials. As an investigation connected to the Japanese Imperial Government Disclosure Act of 2000 showed, receipts for the records returned in these transfers cannot be found anymore, nor could it be ascertained whether or not the U.S. government received a guarantee of access at the time of the transfer. The U.S. Army, Navy, and Air Force had made their approval dependent on such an access clause. It is likely that the Americans simply forgot to insert an access clause in the pertinent paperwork. See Bradsher, "Survey of Disposition of Captured Japanese Records;" Interagency Working Group (IWG), Implementation of the Japanese Imperial Govenrment Disclosure Act and the Japanese War Crimes Provisions of the Nazi War Crimes Disclosure Act. An Interim Report to Congress at http://www.archives.gov/iwg/reports/japanese-interim-report-march-2002-1.html#japan (accessed Feb. 14, 2011).

321 Verbal note to the Ambassadors of the United States, Great Britain and France, Oct. 16, 1956, PA/AA, B118, vol. 510.

322 Fone to Peter Wilkinson, BritEmb Bonn, Jan. 20, 1959, PRO FO 370/2550 LS5/79: "Considerable importance is attached to such [i.e. scholarly; A.E.] right of access and it is now thought that the Germans should be asked to give the same general undertaking as they did in connexion with the return of the archives of the former German Foreign Office."

323 Ullrich to Noble, Sept. 4, 1961, Noble to Ullrich, Oct. 4, 1961; Ullrich, memo for Ref. 305 and Dg11, Nov. 29, 1961; Draft verbal note for the United States, Dec. 14, 1961, all in PA/AA, B118, vol. 123.

their own. If they did not publish collections of World War II era diplomatic records as well, they risked opening *Documents on German Foreign Policy* to the criticism that it was one-sided propaganda ploy.[324] But not only publication policy was affected, the access agreement that the West Germans signed cast an unfavorable light on how the British and Americans were handling access to German diplomatic records at Whaddon Hall, as well as to their very own records in their respective national archives. Whaddon had never functioned as an archive that outside researchers would have been allowed to use. The sources for the years that the publication project was to cover were not to be opened for general research until the respective volume had been published.[325] Every once in a while, historians with good connections succeeded in gaining access to the original sources,[326] while everyone else had to make do with the few microfilms that had been released.[327] As to the British and American diplomatic records, by 1956, the former were accessible up to 1902, the latter up to 1926.[328] During the 1950s, British historians repeatedly criticized the government's hurdles impeding research, especially on World War I.[329] The irony was not lost on Johannes Ullrich, the director of the Political Archives. In 1962, he thought

324 In 1944, planning began for the *Documents on British Foreign Policy, 1919–1939*, edited by E. Llewellyn Woodward and Rohan Butler. See Bialer, "Telling the Truth." On American publications about the war and postwar planning within the FRUS series, see Zala, *Zensur*, 116–26.

325 Minutes Passant to Sir Orme Sargent, Feb. 18, 1949, PRO FO 370/1953 L605: "Under present agreements the documents both of the period after 1918 and of the period 1867–1918 will remain closed to private research during this time [i.e. of the editorial project, A.E.]." See also the original "Charta" of the DGFP from June 19, 1946, NA RG 84, POLAD, entry 2531B, box 100: "It is recommended that the German records to be used for this project should not be released for publication or other use by unofficial persons until the material involved has been approved for publication by the cooperating Powers. The documents should only be made available to the German authorities as and when the editors have completed their work upon them."

326 For example, W. N. Medlicott received permission in 1952 to see records from 1880/81. See Minutes Lambert to Passant, Mar. 17, 1952, PRO FO 370/2273 LS22/2. Medlicott was the author of the official history of Anglo-American economic warfare (*The Economic Blockade*, 1952ff.) and became a member of the British DGFP advisory committee in 1953.

327 On the topic of access for German historians, see Ritter to Aubin, Nov. 10, 1955, BArch, N1166, NL Ritter, vol. 286; Kluke to Aubin, Nov. 22, 1955, IfZ Hausarchiv, ID102, vol. 1; Embassy of the Federal Republic in London to AA, Feb. 23, 1957, Benutzung der Akten des Politischen Archivs in England, Feb. 23, 1957, PA/AA, B118, vol. 6.

328 Meanwhile, the French records were only open up to 1877. In 1967, British records were available up to 1922, and in 1968, the fifty-year-closure period was reduced to thirty years. On the British handling of official material, Lowe, "Archival Report"; and Wilson, "Public Records." Some general thoughts on declassification and access in Kreis, "Die Sperrfristen."

329 James Joll, "German Diplomatic Documents," *TLS*, no. 2695, Sept. 25, 1953, 613; letter to the editor by George P. Gooch, A. J. P. Taylor, F. C. Corrance, and C. Collin Davies to *The Times* (London), Aug. 19–21, 1954; "Diplomacy and Scholarship," *TLS*, no. 2753, Nov. 5, 1954. See also Butterfield, "Official History," 205 (1951); Taylor, "Keeping It Dark" (1959); Watt, "Right to Know" (1963).

that the access guarantee that had been imposed on the West Germans had created

a certain advantage, since we – coerced or uncoerced – have gained a lead by opening the records analogous to that of the major publication of records after the First World War: and in this lies also a certain political opportunity: but one must exploit it cleverly along the lines of saying: now is the time for the 'Free World' to open unconditionally their archives to international scholarship. Should the others not do it, then they will be suspected of having much to hide.[330]

Indeed, British research on World War I did not recover from this structural disadvantage for a long time.[331] Still, Ullrich's analogy to *Die Große Politik* is not entirely accurate because the Federal Republic certainly did not agree to guarantee full access to records out of a conviction that the country could gain any sort of scholarly advantage from this move.

Archival Micropolitics. Once the access guarantee existed on paper, it had to be implemented. Scholars abroad were pessimistic and had low expectations. The time-consuming and costly process of microfilming German records in Great Britain and in the United States had not been undertaken, after all, solely to increase the source material available to researchers: it was also intended to secure German compliance with the promise of access. Creating microfilm copies stripped German archivists of control over the records and bruised their professional egos. The loss of control also meant a loss of power. That new terms of use had to be issued was an externally induced development to which archivists had to submit. In this new situation, old access regulations could not simply be re-implemented, nor could archivists be as arbitrary or imperious in responding to researchers' requests as previously.[332] Given that they were being watched very closely, the German archivists affected by the document return, especially the staff at the Political Archives, knew that they could not afford a single faux pas.

German archivists were initially uncertain about what the access guarantee would mean in practice. In 1959, the Bundesarchiv tried to find out from the Auswärtiges Amt how seriously it had to take the guarantee. The records of the Reich Chancellery had arrived in Koblenz from Whaddon Hall, and the Bundesarchiv sought to coordinate access policy with the Political

---

330 Ullrich to Gerhard Ritter, Apr. 25, 1962, PA/AA, B118, vol. 77.

331 Pogge von Strandmann, "Britische Historiker," 939f. In a 1955 report on research literature about the Second World War in Great Britain, Grunewald, "Travaux," 64, points out the paradoxical situation that, by this time in Great Britain, it was easier to obtain access to primary sources for research on WWII than on WWI.

332 Pöhlmann, *Kriegsgeschichte*, 322–6, describes vividly the highhanded treatment of archive users, who, as a rule, were thought to be bothersome in the Reich Archives.

Archives to avoid potential criticism. The Bundesarchiv, in other words, did not want to appear backward compared with the Political Archives. Officials at the Political Archives advised that the 1956 access stipulation was a commitment that "warranted strict observance" – a view apparently not shared entirely by the director of the Bundesardchiv.[333] In fact, Georg Winter seems to have considered closing the Reich Chancellery records, which would have been ineffective in light of the fact that the records had been microfilmed.[334] However, the Political Archives, under the direction of Johannes Ullrich, consistently insisted that full access be granted to the returned records.[335]

The issue arose again when the first shipment of so-called nonbiographical records were transferred from the Berlin Document Center to the Bundesarchiv. Officials in Koblenz again turned to the Political Archive, asking how to handle applications for access to the newly arrived materials, especially records on individuals still living.[336] This time Ullrich took it upon himself to answer. In clear and unequivocal language, he explained that the guarantee of access had been decisive in overcoming the Allies' hesitancy to return the captured documents. It was binding and applied to both the material that had already arrived and the materials still to come. Even though Bonn had given only a declaration of intent for the latter, Ullrich argued, it would not be befitting "if the responsible German authorities refused to make material that has already been received not available to designees of the three governments and scholarly researchers."[337] Just how inclusive the definition of scholarly access was to be would have to be determined on a case-by-case basis. As long as no significant concerns about the qualification of the reader existed, access to the sources was to be given. The Political Archives, Ullrich added, had not had any negative experiences with private scholarly users. Even Polish and "Soviet zone" researchers were admitted. He recommended "generous accommodation" of foreign visitors in particular. "The Auswärtiges Amt does not exercise censorship, so that misuse in evaluating sources falls back on the reader and

333 Report [on a conversation with archivist Dr. Vogel], Hans Philippi, Political Archive, Aug. 18, 1959, PA/AA, B118, vol. 163. Philippi noted that, if he had understood Vogel correctly, "the head of the Federal Archives does not seem to share this view fully."

334 Ibid.: "It was well known that the mass microfilming of German material in the United States only derives from a latent mistrust of the German archival administrations. The closure of Reich Chancellery records would be a way to augment existing suspicion and, apart from that, is also completely infeasible because the photo series would be freely accessible in London and Washington."

335 Ibid.

336 Wolfgang A. Mommsen to das Politische Archiv, July 8, 1960, PA/AA, B118, vol. 163.

337 Johannes Ullrich to Bundesarchiv, Oct. 5, 1960, PA/AA, B118, vol. 163. Ullrich had presented his letter to the Federal Archives to the legal department to be co-signed. See also VLR I Meyer-Lindenberg, Legal Dept., to Political Archive, Sept. 2, 1960, ibid.

not on the Auswärtiges Amt." Ullrich betrayed his suspicions of the reasons behind the Bundesarchiv's inquiry with his reminder "that it cannot be the business of the German archival administrations to cover up the behavior of functionaries in the Nazi system and to hinder the clarification of facts."

Did the Political Archives adhere to the policies its director recommended to the Bundesarchiv? Given the limited amount of information available about practices at the Political Archives, it is possible to draw only preliminary conclusions. It is clear, however, that the director of the Political Archives has never been able to set policies on use according to strictly archival criteria. Because the Political Archives were – and still are – part of the Auswärtiges Amt, political concerns have always influenced its policies. Ullrich could not simply ignore the ministry's Political Department.

The Political Archives' reading room had barely opened its doors in Bonn when the first press reports denounced the "supposedly antiquated practice of the Political Archives including the renewed classification of returned records."[338] The archive was accused of having immediately locked away the files upon their return. Certainly, the Auswärtiges Amt was very restrictive when it came to personnel records. The Allies had neglected to press for a guarantee of access when those records were returned in 1951. The State Department had filmed only the questionnaires that senior Auswärtiges Amt personnel had been asked to complete to replace personnel files destroyed in a 1944 air raid. The Political Archives was willing to supply information from the personnel files but would not let users view the documents. Even within the ministry, access to personnel files was highly regulated, although the personnel department made irritating exemptions. Nazi-era "Jewish experts" who were brought to trial at in the 1950s and 1960s for their role in the deportation of Jews were granted access to their files in order to prepare their defense.[339] Although this questionable practice was not made public, the Auswärtiges Amt came under suspicion of concealing information about the pasts of its personnel. The Bundestag committee investigating the backgrounds of newly hired high-level diplomats complained time and

---

338 Paul Kluke to LR Dirk Oncken, Political Dept., July 16, 1957, PA/AA, B118, vol. 29. Kluke refered to the article "Archivalisches," *Sonntagsblatt*, May 26, 1957, and pointed out that American historians had already broached the topic with him. See also "So streng sind hier die Bräuche," *Rhein-Neckar-Zeitung*, June 1/2, 1957.

339 Ullrich to Bundesarchiv, Oct. 5, 1960; Dg ZB [i.e. administration], Runderlaß an alle Arbeitseinheiten im Hause [AA], May 20, 1963, PA/AA, B118, vol. 163: AA staff members were not allowed to see pre-1945 personnel records for private scholarly purposes. For offical purposes, they could be consulted only with the consent of the personnel department in the rooms of the Political Archives. Former "Jewish expert" Horst Wagner was granted access to his personnel files in March 1957, his colleague Fritz Gebhardt von Hahn saw files pertaining to his "work" during the war in early 1964. See PA/AA, B100, vol. 2094 and B118, vol. 121.

again about the difficulties it encountered with the Auswärtiges Amt, especially about access to personnel records.[340] Rumors spread quickly, even
abroad, that the personnel files had been tampered with.[341]

Access to other records was also still subject to strict rules. In 1957,
the Political Archives began drafting new guidelines on official and private
use of its files.[342] In connection with this project, Ullrich summarized the
new situation facing archivists: because records were being used and copied
to a "no longer assessable degree," they no longer represented "unique
items."[343] Owing to the access guarantee, the Auswärtiges Amt did not have
any legal means "to influence the editing of a publication based on material
of the [Auswärtige Amt]." The "indiscrete and tactless use of records" could
affect the interests of West Germany, other countries, firms, organizations,
or individuals. Such "unwelcome occurrences" were all the more likely
because it had become practically impossible to unmask individuals feigning
scholarly intentions in order to use records for other ends. Consequently,
the access guarantee prevented the Political Archives from imposing any
"restriction on the user's freedom to publish by way of inserting a stipulation
into the access regulations . . . requiring the submission of the manuscript
to be published, as had previously been the case. The only means left to
the Political Archives is to exert a moral influence on the user, which is
naturally ineffective when dealing with people whose intentions are anyway
dishonest."[344] The terms of use that the archive presented to Secretary of
State Walter Hallstein for approval in April 1957 made no mention of the
access guarantee given to the Allies, thus leaving users in the dark about
their rights.[345]

340 Döscher, *Verschworene Gesellschaft*, 180; see also the hearing with the chief of personnel, Wilhelm
    Haas, ibid. 193, and the first director of the Political Archives, Hanns-Erich Haack, who received
    the personnel records in 1951, Stenographisches Protokoll über die 6. Sitzung des UA 47, Feb. 15,
    1952, BT, Parlamentsarchiv. I thank Dr. Thomas W. Maulucci for this source. The list of personnel
    files that the UA 47 did receive can be found in PA/AA, vol. 487.
341 Alfred Wiener, founder of the Library carrying his name in London, reported to John Wheeler-
    Bennett in May 1952, that the personnel records "show now remarkable gaps." From this, he
    concluded that other records could also be cleaned up "if they are not handed over to the right
    type of people." JCC 46th Meeting, May 7, 1952, PRO FO 370/2269 LS 18/6.
342 Entwurf Benutzungsordnung für das Politische Archiv des Auswärtigen Amtes, Jan. 26, 1957,
    PA/AA, B118, vol. 3. The archivist Hans Philippi reviewed Ullrich's draft and suggested two
    restrictions: "11) Restriction of use in cases in which particular political circumstances and consid-
    eration mandate this. 12) All topics extracted from the records are to be presented upon completion.
    The AA's intention with this measure is not to censor, but only to examine work with regard to
    possible political repercussions." Ullrich did not accept these suggestions.
343 Ullrich, Draft of the Terms of Use, Feb. 13, 1957, ibid.
344 Ibid.
345 Benutzungs- und Lesesaalordnung, Apr, 16, 1957, PA/AA, B118, vol. 163. Only the bulletin of the
    Federal Government mentioned the guarantee in connection with the return of the documents:
    Bulletin des Presse- und Informationsamtes der Bundesregierung, Sept. 20, 1957, no. 175, 1620.

The first "unwelcome occurrence" took place in the autumn of 1957. The Swedish daily *Dagens Nyheter* published a series of articles on the role of King Gustav V during World War II that touched on the topic of collaboration. The series met with criticism in the Political Department and prompted the question about use of the Political Archives by journalists.[346] In his initial statement on the issue, Ullrich came out in support of the continued admittance of journalists if only "for *tactical* reasons . . . with regard to the forthcoming negotiations on the remaining archival holdings." Dirk Oncken, legation councillor at the Political Department, wanted instead to raise the question of "misuse" in the negotiations. He assumed that the Western Allies would be sympathetic once they realized that the archives could be used by "journalists . . . who are manipulated by the East."[347] Ullrich fought vehemently against these plans. In light of the negative press received at the time of the reopening of the Political Archives, he did not consider it wise to adopt a basically negative attitude toward journalists. In the case of the *Dagens Nyheter* articles, the archive users were qualified scholars who chose to publish some of their findings in a newspaper. Ullrich again brought up the key points that the ongoing negotiations could be endangered if access was restricted and that the records were, in any event, accessible on microfilm and, in some cases, in print. He emphasized further that the

danger lies much less in the form and the place of the presentation than in the record material itself. . . . No particular journalistic elaboration is needed at all to make the circumstance seem so serious, it is the stark wording of the records themselves. . . . To prevent all embarrassing discussions, one would need to stop publishing the content of all *those* files that reveal any kind of collaborationism.[348]

Even though the Auswärtiges Amt's press office backed Ullrich, Oncken held to his opinion that the Allied access clause had been intended for scholars and was never meant to apply to journalists. He argued that this

---

Among scholarly articles *about* the PA, Pretsch, 'Politisches Archiv," 301, was the first, in 1979, to mention the access guarantee. He was the director of the archive at the time. Philippi, "Politisches Archiv (I)," 149, did mention in 1958 that all material up to 1945 would be available. However, the explanation he provides only vaguely points to the political turning point of 1945, after which it had become imperative "to reject emphatically the idea of a closed or only partly accessible archive." He did not refer to the access guarantee.

346 LR Oncken, Political Department, report, re: Einsicht in die Aken des AA für in- und ausländische Privatpersonen, Dec. 10, 1957, PA/AA, B 118, vol. 504.

347 Both quotes in ibid. Original emphasis. Scribbled on the file by State Secretary Karl Carstens, Nov. 11, 1957: "I am of the opinion that the Archive should not be made accessible to journalists."

348 Ullrich, Aufzeichnung über die Frage der Benutzung des Politischen Archivs durch Journalisten, Jan 13, 1958, PA/AA, B118, vol. 3. Original emphasis. See also Ullrich, Stellungnahme des Ref. 117 zu der Aufzeichnung des Ref. 200 [Jan. 20, 1958] zur Frage der Benutzung des PA durch Journalisten, Jan. 27, 1958, ibid.

was how the policy should continue to be implemented in order to avoid an "impairment" of foreign relations. "Above all, it is important that a situation be created which enables the Political Archives to exert a strong influence over the selection of its users."[349] Such power seemed all the more important because the Auswärtiges Amt had become a frequent target of accusations from East Berlin, which claimed the ministry had been "renazified" by the many former Nazis on its staff.[350] In the end, Oncken prevailed over Ullrich.[351]

The influence of the Cold War on access policy was even more evident when users came from Poland or East Germany. Ullrich fought repeatedly for equal treatment of all scholarly users and invoked the access guarantee given to the Allies in arguing against the principle of *raison d'état* championed by the other departments of the Auswärtiges Amt. In the end, Ulrich's position was undermined by the Americans, who signaled their approval of a more restrictive interpretation of the access guarantee.

The first application to use the Political Archives was submitted by an East German scholar. In assessing it for his superiors, Ullrich referred not only to the access clause but also to the principle of reciprocity. At the time of the application, West German historians were still able to work in East German archives. A rejection of the East German application, he argued, would play into the hands of "Soviet zone propaganda" and force the researchers to head to London to use the microfilms there.[352] The fact that the Political Department had no problem with approving this first application indicates that the Auswärtiges Amt was not under considerable political pressure. The situation soon changed, however, as the Federal Republic came under accusation, not least from East Berlin, for allowing former Nazis to fill positions of authority. The German Eastern Affairs Desk and the Polish Desk led the resistance to Ullrich's access policies. After the tabloid *Bild* became interested in knowing whether Polish researchers were allowed to

349 LR I Jaenicke, Press Division, Jan 17, 1958, ibid.; LR Oncken, Political Department, report, Frage der Benutzung des Politischen Archivs durch Journalisten, Jan. 20, 1958, ibid.
350 The most sophisticated campaign by the East Berlin "Committee for German Unity" against the West German Foreign Office was launched in March 1959. In 1956, the Committee had already succeeded in forcing Otto Bräutigam, head of the Eastern Department at the AA, to resign by publishing the wartime diary that he kept while serving as Rosenberg's representative for Caucasian affairs. Heilmann, "Kriegstagebuch des Diplomaten Otto Bräutigam"; Lemke, "Kampagnen gegen Bonn."
351 Only "scholars" would be allowed to use the archives. LR Oncken to Ref. 117, Feb. 12, 1958, PA/AA, B118, vol. 474.
352 "It may also be in the interests of the Federal Republic," writes Ullrich here, "that *German* researchers, even those from the Eastern zone, read records of German provenance in German and not in foreign archives." Ullrich to Abt. 2, Mar. 5, 1957, PA/AA, B118, vol. 504. Original emphasis.

work at the Political Archives[353] and State Secretary Karl Carstens began urging that more caution be used in admitting scholars from "the Soviet zone,"[354] the Polish Desk attempted to stop all visits by Polish historians. It urged the negotiation of a "protection clause" with the Allied governments that would ease the obligation of archival access so that the Political Archives could turn down applicants from the Eastern bloc. For archival visits that had already been approved, the Polish Desk suggested that the readers be presented "'presorted' material."[355] A similar approach was advocated in early 1965 with regard to applications from the GDR. It was suggested that the Political Archives turn down the applications on the argument that an insufficient number of work places were available in the reading room.[356]

The German Eastern Affairs Desk – represented in the clash with Ullrich by its director Gotthold Starke[357] – was particularly interested in denying access to the pre-1939 papers of the "Eastern consulates" (*Ostkonsulate*) that had been returned from Whaddon Hall in 1958.[358] Starke, himself a member of the prewar German minority in Poland, feared that Polish researchers would use these records to publish revelations about German

353 Ullrich, report, Die Benutzung des PA durch polnische Gelehrte, Jan. 28, 1960, PA/AA, B118, vol. 163.

354 State Secretary Karl Carstens, memorandum, Oct. 12, 1960, PA/AA, B2, vol. 72: "I am of the opinion that we should use greater caution than we have to date and especially should not make events from the most recent past (such as German-English relations from 1939–1941) accessible to users from the Soviet zone."

355 Ullrich, report, "Die Benutzung des PA durch polnische Gelehrte und die in diesem Zusammenhang von Referat 705 (Ref. 701) vorgeschlagene Einführung einer 'Schutzklausel,'" Apr. 24, 1962, PA/AA, B118, vol. 163.

356 Weinandy, report (concept), Benutzung des PA durch Historiker aus der SBZ und den Ostblockstaaten, Jan. 14, 1965, PA/AA, B118, vol. 291.

357 Gotthold Starke (1896–1968) was born in Runowo, Wirsitz county (administrative district Bromberg/Bydgoszcz), graduated from Gymnasium in 1914, was sent to the front and wounded soon thereafter; later he studied law in Heidelberg, Berlin, and Göttingen. As a participant in the border hostilities with Poland in 1919, he was forced to leave the area and went to Berlin, where he joined the "June Club" associated with Arthur Moeller van den Bruck. He held onto his Polish nationality, although this hindered a career in the Prussian justice system. In 1922, he returned to Bromberg, assumed the post of editor-in-chief of the *Deutsche Rundschau in Polen*, and became one of the founders of the "Kant Club" in 1924. In September 1939, he was interned by the Polish. Upon his release, he entered the Foreign Service. From 1941–1943 he was the head of the Eastern Europe Section of the press department at the Auswärtiges Amt in Berlin. In 1945, he was captured by the Soviets and did not return to West Germany until 1955. See *Deutsche Biographische Enzyklopädie*, vol. 9, 453; Breyer, "Gotthold Starke."

358 The British had drafted a three-step plan for the return of diplomatic records. Although the first step already included consular records, the papers of the German consulates in Memel, Danzig, Poland, Switzerland, and Czechoslovakia were excluded from this. See the return schedule of August 1955 drawn up by Kenneth Duke in PRO FO 370/2431 LS5/82. In a letter to Barclay, BritEmb Bonn, Sept. 30, 1955, PRO FO 370/2432 LS5/102, Fone specifically names Bromberg (Bydgoszcz), Brünn (Brno), Chust (Khust), Danzig, Eger, Geneva, Kattowitz (Katowice), Krakow, Lemberg (Lviv), Lodz, Mährisch Ostrau (Ostrava), Memel (Klaipėda), Pilsen, Posen (Poznań), Preschau (Prešov), Reichenberg (Liberec), Teschen (Cieszyn-Český Těšín), Thorn (Toruń), Warsaw, and Zurich.

prewar sabotage and infiltration activities in Poland, painting the German minority as a "fifth column."[359] Starke had no authority over the Political Archives, which had to take the access guarantee into consideration. The archivists Heinz Buttkus met with Starke and suggested a compromise solution.[360] Buttkus assured Starke that inquiries would be answered with notice that the records had to be reorganized and thus could not yet be made available to researchers. To inquiries that came after the reorganization was complete, the Political Archives would respond that the consulate reports were not available because they were in use – as they were in fact, by Buttkus himself. It was considered archival custom that documents being used by one researcher could not be made available to another. Buttkus would therefore sit on the consulate reports as long as necessary. This practice was part of the repertoire of tricks the Prussian Archival Administration had employed under Albert Brackmann and would have been familiar to Buttkus.[361] The first Polish historians began work in the Political Archives in 1959.[362] It cannot be determined whether the records of the German consulates would have even been relevant to their research. Those records were not, in any event, presented to them.[363]

Arguments between Ullrich's and Starke's departments over archival access for Polish researchers were a regular occurrence. Dr. Karol Grünberg, a Polish scholar who wanted to work on "the social structures of the German population in Upper Silesia," submitted a reader application that prompted

359 At this time, in late 1958, Starke could not have known yet the content of the records, but obviously he divined it. The records were utilized in Kotowski, *Polens Politik*, 338–44, and his findings show that Starke's concern was justified. Particulary the papers from the Consulate General in Toruń yield a good deal on attempts to recruit German saboteurs by the Security Service (SD) and the Gestapo, which recruited geographically in Polish Silesian and politically among the supporters of the *Jungdeutsche Partei* (Young German Party).

360 Report Dr. Buttkus for Ullrich, Nov. 20, 1958, PA/AA, B118, vol. 163. Original emphasis. Buttkus was a graduate of the Institut for Archival Science (IfA) in Berlin-Dahlem. On Oct. 12, 1939, he was transferred from his job at the Magdeburg State Archives by the Prussian Archival Administration to Warsaw, where he worked on securing Polish archives and registries, on determining the locations of depositories and repatriating the holdings. After the invasion of the Soviet Union, he was also deployed to Białystok, Novgorod, Brest and Minsk. See Musial, *Staatsarchive im Dritten Reich*, 126, 135, 162. On the context of the IfA, see Haar, *Historiker im Nationalsozialismus*, 108–10.

361 See Haar, *Historiker im Nationalsozialismus*, 115. The British and Americans did the same thing with German diplomatic records in Whaddon Hall. See n. 325.

362 Leon Grosfeld, Polish Academy of Science, Warsaw; Marian Wojciechowski, Historical Institute, Toruń; Dr. Kulak, West Institute, Poznań; Dr. Jurkiewicz, Institute for International Relations, Warsaw.

363 "In accord with the agreement with Dept. 701 [i.e. Starke; A.E.], to which explicit reference is being made, the Political Archives did not present the Polish scholars the sources from the German Eastern consulates because they had already been released as of 1958 to a member of the Archive [Buttkus himself; A.E.] for scholarly use." Report, Buttkus, Jan. 13, 1960, PA/AA, B118, vol. 163.

Starke to intervene again.[364] Ullrich assigned Grünberg a seat in the reading room for autumn 1961. For the co-signing Eastern desk at the AA, Ullrich providently referred to the reciprocal actions by the Polish archival administration.[365] Apparently, he had foreseen the protest that his accommodating answer would provoke. Starke had accused the head archivist already in the case of the historian Marian Wojciechowski from Torun of having acted against the "earnest objection" of his office.[366] Wojciechowski had been allowed to "take several hundred copies back home" that would now be used against West Germany. Starke expressed his "due respect to the freedom of scholarship, but *only* the freedom of *scholarship* – not the support for the opponent's propaganda!"[367] Wojciechowski himself had been pleasantly surprised to discover that he would be given "*all* available material to read," from which Starke concluded that in Polish archives records were censored before being presented. In Eastern European countries there was "no free scholarship in a Western sense." Grünberg's research on Silesia sounded harmless enough, but there was "unfortunately no way of knowing whether Dr. Grünberg feels called upon to prove the thoroughly incorrect theory of the 'fifth column' that the exemplarily loyal ethnic Germans are said to have formed in prewar Poland [and apply that theory to] Upper Silesia." Starke admitted that Grünberg would be able to see all the records in London, should he decide to go there. Still, argued Starke, this would be easier for the Germans to tolerate "in so far as they were not themselves cutting the branch with which they will be whipped." Starke urged Ullrich not to let Grünberg come to the archive in September, but only six months later. This would give the archive sufficient time to "sort out" the material to be presented to Grünberg.[368]

364 Henryk Altmann, Director General of the Polish Archives, Warsaw, to Ullrich, June 21, 1961, PA/AA, B118, vol. 237. Altmann supervised Grünberg's habilitation thesis. Grünberg, born 1923 in Drohobycze, completed his university study in history at the University of Warsaw in 1951. He earned his PhD in 1958 and completed his habilitation work in 1968. Afterward, he was a lecturer for nineteenth- and twentieth-century history at Copernicus University in Toruń.

365 Ullrich to Altmann, July 31, 1961, draft copy, with notation "cesset!" ibid. The letter was presented to Dept. 701 (German Eastern Affairs) and Dept. 705 (in charge of matters re. Poland) for co-signature. Ullrich had made inquiries beforehand to Eastern European researchers in West Germany about Grünberg. See Ullrich to Werner Philipp, Direktor Osteuropa Institut, FU Berlin, July 11, 1961, ibid.

366 In 1959, Wojciechowski worked on German-Polish relations from 1933 to 1939 at the Political Archives. See Ullrich, report re: Die Benutzung des PA durch polnische Gelehrte, Jan. 28, 1960, PA/AA, B118, vol. 163.

367 VLR Starke, Ref. 701 to Ref. 705, Einsichtnahme von Archivmaterial durch Herrn Dr. Karol Grünberg, Aug. 8, 1961, PA/AA, B118, vol. 237. Ullrich added emphasis to original by underlining.

368 Ibid. Starke wanted to assign a German researcher to this task. Dept. 705 concurred with his comments.

Ullrich used all the means at his disposal to defend the autonomy of the Political Archives on the issue of user access. He did end up making a concession on the timing of Grünberg's archival visit by offering him a slot for April 1962.[369] He never once consented, however, to having presorted material prepared for a particular user. Any attempt to tamper with the materials presented to a researcher could be exposed by checking the microfilms in London and Washington, he repeatedly argued, and evidence of tampering would be far more damaging than any information in the files. The records themselves said nothing about the Federal Republic, as he pointed out, "but always only about political systems . . . that belonged to the past."[370] A "protection clause" as demanded by the Polish Desk could hardly be kept out of the public eye permanently. Not only would it "deliver the fuel for agitation sought by East bloc propagandists," the Federal Republic would come dangerously close to "distorting history" if it engaged in such practices of "obscuration or concealment."[371] Ullrich could not resist a barb against Starke himself, who had spoken "of the exemplarily loyal ethnic Germans in prewar Poland." If Starke's account were accurate, "objectively," then it "remains puzzling that concerns could exist with regard to evidence of a contradictory theory." Moreover, if, as Starke charged, scholarship in Poland was carried out "pseudoscientifically and with bias," Ullrich added, a "Polish falsification of history" could be countered "easily by German objectivity."[372]

Ullrich spoke out against reopening negotiations with the Allies on archival access so as not to endanger the ongoing negotiations on the military records,[373] but State Secretary Rolf Lahr decided otherwise in 1965. West German diplomats were to take up the access questions with the Allies again.[374] Lahr could count on the cooperation of the Americans, because

---

369 Ullrich to Henryk Altmann, Warschau, Aug. 11, 1961; Altmann to Ullrich, Oct. 19, 1961, both in PA/AA, B118, vol. 237.

370 Ullrich, Stellungnahme zu dem Einreiseantrag des polnischen Staatsangehörigen Dr. Karol Grünberg, Jan. 22, 1962, ibid.

371 Ullrich, report, Apr. 24, 1962, PA/AA, B118, vol. 163.

372 Ullrich, Notiz zu der Stellungnahme des Ref. 701 und 705 zum Antrag . . . für Dr. Karol Grünberg, Sept. 6, 1961, PA/AA, B118, vol. 237.

373 Ullrich, report, Apr. 24, 1962, PA/AA, B118, vol. 163; see also Ullrich, report re: die Benutzung des PA durch polnische Gelehrte, Jan. 28, 1960, PA/AA, B118, vol. 163.

374 Ullrich, Aufzeichnung, May 8, 1962 and May 10, 1962, both in PA/AA, B118, vol. 123. The actual wording of Lahr's decision cannot be found. However, it is clear in a letter from Referat II A 5 (in charge of matters re. Poland), dated Oct. 5, 1965, PA/AA, B118, vol. 237, that the decision was made at a directors conference on May 2, 1965. This occasion was also used to stipulate that "East European scholars are to be denied access to the Archives should there be justified grounds to suspect political misuse of research work."

Bernard Noble had already indicated in 1961 that Ullrich's interpretation of the access guarantee was "perhaps somewhat broader than we had proposed." What the State Department had intended was to ensure access "to qualified researchers of friendly Allied powers."[375] Noble thus not only undermined Ullrich in this specific instance but also watered down the access guarantee in general, even though the State Department had originally demanded and fully supported such a guarantee.[376] It is not possible to ascertain precisely what was consequently worked out between West Germany and the Western Allies. However, the Polish desk at the Auswärtiges Amt referred from that point on to a "suggestion made by the Americans to prevent the use of the archive with administrative measures, if need be."[377] In 1964, this "suggestion" was used against both a Czech and a Yugoslavian historian; the latter was referred to the microfilms in London.[378] The British, however, did not share the American distinction between friendly and unfriendly countries. When the head of the research department at the Foreign Office learned of the case, he demanded that all scholars,

375 Noble to Fritz T. Epstein, co-editor of the ADAP at AA, July 27, 1961, PA/AA, B118, vol. 123.
376 A year later, Noble torpedoed the access guarantee once again. In a conflict between the Flick company and the West German government over returning files originating from the Düsseldorf firm, the access guarantee was used by the Auswärtiges Amt, Ministry of the Interior, Political Archives, and Federal Archives to fend off Flick's claim to the papers. The records had been confiscated by the Americans at the end of the war and evaluated for the Nuremberg trial against industrialists (Case 5). In March 1960, the records were returned as part of a routine delivery of German government records. The company filed claims to the papers and let it be known that they would be handled as the company saw fit. This announcement explicitly included the destruction of records. Countering this were the government ministries and institutions mentioned above, who argued instead that the access guarantee included the Flick company papers and that these had been returned to the West German government and not to the company. The aim was to keep the papers available for the newly established Central Office for the Investigation of National Socialist Crimes at Ludwigsburg and for historical research. The Flick company threatened to sue the West German government. In the meantime, the records had been deposited in the Federal Archives. Ullrich went so far as to have a contract prepared to permanently settle the issue of keeping the papers public, which was to be passed by the Bundestag and would strengthen his hand in the future. However, the position of the West German government became untenable once Noble informed Flick's American lawyer "that the United States Government does not insist that such a condition [making the files available for inspection; A.E.] be imposed on those seized German records returned from the United States which the German Federal Government decides to give back to private owners." Flick received the records in November 1962. The Federal Archives microfilmed the most important files beforehand. The entire episode is documented in PA/AA, B118, vol. 237 and vol. 202.
377 Referat II.5 (Poland Desk) to ZB 8 (Political Archives), July 3, 1964, Aktenstudium von Wissenschaftlern aus kommunistischen Staaten im PA, PA/AA, B118, vol. 237.
378 The historians were Bohumil Cerny, Prague, and Tone Ferenc from the Insitute for the History of the Workers Movement in Ljubljana. Ferenc was working on a dissertation about ethnic issues in occupied Yugoslavia during the Second World War. The decision to refuse the request was made by the head of the Political Deptment while Ullrich was on vacation. See verbal note, Nov. 25, 1963, PA/AA, B118, vol. 237.

regardless of their nationality, be granted unconditional access.[379] When similar cases arose later, Ullrich reminded the Eastern desk with great pleasure of the "unpleasantries" that the Auswärtiges Amt had faced because of such attempted restrictions.[380]

In the end, Ullrich was not able to practice at the Political Archives what he had preached to the Bundesarchiv. His faith in "the impeccably researched, scholarly reply [as an] effective weapon against biased publications"[381] was out of step with the times. It had already been recognized early in the Cold War on both sides of the Iron Curtain that history was the "most inexpensive resource in the rivalries between the two systems."[382] The past had become too valuable to be left to archivists and historians alone. By the mid-1960s, restrictive polices enacted in East and West alike put an end to the ideal of unrestricted access to archives.

379 R. W. Mason, FO Library, to Ullrich, Apr. 29, 1964, PA/AA, B118, vol. 237. Ferenc was then allowed to work in the Political Archives for five days in October 1965. See Weinandy to Ferenc, Sept. 16, 1965, ibid.
380 Weinandy (signed by Ullrich), draft report, Benutzung des PA durch Historiker aus der SBZ und den Ostblockstaaten, Jan. 14, 1965, PA/AA, B118, vol. 291. The cases in question were applications to use the archives submitted by the scholars from the GDR Gerhart Haß, A. Anderle, Fritz Klein, and Johanna Schellenberg.
381 Weinandy (signed by Ullrich), draft report, Benutzung des PA durch Historiker aus der SBZ und den Ostblockstaaten, Jan. 14, 1965, PA/AA, B118, vol. 291.
382 Wolfrum, *Geschichtspolitik*, 36.

Conclusion

This study has used the odyssey of the German governmental archives seized at the end of World War II to consider the issue of the documents' return as a facet of the Federal Republic's relations with the Western Allied powers, to illuminate the early West German debate about the recent German past, and to embed an important chapter in archival history within a political framework. Exploring the historiographic dimension of the story of the captured records, this study has also pointed to the role historians played in the negotiations on the documents' return and to their responses to the unprecedented access – or, for German historians, denial of access – to source materials on the very recent past. To explain why the negotiations proved so difficult, it considered the different interests of the parties responsible for deciding what was to be done with the documents. What did these records and the negotiations for their return mean for government policy in West Germany, Britain, and the United States? What did they mean for archivists in West Germany and historians in all three countries?

For the West German government, the negotiations were an element of its policy to disassociate the Federal Republic from the period of Allied occupation. The great symbolic value of records, especially diplomatic records, made the demand for their return a matter of national prestige. For the members of the West German public, the fact that the captured documents were being held abroad and edited for publication by Allied historians was tantamount, as one commentator put it, to a "demolition of our history."[1] From that standpoint, the absence of the records amounted to a loss of history and identity. Arguments about the necessity of having the records on hand for administrative purposes paled in comparison. The Germans did not clamor for the return of the captured documents because

---

1 Dr. K., "Die Demontage unserer Geschichte," *Hamburger Freie Presse*, Oct. 20, 1950.

possession of them would facilitate day-to-day governmental business, but rather because possession would erase a visible reminder of Germany's recent defeat and occupation. The struggle for the files can therefore be considered one facet of Bonn's determined efforts to draw a line under Allied rule. Contemporaries saw progress on the issue of the records as an indicator of the state of West German sovereignty. The issue became all the more urgent after the Soviet Union returned records to the German Democratic Republic in 1955. Bonn and its Western Allies took notice of this deliberate provocation. An exchange of notes between the Auswärtiges Amt and the Allied embassies in March 1956 led to the transfer of diplomatic records from Great Britain later that year, a highly publicized gesture that helped defuse an explosive political issue. Tensions had so evidently receded by the opening of the next round of negotiations – in 1958, on the return of military records – that neither Chancellor Konrad Adenauer nor his foreign minister saw it necessary to remain directly involved.

Given the urgency the Federal Republic sought to bestow upon its demands for the return of the captured records, it is worth reconsidering the two main arguments Bonn put forward in the negotiations, namely administrative necessity and historical research. At no point did Bonn attempt to argue that it needed the records to prosecute Nazi criminals. The British and American governments, which had invested considerable effort in the Nuremberg proceedings and numerous other trials, would probably have been highly receptive to such an argument. In the few cases in which the Auswärtiges Amt did request specific materials from the British and Americans for use as evidence, the petitions were granted promptly.[2]

The importance the West Germans attributed to the records grew in proportion to the apparent unwillingness of the other side to give them back. It took time for German diplomats to get a glimpse of the intricate webs of interests surrounding the issue within the British and American

---

2 One such incident from 1956 is in PA/AA, B118, vol. 32 and NA RG 59, CDF 1954–59, 862.423/3–656. In this case, the German embassy in Washington requested certified copies for a trial at the Bavarian Regional Court Munich I. They were provided two months after the request. Another case concerned preparations for a trial against Holocaust perpetrators involved in mass killings in Bulgaria, Macedonia, and Thrace in 1942/43. See Ullrich to German Embassy London, June 27, 1956, and Ullrich to State Prosecutor Frankfurt, Aug. 11, 1956, PA/AA, B118, vol. 5. See also the preliminary investigation by the Cologne district attorney's office against Eberhardt von Thadden, one of the leading "Jewish experts" in Abteilung Inland II at the Auswärtiges Amt from 1943–45. The material was made immediately available from the records found at Whaddon. The episode is documented in PRO FO 370/2374 LS5/140. State Prosecutor Erwin Schuele, director of the Central Office for the Investigation of National Socialist Crimes set up in late 1958, requested evidence directly from American offices in order to avoid the detour via the Auswärtiges Amt. See Allen B. Moreland, American Consul General, Stuttgart, to State Dept., no. 76, Nov. 27, 1959, NA RG 59, CDF 1955–59, 862.423/11–2759.

governments. Their counterparts in the High Commission were eager to resolve the matter of the captured documents and supported German interests at their foreign ministries, but the subject did not rank high enough on the political agenda in either London or Washington to warrant immediate and sustained attention. It soon became a much resented addendum to the central questions in relations between West Germany and the Western Allies in the early 1950s. Although overshadowed by such emotionally laden problems as the future of war criminals held in Allied prisons, rearmament, and the Paris treaties, the captured documents consumed a great deal of diplomatic energy. In the case of Britain, the reason for this was the policy of deliberate obstruction pursued by the interdepartmental Joint Consultative Committee. There was an element of farce in the maneuvers the JCC members used to delay negotiations on the return of the documents time and again, and they testified to the oft-described power exercised by civil servants vis-à-vis political appointees at the upper echelons of the executive branch of government.[3]

For German archivists, the issue of the captured documents hit a professional nerve. So long as the records remained in British and American possession, the Bundesarchiv and the Political Archives of the Auswärtiges Amt were under pressure to justify their existence. The first director of the Bundesarchiv, Georg Winter, and his deputy director, Wilhelm Rohr, demanded the return of all the captured records in an aggressive, nationalistic tone. There was a dissonance between their frequent appeals to international law in making their demands and their own wartime activities. That they chose to ignore that contradiction does not come as a surprise; that the Allies did not call attention to it can be seen as a missed opportunity to set the record straight at an early date. At the same time, German archivists enjoyed the unqualified support of their foreign colleagues in seeking the return of older historic holdings. The Archivist of the United States Wayne C. Grover, for example, returned eighteenth- and nineteenth-century military papers from the former Reich Archives and Army Archives at the first possible opportunity in order to comply with international professional standards among archivists.

The two most important long-term results of the struggle for the files were the guarantee of access to the records and the comprehensive microfilming project. Both set a precedent for the return of records dislocated through war and, in retrospect, established a largely positive example. The

---

3 Butterfield, "Official History," 203f.; Lowe, "Plumbing New Depths," 241–3; Steiner, "The Historian and the Foreign Office," 44.

German story contrasts with that of Japanese records, for example, which were returned by the United States in the 1950s. Prior to their return, Japanese documents were not microfilmed, nor did the U.S. government secure an access guarantee for researchers. Moreover, the U.S. government cannot fully reconstruct the circumstances surrounding the return of the Japanese records.[4] The Western Allies' return of the captured German records also stands in stark contrast to the difficulties that arose in the 1990s with the successor states of the Soviet Union. Cultural treasures long thought to be lost – including important collections of documents and entire libraries – resurfaced at the end of the East-West conflict in depositories and secret archives. These rediscoveries were greeted with a general sense of relief and joy. Attempts to reunite collections, resolve questions of ownership, or at least guarantee the long-term preservation of cultural properties quickly fell victim to larger political concerns. The failure to resolve the issue remains a thorny legacy of World War II and its aftermath.[5]

In the Federal Republic, neither the immediate advantages of the return agreements nor their success were initially recognized. The access guarantee temporarily overtaxed the Bundesarchiv in the early 1960s. The "precipitous" increase in the volume of records held by the Bundesarchiv resulting from the transfers from the United States, combined with the "serious condition" that the materials were to be "available literally from the hour [of their arrival]," forced archivists there to abandon detailed cataloging and to adopt makeshift arrangements.[6] The archivists also needed a long time to make their peace with the loss of control and power resulting from the access guarantee for material up to the year 1945 and the existence of microfilm copies held outside of Germany. It was years before the Bundesarchiv came to see the liberal access policies imposed upon it as an advantage. In an essay published in 2000, Bundesarchiv archivist Heinz Boberach called particular attention to the "liberal right of access that made archival sources documenting events from the period between 1933 to 1945 available, independent of the thirty-year closure period." Boberach made no mention, however, of the origins of this liberality.[7] Forgotten, too, are the concerns

---

4 See the March 2002 report of the Interagency Working Group (IWG), Implementation of the Japanese Imperial Government Disclosure Act and the Japanese War Crimes Provisions of the Nazi War Crimes Disclosure Act at http://www.archives.gov/iwg/reports/japanese-interim-report-march-2002-1. html (accessed August 2011). The microfilming effort of Japanese records yielded only 163 reels of microfilm that are held at the Library of Congress and at the National Diet Library in Tokyo today.
5 The literature on the topic is immense. See the bibliography by Bruhn, "Trophy Art"; specifically on German archives, Jena, "Rückführung deutscher Akten aus Rußland."
6 Booms, "Bundesarchiv," 22
7 Boberach, "Beteiligung des Bundesarchivs." See also Boberach, "Benutzungsordnung," 67f., where he explains the access regulations of 1970 – again without including an explanation of the relevant paragraphs in the access regulations that made material from 1933 to 1945 available.

about the American Historical Association's microfilming project voiced by many in West Germany, including, for example, historians at the Institute for Contemporary History in Munich. By the time the institute celebrated the fiftieth anniversary of its founding, its position had changed conspicuously. The collection of little blue boxes containing rolls of microfilm was now valued as "an exceptional stroke of luck for the research mission of the institute."[8]

The seizure of the records was of profound importance for historical research. The British and American official histories of the war were the first projects to benefit from the capture of German military records. "Private research," as scholarly research was called at the time, also profited from the bonanza of captured German records. Dagmar Horna Perman, a collaborator on the microfilming project, summarized the American perspective on the issue in 1959:

Seldom are historians suddenly given access to documentary materials covering all aspects of a nation's life during a whole era. Yet this is the opportunity now afforded to historians in America. Within a short time they will have available documents of the Hitler era in Germany reflecting its origins, causes, administrative system, philosophy, policies, military system, propaganda, and almost every other imaginable feature of significance or interest.[9]

The captured records gave a decisive professional boost to several members of an up-and-coming generation of historians in the United States. Whaddon Hall, the War Documentation Project, and the American Historical Association's microfilming project were the conduits that brought a number of ambitious young historians into direct contact with crucial source materials. They lobbied to gain access to the records and took full advantage of it, thereby giving a dynamism to the study of German history in the United States that is evident to this day. As a result, the German past was no longer the province of German historians alone. They had to reckon with scholars from abroad who could speak with the authority bestowed by unrestricted access to primary source materials.

The situation for British historians during the 1950s was somewhat different. For one, Britain did not have a comparable group of émigré German historians who had continued to teach German history in their host country after their arrival. The German émigrés in Great Britain quite frequently

---

8 Röder, Weiß, and Lankheit, "Archiv des Instituts," 112. The complete quote reads: "exceptionally fortunate for the research mission of the institute was finally the microfilming of captured documents from officials and offices of the Third Reich that began in 1956 by the National Archives in Washington."

9 Perman, "Microfilming," 433. Perman succeeded Gerhard L. Weinberg as the head of the microfilming project in Alexandria, Virginia.

took up English history and seldom returned to German topics. Francis L. Carsten was a notable exception.[10] For another, modern and contemporary history – British or German – had not yet established itself as a field of study at the leading universities. Ancient, medieval, and early modern history predominated in both teaching and research. Only slowly did modern history find its way into the curriculum at the major universities.[11] Students could study contemporary history at the University of Manchester, thanks solely to the personal interests of Lewis Namier and A. J. P. Taylor, who taught there during the 1930s.[12] The number of historians at Oxford interested in contemporary history quickly reached a critical mass after 1945.[13] The founding of St. Antony's College at Oxford in 1951, helped along by Alan Bullock and John Wheeler-Bennett, was an important milestone. The college soon established itself as the leading British center for teaching and research on twentieth-century international relations.[14] Of the small number of British historians who published works on contemporary history, only Wheeler-Bennett and, in the following generation, D. C. Watt can be called historians of Germany. Alan Bullock, Geoffrey Barraclough, James Joll, Hugh Trevor-Roper, and Elisabeth Wiskemann wrote on German topics but did not make German history the primary focus of their work.[15] Thus, there was no clearly identifiable group of historians in Great Britain who benefited from having access to German records to the same degree that the Americans did.

Among the German scholars, the person most actively involved in the debate on the captured documents was Gerhard Ritter. Ritter considered himself to be the historical profession's spokesperson on this issue in dealing with officials in Bonn and colleagues abroad. Ritter was also the prime example of a German historian who sought to stem the tide of "foreign" interpretations. His research and publications were particularly embroiled in the controversy over the right to interpret German history. More vehemently than any of his colleagues at home, Ritter insisted that German

10 Alter, *Out of the Third Reich;* Berghahn, "Deutschlandbilder 1945–1965," 244, 251, and Berghahn, "Francis Carsten," 19.

11 As late as 1970, history courses at the undergraduate level at Oxford ended with the year 1939.

12 Kathleen Burk, "Britische Traditionen," 45–59, 48f.; Burk, *Troublemaker*, 126–30.

13 This refers to Hugh Trevor-Roper, Bill Deakin, Robert Blake, Keith Hancock, James Joll, the Seton-Watson brothers, A. J. P. Taylor, Alan Bullock, and John Wheeler-Bennett as an affiliate. See Bullock, [Obituary], "John Wheeler Wheeler-Bennett," 819; Geoffrey Barraclough of University of Liverpool joined the Recent History Group at Oxford as a visitor in 1956. The discussions there provided the seeds for his book *An Introduction to Contemporary History* (London, 1964).

14 Burk, *Troublemaker*, 103–47; Burk, "Britische Traditionen"; Nicholls, *History of St. Antony's*, 27, 59–79. Among those teaching at St. Antony's College were Alan Bullock, James Joll and John Wheeler-Bennett.

15 Berghahn, "Deutschlandbilder," 244.

historians should have priority in interpreting the German past. Foreign scholars, he contended, could have only limited understanding of the Germans' national history. To a degree, his research agenda was reactive, as the following three examples illustrate. First, his book *Europa und die deutsche Frage* (1948) was a general attack on alleged misinterpretations of German history from abroad.[16] Second, the success of John Wheeler-Bennett's book *Nemesis of Power* (1953; German translation, 1954), prompted Ritter to push for the translation of his biography of Carl Friedrich Goerdeler into English to counter Wheeler-Bennett's portrayal of the German resistance to Hitler.[17] Third, the interpretation of the Schlieffen Plan Gordon A. Craig presented in his book *The Politics of the Prussian Army* (1955) prompted Ritter to step up his work on an edition of the plan to counter Craig's argument that it had been intended for a military offensive.[18] Although Ritter held the American historian in high regard, he could not agree with his ascription of aggressive motives to Germany.[19] Ritter's struggle for the files, in other words, was in large part a fight to preserve the larger sweep of German history from the taint of the Nazi era.

Ritter's prominence and many outspoken pronouncements on the issue of the captured documents should not be allowed to overshadow the German historians who took a more conciliatory stance. Many members of the next generation of German historians took a different view of the issue of

16 Gerhard Ritter, *Europa und die deutsche Frage*, Munich, 1948. There is no English translation but see Gerhard Ritter, *The German Problem. Basic Questions of German Political Life* (Columbus, 1965).

17 The Deutsche Verlags-Anstalt (DVA) in Stuttgart solicited funds from the Auswärtiges Amt to publish an English translation of "a work so incredibly important for restoring the respect and honor of the German people." DVA to von Trützschler, AA, May 10, 1955. Ritter explained to von Trützschler on May 17, 1955, how crucial it would be "at last to have a rather major historical work penned by a German, which deals also with a politically important problem, become known word for word in the Anglo-American world and not just by way of the regularly vilifying reviews of the Times Literary Supplement, whose Germanophobic attitude in all issues involving German historiography is certainly known.... I would welcome this in particular with regard to the much-read book by Wheeler-Bennet." See also Ritter to Epstein, May 3, 1955, all in BArch, N1166, NL Ritter, vol. 286. In a long review appearing in the *Frankfurter Allgemeine Zeitung*, Ritter calls Wheeler-Bennett's book a "political calamity." Ritter, "Nemesis der Macht?" in *Frankfurter Allgemeine Zeitung*, Apr. 20, 1955.

18 Craig, *Politics of the Prussian Army*, 283f.; Ritter's positive review of the book in *Die Zeit*, Nov. 17, 1955, 3.

19 Ritter, *The Schlieffen Plan*. On page 8 of the introduction, Ritter refers to Craig without mentioning him by name: "It [the Schlieffen plan] has recently been interpreted even as a plan to conduct a preventive war against France that is said to have been arranged with the head of the Foreign Office, Baron Fritz von Holstein, at the end of 1905." See also Ritter to Prof. Dr. Fuerler, Bundestag Deputy, Jan. 13, 1955: in his publication on the Schlieffen Plan, Ritter maintains that "the main point is especially to test the assertion recently put forward that Count Schlieffen devised his plan for a preventative war against France on orders from Holstein, an assertion that I consider false." A similar statement is found in Ritter to Thilo Vogelsang, IfZ, Oct. 27, 1955, both in BArch, N1166, NL Ritter, vol. 286. On the publication of the book, see also Cornelißen, *Ritter*, 561f., who puts it in another frame of reference, however.

the captured documents. Scholars such as Hermann Mau (born 1913) and
Paul Kluke (born 1908) supported international cooperation. The return of
the records was not, in their view, a matter of national prestige; calling for a
pragmatic solution, they sought to give scholars from all countries the same
access to the records. They discussed the issue with their colleagues in Great
Britain and the United States, and they critically distanced themselves from
the position of their own government. In 1955, Kluke wrote to Ritter:

> By the way, I tend to believe that we will hardly fare any better once the records
> are again in German possession. According to the news reaching me and my own
> personal observations, the tendencies of German archivists to reclassify records are
> growing stronger and will perhaps at some point make a joint effort by historians
> necessary to combat the absurd secretiveness.[20]

Years later, even Ritter put the "source situation" of the postwar period into
a broader perspective without, however, abandoning the view that German
historians should have priority in interpreting the German past:

> Personally, I find it very annoying that our diplomatic records are divulged so
> unscrupulously to the entire world and that every little college in America or
> Australia can photocopy them as much as they like. Well: back then in Paris we
> also copied archival material unscrupulously. Mutual archival theft appears to have
> become part of the modern style of warfare now, and undoubtedly, the historian
> profits from this.[21]

As Dagmar Perman had so vividly argued, the benefit of the Allies' confiscation of German governmental records brought real, lasting gains for historical scholarship. What many West Germans, especially members of the press,
saw in the 1950s as a continuation of occupation-era re-education policies
by other means appears in retrospect as an unprecedented opportunity to
write contemporary history as a transnational project. Even so, it was left
to later generations of historians to appreciate external views of their own
country's histories and to regard external perspectives as an enrichment and
pluralization of opinion. German scholars, archivists, politicians, and officials in the 1950s found this hard to do. Confronted with tough and lengthy
negotiations on the return of the captured documents, they leveled a host of

---

20 Paul Kluke to Gerhard Ritter, Apr. 13, 1955, in BArch, N1166, NL Ritter, vol. 286.
21 Gerhard Ritter to Johannes Ullrich, Apr. 12, 1962, PA/AA, B118, vol. 77. The letter was written
   at the highpoint of Ritter's campaign against Fritz Fischer's book *Griff nach der Weltmacht*. Ritter
   argued here on behalf of Erwin Hölzle, who used records from the French foreign ministry that he
   had collected during the war in an essay. For this reason, Johannes Ullrich advised against publishing
   the essay in *Historischen Zeitschrift*. See Ullrich to Ritter, Apr. 25, 1962, ibid.; Cornelißen, *Ritter*,
   602f. with n. 164.

accusations against the Allies: the confiscation of the records had been a violation of international law, as were the microfilming and sale of microfilms; foreign historians wanted to dominate historical research and neutralize competition from German historians; collecting evidence for Nuremberg left the original arrangement of holdings irreparably destroyed.[22] Emotionally satisfying as such polemics might have been in the short term, they prevented German scholars and officials from recognizing that, in the long run, it was the capture of the documents that saved an immense amount of material for posterity. In the course of denazification and demilitarization, the Allies could have decided in favor of an alternative method of handling such documentary material, namely, the pulping mill. It could have molded away in the ruins of bombed-out buildings or have been used as fuel to keep people warm during the harsh postwar winters. Or some Germans, thinking that the papers contained evidence of past crimes and injustices, might have pressed to have the records destroyed.[23] The preservation, duplication, and publication of the captured documents led to an intense international engagement with German history. By microfilming records, the sources have been transferred from what was often fragile paper to a new and more resilient form of storage and made available worldwide.[24] Had the records not been seized, many of them – to modify the saying *quod non est in actis, non est in mundo*[25] – would probably no longer be in the world.

22 Several "differences of opinion" are referenced subtly in the volume of conference papers by Wolfe, *Captured German Records*, 240f.: "We may be of various opinions about the propriety of seizing and mass-microfilming other peoples records. We do know that the Nazi regime planned to do just that and did so in some cases, so perhaps one can claim retaliation. [B]e that as it may. . . . "

23 Counterfactual arguments are open to discussion, but the ones here are not far-fetched. One needs to look only at the widespread destruction of official records as the war ended, as well as the private *autodafés* that were to erase all traces of approval and accompliceship. See Fritzsche, "The Archive," 32. This behavior was not limited to the end of the war, but perpetuated itself in the postwar period. See the incident described in Schildt, *Ankunft im Westen*, 106, in which the dignitaries in a small town in Lower Saxony burned the denazification papers of their community in what can be called a ritual act.

24 Gerhard L. Weinberg uses this argument often, e.g. in Weinberg, "Zu den deutschen Akten," 520; Weinberg, "End of Ranke's history?," 333f.

25 "What is not in the records is not in the world."

Bibliography

Archival Sources

I. Archives in the United States

National Archives, College Park, Maryland (NA)
Modern Diplomatic Branch
RG 59 Records of the Department of State – Decimal Files
  Central Decimal File, 1945–1949. 840.414, 761.62
  Central Decimal File, 1950–1954. 862.423
  Central Decimal File, 1955–1959. 862.423
  (cited as CDF 1945–49 etc. with decimal figure)
RG 59 Records of the Department of State – Lot Files
  Lot File 60D24: Division of Foreign Activity Correlation. Records regarding
    the Exploitation of Captured German Documents, 1945–48
  Lot File 78D441: Bureau of Public Affairs. Historical Office. Records Relating
    to the German Documents Project, 1944–1983
  Lot File 55D371: Records of the Office of Western European Affairs, 1941–
    1954. Subject Files, 1941–54
  Lot File 56D307: HICOG Policy Files, 1950–52. Subject Files for the Assistant
    Legal Advisor for German Affairs Relating to Germany, 1952–55
  [DeWitt C.] Poole Commission. MF 679, Roll 1–3
RG 84 Records of the Foreign Service Posts of the Department of State
  Entry 2530: POLAD. Top Secret Correspondence of Robert Murphy
  Entry 2531b: Classified Correspondence of the Political Advisor (POLAD),
    1945–1949
  Entry 2544: POLAD Frankfurt, Top Secret Cables
  Entry 2600a: Classified Correspondence, U.S. Embassy London
RG 64 The National Archives
RG 200 Gift Collections. Papers of Ernst Posner
RG 242 Collection of Foreign Records Seized
  AGAR-S Record Series. Selected Documents Concerning the Conference on
    Captured German and Related Records. [Numerically] Compiled by Seymor
    J. Pomrenze (cited as AGAR-S and doc. nr.)

BDC Administrative Records. BDC Directorate Files, 1946–1994
BDC Administrative Records. BDC History and Archives, 1945–1971
Non-Record Material Relating to RG 242. Inventory Disposition Concerning Captured Records from the 1950s (cited as "Non-Record Material")

Modern Military Branch
RG 165 War Department. General and Special Staffs
RG 218 Records of the Joint Chiefs of Staff
   Entry 1: Central Decimal File, 1942–1945
RG 226 Office of Strategic Services (OSS)
   Entry 210: Source & Method File
RG 238 U.S. Counsel for Prosecution of Axis Criminality
   Entry 52a: Records formerly retained by Justice Jackson. Correspondence with European Document Centers, 1945.
RG 260 Records of the U.S. Occupation Headquarters, World War II. (OMGUS) Records of the Executive Office. FIAT, General Records, 1945–47
RG 319 Records of the Army Staff
   Entry 1018: Assistant Chief of Staff. G-2, Intelligence. Captured Records Branch
   Entry 1037: U.S. Army Center of Military History [OCMH]. Administration Files ("Finke Files"), 1943–1984
   Records of the Investigative Records Repository (IRR): Personal Files
   Records of the Investigative Records Repository (IRR): Impersonal Files
RG 331 Allied Operational and Occupation Headquarters. World War II. Supreme Headquarters Allied Expeditionary Forces (SHAEF)
   Entry 11: General Staff. G-2, Intelligence. Decimal File
   Entry 18a: Intelligence Target "T" Sub-Division. Decimal File 1943–1944
   Entry 47: General Staff. G-5 Division, Secretariat. Numeric File, Aug. 1943-July 1945
   Entry 55b: General Staff. G-5 Division, Operations Branch. MFAA Subject File August 1943–1945
RG 338 Records of the United States Army Commands, 1942-
   Entry 33192: USAREUR. The Adjutant General
   FIAT Correspondence Files
RG 407 The Adjutant General's Office, 1917-
   Entry 360: Records of the Administrative Services Division. Records of or Maintained by the Communications Branch. Classified Decimal File, 314.4
   Entry 361: Records of the Administrative Services Division. Records of or Maintained by the Communications Branch. Top Secret Decimal File, 314.4
   Entry 363: Unclassified Decimal File
   Entry 369: Records of the Departmental Records Branch. Classified Decimal Files, 1946-Jan. 1958, 314.4
   Entry 371: Records of the Departmental Records Branch Archivist ("Archival Policy File"), 1954–1957
   Entry 371F: Captured Records Section (formerly GMDS). Classified Chronological File, 1947–1958.
   Entry 375: Department Records Branch. Journal of Significant Events, 1949-Jan. 1958.

Franklin Delano Roosevelt Library, Hyde Park, New York (FDRL)
President's Secretary's File (PSF)
President's Personal File (PPF)
Official File (OF)

Library of Congress, Washington D.C.
Manuscript Division
Records of the Library of Congress Series. The European Mission and Cooperative
    Acquisition Project (cited as LoCM and box nr.)
Records of the Library of Congress Series. Central File. [Archibald] MacLeish to
    [Luther H.] Evans (cited as LoC Central File and box nr.)
Papers of the American Historical Association (cited as LoC AHA and box nr.)
Papers of Verner W. Clapp

Harvard University Library, Cambridge, Massachusetts
Pusey Library
Papers of William L. Langer

Yale University Library, New Haven, Connecticut
Sterling Memorial Library
Papers of Hajo Holborn
Papers of Samuel Flagg Bemis
Papers of Harold D. Lasswell

University of Virginia, Charlottesville, Virginia
Alderman Library
Papers of Oron J. Hale

Columbia University Library, New York, New York
Rare Books and Manuscript Library
Walter L. Dorn Papers

II. Archives in Great Britain

National Archives (formerly Public Records Office, PRO), London
FO 370   Records of the Foreign Office, Library and Research Section
FO 371   Records of the Foreign Office, Political Correspondence
FO 1050   Records of the Control Commission for Germany (British
            Element), CCG(BE)
CAB 21   Cabinet Office and Predecessors. Registered Files
CAB 103   Second World War, 1939–1945. The War Cabinet
CAB 128   Cabinet Minutes (CM and CC Series). 1945–1974
CAB 140   War Cabinet and Cabinet Office. Historical Section
CAB 146   Cabinet Office. Historical Section. Enemy Documents Section
WO 208   War Office. Directorate of Military Operations and Intelligence
            and Directorate of Military Intelligence
PRO 30/90   Papers of Cecil A. F. Meekings

St. Antony's College, Oxford
Papers of Sir John W. Wheeler-Bennett

Bodleian Library, Oxford
Papers of Sir Walter Monckton

Imperial War Museum
Papers of Kenneth Duke

III. Archives in Germany

Bundesarchiv Koblenz (BArch)

B 106	Bundesinnenministerium
B 136	Bundeskanzleramt
B 198	Bundesarchiv, Dienstakten
N 1102	Nachlaß Fritz T. Epstein
N 1166	Nachlaß Gerhard Ritter
N 1188	Nachlaß Theodor Schieder
N 1213	Nachlaß Hans Rothfels
N 1263	Nachlaß Kurt Rheindorf
N 1333	Nachlaß Georg Winter
N 1418	Nachlaß Wilhelm Rohr
N 1422	Nachlaß Fritz Fischer
KLE 586F	Kleine Erwerbungen Erich Eyck
KLE 909	Kleine Erwerbungen Kurt Rosenow
All. Proz. 1	Fall 11 (von Weizsäcker)

Politisches Archiv des Auswärtigen Amtes (PA/AA)

B 2	Büro Staatssekretäre
B 10	Politische Abteilung 2
B 118	Abteilung 1, Referat 117 (Politisches Archiv)
NL Andres	Nachlaß Hans Andres

Hausarchiv des Instituts für Zeitgeschichte München (IfZ)

Bestand ID	(Interne Dokumente) Hausarchiv: Sammlung Stiftung zur wissenschaftlichen Erforschung der Zeitgeschichte
ID1	Geschichte des IfZ
ID34	Zeitungsausschnittssammlung
ID101	Korrespondenz Hermann Mau (1950–1952)
ID102	Korrespondenz Paul Kluke (1953–1956)
ID103	Korrespondenz Helmut Krausnick

Hauptstaatsarchiv Düsseldorf (HStA Dü)

RWN 254	Nachlaß Bernhard Vollmer
BR 2094	Dienstregistratur des Staatsarchivs Düsseldorf

Hauptstaatsarchiv Hannover (HStA Han)
Nds 50 Niedersächsische Staatskanzlei

Landesarchiv Saarbrücken (LA Saarbrücken)
NL MeyerE Nachlaß Eugen Meyer

Geheimes Staatsarchiv Preußischer Kulturbesitz Berlin-Dahlem (GStA)
HA I, Rep 178 B Dienstregistratur des Geheimen Staatsarchivs

Published Sources

Daily newspapers and contemporary news magazine articles are cited in full in the footnotes and do not reappear in the bibliography.

I. Document and Source Editions

Adenauer, Konrad. *Briefe 1949–1951.* Ed. by Hans Peter Mensing. (Rhöndorfer Ausgabe ed. by Rudolf Morsey and Hans-Peter Schwarz). Berlin 1985. [cited as Adenauer, *Briefe*].

Adenauer und die Hohen Kommissare. Akten zur Deutschen Auswärtigen Politik. Ed. by Hans-Peter Schwarz on behalf of Auswärtiges Amt. Munich 1990.

Amtsblatt des Kontrollrats in Deutschland. Nr. 1–14. 1945–1949.

Der Auswärtige Ausschuss des Deutschen Bundestages. Sitzungsprotokolle 1949–1953. Ed. by Wolfgang Hoelscher. Erster Halbband: Oktober 1949–Mai 1952 (Quellen zur Geschichte des Parlamentarismus und der politischen Parteien. Vierte Reihe 13/I). Düsseldorf 1998.

Bonnin, Georges, ed. *Bismarck and the Hohenzollern Candidature for the Spanish Throne. The Documents in the German Diplomatic Archives.* Edited with an Introduction by Georges Bonnin. Translated by Isabella M. Massey. With a Foreword by G. P. Gooch. London 1957.

Deutscher Bundestag. *Verhandlungen des Deutschen Bundestages.* Stenographische Berichte und Drucksachen. Bonn 1949ff.

Documents on German Foreign Policy 1918–1945. From the Archives of the German Foreign Ministry. Series D (1937–1945), vol. I: From Neurath to Ribbentrop (September 1937-September 1938). Washington, D.C. 1949.

Dorn, Walter L. *Inspektionsreisen in der US-Zone. Notizen, Denkschriften und Erinnerungen.* Aus dem Nachlaß übersetzt und herausgegeben von Lutz Niethammer. (Schriftenreihe der VfZ 26). Stuttgart 1973.

Foreign Relations of the United States.
_____. 1944, 1: General. Washington, D.C.: GPO 1966.
_____. 1945, 3: European Advisory Commission; Austria; Germany. Washington, D.C.: GPO 1968.
_____. 1946, 5: The British Commonwealth, Western and Central Europe. Washington, D.C.: GPO 1969.

Gesetzliche Vorschriften der amerikanischen Militärregierung in Deutschland. 1945–1949.

Hofer, Walther, ed. *Der Nationalsozialismus. Dokumente 1933–1945.* Frankfurt 1957.

Holborn, Hajo. *American Military Government. Its Organization and Policies.* Westport, CT 1977.

The Holstein Papers. Vol. I. Memoirs and Political Observations. Ed. by Norman Rich and M. E. Fisher. Cambridge 1955.

Kaehler, Siegfried A. *Briefe 1900–1963.* Ed. by Walter Bußmann (Deutsche Quellen des 19. und 20. Jahrhunderts 58). Boppard/Rh. 1993.

Meinecke, Friedrich. *Ausgewählter Briefwechsel.* Edited and introduced by Ludwig Dehio and Peter Classen. (Meinecke Werke 6). Stuttgart 1962.

Occupation of Germany. Policy and Progress 1945–46. Issued by Department of State. (Publication 2783). Washington, D.C. 1947.

Picker, Henry. *Hitlers Tischgespräche im Führerhauptquartier 1941–1942.* Im Auftrage des Deutschen Instituts für Geschichte der nationalsozialistischen Zeit, geordnet, eingeleitet und veröffentlicht von Gerhard Ritter. Bonn 1951.

Der Prozeß gegen die Hauptkriegsverbrecher vor dem Internationalen Militärgerichtshof. Nürnberg 14. XI. 1945–1. X. 1946 (dt. amtliche Ausgabe). 42 Bde. Nürnberg: 1949.

Ritter, Gerhard: *Ein politischer Historiker in seinen Briefen.* Ed. by Klaus Schwabe and Rolf Reichardt. (Schriften des Bundesarchivs 33). Boppard/Rh. 1984 (cited as Ritter, *Politischer Historiker*).

Ritter, Gerhard A., ed. *Friedrich Meinecke. Akademischer Lehrer und emigrierte Schüler. Briefe und Aufzeichnungen 1910–1977.* Munich 2006.

Seidl, Alfred. *Die Beziehungen zwischen Deutschland und der Sowjetunion 1939–1941. Dokumente des Auswärtigen Amts.* Tübingen 1949.

Sontag, Raymond J. and James S. Beddie, eds. *Nazi-Soviet Relations 1939–1941. Documents from the Archives of the German Foreign Office.* Washington, D.C. 1948.

Thimme, Friedrich. *Friedrich Thimme 1868–1938. Ein politischer Historiker, Publizist und Schriftsteller in seinen Briefen.* Ed. by Annelise Thimme. Boppard/Rh. 1994.

Vollnhals, Clemens, ed. *Entnazifizierung. Politische Säuberung und Rehabilitierung in den vier Besatzungszonen 1945–1949.* (dtv dokumente). Munich 1991.

II. Memoirs and Diaries

Annan, Noel. *Changing Enemies. The Defeat and Regeneration of Germany.* New York 1995.

Bein, Alex. *"Hier kannst Du nicht jeden grüßen." Erinnerungen und Betrachtungen.* Ed. by Julius H. Schoeps. (Haskala. Wissenschaftliche Abhandlungen 14). Hildesheim 1996.

Buchheim, Karl. *Eine sächsische Lebensgeschichte. Erinnerungen 1889–1972.* Ed. by Udo Wengst and Isabel F. Pantenburg. (Biographische Quellen zur Zeitgeschichte 16). Munich 1996.

Cadogan, Alexander. *The Diaries of Sir Alexander Cadogan, 1938–1945.* Ed. by David Dilks. London 1971.

Carsten, Francis L. "From Revolutionary Socialism to German History," in Peter Alter, ed. *Out of the Third Reich. Refugee Historians in Postwar Britain.* London 1998, 25–39.

Clay, Lucius D. *Decision in Germany.* New York 1950.

Ellis, Roger H. "Recollections of Sir Hilary Jenkinson," *Journal of the Society of Archivists* 4 (1971): 261–75.

Gilbert, Felix. *A European Past. Memoirs. 1905–1945.* New York 1988.

Hammond, Mason. "'Remembrance of Things Past.' The Protection and Preservation of Monuments, Works of Art, Libraries and Archives during and after World War II," *Proceedings of the Massachusetts Historical Society* 92 (1980): 84–99.

Hechler, Kenneth W. *The Enemy Side of the Hill. The 1945 Background on Interrogations of German Commanders. As Seen Subjectively by Major Kenneth W. Hechler.* Washington, D.C.: Department of the Army–Historical Division 1949.

Hilberg, Raul. *The Politics of Memory. The Journey of a Holocaust Historian.* Chicago 1996.

Langer, William L. *In and Out of the Ivory Tower.* New York 1977.

Murphy, Robert. *Diplomat Among Warriors. The Unique World of a Foreign Service Expert.* New York 1964.

Pomrenze, Seymour J. "Personal Reminiscences of the Offenbach Archival Depot, 1946–1949. Fulfilling International and Moral Obligations," in J. D. Bindenagel, ed. *Proceedings. Washington Conference on Holocaust Era Assets. Nov. 30–Dec. 3, 1998.* Washington, D.C. 1999, 523–8.

Schnath, Georg. "Drei Jahre deutscher Archivschutz in Frankreich," in Schnath, *Ausgewählte Beiträge zur Landesgeschichte Niedersachsens.* Hildesheim 1968, 341–4.

Strang, Lord William. *Home & Abroad.* London 1956.

Thimme, Annelise. "Geprägt von der Geschichte. Eine Außenseiterin," in Hartmut Lehmann, Otto Gerhard Oexle, eds. *Erinnerungsstücke. Wege in die Vergangenheit. Rudolf Vierhaus zum 75. Geburtstag.* Köln 1997, 153–223.

Woodward, E. Llewellyn. *Short Journey.* London 1942.

Secondary Literature

I. Official Publications

Bell, H. E. and Hilary Jenkinson. *Italian Archives During the War and at Its Close. Ed. by the British Committee on the Preservation and Restitution of Works of Art, Archives and Other Material in Enemy Hands.* London 1947.

Coles, Henry L. and Albert K. Weinberg. *Civil Affairs. Soldiers become Governors. United States Army in World War II.* Special Studies [by the] Office of the Chief of Military History, Dept. of the Army. Washington, D.C. 1964.

Counter Intelligence Corps. *History of the Counter Intelligence Corps. Vol. XX: Germany Overrun.* Baltimore, MD 1959.

Foreign & Commonwealth Office. *British Policy towards Enemy Property during and after the Second World War.* (History Notes Nr. 13). London 1998.

Hinsley, Franics H. et al., eds. *British Intelligence in the Second World War. Its Influence on Strategy and Operations.* Vol. III, Part II. London 1984.

Interagency Working Group (IWG): Implementation of the Japanese Imperial Government Disclosure Act and the Japanese War Crimes Provisions of the Nazi War Crimes Disclosure Act. An Interim Report to Congress. Washington, March 2002. http://www.archives.gov/iwg/reports/japanese-interim-report-march-2002–1.html#japan (accessed May 23, 2010).

Plunder and Restitution. The U.S. and Holocaust Victims' Assets. Findings and Recommendations of the Presidential Advisory Commission on Holocaust

Assets in the United States [Clinton Commission] and Staff Report. Washington, D.C. 2000.

[National Archives]. "Polish Records Returned in White House Ceremony." *Prologue* 24; 3 (1992): 320.

[Roberts Commission]. *Report of the American Commission for the Protection and Salvage of Artistic and Historic Monuments in War Areas.* Washington, D.C. 1946.

SHAEF. *Handbook for Military Government in Germany Prior to Defeat or Surrender.* SHAEF: Office of the Chief of Staff December, 1944.

[War Department]. *Civil Affairs Information Guide. Field Protection of Objects of Art and Archives.* War Department Pamphlet Nr. 31–103.

[War Department]. *Preservation and Use of Key Records in Germany.* War Department Pamphlet Nr. 31–123.

[War Department]. *Archival Repositories in Germany.* War Department Pamphlet Nr. 31–180.

[War Department]. *Military Government Information Guide.* Information on German Records. War Department Pamphlet Nr. 31–217.

Verband Deutscher Soldaten/Bund der Berufssoldaten. *Wenn die Beweispapiere fehlen,* ed. by Wolf Keilig. Munich 21954.

Ziemke, Earl F. *The U.S. Army in the Occupation of Germany 1944–1946.* Army Historical Series. Center for Military History United States Army. Washington, D.C. 1975.

II. Archival Guides and Inventories

The American Historical Association Committee for the Study of War Documents: *Supplement to the Guide to Captured German Records.* Prepared by Gerhard L. Weinberg. Washington, D.C. 1959.

[Berlin Document Center]. *The Holdings of the Berlin Document Center. A Guide to the Collections.* Berlin 1994.

Bruhn, Peter. *Trophy Art. Bibliography of the International Literature on the Fate of the Cultural Treasures Displaced as Trophies by the Red Army from Germany to the USSR in the Result of World War II and Situated Now on the Territory of the Russian Federation and Other Republics of the Former Soviet Union.* 4th, completely revised and enlarged edition, vol. 1: 1990–1999, vol. 2: 2000–2002. Munich 2003.

La France et la Belgique sous l'occupation allemande 1940–1944. Les fonds allemands conservés aux Centre historique des Archives nationales. Inventaire de la sous-série AJ40. Inventaire redigé par Guy Beaujouan, Anne-Marie Bourgoin, Pierre Cézard, Marie-Thérèse Chabord, Élisabeth Dunan, Jean-Daniel Pariset, Christian Wilsdorf, revue par Christine Douyère-Demeulenaere avec la collaboration de Michèle Conchon. Introduction par Stefan Martens et Andreas Nielen. Paris 2002.

Guide to Captured German Documents. (War Documentation Project. Study Nr. 1). Prepared by Gerhard L. Weinberg. Maxwell Air Force Base, Alabama: December 1952.

[The National Archives and Records Service]. *Guides to the Microfilmed Records of the German Navy, 1850–1945, Nr. 1: U-Boats and T-Boats 1914–1918.* Washington, D.C. 1984.

OMGUS Handbuch. Die amerikanische Militärregierung in Deutschland 1945–1949. Ed. by Christoph Weisz. (Quellen und Darstellungen zur Zeitgeschichte 35). Munich 1995.

Preliminary Inventory of the German Records 1679–1945 in the World War II Collection of Seized Enemy Records. Compiled by Martin Rogin. (Preliminary Inventory Nr. 24). Washington, D.C. 1950.

III. Monographs and Articles

Alford, Kenneth D. *The Spoils of World War II. The American Military's Role in the Stealing of Europe's Treasures.* New York 1994.

Alter, Peter, ed. *Out of the Third Reich. Refugee Historians in Postwar Britain.* London 1998.

Aly, Götz and Susanne Heim. *Das Zentrale Staatsarchiv in Moskau ("Sonderarchiv").* Düsseldorf 1992.

Angress, Werner T. and Bradley F. Smith. "Diaries of Heinrich Himmler's Early Years." *Journal of Modern History* 31 (1959): 206–24.

Aretin, Karl Otmar Frh. von. "Der Erfolgsdeutsche. Studie zu einer beklemmenden Gegenwartsfrage." In Aretin, *Nation, Staat und Demokratie in Deutschland. Ausgewählte Beiträge zur Zeitgeschichte.* Mainz 1993, 295–303.

Ash, Mitchell G. "Verordnete Umbrüche – Konstruierte Kontinuitäten: Zur Entnazifizierung von Wissenschaftlern und Wissenschaften nach 1945." *Zeitschrift für Geschichtswissenschaft* 43 (1995): 903–23.

Auerbach, Hellmuth. "Die Gründung des Instituts für Zeitgeschichte." *Vierteljahrshefte für Zeitgeschichte* 18 (1970): 529–54.

August, Jochen. *"Sonderaktion Krakau." Die Verhaftung der Krakauer Wissenschaftler am 6. November 1939.* Hamburg 1997.

Barkin, Kenneth D. "German Émigré Historians in America: The Fifties, Sixties, and Seventies," in Hartmut Lehmann und James J. Sheehan, eds. *An Interrupted Past. German-Speaking Refugee Historians in the United States After 1933.* Cambridge 1991, 149–69.

Barraclough, Geoffrey. "What is the Future of Germany?" *The Listener* [BBC] LI (27. V. 1954): 903f., 923.

Barthel, Konrad. "Zur Problematik zeitgeschichtlichen Verstehens. Bemerkungen zu Wheeler-Bennetts 'Nemesis der Macht.'" *Geschichte in Wissenschaft und Unterricht* 6 (1955): 608–26.

Bauerkämper, Arnd, Martin Sabrow and Bernd Stöver, eds. *Doppelte Zeitgeschichte. Deutsch-deutsche Beziehungen 1945–1990.* Bonn 1998.

Beck, Peter. "Politicians versus Historians: Lord Avon's 'Appeasement Battle' against 'Lamentably Appeasement-Minded' Historians," *Twentieth Century British History* 9 (1998): 396–419.

Beddie, James S. "The Berlin Document Center," in Robert Wolfe, ed. *Captured German and Related Records. A National Archives Conference.* Athens, OH: Ohio UP, 1974, 131–42.

Beer, Mathias. "Im Spannungsfeld von Politik und Zeitgeschichte. Das Grossforschungsprojekt 'Dokumentation der Verteibung der Deutschen aus Ost-Mitteleuropa'." *Vierteljahrshefte für Zeitgeschichte* 46 (1998): 345–89.

———. "Die Landesstelle Schlesien für Nachkriegsgeschichte 1934 bis 1945. Geschichtswissenschaft und Politik im Lichte neuer Aktenfunde," in Matthias Weber and Carsten Rabe, eds. *Silesographia. Stand und Perspektiven der historischen Schlesienforschung. Festschrift für Norbert Conrads zum 60. Geburtstag.* Würzburg 1998, 119–44.

———. "Die Dokumentation der Vertreibung der Deutschen aus Ost-Mitteleuropa. Hintergründe, Entstehung, Ergebnis, Wirkung." *Geschichte in Wissenschaft und Unterricht* 50 (1999): 99–117.

———. "Der 'Neuanfang' der Zeitgeschichte nach 1945. Zum Verhältnis von nationalsozialistischer Umsiedlungs- und Vernichtungspolitik und der Vertreibung der Deutschen aus Ostmitteleuropa," in Winfried Schulze and Otto Gerhard Oexle, eds., *Deutsche Historiker im Nationalsozialismus.* Frankfurt 1999, 274–301.

Behringer, Wolfgang. "Bauern-Franz und Rassen-Günther. Die politische Geschichte des Agrarhistorikers Günther Franz (1902–1992)," in Winfried Schulze and Otto Gerhard Oexle, eds., *Deutsche Historiker im Nationalsozialismus.* Frankfurt 1999, 114–41.

Benninghoven, Friedrich. "Verbleib, Vernichtung und Ersatz Reichs- und preußischer Behördenüberlieferungen." *Der Archivar* 31 (1978): 35–8.

Benz, Wolfgang. "Wissenschaft oder Alibi? Die Etablierung der Zeitgeschichte," in Walther H. Pehle, ed. *Wissenschaft im geteilten Deutschland. Restauration oder Neubeginn nach 1945.* Frankfurt/Main 1992, 11–25.

Berg, Nicolas. *Der Holocaust und die westdeutschen Historiker. Erforschung und Erinnerung.* Göttingen 2003.

Berghahn, Volker. "Deutschlandbilder 1945–1965. Angloamerikanische Historiker und moderne deutsche Geschichte," in Ernst Schulin, ed. *Deutsche Geschichtswissenschaft nach dem Zweiten Weltkrieg 1945–1965.* (Schriften des Historischen Kollegs. Kolloquien 14). Munich: Oldenbourg 1989, 239–72.

Berghahn, Volker and Henry Cohn. "Francis L. Carsten. Politics and History in two Cultures," in Volker Berghahn and Martin Kitchen, eds. *Germany in the Age of Total War. Festschrift für Francis L. Carsten.* London 1981, 7–22.

Bergmeier, Horst J. P. and Rainer E. Lotz. *Hitler's Airwaves. The Inside Story of Nazi Radio Broadcasting and Propaganda Swing.* New Haven 1997.

Bialer, Uri. "Telling the Truth to the People: Britain's Decision to Publish the Diplomatic Papers of the Interwar Period," in Keith Wilson, ed. *Forging the Collective Memory. Government and International Historians Through Two World Wars.* Providence, RI, 1996, 265–88.

Biewer, Ludwig. "Das Politische Archiv des Auswärtigen Amtes" *Der Auswärtige Dienst* 58 (1997): unpaginated [15pp.].

Bindschedler, Rudolf L. "Die völkerrechtliche Stellung Deutschlands." *Schweizerisches Jahrbuch für internationales Recht* 6 (1949): 37–64.

Bing, Harold F. "The Study and Teaching of History in Post-War Germany." *History* 36 (1951): 92–107.

Blasius, Rainer A. "Heißer Draht nach Washington? Die Botschafter der Bundesrepublik Deutschland in Washington 1955–1968." *Historische Mitteilungen der Ranke-Gesellschaft* 11 (1998): 282–305.

Boberach, Heinz. "Das Schriftgut der staatliche Verwaltung, der Wehrmacht und der NSDAP aus der Zeit von 1933–1945. Versuch einer Bilanz." *Der Archivar* 22 (1969): 137–52.

_____. "Die Benutzungsordnung für das Bundesarchiv." *Der Archivar* 23 (1970): 63–9.

_____. "Die schriftliche Überlieferung der Behörden des Deutschen Reiches 1871–1945. Sicherung, Rückführung, Ersatzdokumentation," in Boberach and Hans Booms, eds. *Aus der Arbeit des Bundesarchivs. Beiträge zum Archivwesen, zur Quellenkunde und Zeitgeschichte.* (Schriften des Bundesarchivs 25). Boppard/Rh. 1977, 50–61.

_____. "Angehörige des Reichsarchivs als Opfer der Verfolgung durch das NS-Regime." *Mitteilungen aus dem Bundesarchiv* 2 (1997): 17–19.

_____. "Die Beteiligung des Bundesarchivs an der Verfolgung und Wiedergutmachung nationalsozialistischen Unrechts in den sechziger Jahren," in Klaus Oldenhage, Hermann Schreyer, Wolfram Werner eds. *Archiv und Geschichte. Festschrift für Friedrich P. Kahlenberg.* (Schriften des Bundesarchivs 57). Düsseldorf 2000, 264–74.

Bönnen, Gerold. "Beschlagnahmt, geborgen, ausgeliefert. Zum Schicksal des Wormser jüdischen Gemeindearchivs 1938–1957," in Kretzschmar, *Deutsches Archivwesen und der Nationalsozialismus*, 101–15.

Booms, Hans. "Gesellschaftsordnung und Überlieferungsbildung. Zur Problematik archivarischer Quellenbewertung." *Archivalische Zeitschrift* 68 (1972): 3–40.

_____. "Das Bundesarchiv. Ein Zentralarchiv 25 Jahre nach der Gründung," in Boberach and Booms, eds. *Aus der Arbeit des Bundesarchivs. Beiträge zum Archivwesen, zur Quellenkunde und Zeitgeschichte.* (Schriften des Bundesarchivs 25). Boppard/Rh. 1977, 11–49.

_____. "Georg Winters Weg zum Gründungsdirektor des Bundesarchivs," in Klaus Oldenhage, Hermann Schreyer, Wolfram Werner, eds. *Archiv und Geschichte. Festschrift für Friedrich P. Kahlenberg.* (Schriften des Bundesarchivs 57). Düsseldorf 2000, 240–63.

Born, Lester K. "The Archives and Libraries of Postwar Germany." *American Historical Review* 56 (1950): 34–57.

_____. "The Ministerial Collecting Center Near Kassel, Germany." *American Archivist* 13 (1950): 237–58.

Bourgeois, Émile. "Les Archives d'État et l'Enquete sur les Origines de la Guerre Mondiale." *Revue Historique* 155 (1927): 39–56.

Bradsher, Greg. "A Brief Survey of the Disposition of Captured Japanese Records 1945–1962." National Archives, unpublished typoscript, 2000.

Brandt, Ahasver von. "Schicksalsfragen deutscher Archive." *Der Archivar* 1 (1948): 133–40.

Brather, Hans-Stephan. "Aktenvernichtung durch deutsche Dienststellen beim Zusammenbruch des Faschismus." *Archivmitteilungen* 8:4 (1958): 115–17.

Breit, Gotthard. *Staats- und Gesellschaftsbild deutscher Generale beider Weltkriege im Spiegel ihrer Memoiren.* Boppard/Rh. 1973.

Breitman, Richard, Norman J. W. Goda, Timothy Naftali, and Robert Wolfe. *U.S. Intelligence and the Nazis.* New York 2005.

Breitman, Richard. *Official Secrets. What the Nazis Planned, What the British and Americans Knew.* New York 1998.

Breyer, Richard. "Gotthold Starke – ein Wortführer unserer Volksgruppe." *Jahrbuch Weichsel-Warthe* (1970): 53–9.

Brochhagen, Ulrich. *Nach Nürnberg. Vergangenheitsbewältigung und Westintegration in der Ära Adenauer.* Hamburg 1994.

Brockfeld, Susanne. "Das Beispiel Eckhart Kehr. Reaktionen der preußischen Archivverwaltung auf die Machtübernahme der Nationalsozialisten," in Kretzschmar, *Deutsches Archivwesen und der Nationalsozialismus*, 274–80.

Browder, George C. "Captured German and Other Nations' Documents in the Osoby (Special) Archive, Moscow." *Central European History* 24 (1991): 424–45.

_____. "Update on the Captured Documents in the Former Osoby Archive, Moscow." *Central European History* 26 (1993): 335–42.

Brower, Philip P. "The U.S. Army's Seizure and Administration of Enemy Records up to World War II." *American Archivist* 26 (1963): 191–207.

Brübach, Nils. "Johannes Papritz (1898–1992) und die Entwicklung der Archivwissenschaft nach 1945." *Der Archivar* 51 (1998): 573–88.

Bruchmann, Karl G. "Das Bundesarchiv in Koblenz. Entstehung, Organisation, Aufgaben." *Geschichte in Wissenschaft und Unterricht* 15 (1964): 83–98.

Buchheim, Hans. "Hermann Mau zum Gedächtnis." *Vierteljahrshefte für Zeitgeschichte* 10 (1962): 427–9.

Bullock, Alan. "[Obituary] John Wheeler Wheeler-Bennett, 1902–1975." *Proceedings of the British Academy* 65 (1979): 799–833.

Burk, Kathleen. "Britische Traditionen internationaler Geschichtsschreibung," in Wilfried Loth and Jürgen Osterhammel, eds. *Internationale Geschichte.* Munich 2000, 45–59.

_____. *Troublemaker. The Life and History of A. J. P. Taylor.* New Haven, CT, 2000.

Burleigh, Michael. *Germany Turns Eastwards. A Study of Ostforschung in the Third Reich.* Cambridge 1988.

Buscher, Frank M. "The U.S. High Commission and German Nationalism, 1949–1952." *Central European History* 23 (1990): 57–75.

Butler, J. R. M. "The British Official Military History of the Second World War." *Military Affairs* 22 (1958): 149–51.

Butler, Rohan. *Roots of National Socialism.* London 1941.

Butterfield, Herbert. "Official History: Its Pitfalls and Criteria," in Butterfield, *History and Human Relations.* London 1951, 182–224.

Cline, Catherine Ann. "British Historians and the Treaty of Versailles." *Albion* 20 (1988): 43–58.

Connell, John. "Official History and the Unofficial Historian." *Royal United Service Institute Journal* 110 (1965): 329–34.

Conrad, Sebastian. *Auf der Suche nach der verlorenen Nation. Geschichtsschreibung in Westdeutschland und Japan 1945–1960.* (Kritische Studien zur Geschichtswissenschaft 134). Göttingen 1999.

Cordshagen, Hugo. "Die Aktenvernichtungen beim Mecklenburgischen Staatsministerium, Abt. Inneres, und seinen nachgeordneten Behörden im März und April 1945." *Archivmitteilungen* 6 (1956): 127–30.

Cornelißen, Christoph. "Zeitgeschichte im Übergang von der NS-Diktatur zur Demokratie: Gerhard Ritter und die Institutionalisierung der Zeitgeschichte in Westdeutschland," in Matthias Middell, Gabriele Lingelbach, Frank Hadler, eds. *Historische Institute im internationalen Vergleich* (Geschichtswissenschaft und Geschichtskultur im 20. Jahrhundert 3). Leipzig 2001, 339–61.

Cornelißen, Christoph. *Gerhard Ritter. Geschichtswissenschaft und Politik im 20. Jahrhundert.* (Schriften des Bundesarchivs 58). Düsseldorf 2001.

Costello, John. *Ten Days to Destiny. The Secret Story of the Hess Peace Initiative and British Efforts to Strike a Deal with Hitler.* New York 1991.

Craig, Gordon A. *The Politics of the Prussian Army 1640–1945.* Oxford 1955.

Dehio, Ludwig. "Erfassung von Privatpapieren als Zeugnisse einer untergehenden Gesellschaftskultur." *Der Archivar* 1 (1948): 91.

Demandt, Alexander. *Vandalismus. Gewalt gegen Kultur.* Berlin 1997.

Dietz, Burkhard, Helmut Gabel, and Ulrich Tiedau, eds. *Griff nach dem Westen. Die "Westforschung" der völkisch-nationalen Wissenschaften zum nordwesteuropäischen Raum, 1919–1960.* Münster 2003.

Diestelkamp, Adolf. "Die künftige Behandlung der Personalakten und der bei den Gerichten erwachsenen Akten personengeschichtlichen und erbbiologischen Inhalts." *Der Archivar* 1 (1947/48): 79–91.

Diestelkamp, Bernhard. "Rechtsgeschichte als Zeitgeschichte. Historische Betrachtungen zur Entstehung und Durchsetzung der Theorie vom Fortbestand des Deutschen Reiches als Staat nach 1945." *Zeitschrift für neuere Rechtsgeschichte* 7 (1985): 181–207.

Dillgard, Georg. "Die Zentralnachweisstelle des Bundesarchivs und die Abwicklung wehr- und militärrechtlicher personeller Angelegenheiten aus der Zeit bis zum 8. Mai 1945," in Friedrich P. Kahlenberg, ed. *Aus der Arbeit der Archive. Beiträge zum Archivwesen, zur Quellenkunde und zur Geschichte. Festschrift für Hans Booms.* Boppard/Rh. 1989, 257–69.

Dockrill, Saki. *Britain's Policy for West German Rearmament 1950–1955.* Cambridge 1991.

Döscher, Hans-Jürgen. *Das Auswärtige Amt im Dritten Reich. Diplomatie im Schatten der "Endlösung."* Berlin 1987.

_____. *Verschworene Gesellschaft. Das Auswärtige Amt unter Adenauer zwischen Neubeginn und Kontinuität.* Berlin 1995.

Downey, William Gerald. "Captured Enemy Property: Booty of War and Seized Enemy Property." *American Journal of International Law* 44 (1950): 488–504.

East, Sherrod. "Archival Experience in a Prototype Intermediate Depository." *American Archivist* 27 (1964): 42–56.

Eckert, Astrid M. *Feindbilder im Wandel. Ein Vergleich des Deutschland- und des Japanbildes in den USA 1945 und 1946.* (Studien zur Geschichte, Politik und Gesellschaft Nordamerikas 13). Münster 1998.

_____. Nazi War Crimes Disclosure Act, in: H-Soz-Kult, 30. Juni 2000, http://hsozkult.geschichte.hu-berlin.de/BEITRAG/essays/ecas0600.htm.

Eckert, Astrid M. and Stefan Martens. "Glasplatten im märkischen Sand: Ein Beitrag zur Überlieferungsgeschichte der Tageseinträge und Diktate von Joseph Goebbels." *Vierteljahrshefte für Zeitgeschichte* 52 (2004): 479–526.

Eckert, Astrid M. "The Transnational Beginnings of West German *Zeitgeschichte* in the 1950s." *Central European History* 40:2 (June 2007): 63–87.

———. "Managing Their Own Past. German Archivists between National Socialism and Democracy." *Archival Science* 7:3 (2007): 223–44.

Ehrmann, Howard M. "German Naval Archives (Tambach)," in Robert Wolfe, ed. *Captured German and Related Records. A National Archives Conference.* Athens, OH, 1974, 157–62.

Eichwede, Wolfgang and Ulrike Hartung, eds. *"Betr.: Sicherstellung." NS-Kunstraub in der Sowjetunion.* Bremen 1998.

Eller, Ernest M. "United States Navy Microfilm of German Naval Archives," in Robert Wolfe, ed. *Captured German and Related Records. A National Archives Conference.* Athens, OH, 1974, 163–172.

Endres, Robert. "Zum Verbleib der Luftwaffenakten beim Zusammenbruch 1945 und danach," in *Fünfzig Jahre Luftwaffen- und Luftkriegs-Geschichtsschreibung*, edited by Militärgeschichtliches Forschungsamt. Freiburg/Br. 1970, 25–31.

Engstrom, Eric J. "*Zeitgeschichte* as Disciplinary History: On Professional Identity, Self-Reflexive Narratives, and Discipline-Building in Contemporary German History." *Tel Aviver Jahrbuch für deutsche Geschichte* 29 (2000): 399–425.

Epstein, Catherine. *A Past Renewed. A Catalog of German-Speaking Refugee Historians in the United States after 1933.* Cambridge 1993.

Epstein, Fritz T. "Zur Quellenkunde der Neuesten Geschichte. Ausländische Materialien in den Archiven und Bibliotheken der Hauptstadt der Vereinigten Staaten." *Vierteljahrshefte für Zeitgeschichte* 2 (1954): 313–25.

———. "Die Erschließung von Quellen zur Geschichte der deutschen Außenpolitik." *Die Welt als Geschichte* 22 (1962): 204–19.

Erdmann, Karl Dietrich. "Aktenpublikationen zur Neuesten Geschichte." *Geschichte in Wissenschaft und Unterricht* 3 (1952): 507–11.

———. *Die Ökumene der Historiker. Geschichte der Internationalen Historikerkongresse und des Comité International des Sciences Historiques.* Göttingen 1987.

Ericksen, Robert P. "Kontinuitäten konservativer Geschichtsschreibung am Seminar für Mittlere und Neuere Geschichte: Von der Weimarer Zeit über die nationalsozialistische Ära bis in die Bundesrepublik," in Heinrich Becker, Hans-Joachim Dahms and Cornelis Wegeler, eds. *Die Universität Göttingen unter dem Nationalsozialismus. Das verdrängte Kapitel ihrer 250jährigen Geschichte.* Munich 1987, 219–45.

Ernst, Fritz. "Die Londoner Diskussion über die deutsche Aktenausgabe 'Die Große Politik der Europäischen Kabinette' (G.P.)." *Die Welt als Geschichte* 13 (1953): 274f.

———. "Blick auf Deutschland. Ausländische Stimmen zur neuesten deutschen Geschichte." *Die Welt als Geschichte* 10 (1955): 192–212.

Ernst, Wolfgang. "Das Schweigen des Archivs erzeugt Ungeheuer (When Memory Comes)." *WerkstattGeschichte* 5 (1993): 39–49.

_____. "Archival Action. The Archive as ROM and its Political Instrumentalization under National Socialism." *History of the Human Sciences* 12 (1999): 13–34.

Etzemüller, Thomas. *Sozialgeschichte als politische Geschichte. Werner Conze und die Neuorientierung der westdeutschen Geschichtswissenschaft nach 1945.* Munich 2001.

Evans, Ellen L. and Joseph O. Baylen. "History as Propaganda. The German Foreign Ministry and the 'Enlightment' of American Historians on the War Guilt Question, 1930–1933," in Keith Wilson, ed. *Forging the Collective Memory. Government and International Historians Through Two World Wars.* Providence, RI, 1996, 151–77.

Fahlbusch, Michael. *Wissenschaft im Dienst der nationalsozialistischen Politik? Die "Volksdeutschen Forschungsgemeinschaften" von 1931–1945.* Baden-Baden 1999.

Falter, Jürgen W. "Die 'Märzgefallenen' von 1933. Neue Forschungsergebnisse zum sozialen Wandel innerhalb der NSDAP-Mitgliedschaft während der Machtergreifungsphase." *Geschichte und Gesellschaft* 24 (1998): 595–616.

Farquharson, John. "Governed or Exploited? The British Acquisition of German Technology, 1945–1948." *Journal of Contemporary History* 32 (1997): 23–42.

Faulenbach, Bernd. *Ideologie des deutschen Weges. Die deutsche Geschichte in der Historiographie zwischen Kaiserreich und Nationalsozialismus.* Munich 1980.

Fedorowich, Kent. "Axis Prisoners of War as Sources for British Military Intelligence, 1939–1942." *Intelligence & National Security* 14 (1999): 156–78.

Fiedler, Wilfried, ed. *Internationaler Kulturgüterschutz und deutsche Frage. Völkerrechtliche Probleme der Auslagerung, Zerstreuung und Rückführung deutscher Kulturgüter nach dem Zweiten Weltkrieg.* Berlin 1991.

Fiedler, Wilfried. *Kulturgüter als Kriegsbeute? Rechtliche Probleme der Rückführung deutscher Kulturgüter aus Russland.* (Heidelberger Forum 95). Heidelberg 1995.

_____. "Safeguarding of Cultural Property during Occupation – Modifications of the Hague Convention of 1907 by World War II?" in Martine Briat, Judith A. Freedberg eds. *Legal Aspects of International Trade in Art. International Sales of Works of Art.* Paris/Den Haag 1996, 175–83.

Fitschen, Thomas. *Das rechtliche Schicksal von staatlichen Akten und Archiven bei einem Wechsel der Herrschaft über Staatsgebiet.* (Saarbrücker Studien zum Internationalen Recht 25). Baden-Baden 2004.

Fletcher, Harry R. "The Use of Captured German and Related Records by the United States Air Force," in Robert Wolfe, ed. *Captured German and Related Records. A National Archives Conference.* Athens, OH, 1974, 73–91.

Fox, John P. "German Bureaucrat or Nazified Ideologue? Ambassador Otto Abetz and Hitler's Anti-Jewish Policies 1940–44," in Michael Graham Fry, ed. *Power, Personalities and Politics. Essays in Honor of Donald Cameron Watt.* London 1992, 175–232.

Frankland, Noble. *History at War. The Campaigns of an Historian.* London 1998.

Frei, Norbert. *Amerikanische Lizenzpolitik und deutsche Pressetradition. Die Geschichte der Nachkriegszeitung Südost-Kurier.* (Schriftenreihe der VfZ 52). Munich 1986.

_____. *Adenauer's Germany and the Nazi Past. The Politics of Amnesty and Integration.* New York 2002.

_____. "Farewell to the Era of Contemporaries. National Socialism and its Historical Examination en route into History." *History & Memory* 9:1/2 (Fall 1997), 59–79.

_____. *National Socialist Rule in Germany. The Führer State 1933–1945.* Oxford 1993.

Freitag, Gabriele and Andreas Grenzer. "Der nationalsozialistische Kunstraub in der Sowjetunion," in Wolfgang Eichwede and Ulrike Hartung, eds. *"Betr.: Sicherstellung." NS-Kunstraub in der Sowjetunion.* Bremen 1998, 20–66.

Freitag, Gabriele. "Die Restitution von NS-Beutegut nach dem Zweiten Weltkrieg," in Wolfgang Eichwede and Ulrike Hartung, eds. *"Betr.: Sicherstellung." NS-Kunstraub in der Sowjetunion.* Bremen 1998, 170–208.

Fritzsche, Peter. "The Archive." *History & Memory* 17:1/2 (Fall 2005): 15–44.

Gall, Lothar, ed. *Das Bismarck-Problem in der Geschichtsschreibung nach 1945.* Köln 1971.

Gassert, Philipp and Daniel S. Mattern, eds. *The Hitler Library. A Bibliography.* Westport, CT, 2001.

Gatzke, Hans W. "The Streseman Papers." *Journal of Modern History* 26 (1954): 49–59.

Gatzke, Hans W. "The Quadripartite Project *Akten zur deutschen Auswaertigen Politik 1918–1945*: Experiment in International Historiography," in Alexander Fischer et al., eds. *Russland – Deutschland – Amerika. Festschrift für Fritz T. Epstein zum 80. Geburtstag.* (Frankfurter Historische Abhandlungen 17). Wiesbaden 1978, 333–41.

Geiss, Immanuel. *Studien über Geschichte und Geschichtswissenschaft.* Frankfurt 1972.

Gerlach, Christian. *Kalkulierte Morde. Die deutsche Wirtschafts- und Vernichtungspolitik in Weißrußland 1941 bis 1944.* Hamburg 1999.

Gerstenberger, Friedrich. "Strategische Erinnerungen. Die Memoiren deutscher Offiziere," in Hannes Heer and Klaus Naumann, eds. *Vernichtungskrieg. Verbrechen der Wehrmacht 1941–1944.* Hamburg 1995, 620–29.

Geyer, Martin H. "Im Schatten der NS-Zeit. Zeitgeschichte als Paradigma einer (bundes)republikanischen Geschichtswissenschaft," in Alexander Nützenadel and Wolfgang Schieder, eds. *Zeitgeschichte als Problem. Nationale Traditionen und Perspektiven der Forschung in Europa.* Göttingen 2004, 24–53.

Giesecke, Dagmar. *Ernst Posner 1892–1980. Archivar in Deutschland und Amerika. Eine biographische Skizze.* Potsdam 1997.

Gießler, Klaus-Volker. "Archivalienrückführung aus den USA." *Mitteilungen aus dem Bundesarchivs* 10:2 (2002): 65–7.

Gilbert, Felix. "German Historiography during the Second World War. A Bibliographical Survey." *American Historical Review* 53 (1947/48): 50–8.

Giles, Robert S. *Archival and Library Restitution in the US Zone of Germany. A Preliminary Study.* Washington, D.C.: American University (Typoscript) 1947.

Gimbel, John. "The Origins of the 'Institut fuer Zeitgeschichte.' Scholarship, Politics, and the American Occupation, 1945–1949." *American Historical Review* 70 (1965): 714–31.

_____. *Science, Technology and Reparations. Exploitation and Plunder in Postwar Germany.* Stanford 1990.

Glenn, Bess. "Private Records Seized by the United States in Wartime – Their Legal Status." *American Archivist* 25 (1962): 399–405.

Goldbeck, Hermann G. "The German Military Documents Section and the Captured Records Section," in Robert Wolfe, ed. *Captured German and Related Records. A National Archives Conference* (NA Conference 3). Athens, OH, 1974, 31–61.

Goldman, Aaron. "Germans and Nazis: The Controversy over 'Vansittartism' in Britain during the Second World War." *Journal of Contemporary History* 14 (1979): 155–91.

Goldmann, Klaus. "The Trojan Treasures in Berlin: The Disappearance and Search for the Objects after World War II," in Elisabeth Simpson, ed. *The Spoils of War. World War II and Its Aftermath: The Loss, Reappearance, and Recovery of Cultural Property*. New York 1999, 200–3.

Gossel, Daniel. *Briten, Deutsche und Europa. Die Deutsche Frage in der britischen Außenpolitik 1945–1962*. (HMRG Beihefte 32). Stuttgart 1999.

Grahn, Gerlinde, Helmut Lötzke and Johanna Weiser. "Die Hilfe und Unterstützung der UdSSR für den Schutz und die Sicherung des Staatlichen Archivfonds der DDR." *Archivmitteilungen* 15 (1975): 47–52.

Graml, Hermann and Hans Woller. "Fünfzig Jahre Vierteljahrshefte für Zeitgeschichte 1953–2003." *Vierteljahrshefte für Zeitgeschichte* 51 (2003): 51–87.

Greenfield, Jeannette. "'The Spoils of War'," in Elisabeth Simpson, ed. *The Spoils of War. World War II and Its Aftermath: The Loss, Reappearance, and Recovery of Cultural Property*. New York 1999, 34–8.

Greiner, Bernd. *Die Morgenthau-Legende. Zur Geschichte eines umstrittenen Plans*. Hamburg 1995.

Greve, Michael. *Der justitielle und rechtspolitische Umgang mit den NS-Gewaltverbrechen in den sechziger Jahren*. Frankfurt 2001.

Grimsted, Patricia Kennedy. "The Odyssey of the Smolensk Archive. Plundered Communist Records, Part I – III." *1999. Zeitschrift für Sozialgeschichte des 20. und 21. Jahrhunderts* 12:4 (1997): 71–97; 13:2 (1998): 190–201; 14:1 (1999): 134–51.

_____. *Trophies of War and Empire. The Archival Heritage of Ukraine, World War II, and the International Politics of Restitution*. (Harvard Papers in Ukrainian Studies). Cambridge, MA, 2001.

_____. "Twice Plundered or 'Twice Saved'? Identifying Russia's 'Trophy' Archives and the Loot of the Reichssicherheitshauptamt." *Holocaust and Genocide Studies* 15 (2001): 191–244.

_____. "Roads to Ratibor. Library and Archival Plunder by the Einsatzstab Reichsleiter Rosenberg." *Holocaust and Genocide Studies* 19; 3 (2005): 390–458.

_____. *U.S. Restitution of Nazi-Looted Cultural Treasures to the USSR, 1945–1959. Facsimile Documents from the National Archives of the United States*. CD-Rom. Compiled with an Introduction by Patricia Kennedy Grimsted. Washington, D.C. 2001.

Grunewald, Jacques. "Les Travaux sur l'Histoire de la Seconde Guerre Mondiale en Grande-Bretagne." *Revue d'Histoire de la Deuxième Guerre Mondiale* 5:17 (1955): 58–64.

Haar, Ingo. *Historiker im Nationalsozialismus. Deutsche Geschichtswissenschaft und der "Volkstumskampf" im Osten.* (Kritische Studien zur Geschichtswissenschaft 143) Göttingen 2000.

Hachmeister, Lutz. *Der Gegnerforscher. Die Karriere des SS-Führers Franz Alfred Six.* Munich 1998.

Hadsel, Fred L. "George Peabody Gooch," in S. William Halperin, ed. *Some Twentieth Century Historians. Essays on Eminent Europeans.* Chicago 1961, 255–76.

Hallgarten, George W. *Imperialismus vor 1914. Die soziologischen Grundlagen der Außenpolitik europäischer Großmächte vor dem Ersten Weltkrieg.* Bd. 1. Munich 1963.

Hamerow, Theodore S. "Guilt, Redemption, and Writing German History." *American Historical Review* 88 (1983): 53–72.

Hamilton, Keith. "Historical Diplomacy: Foreign Ministries and the Management of the Past," in Jovan Kurbalija, ed. *Knowledge and Diplomacy.* Malta: Mediterranean Academy of Diplomatic Studies 1999. (http://www.diplomacy.edu/Books/knowledge/Hamilton.htm, accessed May 15, 2010).

Hammerstein, Notker. "Eine verwickelt vielschichtige Zeitgenossenschaft. Kurt Rheindorf und die Frankfurter Universität," Dieter Hein, Klaus Hildebrand, Andreas Schulz, eds. *Historie und Leben. Der Historiker als Wissenschaftler und Zeitgenosse.* Munich 2006, 467–78.

Hansen, Niels. "Ein wahrer Held in seiner Zeit. Zum dreißigsten Todestag von Johannes Ullrich." *Historische Mitteilungen* 9 (1990): 95–109.

Hartung, Ulrike. *Verschleppt und Verschollen. Eine Dokumentation deutscher, sowjetischer und amerikanischer Akten zum NS-Kunstraub in der Sowjetunion (1941–1948).* Bremen 2000.

Heiber, Helmut. *Walter Frank und sein Reichsinstitut für die Geschichte des neuen Deutschlands* (Quellen und Darstellungen zur Zeitgeschichte 13). Stuttgart 1966.

Heilmann, H. D. "Aus dem Kriegstagebuch des Diplomaten Otto Bräutigam." Introduced and edited by H. D. Heilmann. In: *Biedermann und die Schreibtischtäter. Materialien zur deutschen Täter-Biographie.* (Beiträge zur nationalsozialistischen Gesundheits- und Sozialpolitik 4). Berlin 1987, 123–30.

Heimpel, Hermann. "Internationaler Historikertag in Paris." *Geschichte in Wissenschaft und Unterricht* 1 (1950): 556–9.

Heinemann, Ulrich. *Die verdrängte Niederlage. Politische Öffentlichkeit und Kriegsschuldfrage in der Weimarer Republik.* Göttingen 1983.

Heinsius, Paul. "Das Aktenmaterial der deutschen Kriegsmarine. Seine bisherige Auswertung und sein Verbleib." *Die Welt als Geschichte* 13 (1953): 198–202.

Henke, Josef. "Das Schicksal deutscher zeitgeschichtlicher Quellen in Kriegs- und Nachkriegszeit. Beschlagnahme – Rückführung – Verbleib." *Vierteljahrshefte für Zeitgeschichte* 30 (1982): 557–620.

Henke, Klaus-Dietmar. *Die amerikanische Besetzung Deutschlands* (Quellen und Darstellungen zur Zeitgeschichte 27). Munich 1995.

————. *Wann bricht schon mal ein Staat zusammen? Eine Debatte über die Stasi-Akten und die DDR-Geschichte auf dem 39. Historikertag 1992.* Munich 1993.

Herbert, Ulrich. *Best. Biographische Studien über Radikalismus, Weltanschauung und Vernunft 1903–1989.* Bonn 1996.

————. ed. *Wandlungsprozesse in Westdeutschland. Belastung, Integration, Liberalisierung 1945–1980.* (Moderne Zeit. Neue Forschungen zur Gesellschafts- und Kulturgeschichte des 19. und 20. Jahrhunderts 1). Göttingen 2002.

Herrebout Els. *De Duitse Archivschutz in België tijdens de Tweede Wereldoorlog.* Brussels 1997.

————. "Georg Sante und der deutsche Archivschutz in Belgien während des Zweiten Weltkrieges," in Kretzschmar, ed. *Deutsches Archivwesen und Nationalsozialismus,* 208–16.

Herrmann, Matthias. "Archiv(gut)schutz im Deutschen Reich in der ersten Hälfte des 20. Jahrhunderts." *Archivmitteilungen* 42 (1993): 169–82.

Herrmann, Matthias. *Das Reichsarchiv (1919–1945). Eine archivische Institution im Spannungsfeld der deutschen Politik.* 2 vols. Phil. Diss. Berlin 1993.

Herwig, Holger H. "Clio Deceived: Patriotic Self-Censorship in Germany after the Great War," in Keith Wilson, ed. *Forging the Collective Memory. Government and International Historians through Two World Wars.* Providence, RI, 1996.

Herz, Rudolf. *Hoffmann & Hitler. Fotografie als Medium des Führer-Mythos.* Munich 1994.

Heuss, Anja. "Die 'Beuteorganisation' des Auswärtigen Amtes. Das Sonderkommando Künsberg und der Kulturraub in der Sowjetunion." *Vierteljahrshefte für Zeitgeschichte* 45 (1997): 535–56.

————. *Kunst- und Kulturgutraub. Eine vergleichende Studie zur Besatzungspolitik der Nationalsozialisten in Frankreich und der Sowjetunion.* Heidelberg 2000.

Heusterberg, Babett. "Personenbezogene Unterlagen aus der Zeit des Nationalsozialismus. Das Bundesarchiv in Berlin und seine Bestände, insbesondere des ehemaligen amerikanischen Berlin Document Center (BDC)." *Herold-Jahrbuch* N.F. 5 (2000): 149–86.

Heym, Stefan. "Eine wahre Geschichte," in Heym, *Die Kannibalen und andere Erzählungen.* Leipzig 1953, 51–76.

Hockerts, Hans Günter. "Zeitgeschichte in Deutschland. Begriff, Methode, Themenfelder." *Aus Politik und Zeitgeschichte* B29–30/93 (1993): 3–19.

Holmes, Oliver W. "The National Archives and the Protection of Records in War Areas." *American Archivist* 9 (1946): 110–127.

Holzhausen, Rudolf. "Die Quellen zur Erforschung der Geschichte des 'Dritten Reiches' von 1938–1945." *Europa-Archiv* 4 (November 1949): 2585–90.

Hoogewoud, F. J. "The Nazi Looting of Books and its American 'Antithesis.' Selected Pictures from the Offenbach Archival Depot's Photographic History and Its Supplement." *Studia Rosenthaliana* 26 (1992): 158–92.

Hölzle, Erwin. *Die Selbstentmachtung Europas. Das Experiment des Friedens vor und nach dem Ersten Weltkrieg. Unter Verwertung unveröffentlichter, zum Teil verlorengegangener deutscher und französischer Dokumente.* Göttingen 1975.

Hönicke, Michaela. "'Know Your Enemy': American Wartime Images of Germany, 1942/43," in Ragnhild Fiebig-von Hase and Ursula Lehmkuhl, eds. *Enemy Images in American History.* Providence, RI, 1997, 231–78.

Humphrey, Richard A. "War-Born Microfilm Holdings of the Department of State." *Journal of Modern History* 20 (1948): 133–6.

Hutterer, Herbert, Thomas Just. "Zur Geschichte des Reichsarchivs Wien 1938–1945," in Kretzschmar, ed. *Archivwesen und Nationalsozialismus,* 313–25.

Iggers, George G. *Deutsche Geschichtswissenschaft. Eine Kritik der traditionellen Geschichtsauffassung von Herder bis zur Gegenwart.* Köln 1997.

Jacobs, Harry A. "Operation Strakonice: In Pursuit of the Soviet Order of Battle." *Journal of Military History* 65 (2001): 391–400.

Jäger, Wolfgang. *Historische Forschung und politische Kultur in Deutschland. Die Debatte 1914–1980 über den Ausbruch des Ersten Weltkriegs.* (Kritische Studien zur Geschichtswissenschaft 61). Göttingen 1984.

Jarausch, Konrad. "Die Provokation des 'Anderen.' Amerikanische Perspektiven auf die deutsche Vergangenheitsbewältigung," in Arnd Bauerkämper, Martin Sabrow, Bernd Stöver, eds. *Doppelte Zeitgeschiche. Deutsch-deutsche Beziehungen 1945–1990.* Bonn 1998, 432–46.

Jefferies, Matthew. *Contesting the German Empire, 1871–1918.* London 2008.

Jena, Kai von and Wilhelm Lenz. "Die deutschen Bestände im Sonderarchiv Moskau." *Der Archivar* 45 (1992): 457–67.

Jena, Kai von. "Die Rückführung deutscher Akten aus Rußland – eine unerledigte Aufgabe," Klaus Oldenhage et al., eds. *Archiv und Geschichte. Festschrift für Friedrich P. Kahlenberg* (Schriften des Bundesarchivs 57). Düsseldorf 2000, 391–420.

Jenke, Manfred. *Verschwörung von rechts? Ein Bericht über den Rechtsradikalismus in Deutschland nach 1945.* Berlin 1961.

Jessen, Ralph. "Zeithistoriker im Konfliktfeld der Vergangenheitspolitik," in Konrad Jarausch and Martin Sabrow, eds. *Verletztes Gedächtnis. Erinnerungskultur und Zeitgeschichte im Konflikt.* Frankfurt 2002, 153–75.

Kahlenberg, Friedrich. *Deutsche Archive in West und Ost. Zur Entwicklung des Staatlichen Archivwesens seit 1945.* (Mannheimer Schriften zur Politik und Zeitgeschichte 4). Düsseldorf 1972.

Kahn, David. "Secrets of Nazi Archives." *Atlantic Monthly* 223; 5 (May 1969): 50–6.

Kaiser-Lahme, Angela. "Westalliierte Archivpolitik während und nach dem Zweiten Weltkrieg. Die Beschlagnahmung, Sicherung und Auswertung deutscher Archive und Dokumente durch die Amerikaner und Briten 1943–1946." *Der Archivar* 45 (1992): 397–410.

Kaye, Lawrence M. "Laws in Force at the Dawn of World War II: International Conventions and National Laws," in Elisabeth Simpson, ed. *The Spoils of War. World War II and Its Aftermath: The Loss, Reappearance, and Recovery of Cultural Property.* New York 1997, 100–5.

Kehrig, Manfred. "'. . . und keinen Staat im Staate bilden.' Skizzen zur Entwicklung des militärischen Archivwesens 1945–1955," in Friedrich P. Kahlenberg, ed. *Aus der Arbeit der Archive. Beiträge zum Archivwesen, zur Quellenkunde und zur Geschichte. Festschrift für Hans Booms.* Boppard/Rh. 1989, 368–408.

Kempner, Robert. "The Nuremberg Trials as Sources of Recent German Political and Historical Materials." *American Political Science Review* 44 (1950): 447–59.

Kent, George O. "The German Foreign Ministry Archives," in Robert Wolfe, ed. *Captured German and Related Records. A National Archives Conference* (NA Conference 3). Athens, OH, 1974, 119–30.

———. "The German Foreign Ministry Archives at Whaddon Hall, 1948–1958." *American Archivist* 24 (1961): 43–54.

———. "Editing Diplomatic Documents: A Review of Official U.S. and German Document Series." *American Archivist* 57 (1994): 462–81.

Kettenacker, Lothar. *Krieg zur Friedenssicherung* (Veröffentlichung des DHIL 22). Göttingen: V&R, 1989.

_____. "Die Haltung der Westalliierten gegenüber Hitlerattentat und Widerstand nach dem 20. Juli 1944," in Gerd R. Ueberschär, ed. *Der 20. Juli 1944. Bewertung und Rezeption des deutschen Widerstandes gegen das NS-Regime.* Freiburg 1994, 19–37.

Kißmehl, Horst. "Kriegswichtige Zielobjekte – Akten, Archive, Bibliotheken," in Burchard Brentjes, ed. *Wissenschaft unter dem NS-Regime.* Berlin/Bonn 1992, 132–55.

Klein, Fritz. "Über die Verfälschung der historischen Wahrheit in der Aktenpublikation 'Die Große Politik der Europäischen Kabinette 1871–1914.'" *Zeitschrift für Geschichtswissenschaft* 7 (1959): 318–30.

Kleßmann, Christoph. *Die Selbstbehauptung einer Nation. NS-Kulturpolitik und polnische Widerstandsbewegung.* Düsseldorf 1971.

_____. "Verflechtung und Abgrenzung. Aspekte der geteilten und zusammengehörigen deutschen Nachkriegsgeschichte." *Aus Politik und Zeitgeschichte* B29–30/93 (1993): 30–41.

Kleßmann, Christoph. and Martin Sabrow: "Zeitgeschichte in Deutschland nach 1989." *Aus Politik und Zeitgeschichte* B39 (1996): 3–14.

_____. *Zeitgeschichte in Deutschland nach dem Ende des Ost-West-Konflikts.* Essen 1998.

Kluke, Paul. "Die englischen und deutschen diplomatischen Akten." *Historische Zeitschrift* 175 (1953): 527–41.

_____. "Aufgaben und Methoden zeitgeschichtlicher Forschung." *Europa-Archiv* 10 (1955): 7429–38.

Knoch, Habbo. "Der Krieg des Landsers. Populäre Kriegserinnerung in den 50er Jahren," in Jens Baumgarten, Jens Jäger, Martin Knauer, eds. *Inszenierte Wahrheit. Krieg der Bilder – Bilder des Krieges*, Frankfurt 2003, 163–86.

Köhler, Henning. *Adenauer. Eine politische Biographie.* Frankfurt 1994.

König, Helmut. "Das deutsch-sowjetische Vertragswerk von 1939 und seine Geheimen Zusatzprotokolle." *Osteuropa* 39 (1989): 413–58.

Kohn, Hans, ed. *German History. Some New German Views.* Boston 1954.

_____. "Rethinking Recent German History," in Kohn, ed. *German History. Some New German Views.* Boston 1954, 24–43.

Koselleck, Reinhart. "Stetigkeit und Wandel aller Zeitgeschichten. Begriffsgeschichtliche Anmerkungen," in Koselleck, ed. *Zeitschichten. Studien zur Historik.* Frankfurt 2000, 246–64.

Kotowski, Albert S. *Polens Politik gegenüber seiner deutschen Minderheit 1919–1939.* (Studien der Forschungsstelle Ostmitteleuropa an der Universität Dortmund 23). Wiesbaden 1998.

Kreikamp, Hans-Dieter. *Deutsches Vermögen in den Vereinigten Staaten. Die Auseinandersetzung um seine Rückführung als Aspekt der deutsch-amerikanischen Beziehungen 1952–1962.* (Studien zur Zeitgeschichte 14). Stuttgart 1979.

Kreis, Georg. "Die Sperrfristen. Überlegungen und Erfahrungen eines Forschers," *Zeitschrift des Schweizerischen Bundesarchivs* 27 (2001): 249–68.

Kretzschmar, Robert, Astrid M. Eckert, Heiner Schmitt, Dieter Speck and Klaus Wisotzky, eds. *Das deutsche Archivwesen und der Nationalsozialismus. 75. Deutscher Archivtag 2005 in Stuttgart.* Essen 2007.

Kröger, Martin and Roland Thimme. "Das Politische Archiv des Auswärtigen Amts im Zweiten Weltkrieg. Sicherung, Flucht, Verlust, Rückführung." *Vierteljahrshefte für Zeitgeschichte* 47 (1999): 243–64.

Krohn, Claus-Dieter. "Unter Schwerhörigen? Zur selektiven Rezeption des Exils in den wissenschaftlichen und kulturpolitischen Debatten der frühen Nachkriegszeit," in Bernd Weisbrod, ed. *Akademische Vergangenheitspolitik. Beiträge zur Wissenschaftskultur der Nachkriegszeit.* Göttingen 2002, 97–120.

Krüger, Dieter. *Das Amt Blank. Die schwierige Gründung des Bundesministeriums für Verteidigung.* (Einzelschriften zur Militärgeschichte 38). Freiburg 1993.

_____. "Archiv im Spannungsfeld von Politik, Wissenschaft und öffentlicher Meinung. Geschichte und Überlieferungsprofil des ehemaligen 'Berlin Document Center'." *Vierteljahrshefte für Zeitgeschichte* 45 (1997): 49–74.

Krumeich, Gerd. "Vergleichende Aspekte der 'Kriegsschulddebatte' nach dem Ersten Weltkrieg," in Wolfgang Michalka ed. *Der Erste Weltkrieg. Wirkung, Wahrnehmung, Analyse.* Munich 1994, 913–28.

Kurtz, Michael J. *Nazi Contraband. American Policy on the Return of European Cultural Treasures, 1945–1955.* New York 1985.

_____. "The End of the War and the Occupation of Germany 1944–1952. Laws and Conventions Enacted to Counter German Appropriations: The Allied Control Council," in Elisabeth Simpson, ed. *The Spoils of War. World War II and Its Aftermath: The Loss, Reappearance, and Recovery of Cultural Property.* New York 1997, 112–16.

Kwiet, Konrad. "Die NS-Zeit in der westdeutschen Forschung 1945–1961," in Ernst Schulin, ed. *Deutsche Geschichtswissenschaft nach dem Zweiten Weltkrieg 1945–1965.* (Schriften des Historischen Kollegs. Kolloquien 14). Munich 1989, 181–98.

Lambauer, Barbara. *Otto Abetz et les Français ou l'envers de la Collaboration.* Paris 2001.

Lambert, Margaret. "Source Materials Made Available to Historical Resesrach as a Result of World War II." *International Affairs* 35:2 (1959): 188–96.

Leesch, Wolfgang. *Die deutschen Archivare 1500–1945. 2 vols. Vol. II: Biographisches Lexikon.* Munich 1992.

Lehr, Stefan. *Ein fast vergessener "Osteinsatz." Deutsche Archivare im Generalgouvernement und im Reichskommissariat Ukraine.* Düsseldorf 2007.

_____. "Deutsche Archivare und ihre Archivpolitik im 'Generalgouvernement' (1939–1945)," in Kretzschmar ed. *Archivwesen und Nationalsozialismus,* 166–74.

Lemke, Michael. "Kampagnen gegen Bonn. Die Systemkrise der DDR und die West-Propaganda der SED 1960–1963." *Vierteljahrshefte für Zeitgeschichte* 41 (1993): 153–74.

Lenz, Wilhelm. "Die Handakten von Bernhard Lösener, 'Rassereferent' im Reichsministerium des Innern," in Klaus Oldenhage, Hermann Schreyer, Wolfram Werner eds. *Archiv und Geschichte. Festschrift für Friedrich P. Kahlenberg.* (Schriften des Bundesarchivs 57). Düsseldorf 2000, 684–99.

Lepsius, M. Rainer. "Das Erbe des Nationalsozialismus und die politische Kultur der Nachfolgestaaten des 'Großdeutschen Reiches,'" in Lepsius, ed. *Demokratie in Deutschland.* (Kritische Studien zur Geschichtswissenschaft 100). Göttingen 1993, 229–45.

Lipinsky, Jan. "Sechs Jahrzehnte Geheimes Zusatzprotokoll zum Hitler-Stalin-Pakt. Sowjetrussische Historiographie zwischen Leugnung und Wahrheit." *Osteuropa* 10 (2000): 1123–48.

Lötzke, Helmut. "Die Bedeutung der von der Sowjetunion übergebenen deutschen Archivbestände für die deutsche Geschichtsforschung." *Zeitschrift für Geschichtswissenschaft* 3 (1955): 775–9.

_____. "Die Übergabe deutscher Archivbestände durch die Sowjetunion an die Deutsche Demokratische Republik." *Der Archivar* 9 (1956): 31–4.

Lowe, Rodney. "Archival Report. Plumbing New Depths. Contemporary Historians and the Public Records Office." *Twentieth Century British History* 8 (1997): 239–65.

Ludwig, Jörg. "Das Sächsische Hauptstaatsarchiv Dresden in der Zeit des Nationalsozialismus und der Sowjetischen Besatzungszone (1933–1949)," in *Archive und Herrschaft. Referate des 72. Deutschen Archivtags. 18.–21. September 2001 in Cottbus.* (Der Archivar. Beiband 7) Siegburg 2002, 52–68.

Maddrell, Paul. "British-American Scientific Intelligence Collaboration during the Occupation of Germany." *Intelligence and National Security* 15 (2000): 74–94.

Mai, Gunther. *Der Alliierte Kontrollrat in Deutschland 1945–1948. Alliierte Einheit – deutsche Teilung?* (Quellen und Darstellungen zur Zeitgeschichte 37). Munich 1995.

Majer, Diemut. "Grundlagen des Besatzungsrechts 1945–1949," in Hans-Erich Volkmann, ed. *Ende des Dritten Reiches–Ende des Zweiten Weltkriegs. Eine perspektivische Rückschau.* Munich 1995, 141–71.

Manke, Matthias. "Vom Hofhistoriker des Gauleiters zum Militärarchivar des Bundes. Der Archivar Georg Tessin im Staatsarchiv Schwerin und im Bundesarchiv Koblenz," in Kretzschmar ed. *Archivwesen und Nationalsozialismus,* 281–312.

Martens, Stefan. "Frankreich und Belgien unter deutscher Besatzung und das Schicksal der deutschen Akten nach dem Zweiten Weltkrieg," in Martens, ed. *Frankreich und Belgien unter deutscher Besatzung 1940–1944. Die Bestände des Bundesarchiv-Militärarchiv Freiburg.* Bearb. von Sebastian Remus. (Instrumenta 7). Stuttgart 2002, XXIII-LVI.

Maschke, H M. "Die deutschen Akten und das Kriegsrecht." *Der Archivar* 3 (1950): 27–34.

Mau, Hermann. "Die deutschen Archive und Dokumente in den Vereinigten Staaten." *Geschichte in Wissenschaft und Unterricht* 2 (1951): 621–5.

Maulucci, Thomas W. *The Creation and Early History of the West German Foreign Office, 1945–55.* Dissertation, Yale University, 1997.

Meekings, C. A. F. "Germany [Archives 1939–1947]." *The Year's Work in Librarianship* 14 (1947): 314–20.

_____. "Rückgabe von Archiven an Polen." *Der Archivar* 1 (1948): 71–4.

Meinecke, Friedrich. "Irrwege unserer Geschichte?" *Der Monat* 2:13 (1949): 3–6.

Meinert, Hermann. "[Obituary] Albert Brackmann und das deutsche Archivwesen." *Archivalische Zeitschrift* 49 (1954): 127–38.

Melton, James V. H. "From Folk History to Structural History: Otto Brunner and the Radical-Conservative Roots of German Social History," in Hartmut Lehmann and James V. H. Melton, eds. *Paths of Continuity. Central European Historiography from the 1930s to the 1950s.* Cambridge 1994, 263–97.

Menk, Gerhard, Sierk F. M. Plantinga. "'Die Ehre der deutschen Staatsarchivare und Historiker zu wahren.' Bernhard Vollmer und seine Tätigkeit in den Niederlanden," in Kretzschmar, ed. *Archivwesen und Nationalsozialismus*, 217–71.

Meyer, Georg. "Zu Fragen der personellen Auswahl bei der Vorbereitung eines westdeutschen Verteidigungsbeitrages (1950–1956)," in Hanns Hubert Hofmann ed. *Das deutsche Offizierkorps 1860–1960*. (Büdinger Vorträge 1977). Boppard/Rh. 1980, 351–65.

———. "Zur Situation der deutschen militärischen Führungsschicht im Vorfeld des westdeutschen Verteidigungsbeitrages 1945–1950/51," in Roland G. Foerster, Christian Greiner, Georg Meyer, Hans-Jürgen Rautenberg, and Norbert Wiggershaus, eds. *Von der Kapitulation bis zum Pleven-Plan*. (Anfänge westdeutscher Sicherheitspolitik. Vol. 1) Munich 1982, 579–735.

———. "Soldaten wie andere auch? Zur Einstellung ehemaliger Angehöriger der Waffen-SS in die Bundeswehr," in Harald Dickerhof, ed. *Festschrift für Heinz Hürten*. Frankfurt 1988, S. 545–94.

Meyer-Landrut, Joachim. "Die Behandlung von staatlichen Archiven und Registraturen nach Völkerrecht." *Archivalische Zeitschrift* 48 (1953): 45–120.

Möller, Horst. "Das Institut für Zeitgeschichte und die Entwicklung der Zeitgeschichtsschreibung in Deutschland," in Möller and Udo Wengst, eds. *50 Jahre Institut für Zeitgeschichte. Eine Bilanz*. Munich: Oldenbourg, 1999, 1–68.

Möller, Horst and Udo Wengst, eds. *50 Jahre Institut für Zeitgeschichte. Eine Bilanz*. Munich 1999.

Mommsen, Wolfgang A. "Deutsche Archivalien im Ausland." *Der Archivar* 3 (1950): 33–8.

———. "Die Akten der Nürnberger Kriegsverbrecherprozesse und die Möglichkeit ihrer historischen Auswertung." *Der Archivar* 3 (1950): 14–25.

———. "Ernst Posner. Mittler zwischen deutschem und amerikanischem Archivwesen." *Der Archivar* 20 (1967): 217–30.

Mühle, Eduard. *Für Volk und deutschen Osten. Der Historiker Hermann Aubin und die deutsche Ostforschung*. Düsseldorf 2005.

Müller, Claus M.: *Relaunching German Diplomacy. The Auswärtiges Amt in the 1950s*. Münster 1994.

Müller, Wolfgang. "Georg Winter und das Bundesarchiv." *Archivalische Zeitschrift* 58 (1962): 129–37.

Helmut Müller-Enbergs. *"Rosenholz"* – *Eine Quellenkritik*, ed. by The Office of the Federal Commissioner, BStU (Series BF Informiert Nr. 28); http://www.bstu.bund.de/DE/Wissen/Aktenfunde/Rosenholz/rosenholz inhalt.html (accessed August 2011).

Musial, Torsten. *Staatsarchive im Dritten Reich. Zur Geschichte des staatlichen Archivwesens in Deutschland 1933–1945*. (Potsdamer Studien 2). Potsdam 1996.

Naylor, John F. "The Establishment of the Cabinet Secretariat." *Historical Journal* 14 (1971): 783–803.

Nicholas, Lynn H. *The Rape of Europa. The Fate of Europe's Treasures in the Third Reich and the Second World War*. New York 1995.

Nicholls, C. S. *The History of St. Antony's College, Oxford, 1950–2000*. London 2000.

Oldenhage, Klaus. "Das Schicksal deutscher zeitgeschichtlicher Quellen nach dem Zweiten Weltkrieg." *Archivum* 32 (1986): 303–9.

_____. "Archivbeziehungen zur DDR," in Friedrich P. Kahlenberg, ed., *Aus der Arbeit der Archive. Beiträge zum Archivwesen, zur Quellenkunde und zur Geschichte. Festschrift für Hans Booms.* Boppard/Rh. 1989, 135–41.

Overesch, Manfred. *Hermann Brill in Thüringen, 1895–1946. Ein Kämpfer gegen Hitler und Ulbricht.* Bonn 1992.

Overmans, Rüdiger: *Deutsche militärische Verluste im Zweiten Weltkrieg* (Beiträge zur Militärgeschichte 46). Munich 1999.

Papen, Patricia von. "Schützenhilfe nationalsozialistischer Judenpolitik. Die 'Judenforschung' des 'Reichsinstituts für Geschichte des neuen Deutschland' 1935–1945," in *"Beseitigung des jüdischen Einflusses. . . . " Antisemitische Forschung, Eliten und Karrieren im Nationalsozialismus. Fritz Bauer Institut. Jahrbuch 1998/99 zur Geschichte und Wirkung des Holocaust.* Darmstadt 1999, 17–41.

Passant, E. James. *A Short History of Germany, 1815–1945.* Cambridge 1959.

Perman, Dagmar Horna. "Microfilming of German Records in the National Archives." *American Archivist* 22 (1959): 433–43.

Petropoulos, Jonathan. *The Faustian Bargain. The Art World in Nazi Germany.* Oxford 2000.

_____. *Royals and the Reich. The Princes von Hessen in Nazi Germany.* New York 2006.

Pfeil, Ulrich. "Archivraub und historische Deutungsmacht. Ein anderer Blick in die deutsche Besatzungspolitik in Frankreich." *Francia* 33 (2006): 163–94.

Philippi, Hans. "Das Politische Archiv des Auswärtigen Amtes [I]." *Der Archivar* 9 (1958): 139–50.

_____. "Das Politische Archiv des Auswärtigen Amtes [II]. Rückführung und Übersicht über die Bestände." *Der Archivar* 13 (1960): 199–218.

Piontkowitz, Heribert. *Anfänge westdeutscher Außenpolitik 1946–1949. Das Deutsche Büro für Friedensfragen.* (Studien zur Zeitgeschichte 12). Stuttgart 1978.

Piskorski, Jan M., Jörg Hackmann, and Rudolf Jaworski, eds. *Deutsche Ostforschung und polnische Westforschung im Spannungsfeld von Wissenschaft und Politik: Disziplinen im Vergleich.* Osnabrück 2002.

Pöhlmann, Markus. *Kriegsgeschichte und Geschichtspolitik: Der Erste Weltkrieg. Die amtliche deutsche Militärgeschichtsschreibung 1945–1956.* (Krieg in der Geschichte 12). Paderborn 2002.

Pogge von Strandmann, Hartmut. "Britische Historiker und der Ausbruch des Ersten Weltkrieges," in Wolfgang Michalka, ed. *Der Erste Weltkrieg. Wirkung, Wahrnehmung, Analyse.* Munich 1994, 929–52.

_____. "The Role of British and German Historians in Mobilizing Public Opinion in 1914," in Benedikt Stuchtey and Peter Wende, eds. *British and German Historiography 1750–1950. Traditions, Perceptions and Transfers.* London 2000, 335–71.

Poll, Bernhard. "Vom Schicksal der deutschen Heeresakten und der amtlichen Kriegsgeschichtsschreibung." *Der Archivar* 6 (1953): 66–75.

Pomrenze, Seymour J. "Policies and Procedures for the Protection, Use, and Return of Captured German Records," in Robert Wolfe, ed. *Captured German and Related Records. A National Archives Conference* (NA Conference 3). Athens, OH, 1974, 5–30.

Posner, Ernst. "Public Records under Military Occupation." *American Historical Review* 49 (1944): 213–37.

Poste, Leslie I. "Books Go Home From the Wars." *Library Journal* 73 (1948): 1699–704.

_____. *The Development of U.S. Protection of Libraries in Europe during World War II.* Fort Gordon, GA 1964.

Poyser, Elisabeth R. "Review [of the Guide to Captured German Records]." *Journal of the Society of Archivists* 1 (1955–59): 53–4.

Pretsch, Hans Jochen. "Das Politische Archiv des Auswärtigen Amtes." *Der Archivar* 32 (1979): 299–302.

Prott, Lyndel V. and P. J. O'Keefe. *Law and the Cultural Heritage.* 5 vols., here: vol. 3: Movement (1989). London 1984ff.

Ramscheid, Birgit. *Herbert Blankenhorn (1904–1991). Adenauers außenpolitischer Berater.* Düsseldorf 2006.

Rantzau, Johann Albrecht von. "Individualitätsprinzip, Staatsverherrlichung und deutsche Geschichtsschreibung." *Die Sammlung* 5 (1950): 284–99.

Rauh-Kühne, Cornelia. "Die Entnazifizierung und die deutsche Gesellschaft." *Archiv für Sozialgeschichte* 35 (1995): 35–70.

Ray, Roland. *Annäherung an Frankreich im Dienste Hitlers? Otto Abetz und die deutsche Frankreichpolitik 1930–1942.* (Studien zur Zeitgeschichte 59). Munich 2000.

Reusch, Ulrich. "Die Londoner Institutionen der britischen Deutschlandpolitik 1943–1948. Eine behördengeschichtliche Untersuchung." *Historisches Jahrbuch* 100 (1980): 318–443.

_____. *Deutsches Berufsbeamtentum und britische Besatzung 1943–1947. Planung und Politik 1943–1947* (Forschungen und Quellen zur Zeitgeschichte 6). Düsseldorf 1985.

Reynolds, David J. "Churchill's Writing of History: Appeasement, Autobiography and *The Gathering Storm,*" in: *Transactions of the Royal Historical Society. Sixth Series*, vol. 11. Cambridge 2001, 221–47.

_____. *In Command of History. Winston Churchill and "The Second World War".* London 2004.

Reynolds, Nicholas. "Der Fritsch-Brief vom 11. Dezember 1938." *Vierteljahrshefte für Zeitgeschichte* 28 (1980): 358–71.

Ritter, Gerhard. *Europa und die deutsche Frage. Betrachtungen über die geschichtliche Eigenart des deutschen Staatsdenkens.* Munich 1948.

_____. "Gegenwärtige Lage und Zukunftsaufgaben deutscher Geschichtswissenschaft. Eröffnungsvortrag des 20. Deutschen Historikertages in München am 12. September 1949." *Historische Zeitschrift* 170 (1950): 1–22.

_____. "Ergebnis meiner Archivreise nach Berlin (11.-18. Oktober)." *Der Archivar* 4 (1951): 49–55.

_____. "Der X. Internationale Historikerkongreß in Rom (4.-11. September 1955)." *Historische Zeitschrift* 180 (1955): 657–63.

_____. *The Schlieffen Plan: Critique of a Myth*. London 1958. (German edition: *Der Schlieffenplan. Kritik eines Mythos. Mit erstmaliger Veröffentlichung der Texte und 6 Kartenskizzen*. Munich 1956.)

Röder, Werner, Hermann Weiß and Klaus A. Lankheit. "Das Archiv des Instituts für Zeitgeschichte," in Horst Möller and Udo Wengst, eds. *50 Jahre Institut für Zeitgeschichte. Eine Bilanz*. Munich 1999, 105–25.

Rohr, Wilhelm. "Die zentrale Lenkung deutscher Archivschutzmaßnahmen im Zweiten Weltkrieg." *Der Archivar* 3 (1950): 105–22.

_____. "Schicksal und Verbleib des Schriftguts der obersten Reichsbehörden." *Der Archivar* 8 (1955): 161–74.

_____. "[Obituary] Ernst Zipfel." *Der Archivar* 20 (1967): 206–10.

_____. "[Obituary] Georg Winter." *Der Archivar* 14 (1961): 179–90.

_____. "Mikroverfilmung und Verzeichnung deutscher Akten in Alexandria, USA." *Der Archivar* 19 (1966): 251–60.

Rose, Norman. *Lewis Namier and Zionism*. Oxford 1980.

Roth, Karl Heinz. "Eine höhere Form des Plünderns. Der Abschlußbericht der 'Gruppe Archivwesen' der deutschen Militärverwaltung in Frankreich 1940–1944." *1999 Zeitschrift für Sozialgeschichte des 20. und 21. Jahrhunderts* 4:2 (1989): 79–122.

_____. "Klios rabiate Hilfstruppen. Archivare und Archivpolitik im deutschen Faschismus." *Archivmitteilungen* 41 (1991): 1–10.

_____. "'Richtung halten': Hans Rothfels und die neo-konservative Geschichtsschreibung diesseits und jenseits des Atlantik." *Sozial.Geschichte* 18 (2003): 41–71.

Rothfels, Hans. "Zeitgeschichte als Aufgabe." *Vierteljahrshefte für Zeitgeschichte* 1 (1953): 1–8.

Rupieper, Hermann-Josef. *Der besetzte Verbündete. Die amerikanische Deutschlandpolitik 1949–1955*. Opladen 1991.

Sabrow, Martin. "Ökumene als Bedrohung. Die Haltung der DDR-Historiographie gegenüber den deutschen Historikertagen von 1949 bis 1962." *Comparativ* 6:5/6 (1996): 178–202.

_____. *Das Diktat des Konsenses. Geschichtswissenschaft in der DDR 1949–1969*. (Ordnungssysteme 8). Munich 2001.

Sandhofer, Gert. "Rückführung deutscher Archivalien an das Bundesarchiv." *Der Archivar* 32 (1979): 88.

Sante, Georg W. "Die Archive Großhessens. Bericht über die Tagungen zu Wiesbaden vom 25. Oktober und 10. Dezember 1946." *Der Archivar* 1 (1947): 5–9.

Schildt, Axel. *Ankunft im Westen. Ein Essay zur Erfolgsgeschichte der Bundesrepublik*. Frankfurt 1999.

Schlie, Ulrich. "Das Ausland und die deutsche Opposition gegen Hitler. Widerstandsforschung und politische Gegenwart seit 1945." *Militärgeschichtliche Mitteilungen* 52 (1993): 153–68.

Schneider, Konrad: "Das Stadtarchiv Frankfurt," in Kretzschmar, ed. *Archivwesen und Nationalsozialismus*, 372–84.

Schöllgen, Gregor. *Die Außenpolitik der Bundesrepublik Deutschland. Von den Anfängen bis zur Gegenwart.* Munich 1999.

Schönwalder, Karen. *Historiker und Politik. Geschichtswissenschaft im Nationalsozialismus.* Frankfurt 1992.

Schöttler, Peter, ed. *Geschichtsschreibung als Legitimationswissenschaft 1918–1945.* Frankfurt 1999.

_____. "Geschichtsschreibung als Legitimationswissenschaft 1918–1945. Einleitende Bemerkungen," in Schöttler, ed. *Geschichtsschreibung als Legitimationswissenschaft 1918–1945.* Frankfurt 1999, 7–30.

Schornstheimer, Michael. *Bombenstimmung und Katzenjammer. Vergangenheitsbewältigung: Quick und Stern in den fünfziger Jahren.* Köln 1989.

_____. *Die leuchtenden Augen der Frontsoldaten. Nationalsozialismus und Krieg in den Illustriertenromanen der fünfziger Jahre.* Berlin 1995.

Schrenk, Christhard. *Schatzkammer Salzbergwerk. Kulturgüter überdauern in Heilbronn und Kochendorf den Zweiten Weltkrieg.* (Quellen und Forschungen zur Geschichte der Stadt Heilbronn 8). Heilbronn 1997.

Schroll, Heike. *Spurensicherung. Die Bestände des Stadtarchivs Berlin und ihr Schicksal durch den Zweiten Weltkrieg.* (Schriftenreihe des Landesarchivs Berlin 5). Berlin 2000.

Schulin, Ernst. "Deutsche und amerikanische Geschichtswissenschaft. Wechselseitige Impulse im 19. und 20. Jahrhunderts," in Schulin, ed. *Arbeit an der Geschichte. Etappen der Historisierung auf dem Weg zur Moderne.* Frankfurt 1997, 164–91.

_____. "Weltkriegserfahrung und Historikerreaktion," in Wolfgang Küttler, Jörn Rüsen, Ernst Schulin, ed. *Geschichtsdiskurs 4: Krisenbewußtsein, Katastrophenerfahrung und Innovation 1880–1945.* Frankfurt 1997, 165–88.

Schulze, Winfried. *Deutsche Geschichtswissenschaft nach 1945.* Munich 1993.

Schulze, Winfried and Otto Gerhard Oexle, eds. *Deutsche Historiker im Nationalsozialismus.* Frankfurt 1999.

Schumann, Peter. "Gerhard Ritter und die deutsche Geschichtswissenschaft nach dem Zweiten Weltkrieg," in *Mentalitäten und Lebensverhältnisse. Beispiele aus der Sozialgeschichte der Neuzeit. Rudolf Vierhaus zum 60. Geburtstag,* edited by his colleagues and students. Göttingen 1982, 399–415.

Schwarz, Hans-Peter. "Die neueste Zeitgeschichte." *Vierteljahrshefte für Zeitgeschichte* 51 (2003), 5–28.

Schwengler, Walter. "Der doppelte Anspruch. Souveränität und Sicherheit. Zur Entwicklung des völkerrechtlichen Status der Bundesrepublik Deutschland 1949 bis 1955," in Werner Abelshauser and Schwengler: *Wirtschaft und Rüstung, Souveräntität und Sicherheit.* (Anfänge westdeutscher Sicherheitspolitik 1945–1956, vol. 4). Ed. by Militärgeschichtlichen Forschungsamt. Munich 1997, 187–566.

Searle, Alaric. "'Jetzt dürfen sie reden': Basil Liddell Hart, die Wehrmachtsgeneralität und die Militärgeschichte im Dienste der Wiederbewaffnung." *Newsletter des Arbeitskreises Militärgeschichte* 9 (Mai 1999): 20–3.

_____. "A very special relationship: Basil Liddell Hart, Wehrmacht Generals and the Debate on West German Rearmament, 1945–1953." *War in History* 5 (1998): 327–57.

Seier, Hellmut. "[Obituary] Paul Kluke (1908–1990)." *Historische Zeitschrift* 252 (1991): 212–15.

Sharp, Alan. "Some Relevant Historians – the Political Intelligence Department of the Foreign Office 1918–1920." *Australian Journal of Politics and History* 34 (1988): 359–68.

Simpson, Elisabeth, ed. *The Spoils of War. World War II and Its Aftermath: The Loss, Reappearance, and Recovery of Cultural Property.* New York 1995.

Smith, Bradley F. "Die Überlieferung der Hoßbach-Niederschrift im Lichte neuer Quellen." *Vierteljahrshefte für Zeitgeschichte* 38 (1990): 329–36.

Sontag, Raymond. "The German Diplomatic Papers. Publication after Two World Wars." *American Historical Review* 68 (1962/63): 57–68.

Später, Jörg. *Vansittart. Britische Debatten über Deutsche und Nazis 1902–1945.* Göttingen 2003.

Spring, Derek. "The Unfinished Collection. Russian Documents on the Origins of the First World War," in Keith Wilson, ed. *Forging the Collective Memory. Government and International Historians through Two World Wars.* Providence, RI, 1996, 63–86.

Stein, Wolfgang Hans. "Die Inventarisierung von Quellen zur deutschen Geschichte. Eine Aufgabe der deutschen Archivverwaltung in den besetzten westeuropäischen Ländern im Zweiten Weltkrieg," in Stein, ed. *Inventar von Quellen zur deutschen Geschichte in Pariser Archiven und Bibliotheken.* (Veröffentlichungen der Landesarchivverwaltung Rheinland-Pfalz 39). Koblenz 1986, XXVII–LXVII.

———. "Archive als Objekt von Kulturimperialismen: Französische Archive in Deutschland – deutsche Archive in Frankreich," in Michel Espagne, Katharina Middell, Matthias Middell, eds. *Archiv und Gedächtnis. Studien zur interkulturellen Überlieferung.* Leipzig 2000, 89–121.

———. "Georg Schnath und die französischen Archive unter deutscher Besatungsverwaltung," in Kretzschmar, ed. *Archivwesen und Nationalsozialismus,* 175–94.

Steiner, Zara. "The Historian and the Foreign Office," in Christopher Hill and Pamela Beschoff, eds. *Two Worlds of International Relations. Academics, Practitioners and the Trade in Ideas.* London 1994, 40–53.

Stieg, Margaret F. "The Postwar Purge of German Public Libraries, Democracy, and the American Reaction." *Libraries and Culture* 28 (1993): 143–64.

Stumpf, Reinhard. "Die Wiederverwendung von Generalen und die Neubildung militärischer Eliten in Deutschland und Österreich nach 1945," in Manfred Messerschmidt et al., eds. *Militärgeschichte. Probleme – Thesen – Wege. Im Auftrag des Militärgeschichtlichen Forschungsamtes aus Anlaß seines 25jährigen Bestehens.* (Beiträge zur Militär- und Kriegsgeschichte 25). Stuttgart 1982, 478–97.

Sweet, Paul R. "Der Versuch amtlicher Einflußnahme auf die Edition der" Documents on German Foreign Policy, 1933–1941." *Vierteljahrshefte für Zeitgeschichte* 39 (1991): 265–303.

———. "The Windsor File." *Historian* 59 (1997): 263–79.

Taylor, A. J. P. "Keeping It Dark. Half-Century Secrets." *Encounter* 13 (1959): 40–5.

Thimme, Annelise. "Friedrich Thimme als politischer Publizist im Ersten Weltkrieg und in der Kriegsschuldkontroverse," in Alexander Fischer et al., eds. *Russland-Deutschland-Amerika. Festschrift für Fritz T. Epstein zum 80. Geburtstag* (Frankfurter Historische Abhandlungen 17). Wiesbaden 1978, 212–38.

Thimme, Roland. "Das Politische Archiv des Auswärtigen Amts. Rückgabeverhandlungen und Aktenedition 1945–1995." *Vierteljahrshefte für Zeitgeschichte* 49 (2001): 317–62.

Trevor-Roper, Hugh. *The Last Days of Hitler.* New York 1962.

Trommler, Frank. "Neuer Start und alte Vorurteile. Die Kulturbeziehungen im Zeichen des Kalten Krieges 1945–1968," in Detlef Junker, ed. *Die USA und Deutschland im Zeitalter des Kalten Krieges. Ein Handbuch.* 2 vols. Vol. I: 1945–1968. Stuttgart 2001, 567–89.

Umbreit, Hans. "Towards Continental Domination," in Bernhard R. Kroener, Rolf-Dieter Müller and Hans Umbreit: *Organization and Mobilization of the German Sphere of Power. Part I: Wartime administration, economy, and manpower resources 1939–1941* (Germany and the Second World War, vol. 5:1). Oxford 2000, 9–404.

Urbach, Karina. "Zeitgeist als Ortsgeist. Die Emigration als Schlüsselerlebnis deutscher Historiker?" in Hermann Joseph Hiery, ed. *Der Zeitgeist und die Historie.* Dittelbach 2001, 161–79.

Vismann, Cornelia. *Akten. Medientechnik und Recht.* Frankfurt 2000.

Volkert, Natalia. *Kunst- und Kulturraub im Zweiten Weltkrieg. Versuch eines Vergleichs zwischen den Zielsetzungen und Praktiken der deutschen und der sowjetischen Beuteorganisationen unter Berücksichtigung der Restitutionsfragen.* Frankfurt 2000.

Volkmann, Hans-Erich. "Deutsche Historiker im Umgang mit Drittem Reich und Zweitem Weltkrieg 1939–1949," in Volkmann, ed. *Ende des Dritten Reiches – Ende des Zweiten Weltkriegs. Eine perspektivische Rückschau.* Munich 1995.

Vollmer, Bernhard. "Die Lage des deutschen Archivwesens nach dem Kriege." *Europa Archiv* 3 (1948): 1623–8.

_____. "Deutsche Archivalien im Nationalarchiv Washington." *Der Archivar* 2 (1949): 23–4.

Waite, Robert G. "Returning Jewish Cultural Property: The Handling of Books Looted by the Nazis in the American Zone of Occupation." *Libraries & Culture* 37 (2002): 213–28.

Walther, Peter Th. "Emigrierte deutsche Historiker in den Vereinigten Staaten, 1945–1950," in Chr. Cobet, ed. *Einführung in die Fragen an die Geschichtswissenschaft in Deutschland nach Hitler 1945–1950.* Frankfurt 1986, 41–50.

_____. "Die deutschen Historiker in der Emigration und ihr Einfluß in der Nachkriegszeit," in Heinz Duchhardt and Gerhard May, eds. *Geschichtswissenschaft um 1950.* Mainz 2002, 37–47.

Watt, D. C. "Sir Lewis Namier and Contemporary European History." *Cambridge Journal* 7 (1954): 579–600.

_____. "Foreign Affairs, the Public Interest and the Right to Know." *Political Quarterly* 34 (1963): 121–36.

Watt, D. C.. "Perceptions of German History among the British Policy-Making Elite, 1930–1965, and the Role of British and German Emigré Historiography in its Formation," in Henning Köhler, ed. *Deutschland und der Westen. Vorträge und Diskussionsbeiträge des Symposiums zu Ehren von Gordon A. Craig.* Berlin 1984, 140–58.

Watt, D. C.. "British Historians, the War Guilt Issue, and Post-War Germanophobia: A Documentary Note." *Historical Journal* 36 (1993): 179–85.

Weber, Hermann. "Gefahr der Aktenvernichtung." *Deutschland-Archiv* 32 (1999): 828–30.

Wegner, Bernd. "Deutsche Aktenbestände im Moskauer Zentralen Staatsarchiv. Ein Erfahrungsbericht." *Vierteljahrshefte für Zeitgeschichte* 40 (1992): 457–67.

Weidemann, Diethelm. "Das Schicksal der Akten der Deutschen Gesandtschaft Kabul, Afghanistan." *Archivmitteilungen* 40 (1990): 81–3.

Weinberg, Gerhard L. "Critical Note on the Documents on German Foreign Policy, 1918–1945." *Journal of Modern History* 23 (1951): 38–40.

_____. "Zu den deutschen Akten in den Vereinigten Staaten." *Historische Zeitschrift* 194 (1962): 519–26.

_____. "German Records Microfilmed at Alexandria, Virginia, in Collaboration with the American Historical Association," in Robert Wolfe, ed. *Captured German and Related Records. A National Archives Conference* (NA Conference 3). Athens, OH, 1974, 199–210.

_____. "The End of Ranke's History? Reflections on the Fate of History in the Twentieth Century," in Weinberg, ed. *Germany, Hitler & World War II. Essays in Modern German and World History.* Cambridge 1995.

_____. "German Documents in the United States." *Central European History* 41:4 (2008): 555–67.

Weinreich, Max. *Hitler's Professors. The Part of Scholarship in Germany's Crimes Against the Jewish People.* New York 1946.

Weisbrod, Bernd. "The Moratorium of the Mandarins and the Self-Denazification of German Academe: A View from Göttingen." *Contemporary European History* 12;1 (2003): 47–69.

Weiser, Johanna. *Geschichte der preußischen Archivverwaltung und ihrer Leiter. Von den Anfängen unter Staatskanzler von Hardenberg bis zur Auflösung im Jahre 1945.* Köln 2000.

Weiß, Petra. "Die Bergung von Kulturgütern auf der Festung Ehrenbreitstein." *Jahrbuch für westdeutsche Landesgeschichte* 26 (2000): 421–52.

Wengst, Udo. *Staatsaufbau und Regierungspraxis 1948–1953. Zur Geschichte der Verfassungsorgane der Bundesrepublik Deutschland.* (Beiträge zur Geschichte des Parlamentarismus und der politischen Parteien 74). Düsseldorf 1984.

_____. *Beamtentum zwischen Reform und Tradition. Beamtengesetzgebung in der Gründungsphase der Bundesrepublik Deutschland 1948–1953.* (Beiträge zur Geschichte des Parlamentarismus und der Politischen Parteien 84). Düsseldorf 1988.

W[erner], W[olfram]. "Rückführung deutscher Marineakten." *Der Archivar* 31 (1978): 98.

Wiggershaus, Norbert. "Die amtliche Militärgeschichtsforschung in der Dienststelle Blank und im Bundesministerium für Verteidigung 1952 bis 1956." *Militärgeschichtliche Mitteilungen* 30:2 (1976): 115–21.

Wilson, Duncan. "Public Records. The Wilson Report and the White Paper." *Historical Journal* 25 (1982): 985–94.

Winter, Georg. "[Das Bundesarchiv in:] Auszug aus dem Protokoll des 31. Deutschen Archivtags." *Der Archivar* 5 (1952): 106–7.

Winter Jay and Emmanuel Sivan. "Setting the Framework [Introduction]," in Winter and Sivan, eds. *War and Remembrance in the Twentieth Century.* Cambridge 1999, 6–39.

Wisotzky, Klaus. "Die rheinischen und westfälische Stadtarchive im Nationalsozialismus," in Kretzschmar, ed. *Deutsches Archivwesen und Nationalsozialismus,* 354–71.

Wittgens, Herman J. "Senator Owen, the *Schuldreferat*, and the Debate over War Guilt in the 1920s," in Keith Wilson, ed. *Forging the Collective Memory. Government and International Historians Through Two World Wars.* Providence, RI, 1996, 128–50.

Wolfe, Robert, ed. *Captured German and Related Records. A National Archives Conference* (NA Conference 3). Athens, OH, 1974.

_____. "Sharing Records of Mutual Archival Concern to the Federal Republic of Germany and the United States of America." *Archivum* 33 (1984): 292–302.

_____. "United States Exploitation of Captured German Records. Theory and Practice," in George O. Kent, ed. *Historians and Archivists. Essays in Modern German History and Archival Policy.* Fairfax, VA, 1991, 15–25.

_____. "A Short History of the Berlin Document Center," in *The Holdings of the Berlin Document Center. A Guide to the Collections.* Berlin 1994, xi–xxii.

Wolfrum, Edgar. *Geschichtspolitik der Bundesrepublik Deutschland. Der Weg zur bundesrepublikanischen Erinnerung 1948–1990.* Darmstadt 1999.

Wright, Jonathan and Paul Stafford. "Hitler, Britain and the Hoßbach Memorandum." *Militärgeschichtliche Mitteilungen* 41:2 (1987): 77–116.

Zala, Sacha. *Geschichte unter der Schere politischer Zensur. Amtliche Aktensammlungen im internationalen Vergleich.* Munich 2001.

_____. "Coloured Books. The Censorship of Diplomatic Documents," Derek Jones, ed. *Censorship. A World Encyclopedia.* Vol. I. 1London 2001, 551–3.

_____. "Dreierlei Büchsen der Pandora. Die Schweiz und das Problem der deutschen Archive," in Antoine Fleury, Horst Möller and Hans-Peter Schwarz, eds. *Die Schweiz und Deutschland 1945–1961.* Munich 2004, 119–34.

Zarusky, Jürgen. "Bemerkungen zur russischen Archivsituation." *Vierteljahrshefte für Zeitgeschichte* 41 (1993): 139–47.

Zibell, Stephanie. "Ludwig Bergsträßer und das deutsche Archivwesen." *Archivalische Zeitschrift* 87 (2005): 7–38.

Zimmermann, Ludwig. *Frankreichs Ruhrpolitik. Von Versailles bis zum Dawesplan.* Ed. by Walther Peter Fuchs. Göttingen 1971.

Index

Acheson, Andrew B., 197, 199, 200, 204, 208, 216
  industrial documents, 204
Acheson, Dean, 149
Adenauer, Konrad, 2, 123, 339, 340
  Germany treaty negotiations, 207
  ownership of records, 235
  records relocation proposal, 256
  records return request, 137, 146, 156, 166, 196, 203, 206, 210, 213, 234, 241, 263
  reelection, 238
Air Ministry, 266
  Luftwaffe records, 262
Alfred Six, Franz, 127
Allen, Roger, 242
Allied Control Commissions on the Continent, 25
Allied Control Council
  Directive No. 18, 30
  Order No. 2, 30
  Order No. 34, 30
  Order No. 4, 174
  Proclamation no. 2, 106
Allied Headquarters, Algiers, 18
Allied High Commission, 3, 146
  access to files, 360
  ownership of papers, 220
  return of records, 137, 138, 155
Allies
  access to archives, 372
  May 1955 offer, 244

  October 1954 offer, 240
  records return disputes, 240
  response to Adenauer, 258
American Committee for the Protection and Salvage of Artistic and Historic Monuments in War Areas. *See* Roberts Commission
American Committee for the Study of War Documents, 343, 344
American Council of Learned Societies, 17
American Defense Harvard Group, 17
American Field Intelligence Agency, Technical, 30
American High Commission, 224
American Historical Association, 348
  Conference Group for Central European History, 349
American Liberation Law of March 1946, 114
American Library Association, 180
Amt Blank, 187, 265
Andres, Hans, 132, 133, 163, 225, 237, 312, 314, 323, 359
Anti-semitism, 158
Appeasement, 326
Archival protection, 27
Archivists
  wartime deployment, 18
Arendt, Hannah, 340
Army Research Institute for Military History, 135

Association of German Historians, 150,
    206, 315, 357
Aubin, Hermann, 247, 315, 331
Auswärtiges Amt, 2, 33, 35, 43, 59, 60, 62,
    105, 122, 156, 164
    Archive Commission, 135, 161
    Documents on German Foreign Policy
        response, 301
    interdepartmental disputes, 279
    Legal Division, 239
    microfilming, 356
    Political Archives 156. *See* Political
        Archives
    Political Department, 132, 220
    press relations, 295
    records storage, 237
    War Guilt Office, 135, 316
Auswärtiges Amt records, 37, 73, 94, 149,
    152, 154, 206, 215, 244
    archives access, 360
    diplomatic, 222, 223, 261
    French Access, 80
    immigration, 192, 193
    legal status, 220, 227, 235
    publication, 88
    relocation, 323
    return of, 209, 213, 240, 276, 285
    Soviet access, 81
    storage, 96

Barclay, Kit, 209
Barraclough, Geoffrey, 329, 380
Basic Law, 187
    Article 33, 190, 262
Baumont, Maurice, 251, 254, 307
Becker, Otto, 310
Beddie, James, 93
Bein, Alex, 117
Beneš, Edvard, 49, 50
Bergsträßer, Ludwig, 123–127, 128, 140
Berlin Document Center, 44, 53, 97, 126,
    187, 192, 282, 341
Berlin Wall, 10, 358
Bernstein, Bernard, 42
Bevin, Ernest, 46
Bidault, George, 250
Bild, 368

Bismarck, study of, 308
Bissell, Clayton, 24
Bissell-Sinclair Agreement, 23, 96, 171,
    264, 268, 272, 274
Blankenhorn, Herbert, 137, 159, 225, 233
Blücher, Wibert von, 301
Board of Trade, 203
Boberach, Heinz, 378
Bonn Convention, 234, 235
Brackmann, Albert, 100, 101, 115
Brentano, Heinrich von, 282
Brill, Hermann, 43, 140, 141, 144
British Army of the Rhine, 29
British Control Commission, 29
British High Commission, 159, 232
    diplomatic records, 215
    records return policy, 193
    return of records, 196
British Intelligence Objectives
        Sub-Committee, 30, 202
British Joint Services Mission, 273
Brower, Philipp, 198
Brown, William D., 45
Bruchmann, Karl G., 104, 118
Brückner, Hardo, 239, 260
Buchheim, Karl, 338
Buck, Solon J., 15
Bullock, Alan, 380
Bundesamt für Verfassungsschutz. *See*
        Federal Office for the Protection of
        the Constitution
Bundesarchiv, 9, 120, 121, 132, 166, 193,
    237, 277, 282
    access to archives, 363
    interdepartmental disputes, 279
    leadership, 125
    microfilming, 356
    military archive, 283
    negotiations, 350
    record return strategy, 278
    Soviet return of records, 246
Bundestag, 2
    campaign, 1953, 238
    Committee on Cultural Affairs, 141
    debate of May 1950, 210
    resolution on records, 140–146
Bundeswehr, 263

Butler, J.R.M., 253
Butler, Rohan, 322, 326
Buttkus, Heinz, 370
Byrnes, James, 72

Cabinet Office, British, 197
Cadogan, Alexander, 77
Camp King, 268
Camp Ritchie, 23, 24, 96, 171
Carpenter, Gardner C., 47, 62, 65
Carroll, E. Malcolm, 91
Carsten, Francis L., 303
Carstens, Karl, 369
Cavendish-Bentinck, William, 66, 68
Central Department, 194
    records return policy, 193, 207, 208
Central Immigration Office, 190
    records, 191, 192
Central Intelligence Agency, 292
    Operation Rosewood, 11
    return of records policy, 181
Child, B., 20, 45, 56
Churchill, Winston, 70, 212, 250, 252, 327
Cilivian Archivists, 17
Clay, Lucius D., 78, 81, 94
Clemm, Ludwig, 111, 123
Clinton administration, 291
Cold War, 349
Collins, Ralph, 62, 63
Color Books of the First World War,
    9
Columbia University, 176
Combined Advance Field Teams, 32
Combined Chiefs of Staff, 30, 32
Combined Intelligence Committee, 32
Combined Intelligence Objectives
    Sub-Committee, 30–33, 37, 67, 202,
    204
    Black List, 31
    Gray List, 31
Conant, James B., 238, 242
Congress, U.S., 227
Contemporary history, 332
    study of, 380
Conze, Walter, 166
Cooperative Acquisition Project,
    174

Copyright, 229, 232
Counter Intelligence Corps, 1, 60
Craig, Gordon A., 381
Czechoslovakia
    archives, 128

Dagens Nyheter, 367
Daily Mail, 324
Daily Telegraph, 267
Dalton, Hugh, 267
Declassification, 345
Defense Department, U.S.
    German army records, 264
    records legal status, 229
Defense Ministry
    military document center, 283
Dehio, Ludwig, 118, 305, 310
Denazification, 29, 102, 110, 114, 116,
    302
Department for Industrial and Scientific
    Research, 203
Department of Commerce, U.S., 173
Departmental Records Branch, 175, 176,
    177, 197, 269, 272, 275, 339, 345
    relations with France, 274
    rescue of records, 187
    return of records, 264, 268
Der Archivar, 108
Der Spiegel, 246, 298
Deutsch, Harold, 303
Deutsches Auslands Institut, 43
Deutsches Institut für Geschichte der
    nationalsozialistischen Zeit, 334
Die Große Politik der europäischen Kabinette,
    248, 295, 315–324, 352
Die Sammlung, 305
Diestelkamp, Adolf, 126
Diestelkamp, Bernhard, 226
Diplomatic records, 33, 221, 376
    access to, 360
    publication of, 295
Displaced Persons Program, 191
Document Activity Reports, 29
Document centers, 51–54
    American, 52
    British, 52
Documents on British Foreign Policy, 38

Documents on German Foreign Policy, 34,
    87–92, 131, 134, 136, 137, 138, 148,
    149, 150, 151, 152, 153, 155, 156,
    162, 195, 196, 202, 207, 294
  financing, 238
  first volume, 96
  German participation, 162, 308, 311,
    316
  legal status, 233
  political purpose of, 295
  reaction to, 297
  relocation, 164, 236, 240, 248, 251, 255,
    259, 320
  Windsor file, 250
Dorn, Walter L., 302, 310, 311, 344
Duke, Kenneth H. M., 91
Dulles, 225
Dzhugashvili, Yakov, 47, 48

East German Ministry for State Security, 11
East, Sherrod, 175, 178, 286, 345
Eden, Anthony, 68, 214, 257
Ehard, Hans, 340
Einsatzstab Reichsleiter Rosenberg, 103,
    105
  Special Task Force on Arches, 113
Eisenhower, Dwight D., 72, 163, 250
Ellis, Major R. H., 21
Enemy Document Section, 197, 199
Enemy Property Act, 232
Epstein, Fritz T., 91, 302, 338, 344, 347,
    351, 355
Erdmann, Karl Dietrich, 300, 312
Erler, Fritz, 167
Ernst, Fritz, 309, 310, 323, 337
Ernst, Wolfgang, 103
Europa und die deutsche Frage, 329, 381
Europa-Archiv, 299
European Advisory Commission, 36, 37
European Defence Community, 201
  treaty, 263
Executive Order No. 12958, 291
Eyck, Erich, 308

Federal Office for the Protection of the
    Constitution, 158, 159, 340
Federal Records Disposal Act, 228

Federal Republic, 2
  historians, 136
  rearmament, 178, 263
  reclaimation of records, 97
  sovereignty, 247, 298
  study of recent past, 307
Fischer, Fritz, 305, 309, 311, 331
Fisher, M.H., 232, 317
Flensburg, 95
Fone, Charles Henry, 216, 360
Ford Foundation, 345, 348
Foreign Affairs Office, 131, 132
Foreign Ministers Conference, 93
Foreign Ministry Archives, 233
Foreign Office, 4, 33, 34, 37, 38, 205
  access to archives, 373
  Central Department. *See* Central
    Department
  diplomatic records, 222
  industrial records, 204, 205
  internal debate, 258
  Loesch microfilms, 68
  records legal status, 233
  records publication, 85, 89
  records return policy, 193
  response to Adenauer, 242
  return of records, 150
  Windsor file, 71
Foreign Office Library, 91, 206
  access to records, 360
Four-Power government, 53, 68, 74, 79, 82
  records publication, 86
Frame, T.H., 58
France, 3
  access to records, 76
  archives, 40
  Foreign Ministry, 161
  records, 161
  records legal status, 235
  records publication, 90
  records return involvement, 274
  return of military records, 266
  wartime archives, 111
François-Poncet, André, 235
Frank, Walter, 115, 304
Frankfurter Allgemeine Zeitung, 282, 298
Franklin D. Roosevelt Library, 16

Franklin, Bill, 289
Franz, Günther, 304, 310
Frei, Norbert, 102
Friedrich Goerdeler, Carl, 303
Friedrich, Carl J., 344
Friedrichsen, George W.S., 197, 198, 274
Fürstenhagen, 78

G-2 Document Section. *See* U.S. Army
Gatzke, Hans, 319
German archivists, 99
    denazification, 110
    genealogical research, 103
    Nazi ideology, 100, 101, 109
    post-war, 104
    reclaimation of records, 136
German-Czechoslovak archive treaty, 128
German Democratic Republic
    access to records, 368
    return of records, 246, 376
    Soviet return of records, 260
German Documents Panel, 27
German Eastern Affairs Desk, 368, 369
German Foreign Ministry records, 38
German Institute for the History of the National Socialist Period. *See* Institute for Contemporary History
German Military Document Section, 23, 270
German navy files, 95
German Occupation
    "Eclipse" plan, 29
    "Talisman" plan, 29
German Office for Peace Issues, 131
German Reich
    post surrender existance, 226
German-Soviet Relations
    documents, 93
Germany
    Allied occupation, 13
Germany Treaty, 191, 245
    ratification of, 214
    return of documents, 207
Germany's Aims in the First World War, 311
Gestapo, 103

Gilbert, Felix, 303
Goebbels, Joseph, 202
Goldbeck, Herman, 8
Goldschmidt, Hans, 117
Gooch, George P., 325, 326
Granzin, Martin, 105
Great Britain
    access to archives, 373
    historians, 379
    records legal status, 227
    records return policy, 151
    return of military records, 265
Grewe, Wilhelm, 132, 244, 280
Griesheim, Witilo von, 61
Griff nach der Weltmacht, 331
Gronich, Lieutenant S.F., 22
Grover, Wayne, 173, 229, 230, 232
Grünberg, Karol, 370
Grunwald, Jacques, 320
Gruppe Archivwesen, 105
    final report, 40
Gruppe Archivwesen final report, 39–41
Guide to Captured Records, 122
Gusev, Feodor T., 48, 76
Gymnich Castle, 237, 240, 256

Haack, Hanns-Erich, 132, 133, 139
Haeften, Hans-Bernd von, 239
Hague Regulations of Land Warfare, 179, 183, 220, 225
Hale, Oron J., 303, 346
Halifax, 228
Hallgarten, George W., 303, 344
Hallstein, Walter, 164, 234, 366
Hancock, Francis, 209, 240, 249, 253, 256
Hannoversche Allgemeine, 295
Hartung, Fritz, 310
Harz castles, 1, 61
Headlam-Morley, Agnes, 321
Heeresachiv, 230
Heeresgruppe Mitte, 48
Heinemann, Gustav, 124, 126
Henke, Josef, 9, 278
Herzfeld, Hans, 306, 354
Heusinger, Adolf, 288
Himmler, Heinrich, 190
Hinrichs, Carl, 310

Historical Advisory Committee, 239, 258
Historische Zeitschrift, 299, 305
Hitler, Adolf
assassination attempt, 56
Last Will and Testament, 46
records, 339
Hitlers Tischgespräche im Führerhauptquartier 1941–1942, 339, 352
Hitler-Stalin Pact
documents, 93
Hoch, Anton, 336
Hoffmann Photo Collection, 290
Holborn, Hajo, 310, 311
Holldack, Heinz, 310
Holstein papers, 232
Holstein, Friedrich von, 232
Holzhausen, Rudolf, 299
Hölzle, Erwin, 161
Hoßbach Memorandum, 59
Huber, Hans, 45
Hübinger, Paul Egon, 165

Industrial records, 203
Institute for Archival Science, 100
Institute for Contemporary History, 3, 140, 144, 165, 282, 283, 294, 310, 334, 352
Intelligence, 21
Intelligence Division of the European Command, 187
Interagency Conference on Captured Enemy Documentation, 169, 170–175, 178–183, 198, 229
policy paper, 183–185
Interior, Ministry of, 124
microfilming, 356
records, 339
records request, 189, 191
International Congress of Historical Sciences, 331
Italy, 19
archival protection, 17

Jackson, Robert H., 42
JCS 29, 263
Jenkinson, Hilary, 16, 18, 20, 28
Jewish archivists, 117

Johannmeier, Willi, 46
Joint Chiefs of Staff, 179
Joint Consultative Committee, 151, 194–218, 377
Admiralty, 199, 217
Air Ministry, 199, 201, 217
Cabinet Office, 195, 197
consultation with America, 210
coordination with France, 273
document return policy, 194
military records, 210
policy paper, 206, 210
policy paper, fourth, 216
policy paper, second, 214
policy paper, third, 215, 217
records return policy, 208
response to American declassification, 271
return of military records, 265
Joint Intelligence Committee, 201
return of military records, 265
Joint Intelligence Sub-committee, 27
Joll, James, 309, 319, 322, 380
Justice Department, U.S., 181
Office of Alien Property, 172, 230
Justice, Ministry of records, 339

Kaehler, Siegfried, 310
Kahlenberg, Friedrich, 126
Kaltenbrunner reports, 56
Kassel-Fürstenhagen, 84
Kempner, Robert M.W., 292
Kent, George O., 319
King Edward VIII, 70
King Gustav V, 367
Kirkpatrick, Ivone, 138, 151, 193, 206, 207, 214, 234, 248
military records return, 265
Klassen, Peter, 134, 135, 156, 157, 158, 159, 164, 239, 301, 314
Klaus, Samuel, 42
Klein, Arthur G., 345
Kluge, Paul, 299
Kluke, Paul, 145, 282, 300, 303, 306, 333, 335, 343, 354, 382
microfilming, 356
Koblenz, 121

Kohn, Hans, 306, 311, 344, 354
  microfilming, 351
Korean War, 4, 170, 175, 344
Kothe, Wolfgang, 126
Krausnick, Helmut, 161, 335
Krekeler, Heinz, 185
Kristallnacht, 103
Kroll, Gerhard, 336
Kulturpolitik, 34

Lacy, Dan, 178
Lahr, Rolf, 372
Lambert, Margaret, 248, 251, 256, 301, 320, 354
Langer, William L., 294, 304
Lasswell, Harold D., 344
Laval, Pierre, 76
Law for the Restoration of the Professional Civil Service, 102
Lehr, Robert, 126
Leishman, Frederick, 274
Library of Congress, 181, 339
  return of documents, 173
Library of Congress Mission, 174, 180
Liddell Hart, Basil H., 212
Loesch microfilms, 64, 67, 92
Loesch, Karl von, 62–67
London Declaration of 1943, 111
London Military Document Center, 23
Lord Halifax, 68, 71
Lorenz, Heinz, 46
Lovett, Robert A., 182, 229
Luftwaffe files, 95, 213, 262

Madrid embassy records, 220
Marburg castle, 1, 73
Marshall-Cornwall, James, 138, 150
Masaryk, Jan, 50
Masigli, René, 80
Massey, Isabella M., 322
Mau, Hermann, 142, 310, 312, 335, 338, 341, 382
McCloy, John J., 235, 336, 345
Meddlicott, W.M., 253
Meier-Welcker, Hans, 283
Meinecke, Friedrich, 303
Melchers, Wilhelm, 132

Melland, Brian, 197, 198, 272, 275, 276, 285
Mende, Dietrich, 307, 308
MI 14, 197
MI 3, 26
Microfilming, 347, 350, 354, 379, 383
Military History Research Office, 289
Military Intelligence Records Section, 21, 22
  split, 23
Military records, 261, 264, 361, 372, 376
Ministerial Collecting Center, 27, 45, 52, 74, 79, 81, 84
Ministerial Document Branch, 53, 84, 97
Molotov-Ribbentrop Pact, 64, 93
Mommsen, Wilhelm, 310
Mommsen, Wolfgang A., 104, 112, 122, 126
Monckton, Walter, 254
Monuments, Fine Arts and Archives division, 17, 19
  reorginization of German archivists, 108
  sub-comission, 18
Mosler, Hermann, 156, 235, 312
Mühlhausen, 62
Munich Agreement, 128
Murphy, Robert, 40, 43, 49, 65, 68, 74, 78, 83, 84, 91

Namier, Lewis, 35, 253, 324, 326, 380
National Archives, 17, 20, 35, 122, 271
  1968 conference, 8
  copyright, 229, 232
  microfilm, 347, 348
  return of records, 148, 173
National Archives, U.S., 15
National Institute for the History of New Germany, 304
National Security Agency, 291
National Socialism
  party records, 44, 97, 185, 261, 270, 281, 336, 339
  study of, 144, 146, 293, 302, 328, 331, 333
  transition from, 142
Naumann affair, 202
Naumann, Werner, 202

Nazi party. *See* National Socialism
Nazi War Crime Disclosure Act, 291, 292
Nazi-Soviet Relations, 91
Nazi-Soviet Relations, 1939–1941, 93
Nemesis of Power, 159, 327, 381
Netherlands, 111
New York Times, 343
Newton, Henry C., 81
Noack, Ulrich, 310
Noble, Bernard, 94, 148, 153, 154, 156,
     170, 178, 181, 197, 238, 249, 252,
     253, 256, 259, 274, 286, 305, 307,
     310, 318, 338, 341, 342
  access to archives, 373
  Die große Politik der europäischen
     Kabinette, 318
  financial cost, 163
  German editor, 162
  german visitors, 343
  microfilming, 351
  relocation of records, 178
  response to Adenauer request, 213
Nuremberg Laws, 102
Nuremberg Trials, 2, 47, 58, 72, 277, 292,
     383
Nutting, Anthony, 267

O'Neill, Con, 360
Offenbach Archival Depot, 54
Office of Strategic Services, 43
Office of the High Commission, 194
Office of the High Commissioner for
     Germany, 149, 192, 238
Office of the Political Advisor, 45
Oncken, Dirk, 367, 368
Operation Goldcup, 53
Ostforschung, 100, 101, 115

Papritz, Johannes, 100
Paris Agreements, 246
Paris Treaty, 344
Parrott, Cecil C., 210, 216
Passant, James, 150, 154, 157, 162, 205,
     233, 245, 252, 257, 259, 305, 307,
     317
  Foreign Office, 205–208
  Institute for Contemporary History, 341

JCC, 195–197
  response to Adenauer, 242
Patents, 203
Patton, George, 48
Pearson, Drew, 89
Perkins, E. Ralph, 38, 67
Perman, Dagmar Horna, 379, 382
Pers. Z, 290
Persilscheine, 114, 116, 134
Pétain, Philippe, 76
Pflanze, Otto, 319
Phelps, Reginald H., 344, 353
Philippi, Hans, 260
Pink Book, 22
Pinson, Koppel, 344
Polish Desk, 368
Political Archives, 130, 132, 134, 161, 261,
     300
  access, 364, 368
  Allies access, 359
  Eastern bloc access, 369
  journalists, 367
Pomrenze, Seymour J., 8, 273
Posner, Ernst, 15, 16, 18, 108, 110, 118,
     124, 229, 304
Potsdam Conference, 47, 79
Prague, 48, 50
Press and Information Office, 130
Preußischen Archivverwaltung. *See* Prussian
     Archival Administration
Propaganda, Ministry of records, 339
Propaganda, Ministry of, 202
Prussian Archival Administration, 15, 100,
     101, 115, 118, 123
Prussian Privy State Archive, 120
Prussian State Archive, 113
Public Record Office, 16, 20
Public Record Office, British, 15
Publikationsstelle Dahlem, 100

Quisling, Vidkun, 76

Raiser, Ludwig, 161
Randt, Erich, 113
Rantzau, Johann Albrecht von, 305
Red Army, 4, 26, 48
Refugee Relief Act, 192

Reich Archives, 120, 127
Reich Chancellery records, 339, 363
Reich Civil Service Act, 102
Reich Commissioner for the Strengthening
of Germanism, 190
Reich Security Main Office records, 339
Reichsnährstand records, 282
Reichssicherheitshauptamt, 54
Renouvin, Pierre, 91
return of records policy
cost, 182
Rheindorf, Kurt, 133, 159, 163, 304,
312
Ribbentrop, Joachim von, 60, 62, 70
Rich, Norman, 232, 317, 318, 319
Ritter von Lex, Hans, 124
Ritter, Gerhard, 136, 293, 303, 305, 308,
311, 312–315, 328, 330, 337, 340,
380, 382
Roberts Commission, 17
Roberts, Frank, 208, 240, 249, 254,
256
Roberts, Owen J., 17
Rogge, Helmuth, 127, 128, 129, 130
Rohr, Wilhelm, 104, 115, 117, 126, 277,
377
Roosevelt, Franklin D., 16, 57
Rosenberg, Alfred, 277
Rosenberg, Einsatzstab Reichsleiter, 277
Rosenow, Kurt, 341
Rothfels, Hans, 125, 308, 332, 347

Safehaven Program, 42
Salisbury, Lord, 250, 253, 254
San Francisco Conference, 228
Sandys, Duncan, 62
Sasse, Heinz Günter, 135
Saunders, Malcolm, 199, 287
Schieder, Theodor, 331, 356
Schlieffen Plan, 381
Schmidt box, 47, 64, 69
Schmidt, Paul Otto, 47, 62
Schmieden, Werner von, 137
Schmitt, Bernadotte, 307, 316, 354
Schnabel, Franz, 308, 310, 312
Schnath, Georg, 105, 111, 112, 116
Schramm, Percy Ernst, 304, 309, 310

Schröder, Gerhard, 282
Schwerdtfeger, Max, 265
Secretary of Defense, 182
Settlement Convention 1952, 231
Seventh Army, 44
Shafer, Boyd C., 344, 354
Shipman, Fred, 16, 18, 20, 35
Sicherheitsdienst, 103
Sinclair, John Alexander, 24, 25
Smolensk party archives, 184
Smyth, Howard M., 354
Sontag, Raymond, 59, 89, 91, 93, 152,
344
Soviet Union, 94
access to files, 76
Documents on Germany Foreign Policy, 90
post-war internments, 112
return of records, 246, 376
study of, 349
Spain, 219
Spaulding, E. Wilder, 35, 36, 37
Spruchkammern, 114, 116
St. Antony's College, 380
Stalin, Josef son, 47
Starke, Gotthold, 369, 371
Stasi
records, 358
State Archive Düsseldorf, 111
State Department, 3, 33, 34, 35, 37, 181
access to records, 361, 373
Department of State Bulletin, 86
diplomatic records, 221, 223
Historical Office, 35, 91, 147, 163
Hitler's will, 46
Loesch microfilms, 68
Office for Foreign Activity Correlation,
88
records legal status, 228
records publication, 85, 86
records retained, 289
records return policy, 169
return of records, 147, 148, 186, 342
statement on Adenauer request, 213
State Department-Foreign Office team, 33,
39, 41, 47, 58, 61
Loesch incident, 67
Windsor file, 72

Steel, Christopher, 94, 216
Steinhardt, Laurence A., 49
Stettinius, Edward R., 69, 71, 228
Stone, Isaac A., 193
Stone, Shepard, 341, 345
Strang, William, 36, 75, 195, 249, 250, 255
Süddeutsche Zeitung, 298
Sunday Chronicle, 77
Supply, Ministry of, 203, 204
Supreme Headquarters Allied
    Expeditionary Forces, 14, 19, 20, 22,
    23, 27, 30, 33, 95
    Goldcup, 27
Sweet, Paul, 251, 253, 299, 318
Switzerland, 221

Tambach, 95
Taylor, A.J.P., 321, 327, 380
Tempelhof, 91
Temperly, Harold, 325
Tenth International Congress of the
    Historical Sciences, 353
T-Forces, 26, 32
The Mediterranean and Middle East, 199
The Politics of the Prussian Army, 381
Thimme, Friedrich, 248
Thompson, Robert, 301
Thomson, Robert, 38, 58, 62, 63, 65, 72,
    80
Times Literary Supplement, 321, 323
Trading with the Enemy Act, 172, 230
Transport Ministry, 189
Treasury Department, 42
Treaty of Versailles, 100, 325
Trevor-Roper, Hugh, 380
Truman, Harry S., 93
Trützschler, Heinz von, 237

U.S. Air Force, 176
U.S. Archivist, 229
U.S. Army, 44, 345
    archival officers, 20
    archivist, 20
    British discussions, 198
    declassification, 345
    Departmental Records Branch, 96
    diplomatic records, 224

G-2 Document Section, 22
    records return policy, 177, 182
    records return process, 269
    return of records, 148, 171, 174, 261,
    268
U.S. Navy, 95
Ullrich, Hans, 105
Ullrich, Johannes, 105, 133, 135, 244, 278,
    280, 282, 285, 362, 364, 366, 367,
    371, 372, 374
United Nations, 69
United States
    records legal status, 227
USGCC, 20

Valentin, Heinrich, 61, 132, 137, 164, 300
Verband Deutscher Historiker, 136
Verein deutscher Archivare, 108
Verein Deutscher Ingenieure, 43
Victory in the West, 199
Vierteljahrshefte für Zeitgeschichte, 185, 352
Vogel, Walther, 126
Volksdeutsche, 190
Volksmentalität, 164
Vollmer, Bernhard, 111, 121, 126, 136

Wagner, Fritz, 306
Wallach, Sidney, 345
War booty, 179, 229
War crimes trials
    evidence, 21
War Department, 24
    archival practices, 18
    G-2 division, 96
    MFAA, 17
    use of captured documents, 22
War Department, U.S., 21
War Documentation Project, 176, 347
War guilt, 86, 315, 325, 331
War Office, British, 21
    military intelligence department, 24
War trophies, 57
Watt, D.C., 324, 380
Wehrmacht, 30, 217
    personnel records, 262, 265, 268
Weinberg, Gerhard L., 319, 347
Weise, Erich, 101

Weizsäcker, Ernst von, 70
Wende, Erich, 124
Wendland, Ulrich, 113
Whaddon Hall, 94, 96, 134, 150, 151, 155, 156, 196, 232, 249
   diplomatic records, 222
Wheeler-Bennett, John W., 91, 151, 159, 194, 207, 248, 253, 308, 316, 326, 380
   JCC, 195–197
Wiener, Alfred, 160
Winant, John G., 36
Windsor File, 70, 71, 92, 228, 250
Winter, Georg, 112, 115, 116, 117, 121, 122, 124, 125, 127, 128, 129, 261, 277, 278, 280, 281, 284, 295, 364, 377
   microfilming, 350, 356
Wiskemann, Elisabeth, 380

Wodehouse, P.G., 64
Wojciechowski, Marian, 371
Wolfe, Robert, 8
Woodward, E. Llewellyn, 35, 38, 195, 253, 322, 326, 328
World War I, 33
   origin, 327, 329

Yalta Treaty, 1

Zala, Sacha, 9
Zander, Willhelm, 46
Zechlin, Egmont, 310
Zentralarchiv, 107
Zentralnachweisstelle, 336
Zimmermann, Ludwig, 161
Zipfel, Ernst, 104, 109, 112, 115, 117, 119

Printed in Great Britain
by Amazon.co.uk, Ltd.,
Marston Gate.